Wodehouse

Also by Robert McCrum

Fiction
In The Secret State
A Loss of Heart
The Fabulous Englishman
Mainland
The Psychological Moment
Suspicion

Non-fiction
The Story of English (with William Cran and Robert MacNeil)
My Year Off: Rediscovering Life After a Stroke

For Children
The World Is A Banana
The Brontosaurus Birthday Cake

Wodehouse

A Life

ROBERT McCRUM

VIKING
an imprint of
PENGUIN BOOKS

VIKING

Published by the Penguin Group
Penguin Books Ltd, 80 Strand, London wc2r 0rl, England
Penguin Group (USA) Inc., 375 Hudson Street, New York, New York 10014, USA
Penguin Books Australia Ltd, 250 Camberwell Road, Camberwell, Victoria 3124, Australia
Penguin Books Canada Ltd, 10 Alcorn Avenue, Toronto, Ontario, Canada m4v 3b2
Penguin Books India (P) Ltd, 11 Community Centre, Panchsheel Park, New Delhi – 110 017, India
Penguin Group (NZ), cnr Airborne and Rosedale Roads, Albany, Auckland 1310, New Zealand
Penguin Books (South Africa) (Pty) Ltd, 24 Sturdee Avenue, Rosebank 2196, South Africa

Penguin Books Ltd, Registered Offices: 80 Strand, London wc2r 0rl, England

www.penguin.com

First published 2004

1

Set in 11.5/14pt Monotype Bembo
Typeset by Palimpsest Book Production Limited, Polmont, Stirlingshire
Printed in Great Britain by Clays Ltd, St Ives plc

A CIP catalogue record for this book is available from the British Library

ISBN 0-670-89692-6

To Michael McCrum

pater optime

with love and gratitude

Contents

List of Illustrations

Childhood and Youth

Writing and Hollywood

War

The Post-war Years

The author and publisher are grateful to the following for permission to reproduce photographs: pages 1-5, 11-13, 15, 20, 21, 26, 27, 29, 32, 37-41, Wodehouse Estate; pages 6 and 7, by kind permission of the Governors of Dulwich College; page 8, by kind permission of the Wodehouse Estate and the Governors of Dulwich College; page 9, HSBC Archives; page 10, Rex Features Limited; page 14, Museum of the City of New York; page 18, The Raymond Mander & Joe Mitchenson Theatre Collection; page 19, Courtesy of the Academy of Motion Picture Art and Sciences; page 22, *LA Times* 1931; page 25, *The Times* 1939/NI Syndication; page 28, A. Wells Collection/J. Fox Archives; pages 30 and 42, Associated Press; page 31, Keystone Press Agency, Hamburg; page 33, Reinhild Maxtone-Miller; page 34, Getty Images – Kurt Hutton/Stringer; page 35, Joanna Vallance; page 36, Mirrorpix.

Acknowledgements

In the long and crowded life of P. G. Wodehouse, there are six biographical pioneers whose invaluable work I gratefully acknowledge. First, in Britain, there is the founding father of Wodehouse studies, Richard Usborne, author of *Wodehouse at Work*. In the United States, David Jasen published the first biography, with his subject's approval, and in doing so accumulated an archive of original manuscript and interview material that makes his work almost a primary source. Frances Donaldson's 'authorized' life was the first to benefit from full access to the Wodehouse archive, and to begin the illumination of Wodehouse's war years. Subsequently, Norman Murphy, who has also made many helpful contributions to my own work, transformed our appreciation of Wodehouse's childhood and youth. Barry Phelps, following in Murphy's footsteps, researched many neglected aspects of Wodehouse's life, shedding light on previously contentious matters. Finally, in America, Lee Davis, Wodehouse's Long Island neighbour, showed, for the first time, the importance of Wodehouse's Broadway career and of his friendship with Guy Bolton. To all of these, I offer heartfelt thanks.

Next to the trailblazers, there are the dedicated Wodehousians: Joseph Connolly, Murray Hedgcock and Iain Sproat, who all spoke up for their special interests and supplied useful information. Tony Ring, the indefatigable editor of *Wooster Sauce*, and his wife Elaine also made some vital suggestions about *Wodehouse: A Life*, and saved me from some egregious errors. Rex Bunnett, Barry Day and Miles Krueger have been equally indispensable to my understanding of Wodehouse's Broadway years. Steven Blier, whom I met during the New York blizzard of 2002, infused my grasp of the American musical with his infectious passion for Wodehouse the lyricist.

Just as important as any of these Wodehouse experts are the various witnesses who agreed to be interviewed about their personal experience of Wodehouse. A special thank you goes to Peter Brown, Frances Ershler, Lynn Kiegiel, Christopher MacLehose, John Millar, Tom Mott, Philip Norman, John Julius Norwich, Jacqueline Powell (née Grant), Naomi Roberts (née Ziman), Hilary Rubinstein, Peter Schwed, Anne Smith, Michael Vermehren, R. E. Whitby, Patrick Wodehouse and Margaret Zbrozak. Adam Phillips gave me the exceptional benefit of his long experience as a child psychotherapist. Bill and Dee Bourne were instrumental in the swift transcription of my tape recordings. Artemis Cooper kindly shared pages of her grandfather Duff Cooper's unpublished diary; Nigel Nicolson let me consult previously unseen folios from his father's journal. Reinhild Maxtone Miller (née von Bodenhausen) generously shared her fascinating unpublished memoir of her 'Oncle Plummie', a manuscript that surely deserves a wider audience.

I have been exceptionally fortunate in my association with the Trustees of the Wodehouse Estate. Edward and Camilla Cazalet have been generous towards, and supportive of, me in ways I can never repay. The Cazalet family's housekeeper Esther Valdez provided a sustaining menu of delicious meals. Hal Cazalet has been an enthusiastic and persuasive champion of his step-grandfather's lyrics. I have listened to Lara Cazalet's recording of 'Bill' more times than is sensible.

Several friends and acquaintances contributed to my understanding of this subject: Glen Baxter, Peter Bazalgette, Linda Blandford, John Bodley, Craig Brown, Cressida Connolly, Peter Conrad, Michael Davie, Nick Dennys, Timothy Garton Ash, Malcolm Gladwell, Geordie Greig, Jaco Groot, Selina Hastings, Philip Hensher, Julie Kavanagh, Anthony Lane, Edmund Morris, Orhan Pamuk, Roland Phillips, Christopher Sylvester, D. J. Taylor, Michael Whitehall and Simon Winder. My thanks to all of these.

From among the staff of libraries and archives I have consulted in Britain, Europe and the United States, I particularly want to acknowledge the kind assistance of Barbara Hall (Academy of Motion Picture Arts and Sciences); Hazen Lutaaya (BBC, Caversham); Dr Isaac Gewirtz and Diana Berman (Berg Collection); Michelle Simpson and David Gadsby (A. & C. Black); John White (Chapel Hill); Henry Rowen (Columbia); Tessa Daines (Emsworth); Edwin Green (HSBC); Philippe Dejaive (Huy); Rosalind Moad (King's College, Cambridge); Sally Muggeridge (Muggeridge Collection); Nick Roberts (Punch Library); Tara Wenger (Ransom); Julie Graham (UCLA); Ned Comstock (USC); with a special thank you to Jan Piggott, keeper of the Wodehouse archive at Dulwich. In Berlin, Bettina von Hase was invaluable, while Theresa von Eltz combed the German Foreign Office archives. In British newspaper files, thanks are also due to Fatema Ahmed and Ben Cooper. In the United States, Major Thomas L. Smith guided me through the maze of State Department papers.

Work on *Wodehouse* got a timely boost from the BBC with a documentary based on my research. In the shooting of *Wodehouse: The Long Exile*, I am especially grateful to my old friend William Cran, the director Ian Denyer, his assistant Erica Dodd, who organized our visit to Toszek (Tost), and Clive Syddall. Among Corporation executives, past and present, a special thanks to Roly Keating, Jane Root, Roger Thompson and, above all, to Nigel Williams.

The best ideas spring from a single seed. This one came from the tireless imagination of Kate Jones at Penguin Books who, before she went out on her 'wild lone' as a literary agent, identified that the time was ripe for a new Wodehouse biography, and who understood that some important personal testimony was in danger of being lost. In the negotiations that followed, I have depended, as ever, on the wisdom and counsel of Binky Urban, Michael Sissons and James Gill. At W. W. Norton, Star Lawrence has provided a patient ear and a shrewd editorial eye. At Viking, I am especially grateful to Juliet Annan, Mary Mount, Joanna Prior and Katherine Stroud for their smart and sympathetic professionalism. Closer to home, Sarah Lyall raked through at least two drafts of the book with the merry zeal known only to those raised on *Strunk and White*.

Long before the manuscript reached the publishers and I had completed my research I received an almost daily flow of unsolicited help from well-wishers and Wodehouse aficionados who offered copies of letters, photographs and biographical titbits. I am particularly grateful to Anthony Andrews, Marjorie Barton, Patrick Carroll, Michael Cockerell, David Conville, Alan Crisp, Michael Forster, Jimmy Fox, John Maxtone-Graham, Jane Greenwood, P. D. Hancock, Christobel Haward, Rex King-Clark, Michael Leapman, Michael Meakin Lestrange, Gavin Marmoy, Margo Miller, Gunner Pedersen, Robert Robinson, Judy Ryland, Margaret Slythe, Kris Smets, J. W. Smurr, Tony Staveacre, John Stubbs, Christopher Sylvester, Richard and Rosemary Wells, and James Young.

Among those who have helped with specific aspects of Wodehouse's life, I record a special gratitude to Mary Able, Dr Bernard Berger, Hilary Bruce, Jonathan Cecil, Baroness Charlotte De Serdici, David Emms, John Green, Peter Hollingsworth, Sofia Kitson, Ulrike Lange, Richard Perceval Maxwell, Joanna Nowak, Ed Ratcliffe, Nathan and Debbie Rosenblatt, Dr Anna Russek, Philippe Sands, Kristin Thompson, Helen Townend, Professor Gavin Townend and Joanna Vallance. Elisabeth and Vincent Mayer provided the perfect sanctuary to begin the writing.

I would like also to pay tribute to my friends at the *Observer*. Roger Alton, the editor, was characteristically generous in giving me leave to write the main draft of the book; John Mulholland and Paul Webster, his deputies, were both wonderfully understanding and supportive. Martin Bright and Vanessa Thorpe helped me track down the elusive Townend family. Among other colleagues who have assisted this project in different ways, Jeannette Hyde, Jane Ferguson, William Keegan (and his friends at the National Office of Statistics), Andy Malone and Lisa O'Kelly have all played a part. The staff of the *Observer* books department, Teresa Goodman and Stephanie Merritt, have been tolerant and sympathetic during my absences, and have cheerfully fielded some apparently bizarre inquiries from enthusiastic Wodehousians around the world.

A special thank you also goes to Jonathan Bouquet and Katherine Bucknell for their editorial wisdom, insight and experience: my debt to them is profound. Tom Sharpe was an inspiration when the biographical labour seemed particularly daunting. I shall never forget his encouragement and support. At the end, David Cornwell's frank and generous scrutiny seemed like a very special benediction.

Finally, to my wife Sarah, and our daughters, Alice and Isobel, thanks and blessings, and boundless love. Without their unfailing support and understanding this book would have taken twice as long.

PROLOGUE
'Does aught befall you? It is good'

'I wonder if I might call your attention to an observation of the Emperor
Marcus Aurelius? He said: "Does aught befall you? It is good. It is part
of the destiny of the Universe ordained for you from the beginning. All
that befalls you is part of the great web."'
    I breathed a bit stertorously.
'He said that, did he?'
'Yes, sir.'
'Well, you can tell him from me he's an ass.' (*The Mating Season*)

In the clear blue days of May 1940, a middle-aged Englishman and his
wife, living in the French seaside resort of Le Touquet-Paris Plage with
their Pekinese and pet parrot, found themselves faced with the threat
of the invading Nazi army. Nothing could have prepared them for this
moment. They were rich, upper-middle-class expatriates accustomed to
leisurely breakfasts, walks on the beach, afternoon golf, a preprandial
martini or two, and evenings with the wireless, listening to the BBC,
before a good night's sleep.

    Now they were faced with the alarm call of their lives. The
Wehrmacht was massed on their doorstep and they were 'alien nationals'.
Should they fight, flee or lie low? The Englishman was nearly sixty,
and although his wife had a reputation for taking on all comers, neither
of them was belligerent. Flight was out of the question. They had already
tried that. Their car had broken down and, besides, the Normandy roads
were jammed with refugees. To organize a daring escape by sea was
beyond their repertoire. In the end they decided to go shopping for
vegetables.

    This stoic, practical decision was typical of the Englishman and his
generation. The consequences of it were not. Setting off for the farmers'
market in a van with the parrot and their dogs, the couple drove straight
into a German patrol. It must have been a terrifying moment. Everyone
was jumpy and the fully armed troops, high on victory, were also being

threatened with air attack from RAF fighters. An Englishman driving an unmarked van could easily have been arrested or shot. In the event, almost the only violence came from the parrot, which gave the German lieutenant in charge of the patrol an angry nip as he searched the van. Almost, but not quite. The investigating officer had yet to meet Wonder, the Pekinese. There was a sharp, indignant yap, then the cry of a strong man in agony echoed over the dunes; and the lieutenant staggered back, sucking his hand.

We have this cameo of life in occupied France because the Englishman driving the van was a writer who left an account of his rendezvous with Hitler's army. And because that Englishman was P. G. Wodehouse, his account is naturally amused, even carefree, and above all nonchalant:

There for awhile [he went on], the matter rested.

What would have been the upshot, had the lieutenant been at liberty to go into the thing, one cannot say. He had the air of a man who was about to call for hollow squares and firing squads. But at this moment there came a droning overhead and the entire strength of the company vanished into the thicket at the side of the road like eels into mud. Some British aeroplanes were circling over us.

It was a tense situation. The probability seemed to be that a brisk combat would now break out, with machine guns firing from the thicket and machine guns firing from the planes and us in the middle of it all. But there did not appear to be much we could do but wait, so we waited. We could only hope that the occupants of the thicket, trusting to have escaped notice, would maintain a dignified reserve, and this, fortunately, they did. Presently the planes moved away and the troops emerged, dusting their uniforms and trying to look as if they had gone into the thicket merely to see if there were any mushrooms there.

Wonder, I could see, would have been glad to take up the argument at the point where it had been broken off, for the battle light was in her eyes, and she was swearing softly to herself in Chinese.

There is no mistaking the voice of a great comic writer. As much as his mastery of a farcical situation, or his picture of gentlemen's gentlemen and young men in spats, it is Wodehouse's unique voice that has continued to hold his readers, for whom spats and valets are as remote as halberds and yeomen, under his spell. In 1940 he was at the height of his powers. 'In the forty years in which I had been writing,' he observed with hindsight, 'I had sometimes caught myself wishing that life were not just one damned book after another. And here at last was something that was not on the routine. What the future held in store might turn out to be unpleasant, but at any rate it was going to be brand new.' At the moment he bumped into Hitler's army, Wodehouse had already written most of the books for which he is remembered today – *The Inimitable Jeeves*, *Leave It to Psmith*, *Right Ho, Jeeves*, *Heavy Weather*, *The Code of the Woosters* and *Uncle Fred in the Springtime* – and been celebrated across the English-speaking world for his achievement in a way known to few writers of his century. But it was his success that had placed him in France, and his fame that would expose him to a test no other English writer of his generation had to face, a test that proved beyond him. It is the cruel irony of Wodehouse's story that it was the thing with which he was blessed, and which he had worked so hard to perfect, his inimitable lightness of spirit and self-protective flippancy, that betrayed him. 'This diversion', he continued, in his un-ruffled way,

seemed to have taken the Lieutenant's mind off us. So we turned and . . . just as we got into the Avenue du Golf bless my soul if here didn't come the same platoon and the same lieutenant. It was one of those awkward moments. Once more we halted and looked at them, and they halted and looked at us, and this time the sense of strain was even more pronounced. You could see what was passing in the lieutenant's mind. He and his men were being dogged by a mystery car. He was not at all sure that it had not been our secret signals that had attracted those planes, and he was now certain that we had got soldiers aboard.

But he kept his head. This time he stood at a safe distance and told the Sergeant to search the car. The Sergeant, a man of sound intelligence, merely looked in through the window, paling a little as Wonder hurled herself at it. He gave us a clean bill, and we were allowed to return home.

But it had been an unpleasant incident, and we felt that we had not made a good first impression.

Wodehouse's inability to take seriously what was happening to him, or rather, because he was obviously scared, instinctively to look for the joke in a bad situation, was typical of his class, and of his generation.

The stiff upper lip for which the English are still renowned was second nature to him and his characters. What he could not know was that his fateful collision with the twentieth century was about to place him in a succession of circumstances that were beyond a joke, for which he was inappropriately equipped, and to which his relaxed, seemingly frivolous, response was hopelessly misconceived. His encounter with the German patrol is symbolic of everything that would follow, and marks the first act of a personal tragedy that has at times threatened to obliterate his literary genius.

The Second World War finished Wodehouse. If it did not actually take away his life, his involuntary detention in Nazi Germany and its contentious aftermath wrecked it for ever. For the rest of his career, he would be tarred with a variety of cruel, and wholly inaccurate, labels: 'Nazi', 'collaborator', 'traitor', 'Goebbels' stooge' and so on. Puzzled, ashamed and embarrassed, he went into exile in America and died there, thirty years later, loved for his work, largely unknown for himself, imprisoned by his enemies in his wartime reputation and by his fans in the worldwide adulation expressed in their soubriquet, 'The Master'.

In the generation since his death, the name Wodehouse has become attached to two kinds of headline: first, a medley of ill-informed stories recycling aspects of his wartime disgrace; and secondly, some equally uncritical celebrations of his silly ass heroes and the charmed, lost world of upper-class Edwardian England. Between the cacophanies of these two factions, the enemies and the cult, the man himself has quietly slipped away, as he liked to do when he was alive. In the process, the range and complexity of his achievement, and the importance of his contribution to English and American literature, has been overlooked, even neglected.

This is not for want of popularity. His books, which, including posthumous editions, number more than a hundred, are almost all in print, and are still selling, from China to Peru. For the cognoscenti, there are Wodehouse Societies in the United Kingdom, Russia, Sweden, Holland and the United States. Belgium has its Drones Club. On the Indian subcontinent, admiration for his works transcends politics. In Britain and across the English-speaking world, his fans range from the idolatrous to the merely obsessed. In the past hundred years, his admirers have included T. S. Eliot, Kaiser Wilhelm, W. H. Auden, Dorothy Parker, Arthur Balfour, Hilaire Belloc, Evelyn Waugh, Ludwig Wittgenstein,

Eudora Welty, Ogden Nash, John le Carré, H. L. Mencken, Cardinal Basil Hume, Salman Rushdie, and two contrasting Adamses, Douglas and Gerry. To all his readers, high and low, Wodehouse still promises a release from everyday cares into a paradise of innocent comic mayhem, narrated in a prose so light and airy, and so perfectly pitched, that the perusal of a few pages rarely fails to banish the demons of darkness, sickness and despair.

Now, at the beginning of the twenty-first century, a hundred years after the publication of his first novel, it is a good time to consider again his extraordinary versatility — as a journalist, an essayist, a playwright, a librettist, a novelist, and a poet of light verse — to re-examine the making of this *oeuvre*, and to rediscover the man himself, whose best work is timeless and who remains surprisingly modern, an Englishman for all seasons.

PART ONE

Getting Started

(1881-1914)

1. 'My childhood went like a breeze'
(1881-1894)

'Golly, Jeeves,' I said . . . 'there's some raw work pulled at the font from time to time, is there not?' (*Jeeves and the Feudal Spirit*)

Wodehouse is a funny Old English name that has become synonymous with the kind of humour that involves silly young men, dotty peers, and a regiment of all-powerful aunts and butlers. It is a universal label, a guarantee of a certain kind of Englishness: even those who have never read a line of Wodehouse know what he represents. Rooted in the English past, its pronunciation (WOOD-house) also puts it into that category of ancient surnames, like Cholmondeley (Chumley) and Featherstonehaugh (Fanshawe), which do not sound as they look. This is appropriate because the name Wodehouse, whose primary meaning relates to trees, has a secondary, comic derivation, 'out of one's mind, insane, lunatic'. This sense appears punningly in *A Midsummer Night's Dream* and is echoed in the Old English term *woodwose* (or *wude-wusa*) for which the *Oxford English Dictionary* gives 'a wild man of the woods, a satyr, a faun'.

The child who would bear this antic name, and make it famous, the third son of Ernest and Eleanor Wodehouse, was born at 1 Vale Place, Epsom Road, Guildford, on 15 October 1881. He was christened Pelham Grenville, after a godfather, a 'frightful label', in his own words, that came out, in his childish pronunciation, as 'Plum'. He remained, for family, friends and admirers, 'Plum', or 'Plummie', for the rest of his life. 'If you ask me to tell you frankly if I like the names Pelham and Grenville,' he wrote in 1968, 'I must confess that I do not.'

Wodehouse and the world into which he was born would eventually be subjected to violent change. But at the end of the nineteenth century, in the twilight of a golden age, there was hardly a hint of the volcanic upheavals to come. Apart from remote imperial adventures in Afghanistan or the Sudan, and occasional outrages in Ireland, Liberal Britain was at peace. 'Votes for Women' was a slogan still confined to the political fringe. Everyone knew his place, more or less: British socialism was still in its infancy. If, like Wodehouse, you were born into a good family of colonial administrators, you were joining perhaps the most stable and most conservative part of British society. Here, the hushed calm of everyday life was broken only by the ticking of grand-father clocks, the rattle of crockery on trays, and the occasional booming of a distant dinner gong. Encompassed by near-feudal attitudes, servants waited at table, clergymen preached sermons and schoolmasters disci-plined ebullient younger sons.

Families like the Wodehouses were the people who ran the country, and who served as MPs, admirals and District Officers. As boys, they went to the public schools which had been set up for their prepara-tion in the duties of empire. As grown men, they enlisted in regiments and the imperial civil service, and joined clubs in Pall Mall where they read *The Times*, and relaxed over coffee, cigars and copies of *Punch*, the Victorian magazine which perfectly expresses the mandarin hierarchy in which they were so comfortably at home. In *Punch*, there are only three classes: the frivolous toffs, who wear top hats, and put up with the lower orders; the respectable middle classes, who aspire to better things; and the aitch-dropping working classes, who throw half-bricks at their superiors. This hierarchy was part of Wodehouse's unconscious inheritance, inspiring his characterization, in 'The Metropolitan Touch', of the audience for Bingo Little's village hall production of *What Ho, Twing!!*: 'The first few rows were occupied by the Nibs . . . then came a dense squash of what you might call the lower middle classes. At the back . . . we came down with a jerk in the social scale, this end of the hall being given up almost entirely to a collection of frankly Tough Eggs.' Wodehouse slyly describes the Nibs 'whispering in a pleased manner to each other', observes the middle classes 'sitting up very straight, as if they'd been bleached', and caricatures the Tough Eggs exchanging 'low rustic wheezes'. In his fiction, Wodehouse would make this world farcical, but he understood its infinite nuances of accent, dress and antecedent in his bones.

Wodehouse was born a Victorian, but matured as an Edwardian, and would flourish during the twentieth century. He was two years younger than Einstein, Trotsky and E. M. Forster. Picasso and Bartók were his exact contemporaries. Virginia Woolf and James Joyce were born one year later. So he was part of a generation that would challenge every aspect of the world around them: language, perspective, even time itself. But Wodehouse, who transformed comic prose into a kind of poetry, with a profound instinct for the music of English, was not a revolutionary, either by temperament or inheritance. First and last, he was an Englishman, who gave England an infectiously lunatic version of itself that owed everything to his genius but was also, in part, derived from his peculiar heritage.

Wodehouse himself had no title, nor ever any real prospect of one, but he came from a family of long-established Norfolk knights with centuries of royal service. One branch was directly descended from Lady Mary Boleyn, the unfortunate sister-in-law of Henry VIII. Further back, Sir Constantine Wodehouse, knighted by Henry I, held land at Kimberley, outside Norwich, which remained the family seat until recently. Bertram de Wodehouse served with Edward I in the wars against the Scots, and it is Bertie Wooster who remembers that 'his ancestors did dashed well at the Battle of Crécy'. According to *Burke's Peerage*, Bertram's descendant Sir John Wodehouse was made Constable of Castle Rising in 1402, having married the daughter and heir of Sir John Fastolf of Kimberley, who possibly inspired Shakespeare's Falstaff. Their son John fought at the Battle of Agincourt and received a knighthood from Henry V. Later Wodehouses were also knighted by Henry VI and Elizabeth I; one was elevated to a baronetcy in 1611, another secured a peerage in 1797; and, finally, a third was rewarded with the earldom of Kimberley in 1866. (The barons Wodehouse support their coat of arms with two 'woodwoses'.) The characters in Wodehouse's fiction, for whom 'Earls are hot stuff', display a lively interest in the nuances of noble rank:

'Is an Earl the same as a Duke?'
  'Not quite. Dukes are a bit higher up.'
  'Is it the same as a Viscount?'
  'No. Viscounts are a bit lower down. We Earls rather sneer at Viscounts. One is pretty haughty with them, poor devils.'

Members of the cadet branch of the family to which his father Ernest Wodehouse belonged typically served in the Victorian army and navy, or in the colonial and diplomatic services. Ernest's father, Colonel Philip Wodehouse, fought at Waterloo. Wodehouse himself was familiar with his lineage; he referred knowingly to 'the manly spirit of the Wodehouses (descended from the sister of Anne Boleyn)'. In *Uncle Fred in the Springtime*, Lord Ickenham, one of the many eccentric peers who flit through the pages of Wodehouse, rebukes his nephew Pongo Twistleton for wanting to run away from a tricky situation:

Clear out? That is no way for a member of a proud family to talk. Did Twistletons clear out at Agincourt and Crécy? At Malplaquet and Blenheim? When the Old Guard made their last desperate charge up the blood-soaked slopes of Waterloo, do you suppose that Wellington, glancing over his shoulder, saw a Twistleton sneaking off with an air of ill-assumed carelessness in the direction of Brussels? We Twistletons do not clear out, my boy. We stick around, generally long after we have outstayed our welcome.

The real Waterloo veteran, Colonel Philip Wodehouse, married late, aged forty-four, in 1832, an heiress named Lydia Lea from a wealthy Birmingham family. They had three daughters and six sons, including Henry Ernest, born on 14 July 1845. When Colonel Wodehouse died in December the following year, his widow took her large Victorian family to live at Ham Hill, in Powick, just outside the county town of Worcester. It was here, deep in the traditional English countryside, that Wodehouse's father grew up. After schooling at Repton, he became a colonial civil servant and in 1867 was posted to Hong Kong as a magistrate, where he served until his return in 1895.

An undemonstrative, tall, good-natured man, Ernest – borrowing from George Bernard Shaw – humorously liked to describe the cadet branch of his family as 'downstarts'. Ernest was an indulgent father and a keen walker. From him Wodehouse inherited both his imposing physique and his apparently easygoing nature. Ernest's influence as a late-Victorian imperialist is important; it is from his father's society that Wodehouse would have picked up the 'Bohea', 'purdah', 'tofah', 'boodle' and 'Oolong' that litter his mature comic writing. To be a judge in Victorian Hong Kong was to serve the imperial ideal at one of its nerve centres. As the historian David Cannadine has shown, British colonial servants were 'concerned to replicate the layered, ordered, hierarchical society they believed they had left behind at home'. The 'widespread eagerness for honours and hereditary distinctions' that typified these expatriates excluded any doubts or anxieties about the imperial project, and it was from his family that the young Wodehouse absorbed his amused fascination with the infinite nuances of class. Ernest was also supremely English in his quiet nonchalance towards his professional duties. Somewhere in his oriental career he had acquired the ability to nap at will, a habit he practised long into his retirement.

Wodehouse's mother was a more formidable proposition, a strong-willed matriarch whose imperious traits can be detected in many of Wodehouse's fictional women, and perhaps in his own stubborn determination to write. Tall and angular, Eleanor Deane, known as 'Lil', came from a family that could trace itself back as far as, if not further than, the Wodehouses, one that displayed a similar riot of ancestry and an equal rootedness in the 'county' life of England. Her father, the Revd John Bathurst Deane, absentee vicar of the parish of St Helen's, Bishopsgate, in London, lived in a Regency house in Bath and devoted his energies to genealogy, demonstrating that the Deanes were descended from Roberto de Dena, a Norman noble at the court of Edward the Confessor, and numbered among their forebears an Archbishop of Canterbury in the sixteenth century. In a tight situation, Bertie Wooster always alludes to his heritage:

One doesn't want to make a song and dance about one's ancient lineage, of course, but after all the Woosters did come over with the Conqueror and were extremely pally with him: and a fat lot of good it is coming over with Conquerors, if you're simply going to wind up by being given the elbow by Aberdeen terriers.

The Deanes were a Victorian family with mildly bohemian inclinations. Eleanor, the tenth of thirteen children, exploited family connections to visit her brother Walter in Hong Kong with the so-called 'fishing fleet' in search of a husband, promptly snagged Ernest and married him in 1877, becoming known to her immediate family as 'Shanghai Lil'. Before her marriage, Eleanor had shown some talent as an artist; her rebellious younger sister Emmeline (Nym) was a Paris-trained painter who exhibited seven times at the Royal Academy and whose portrait of Cardinal Newman, a distant uncle on her mother's side, is still in the collection of the National Portrait Gallery; her sister Mary had a dozen volumes of poetry and romantic fiction to her name, and another Deane uncle published a book on whist.

Wodehouse was never close to his mother, whom even her family referred to as 'the Memsahib' for her peremptory manner and forbidding personality. In later life he saw her rarely, and then preferably with his brother Armine along for moral support. He used to say that she was 'guvvy', and hard on her servants. Wodehouse's portrait of a mother blighting the independence of a young Englishman at the opening of his novel *Jill the Reckless*, a chapter entitled 'The Family Curse', seems to be drawn as much from life as from imagination. His memoirs are noticeably reticent about his feelings towards Eleanor, but the fact that, in the ten years of her widowhood, he visited her only once has its own eloquence.

Once married, Ernest and Eleanor Wodehouse were typical Victorians of their class and generation. They settled down to raise a family of eccentrically named sons – Philip Peveril ('Pev') in 1877; Ernest Armine in 1879, born after twins lost in childbirth; Plum himself; and finally Richard Lancelot Deane ('Dick'), in 1892 – but then, coerced by the discipline of colonial service overseas, they abdicated from parental involvement. From the day he was born, Wodehouse's parents were at best remote, at worst utterly foreign. There are extraordinarily few mothers and fathers in his writing. Parents are usually portrayed as cold and aloof, and their attitude towards children, in his fiction, is generally stern, not loving. The lack of feeling is mutual. When Wodehouse writes, of Lord Emsworth's son, that 'The last thing in the world which the Hon. Freddie wanted was to see his parent', the gulf of emotion reflects his own experience.

In 1881, having given birth to baby Plum unexpectedly early at a sister's house in Guildford, Eleanor took her new child to join his brothers in Hong Kong where, according to custom, he was raised by a Chinese nursemaid. In 1883, when Wodehouse was still an infant, Ernest and Eleanor came home on leave, and shipped him and his two older brothers to Bath. They were placed in the care of a Miss Roper, a stickler for order and cleanliness who finds her fictional counterpart in the Nanny Wilks of Wodehouse's story 'Portrait of a Disciplinarian', of whom Wodehouse writes: 'it is a moot point whether a man of sensibility can ever be entirely at his ease in the presence of a woman who has frequently spanked him with the flat side of a hairbrush.'

Once in the care of Nanny Roper, the Wodehouse boys did not see either Ernest or Eleanor again for three years. Placed under a kind of house arrest in the nursery, they became middle-class colonial internees, typical of imperial Britain at the end of the nineteenth century. In total, Wodehouse saw his parents for barely six months between the ages of three and fifteen, which is by any standards a shattering emotional deprivation. In old age, he remembered: 'We looked upon mother . . . [as] a stranger.' At the time, it was considered normal to orphan one's children in this way. Today, it seems irresponsible, even heartless. The psychological impact of this separation on the future writer lies at the heart of his adult personality.

It is at this point that many commentators have drawn parallels between the respective childhoods of Wodehouse and Kipling. Despite the age difference (Kipling was sixteen years older), there are some superficial similarities. Both grew up in late-Victorian England; like many middle-class children, both had parents away in the East; both were raised by strangers; and both developed precocious storytelling powers. But Wodehouse seems to have been much better adjusted towards, and far more successful at coping internally with, quasi-orphan distress, perhaps because he simply did not feel it, or did not allow himself to.

Most writers draw inspiration from some inner hurt. Compared with psychologically wounded men like Kipling, 'Saki' (H. H. Munro), Somerset Maugham or George Orwell, whose childhoods have something in common with his, Wodehouse was fortunate in having the damage inflicted on him in childhood counterbalanced by his exceptional good nature, and the light, personal sweetness that all those who knew him comment on. His childhood made him solitary, but his genius – the word is not too strong – made the solitude bearable and transformed its fantasies into high comedy. It was always in his nature to explore the dimensions of absurdity. That was all part of a defensive strategy, too. Wodehouse took his writing very seriously, but the irony of his work is that, like all comedy, it rebuffs serious analysis. In his adult life, he never allowed emotional pain to get too close, and his family went to extraordinary lengths to insulate him from emotional distress. There is a revealing moment, during his wartime imprisonment, when he confessed to his diary that, threatened by unbearable thoughts, 'one has deliberately to school oneself to think of something else quick'. In considering 'the psychology of the individual', Jeeves's watchword, Wodehouse's adoption of an idealized picture of his parents is a textbook case of what psychoanalysts call 'splitting'. Looking back in old age, he said, 'my father was very indulgent to us boys, my mother less so . . . With my father . . . I was always on very good terms, though never in any sense very close.' Such admissions are rare. Wodehouse was a master of evasion. During his adult life he also perfected the art of escape, in constant travel. A Freudian would say that this was the fulfil-ment of a childhood wish to escape the family, but Wodehouse's published and unpublished writings give nothing away. In his memoirs he continued, as Bertie Wooster puts it, to 'wear the mask':

The three essentials for an autobiography are that its compiler shall have had an eccentric father, a miserable misunderstood childhood and a hell of a time at his public school . . . I enjoyed none of these advantages. My father was as normal as rice pudding. My childhood went like a breeze from start to finish, with everybody I met understanding me perfectly, while as for my schooldays at Dulwich they were just six years of unbroken bliss.

But it was a solitary experience, cut off from emotion, and it taught him to withdraw, instinctively to cultivate an unflappable detachment, to be satisfied with his own company and to find comfort in a parallel, imaginative world. He always said he wanted to be a writer. The completeness of his fantasy world reflects the intense and lonely bleak-ness of the inner world created by his early life.

So Wodehouse, the perfect Englishman, developed a preference for keeping the lid on things. He also acquired the habit, which stayed with him for the rest of his life, of looking on the bright side of life, and of accepting philosophically whatever fate (which features throughout his work) should hand out. With the wisdom and the vocabulary of hind-sight we should say that, when he observed 'I can't remember ever having been unhappy in those days', he was in denial, a state of mind he sustained throughout his life. In 1924 he wrote:

As a writer of light fiction, I have always . . . been handicapped by the fact that my disposition was cheerful, my heart intact, and my life unsoured. Handicapped, I say, because the public likes to feel that a writer of farcical stories is piquantly miserable in his private life, and that, if he turns out anything amusing, he does it simply in order to obtain relief from the almost insupportable weight of an existence which he has long since realised to be a wash-out.

Innate or cultivated it is impossible to determine, but this skill at keeping distant from the worst that life could throw at him would stand him in good stead, and inspired the insouciant mood of his writing.

The child psychotherapist Adam Phillips has commented, 'The question [for Wodehouse] would be, as it is for any abandoned child, what is it about me that is so unbearable my parents don't want to be with me? Why are other people required to look after me?' Psychotherapists would identify at least three likely responses to the infant experience of parental absence. In the first place, the boy Wodehouse would have been made acutely attentive to the adult world, learning to listen intently to the conversations that were going on over his head. He would have been preoccupied by the circumstances that had separated him from his parents and he would have wanted to improvise a narrative to account for an inexplicable absence. In later life, Wodehouse developed an addiction to plots and stories of all kinds. Second, he would have grown up to dread instability and to crave the continuity of a boring life and the solace of daily rituals. In his working life he adhered, whenever possible, to an iron routine. Third, deprived so early of his mother, he would have been wary of the opposite sex, preferring brotherly relations with men. Even a casual reading of his collected work reveals a consistent strain of circumspection (even misogyny) towards aunts, sweethearts, bluestockings and lady novelists. Describing William ('Bill') West's 'volcanic but steadfast' love for Alice Coker in *Bill the Conqueror*, he writes that 'here she was jabbing spikes into his head'. He comments, 'Women are like that', a refrain echoed in all his writings. 'Show me a delicately nurtured female,' says Bertie Wooster in *Stiff Upper Lip, Jeeves*, 'and I will show you a ruthless Napoleon of crime.' Vis-à-vis the women in Wodehouse's life, Phillips says that it would feel dangerous for him to begin to trust, or to form a close and loving relationship with, a woman. To the young Wodehouse, women would seem to be excessively powerful, and unbearably organizing. Phillips notes that 'organizing' in this context becomes 'a refusal to know them, a way of not listening to [the child's] needs and wishes. So, from a child's point of view, being over-organized equals being ignored.'

The irony is that, in the absence of parents, there was no shortage of women. On his mother's side, there were no fewer than eight aunts living in England, of whom Mary and Louisa would play an important role in Wodehouse's childhood. Mary, 'the scourge of my childhood', never married, quarrelled with almost all her family and inspired both Ukridge's fearsome Aunt Julia and Bertie Wooster's celebrated Aunt Agatha, the 'pest of Pont Street'. Wodehouse condensed his memory of the women responsible for his upbringing into a variety of unflattering descriptions: 'There's about five-foot-nine of Aunt Agatha, topped off with a beaky nose, an eagle eye and lots of grey hair, and the general effect is pretty formidable.' This is a consistent picture. Even on her first appearance, Aunt Agatha 'has an eye like a man-eating fish, and she has got moral suasion down to a fine point'. By contrast, the eldest Deane daughter, Aunt Louisa, known as 'Looly', Wodehouse's favourite, was a kind of proxy-mother who, in her turn, suggested some aspects of Bertie's Aunt Dahlia, described as 'a large, genial soul, the sort you see in dozens on the hunting field'. Among the Wodehouse uncles, there were four clergymen (uncles Philip, Frederick, Edward and Henry) scattered across the south and west of England from Bratton Fleming in Devon to Hanley Castle in Worcestershire, villages whose names recall the ecclesiastical livings affectionately referred to in 'The Great Sermon Handicap' and one of his best stories, 'Anselm Gets His Chance'. There are moments, even in his most inspired comic writing, when Wodehouse, who had absorbed the rituals of the rural English parish into his consciousness, will happily digress into a fictional evocation of these clergified years:

There's something about evening service in a country church that makes a fellow feel drowsy and peaceful. Sort of end-of-a-perfect-day feeling . . . They had left the door open, and the air was full of a mixed scent of trees and honeysuckle and mildew and villagers' Sunday clothes . . . The last rays of the setting sun shone through the stained-glass windows, birds were twittering in the trees, the women's dresses crackled gently in the stillness. Peaceful. That's what I'm driving at. I felt peaceful.

In 1886, when he was just five, Wodehouse's infant world of aunts and clergymen was temporarily interrupted by his first significant encounter with his parents, who returned home for a few weeks' leave. Ernest had been awarded a CMG (Companion of the Order of St Michael and St George) for his work on the Chinese pavilion in the Colonial and Indian Exhibition. Family legend holds that the regime of Miss Roper, the nanny, reached a stormy end when Ernest and his boys came back from a country ramble, muddy and dishevelled, an outrage that prompted her instant resignation. The Wodehouse brothers had outgrown their nanny, and it was time for them to be packed off to boarding school. Elmhurst School (as it is today) in Croydon was one of many late-Victorian establishments 'for Indian children' (meaning those with parents abroad in the East), catering for the families of colonial civil servants. It was a new school with just six pupils, run by two spinster sisters, Clarissa and Florence Prince (Cissie and Florrie), on behalf of their father, a retired 'railway director' in his seventies. It was housed in The Chalet, 43 St Peter's Road, a cramped, ugly, Swiss-style suburban residence on the slopes of south-west Croydon. In those days, Croydon was on the edge of rolling Surrey countryside. Food was scarce and Wodehouse later recalled getting into trouble for stealing a turnip from a nearby field. Among many family tales of the Prince sisters' regime, there are stories of a boiled egg shared six ways by the pupils and a bag of biscuits, intended for the local road-sweeper, guiltily consumed by Wodehouse and his brothers. Memories of Victorian Croydon inspired Wodehouse's rendering of Uncle Fred's reminiscences of 'Mitching Hill' in the preamble to his afternoon in the suburbs in 'Uncle Fred Flits By': 'It is many years since the meadows where I sported as a boy were sold and cut up into building lots. But when I was a boy Mitching Hill was open country . . . I have long felt a sentimental urge to see what the hell the old place looks like now. Perfectly foul, I expect.'

Life in The Chalet was part school, part foster-home in which the Prince sisters and their charges (three Wodehouse boys, two Atkinsons and one other) lived cheek by jowl. On one occasion the young Wodehouse, hiding behind a sofa, like a character in one of his stories, was forced to eavesdrop on an ardent proposal of marriage to Miss Florrie from a Mr George Hardie Scott, who not only secured her hand but also the headmastership of the school. The boys were allowed few treats. The only surviving letter home from this time, from Armine to his parents, ends with a sad little postscript ('Pev has written to father. I am so sorry he is not coming home yet') and describes a pre-Christmas outing to Barnum's Circus at Olympia.

From 1886, the classic late-Victorian routine of long boarding-school terms interrupted by school holidays spent in the company of aunts ('formidable Victorian women') became an established part of Wodehouse's life. He never forgot counting the days until 'the great

event of the year', the two idyllic weeks in the summer when the boys
would stay at their grandmother's house in Powick, Worcestershire, a
part of England to which the adult Wodehouse would return for isolated
bursts of writing. So it was that, from boyhood, Wodehouse's solitary
habits, and reticent self-suffiency, became a way of life. At Croydon,
there was the discipline of the school to escape; in the holidays there
was the benign neglect of the adult world. 'We were left very much to
ourselves at Ham Hill,' he recalled. 'Once a day we were taken in to
see our grandmother – a wizened lady who looked just like a monkey.'
When the Wodehouse boys were not at Ham Hill, they would be
dispatched to stay with Uncle Philip in the West Country, or with
Uncle Edward and their cricket-loving cousins at Hanley Castle.

Even at that age Wodehouse's future path was clear. 'I had always
wanted to be a writer,' he wrote in his memoirs, *Over Seventy*. 'I started
turning out the stuff at the age of five.' He was also a precocious reader,
steeped in late-Victorian classics such as F. Anstey's *Vice Versa*, Stevenson's
Treasure Island and Richard Jefferies' *Bevis: The Story of a Boy*, and
devoured Pope's translation of the *Iliad* at the age of six. Like many
solitary children, he filled the void by making up his own poems and
stories. Two examples can be traced to his early years. The first, 'a bit
of poertory I made up', is said to have been written when he was just
five:

> O ah, that soryful day
> when on the battel
> field the pets did
> lay in sorryful
> disgrace.
> With red blud
> streaming past
> there life was
> pasing fast
> And in the
> camp there lay
> Thousands of dead
> men.
>
>   P. G. Wodehouse

The second, a short story, with cadences reminiscent of the Book of Common Prayer and the Authorized Version, whose sentences he would have heard in church every Sunday, survives from the age of seven:

About five years ago in a wood there was a Thrush. who built her nest in a Poplar tree. and sang so beautifully that all the worms came up from their holes and the ants laid down their burdens. and the crickets stopped their mirth. and moths settled all in a row to hear her. she sang a song as if she were in heaven – going up higher and higher as she sang.
at last the song was done and the bird came down panting.
Thank you said all the creatures. Now my story is ended. Pelham G. Wodehouse

In 1887 Wodehouse's maternal grandfather, John Bathurst Deane, died in his ninetieth year. His widow moved with her unmarried daughters – Louisa, Mary, Anne and Emmeline – down the Bath road to the little village of Box where they took Cheney Court, a fine old Elizabethan country house with a shady driveway, rolling grounds, stables, rose gardens and good views of the surrounding Wiltshire countryside. Memories of Cheney Court and its auntly ménage certainly inspired one of Wodehouse's best novels, *The Mating Season*. Bertie Wooster goes to stay with young Esmond Haddock at Deverill Hall, King's Deverill, and finds himself in the company of 'a surging sea' of no fewer than five aunts.

'*Five?*'
   'Yes, sir. The Misses Charlotte, Emmeline, Harriet and Myrtle Deverill . . .'
   On the cue 'five aunts' I had given at the knees a trifle, for the thought of being confronted with such a solid gaggle of aunts, even if those of another, was an unnerving one.

Cheney Court, whose immutable social geography (upstairs, downstairs, and green baize door) the young Wodehouse never forgot, had a cavernous and impressive Tudor domesticity. It was during the holidays at Cheney Court that Wodehouse now entered what he described as 'the knickerbocker age', the years in which he would be passed from aunt to aunt. In his seventies, recalling these solitary, parentless years, Wodehouse often characterized himself as a 'dumb brick', a typically self-deprecating formula. The surviving photographs show a chunky, precocious-looking and well-scrubbed lad with a clear, wide-apart gaze and the beginnings of the square, determined jaw that cartoonists would later single out as a key to the mature man. It is not difficult, looking at these photographs, to imagine some imperious aunt, standing behind the camera, ordering the boy to compose himself.

In addition to the aunts, the clergymen and the nautical uncles, there was one other, more approachable, kind of adult to contend with: the family servant. The largest occupational group among nineteenth-century women in England was the servant class. In 1891 there were nearly one and a half million women of all ages 'in service', the foot-soldiers of a domestic army led by an officer corps of butlers. The young Wodehouse and his brothers lived, as he put it, 'on the fringe of the butler belt'. He became intimately familiar with the below-stairs life of the country houses to which, in the holidays, he would be taken by one of his clergyman uncles or their wives. This was a rite of passage he would remember in old age: 'There always came a moment when my hostess, smiling one of those painful smiles, suggested that it would be nice for [me] to go and have tea in the servants' hall.' In the company of footmen and chambermaids, the 'dumb brick' would become liberated. 'In their society,' wrote Wodehouse, 'I forgot to be shy and kidded back and forth with the best of them.'

In 1889, after three years at Croydon, 'Pev', the eldest Wodehouse boy, was found to have a weak chest, for which the Victorian remedy was always sea air. Their parents decided to send the Wodehouse brothers to Elizabeth College, in Guernsey in the Channel Islands. 'Why Armine and I had to go too I can't imagine,' Wodehouse remarked to David Jasen, his first biographer, 'but my parents seemed to like these package deals.' Wodehouse says he was content at Elizabeth College, remembering that 'we were allowed to roam where we liked . . . [and] life was very pleasant', but has left few other recollections of his two pre-adolescent years at the College, an imposing early Victorian establishment overlooking St Peter Port.

Nothing is known of Wodehouse's friends at Elizabeth College. With Peveril and Armine alongside him in the school, he had all the limited companionship he required. 'Brotherly love' is a recurrent theme in his later comedies of ecclesiastical life, but despite these childhood years spent in his brothers' company, there was no real closeness, and their paths soon diverged. As a young man Peveril grew up to be an Edwardian boulevardier who later followed his father out East and joined the Hong Kong police, lost an eye to an insect bite, and settled into middle-aged expatriate comfort. With his glass eye and Chinese butler, whose brass buttons bore the Wodehouse crest, he was the very model of the colonial civil servant: pompous, dull and exceedingly conservative.

If Wodehouse expressed any complex fraternal love it was towards Ernest Armine, two years his senior and in some conventional ways quite as gifted. Armine is a name that occurs in Norfolk families from the seventeenth century on. Wodehouse's second brother was an outstanding scholar who, at Oxford, won the Newdigate Prize for poetry and took a double first in Mods and Greats. Tall and self-possessed, he was an excellent sportsman, a good piano player and an accomplished poet, with a gift for light verse. After Oxford, he followed the family tradition and went out East, to India, where he became a professor at Deccan College in Poona. There he was attracted to theosophy and went to Annie Besant's college, serving briefly as a tutor to Krishnamurti, the young messiah of the theosophical movement. After service in the Scots Guards during the First World War, he published *On Leave*, a volume of war poetry, married, went back to India and eventually retired to England in 1935. Lazy, fat, chatty and highly intelligent, he died in 1936 from the effects of a lifetime of heavy smoking. His relationship with his remarkable younger brother was problematic, but their shared childhood was always a bond. After his death Wodehouse wrote to his widow, Nella: 'I always felt so near to poor Armine and looked up to him so enormously.' He added with an instinctive sweetness that 'he and I had always seemed so particularly close to one another', but it was a closeness that involved absence. 'Ours was one of those attachments which are not dependent on close contact. I always felt that we could pick up the thread even after not seeing each other for years.'

Dick, the baby of the quartet, and his mother's favourite, hardly featured in Wodehouse's life. His attitude to his baby brother is not known, but perhaps something can be discerned in his fictional portraits of the small boys – Oswald Glossop, Edwin the boy scout, Bonzo Travers, or Thomas ('young Thos.') Gregson – who later torment Bertie Wooster. After school, Dick went out to India and then China, where he worked for the insurance arm of the Hongkong and Shanghai Bank. He died of leukaemia, aged 48, in May 1940, just as his elder brother was caught up in the fall of France.

Once he turned ten, it was customary for the Victorian middle-class boy to face up to his future. Wodehouse was typical of his class and his generation in being groomed for the services. In 1892 he was sent to a naval preparatory school at Malvern House, in Kearsney, just outside Dover. The school specialized in getting boys into the Royal Naval College in Dartmouth, and was a very bad choice for a dreamy, impractical boy who loved reading. The regime was harsh and the curriculum was geared to the needs of future midshipmen and commodores. Wodehouse escaped, as he did throughout his life, by taking himself off on long, solitary walks. Leaving aside his burgeoning literary disposition, it was also increasingly obvious that his poor eyesight would disqualify him from any active service involving the speedy interpretation of distant signals so essential to the career of a Victorian naval officer. Wodehouse took his revenge on Malvern House by sending Bertie Wooster to preparatory school there under the fearsome tutelage of the Revd Aubrey Upjohn, a man with 'a soup-strainer moustache and a face like a cassowary'.

In 1893 Wodehouse's dislike for Malvern House was intensified by the knowledge that Armine was now happily established at Dulwich College. Apparently their father, Ernest, had glimpsed this ancient foundation from a suburban train during one of his rare visits to London and, already on the lookout for a good public school within his means at which to educate the academically precocious Armine, promptly enrolled the boy there. Wodehouse, who visited his brother at Dulwich during one bleak vacation, fell for its tranquil grounds and ordered serenity. After his rootless, solitary childhood, the attractions of somewhere settled and well run, with plenty of other boys for companionship, were obvious. When Wodehouse set his mind on something, he generally got it. Now he badgered Ernest for a transfer. In the spring of 1894, he set off for Dulwich. The second formative phase of his early life was about to begin.

2. 'The Boy, What Will He Become?'
(1894–1900)

'Are you the Bully, the Pride of the School, or the Boy who is Led Astray and takes to Drink in Chapter Sixteen?' (*Mike*)

Wodehouse entered Dulwich College on 2 May 1894. He was twelve-and-a-half years old, and both his parents were still absent in Hong Kong. The school ledger lists the Revd E. H. Sweet-Escott, housemaster of Ivyholme, as his 'parent or guardian'. So, from the first, the school gave him the home he had missed as a child. In one sense, he would remain a Dulwich boy for the rest of his life. He idealized his 'six years of unbroken bliss' in all his recollections, and told his best friend there that 'the years between 1896 and 1900 seem like Heaven'.

Dulwich was a countrified late-Victorian London suburb, just five miles from Piccadilly Circus, with even a glimpse of St Paul's, and connected to the capital by the railway. The college, some sixty-five acres of playing fields, stately avenues of chestnut trees and red-brick Italianate buildings, was in the leafy part of West Dulwich that Wodehouse would pastoralize in his fiction as 'Valley Fields'. In Wodehouse's imaginative landscape, next to the Elysium of Blandings Castle, Valley Fields was *rus in urbe*, a 'fragrant oasis' amid the stench, noise and threatening chaos of London life. He never lost his love of the suburbs; 'Valley Fields' was always near the front of his mind. Writing at the very end of his life, in the preface to the 1972 edition of *Sam the Sudden*, one of his favourite books, Wodehouse expressed the hope that 'in the thirty-three years since I have seen it Valley Fields has not ceased to be a fragrant backwater'. Map the world of Wodehouse through such published comments, and you find his Alma Mater at the heart of a romanticized suburban paradise.

This south London veneer, overlaid on the sturdy English oak of Wodehouse's family background, is integral to an understanding of his work and his character. South London is a place of genteel, sorrowful aspiration, a place of servants and landladies. It is both of the metropolis and not of it. The south London of Herne Hill, Brixton, Clapham and Dulwich, and even Wimbledon, is inferior to the London of Knightsbridge and Mayfair, as Ukridge is inferior socially to Bertie Wooster. At the same time, 'Valley Fields' connects the Wodehouse of the shires to a mass audience of clerks, insurance salesmen and minor civil servants. In 'Valley Fields', country houses become semi-detached villas like 'stucco Siamese twins'. Here, rhododendrons become laurels; broad acres become 'apologetic flower beds with evergreens', and even the fences that separate Mon Repos from San Rafael become a hideous parody of the honest English five-barred gate. Wodehouse, the child of empire who, until he found Dulwich, felt cast out of the English paradise his family had inhabited for centuries, is secure here. Where others might sneer at the suburbs, to the end of his life Wodehouse was always particularly at home in places that to others would have seemed nondescript, bland and incorrigibly suburban. Here he could connect to another invented version of the English past.

Established in 1619, Dulwich College was a Jacobean foundation, the work of Shakespeare's contemporary, the actor-manager Edward Alleyn. In 1857, it had become divided by Victorian public school reform into the Upper School (Dulwich College) and the Lower School (Alleyn's). This unusual educational pedigree set it apart from what it perceived as the common run of London schools. Wodehouse expressed the 'Alleynian' sensibility in his first novel, *The Pothunters*: 'The most deadly error mortal man can make, with the exception of calling a school a college, is to call a college a school.' Dulwich was both a London day school and a boarding school, with Sir Charles Barry's magnificent new palazzo (1866–70) imparting that air of dynamic respectability to which it aspired. Like its competitors on the playing field, Tonbridge, Charterhouse and Sherborne, Dulwich was neither Eton nor Winchester, any more than the London suburb in which it was situated would ever be a provincial market town, but it offered an excellent education for the sons of the imperial civil servant. Speaking of Dulwich, Wodehouse himself never lost the English public schoolboy's instinctive grasp of such class distinctions. 'It was', he said, towards the end of his life, 'what you would call a middle-class school. We were the sons of reasonably solvent but certainly not wealthy parents, and all had to earn our living later on. Compared with Eton, Dulwich would be something like an American state university compared with Harvard or Princeton. Bertie Wooster's parents would never have sent him to

Dulwich, but Ukridge could very well have been there.' Dulwich may
have been petit-bourgeois and suburban; it was also literary and artistic,
with a higher proportion of writers than most public schools, including
the best-selling writer Dennis Wheatley, who hated the place and was
expelled; Raymond Chandler, who was there shortly after Wodehouse;
C. S. Forester, author of the Hornblower stories; and, much later, the
novelists Michael Ondaatje and Graham Swift.

Wodehouse began his Dulwich career as a day-boy, lodging for that
first summer term of 1894 with an assistant master whose home was
in East Dulwich. He might have been short-sighted and diffident, but
he was big for his age. Moreover, he was following in Armine's footsteps, and would never quite throw off the sense that his older brother
was watching over his conduct 'like a policeman'. Dulwich boarders
looked down on day-boys, but once the autumn term of 1894 began,
Wodehouse was installed in Ivyholme, one of four boarding houses.
Now, at last, he achieved that place in the community he craved and
the stability that had been so lacking in his childhood. Being a boarder,
he recalled, offered much more opportunity for making friends, and
made his experience of school central to his imagination. The stories
he published after leaving Dulwich are rich in affectionately observed
detail of everyday public school life, and according to his best friend
and contemporary, William Townend, give a faithful picture of his time
there: 'elderly men who were at Dulwich between the years 1895 and
1901 will recognise and appreciate Plum's masterly delineation of the
life we lived so long ago.' To those schoolfellows, of course, he would
have been, in the terminology of the school, not 'Plum', but 'Wodehouse
minor'. In due course, he acquired another nickname, 'Podge', derived
from his initials, and perhaps because he was a chubby teenager. 'I was
pretty friendly with everybody,' he said later, 'but I had no intimate
friends.'

Ivyholme was a mixture of surrogate family, prison camp and adolescent mayhem, and provided the base around which the school routine
(morning lessons with a break at a quarter to eleven, afternoon school
from two to four, followed by games and two hours of evening prep)
was organized. Beyond the door separating the private house from the
boys' side lived the housemaster, his family and servants. For a new boy
like Wodehouse, the boys' domain consisted of the house dining room,
the senior and junior day-rooms, and the dormitories, which generally

slept five to twenty in narrow iron bedsteads with bright red institutional
blankets. These were formative experiences. In 'The Bishop's Move', when
an eminent bishop returns to his Alma Mater as a distinguished old boy,
he begins to feel like a schoolboy again and, after a glass of Mulliner's
wonderful tonic, Buck-U-Uppo, becomes 'conscious of an extraordinary
feeling of good cheer . . . He felt a youngish and rather rowdy fifteen'
– the emotional age of Wodehouse's fictional young men.

Within the raucous boarding house eco-system, the study was the
senior boy's sanctuary, with a fireplace for toasting bread or muffins, a
kettle for brewing tea or cocoa, and perhaps a greasy pan for fry-ups.
Each study expressed its owner's personality. The study-dweller might
also pass his leisure time reading magazines like the *Boy's Own Paper* or
the *Captain*, and his books would be boys' adventure stories by writers
like G. A. Henty, H. Rider Haggard and Arthur Conan Doyle. The
highlight of Wodehouse's month was the arrival at the West Dulwich
station bookstall of the latest edition of the *Strand*, with the new Conan
Doyle serial.

It was a male world. There were no girls, apart from the housemaids
or, if the housemaster was married with children, his daughters. Girls
rarely appear in Wodehouse's early fiction, and then usually as an unfath-
omable embarrassment. Without the civilizing influence of women, the
extracurricular life of the public schoolboy tended to revolve around
either the authorized rough-and-tumble of the sports field, or the illegal
delights of 'breaking out' after ten o'clock house lock-up, by way of
drainpipes and open windows. In *The White Feather*, the boys break out
to play billiards or smoke Turkish cigarettes, while in *Mike*, the eponymous hero expresses his disaffection by sneaking downstairs to listen to
his housemaster's gramophone in the small hours. The incipient anarchy
of this society was channelled into organized games, and, when sports
failed, would be regulated by the house prefects, who had the power
to cane miscreants with a swagger-stick, a process known as 'touching
up'.

Sports involved all kinds of physical exercise from fives and cross-
country running to boxing and cricket. Wodehouse was an exceptional
games player, proud of his prowess on the field, who ended his Dulwich
career in both the 1st XV (rugby football) and the 1st XI (cricket). He
was also a keen boxer, though his poor, and deteriorating, eyesight made
him vulnerable. Wodehouse's passion for sport, which lingered long after

school, offers a window onto the inner life of a man for whom emotions were always dangerous. Sport was where he found uninhibited self-expression. Sport was an acceptable, sublimated kind of body contact. In sport, Wodehouse could have physical relationships with other boys but in a pursuit that was not sex. In a childhood starved of love, sport became his version of intimacy. Sport was one love; Dulwich College was another. The two were always linked in his mind. If there was one theme, apart from writing, that always engaged his passionate interest throughout his life, it was the performance of his school team. His first appearance in print was an article in 1894 entitled 'Junior Cup Matches'.

Wodehouse continued to attend first team matches, habitually clad in grey plus fours, a grey overcoat and a grey felt cap, well into middle age. In 1938, aged fifty-seven, he rewarded the unbeaten cricket XI with a dinner in the West End and a show at the Palladium. Throughout the 1930s, he corresponded with the Dulwich and England cricketer S. C. 'Billy' Griffith, taking a deep personal interest in his career, sending him money and copies of his books, and on one occasion inviting him to dinner at the Savoy Grill. In 1946, after spending seven dreadful years in Nazi-occupied Europe, he wrote to another friend, 'Isn't it odd, when one ought to be worrying about the state of the world and one's troubles generally, that the only thing I can think of nowadays is that Dulwich looks like winning all its school matches and surpassing the 1909 record.' Wodehouse's identification with this peculiar society would remain wholehearted. In a famous essay, George Orwell claimed that Wodehouse was '"fixated" on his old school'. Wodehouse protested at Orwell's analysis, but elsewhere frankly acknowledged he was 'a bad case of arrested mental development . . . Mentally, I seem not to have progressed a step since I was eighteen.'

In common with most clever and ambitious boys of his time, Wodehouse joined the college on 'the Classical side', and in later life he believed that this was 'the best form of education I could have had as a writer'. Wodehouse's school career was progressive instruction in the classical greats, from Aeschylus to Thucydides (also known, in public school slang, as 'Thicksides'). Throughout his career, Wodehouse affected a characteristic insouciance towards well-meaning attempts to find parallels between his works and the classics. In 1969 a young Oxford classicist wrote to ask whether he was conscious of having been influenced by Plautus or Terence (there is a similarity between a passage in Terence's

Heauton Timorumenos ('The Self-Tormentor') and one in *The Luck of the Bodkins*). Wodehouse replied:

There certainly is a close resemblance between the two passages, and it can only be explained by a similarity of thought between Plautus and me, for though in my time at Dulwich we read a great many authors, for some reason neither Plautus nor Terence came my way. Why would this be? Because P and T were supposed to be rather low stuff? . . . But we read Aristophanes, who was just as slangy as either of them.

Wodehouse always had a heavy investment in normality and self-sufficiency, and he was the kind of boy who was rarely without a book. Allusions in the school stories he published as a young man suggest that his adolescent library included Browning's and Tennyson's poetry, some Dickens, Kipling, Conan Doyle, Jerome K. Jerome, and the now-forgotten popular writers of late-Victorian England such as Barry Pain and James Payn. He also had a passion for Gilbert and Sullivan. Quotations from the Savoy operas permeate his early writing. The first stage show he ever saw, a production of *Patience* at the Crystal Palace, made him, he recalled, 'absolutely drunk with ecstasy. I thought it the finest thing that could possibly be done.' In the schoolroom, he studied English literature – from *The Knight's Tale* to *The Faerie Queene*. Dulwich records show that he was generally placed in the middle of most classes.

Three of his teachers were to have a profound influence on his development as a writer. William Beach Thomas, Wodehouse's form master in the Upper Fourth in 1897, was one of those rarities who make a successful transition from teaching to journalism. In 1898 Beach Thomas left Dulwich to join the *Globe*, the leading London evening paper of the day, eventually becoming a distinguished war correspondent, for which he was knighted. Wodehouse must have made an impression in class as well as in the *Alleynian* because in 1903 Beach Thomas would give his ex-pupil his first newspaper job. In the Upper School, the young Wodehouse also came under the influence of the Librarian, Philip Hope, who was the kind of schoolmaster who liked to make an entrance, striding about with a pile of books under his arm. Hope was an exceptional teacher whose lessons, one of his students remembered, were 'a new and exhilarating experience . . . Few could have rivalled him in teaching boys to compose in prose and verse, and we were often spellbound by the speed and brilliance with which he gave version after version of the ways in which a sentence or line could be turned in Greek or Latin.' Wodehouse learned to write Latin and Greek as rapidly as he wrote English. It is hard to overemphasize the importance of this training. Throughout his writing, he would always display a passion for grammar and a virtuoso assurance over the perils of the most sophisticated English sentence, for example the opening to *The Luck of the Bodkins*:

Into the face of the young man who sat on the terrace of the Hôtel Magnifique at Cannes there had crept a look of furtive shame, the shifty, hangdog look which announces that an Englishman is about to talk French.

    Beach Thomas and Hope were impressive men, but there was yet a higher and more daunting presence in the life of the schoolboy Wodehouse. Presiding over Dulwich's golden age was the imposing figure of Arthur Herman Gilkes, described by Wodehouse as 'one of the recognised great headmasters'. Gilkes had become Master of Dulwich in 1885, and the 1890s were his finest years. A big man with a white beard, who personified the Victorian idea of the Almighty, Gilkes once told a prefect that he would rather see him dead than hear him utter a profanity. Even when they are made to look ridiculous, headmasters in Wodehouse's fiction remain awe-inspiring – in the words of Mr Mulliner, 'a sort of blend of Epstein's Genesis and something out of the Book of Revelations'. Gilkes could be as thrilling as Philip Hope, and was an Olympian figure who could in one breath declare war on vulgar abbreviations like 'exam' or 'quad', before turning to declaim 'City of Dreadful Night' from Carlyle's *Sartor Resartus*. 'It was terrific,' Wodehouse remembered, 'but he also always scared the pants off me.'

    There was only one other person who frightened the young Wodehouse as much: his mother. In 1895, after he had been at the school for a year, his happy new life was overshadowed by his parents' return from Hong Kong. At the age of forty, Ernest Wodehouse was coming home; he and Eleanor took a house in Dulwich, at 62 Croxted Road. Armine and Plum became day-boys again, lodging with parents they had hardly seen in fifteen years and scarcely knew. Propinquity did not lend enchantment. Wodehouse discovered to his horror that Ernest suffered from constipation; there was a daily morning race to 'get to the only gents' lavatory in the house before Father, as he invariably occupied it for two hours'. Further to complicate the life of the two teenagers (Peveril was still boarding at Elizabeth College), Eleanor had recently given birth to a fourth child, Richard Lancelot Deane ('Dick'). There are few mothers or fathers in Wodehouse's fiction, but babies get even shorter shrift. Freddie Widgeon's attitude towards babies in *Young Men in Spats* is typical:

It would be paltering with the truth to say that he likes babies. They give him, he says, a sort of grey feeling. He resents their cold stare and the super-cilious and up-stage way in which they dribble out of the corner of their mouths on seeing him. Eyeing them, he is conscious of doubts as to whether Man can really be Nature's last word.

The move to Croxted Road, a shabby, insalubrious milieu, was not a success, and the experiment in family life was short-lived. Ernest was sweetly paternal, and Wodehouse was fond of him, but Eleanor was forbidding in her demeanour and strict in her attitude towards her dreamy, impractical adolescent son. In the summer of 1896, at the end of the school year, the Wodehouses, like many London middle-class parents oppressed by teenage children, began to explore the possibili-ties of living in the country, and eventually settled on The Old House, a pleasant, former Royalist, seventeenth-century house of russet sand-stone on the edge of Stableford, a scattered hamlet near Bridgnorth, in south-east Shropshire. If Dulwich was 'a fragrant oasis', Shropshire was, and would remain, a rural English paradise to which Wodehouse would return time after time in his fiction, conjuring 'visions of shady gardens and country sounds and smells, and the silver Severn gleaming in the distance through the trees'. Stableford is surrounded by several country houses whose spacious and well-appointed grounds would later inspire his vision of Blandings Castle. As he later wrote in the preface to his first Blandings novel, 'my happiest days as a boy were spent near Bridgnorth'. To the end of his days he always hankered after the English countryside.

Up to this point in his life – he was now fourteen – Wodehouse had been shuttled from aunt to grandparent to ecclesiastical uncle. The Old House, Stableford, gave him, for the first time, a place he could identify as home. But his lonely, dislocated childhood had left its mark.

At school, he wrote, 'troubles are things to be worried through alone', and at home he would never be close to his family. Dulwich gave him all he needed. 'The part played by relations in school life', he observed, 'is small but sufficient.' At home, according to his own account, 'I was completely inarticulate. Picture to yourself a Trappist monk with large feet and a tendency to upset tables with priceless china on them, and you will have the young Wodehouse.' Appropriately enough, it was at Stableford that he acquired his first dog, a mongrel named Bob. For the rest of his life, dogs of all kinds, especially Pekinese, would be the constant first objects of his affectionate heart.

The new regime at Stableford meant that he could become a Dulwich boarder again, and in the autumn of 1896 he moved to Elm Lawn, an attractive, red-brick, eighteenth-century house facing the main school playing fields. His new housemaster was T. G. Treadgold, a walrus-moustached disciplinarian. Under his direction, Wodehouse rapidly became one of those all-rounders, thriving in sports as much as school work, who stride across the pages of his school stories. In the surviving school photographs, he is tall and beefy-looking, often standing slightly apart, with an air of detachment that seems to reflect his attitude to life. Academically, he flourished now as never before. In the summer of 1897, he was awarded a senior classical scholarship (a valuable £10 per annum), entering the Classical Sixth (under Philip Hope) in 1898. He also began sharing a little attic study with William 'Bill' Townend, forming an important relationship that lasted until Townend's death in 1962, one that gives a unique insight into Wodehouse's life and work.

In 1899, as well as sharing a study, Wodehouse and Townend also slept in the same small dormitory at the top of Elm Lawn. Townend idolized Wodehouse as 'one of the most important boys in the school' who, for his part, played the role of mentor, counsellor and moral support to his rather hopeless friend. They were both born in 1881, but if they had anything in common, apart from a shared love of books and literature, it was spectacles: they were equally near-sighted. Wodehouse's relationship with Townend is highly revealing for its simplicity and innocence. Much of it was articulated on paper in a colossal correspondence which is fascinating, principally, for what it does *not* express, as well as for its portrait of Wodehouse's creative mind at work. Of the two, it is Townend who is more candid, but, in a rare confession,

Wodehouse once wrote, 'I pour out my heart to you, without stopping to weigh what I am writing', and he worried that these letters were 'infernally intimate . . . full of stuff that I wouldn't want anyone but you to see', but by the standards of most literary correspondence there are few sensations or revelations. 'Old Bill Townend' was important to Wodehouse, and he felt responsible for him. 'Bill' became part of the Wodehouse unconscious. The solid, likeable young men who have to make their way in the world of his later stories are often called 'Bill' (Bill Brewster, Bill Bailey, and Bill West in *Bill the Conqueror*). Then there's 'Bill' Shannon, in *The Old Reliable*, who is actually a girl. The offbeat love song for which Wodehouse is still remembered in the musical world is 'Bill' from *Show Boat*:

> He's just my Bill – an ordinary boy
> He has no gifts at all . . .
> It's surely not his brain
> That makes me thrill.
> I love him because he's – I don't know,
> Because he's just my Bill.

To the dispassionate observer, Townend does not cut an attractive figure. Tall, pale, undernourished and eventually quite deaf, he attached himself to Wodehouse, repaying his friend's money and literary counsel over the years with a dogged, slightly pathetic hero-worship. After Dulwich, with the contrarian obstinacy that would characterize his later life, Townend rejected the opportunity to go to Cambridge. He enrolled in a London art school, whence he tried, and failed, to have a career as a commercial artist of the kind that pop up throughout Wodehouse's stories. To help his friend, Wodehouse commissioned him to draw the (rather wooden) illustrations to his sixth novel, *The White Feather*, and went to elaborate lengths to involve him in his own early successes. Thereafter, Townend became an itinerant freelance writer, working on a lemon farm in California, knocking about the American West, and ending up in Vancouver, where he met Irene Ellam, known as 'Rene', whom he married in 1915. His first novel, *A Light for His Pipe*, was published in 1927. Throughout the 1930s he published a book a year, pursuing a career as an indigent literary man whose novels and short stories of sea-going adventure (*The Tramp*, *The Ship in the Swamp*) teetered on the brink of popularity but never found a public. In secret, Wodehouse supported Townend financially throughout these years, and in other ways too, with hundreds of little kindnesses. He confessed to his literary agent Paul Reynolds that 'I feel sort of responsible for him, as I egged him on to be a writer'. During Wodehouse's disgrace in the Second World War, and immediately after, Townend loyally stood up for his friend and attempted to play a role as his champion. He also kept up a correspondence with Raymond Chandler, occasionally quoting the two famous Alleynian writers to each other.

It is Townend who provides the first authentic picture of Wodehouse, the aspiring young writer, revealing the real clue to the basis of their friendship. 'We talked incessantly about books and writing,' he remembered. 'Plum's talk was exhilarating. I had never known such talk. Even at the age of seventeen he could discuss lucidly writers of whom I had never heard . . . And from the first time I met him, he had decided to write. He never swerved.' Townend also provides a tantalizing glimpse of Wodehouse's beginnings as a comic writer, remembering that his friend wrote 'a series of plays after the pattern of the Greek tragedies, outrageously funny, dealing with boys and masters'. Wodehouse was never funny to meet, but Townend also has a memory of a house photograph (prefects on chairs, junior boys cross-legged on the ground) in which the participants were reduced to helpless laughter by a low-voiced comment from Wodehouse at the moment the photographer, emerging from beneath his black cloth, asked for the formal pose.

In the written word, the humorist was still an apprentice. In 1899 Wodehouse succeeded his brother Armine as one of the five editors of the *Alleynian*. Many of his youthful contributions are unsigned, but two poems do bear his initials. The first, in February 1899, is a celebration of the levelling of a new rugby football pitch. This is followed in the *Alleynian* of June 1899 by 'On Purely Hypothetical Subjects', a defence of the five-shilling subscription to the Alleyn Club, in the style of Wodehouse's literary hero W. S. Gilbert, which begins:

> If a person decides that a fee of five shillings
> For joining a club is immense,
> And states in the press that he's very unwilling
> To go to such fearful expense . . .

Wodehouse could also sing. According to the *Alleynian*, he performed solo three times in Great Hall school concerts, notably on 31 July 1899, when he sang Thomas Campbell's 'Song of Hybrias the Cretan'. In later life, Wodehouse hated to perform in public, and was said by his stepdaughter to be a poor singer with no ear for music. Yet the Dulwich records show that, as well as the solos, he also appeared as a member of the Chorus in a production of Aristophanes' *The Frogs*, performed in Greek. And at the end of his last term, on Founder's Day in June 1900, Wodehouse played the part of Guildenstern in W. S. Gilbert's *Rosencrantz and Guildenstern*, a role in which he improvised some memorably comic stage business with a revolver.

Wodehouse's final year at Dulwich confirms Townend's description of him as one of the most important boys in the school. In the jargon of the times, he was 'a blood'. He was a dominant member of the classical Upper Sixth; a school prefect; a 'heavy forward' in the 1st XV, and a useful 'fast right-hand bowler with a good swing' in the 1st XI. The logical next step was an Oxford or Cambridge scholarship. In September 1899 he told his friend Eric 'Jimmy' George, 'that scholarship at [Oriel] . . . is a certainty. I *am* a genius. I always knew it.' His brother Armine had already blazed this path, and had got a scholarship to Corpus Christi College, Oxford, and 'the idea', Wodehouse remembered, 'was that if I got a scholarship too, I would join him there'. On the face of it, there was nothing to stop an inexorable progression to Oxford or Cambridge ('the Varsity'), and thence perhaps to the Foreign Office or the imperial civil service, following in his father's footsteps.

But it was not to be. Inexplicably, Ernest Wodehouse told his third son that, with or without a scholarship, Oxford was out of the question. With three other boys to educate, he said he could not afford it. Wodehouse at once broke this news to his contemporary, Jimmy George: 'Friend of me boyhood, here's some dread news for you. My people have not got enough of what are vulgarly but forcibly called "stamps" to send me to Varsity . . . Oh! money, money, thy name is money! (a most lucid remark).' Despite his insouciance, it was a terrible blow, as much to his pride and self-confidence as to his academic self-esteem. The pain of this exclusion was not something that Wodehouse, temperamentally, would have wanted to brood on. Throughout his life, he was the master of the stiff upper lip. Only in old age was he fully reconciled to his exclusion from this avenue of privilege, and told the novelist

Tom Sharpe that, if he had gone to Oxford, he would 'definitely not' have become a writer. But the wound was there. In its way it cut as deep as the exclusion from his mother's love. A poem published the following year expresses his dismay in a telling stanza:

> For he heard the voice of his father say
> > In tones devoid of pity:
> You aren't going up to the 'Varsity,
> > For I've got you a place in the City.

In the narrative of Wodehouse's life, that was not the end of the matter. He had to make farce out of his pain. It was not enough that Ernest's pension should be deemed inadequate to send two sons to Oxford; there had to be a larger, and ideally comic, explanation. Enter the rupee, the currency in which Ernest's pension was paid. In late-Victorian England, the rupee and its fluctuations were something of a national joke, as Oscar Wilde recognized in *The Importance of Being Earnest*. When he came to rationalize his youthful disappointment, Wodehouse was too good a writer to miss the comic opportunities presented by this currency: 'The rupee . . . was always jumping up and down and throwing fits, and expenditure had to be regulated in the light of what mood it happened to be in at the moment. "Watch that rupee!" was the cry in the Wodehouse family.'

The mystery remains. There is no question that Ernest Wodehouse believed he was hard up. He had only just retired, and was perhaps uncertain about living on an unreliable pension. Ernest and Eleanor certainly had rows about money. When he was married, Wodehouse, with painful memories of these scenes, always left the day-to-day administration of the family purse to his wife. An examination of the costs of university, however, does not explain why the trouble with his pension persuaded Ernest to deny his third son the opportunity of going to Oxford. Allowing for exchange-rate fluctuations in the value of the rupee, Ernest's pension translated to about £900 per annum, and he had no difficulty in giving Wodehouse an £80 allowance in the City. Besides, Dulwich boys going up to Oxford or Cambridge automatically received as much as £30 per annum from a proud and well-endowed college. It is inconceivable that such a successful schoolboy as Wodehouse would not have received the maximum support from the college. To put the figures in perspective, the annual salary of an assistant master at Dulwich was £150. Armine already had a scholarship; his annual college bills, for which Ernest was responsible, never surpassed £100. How difficult would it have been to sustain two sons at the 'Varsity'? Was Ernest cruelly arbitrating some sibling rivalry with Armine that is now lost to view? Did overbearing Eleanor support her husband's decision as a stern reminder to her shy, vague and impractical son about the realities of earning a living?

Wodehouse, of course, gives nothing away. In the laconic account of his final Dulwich year presented in his autobiography, he says that 'during my schooldays my future was always uncertain. The Boy, What Will He Become? was a question that received a different answer almost daily.' Typically, he took refuge in his work and devoted himself to his scholarship studies with all his formidable powers of application. 'All through my last term at Dulwich,' he remembered, 'I sprang from my bed at five sharp each morning, ate a couple of petit beurre biscuits and worked like a beaver at my Homer and Thucydides.' Then the blow fell. 'Just as scholarship time was approaching,' he wrote, 'the rupee started creating again, and it seemed to my father that two sons at the University would be a son more than the privy purse could handle. So Learning drew the loser's end, and Commerce got me.'

A passage in *Psmith in the City*, a novel published in 1910, evokes Wodehouse's dreadful heartbreak. The hero, Mike Jackson, is summoned to his father's study. After some awkward conversation, Mike's father breaks the bad news:

Mike looked at him blankly. This could only mean one thing. He was not to go to the Varsity. But why? What had happened? . . .

'Aren't I going up to Cambridge, father?' stammered Mike.

'I'm afraid not, Mike . . . I won't go into details . . . but I've lost a very large sum of money since I saw you last. So large that we shall have to economise in every way . . . I'm afraid [you] will have to start earning your living. I know it's a terrible disappointment to you, old chap.'

'Oh, that's all right,' said Mike thickly. There seemed to be something in his throat, preventing him from speaking.

'If there was any possible way –'

'No, it's all right, father, really. I don't mind a bit. It's awfully rough luck on you losing all that.'

Ernest Wodehouse had arranged, through his Hong Kong connections, for his son to join the Lombard Street branch of the Hongkong and Shanghai Bank ('the Honkers and Shankers' of ex-pat jargon), in the City of London. 'I didn't want to do it,' said Wodehouse later, 'but my hand was forced.' This is as close as he ever comes to reproaching his father, or indeed Armine, for this decision, but there's strong evidence in his fiction how keenly he felt the banishment from the 'unbroken bliss' of Dulwich. In *Psmith in the City*, Mike Jackson explores the school grounds near the vile lodgings he has just taken in 'Acacia Road', Dulwich:

He sat down on a bench beside the second eleven telegraph-board, and looked across the ground at the pavilion. For the first time that day he began to feel really home-sick . . . The clock on the tower over the senior block chimed quarter after quarter, but Mike sat on, thinking. It was quite late when he got up, and began to walk back to Acacia Road. He felt cold and stiff and very miserable.

In correspondence with Jimmy George, Wodehouse shows none of this self-pity. His determination to succeed is quite unambiguous. 'I will have 2 yrs to establish myself [*illegible*] on a pinnacle of fame as a writer . . . Let us hope the boodle will flow in.'

In fact, the boodle was already flowing. He had begun to focus on his ambition to be a writer even before he left Dulwich. In February 1900, the month in which he won a half-guinea prize for an essay entitled 'Some Aspects of Game Captaincy' from the *Public School Magazine*, the eighteen-year-old Wodehouse started to keep a kind of freelancer's journal entitled 'Money Received for Literary Work'. To this meticulous inventory he appended an epigraph from W. S. Gilbert's *Iolanthe*:

> Though never nurtured in the lap
> Of luxury, yet, I admonish you,
> I am an intellectual chap,
> And think of things that would astonish you.

In many respects, young Plum Wodehouse was a conventional English public schoolboy (diffident, games-mad, awkward with girls, over-educated in the classics), but he was determined to succeed as an artist and had no lack of self-belief when it came to his future career. Quiet, thoughtful, ambitious and single-minded, he was ready to make his way in the world as a writer. His memoirs accurately reflect this new mood of determined realism: 'Better, I think, to skip childhood and adolescence and go straight to the Autumn of 1900.'

3. 'First-fruits of a GENIUS'
(1900–1902)

London was too big to be angry with. It took no notice of him. It did not care whether he was glad to be there or sorry, and there was no means of making it care. (Psmith in the City)

'Banks', Wodehouse later wrote, 'have a habit of swallowing their victims rather abruptly.' His employment by the Hongkong and Shanghai Bank was a double exile. Once the summer holidays in Shropshire were over, he was not only cut off from the hoped-for career at the 'Varsity' but also from Dulwich. Throughout the fiction inspired by the bank, Wodehouse, usually a master of calculated unconcern, cannot conceal his alienation. In *Psmith in the City*, Wodehouse writes that, 'The whole system of banking was a horrid mystery'; the City exhibits 'aloofness'; the bank is 'a blighted institution'; its business is 'irksome', and its 'monotony' appalling. 'We are', concludes Mike Jackson, before Psmith, the suavest of Wodehouse's many suave metropolitan fixers, begins to work his magic, 'in for a pretty rotten time of it in this bally bank.'

This is an apt summary of the writer's feelings. In old age, Wodehouse told a former fellow trainee that he often felt very lost and forlorn when he first got there. But it was not in his nature to be overwhelmed by circumstances, and 'for the last twenty-odd months of my two years there I had a fine time'. Typically, it was the collegiate side of the bank to which he responded; 'I liked the companionship – we had an awfully nice crowd.' It is characteristic of Wodehouse that, whatever his private views, in subsequent correspondence with his contemporaries he idealized his City experience, claiming in hindsight to have 'enjoyed my two years in the bank enormously'. His relationship with the Hongkong and Shanghai Banking Corporation was complicated. To the end of his life, he kept a private account there, using it to disburse small amounts to needy friends like Bill Townend.

And so, early one morning in September 1900, crammed into his clerk's suit, lace-up boots and stiff white collar, Wodehouse followed the hectic stream of suburban commuters and overworked office clerks disgorging from the recently opened Bank tube station, and walked down Cornhill in the shadow of the Mansion House, eventually finding himself outside the massive building of the Hongkong and Shanghai Banking Corporation. In the chaotic, overcrowded offices of 31 Lombard Street, business was booming. The 'local bank' founded by Hong Kong taipans in 1865 had become one of the great, and most idiosyncratic, imperial finance houses of the City of London; Wodehouse joined during a period of rapid change. It was said that, whereas the City was full of bankers pretending to be gentlemen, the staff at the Hongkong and Shanghai Banking Corporation were gentlemen pretending to be bankers. Wodehouse was always a good reporter. Many of the bank's Edwardian employees later confirmed the worm's-eye view he gave of the institution he called 'the New Asiatic' and his rendering of Mike Jackson's arrival at his first job:

The difficulty now was to know how to make an effective entrance. There was the bank, and here was he . . . Inside the bank seemed to be in a state of some confusion. Men were moving about in an apparently irresolute manner. Nobody seemed actually to be working. As a matter of fact, the business of a bank does not start very early in the morning. . . . As he stood near the doorway, one or two panting figures rushed up the steps, and flung themselves at a large book which stood on the counter near the door . . . It was removed at ten sharp to the accountant's room, and if you reached the bank a certain number of times in the year too late to sign, bang went your bonus.

As well as persuading junior clerks to turn up on time (late comers had to report in; frequent offenders had their pay docked), the bank's managers issued repeated instructions against smoking and newspaper-reading during office hours; against overlong tea-breaks; and even against 'the practice of throwing pellets of paper about the office'. To juniors like Wodehouse, these restrictions were as tiresome as the men who attempted to uphold office discipline were comical. The 'home staff' during those years, some of whom are recognizable in *Psmith in the City*, included H. C. Carruthers, a short man with a grey beard, known as 'the Flea'; H. L. Rowett ('Uncle'), a Victorian character in frock coat and silk hat, suffering from senility and prone to weeping when crossed; S. Broadbent ('the Skipper') given to sudden, gnomic utterances, for example, 'Rumjohn, will the night soon pass?'; and, among the uniformed staff members in their top hats and chocolate-coloured tailcoats, William, an ex-railway signalman who would tap out messages with his spoon at teatime.

Tea-breaks, for a quick smoke, and meals were serious concerns. 'Conversation in a city office', noted Wodehouse the novelist, 'deals in the morning, with what one is going to have for lunch, and in the afternoon with what one has had for lunch.' Clerks would creep back from their breaks with heads bent below the counter to avoid the eagle eye of the department chiefs. Lunch was a milestone, 'an oasis in a desert of ink and ledgers'. Initially, the young trainee could only dream of outings to the local chophouse, where steaks were ninepence and potatoes a penny. 'I can still remember my dismay,' Wodehouse wrote in 1954, 'when I realised on the first morning that all I would be able to afford in the way of lunch was a roll and butter and a cup of coffee. I had come straight from school, where lunch was a solid meal.'

Wodehouse also recalled that the London office was 'a sort of kindergarten'. When, after two years, the ex-public school clerks of Lombard Street were sent out East, this was known as 'getting one's orders', a prospect that terrified Wodehouse. In the 1900s, there were forty-eight juniors in the London office, learning their trade under the headmasterly eye of the chief manager Sir Thomas Jackson ('TJ'), a fiery and eccentric Irishman given to impromptu renderings of 'The Wearin' o' the Green'. In one of his notebooks, Wodehouse records an exchange between Charles, the bank's messenger, and a customer who had come in to complain. 'Ah, you see, sir. This ain't a regular bank. It's a place where they prepare young gentlemen for the East.' Wodehouse remembered that 'Everybody except me was counting the days till he would be able to "give a Langdon" which was the term for the party you gave at the Langdon public house when you "got your orders"'.

A substantial income, 'a big screw', was never off his mind. With a weekly £3 3s. 10d. in his pocket, topped up with an allowance from his father, Wodehouse was better off than many lower-middle-class families, but money would always be a worry. 'Money' would animate the plots of many later novels and stories, and appear explicitly in the titles of four books (*Uneasy Money*, *Money for Nothing*, *Big Money* and *Money in the Bank*). Practically speaking, as a young man in a hurry, he now had to make enough, through his writing, to justify leaving the bank and becoming a freelance writer. He had to put himself in a position where he would never again be at the mercy of the dreaded rupee. On Sunday evenings, to save money, he would stride down to Townend's digs on Clapham Common for buttered toast and hot, sweet cocoa. The meticulous monthly record of his freelance earnings he kept for the years 1900–1908 suggests a young man driven, even obsessed, by the need for complete financial independence. In the short term, however, he was forced to sacrifice his individuality to the routine of the City, and become one of those 'mussels' who, as he wrote in *The Girl on the Boat*, 'has his special place on the rock and remains glued to it all his life'.

Although Wodehouse disdained the City, he probably owed rather more to the clerks in the bank than he acknowledged. *Psmith in the City* was written a decade after its author had left the Square Mile, but its dialogue shows that Wodehouse's years as a nine-to-fiver had left their mark. The Pooterish Edwardian slang of 'give me the pip' (irritate), 'restore the tissues' (take alcoholic refreshment), 'off his onion/chump' (unbalanced), 'old oil' (flattery), 'pure applesauce' (fanciful nonsense), 'perfect rot' (utter rubbish), 'friendly native' (useful ally) and 'toodle pip' (goodbye) had become part of his conversational repertoire and would be recycled in the interior monologues of Bertie Wooster and, to a lesser extent, in Wodehouse's own correspondence with friends like Bill Townend, for decades to come.

In the office, the newly arrived junior was automatically sent to the 'postage' desk, stamping and entering letters in the appropriate ledger. 'The work in the postage department was not intricate,' Wodehouse wrote. 'There was nothing much to do except enter and stamp letters, and, at intervals, take them down to the post office at the end of the street.' He would always look for the joke against himself in even the most unpromising situations. When he came to recall his Lombard Street beginnings in his memoirs, he stressed, not his unhappiness at the move, but his incompetence there. 'I was just a plain dumb brick,' he writes, using a favourite formula, 'the most inefficient clerk whose trouser seat ever polished the surface of a high stool. . . . If there was a moment in the course of my banking career when I had the foggiest notion of what it was all about, I am unable to recall it.' He claimed, 'I couldn't have managed a whelk stall.'

In fact, Wodehouse progressed steadily through the bank. From 'postage' in October 1900 to 'correspondence' to 'shares' to 'deposits' to 'cashiers' in February 1901, his clerkship proceeded with a smoothness that refutes his claims of incompetence. Some aspects of banking life, like the informal choral society in Progressive Ledgers, from which emerged the soft strains of selections from Gilbert and Sullivan, would have been surprisingly congenial. But his heart was elsewhere. From the first, he was devoting all his spare time to writing, usually into the small hours. In 1901, the bank's ledger reveals that Wodehouse was guilty of late morning attendance some twenty times, a record surpassed by only one other trainee. 'One of the great sights in the City in the years 1901–2,' he wrote later, 'was me rounding into the straight with my coat-tails flying and just making it across the threshold.' Fellow clerks detected the late-rising Wodehouse's pyjamas habitually peeping from beneath his trouser leg. There is also an apocryphal tale that, on one occasion, wearying of balancing the books, he simply walked down to London Bridge and chucked a sheaf of cheques and papers into the Thames.

The bank was keen on sports, and kept playing fields and squash courts in Beckenham. Wodehouse was recruited into both its rugby football (yellow jerseys with a black dragon) and cricket teams and found that he was playing alongside men from Tonbridge, Bedford and St Paul's familiar to him from his Dulwich days. There were not as many games as he wanted. The notebooks he kept during these years contain fragments of fiction eloquent of his feelings:

Opening words of novel. Interview between new hand at bank and bank manager.

    Bank manager: 'Sportsman?'
    New hand: 'Yes, sir.'
    Bank manager: 'Play cricket?'
    New hand: 'Yes, sir.'
    Bank manager: 'Tennis?'
    New hand: 'Yes, sir.'
    Bank manager: 'Everything?'
    New hand: 'Yes, sir.'
    Bank manager: 'Had a good deal of it?'
    New hand: 'Yes, sir.'
    Bank manager: 'Good. You won't get any more now.'

Wodehouse the sportsman is the Wodehouse his contemporaries remember, and the sports field was the place where Wodehouse made friends. Like many Edwardian clerks, Wodehouse was not just an enthusiastic weekend and country-house cricketer. He used also to cut across the Thames down to the Oval to follow the game during his lunch hour. On one rainy, overcast August morning, towards the end of his time at the bank, he witnessed the first shots of a legendary test match innings – Jessop's 104 against Australia, struck in just over an hour – that gave England a one-wicket victory as the light worsened and the rain set in. To his lasting regret, the tedious call of his duties at the bank prevented Wodehouse from watching the electrifying climax to 'Jessop's Match'.

The eccentric, and surprisingly collegiate, atmosphere of the Hongkong and Shanghai Bank did not allow the reluctant banker to overstay his lunch hour, but Mr Moore, the Head Cashier, was apparently lenient towards Wodehouse's shortcomings as a clerk. It was Moore who presided over the supreme crisis in his business career. In press interviews and reminiscences at the end of his life, Wodehouse would repeat a well-crafted account of himself as 'virtually an imbecile':

A new ledger came into the office, and was placed in my charge. It had a white, gleaming front page, and suddenly, as I looked over it, there floated into my mind like drifting thistledown the idea of writing a richly comic account of the celebrations and rejoicings marking the Formal Opening of the New Ledger.

It was great stuff . . . There was a bit about my being presented to the King . . . which makes me laugh to this day . . . I simply gloated over it. And then came the reaction . . .

Having defaced the New Ledger with comic prose, and suddenly fearful of the Head Cashier, he liked to say he lost his nerve and cut out the inscribed folio. When Moore discovered the front page missing, he summoned the bank's stationer, with whom he had been having a feud, and angrily accused him of supplying imperfect stationery. The man is said to have replied that someone must have cut out the page. Wodehouse now brings the anecdote to its triumphant conclusion:

'Absurd,' said the Head Cashier. 'Nobody but an imbecile would cut out the front page of a ledger.'

'Then you must have an imbecile in your department,' said the stationer, coming right back at him. 'Have you?'

The Head Cashier started.

'Why yes,' he said, for he was a fair-minded man. 'There is P. G. Wodehouse.'

Wodehouse occasionally implied, in some versions, that after this episode he was summarily fired from the bank, and was then 'at liberty to embark on the life literary'. This is not so. He left the bank of his own volition in September 1902. Exactly two years since he first went to the City, he had achieved the goal he had first expressed to his school-friend Jimmy George in the black days of 1899 when he had been denied his 'Varsity' career. Through a remarkable act of will-power, Wodehouse had established himself in his spare time as a successful free-lance writer, quite at home in Edwardian literary London.

The first decade of the new century was a golden age for the free-lance journalist. New magazines, exploiting new printing technology, offered any number of opportunities. 'Never before had there been such reading masses,' wrote H. G. Wells, a spokesman for the bank clerks, estate agents and Mr Pooters who were so hungry for magazines like *Tit-Bits*. Short stories, a reaction against mid-Victorian long-windedness, were in vogue and would become an essential element of Edwardian reading. 'How on earth does a young writer of light fiction get going these days?' Wodehouse exclaimed to Bill Townend in the much tougher circumstances of the 1940s. 'Where can he sell his stories? We might get turned down by the *Strand*,' he recalled, 'but there was always hope of landing with *Nash's*, the *Storyteller*, the *London* . . . and probably a dozen more I've forgotten.'

The Education Act of 1870 had created a literate adult population eager for entertainment and self-improvement, a new audience charac-terized by G. B. Shaw as 'readers who had never before bought books, nor could have read them if they had'. This was a market exploited by the successful newspaper and magazine proprietors of Edwardian England such as George Armstrong, George Newnes, and especially Alfred Harmsworth, an autocratic and slightly mad press baron. Wodehouse knew Harmsworth, who endeared himself to the struggling freelancer by paying promptly. 'If Harmsworth pays *before* publication,' Wodehouse noted in 1901, 'then he *must* be my long lost brother.' Ennobled as Lord Northcliffe, he became a model for Wodehouse's

Lord Tilbury, the short-tempered proprietor of the Mammoth Publishing Company in *Heavy Weather* and *Service with a Smile*.

These favourable conditions do not diminish Wodehouse's achievement. When he started work at the bank, he had found 'horrible lodgings', a bed-sittingroom in Markham Square, Chelsea, the 'dismal backwater' in which he later situated the impecunious Stanley Featherstonehaugh Ukridge. At the end of each day in the City, he would hurry home, often on foot, to settle down to an evening of solitary composition, glued to his chair and taking no part in London's nightlife except for a weekly dinner – half a crown and sixpence for the waiter – at the Trocadero grill-room. At first, like most freelancers, he received many rejection letters, with which, he wrote, 'I could have papered the walls of a good-sized banqueting hall', but he was not discouraged. In his determination to make his way, and with one eye firmly on the clerks' market that had made such a success of *Three Men in a Boat*, Wodehouse would write for anyone. 'I wrote everything in those days,' he recalled, 'verses, short stories, articles for the lowest type of weekly paper.' Nothing was beneath his notice. Later, as a famous writer, he was dismissive of these efforts – 'Worse bilge than mine may have been submitted to the editors of London in 1901 and 1902, but I should think it unlikely' – but at the time, with the deadline of his 'orders' looming, he could not afford to be choosy. His sole concern was to escape the bank.

Simultaneously, he was prowling the crowded streets of London for material, idling past flaring naphtha lamps, and filling his notebook with all kinds of journalistic observations and scraps of overheard conversation:

169. *Bus driver*. Been 17 years in the Army (Bodmin, India, Burmah, India, Burmah, Malta, Gibraltar, Soudan – relief of Gordon – and Transvaal): says that a bus driver could write a 'reel 'istory' of the things he sees from his box seat . . . His appearance was rugged and battered: his manner independent yet very civil: his nose broken: short moustache: short scar over right eye.

285. *Brutal speeches*:
a) Cabman to cyclist whom he has knocked down; 'Ah, now, if you'd taken a keb, this 'ere wouldn't 'ave 'appened.'
b) Hearty voyager to pale friend on ship; 'What you *want* is a pork chop.'

Wodehouse's ambition to be a writer was still unfocused. His literary heroes were W. S. Gilbert, Conan Doyle, Kipling and J. M. Barrie, whose highly influential novel *When a Man's Single*, the autobiographical tale of a Scotsman's quest for literary success in London, is full of practical advice for Edwardian freelance writers. For Wodehouse, the fruits of his flirtation with Barrie's belief that one should tailor one's work to the editor's tastes were inevitable: 'I avoided the humorous story, which was where my inclinations lay, and went in exclusively for the mushy sentiment which, judging from the magazines, was the thing most likely to bring a sparkle to an editor's eye. It never worked.'

Gradually he found his voice. His first comic article, 'Men Who Have Missed Their Own Weddings', appeared in the November 1900 issue of *Tit-Bits*:

At Ipswich recently a marriage was about to take place when it was discovered that the bridegroom was not present. Nobody had seen or heard anything of him, and the greatest confusion reigned until, some twenty minutes after the hour appointed for the service, his brother appeared on a bicycle with the news that the missing gentleman was too busy to come, but would present himself at church on the following day.

Despite the gusto with which Wodehouse conducted his assault on the editorial offices of publications like the *Public School Magazine*, *Pearson's Weekly* and the rest, the first half of 1901 did not go well. In February, he stoically noted 'rather a bad time', during which *Fun* had 'rejected ten contributions running'. In June, he contracted mumps. Orchitis is a serious condition for an adult: it may have made him infertile, and possibly explains a diminished sexual appetite, though this subject remains opaque. He was obliged to spend three weeks convalescing in Stableford. In his memoirs, he says he used this time 'in the bosom of my family' to write nineteen short stories.

On his return to the City, still employed by the bank, things began to look up. On 16 August, having made an approach to his old school-master William Beach Thomas, now a successful journalist with the *Globe*, who remembered his work on the *Alleynian*, Wodehouse began contributing to the daily 'By the Way' column, and also to 'Men and Matters'. The *Globe and Traveller*, the most popular of some eight London evening broadsheets, was printed on pink paper. The 'By the Way' column, on its front page, was one of those newspaper institutions whose readership and popularity guaranteed considerable prestige for its (anonymous) authors.

The *Globe*'s address was 397 Strand. In turn-of-the-century London, the Strand, jammed with omnibuses and hansom cabs, was the heart of the metropolitan theatrical and journalistic community. Until the building of Shaftesbury Avenue was completed, it was the Strand, with its restaurants, pubs and sixteen theatres, where the clerk from the suburbs, or the imperial subaltern on leave, or the young man about town, went in search of a night out. Located east of Trafalgar Square, and west of Temple Bar, between the fashionable society of St James's and the legal world of the Inns of Court, the Strand was a raffish thoroughfare peopled by barristers, actors, journalists, bookies, 'Gaiety girls' from the Gaiety Theatre, and silly young men heading for Romano's, the restaurant on which so much Edwardian London nightlife centred. The Strand sustains and inspires the lives of many early Wodehouse characters, and the *Strand* was the Edwardian magazine, celebrated for its Sherlock Holmes stories, to which the freelance Wodehouse aspired. Once his work was accepted there, he remained loyal to it for nearly forty years, and it published more than two hundred of his articles. To appear in those pages, he wrote, was 'roughly equivalent to being awarded the Order of the Garter'.

This was the Edwardian world whose slang – 'old man', 'cove', 'blighter', 'snifter' and 'chump' – subtly transposed, would pepper the conversations of Bertie Wooster and Bingo Little, and whose landscape, subtly reconfigured, would provide the backdrop to the youthful adventures of Galahad Threepwood and Frederick Altamont Cornwallis Twistleton, 5th Earl of Ickenham ('Uncle Fred'). There are, as Norman Murphy has suggested in *In Search of Blandings*, two Londons to be found in Wodehouse – the society neighbourhoods of Belgravia and Kensington, and the commercial, down-at-heel London of Covent Garden, Fleet Street and Holborn. Wodehouse, the Dulwich outsider, always aspired to Mayfair, but his London street-references suggest he was also creatively at home in the backstreets and byways of Chelsea, Piccadilly and the Strand.

The *Globe* was something of a nursery for comic writers. E. V. Lucas had worked there. So had Charles Lamb, the author of *Essays of Elia* and *Tales from Shakespear*. From a freelance point of view, working for 'By the Way' was ideal. The freelance contributor simply presented

himself at the *Globe* at nine o'clock in the morning, and completed his
humorous skits on the current affairs of the day, either in verse or prose,
by midday at the latest. It was work which Wodehouse loved, and to
moonlight at the *Globe* he would plead 'non-existent attacks of neuralgia'
with the bank. A hundred years on, the 'By the Way' column seems
stiff and unfunny, but it was good training, and gave him the useful
knack of being able to write under almost any conditions. Typical 'By
the Way' paragraphs read:

Herr Nyman, a poet of the Young Finnish School, has been expelled from
his native town by the Russian authorities. Their idea is to make him a young
Finished poet.

or,

After forty-six years the widow of an Indian Mutiny veteran has just obtained
her husband's share of the Lucknow prize money. He was in Lucknow; she is
in luck now.

Wodehouse's probation went well. 'They printed 7 of my pars [para-
graphs],' he noted in his account book in September 1901. 'Good! There
is a reasonable hope of my getting this post permanently. Let the good
work go forward!' Shy, short-sighted and socially awkward he may have
been in person, but on the page he had (he wrote) 'the most complete
confidence in myself. I knew I was good.'

    He was not only good, he was a supremely hard worker. As well as
occasional paragraphs for the *Globe*, he produced in these two formative years at the bank some eighty stories and articles. The habit of
writing to a deadline never left him. His pride in his craft remained to
the end. 'When in due course Charon ferries me across the Styx and
everyone is telling everyone else what a rotten writer I was, I hope at
least one voice will be heard piping up, "But he did take trouble."' As
well as his remarkable powers of application, there was also the dawning
recognition of his true *métier*. A year after he joined the bank, he item-
ized an article called 'The Language of Flowers', noting that it was
''Ighly yumorous'. The steady increase in his monthly earnings meant
that he would soon reach the magical point at which his freelance
earnings surpassed his bank salary.

Write what you know about is good advice for the would-be novelist. During this first year in Lombard Street, Wodehouse's public school experience was his main inspiration. Throughout 1901 he wrote a series of articles for a column in the *Public School Magazine* entitled 'Under the Flail', breezy editorial commentary on public school topics such as the lack of forks in the Dulwich dining hall or the absence of vanilla chocolate in the Dulwich buttery. At the same time, he was also beginning to explore the literary potential of public school fiction, novels like *Eric, or, Little By Little, Tom Brown's Schooldays* and *Stalky & Co.* In August 1901, in an essay entitled 'School Stories', he announced that 'the rules governing school stories should be similar to those of Greek Tragedy'. There would, however, never be any deaths in Wodehouse, nor any serious emotional pain. 'The worst thing', he wrote, 'that ought to happen to your hero is the loss of the form-prize or his being run out against the MCC.' When Wodehouse sat down to write his first school story, *The Pothunters*, shortly after leaving Dulwich, he did so because school was the only subject he knew and understood. He was prompted to write, in fact, by another school story, *Acton's Feud* by Fred Swainson, published in the *Captain*, a rival magazine edited by the Old Fag (R. S. Warren Bell). 'Awfully funny how something like that gives you a kick-off,' he remembered.

The Pothunters, serialized in monthly instalments in the *Public School Magazine* from January to March 1902, was a school story, typical of the five that were to follow. It is set in 'St Austin's', the first of several fictional schools (Beckford, Sedleigh, Eckleton and, most notably, Wrykyn) based on Dulwich College. Wodehouse's all-purpose public school is, however, a Dulwich translated into an English pastoral setting. When the story opens there has been a mysterious robbery from the school pavilion in which thieves have made off with a shelf of silver sporting cups (the 'pots' of the title). In the quest for the missing trophies that follows, Wodehouse displays natural storytelling gifts, depicting the life and the characters of his imaginary public school with what the reviewer in the *World* characterized as 'insight and humour'. Wodehouse's 'easy attractive style' was also singled out for praise. His work had a freshness of observation and a lack of sentimentality that sets his early fiction apart from contemporaries like Ian Hay, author of the saccharine *Pip*. Students of his later work will detect several stylistic traits: effortless literary allusion (to Aeschylus, Thucydides, Dickens and

Tennyson); witty manipulation of cliché ('touch these notes and you rouse the British Lion'); lively similes ('Robinson ran like a cow') and incongruous metaphors ('the champagne of the Head's wrath, which had been fermenting steadily during his late interview, got the better of the cork of self-control, and he exploded'); absurd images ('an expression on his face a cross between a village idiot and an unintelligent fried egg'); and extensive misquotation ('How sweet the moonlight sleeps on yonder haystack'). Soon he would be acknowledged, not merely by public schoolboys, as a young English writer to watch. He was still only twenty.

The serialization of *The Pothunters* was cut short by the closure of the *Public School Magazine* by its publishers, A. & C. Black. But in March, anxious to keep a promising author under contract, the firm agreed to bring out the novel in book form. Wodehouse was still turning out potboiling articles – a comic piece about 'The Split Infinitive', a contribution to *Tit-Bits*, 'Single Day Marriages', and a boxing piece for *Sandow's*, 'The Pugilist in Fiction' – but increasingly it was light verse and stories that occupied his attention. He was still primarily a journalist and had become so much part of the London magazine world that fellow clerks would recall his organizing a team of journalists to play cricket against the bank. Team photographs taken at this time show a tall, serious-looking young man, with cropped dark hair, a square, and slightly forbidding, jaw – and that air of detachment that always characterizes his demeanour.

A solitary, withdrawn young man of English gentry origins, dreaming of literary success, often dressed in his brother's cast-off frock coat and trousers, he dedicated *The Pothunters* not to his mother or father, nor to a sweetheart, nor to any of his brothers, but to some family friends, the Bowes-Lyon granddaughters of the 13th Earl of Strathmore, Joan (thirteen), Effie (twelve) and Ernestine, 'Teenie' (ten). These were the 'naughty cousins' of the Elizabeth Bowes-Lyon who eventually became Queen Elizabeth, wife of George VI. As an old lady, Effie recalled that she and her sisters had first met 'PG' in Shropshire, and then in London, where 'he used to come around to tea with us three sisters'. Wodehouse's role in the Bowes-Lyon household was avuncular, and it was here, not Shropshire, that he felt at home. He told the girls' mother that 'I occupy in your house a position equivalent to that of cold beef . . . If there is nobody new to talk to, the Lyon cubs talk to me.' Effie tried to shock him by saying that she would 'marry a rich man, however much of a beast he was, simply to get a horse'. The Bowes-Lyons liked to tease their diffident young literary friend. Effie remembered that 'he used to propose to us in turn and we always made him go down on his knees and propose in proper fashion . . .' adding the revealing comment that 'I think he could be friends with us because we were little girls'. All his life, Wodehouse had a special gift for these kinds of asexual friendships. Effie paints a charming picture of shy young 'PG' relaxing in play with her sisters in a society drawing-room in 22 Ovington Square, Kensington. 'He had already had some stories published . . . and he asked our advice as to whether he should give up his job and take up writing as a full-time career.'

By the end of the summer of 1902, with the publication of *The Pothunters* imminent, and two years to the day since he had crossed the threshold of Lombard Street, he was bursting with self-confidence, and ready to answer his own question. The dedication he inscribed in the copy of *The Pothunters* he set aside for Bill Townend suggests a new exuberance, a kind of exhilarated determination:

To Villiam [*sic*] Townend
these first-fruits
of
a
GENIUS
at which
the
WORLD
will
(shortly)
be
AMAZED
(You see if it won't)
from
the author
Sep 28. 1902 P.G. Wodehouse

There was a reason for this ebullience. Three weeks before, his mentor Beach Thomas had suddenly announced his annual holiday from the

Globe, and had asked Wodehouse, at very short notice, to fill in. If he wouldn't take the job, Beach Thomas said, the *Globe* would find someone else. For more than a year Wodehouse had somehow managed to keep his freelance work coexisting with his banking duties. Now he had reached the limits of literary escapology. Even the chaotic Hongkong and Shanghai Bank would not allow the reluctant bank clerk to have his 'non-existent neuralgia' for five weeks. It was time to choose.

4. 'My wild lone'
(1902-1904)

To write – the agony with which he throatily confessed it! – to be swept into the maelstrom of literary journalism, to be en rapport with the unslumbering forces of Fleet Street – those were the real objectives. (Not George Washington)

Wodehouse did not flinch from the opportunity before him. 'On September 9th,' he wrote in his account book, 'having to choose between the Globe and the bank I chucked the latter, and started out on my wild lone as a freelance.' It was a daunting moment, one quite alien to the countrified, conservative, and professional upper-middle-class world in which he had grown up; as he put it later, 'a young man's cross-roads'. Henceforth, Wodehouse would live by his typewriter. 'This month starts my journalistic career,' he noted, adding that his earnings for September (£16 4s.) amounted to 'the record so far'.[*]

Whatever his later triumphs and achievements as a writer of plays, musical lyrics, short stories and comic novels, Wodehouse never quite lost the journalist's taste for a story, a deadline or the promise of a cheque. Money would dominate his professional horizons throughout these first months as a freelancer, but he was such a compulsive writer that his creativity always came first. 'I should think it extremely improbable', he wrote in *Over Seventy*, 'that anyone ever wrote anything simply for money. What makes a writer write is that he likes writing. Naturally, when he has written something, he wants to get as much for it as he can, but that is a very different thing from writing for money.'

After a flying start, in which he sold his first piece to *Punch*, a droll smoking-room anecdote about the death of a freelance writer, he made

---

[*] Wodehouse was always a big earner; exactly how big is sometimes difficult to quantify. To establish contemporary equivalents for the money Wodehouse earned before the First World War, it is necessary to multiply his remuneration by a factor of approximately 20. For the inter-war years, when he was very rich, the dollar–pound rate was about 4:1; his earnings should, similarly, be multiplied by a factor of 20 to establish an approximate equivalent.

£19 13*s.* 6*d.* in October, another record. In November, he sold work to the *Globe*, the *Captain*, the *Onlooker* and the *Daily Chronicle*, but had 'nothing!' in *Punch*. By December, *The Pothunters* had sold 396 copies and earned £6 18*s.* 7*d.*, a respectable sale for a novel that had already been serialized. He had already completed a second novel, provisionally entitled 'The Bishop's Uncle', and was negotiating a new contract with A. & C. Black. Adopting his usual modesty, he assured his publisher that 'I can generally improve on my work at a second attempt'.

The quality of his life as a freelancer was solitary and unremitting. He hardly ever went out. He was working too hard. After the *Globe* in the morning, he would walk back to his lodgings and start work right away. Occasionally, he would break off to play cricket, but he was too keen on his work to leave his desk for long. For relaxation, he would read anything that came along. Wodehouse would later disdain the dedicated slogging of these first years, but the unguarded asides of his early fiction betray his true feelings. In *Not George Washington*, his neglected but highly autobiographical novel, Wodehouse describes his hero's career in words inspired by these apprentice years: 'The early struggles of the writer to keep his head above water form an experience which does not bear repetition . . . The hopeless feeling of chipping a little niche for oneself out of the solid rock with a nib is a nightmare even in times of prosperity.' By the end of the year, Wodehouse's single-minded dedication paid off, and he felt secure enough in his work to move out of his dingy, dark lodgings in Markham Square, and migrate a few streets in the direction of Sloane Square to superior rooms in 23 Walpole Street. This was an early Victorian white stucco, three-storey, terraced house adjoining Royal Hospital Gardens that would later become popularized in his friend Denis Mackail's inter-war domestic comedy, *Greenery Street*. It was a good address, but Wodehouse's habit of misremembering the number of his house suggests that he was more at home in a workplace like the offices of the *Globe and Traveller*, where he was free from the irritating chatter of his land-lady and her daughter.

The *Globe* was roughly an hour's walk away at 367 Strand, but for the moment Wodehouse was holed up in Walpole Street, sending out his work each morning and sometimes receiving as many as eight rejected manuscripts a day in return. Throughout his later work, particularly in the Ukridge stories, there are countless references to the struggling young writer in his under-heated bed-sittingroom, tyrannized by an unsympathetic landlord, and trying to sell his work in Grub Street. As always with Wodehouse, this intoxicating mixture contains high, even reckless, levels of fantasy, but it is nonetheless distilled from reality. It was here, in the early weeks of 1903, that he was visited by a young man named Herbert Westbrook, an ambitious but lazy schoolmaster with literary aspirations. Westbrook, a charmer and a chancer, who had been given an introduction to Wodehouse by one of his former colleagues at the bank, turned up one day at Walpole Street to find the author of *The Pothunters* sitting at a table, a woollen sweater wrapped around his feet, working on a poem for *Punch* by the light of a green-shaded oil lamp.

Westbrook, who had just graduated from Cambridge, was teaching Latin and Greek at a small private preparatory school in Emsworth, Hampshire. Perpetually broke, handsome, amoral and persuasive, an inveterate ladies' man, he blew into Wodehouse's solitary life in a cloud of breezy conversation, like a character from Jerome K. Jerome. In no time at all, he had not only wangled 'some good advice and . . . sincere encouragement' from Wodehouse but had also convinced his new best friend to come and live at the school (in a room above the stables). This surprising move from London is explained by Wodehouse's lifelong love of rural seclusion, and perhaps by the chance to play football and cricket with the boys. Emsworth House, like so many English private schools, then and now, was an idiosyncratic institution catering to the education of middle-class boys of the kind only too familiar to the young Wodehouse. Like Malvern House, it specialized in preparing boys for the navy; unlike Malvern House, it did this with charm and humanity.

The school, 'King-Hall's' to its inmates, was run by Baldwin ('Baldie' or 'Bud') King-Hall and his sister Ella, assisted in the kitchen by Ma Brown, the cook. The big house, with its inviting grounds and shady cedars, on the outskirts of the picturesque oyster-fishing town of Emsworth, would also have seemed familiar to Wodehouse, and reminiscent of all those mansions he had been dragged round as a child. Westbrook was in love with Ella King-Hall, who was fifteen years older (Wodehouse called the pair 'Stinker' and 'Sport'), and eventually married her in 1912. His invitation suited Wodehouse perfectly. Eleanor and Ernest Wodehouse had just moved from Stableford to 'beastly'

Cheltenham. Emsworth House, Hants, provided an ideal substitute for The Old House, Salop. Wodehouse became so much a fixture that some of the pupils later claimed, erroneously, to have been taught by P. G. Wodehouse. This is not so; he was never a schoolmaster.

He seems to have clicked with Bud from the start. They had plenty in common. Both had been groomed for naval careers, both suffered from poor eyesight, both loved cricket, and shared a tolerant attitude to the vicissitudes of existence. Bud was in many ways a character made for fiction; Mr Abney in *The Little Nugget* is an affectionate portrait of the maverick schoolmaster. Emsworth House boys later recalled their headmaster breakfasting in bed each morning while conducting a 'seminar on life in general', or announcing a sudden half-day and taking the school on a picnic. In this eccentric establishment, Wodehouse soon found himself playing football and cricket with the boys, or helping Ella King-Hall to put on musical plays. He was always at home with servants and, when he was not working, could often be found sitting on the kitchen table below stairs, chatting to Ma Brown. One old boy of the school remembered Wodehouse helping to stir a Christmas pudding, but, apart from organized games and below-stairs relaxation, 'Wodehouse appeared to keep very much to himself,' he recalled, '[and] seldom spoke to the boys. He gave me the impression of observing everything in his own quiet way, but he was not the jovial man one might have expected.'

The life of Emsworth House was highly congenial: the King-Halls treated Wodehouse as family; the school answered his need for routine and recreation; and there was more than enough unspoilt country to satisfy his passion for long walks. In later life, Wodehouse often stayed at Emsworth House, usually on the way to one of his habitual New York liner crossings from the Empress dock in Southampton; he wrote *The Little Nugget* at the school, and dedicated *Indiscretions of Archie* to Bud King-Hall. Not for the last time, Wodehouse had found a secluded rural community in which he could relax and write. He also remained free to pop up to London on the train whenever called upon by the *Globe,* or by the demands of his numerous other commissioning editors.

Wodehouse's London was a place where aristocrats chased actresses, where American money pursued British class, where bookmakers and barmaids mixed on equal terms with Cabinet ministers and newspaper editors, and where everyone read the *Sporting Times,* better known as the 'Pink 'Un', one of the most popular newspapers of the day. In his fiction, the archetypal representatives of this fun-loving society are the Earl of Ickenham and Galahad Threepwood, 'a short, trim, dapper little man of the type one associates automatically in one's mind with checked suits, tight trousers, white bowler hats, pink carnations, and race glasses bumping against the left hip'. Uncles Gally and Fred are known to the maître d' of Romano's and have been thrown out of the old Gardenia; they have lost their shirts at Goodwood; they are life members of the Pelican Club; they have heard the chimes at midnight and tasted onion soup at dawn in Covent Garden. They always wear a hat, and in matters of dress they are obsessively concerned with appearance: full evening dress for the theatre or dining in the club, spats for the city streets, frock coats for business, and loud check tweeds for weekends in the country. Nothing would induce them to settle their tailors' accounts – or place a bet with Mustard Pott. Their scandalous reminiscences, if ever published, would inspire panic among scores of the best families in the kingdom.

The Edwardian London of the great hotels, brilliantly lit restaurants, gentlemen's clubs and department stores, where Wodehouse came of age and first published his early work, was a truly imperial capital: a hedonistic, chaotic, reckless society that was finally killed off in the fields of France during the First World War. But it shaped Wodehouse, in its way, as completely as Dulwich had done. Much of his later work would seem inaccessible without an appreciation of this spendthrift society at whose revels he was an impressionable and sharp-eyed bystander. And when it was all too overwhelming, he could escape to his second home in the sunshine and tranquillity of the south coast, to Emsworth.

As much as Edwardian London, Emsworth pervades Wodehouse's work in character, landscape and allusion. Clarence, 9th Earl of Emsworth ('a mild, dreamy, absent-minded sort of old bird'), a kind of alter ego, was always his personal favourite among all his characters. Emsworth's heir, Lord Bosham, takes his name from the historic Saxon village on the coast near Emsworth. Threepwood, the cottage Wodehouse rented in Record Road, adjoining the Emsworth House grounds, gives its name to Clarence's vacuous second son, Freddie. Nearby Beach Road, which runs down to the seashore, contributed Wodehouse's first and archetypal butler, Sebastian Beach, while the surrounding Hampshire landscape features regularly in the adventures of Bertie Wooster, often bowling along the Portsmouth road in the 'old two-seater', on his way to yet another disastrous imbroglio. Wodehouse commentators have had a field day hunting down countless obscure Emsworth connections in the later fiction, but their significance is simply that they are place-names borrowed from a part of the world Wodehouse knew and loved. Long before the invention of Blandings Castle and the 9th Earl, there are several specific allusions to Emsworth in his early work. The most notable appears in *Mike*, when the eponymous hero is asked about his pre-Wrykyn schooling:

'A prep school in Hampshire,' said Mike. 'King-Hall's at a place called Emsworth.'

'Get much cricket there?'

'Yes, a good lot. One of the masters, a chap called Westbrook, was an awfully good slow bowler.'

Wodehouse always described Emsworth as an ideal place to work. His first year on his 'wild lone', 1903, was a bumper year in which he earned a total of £215 18s. 1d., and, most significant of all, one in which he mastered the art of writing for *Punch*, the supreme mirror of Edwardian establishment taste and opinion, with verses, sketches and contributions to 'Charivaria'. During the following year, he contributed almost weekly, and rapidly made a name for himself as the witty and accomplished author of ephemeral light verse in the style of W. S. Gilbert. The editor of *Punch*, Owen Seaman, particularly liked verses pegged to newspaper items or current events. When Buffalo Bill Cody and his Wild West Show made a triumphant Christmas holiday visit to London, for instance, Wodehouse celebrated the occasion in verse (rhyming 'tomahawk' with 'from a hawk') and closing:

> Still, when your ochred and plume-covered savages
> Make preparations for raising the hair,
> And when your cowboys are stemming their ravages,
> I, may it please you to know, shall be there.
> One, if no more, of the thousands who pen you in
> Looks on your feats with a pleasure that's genuine.

Of the forty-seven items Wodehouse published in *Punch* in 1903, no fewer than eighteen were in verse, much of it sparkling and memorable. When the novelist Hall Caine announced, in a self-promoting way, that he was off to Iceland to collect material for his new novel, Wodehouse, always alert to literary pretension, thoughtfully listed some items of local colour, ending with a pointed rebuke:

> Though other things he will not miss,
>   Those mentioned are enough
> To suit the purposes of this
>   Preliminary puff;
> Others will follow, for we know
>   A chance will not be lost
> To save this Saga of the Snow
>   From turning out a 'frost'.

Wodehouse's light verse, as much as his youthful prose, shows a writer revelling in the allusive music of English, learning to make the words dance on the page while presenting a succession of clear, completely intelligible, images organized into a compelling narrative. The same can be said, in a less quotable way, of his journalism. In the spring of 1903, he also published articles in the *Royal Magazine*, the *Windsor Magazine*, *Punch*, the *Daily Chronicle*, the *Illustrated Sporting and Dramatic News* and *Vanity Fair*, and in July, an interview with his literary hero, Sir Arthur Conan Doyle, in *V.C.* As his reputation spread, he became increasingly familiar with some of the other literary giants of the day. He was invited to lunch with W. S. Gilbert at Grim's Dyke, his home in Harrow Weald, but was so overcome with awkwardness that he laughed in the wrong place during one of his host's interminable stories. Having killed the punchline, he caught his host's eye. 'I shall always remember the glare of pure hatred which I saw in it,' he recalled. Wodehouse was a rising star of the new generation, and Gilbert, whose days were done, must have realized this.

As well as the pleasures of Emsworth, Wodehouse seems also to have been fascinated by Herbert Westbrook. His notebooks, previously devoted to faithful transcriptions of overheard conversations and titbits from the news, suddenly overflow with Westbrook's *obiter dicta*: 'I tell Westbrook I am going to write a story called The Portrait With Awful

Eyes. Ah, he says, an autobiography!' and again, 'Herbert Westbrook: "It is impossible to pass by a barracks without finding a hairpin on the ground."' Occasionally these notebooks capture the tenor of their conversation:

PGW: We have crushed the grapes of life against our palates.
HW: – and spat out the pips! That's the sort of thing that brings the house down if said in a play. It means nothing but sounds well.

Westbrook, 'Westy' or 'Brook', became a central figure in Wodehouse's circle, joining Bill Townend as the dominant third member of a close-knit band of freelancers, now living in the neighbourhood of Piccadilly Circus. A self-centred, outrageous but likeable rogue, he was one of those engaging inveterate hustlers who seem permanently trapped between his last disgraceful misdemeanour and his next grovelling apology. Westbrook was persuasive enough to sustain various literary and theatrical collaborations with Wodehouse, on and off, during the next ten years, until they parted company for good. In later life, Wodehouse spoke with irritation of Westbrook's exasperating ways, and also exacted an affectionate revenge in the character of Ukridge, the fictional embodiment of their long association.

In the summer of 1903 Beach Thomas resigned from 'By the Way'. The new editor of the column was Harold Begbie. His promotion created a vacancy for a full-time staff member on the *Globe* and Wodehouse quickly filled it. According to Beach Thomas, Begbie was 'probably the best hand at the humorous paragraph in prose or verse' since Charles Lamb. Begbie's facility in this genre was 'scarcely credible: verse came from his pen almost at the speed of prose', and Wodehouse, who had already imitated the light verse of W. S. Gilbert in the *Alleynian*, would soon be inspired to emulate his new boss. Even for a member of staff, the hours on the *Globe* were ideal and the work undemanding. By noon, with the day's work done, Wodehouse could concentrate on his own writing, secure in the knowledge that he was getting a solid three guineas a week, a remuneration that was paid every Saturday in a little bag of gold sovereigns.

Work breeds work: 1903–4 saw Wodehouse absorbed in an astonishing output of verses, squibs and short stories, together with a new school serial entitled *The Gold Bat*, for which the *Captain*, a magazine that

catered exclusively for current and former public schoolboys, advanced
£50. *The Gold Bat* is set in Wrykyn, Wodehouse's Shropshire Dulwich,
and, as in *The Pothunters*, the plot turns on a crime – the theft of a
gold replica bat. However, the pleasure for his modern readers comes
not so much from the story, which is efficiently handled, but in the
light, authentic picture of public school life and the hints of the prose
to come. In chapter nineteen, Wodehouse satirizes the practice of his
own headmaster, Gilkes, in having his scholarship pupils read their essays
aloud to him:

[Trevor] was looking forward to the ordeal not without apprehension. The
essay subject this week had been 'One man's meat is another man's poison',
and Clowes, whose idea of English Essay was that it should be a medium for
intempestive frivolity, had insisted on his beginning with 'While I cannot
conscientiously go so far as to say that one man's meat is another man's poison,
yet I am certainly of the opinion that what is highly beneficial to one man
may, on the other hand, to another man, differently constituted, be extremely
deleterious, and, indeed, absolutely fatal.'

It would be another ten years before the sober intervention of Jeeves,
gravely instructing his young master, would give to those concluding
clauses the comic intonation for which Wodehouse would become
renowned. But even Jeeves might have balked at 'intempestive'.
Wodehouse, meanwhile, was experimenting with different voices. Only
a year after he had quit the bank, he was sufficiently well established
to seek a new, national audience, and to do it in a vein rivalling his
colleague Harold Begbie. Enter 'The Parrot'.

In the aftermath of the Boer War (1899–1902), the political question
of the day was the means by which a secure future for the British
Empire could be guaranteed. The argument centred on free trade versus
protection. Joseph Chamberlain, an ambitious Conservative politician
and former Minister for the Colonies, believed that the Empire would
best be united by imperial free trade upheld by 'imperial preference',
a tariff barrier erected against countries outside the Empire. So he
embarked on a barnstorming campaign, up and down the country,
dividing the electorate. 'If you are to give preference to the colonies,'
he told the House of Commons, 'you must put a tax on food.' The
Liberal Party, which believed that 'imperial preference' would mean that

the cost of food would rise, countered with arguments for free trade, and would shortly come to power on the issue.

It was during this intense national debate that, on 30 September 1903, an anonymous poem entitled 'The Parrot', the first of several, appeared on the front page of the *Daily Express*, a pro-Chamberlain conservative paper in favour of 'imperial preference', poking fun at the Liberal Party's objections:

> Where the Cobden Club relaxes into grief at 'stomach taxes',
>> A parrot perches daily just above the entrance door.
> He doesn't mind what's said to him, or sung to him, or read to him,
>> For he can answer nothing but: '*Your food will cost you more.*'

There were five more stanzas in a similar vein, followed by an announcement: 'This wonderful parrot will give his views on fiscal matters tomorrow.'

'The Parrot' was a huge success. The polemical bird gave his opinions on free trade and imperial preference, six days a week, throughout October, the first half of November, and then sporadically into mid-December, printed alongside the *Daily Express*'s sustained and partisan support for Chamberlain. Within the garrulous fraternity of Fleet Street the young Wodehouse's authorship of these verses became an open secret that would give him an entrée into the dazzling world of the theatre. The inventive brilliance of Wodehouse's comic verse now transcended the domestic political issue it was ostensibly addressing:

> Up at Oxford, wrapped in slumber,
> Sits a parrot, and a number
> Of enormous dictionaries
> On the tables and the floor
> Are the treasures which surround him.
> He was dozing when I found him,
> But he opened one eye slowly,
> Saying '*Food will cost you more.*'

> And I said: 'Your classic knowledge
> Is a credit to your college;
> In an Aeschylean chorus
> None deny that you can score;
> Make some sensible suggestion
> On the vexed Homeric question,
> But don't touch that other problem
> Of '*Your food will cost you more*.'

Against the widely held view that Wodehouse was never a political writer, the 'Parrot' verses, on all manner of contemporary political topics, as well as imperial preference, suggest a youthful interest in, and command of, contemporary political debate. The phrase 'Your food will cost you more' became the catchy slogan on which the Liberals would sweep to power in the general election of 1906.

For a few heady weeks, the *Daily Express* had a particularly wonderful time with the popularity of its poetical parrot. On 9 November it reported that 'the King's Jester' Dan Leno, a much-loved music-hall and pantomime star, had acquired two parrots and was training them to repeat, 'Your food will cost you more.' Two days later, the paper was offering a £25 prize to anyone who could teach their parrot the slogan. The next day, 12 November, the *Daily Express* informed its readers that many parrot-owners had begun to instruct their pets and, better yet, that there were even some dealers selling parrots which could repeat the now-celebrated jingle. A few weeks later, the paper announced that so many parrots had been entered for the prize that a competition, sponsored by the *Express* and adjudicated by several show-business celebrities, would be held in the St James's Restaurant on 17 December. 'The Parrot' saluted the imminent contest with:

> Parrots young and parrots mellow
> Parrots grey and parrots yellow
> Welcome to the competition
> Which you now have entered for!

'Screech Day', the *Daily Express* news story, appeared the next day, with Wodehouse, in reporter mode, describing the unaccountable shyness that paralysed these prize birds in public:

There can be no doubt that the absurdity of the phrase which they were set to learn had a depressing effect on the spirits of the birds. They were evidently bored; and no wonder! Most of them had been practising without a break for a month. A few wore a hard-bitten, worried look which spoke eloquently of phonographs and dark rooms . . . there was one parrot which . . . should have walked away with the prize. In private life, it appeared, the talented fowl could not only say 'Your food will cost you more', but make long speeches and sing snatches of song. Yet in the hour of need not one syllable proceeded from its beak. 'Pretty Polly,' shouted its owner, hitting it on the nose to quicken its wits . . . 'Fiscal policy! Fiscal pol-icy!'

He ended his report with a characteristic flourish. 'One owner struck a sinister note. "You can bet your life your food will cost you more," he said grimly to his speechless pet, as he took it back to the ante-room.' A few days later, the *Express* reported with some relief, 'The parrot is dead. He has succumbed to ridicule.' Wodehouse always delighted in the comic potential of the parrot, for example in 'Ukridge Rounds a Nasty Corner' and 'Uncle Fred Flits By', but he was fond of them, too, and kept pet parrots on and off throughout the 1920s and 1930s.

It had been a wonderful autumn. *The Gold Bat* was running in the *Captain*; Wodehouse's second novel, *A Prefect's Uncle*, published in September, was selling steadily; and a collection of school stories, previously published only in magazines, had appeared in November under the title *Tales of St Austin's*. In addition to his success as a freelancer, his *Globe* salary took care of his day-to-day living expenses. He was well paid and popular with his contemporaries. It was with a new self-confidence that, in the new year, 1904, Wodehouse arranged to rent a house called Threepwood, adjoining Emsworth House and its games fields, and perfectly situated for his needs. Now, if Wodehouse wanted to watch the boys playing cricket, or have a spell of bowling in the nets himself, he had only to walk out through the garden of Threepwood. This ugly, red-brick, Victorian seaside dwelling became an essential part of his life from 1904 to 1914. The house was kept during his visits, and in his absence, by Lillian 'Lily' Barnett (née Hill), with whom he would make a close, lifelong friendship, and to whom he expressed, with rare candour, the intense happiness he always felt about Emsworth generally. His new prosperity also meant that he could now fulfil his long-held ambition: a trip to the United States of America.

5. 'I have Arrived'
(1904–1909)

> It would be interesting to know to what extent the work of authors is influenced by their private affairs. If life is flowing smoothly, are the novels they write in that period of content coloured with optimism?
> (*Love among the Chickens*)

'Why America?' is a question Wodehouse addresses in his memoirs, though he never acknowledges the obvious point that it liberated him, once and for all, from his family. He had, he says, 'always yearned to go there'. During his childhood it was 'a land of romance'; and while still at Dulwich he had already told his contemporaries of his intention to visit Philadelphia, the home of the *Saturday Evening Post*, the magazine to which as a young man he most longed to contribute. Once he realized that he was 'sufficiently well fixed to do what I had always dreamed of doing', he was on his way. When the moment came, it was not precisely literature, wanderlust or ambition that prompted the move, though all of these played their part. It was boxing. Wodehouse, an enthusiastic amateur boxer, had secured an introduction to the celebrated former heavyweight champion James 'Gentleman Jim' Corbett. Wodehouse would cross the Atlantic in the hope that he could 'shake the hand that had kayoed John L. Sullivan'.

The decision to visit America was the making of Wodehouse, as momentous in its way as his departure from the bank. After a slow start, he became as much at home in New York as in London, forging a transatlantic literary career long before jet-travel made such a proposition commonplace. On a strict calculation of the time Wodehouse eventually spent in the United States, and the lyrics, books, stories, plays and films he wrote there, to say nothing of his massive dollar income, he should be understood as an American *and* a British writer. Indeed, the notorious crisis in his career, the Berlin broadcasts, occurred as a direct consequence of his deep American, not British, connections.

Wodehouse sailed for New York on the SS *St Louis* on 16 April

1904, sharing a second-class cabin with three others. He arrived in Manhattan on 25 April, staying on Fifth Avenue with a former colleague from the bank. Like many young Englishmen, before and since, he found it an intoxicating experience. To say that New York lived up to its advance billing would be the baldest of understatements. 'Being there was like being in heaven,' he wrote, 'without going to all the bother and expense of dying.'

'Gentleman Jim' Corbett was out of town, but Wodehouse managed to arrange an encounter with the light-heavyweight Kid McCoy, famous for his 'corkscrew' punch, at his training camp in White Plains. McCoy was preparing to fight 'Philadelphia Jack' O'Brien, and Wodehouse claims to have been offered a sparring bout, an opportunity he prudently declined. He did, however, familiarize himself with the American boxing scene, and also picked up from the local press a good working knowledge of New York's gangland culture which he would exploit in *Psmith Journalist*. No experience was ever wasted with Wodehouse. Shortly after this trip he began a series of stories about a boxer named 'Kid' Brady. In his account book, he noted that the trip to Manhattan would be 'worth many guineas in the future, but none for the moment'. Wodehouse returned to London on 20 May and immediately discovered that he had done wisely in going to New York for even so brief a visit. Overnight, he had become an authority on the United States: 'In 1904 anyone in the London writing world who had been to America was regarded with awe. . . . My income rose like a rocketing pheasant.' Now he could charge more for his work, and he had also added another string to his bow. A summer issue of *Punch* finds him writing 'Society Whispers from the States'.

In August, coinciding with the busy aftermath of his American trip, his journalistic fortunes took another upward turn. Harold Begbie resigned from the *Globe* to move to the *Daily Mail* and Wodehouse was promoted again – to the editorship of the 'By the Way' column, with an increased weekly salary of £5 5s. The strength of Wodehouse's identification with the *Globe* was now so complete that he gave The Globe, 367 Strand, as his 'permanent address'. Editorship of the 'By the Way' column might have tempted Wodehouse to ease up. Instead, he made Herbert Westbrook his deputy, with Bill Townend doing occasional stints of holiday cover, and, with his friends in place, was able to keep up his freelance work-rate. In October he began a new serial novel, *The Head of Kay's*, in the *Captain*, for which he was paid £60, and then in November published *William Tell Told Again*, a witty reworking of the Swiss legend, his one and only children's book. By the end of 1904, money worries were at last receding. His year's total was £411 14s. 10d. Wodehouse was certainly wealthy for his age. As he said to Richard Usborne, 'if you had £1 10s. [in the 1900s] you went out and bought a yacht'. To cap it all, that Christmas Wodehouse brought this season of achievement to a climax with an unexpected hit in the West End.

The details of Wodehouse's early involvement with the theatre are obscure, but the Edwardian theatre, in which amateurs and professionals mixed easily, had a special allure for the freelance writer, and he had always been stage-struck. As Wodehouse's prowess as a lyricist of natural grace and invention was becoming more widely known, he had extended his grasp of theatrical technique by enrolling briefly in Mrs Tickell's school of dramatic art in Victoria Street. Towards the end of 1904, he was approached by Owen Hall, the *nom de guerre* of the eccentric and spendthrift playwright James Davis, known in theatrical circles as 'Owing All', to contribute a lyric to his forthcoming musical *Sergeant Brue* at the Strand Theatre. Wodehouse came up with the highly Gilbertian 'Put Me in My Little Cell'. He noted with pride that he 'went and heard it sung on Sat Dec 10 and Monday Dec 12. Encored both times. Audience laughed several times during each verse. This is Fame.'

It was barely two years since he had 'chucked' the bank. He was now just twenty-three, a tall, boyish-looking bachelor with a trim, athletic figure, dark, receding hair and a good-natured shyness that recommended him to everyone he met. He was, he noted in one of his notebooks, 'always quite at my ease (a) with people whose liking I don't want to win, (b) with people who are clever in a way that doesn't impress me e.g. professors etc., (c) with anybody manifestly host-like'. Behind his easygoing diffidence, as those (like Westbrook) who collaborated with him quickly discovered, was a steely determination to succeed and an ambition to make his way in the literary world. In the light of what was to come, his contribution to the opening of *Sergeant Brue* was a comparatively modest beginning, but in the evolution of his genius it was a milestone.

The night after Wodehouse had savoured the sweet sound of those tumultuous encores, he indulged in a rare moment of personal candour, proudly summarizing his achievements at the end of 1904:

On this, the 13th December 1904, time 12pm, I set it down that I have Arrived. Letter from Cosmo Hamilton [playwright] congratulating me on my work and promising [a] commission to write lyrics for his next piece. I have a lyric in 'Sergeant Brue', another − probably − in 'Mr Cingalee', a serial in the 'Captain'. 5 books published, I am editing 'By the Way', *Pearson's* have two stories and two poems of mine, I have finished the 'Kid' Brady stories, I have a commission to do a weekly poem for 'Vanity Fair', and [R. Noel] Pocock [an illustrator of PGW's novels] has just got permanently onto *Pearson's* staff, so in future he will be on the spot.

Here, in sketch form, is Wodehouse's pattern of writing for the next several years − a non-stop juggling of literary work for a variety of patrons in any one of three or four genres: novels, short stories, lyrics and plays, both in London and in New York. Not only was he beginning to explore the art (at which he would later excel) of selling a literary version of Britain to America, and vice versa, in the ten years from 1905 to 1915 his writing also reached a new confidence. Now he began to identify his themes, find his voice, and address an Anglo-American audience for the first time. His later flowering is rooted in the hothouse world of Edwardian magazines and musical theatre; as Evelyn Waugh wrote in a retrospective appreciation, 'the light is kindled which has burned with growing brilliance for half a century'.

After the apprentice years of 1900–1904, Wodehouse, sustaining a prodigious output, was still prowling the streets of London in search of material. His ambitions to social realism can be seen in his account of a conversation with a homeless man in West Kensington reported in his notebook:

70. A shabby man stops me in the Cromwell Road (December 28th 1904) and asks for a light. Says he's 56 and was once at Bedford Grammar school . . . 'I little thought when I sang that old chant "*concinamus o sodales*" that I would come to this. I lost everything in the Liberator. I lost my wife. She's buried at Kensal Green. We have a private grave there (!). I keep it up. I spent my Xmas Day sitting on Barnes Common like a fool, and crying like a baby. I haven't been racketty [*sic*]. Once I thought *nothing* of playing half-crown pool. I was in the City and the firm went to smash. That was 16 months ago, and now I'm wandering through the streets entirely *sine pecunia*.' I gave him a shilling, all I had on me, and wished him luck. Note the interlarding of Latin

phrases, and also the fact that, like a pleasant fellow, he retained his pipe in his poverty. He had an honest, humorous eye, and a cheerful expression.

Like Bertie Wooster's friend Bingo Little, the young Wodehouse was also delighted to converse with waitresses:

213. Miss Congreve, met at Miss B-Ws: charming ladylike girl with sense of humour: is a waitress at Ceylon Kiosk in Dover St: hours 3 to 6.30, but has to stop late if people come: wears dress that cost £6, belongs to proprietor, but is given it at the end of season: if people put her back up, she doesn't give them sugar or forks or napkins next time: hot water and chocolate is served in the same jugs, once she took h.w. to man who wanted chocolate and vice versa, and second man complained wildly that he had poured choc into his tea!

The Cromwell Road is an easy walk from Chelsea. Wodehouse still kept lodgings at the top of 23 Walpole Street, but it is a mark of his new self-assurance and prosperity that he would often repair to Threepwood for bursts of concentrated writing. It was here in the spring of 1905 that he began to work on his first full-blown comic novel, using an idea supplied by Bill Townend about the adventures of an eccentric friend, one Carrington Craxton, on a Devonshire chicken farm.

Love among the Chickens marks Wodehouse's real debut as a comic novelist. Only a few notches above juvenilia, it is a sketch that hints at the work to come. Wodehouse's dedicatory note, a minor art form with him, teasingly blamed Townend for the idea, but the compulsion to write it surely came from his ambition to succeed as a novelist. There was, too, some youthful rivalry with Herbert Westbrook, who appears also to have had designs on Townend's marvellous tale, rashly boasting that he would be the first to reap the rewards in print. Townend had first narrated the story of Carrington Craxton's adventures during a visit to Westbrook's Rupert Street lodgings, subsequently developing the material in a thirty-page letter to Wodehouse. Westbrook appears to have claimed copyright in the material.

On 3 March 1905 Wodehouse wrote to Townend, in the first surviving letter of their lifelong correspondence, angrily asking 'What gory right has he [Westbrook] got to the story any more than me? Tell him so with my love.' His own determination is clear: 'As for me, a regiment of Westbrooks, each slacker than the last, won't stop me. I have the thing mapped out into chapters, and shall go at it steadily.' A restless note of self-criticism was always present in his correspondence with Townend, and he confessed that it wasn't coming out quite as funny as he wanted: 'Chapter one is good, but as far as I have done of Chapter two, introducing Ukridge, doesn't satisfy me. It is flat. I hope, however, to amend this.' He closed by asking Townend for 'more Craxton stories (not improper ones)', taking his best friend into his confidence. 'I have locked up your MS in case of a raid by Westy. Don't give him all the information you've given me.'

Wodehouse's narrative about a struggling young writer, Jeremy Garnet, who, tired of sweating away at his novel in the summer heat of London, accepts an invitation from an old friend, Stanley Feather-stonehaugh Ukridge, to participate in a get-rich-quick scheme, a chicken farm, did not quite succeed in transforming the original anec-dote with the exhilarating lunacy of his later books. Ukridge himself, a disreputable Wrykyn old boy, is described by Garnet as 'the sort of man who asks you out to dinner, borrows the money from you to pay the bill, and winds up the evening by embroiling you in a fight with a cabman'. This is a turning point: never before had Wodehouse found the confidence to place such a character centre-stage in one of his novels. Ukridge is a superannuated public schoolboy for whom life is a 'rag', but he is also a grown-up who, on this debut, even has a wife, Millie, though she is a cipher with little more than a walk-on function.

The genesis of Wodehouse's first comic novel provides a window onto the marginal world of the Edwardian freelancer living in rented rooms on the edge of Soho. The carefully numbered entries in Wodehouse's notebooks, reminiscent of Jerome K. Jerome, convey the atmosphere of his life in and around Leicester Square (especially Rupert and Arundell streets). With their straw hats, pipes and striped blazers, these are the young Edwardians who will populate the pages of Wodehouse's first adult fiction:

73. Westbrook asks me whether reading some English classic did me any good. I say 'Well, I suppose it was like meat going into the sausage mill. It will come out in the form of sausages sometime.'

269. Westbrook is always writing to Dulcimer Moore to get him onto the stage. I say that when he gets into Who's Who he'll put that down under recreations.

357. My suggestions for treating Temple when Westbrook and I are on the go. When T tells a joke, I say to W, 'It's your day for laughing at T's jokes today.' 'No, I laughed yesterday,' says W. We discuss it heatedly. 'Well, look here, who laughed on Friday week?'

Westbrook, the life and soul of the 'Plum–Bill–Brook' trio, was all mouth and no trousers, a 'Prince of Slackers'. In the exploitation of the Craxton story, he never really had a chance. When he set his mind to something, Wodehouse was formidable. It is clear from his manuscript notes that the novel, originally called 'Sunshine and Chickens', sprang to his mind both fully autobiographical and fully formed. The commonplace book, in which, like Jeremy Garnet, he jotted 'memos to self', contains this draft outline: '1. I'm a thorough Londoner. Keen on finishing a novel. While I am sitting in my rooms one June morning, X and his wife come in, are starting chicken farm in Devon. Persuade me to go down. Travel down in same carriage as pretty girl, who is very quiet, but looks as if she had a sense of humour.' On the next page, Wodehouse jots down a rudimentary dramatis personae: 'Hero: Jerry Garnet. X: Ukridge. Servant: Beale . . .' Jeremy Garnet is characterized as 'Old young' by the 'pretty girl' (Phyllis), and he is clearly modelled on the twenty-five-year-old Wodehouse, with his receding hair and grave, rather dry manner. Garnet will become the James Corcoran/Corky of later Ukridge stories.

Ukridge, 'an anecdotal sort of man', and the first in a long line of loquacious bounders that includes Psmith and Uncle Fred, was inspired by Carrington Craxton, but also invokes Herbert Westbrook, larger-than-life sparring partner and friend. At least, this is what Wodehouse himself, never the most reliable of witnesses, subsequently told his French translator in 1952. Townend's own recollection always stressed the importance of Craxton, whom 'I told you about that day in Brook's digs in Rupert Street', a character who 'drank too much and sponged . . . on people'. Townend's account of these early years suggests that he was the junior member of the group and somewhat overawed by 'Westy' who, in his blustery way, always called him 'Tom', not 'Bill'. Townend later told Wodehouse that he could 'write a book about our life in 1906 . . . [Westbrook] used to amuse me immeasurably. He was a much funnier character than Craxton, the prototype of Ukridge . . . Do you remember his "Wude, old man, there's a rabbit under my bed." . . . ? Do you remember his: "Let's go somewhere and have a bit of sammy supper"!'

Ukridge is a charming, fantastical rogue, speaking in a vivid, egotistical, Edwardian slang, habitually dodging an army of red-faced creditors while building castles of imminent prosperity in the air:

I've thought it all over, laddie and it's as clear as mud. No expenses, large profits, quick returns. Chickens, eggs, and the money streaming in faster than you can bank it. Winter and summer underclothing, my bonny boy, lined with crackling Bradbury's. It's the idea of a lifetime. Now listen to me for a moment. You get your hen –

Near-ludicrous in his yellow mackintosh, addressing one and all as 'Old horse', with his pince-nez spectacles precariously attached to his ears by 'ginger-beer wire', and his detachable collar permanently unmoored from its stud, S. F. Ukridge is not as intelligent as Psmith, nor as wool-gathering as Lord Emsworth, nor as effete as Bertie Wooster, but with his 'big, broad, flexible outlook' he is nearly as memorable, though not, perhaps, as universal. To Evelyn Waugh he is too contrived; to many other readers he is too crooked, amoral and self-centred. Where those other Edwardians – Psmith and Jeeves – are memorialized, together with Mr Mulliner and Blandings Castle, on Wodehouse's tombstone in Remsenburg, Long Island, Ukridge is absent. This might not have been his creator's choice. Wodehouse remained fond of him, and published a valedictory Ukridge story ('Ukridge Starts a Bank Account') as late as 1967. Whatever his faults, Ukridge has one great virtue to Wodehouse readers: he is the first in a long line of comic creations and, in the margins of a comic narrative about a West Country chicken farm, his adventures reveal much about the young life of his creator.

The work went well, and soon the manuscript, now entitled *Love among the Chickens*, was ready to be offered to a literary agent. This was a new profession in the world of books, and its pioneer was whispering J. B. Pinker, a rubicund, round-faced, grey-haired sphinx of a man with a protrusive under-lip. Pinker's clients included many of the contem-

porary greats – Wilde, James, Conrad and Wells – but he boasted that
he made a special point of helping young authors in the early stages
of their career. Accordingly, on 1 June 1905 the ambitious young writer
made his first submission of the new manuscript, writing from his offices
at the *Globe* that he would be glad if Pinker would try and place it as
a serial first. This, explained the veteran of the *Captain*, was how he
had planned the work, though he conceded that the editor of *Fry's
Magazine* did not want it.

The idea of selling serial rights before publishing the novel in book
form had a sentimental as well as a commercial motive, one that is
revealing of the threadbare artistic milieu in which the young
Wodehouse was operating. If *Love among the Chickens* was sold as a
serial, Wodehouse hoped that Bill Townend – who was now struggling
to make his way as a commercial artist – could do the illustrations. This
turned out to be impossible, but he did share half the advance with his
friend. Wodehouse, who could be stingy in small things, was unfailingly generous to those for whom he felt responsible.

Perhaps Pinker was discouraged by C. B. Fry's reported coolness,
because he appears not to have responded to the first approach;
Wodehouse was obliged to write again six months later, introducing
himself afresh. During this hiatus, Wodehouse continued to work at his
usual pace. In July he had another important breakthrough, for the first
time selling a cricket story to the *Strand*. In September his sequence of
stories about the fictional American boxer, 'Kid' Brady, began to appear
in print. In October *The White Feather*, the sequel to *The Gold Bat*,
began its serialization in the *Captain*. In December Wodehouse logged
his total freelance earnings for the year 1905 at a grand total of £500.
So it was with renewed self-confidence that he addressed himself to
Pinker in the new year. This time, he underlined his literary creden-
tials, telling Pinker that 'I have made a sort of corner in public-school
stories, and I can always get them taken either by the *Windsor* or one
of the *Pearson* magazines or the *Captain*'. He did not disguise his larger
ambitions. 'I have also written a novel of about 70,000 words,' he wrote,
and informed Pinker that 'a friend of mine on the "New York *World*"
is handling the typed copy in America'.

Now the great literary agent responded with alacrity and had soon
sold *Love among the Chickens* to George Newnes Ltd., breaking with A.
& C. Black, who would nonetheless continue to publish Wodehouse's

school stories. The novel was published in June 1906, and a reprint followed within the year. Money flowed in. Part of the royalties went to pay for Townend's digs in Arundell Street; Townend later recalled a 'wonderful summer'. For Wodehouse, too, the year 1906 would always stand out as an *annus mirabilis* of youthful achievement.

Despite his success, Wodehouse allowed himself few distractions from his routine. There are no significant references to women friends in any of his notebooks, and his emotional life remains obscure. He could always be counted on to watch or play cricket. This recreation had its literary side: he would play for either the *Punch* XI (which included the young A. A. Milne and the light essayist E. V. Lucas) or J. M. Barrie's XI, the Allahakbarries, whose name, said Barrie, derived from the Arabic invocation meaning 'Heaven help us' ('God is great' would be a more accurate translation). The Allahakbarries were an ad hoc team of writers, artists and actors, and their schedule reflected the Edwardian male's obsession with cricket.

Every summer weekend during this opulent decade, young men from the City, or the imperial civil service, or the newspaper and magazine world of Fleet Street and the Strand, would take the train to some nearby provincial town, Tunbridge Wells, perhaps, or Stevenage. There, they would throw their heavy cricket bags into the horse-drawn carriage awaiting them at the station, then rattle through leafy summer lanes to the ground, change into white flannels, play from midday to sundown, breaking only for a cold lunch and a pint or two in the pavilion, before returning to the City in the fading light of summer. In this reassuring, quasi-fraternal society, Wodehouse could wear his school colours, win admiration for his medium-pace bowling, and exchange gossip about the literary world or the fortunes of the *Globe*. He also took his own cricket XI back to Dulwich, occasionally bowling for the Old Alleynians, and fulfilled every cricketer's ambition of playing at Lord's. His team, the Actors vs. Authors, included Arthur Conan Doyle and E. W. Hornung, the creator of Raffles. He also turned out alongside the actor Charles Aubrey Smith, with whom he began a lifelong friendship. Separately, Wodehouse also played with Conan Doyle, joining him in Surrey at his Hindhead country house for long cricketing weekends. He was sufficiently renowned for his cricket and cricket fiction that, on their first meeting, H. G. Wells remarked in a slightly desperate conversational gambit: 'My father was a professional cricketer.'

Wodehouse's cricketing days were almost his only real moment of relaxation in a relentless weekly schedule. Occasionally he would stage impromptu bouts of boxing, describing to Townend how one opponent 'put it all over me. In the second round he was giving me particular Hell.' Throughout his life, Wodehouse relished vigorous physical activity, and part of his daily routine in London included the long, stimulating walk from his Chelsea lodgings to the *Globe*. Wodehouse took his work seriously, but his taste was popular, his audience was made up of clerks and public schoolboys, and it was always his dearest ambition to succeed in the world of musical theatre. By the middle of the Edwardian decade, after 'The Parrot' and *Sergeant Brue*, and in addition to his freelance journalism, he was beginning to fulfil his dream, enjoying considerable *réclame* as a theatrical lyricist. In March 1906, with *Love among the Chickens* at the printers', he was taken on by the celebrated playwright and actor-manager Seymour Hicks, as the resident lyricist at the Aldwych. To be signed up by Hicks was the ultimate accolade, and the commission, according to Westbrook, left Wodehouse so stunned with joy and excitement that, after leaving the stage door at the Aldwych, he walked down the Strand in a mute daze of exhilarated happiness. His first assignment was to contribute a set of topical verses for Hicks's production of Cosmo Hamilton's *The Beauty of Bath*, including 'Mister Chamberlain', a song reminiscent of his 'Parrot' poems, satirizing the apostle of tariff reform.

> He plays for Aston Villa by way of keeping fit
> He runs the mile in four fifteen and wrestles Hackenschmidt.

The new job at the Aldwych, adapting the show's lyrics to the events of the day, paralleled his work on the *Globe*, but now, for the first time, he had to learn to collaborate with an equally gifted musical partner. This, by chance, was the brilliant young American composer who had been shipped over for the run, Jerome D. Kern.

The precocious son of Fannie and Henry Kern, well-to-do New Yorkers with a love of music and theatre, 'Jerry' Kern could hardly have had a more different childhood and upbringing from 'Plum' Wodehouse's. His youthful and approachable parents had been unfailingly supportive of their much-loved son; he himself was bursting with confidence, charm and a sharp intelligence. A schoolboy pianist known as 'the little genius', he had made his first stage appearance in March 1901, riding a velocipede, circling the stage before settling down at the keyboard to treat an enthusiastic audience to a medley of ragtime music. By 1906, the curly-headed kid with glasses, barely twenty-one, who had already made his London debut in 1903 with his contribution to *An English Daisy*, was now commuting across the Atlantic between Broadway and the West End. He had a three-year contract with Seymour Hicks and his American partner, Charles Frohman, to write twelve songs a year. In March 1906, as part of his contract, he was summoned by Hicks to interpolate three songs into the score of his latest venture, *The Beauty of Bath*. Wodehouse recalled meeting the New York prodigy at the Aldwych. Kern, in shirtsleeves, was sitting apart, playing poker with some members of the cast. When the shy lyricist finally managed to get him away from the card table and was able to talk with him, he was impressed: 'Here, I thought, was a young man supremely confident of himself – the kind of person who inspires people to seek him out when a job must be done.' Kern, for his part, did not forget the happy experience of working with the bespectacled Englishman who could accurately remember any tune he'd heard and who, less demanding than many lyricists, preferred to fit the words to music already composed.

'Mister Chamberlain' was a hit, wildly encored in the theatre and enthusiastically written up in the London press. Wodehouse's budding career as a theatrical lyricist was also helped by his friendship with Seymour Hicks and his wife, the actress Ellaline Terriss. They were fond of the young man, and would often invite him to stay with them in the country. Even here, Wodehouse was always writing. Hicks and Terriss teasingly called him 'the Hermit' but were impressed by his self-discipline. His devotion to his work, however, does not seem to have made him remote or unapproachable, but rather innocent and harmless. He was 'like a rather large boy, with an open and happy nature', Terriss later remembered.

Wodehouse's surviving notebooks from this time contain many scenes from the lives of Seymour Hicks and Cosmo Hamilton, suggesting that the 'boy' Wodehouse was more than a little stage-struck:

127. Behind scenes at Chelsea Palace Music Hall. Lanes of cloth stretched to ceiling, ending in brightly-lit stage. bare white-washed walls with hot water pipes (in wire case) and hose and red buckets. Above stage rows of electric

lights in coloured glasses with wires over them. Tattered notice on wall relating to Music-Hall Benevolent Fund (some pro's 'Appeal' to the Profession, stating how reluctantly he had taken charge of the thing).

Occasionally, he would experiment with a clumsy approximation to a Wildean *pensée*.

131. We all act through life, and each of us selects the special audience he wishes to impress. When this audience is not looking at us we are never really happy, however many other people are applauding.

Wodehouse seems also to have wanted to imitate his theatrical mentor. In November 1906, with some trepidation, he bought Hicks's Darracq motor car for the colossal sum of £450. Like Conrad and Kipling, he was entranced by the new century's first great invention but, unlike theirs, his dream ended in a ditch. He crashed the Darracq within a week. For the rest of his life he greatly preferred to be driven, though he did manage a spell behind the wheel in the streets of New York City in the 1920s ('motoring', with 'cricket, boxing, football, swimming' were the hobbies he listed in his *Who's Who* entry). Hicks, meanwhile, took his star lyricist with him to the newly opened Hicks Theatre (now the Gielgud) in Shaftesbury Avenue for the premiere of *The Beauty of Bath* during the Christmas season of 1906.

The experience of writing for the theatre left a profound mark on Wodehouse, one that he always acknowledged, to the point, he once said, that he classed his characters as if they were living, salaried actors. He wrote to Townend:

I'm convinced that this is a rough but very good way of looking at them. The one thing actors – important actors, I mean – won't stand is being brought on to play a scene which is of no value to them in order that they may feed some less important character, and I believe this isn't merely vanity but is based on an instinctive knowledge of stagecraft. You must never, never subordinate your hero.

On the Broadway of Wodehouse's imagination, the traffic went in both directions. Many of his novels (notably *A Gentleman of Leisure*, *A Damsel in Distress* and *Leave It to Psmith*) became plays. The novel *Hot Water* was retitled as a play, *The Inside Stand*. *If I Were You* began as a play, became a short novel, and was rewritten as a play, *Who's Who*. In one exceptional case, *Spring Fever* was adapted for the stage, rewritten as a new novel, *The Old Reliable*, and then revised as a play (though never performed). Indeed, Wodehouse was in his seventies before he finally retired from the provisional, rackety world of theatrical touring he had first glimpsed with Seymour Hicks in 1906.

The story of these years is work, work and more work. His child-hood had left its mark. Better to be alone than take the risk of company. Better to enjoy the fiendish complexity of plot than the troubling complexity of everyday life. Better to exert control over an imaginary world and keep the demons at bay than suffer the manipulations of fate and allow the intrusion of melancholy. Wodehouse's youthful appetite for literary activity was insatiable. As the year turned, he settled down in Threepwood for a fresh burst of writing: a new school story and another collaboration with Herbert Westbrook, with whom Wodehouse appears to have patched up his friendship.

Not George Washington, now a very rare book, owes something to *The Moonstone* (it has no fewer than four different narrative points of view) and a great deal to the freelance literary lives of its co-authors. The novel's protagonists, Julian Eversleigh and James Orlebar Cloyster, are thinly disguised self-portraits. Eversleigh, for instance, has a top-floor flat over a baker's shop on the corner of Rupert Street, just like Westbrook. Young Cloyster works for a newspaper, the *Orb*, writes a column called 'On Your Way', burns to succeed as a writer, and actually lives at 23 Walpole Street. Cloyster wants to achieve enough literary success to marry his Guernsey sweetheart, Miss Margaret Goodwin. The plot turns on his cunning plan to maximize the sale of his writing by persuading four complete strangers to put their names to his work. Cloyster, exercised by the conflict between the demands of love (he wants to marry Margaret) and the call of literature, resolves, he says, 'to be a Bohemian, but a misogynist'. At times, the autobiographical quality of Cloyster's narrative is eerie in its confessional specificity: 'In addition to verses, I kept turning out a great quantity of prose, fiction and otherwise, but without much success . . . I worked extraordinarily hard at that time. All day sometimes.'

There is much that is silly and forgettable about *Not George Washington*, but for Wodehouse it was supposed to be the beginning of a long-term collaboration. When he wrote in January 1907 to urge Pinker to 'close with Cassell's offer' he announced, apropos future contracts, that 'Westbrook and I are going to do a series'. Inevitably, the bulk of the writing had fallen to Wodehouse, the willing workhorse (in correspondence with Pinker he is distinctly proprietorial about the 'things I should like to alter in the MS of *NGW*'), but once the book was in production, it pleased him to play second fiddle to Westbrook. In a fierce letter to Cassells complaining that he and Westbrook had been credited in the wrong order on the title page, he wrote, 'I absolutely refuse to give people the impression that I wrote the book with some slight help from Mr Westbrook when my share in it is really so slight.' In a draft press-release, he added, 'The central idea, the working out of the plot and everything that is any good at all in the book are by "H. Westbrook". The rest is by "P. G. Wodehouse".' Such apparent contradiction is of a piece with Wodehouse's character during his long literary apprenticeship. Like many young writers of immense talent, but with everything to prove, he believed in himself, and yet had no confidence. He was bold and timid; light-footed and awkward; single-minded and uncertain.

Throughout the long, 287-performance, run of *The Beauty of Bath* and the writing of *Not George Washington*, Wodehouse kept up his daily schedule of work on the *Globe* and ceaseless freelance contributions. He was also planning a new school story, though he confessed to Pinker that he was tiring of 'my boys' work'. By the spring of 1907 he felt he had gone 'as far in that direction now as I am ever likely to get'. Certainly, most of his freelance interest and energy this year was focused on journalism and the stage. In March he supplied additional lyrics to *My Darling*, a new show at the Hicks Theatre, followed by an extra number for a Footlights May week musical, *The Honorary Degree*; and then, in September, he contributed two lyrics to *The Gay Gordons*, another Hicks production at the Aldwych. He also had a walk-on part as a butler in a one-off, copyright performance of a play by Duncan Tovey which did not reach commercial production. In November he and Westbrook put on *The Bandit's Daughter*, a 'musical sketch' with a score by Ella King-Hall, at the Bedford Theatre in Camden Town. This theatrical venture was, he reported, 'a frost!', closed swiftly and left no trace in the stage records of the time.

The flop in Camden seems not to have hurt Wodehouse's reputation. In December 1907 he was poached as a lyricist by the Gaiety Theatre. He took the separation from Hicks in his stride. With a rare display of self-confidence, he advertised his prowess as a theatre lyricist in the gaudy new personalized writing paper he had had printed for his freelance correspondence. Beneath his name, in a bold, scarlet gothic script, he described himself, in stage and newspaper terms, as not only 'Editor "By the Way" column, The Globe' but also 'Writer of Lyrics to the Gaiety Theatre'. In addition to his books, he listed several recent 'song successes'.

He had not abandoned novels. Far from it. Before he bade farewell for ever to the school stories that had served him so well, there was a swansong, a serial in the *Captain*, that was later identified by Evelyn Waugh and George Orwell, among many, as a crucial turning point in the development of his writing. *Jackson Junior* (the first part of the novel *Mike*) brings together the two main strands of his fiction so far. There are the adolescent adventures of the bolshie but gifted schoolboy cricketer, Mike Jackson, the youngest of five brothers, probably inspired by the Worcestershire cricketing brothers Foster. This is the kind of straightforward school yarn, with 'breaking out' and 'rags', punctuated by some brilliantly narrated cricket matches, scenes at which Wodehouse was the master. And then there are the elements of the story drawn from Wodehouse's life: the school holidays in Shropshire; the high-spirited trio of baby sisters reminiscent of the Bowes-Lyon girls; the sibling rivalry between Mike and brother Bob; and the disapproving father dishing out fateful decisions to his wayward son like a remote deity.

Jackson Junior, as its title implies, concerns the education (through cricket and other equally hard knocks) of young Mike. On first encounter, about to go to Wrykyn, Mike is an insufferably precocious schoolboy cricketer. When the story ends, Mike is a triumphant cricketer but a poor scholar, deeply at odds with the authorities. Mike's comeuppance occurs in the sequel, *The Lost Lambs*. Again, the story starts during the holidays, at the Jackson family home. This time Mike is in real trouble. His father has decided to take him away from Wrykyn and send him to Sedleigh to get a proper education. There, a reluctant new boy, mourning his expulsion from the paradise of Wrykyn, he meets a fellow exile, another 'lost lamb', an Old Etonian, recently converted to Socialism – enter Rupert (later, Ronald) Psmith, a recognizably grown-up character, far more complex and original than Ukridge.

Psmith ('the p . . . is silent, as in ptarmigan, psalm and phthisis') is one of Wodehouse's most popular creations, a character, crucially, who appealed to an adult as well as a schoolboy readership, a 'grown-up among boys'. Indeed, until the 1920s Wodehouse's nascent literary fame rested not on Jeeves and Wooster, nor Lord Emsworth, but on Psmith. More lovable than Ukridge, more self-confident than Bertie Wooster, at times more potent even than Jeeves, Psmith is the most eloquent and commanding of all Wodehouse's creations. Until the end of the First World War, Psmithisms ('Psmith is baffled'; 'Psmith is himself again') were an essential part of the conversational currency of the English public schoolboy.

Like his creator, Psmith is through with school. He would rather have supper at the Savoy than meat and two veg in the college dining hall. Where Wodehouse's schoolboy protagonists slog manfully through life on foot, Psmith prefers to take a taxi. Like many Wodehouse heroes, he is embroiled in plot, flirting with danger and hovering on the brink of catastrophe, but where Ukridge is eloquent but flustered, Psmith is loquacious but nonchalant. 'Don't talk so much! I never met a fellow like you for talking!' says Freddie Threepwood in *Leave It to Psmith*. 'Psmith', as Richard Usborne has written, 'is the Knut.'

A knut, preceded by the 'masher' of the 1890s, was quintessentially Edwardian, a 'fashion-eddy' with antecedents in the fops and dandies of Restoration comedy and the plays of Sheridan. A knut was a figure of fun in the Edwardian editions of *Punch*, an amiable cove you could laugh at but hardly despise, given to absurd expressions like 'Oojah-cum-spiff' and 'Tinkerty-tonk'. Wodehouse himself wrote that the knut was descended from 'the Beau, the Buck, the Macaroni, the Johnnie, the Swell, and the Dude' and should be distinguished from 'the Blood', a young man who causes riots in restaurants. The knut is 'too listless to do anything so energetic'. Wodehouse also noted that the knut 'speaks a language of his own. Pleasant happenings "brace him awfully": unpleasant happenings "feed" him: a friend is a "stout fellow": an enemy a "tick".' It is in language that Psmith displays his knutishness. Irrepressibly verbal, Psmith will never admit to being 'in the soup', though he might refer to '*consommé* splashing about the ankles', or concede to being 'knee-deep in the *bouillon*'. Psmith, the knut, provides the essential link to the innocent persiflage of Bertie Wooster and even to the mandarin omniscience of Jeeves. Like Wodehouse himself, the range of his vocabulary is matched by an instinctive love of quotation from the classics ('*solvitur ambulando*') and from the kind of English poetry learned at public school. Psmith is never lost for words – either his own, or other people's.

Faultlessly dressed, with impeccable manners, and perfect breeding, Psmith is also a natural star. 'Psmith is a major character,' Wodehouse wrote to Townend in 1936. 'If I am going to have Psmith in a story, he must be in the big situation.' Psmith, like Ukridge, is pure Edwardian, but, in contrast to Ukridge, there is no controversy about Psmith's origins. Wodehouse was always straightforward about having based him on Rupert D'Oyly Carte, the son of the Gilbert and Sullivan impresario, claiming that D'Oyly Carte was the Wykehamist friend of a cousin, and 'the only thing in my literary career which was handed to me on a plate with watercress around it'. Wodehouse, who often said he preferred not to know too much about the characters he was inventing, romanticized the attribution. D'Oyly Carte, he would say, was tall, slender, always beautifully dressed and very dignified. He habitually addressed his fellow Wykehamists as 'Comrade' and if one of the masters chanced to inquire as to his health, would reply, with camp affectation, 'Sir, I grow thinnah and thinnah.'

Jackson Junior was serialized in the *Captain* from April 1907. *The Lost Lambs* did not begin serialization in the *Captain* until April 1908, but both did very well. 'I have made a big hit with my serial,' Wodehouse boasted to Pinker. 'I have had golden opinions from all sorts of men.' Now he linked his success with a hard-headed demand for an adult edition. 'I want to run it as a 6/- novel and not as a boys' story.' Pinker arranged to have the two serials published as *Mike*. Wodehouse quickly followed up with another Psmith story, entitled *The New Fold*, a comic novel based on his experiences at the Hongkong and Shanghai Bank that also cast a satirical eye over Edwardian socialism, and is probably one of the best exposés of office life of its kind. Although this was in no sense a school story, it continued the adventures of Mike and Psmith and appeared in the *Captain* from October 1908 to March 1909, and it was later published as *Psmith in the City*.

Having completed the manuscript of *The Lost Lambs* 'with incredible sweat', Wodehouse returned to his journalism and was soon responding to another lucrative commission. 'Here's a go,' Wodehouse wrote to Townend on 6 May 1908. 'I've been commissioned by "*Chums*" to do a serial (70,000 words) by July. They want it not so public-schooly as my usual, with rather a lurid plot.' This time, possibly because he felt obliged to help Townend, he proposed a collaboration, a modus operandi that satisfied his insatiable appetite for work as well as the constant need for companionship. As usual, Wodehouse did all the work. A 'story of fun and adventure at school', *The Luck Stone* owes everything, as Richard Usborne has identified, to three late-Victorian best-sellers that Wodehouse knew well: Wilkie Collins's *The Moonstone*, Conan Doyle's *The Sign of Four* and F. Anstey's *Baboo Jabberjee*. Wodehouse probably knew his book was derivative. When *The Luck Stone* first appeared in *Chums* in September 1908, its authorship was ascribed, pseudonymously, to 'Basil Windham'.

Wodehouse took the work because he was nervous about his regular income. In the new year of 1908, the *Globe*, the anchor of his free-lance life, was sold by its proprietors, the Armstrong family, to Hildebrand Harmsworth, brother of Alfred, Lord Northcliffe. The new proprietor, inspired by his brother's example, began to flex his muscles by ordering changes of style and tempo. Wodehouse and Westbrook were instructed to popularize the 'By the Way' column and compile a one-shilling promotional paperback, *The Globe By the Way Book*, 'A Literary Quick Lunch for People Who Have Only Got Five Minutes', an anthology of extracts from the column. This was one of Wodehouse's last literary co-productions with Westbrook and unques-tionably the worst. He was all too ready to leave the world of jour-nalistic collaboration, but before he finally made the break with the *Globe* and the world of deadlines, he could not resist yet another potboiling commission to write one of the paper-covered shilling books so popular around 1909, a topical spoof partly inspired by his career as a newspaperman.

Wodehouse the novelist was detached from day-to-day concerns, but Wodehouse the topical lyricist and Wodehouse the journalist were only too well aware of contemporary affairs. In the late 1900s anti-German feeling, provoked by alarmist stories in the popular press about the German dreadnought programme, had inspired a vigorous 'invasion-scare' literature. The appetite for war fantasies among a new generation of popular magazine readers was not lost on Alfred Harmsworth, a rabid germanophobe, who commissioned William Le Queux to write *The Invasion of 1910* for serialization in the *Daily Mail*, and then advertised the story throughout London with sandwich-men dressed in Prussian-blue uniforms and spiked helmets. Le Queux's sensational effort inspired all kinds of responses, from cartoons to a Guildhall speech by Winston Churchill.

For Wodehouse, the subject was topical but it was not new. He had satirized invasion scares in *Punch* six years before. Nonetheless, early in 1909 he sat down and by his own, never trustworthy, account, dashed off *The Swoop!*, a satirical novella of some 25,000 words, in five days flat, having 'a great deal of fun writing it'. Subtitled 'How Clarence Saved England', *The Swoop!* describes how England falls beneath 'the heels of nine invaders' – Russian, German, Chinese, Moroccan, Turk, Swiss, Monégasques of Monaco, a Mullah from Somaliland and the 'Bollygollans'. Wodehouse's basic joke, a good one, is that the English are indifferent to international politics until they impinge on the nation's sporting prospects, for example threatening to disrupt a forthcoming test match against Australia.

The Swoop! is a curiosity, but a revealing one. It deftly subverts the conventions of an odd little genre. In place of the customary North Sea naval engagement, the invaders arrive like day-trippers at Brighton, Lyme Regis and 'the little Welsh watering place, Llgxtpll'. The 'bombardment of London' is not the blood-curdling set piece readers had come to expect, but a three-line chapter, exhibiting all Wodehouse's distaste for violence. In *The Swoop!*, England becomes a loony paradise in which the boy scout hero, Clarence Chugwater, 'a sturdy lad of some fourteen summers' who 'could spoor, fell trees, tell the character from the boot-sole, and fling the squaler', vanquishes Prince Otto of Saxe-Pfennig, Captain von Poppenheim and the Grand Duke Vodkakoff. It is an ebullient satire on Edwardian imperial pretensions, whose targets include politicians, generals, journalists and judges, all of whom will later become regular victims of Wodehouse comedy.

Most farcical of all, that absurd sub-imperial figure Clarence Chugwater saves England by the simple device of making the rival Russian and German commanders jealous of their respective music-hall fees. As it hurtles towards its denouement, showing every sign of hasty composition, the plot of *The Swoop!* now turns on Wodehouse's familiarity with Edwardian music halls and the Edwardian popular press. While it remains outside the mainstream of his work, he did not disown it, and artistically it unites the two main strands of his youthful creativity during the Edwardian years. *The Swoop!* was published in April 1909 and did not sell well: 'the people who read it, if placed end to end, would have reached from Hyde Park Corner to about the top of Arlington Street,' Wodehouse self-mockingly remembered. He was not destined to become a satirist, although a vein of gentle satire certainly does run through his later work.

Meanwhile, Wodehouse had not forgotten *Love among the Chickens*, the novel that, in 1906, he had believed would put him on the literary map in America. Thanks to the vicissitudes of youthful literary endeavour, this had turned out to be a circuitous route. His friend on the *World*, Norman Thwaites, eventually placed the manuscript with a New York literary agent, A. E. Baerman, an 'author's representative' whose technique Wodehouse described in a neglected essay, 'The First Time I Went to New York':

Most people bring back certain definite impressions from their first visit to New York . . . My whole attention throughout my visit was absorbed by Jake Skolsky [A. E Baerman], the capable and enthusiastic literary agent . . . I had sent the MS of . . . 'Love Among The Chickens,' to an English friend living in New York. Pressure of business compelled him to hand it over to a regular agent. He gave it to Jake. That was the expression he used in writing to me – 'I am giving it to Jake Skolsky' – and I think Jake must have taken the word 'giving' literally. Certainly, when the book was published in America, it had on its title page 'Copyright by Jacob Skolsky', and a few years later, when the story was sold for motion pictures, I was obliged to pay Jake two hundred and fifty dollars to release it.

Skolsky/Baerman did at least get the book published, and did raise from the publisher the 'fantastic' sum – to Wodehouse – of $1,000. 'It was great gravy,' he writes. 'There was just one flaw in my happiness. The money seemed a long time in coming . . .' Eventually, after many vicissitudes (and no cheque), the young Wodehouse decided to head across the Atlantic. 'In several of his letters Jake had told me I was a coming man. I came.' Actually, a typical Wodehouse elision of facts, this was his *second* visit to New York, but this time he stayed.

6. 'I want to butt into the big league'
(1909–1914)

'Hang it!' said Bill to himself in the cab, 'I'll go to America!' . . . Bill's knowledge of the great republic across the sea was at this period of his life a little sketchy . . . Of American cocktails he had a fair working knowledge, and he appreciated ragtime. But of the other great American institutions he was completely ignorant. (*Uneasy Money*)

Wodehouse later claimed that he did not intend to linger in America but, as in 1904, would just take a holiday from the *Globe*, anticipating that 'after nineteen days I would have to . . . go back to the salt mines'. He did, however, arrive in Manhattan with two completed short stories and, denouncing the devious Baerman to his friends, acquired a new literary agent, Seth Moyle, who rapidly sold both stories for the incredible sum of $500, a sudden infusion of money that transformed Wodehouse's circumstances. So perhaps he had hoped to strike gold.

Whatever his secret expectations, the discovery, while his stories were commanding less than ten guineas in London, that American editors were prepared to pay on such a stupendous scale was, he wrote many years later, 'like suddenly finding a rich uncle from Australia. This, I said to myself, is the place to be.' Bubbling over with hope and ambition, he immediately cabled his resignation to the *Globe* and took a room in what he described as 'a seedy rookery' at the corner of Washington Square, inhabited by a group of young writers as impecunious as himself. He was exaggerating, as usual. The recently built Hotel Earle, 103 Waverly Place, on the edge of Greenwich Village, a short walk from Bleecker, Delancey and Wooster streets, was a fine eight-storey establishment with a tradition of artistic patronage; it would be his regular New York base until 1913.

Abe Baerman remained as slippery as ever. Then as now, good literary agents were hard to find in New York, and even Moyle, Wodehouse's new representative, turned out to be cut from the same cloth, combining Baerman's evasiveness on questions of money with an extraordinary knack of fast-talking an editor into taking a story. There was no mistaking Moyle's energy ('all that day we were dashing into elevators, dashing out, plunging into editorial offices . . . plunging out, leaping into street cars'), but Moyle's weakness, Wodehouse soon discovered, was that 'although he could always sell *one* story to any editor he'd also sell a lot of rotten stuff'. Magazine editors became wary of Moyle, and clients like Wodehouse suffered as a result. His unflattering portrait of 'Jake Skolsky', a busy little man wreathed in clouds of cigar smoke, was inspired by Baerman, but it owed something to Moyle, too. Looking back on his dealings with these literary jackals, Wodehouse concluded:

There is no question of the value of an association with Jake in the formative years of an author's life. Mine was the making of me. Critics today sometimes say that my work would be improved by being less morbid, but nobody has ever questioned its depth. That depth I owe to Jake. (He owes me about two thousand dollars.)

Now resident in Manhattan, Wodehouse could pursue Baerman for the advance due on *Love among the Chickens*; he could also celebrate its American publication, on 11 May. It was an auspicious debut, saluted by the *New York Times* as 'the slightest, airiest sort of a tale . . . cleverly told, and never lacking in good taste'. To his writing friends at the Hotel Earle, the young English novelist quickly became known, with teasing irony, as 'Chickens'. Once again, he had found himself at home in a circle of struggling freelancers, and, once again, he set about writing for the 'pulps'. Here, as in London, it was a golden age for magazines, and he was an old hand at the art of catering to the tastes of rival editors.

With the money from *Cosmopolitan* and *Collier's*, he bought a second-hand Monarch typewriter, a temperamental beast of a machine that required constant maintenance, and settled into his room at the top of the Earle, with paper, pencils and his trusty copy of *Bartlett's Familiar Quotations*, exciting much amazement among the resident Americans by his habit of walking up and down the hotel stairs in preference to taking the elevator. Breaking only for meals, he would write all day: stories, reviews and a novel about an Englishman in America, provisionally entitled 'The Black Sheep'. There is no reason to question his assertion that life was hard. After Moyle's golden start, both *Collier's* and

Cosmopolitan rejected his later submissions. Without the pulps, Wodehouse said afterwards, he would 'soon have been looking like a famine victim'. But he put the best face on things in his letters home. George Wilson, his editor at A. & C. Black, wrote that he was very glad to hear his author was becoming so prosperous: 'I have no doubt we shall be hearing of you in the public prints as the "Millionaire humorist of the States",' a reference to the latest Psmith serialization, Wodehouse's shrewd exploitation of Psmith's popularity.

Psmith Journalist, originally 'Psmith USA', reveals a new side to Wodehouse. It still features Mike and Psmith (he could not risk losing his public-school readers) but, for the first time, the action is set exclusively in the magazine and boxing world of New York City with which its author had become so familiar. As well as being set in a grown-up world, *Psmith Journalist* also has ambitions to social realism. The Lower East Side gangsterism with which Psmith becomes farcically embroiled is based on Wodehouse's reading of the newspapers in 1904, a fact he was at pains to stress in his preface: 'The "gangs" of New York exist in fact. I have not invented them. Most of the incidents in this story are based on actual happenings.' Bat Jarvis, the cat-loving hoodlum from 'Groome Street' who comes to Psmith's aid, bears a striking resemblance to Monk Eastman, the leader of a gang of twelve hundred hoodlums, who had attracted widespread New York newspaper coverage throughout the 1900s. Eastman was a gangster straight out of the movies, but no picture himself, with a bullet-shaped head, a bull neck and scarred cheeks. Like many thugs, Eastman was soft-hearted towards animals, kept a bird and animal store on Broome Street, and would often venture out with a cat under each arm, a blue pigeon happily perched on his shoulder. 'I like de kits and boids,' he reportedly said. 'I'll beat up any guy dat gets gay wit' a kit or a boid in my neck of de woods.' Like Eastman, Jarvis 'wore his hair in a well-oiled fringe almost down to his eyebrows, which gave him the appearance of having no forehead at all'. Jarvis is also partial to cats: 'Fond of de kit, I am.' As the thrillerish comic plot of *Psmith Journalist* unfolds, Wodehouse displays a steadily more confident knowledge of New York gang life, but as in *The Swoop!* his ambition for social satire is thwarted by the innocence of his vision, his distaste for violence and his reluctance, as he would put it later, to go 'right deep down into life . . . not caring a damn'.

To celebrate its serialization of a new Wodehouse novel, the *Captain* commissioned an article about Wodehouse from L. H. Bradshaw, a young freelance writer. Wodehouse turned up for the interview in a stripey black and purple Incogniti cricketing blazer with the thin gold stripe. He was still the tall, dark-haired, well-built young man with the vigorous handshake, the genial manner and the hearty laugh familiar in London literary, theatrical and journalistic circles. There was the same detached thoughtfulness, too. Wodehouse, Bradshaw wrote, 'makes you feel that he is very carefully considering what you are saying . . . [and is] un-usually well-read and well-informed'. Bradshaw's profile conveys a convincing impression of 'Chickens' in his new habitat, and reported that the magazine's star author was in America 'getting local colour for a new tale'. As usual with Wodehouse, the conversation quickly turned to writing, a discussion of the *Captain*'s interest in his stories, and his own preference for 'light compositions'. There was, inevitably, also talk of boxing, rugby football, soccer and cricket. This was the first time Wodehouse had submitted to journalistic analysis, but it was hardly searching. Bradshaw, for whom Wodehouse was 'a fine specimen of the public school man at his best', told the *Captain*'s readers that the author of *The Gold Bat* and *The Lost Lambs* was being spoken of as 'a second O. Henry', and that he had 'already made a big reputation here as an original humourist of the first water'.

Wodehouse, described as 'a person who likes most people and whom most people like', quickly made a friend of a journalist sent to interview him, encouraged Bradshaw's own ambitions to be a writer, signed his letters 'Chickens', and was soon offering him the use of his notebooks ('Use any public-school stuff you like,' he wrote, 'but don't swipe me other notes!'). He also wrote frankly of his literary ambitions. 'So far from wanting my boys' books published this side,' he confided to Bradshaw,

I look on them as a guilty past which I must hush up. I want to start here with a clean sheet as a writer of grown-up stories. The *Captain* books are all right in their way, but the point of view is too immature. They would kill my chances of doing anything big. I don't want people here to know me as a writer of school stories. I want to butt into the big league.

Wodehouse repeated the theme already broached the year before with Pinker: 'The school stories have served their turn, and it would hurt my chances of success to have them bobbing up when I'm trying to do bigger work. I have given up boys' stories absolutely.' To make this transition to what he would later call 'my middle period' was an arduous process to which Wodehouse applied himself with his usual single-mindedness.

In the latter part of 1909, with *Psmith Journalist* serialized in the *Captain*, he concentrated on his assault on 'the big league', starting work on *The Black Sheep*, followed by *The Prince and Betty* and *The Little Nugget*. Then, early in 1910, Wodehouse returned to England. His second New York adventure had lasted longer than the first, but it had not been an un-qualified success. Was he homesick? There is no record of this, though it would have been quite out of character to concede defeat. Was he broke? Apparently not. He seems to have renewed his lease on Threepwood and to have taken up at Emsworth where he had left off. Was he returning to pursue a romance with a lonely widow? In the remote and well-camouflaged world of his emotions, there are strong suggestions of a liaison with a Mrs Lillian Armstrong, whose daughter 'Bubbles' corresponded with Wodehouse until his death, and who believed her mother had spurned his proposal of marriage. Again, apart from a tantalizing reference to a children's tea party in Battersea, nothing reliable about this relationship survives. He was, however, able to return to his post on the *Globe* and to resume his old working habits. Shortly after his return, a new story, 'The Man Upstairs', appeared in the *Strand*.

His second visit to New York had given him an important insight into his marketability in America. Handicapped by knowing so little about American life, he now resolved to write about England. 'I knew quite a lot about what went on in English country houses . . .' he reflected later. 'In my childhood in Worcestershire and later in my Shropshire days, I had met earls and butlers and younger sons in some profusion.' At last he was beginning to explore the possibility of using this English material in a way that would appeal to an American reader-ship, in a novel that would be the prototype of the house-party com-edies of his prime. Now he quickly completed *The Black Sheep*, a tale about an English ex-newspaperman with hardly a reference to public schools, and sold it to W. J. 'Billy' Watt, a maverick New York publisher, who retitled it *The Intrusion of Jimmy*.

Published in Britain later the same year as *A Gentleman of Leisure*, this new novel precisely reflects Wodehouse's recent American experi-ence. When the story starts, Jimmy Pitt, a square-jawed young

Englishman of the Mike Jackson variety, has just returned to New York, as Wodehouse often did, on the *Mauretania*. In addition to a full complement of Wodehouse blessings (he is single, with independent means, perfect health and 'no relations'), Jimmy has just fallen in love – at a distance – with a girl on the boat. In the rowdy, late-night atmosphere of his club, popular and self-confident young Jimmy bets an actor friend who is playing the lead in a new 'Raffles' drama, then in vogue, that any fool could burgle a house and, what is more, that he would do it himself that very night. He enlists the services of a Lower East Side professional burglar, Spike Mullins, but then has the misfortune to select for his break-in the property of a corrupt police captain, John McEachern, who turns out to be the father of Molly, the girl on the boat.

Amid the multiplying improbabilities of the plot (touches of the later comic mayhem but none of its effortlessness), the turning point in the book, a crucial one in Wodehouse's literary career, occurs when the scene dissolves cinematically from turn-of-the-century Manhattan to Dreever Castle, Shropshire, 'nominally ruled over by Hildebrand Spencer Poyns de Burgh John Hannasyde Coombe-Crombie, twelfth Earl of Dreever ("Spennie" to his relatives and intimates), but in reality the possession of his uncle and aunt, Sir Thomas and Lady Julia Blunt'. Here the devoted Wodehouse reader discovers an early sketch for a picture that will become all too familiar: a country house of immemorial ancestry, infested by a tyrannical aunt, a paternal butler and a hopeless but amiable young peer intent on marrying against his uncle's wishes. Throw in a diamond necklace, Spike Mullins and a private detective and you have most of the ingredients of a Blandings story.

A Gentleman of Leisure took 7,000 copies in pre-publication orders. It did not transform Wodehouse's prospects, but it did attract the attention of the American theatrical producer William A. Brady, who invited the author to adapt it for the stage in collaboration with the playwright John Stapleton. Wodehouse accepted the commission gladly, in part for the excuse it gave him to make another trip to New York in April–May 1910. Summarizing his life at this time, he later commented that 'I sort of shuttled to and fro across the Atlantic'. At £10, the passage was relatively cheap. His fondness for ocean travel left its mark in his early fiction:

In the dim cavern of Paddington Station the boat train snorted impatiently, varying the process with an occasional sharp shriek. The hands of the station clock pointed to ten minutes to six. The platform was a confused mass of travellers, porters, baggage, trucks, boys with buns and fruit, boys with magazines, friends, relatives and Bayliss the butler, standing like a faithful watchdog beside a large suit case.

Transatlantic crossings with Cunard or the White Star line became an integral part of Wodehouse's life. After the bustle of the customs sheds, there were the soothing on-board rituals of mid-morning bouillon, afternoon tea and dressing for dinner. The monotony of life at sea suited Wodehouse. If the weather was good and the voyage calm, he could enjoy long, solitary days of work, with no interruptions from the telegraph boy or, increasingly, the telephone. He could break off at will, and take a turn or two on deck before immersing himself in fiction, bent over the typewriter once more. *Piccadilly Jim* and, later, *The Luck of the Bodkins*, are among many novels that reflect these shipboard experiences:

There was a long line of semi-conscious figures in chairs, swathed in rugs and looking like fish laid out on a slab, and before their glassy gaze the athletes paraded up and down, rejoicing in their virility, shouting to one another 'What a morning!'

When *Psmith in the City* was published in September 1910, Wodehouse, the Anglo-American literary operator, had moved on from his old association with Townend, school and Westbrook. The new novel placed Mike Jackson and Rupert Psmith in a go-getting, adult world – a great London bank, 'the New Asiatic' – and in a plot that shows Wodehouse at his best, skilfully weaving together his love of cricket, his experience of banking, and his newspaperman's view of English politics, especially the rise of British socialism. Even more significant of its author's belated maturity, perhaps, was its dedication to Leslie Havergal Bradshaw.

By the end of 1910, the peripatetic writer was back in London, staying at his favourite club, the Constitutional on Northumberland Avenue, an underpopulated, sepulchral place, which he liked for its anonymity and its guarantee of a school-like routine. Among the well-regulated world of clubs, hotels and ocean liners, Wodehouse could sustain his remarkable work-rate. In the new year of 1911, he told Bradshaw that he had started yet another new novel: 'It's going to be a corker – good love interest – rapid action from the first chapter – length about 100,000 words. W. J. Watt is bringing it out in the fall . . . *All* the characters are American . . . The title is "A Prince at Large".'

The novel that would be published in America as *The Prince and Betty* is a Ruritanian romance after Anthony Hope's *The Prisoner of Zenda*. Its composition says a lot about Wodehouse's attitude to his material. He freely admitted to Bradshaw that, halfway through the narrative, it merged into the plot (with variations) of *Psmith Journalist*. Boasting to Bradshaw that he could get it done by the middle of February, Wodehouse cheerfully cannibalized his own work, combining a novelettish love story with the plot of *Psmith Journalist*, and using different protagonists, including a character called 'Smith'. As the writing gathered momentum, and his self-imposed deadline loomed, he repaired from the club to Emsworth, his other favourite working environment. He told Bradshaw, who had replaced Townend (absent in California) as his confidant, that he was getting good exercise playing soccer with the boys. By April, *The Prince and Betty* was done. He was eagerly awaiting a voyage to New York, and had booked a berth on the *Lusitania*. 'It will be ripping being back in New York,' he wrote.

There could hardly be a bolder indication of Wodehouse's new-found self-confidence and prosperity. When the *Lusitania*, the pride of the Cunard line, had made her maiden voyage to New York a few years before, she was celebrated as 'more beautiful than Solomon's Temple and big enough to hold all his wives'. According to the *Philadelphia Inquirer*, 'the man who came over on the *Lusitania* takes precedence of the one whose ancestors came over in the *Mayflower*'. As much as her grandeur and luxury, the new liner 'like a skyscraper adrift' was a marvel of speed, making the crossing in less than five days.

Wodehouse, too, was now setting an ever-accelerating pace for himself. 'Got to pop down town and whack up some money from my bankah!' he boasted to Bradshaw on disembarking from the *Lusitania*. Occasionally, his work habits took their toll. Returning to London in the blazing June of 1911, the hottest in a generation, in time to witness the coronation of George V, he stood Westbrook dinner at the Café Royal (a far cry from their Soho days of four courses with coffee for a shilling) and promptly fainted in the middle of one of Westbrook's anecdotes. His old sparring-partner bundled him into a taxi in some alarm, but it turned out to be nothing more than a severe chill.

Once recovered, Wodehouse played regularly throughout the cricket season, notably on 22 August when he turned out at Lord's for the Authors against the Publishers and scored sixty runs. On 24 August there was another milestone: *A Gentleman of Leisure*, the first theatrical adaptation of his work, opened on Broadway, with Douglas Fairbanks senior playing Jimmy Pitt, and ran for a modest seventy-six perform-ances. Retitled *A Thief for a Night*, and starring a young John Barrymore, the show enjoyed its first revival in Chicago in 1913, introducing Wodehouse to the American theatrical world.

Wodehouse continued to publish stories in successive issues of the *Strand* from July to September. By January 1912 he was back in Emsworth, urging Bradshaw to 'ginger up' Seth Moyle while he worked hard at a farcical crime story actually set in Emsworth, 'The 18-Carat Kid'. The new book juxtaposed the clashing cultures of English prepara-tory school and American gangster, and was finally published (in August 1913) as *The Little Nugget*. This was an oblique kind of valediction. The Emsworth part of his life was changing irretrievably. Herbert Westbrook was about to marry Ella King-Hall. Wodehouse always had mixed feel-ings about Westbrook, but he was attached to Ella. In a letter to Bradshaw, written in May 1912, he signalled their elopement and subsequent wedding, which caused a minor Emsworth scandal, with a laconic, cryptic '!!!'. He continued to play a role in Westbrook's life as the unac-knowledged breadwinner. After her marriage, Ella King-Hall became his literary agent for all his British contracts and remained so until her retirement through ill-health in 1935.

As the world which had inspired his school stories was breaking up, Wodehouse began to explore new avenues. Shuttling back to London, he became absorbed in another theatrical venture, a music-hall sketch entitled *After the Show*, featuring the Hon. Aubrey Forde-Rasche and his valet Barlow. Simultaneously, Wodehouse began to experiment with a new kind of narrator for the humorous stories he was selling to the *Strand*, Reggie Pepper, a silly ass who has inherited a lot of money from a rich uncle, partly inspired by the English 'dude' parts Wodehouse had seen on the New York stage. Crucially for the evolution of his author's work, Pepper narrates his own adventures and describes himself as 'a chap who's supposed to be one of the biggest chumps in London'.

The dim-witted upper-class stereotype had been a popular English figure of fun since early Victorian times, as Jonathan Cecil has observed. At first Wodehouse simply appropriated the stock comic aristocrat of Edwardian musical comedy, a role popularized by George Grossmith the younger, and gave him a new name. Reggie Pepper made his first appearance in a *Collier's* story in April 1912, 'Disentangling Old Duggie', a piece that Wodehouse reworked for the August number of the *Strand* as 'Disentangling Old Percy'. In the course of this episode, Reggie meets a certain Florence Craye, a platinum blonde with fearsome intellectual pretensions whose favourite reading is 'Types of Ethical Theory', and to whom another English 'drone', Bertie Wooster, would find himself engaged in 1916. But Reggie is not Bertie. He's a rougher and more selfish character; he lacks Bertie's baffled inner monologue and, perhaps as importantly, he attempts to make sense of his life without the sublime agency of Jeeves. Nonetheless, Wodehouse completed seven Reggie Pepper stories, developing the new narrative voice to the point at which an earthbound fiction took wings and became transformed into that tall, debonair Edwardian butterfly, Bertie Wooster. In later life, Wodehouse always maintained that his London was 'full of Berties'.

Such, then, were the first stirrings of the immortal character for which Wodehouse would become internationally renowned and with whom he is for ever associated. For the moment, however, Reggie Pepper's star seemed to be in the ascendant. As 1912 drew to a close, Lawrence Grossmith, son of the comedian George, commissioned Wodehouse to write a one-act play based on a Pepper story 'Rallying round Old George'. The Grossmith play would be called *Brother Alfred* and it occupied Wodehouse's attention throughout the first four months of 1913, while he was simultaneously moonlighting for *Punch*'s 'Charivaria' column. *Brother Alfred* was an unhappy experience, made worse by the fact that Lawrence Grossmith was investing part of an inheritance in the show, and could not resist making Wodehouse write and rewrite till all the punch was lost. The show, 'a ghastly frost', ran for just two weeks at the Savoy. 'I never saw such notices,' Wodehouse reported to Bradshaw, 'all thoroughly well deserved.'

More than ever, as Edwardian society drifted towards war, Wodehouse was convinced that writing stories for magazines, a world he understood and could control, was his *métier*. Mistakenly, as he admitted later, he had mastered the deadly practice of 'slanting', that is, providing what his editors wanted. He went back to New York, and focused his efforts on writing for Bob Davis, the workaholic editor of *Munsey's*, who, famous for pacing his office at the top of the Flatiron Building, never failed to come up with fifty-dollar plots for his writers. 'I have started in already on a new novel for Bob Davis,' Wodehouse informed Bradshaw in May. 'I haven't mapped it out properly yet, but it is coming, I think. He asked me if I could have it finished by July 1. I said "Oh, yes". I don't know how many thousand words a day these guys think I can write!' Davis was hungry for Wodehouse material: in August he serialized *The Little Nugget* in *Munsey's*, but Wodehouse had already fled New York's summer heat. Back in London in the autumn of 1913, he plunged into yet another collaboration.

Charles Bovill, a former colleague from *Globe* days, with whom Wodehouse had co-written *The Gay Gordons*, had come up with an idea – the adventures of a young man who had just inherited a lot of money – that appealed to Wodehouse, and which, they both felt, could be made simultaneously into a theatrical show *and* a magazine series, entitled 'A Man of Means', in what would now be termed synergy. With Westbrook married, Wodehouse had to look elsewhere for lodgings and moved into Bovill's flat in Prince of Wales Mansions, Battersea, just south of the Thames. Their show, *Nuts and Wine*, opened on 4 January 1914 at the Empire Theatre, but closed after only seven performances.

The failure of the show matched the break-up of the old Arundell Street circle. Increasingly restless, Wodehouse returned to New York, where he made a psychologically important move from the Hotel Earle to the Algonquin. It would be another decade before the Round Table became fully established here, but the hotel's hushed dignity and mid-town location suited him far better, and it is here that we get one of those rare, and tantalizing, glimpses into Wodehouse's emotional life. He told Bradshaw that, on his return, two actresses, Alice Dovey and Louise Kelly, 'welcomed me with open arms. I have got over my little trouble with the first-named and we are the best of friends. She's too devoted to Hamilton King for me to form a wedge and break up the combination, and I gracefully retire.' He had earlier described Alice Dovey as 'the nicest girl I ever met', but the 'little trouble' remains a matter for speculation. Wodehouse seems to have been the kind of young man who, like Bingo Little, falls in love easily, but lightly, not letting real emotions interfere.

The examination of Wodehouse's libido is a subject that would have horrified him, but its apparent absence from his life is intriguing. George Orwell famously observed that, as a writer of farce, Wodehouse made the 'enormous sacrifice' of excluding from his country house comedies 'anything in the nature of a sex joke'. Similarly, in his biography, a deafening silence surrounds his sexual life. Not only is there hardly any reference, in Wodehouse's private papers, to intimacy or love; it is also noticeable that those few who were close to him, men like William Townend, Guy Bolton and Denis Mackail, never describe their friend 'Plum' in sexual terms, or comment on his sexual nature. Even allowing for the reticence of the times, Wodehouse seems to have been recognized as a man for whom sex was simply not important. As a young man, he appears to have sublimated his libido in violent exercise like boxing or rugby football and later, throughout his adult life, in non-stop literary work, the thing he most loved to do.

There are two possible explanations for this, both speculative. The first lies in nature, and the second in nurture. Even as a mature man, Wodehouse was emotionally backward. The word that people always found to describe him on first meeting was 'boy'. This derived partly from his lonely and loveless childhood, and partly from his natural character. Then, secondly, there are the exceptional circumstances of the last decade of the Victorian century in which he reached maturity. To quote Orwell again, in his well-known essay on 'Boys' Weeklies': 'sex is completely taboo, especially in the form in which it actually arises in public schools.' Boys of Wodehouse's generation learned to censor their thoughts and feelings. Wodehouse was certainly familiar with the 'fleshly poet' Reginald Bunthorne of Gilbert and Sullivan's *Patience*. But, as the critic Christopher Hitchens has acutely noted, the one late-Victorian writer to whom Wodehouse, the most allusive of writers, never refers is Oscar Wilde.

In 1895, the year Wilde was sentenced to two years' hard labour for 'acts of gross indecency', in a sensational case whose lurid details were widely reported, Wodehouse was an impressionable adolescent of fourteen. When Wilde died, a broken man, in Paris in January 1900, Wodehouse was approaching twenty. It does not require a great leap of imagination to picture the unconscious effect of this cautionary tale on the generation of English schoolboys who grew up in the shadow of the Wilde case. The lesson was clear: intimacy could be dangerous, even fatal. It was safer to concentrate on romantic love for 'the fair sex', the kind of frankly adolescent, courtly wooing that animates Bingo Little and Bertie Wooster, for whom marriage is 'not a process for prolonging the life of love'. In this way, Wodehouse silently borrows the aunts, butlers and young Mayfair lounge lizards of Wilde's plays, but pastoralizes them in his own lunatic Eden, cunningly placing them beyond the reach of serious analysis.

Just occasionally, Wodehouse's Edwardian work leaves a tell-tale clue about his inner life. *The Man Upstairs*, the first volume of his adult stories from the *Strand*, published at the end of January 1914, faithfully reflects his experiences in London and New York during the years 1909–12, though generally without giving much away. There is one story, however, 'In Alcala', which is the exception, and of special interest. Broadly autobiographical, this story conveys something poignant about the aching void in Wodehouse's emotional life, evidence that is masked elsewhere in his work by flippancy and farce.

'Alcala' is a New York lodging house, not unlike the Earle, in which an Englishman, Rutherford Maxwell, a younger son who works as 'one of the numerous employees of the New Asiatic bank', has a cheap 'hall-bedroom' − a bedsit furnished with 'a plain deal table, much stained with ink' at which night after night he sits and writes stories. Once again, Wodehouse draws obsessively on his brief career with the Hongkong and Shanghai Bank:

Rutherford [Maxwell]'s salary was small. So were his prospects − if he remained in the bank. At a very early date he had registered a vow that he would not. And the road that led out of it for him was the uphill road of literature . . . Fate . . . had dispatched him to New York, the centre of things . . . So every night he sat in Alcala, and wrote.

The impoverished Maxwell is lonely and isolated, but then, one hot night in July, there is a knock at the door and a tall and sleepy-eyed girl 'in a picture hat' asks for a cigarette. She is interrupted by a second girl, identified as Peggy Norton, whose voice Maxwell has often heard in the hallway outside, who apologizes for the intrusion and who, having dragged her friend away, strikes up an awkward conversation. Peggy asks his name, laughs at it ('Wants amputation a name like that'), decides she will call him 'George', and rags him for his uptight Englishness:

'Why don't you make your fortune by hiring yourself out to a museum as the biggest human clam in captivity? That's what you are. You sit there just saying "Thanks," and "Bai Jawve, thanks awf'lly," while a girl's telling you nice things about your eyes and hair, and you don't do a thing.'

Rutherford threw back his head and roared with laughter.

'I'm sorry!' he said. 'Slowness is our national failing, you know.'

As she is leaving, Peggy spies a photograph of Maxwell's school football team on the mantelpiece and, next to it, a picture of a girl. More cross-questioning reveals that 'the biggest human clam in captivity' loves an English girl called Alice Halliday (a favourite Wodehouse surname). On this awkward note of potential infidelity, repressed desire and half-acknowledged mutual attraction, the encounter ends.

For a would-be humorist, 'In Alcala' is painfully lacking in laughs. It is, rather, a bold exercise in popular, sentimental realism and is notable for Wodehouse's virtuoso rendering of the everyday conversation of a twenty-something New York actress who may, or may not, have been modelled on Alice Dovey. As Peggy Norton gets to know her emotionally backward neighbour she teases him in a way that the American women of his acquaintance may have joshed 'Chickens' Wodehouse, criticizing his workaholic lifestyle ('Don't you ever let up for a second? Seems to me you write all the time') and accusing him of hankering after a 'little old Paradise' in England. Maxwell, against his will, finds himself depressingly lovesick. When Peggy goes on tour to Chicago, he hits rock-bottom: 'night after night he sat idle in his room; night after night went wearily to bed, oppressed with a dull sense of failure . . . For the first time since he had come to New York he was really lonely. Solitude had not hurt him until now.' Then Peggy returns. Maxwell takes her out to dinner, lavishes luxury on her that he can ill afford, and on the way home in the taxi, he loses control: 'Suddenly an intense desire surged over him to pick her up and crush her to him . . . And then his arms were around her, and he was showering her upturned face with kisses.'

Later, in *The Inimitable Jeeves*, Wodehouse will mercilessly satirize this kind of writing in mocking quotations from the work of Rosie M. Banks. This story, however, is not light-hearted or ironic; it is for real. As time passed, Wodehouse would disown plenty of apprentice work but not 'In Alcala'. Not only did he authorize many reprints of the story in the subsequent editions of *The Man Upstairs*, in 1971 he added an introduction, referring nostalgically to the solitary hours of composition 'in a bedroom at the Hotel Earle', the real-life Alcala.

When the story continues, after Rutherford Maxwell's embarrassing declaration, Peggy Norton becomes a kind of muse, urging her 'George' to new and better work. He settles down to write her a play, at her suggestion investing the hero 'Willie' with all the qualities that will make the role appealing to the matinée idol Winfield Knight, who, they hope, will take the part. It is only when Maxwell gives the script to the star (over cigars in the Players Club) that he realizes why Peggy seems to understand so well what will best appeal to Winfield Knight. She is his mistress. Maxwell's play is a triumph. In the heady aftermath of the first-night party, Maxwell finds himself, in desperation, proposing to Peggy ('I love you, Peggy! Peggy, will you be my wife?'). She, horrified at what she has encouraged, turns him down, sorrowfully admitting her unfitness for him and correctly identifying that he is in love with a fantasy – 'a Broadway dream' – and implying that he is not really the marrying kind. The story ends with Rutherford Maxwell, now 'stiff and cold', contemplating a photograph of Alice Halliday in faraway Worcestershire.

It is impossible to say, with a character as elusive as Wodehouse, exactly how this strange, sentimental story relates to the facts of his own romantic life, which was and always will be tantalizingly opaque. There is no doubt, however, that its mood of depressed melancholy echoed its author's own state of mind during these New York years. The atmosphere of 'In Alcala' pervades his few surviving letters. 'Life at present', he wrote to Bradshaw in September 1914, is 'infernally monotonous. I get up, try to work, feed and go back to bed again. As long as I'm working, I feel all right, but in between stories it's rotten.' Such an admission from Wodehouse is almost unprecedented. In a writer less stoical and self-disciplined, such a story might indicate a profound personal crisis, and perhaps even hint at a severe romantic disappointment.

By the summer of 1914, with a European war threatening, Wodehouse had been working non-stop with dogged persistence for more than a decade, establishing himself as a literary figure of promise and originality in London and New York. He had also, at the age of thirty-two, reached a belated kind of maturity and, as 'In Alcala' shows, a measure of self-knowledge. His quest for intimacy, which had been thwarted in childhood and carefully disciplined during his long literary apprenticeship, was ready to find expression. As the society in which he had grown up drifted towards oblivion, he was poised to transform his bachelor world of gentlemen's clubs, college football and boxing matches into something more grown-up. He was ready to make the biggest – perhaps the only – real emotional commitment of his life, and then embark on the work that would place him once and for all in 'the big league'.

PART TWO

Something New

(1914–1929)

7. 'An angel in human form'
(1914–1915)

In New York, I have always found, one gets off the mark quickly in
matters of the heart. This, I believe, is due to something in the air.
(*Thank You, Jeeves*)

Wodehouse hardly ever referred to the First World War, but he did
acknowledge the Edwardians' fatal nonchalance towards the gathering
European crisis in 'Jeeves in the Springtime', a story first published in
1921:

'How's the weather, Jeeves?'
   'Exceptionally clement, sir.'
   'Anything in the papers?'
   'Some slight friction threatening in the Balkans, sir. Otherwise, nothing.'

Wodehouse's behaviour during the countdown to the declaration of war
on 4 August 1914 was similarly disengaged. He was on a German liner
crossing to New York, fulfilling a commission from *McClure's Magazine*
to interview John Barrymore, the rising young actor who had recently
starred in *A Thief for a Night*, the Chicago revival of *A Gentleman of Leisure*.
The war that would sweep Edwardian England away had been a long
time coming, but no one seemed to take the threat very seriously.

   The air of unreality in England in the weeks leading up to the declaration of war might have come from *The Swoop!* On the day war broke
out – a bank holiday – a party of senior army officers, summoned to
the Suffolk coast by a false invasion alarm, came under fire from a
golfing four, a party of emancipated women, one of whose drives nearly
brought down a general. Furious, the officer called them over. 'My dear
young ladies,' he asked in outrage, 'the Germans are expected to land
this afternoon. Do you know what rape is? I advise you to head for
home.' The first mobilization order was given at teatime. Army officers
playing tennis or cricket on that sunny afternoon were notified by the

waving of white handkerchiefs. In the days that followed, there was a rush to enlist among the public, many of whom appeared to treat the war as a thrilling away match; the British Expeditionary Force was soon disembarking at French ports. Unmoved by this excitement, and working as hard as ever, Wodehouse stayed on in America.

War fever had not yet touched New York, where the events in Europe seemed remote and unreasonable. 'This is a war of kings,' wrote William Randolph Hearst in a signed editorial, 'brought on by the assassination of a king's nephew, who is of no more actual importance to modern society than the nephew of any other individual.' Wodehouse, who fell out briefly with A. & C. Black over his unpatriotic absence in America, was sensitive to charges of cowardice. After conscription was introduced in 1916, he did belatedly register for the draft in New York, as an 'author and playwright' or, as he joked to Bill Townend, 'age sixty-three, sole support of wife and nine children, totally blind'.

Wodehouse's failure to enlist in England was in character. On the outbreak of both world wars, he watched from the sidelines, and carried on writing about an imaginary world that seemed far more vivid to him than the reality of his own times. He took a quiet pride in being English, but he was utterly lacking in chauvinism or a taste for real danger, or a desire to disrupt his cosy little world. Perhaps he was shirking his patriotic responsibility, but, practically speaking, his sense of duty was tempered by the knowledge that his poor sight would have disqualified him from active service. Besides, he was caught up in a more personal kind of turmoil – he was in love.

On 3 August, the day after his ship had docked in New York, he had gone out for the evening with Norman Thwaites, his journalist friend from the *World* in whose 27th Street apartment he was staying. Thwaites had proposed bringing his girlfriend and, knowing that Wodehouse was single, had thoughtfully suggested that his sweetheart should bring *her* best friend, a recently widowed Englishwoman named Ethel Wayman, to make up the foursome. Mrs Wayman was an actress visiting New York with a touring repertory company, and should have been an alarming blind date for the shy, emotionally backward, thirty-two-year-old bachelor, but it was a perfect match.

The nervy, extrovert woman who turned up the following evening would soon become quite as much of a character in Wodehouse's life as any of the women who populate his fiction. Memorably described by Malcolm Muggeridge as combining Mistress Quickly and Florence Nightingale, 'with a touch of Lady Macbeth thrown in', Ethel was flirtatious, frivolous and fun. She was not beautiful, but she had a very good figure, an excellent dress sense and wonderful legs. A high-spirited party-goer with a passion for dancing, whose life was a whirlwind quest for distraction, she was, at the moment she came into Wodehouse's life, insecure, vulnerable and in search of a husband. But she was not just a flapper or a good-time girl. As Wodehouse soon discovered, her indomitable spirit had been forged by a succession of personal tragedies, any one of which might have overwhelmed a less remarkable woman.

Ethel Newton was born in King's Lynn on 23 May 1885, the illegitimate daughter of John Newton, a Norfolk farmer, and a local milliner named Anne Green. Her childhood was unhappy. She never knew her father, and her mother, by her own report, was an alcoholic. Taken into care, she was raised first by a Mary Wilson and then by a family called Walker. At the age of eighteen, she had a holiday fling in Blackpool with Leonard Rowley, a respectable, young, middle-class mining engineer from Cheshire, and became pregnant. Edwardian propriety demanded an immediate wedding, and Leonard married her in Nottingham, where he was a student, on 15 September 1903. Their baby, Leonora, was born on 12 March 1904. A year later, a disgraced Leonard Rowley took his young wife and their daughter to India, where he worked as chief engineer at a mine near Mysore. Four years later, he died in obscure circumstances, probably succumbing to tropical illness.

Ethel seems to have had a pragmatic view of marriage. Shortly after her husband's death, as Mrs Rowley, and now back in England, she married again, this time a London man named John Wayman, a Jermyn Street tailor. When he tried to transform his business into a gentlemen's club, Wayman went bankrupt in 1912, and then committed suicide by throwing himself to his death. As a single parent, Ethel was forced, possibly with help from one of Rowley's sisters, to place Leonora, now aged seven, in boarding school, and seek her fortune in America. When Wodehouse met her, she was living at the unfashionable end of Broadway, making ends meet in New York repertory circles; after they were married, some of Ethel's lines became a standing joke between them. There is a glancing allusion to Ethel's situation in the story 'Extricating Young Gussie', written the year after she and Wodehouse first discovered each other:

It's a known fact that my aunt Julia, Gussie's mother, was a vaudeville artist once, and a very good one . . . the family had made the best of it, and Aunt Agatha had pulled her socks up and put in a lot of educative work, and with a microscope you couldn't tell Aunt Julia from a genuine, dyed-in-the-wool aristocrat. Women adapt themselves so quickly!

Wodehouse and his future wife were opposite in so many obvious ways; he was quiet and elusive, she was noisy and demonstrative; he was intellectual and solitary, she was relatively uneducated and sociable; he was repressed, she was highly sexed; and where he was fanatically prudent, she was extravagant with money. Their relationship finds an unconscious echo in many aspects of Jeeves and Bertie's rapport. But Wodehouse and Ethel had one thing in common. They both knew what it meant to be abandoned in childhood: they were emotional orphans. The combination of Ethel's ebullient personality and the tragedies of her early life seems to have touched a chord with Wodehouse. Here was a woman who was both commanding and fragile, outwardly strong, but inwardly in need of a man's support, in search of a husband on whom to lavish her considerable affections. We cannot know if he understood Ethel's vulnerability, or how it spoke to him. Such revelations were never part of his or his generation's repertoire, even with intimate friends, but he responded to her forcefulness, and allowed himself to be swept off his feet. Soon after their first meeting, they were caught up in a summer romance, orchestrated by Ethel, who seems to have spotted that the way to Wodehouse's well-defended heart was through shared physical exercise like swimming, one of his favourite pursuits. With two marriages behind her, Ethel was the more experienced sexually, and definitely in charge.

Wodehouse later recalled their courtship with its romantic visits to Long Island during August and the first half of September. They used to go down to the Pennsylvania Station, take the LIRR (Long Island Railroad) and ride down to Long Beach, where they would swim and have lunch, and then come back on the train. For both, it would be the beginning of a lifelong love of the South Shore. The tenor of their burgeoning relationship is expressed in Wodehouse's memories of that summer of 1914: 'I remember bathing once, the ocean being particularly rough that day and Ethel said, "Hold on to me" – and I was then swept away from her by a huge wave. But she always said I let go of her . . .' To Wodehouse, letting go of a woman, even one you loved, came quite naturally. It was 'holding on' that was unfamiliar and scarcely imaginable. In old age, Wodehouse did brag to the worldly wise Guy Bolton about the youthful agonies of 'clap', but he was never a man for whom sex was important – in life or in literature. He did, however, have some unfinished business with female acquaintances in New York. A woman, referred to as 'Pinkie', seems to have taken his sudden relationship with Ethel amiss, cutting him dead on 34th Street one day. 'The funny part', Wodehouse confessed to Bradshaw, 'is that I hardly miss her at all. I really believe that, unless you're in love with her, you can dispense with any woman – in other words one's real friendships are never with them.'

But he was in love with Ethel. Somehow, between the trips on the Long Island Railroad and intermittent deadline pressure from *Vanity Fair*, his chief source of income during these tumultuous weeks, their unlikely relationship survived, flourished and swiftly grew into something with a future. She needed him for the benign security he offered. He needed her to organize his life and to give him peace and quiet in which to write. Wodehouse always had the Englishman's aversion to fussing. Family tradition says that he realized Ethel was the wife for him when she left him, suffering from a bad cold, to his own devices during one of their many train journeys. Much of Wodehouse's later work would exploit the comedy of young bachelors like Bertie Wooster who are petrified by the prospect of matrimony. One of the light novels Wodehouse wrote in the 1920s, *The Adventures of Sally*, evokes the awkwardness of a shy young Englishman wrestling with the excruciating embarrassment of a marriage proposal:

'Look here,' exploded Ginger with sudden violence, 'you've got to marry me. You've jolly well got to marry me! I don't mean that,' he added quickly. 'I mean to say I know you're going to marry whoever you please . . . but *won't* you marry me? Sally, for God's sake have a dash at it! I've been keeping it in all this time because it seemed rather rotten to bother you about it, but now . . . Oh, dammit, I wish I could put it into words. I always was rotten at talking. But . . . well, look here, what I mean is, I know I'm not much of a chap, but . . . I've loved you like the dickens ever since I met you . . . I do wish you'd have a stab at it, Sally. At least I could look after you, you know, and all that . . .'

Within two months of first meeting, Wodehouse and Ethel were married. On 30 September 1914, the experienced bride and the novice groom met on 29th Street, at the Little Church Around the Corner, an Italianate church nestled between Fifth and Madison Avenues, just two blocks from Thwaites's apartment. Ethel, admitting to both her former husbands, gave her name as Ethel May Wayman but slyly shaved a year off her age. The occasion was more romantic and regular than her previous weddings, but only just. Wodehouse, who described himself as an 'Author', found that his nerves got the better of him and succumbed to a violent sneezing fit at the moment of solemnization. As usual, he found the joke in the occasion, and liked to recall that the priest, arriving out of breath and late for the service, excused himself by claiming to have just made a killing on the stock market. Thereafter, Wodehouse would always set his fictional New York weddings here, and celebrated it in a sentimental lyric:

> Dear little, dear little Church 'Round the Corner
> Where so many lives have begun,
> Where folks without money see nothing that's funny
> In two living cheaper than one.

Weddings are often peculiar, but this was odder than most. Not only was Wodehouse marrying a woman whose ten-year-old daughter, away at boarding school in England, he had yet to meet; dreamy, jittery or detached, he was also, apparently, so removed from the events that were unfolding around him that he could not even remember his new wife's full name. He wrote to his friend L. H. Bradshaw from the Hotel Astor on the first day of his honeymoon: 'Excuse delay in answering letter. Been busy getting married to Ethel Milton!'

The Wodehouses' marriage was unconventional. Early in their married life, in deference to his working habits and to his asexuality, Ethel and Wodehouse established separate bedrooms. When they stayed in hotels, their suites were often on separate floors. Wodehouse was, nonetheless, a devoted husband. He missed Ethel when she was absent, relied upon her for everything, and trusted her with the freedom she needed. In sexual matters, Wodehouse seems to have recognized that he was not his wife's equal and that, so long as she did not embarrass or neglect him, she should be free to socialize as she chose. Self-control came naturally to him and was part of his upbringing. In his relationship with Ethel, he exercised it by ignoring her various liaisons, none of which appear to have amounted to anything much beyond excessive flirtation. Every marriage has its mysteries. What is not in doubt is that the Wodehouses' was a highly successful partnership that lasted some sixty years and survived crises that would have destroyed a less affectionate couple. Ethel found in her husband's tolerance, affability and dedicated breadwinning the kind of comfort she had never known. As several have testified, she could be 'a terror to work for', 'very difficult' and 'impossible', but he was oblivious – happy to let her organize things, take charge of day-to-day concerns, spend his money, gamble and throw parties. Wodehouse expressed his attitude to marriage in one of the novels he wrote during these first years of their relationship. 'The right way of looking at marriage', says Ann Chester, the heroine of *Piccadilly Jim*, 'is to . . . pick someone who is nice and kind and amusing and full of life and willing to do things to make you happy.' Lord Ickenham, 'Uncle Fred', later expresses a practical version of this approach to matrimony that is adjacent to Wodehouse's own preference: 'The only way of ensuring a happy married life is to get it thoroughly clear at the outset who is going to skipper the team. My own dear wife settled the point during the honeymoon, and ours has been an ideal union.' Whatever Wodehouse's deepest feelings about women in general, and his preference for brotherly male companionship, he idolized and possibly idealized Ethel. She was, he wrote in the preface to the first novel he completed after their marriage, 'an angel in human form'. More than giving his life a new coherence, she also gave it joy. She gave him her daughter Leonora, whom Wodehouse formally adopted and loved as his own.

After his childhood, Wodehouse was never a man for whom the expression of love was either natural or easy. Yet Leonora, whose relationship with her mother was stormy, became as close to him as anyone alive, and, when she reached adulthood, a true confidante, more companion than daughter. By Christmas 1914, he had still not met her, but in the spring of 1915 Leonora joined her mother and new stepfather in New York and rapidly became Nora, S'nora, then Snorky and finally, most intimate, 'dearest darling Snorkles'. Wodehouse always treated her as a kind of 'Bill', a privileged fellow inmate of a select dormitory. To Leonora, 'my best pal and severest critic', he confided the nitty-gritty of his professional life with the directness and candour he bestowed on Townend and Bradshaw. Leonora would grow up to be a kind of fascinating muse to many men: sympathetic, fun and unforgettable.

Looking back on their early married days, Wodehouse liked to say that their joint assets were just $125. His only regular income was from the newly founded *Vanity Fair*, which put him in its Hall of Fame in the same month as Stephen Leacock. For *Vanity Fair*, the workaholic young husband would disguise his numerous contributions under a variety of pseudonyms, including J. Plum, P. Brooke-Haven, Pelham Grenville, Melrose Grainger, J. Walker Williams and C. P. West. At first, to save money and to live a simple life together, the newly weds moved away from the heat and clatter of New York and rented a bungalow in Bellport, Long Island, a quiet, pretty and secluded oceanside town whose wooden jetties and muddy seashore were strongly reminiscent of Emsworth. Here they set up home and here, like any newly married man, Wodehouse came to terms with the realities of shopping, dish-washing and housework. In other ways, his life did not change much. He could write every day, and there were plenty of opportunities to go on long walks. His new home was two and a half miles from the station and a mile from the nearest post office. From time to time, he would make 'hasty dashes' to New York to attend to business there, coming home to find 'a fine dinner and a blazing fire, and E. fussing over me'. If this was marriage, he reported to Bradshaw, it was 'perfectly ripping'.

As they would throughout their married life, the Wodehouses soon collected around them a domestic menagerie. Their joint love of animals, especially strays, was a special bond, possibly attributable to their difficult childhoods. 'We have two cats, a dog and a puppy here,' Wodehouse wrote to Lily, his Emsworth housekeeper, 'and however many of them we turn out of the dining room at mealtimes, there always seems to be one left, shouting for food. I gather them up in armfuls and hurl them into the kitchen.' Married life, he told Lily, in a refrain that recurs throughout his letters, 'is certainly the only life, if you are suited to each other, as we are'. He described his bride as an Englishwoman who claimed to have spent 'several years in America'. This, he explained, gave her a special understanding of the English and American sides of his life. Ethel's love of animals helped, too. 'Knowing me,' he wrote, 'you will understand the importance of my marrying somebody who was fond of animals.'

If he had a complaint, it was that they had only just been able to hire a maid; he also asked Lily, whom he vainly tried to lure to America, to send him his sweater, his heavy boots and a favourite woollen waist-coat. He decided that it would be too difficult to ship his bicycle. Although he was 'frightfully home-sick at times', these first wartime months in Bellport were a season of wedded bliss, a wonderful contrast to the angst he had suffered in the spring. This new happiness only sharpened his appetite for work – 'The knowledge that it is up to one to support someone else has a stimulating effect.' After the publication of *The Man Upstairs*, his work had been in the doldrums throughout 1914. But now the combination of war ('the war has sent my English money all to pieces') and marriage ('Ethel has come out very strong with three fine plots!') focused his thoughts. It was in the bungalow in Bellport that he began to write *Something Fresh*, the novel that would transform his career.

From the moment, in December 1914, that he typed '*Something Fresh* by Pelham Grenville Wodehouse' onto a clean white page, he had the feeling he was going to hit the jackpot. He had written about a crumbling English country house in *A Gentleman of Leisure*, but he had not peopled it with characters worthy of the setting. Now, perhaps because he was missing England, and perhaps because he wanted to appeal to the American reading public's fascination with the Old World and its peculiar ways, he began, in a tentative sort of way, to write about Clarence, 9th Earl of Emsworth, his son the Hon. Freddie Threepwood, and his butler, Beach.

The work flew; Wodehouse found he was inspired. It was, he said later, 'the time of my life'. By 20 January, he had nearly finished a first draft. 'I have been working like a navvy for about two weeks,' he reported to Bradshaw, 'in which time I must have written very nearly forty thousand words of my novel.' He was convinced it was 'the best long thing I have done, and I have great hopes of landing it somewhere good'. As usual with Wodehouse, he was impatiently planning further improvements. 'I have got about another ten thousand [words] to do, and then there will be some revision. I am divided between the desire to get action on it right away and a wish to keep it back and polish it up to the limit.' For possibly the first time in nearly fifteen years of writing for a living, he was in no doubt about the quality of what he had done, boasting to Bradshaw: 'There is some of the funniest knock-about stuff in this book that I have ever written.'

Something Fresh is a comedy about a country house party, a gath-ering together of the Emsworth family to celebrate Freddie Threep-wood's engagement to Aline Peters, the daughter of the dyspeptic American millionaire J. Preston Peters. When the happy event becomes overshadowed by Lord Emsworth's absent-minded appropriation of a priceless Egyptian scarab, various house-guests get drawn into a head-long quest for the ancient relic. Then the 'laughing Love God' inter-venes and when order is restored there is more than one wedding in prospect.

Something Fresh is a comic novel, but it is also a work of nostalgia, and reflects the honeymoon atmosphere in which it was conceived. The story opens with an affectionate picture of the Leicester Square neighbourhood in which Wodehouse had passed his formative years with Townend and Westbrook. It recalls the London restaurants of his youth: 'From the restaurant which makes you fancy you are in Paris to the restaurant which makes you wish you were . . . palaces in Piccadilly, quaint lethal chambers in Soho, and strange food factories in Oxford Street and the Tottenham Court Road.' Evoking the old country, the novel places Lord Emsworth firmly in pre-war Edwardian London, and subtly announces Wodehouse's literary manifesto:

Wafted through the sun-lit streets in his taxi-cab, the Earl of Emsworth smiled benevolently upon London's teeming millions. . . . Other people worried about all sorts of things – strikes, wars, suffragettes, diminishing birth-rates, the growing materialism of the age, and a score of similar subjects. Worrying, indeed, seemed to be the twentieth century's speciality. Lord Emsworth never worried.

Not only does Wodehouse want to banish dull cares, he celebrates the English aristocracy's extraordinary resilience:

We may say what we will against the aristocracy of England; we may wear red ties and attend Socialist meetings; but we cannot deny that in certain crises blood will tell. An English peer of the right sort can be bored nearer to the point where mortification sets in, without showing it, than anyone else in the world.

As an ironic advocate for aristocratic England, Wodehouse is also a keen student of its social structure. This, too, he evokes in affectionate detail with Joan Valentine's explanation of life below stairs:

Kitchen maids and scullery-maids eat in the kitchen. Chauffeurs, footmen, under-butlers, pantry-boys, hall-boys, odd man, and Steward's room footmen take their meals in the Servants' Hall, waited on by the hall-boy. . . . The housemaids and nursery-maids have breakfast and tea in the housemaids' sitting room and dinner and supper in the Hall.

The thriller-writer hero of *Something Fresh*, Ashe Marson, is a young man who has just been turned inside out by the love of a good woman. 'Listen to me, Joan,' he exclaims at one point. 'Where's your sense of fairness? You crash into my life, turn it upside down, dig me out of my quiet groove, revolutionise my whole existence . . .' Behind the comedy, *Something Fresh* is a celebration of Wodehouse's own marriage. This was further blessed when A. & C. Black, which had miraculously forgotten its patriotic disapproval of his absence in America, wrote from England to say they were ready to publish the long-delayed edition of *Psmith Journalist*. In his response to his editor George Wilson's routine inquiry about any author's revisions to the text, Wodehouse replied airily that 'it seems to be one of those masterpieces you can't alter a comma of'.

It was time for Wodehouse, whose work was still represented in Britain by Ella Westbrook (née King-Hall), to acquire a first-class New York agent. Now he arranged to meet Paul Reynolds, proprietor of the Paul Reynolds Agency, 'a very good sort' who was, he found, pleasantly different from Seth Moyle. Reynolds had already made a name for himself as literary agent for William James, Jack London, George Bernard Shaw and Winston Churchill, and later became one of the most powerful men in the American book world during the inter-war years. In his report to Bradshaw, Wodehouse noted with approval that Reynolds 'didn't make one windy promise of selling my stuff for millions. He just said that he hoped he would make good on it, and declined to prophesy.' Wodehouse, the reclusive London clubman, was also taken with Reynolds's assured position in his New York club and by the 'respectful chumminess' with which he was greeted by fellow members, publishers like Charles Scribner. After Seth Moyle, who 'might disappear into nowhere with a lot of one's money and never appear again', it was a relief to sign up with 'one of the aristocrats of the profession'. Reynolds was the kind of agent who did everything for his authors. His massive correspondence with Wodehouse shows him settling taxi bills, paying golf-club subscriptions, sending flowers to Ethel, and even meeting her off the boat. Wodehouse would stay with the agency through a series of hits, and a long and tedious spell of tax trouble, until Reynolds's death in 1944.

His breakthrough novel was complete. He had a new literary agent. Now he had to place his work with the best editor in town. In 1915, for ambitious writers in New York there was only one port of call. Reynolds's first move was to take the manuscript (the title would be modified to *Something New* because of the racy associations of 'fresh' in American English) to George Lorimer at the *Saturday Evening Post*, with whom Wodehouse already had an informal understanding. Lorimer, a tough-minded conservative from Kentucky, was renowned for his instinctive eye for stories that would appeal to the tastes of the American middle-class reading public, attracting work by Rudyard Kipling, Jack London, Stephen Crane, H. G. Wells and G. K. Chesterton.

To his admirers, George Lorimer was more than just a magazine editor. He was one of those rare literary midwives who placed the repu-tation of his magazine above the reputation of the writers he published. Lorimer's writers believed that he always demanded the highest standards and would not hesitate to reject stories, even by big names, if he felt the work was inferior. Wodehouse later told Townend that Lorimer was 'an autocrat all right, but my God, what an editor to work for. He kept you on your toes. I had twenty-one serials in the *Post*, but I never felt safe till I got the cable saying each had got over with Lorimer.' The editor of the *Saturday Evening Post* had no special liking for England and he was unfamiliar with Wodehouse's work, but the novel amused him and, after a contractual row about terms, he acquired it as a substan-tial *Post* serial for $3,500, a dazzling figure to Wodehouse that estab-lished a mutually beneficial connection lasting some twenty years. The thirty-three-year-old writer's situation was transformed overnight. Wodehouse had persevered since 1900, but now, with the *Post*'s cheque in the bank, 'these struggles ceased abruptly'. Throughout his heyday, Wodehouse could always count on selling his work twice over, first in magazine and then in book form, on both sides of the Atlantic.

Wodehouse had long dreamed of selling his work to the *Saturday Evening Post*. Now that he had clicked with Lorimer, and with the eagerness to please that never left him, he raced to complete another novel, entitled *Uneasy Money*, even as his literary agents were finalizing book contracts for *Something Fresh* in London and New York. Simultaneously, Frank Crowninshield, the editor of *Vanity Fair*, appointed Wodehouse the magazine's drama critic. It was in this capacity that, some time during the early spring of 1915, Wodehouse went to the Knickerbocker Theater to see *90 in the Shade*, a new musical by Jerome Kern, his former partner on *The Beauty of Bath* from as long ago as 1906. Kern, who had cemented his position as the coming man of American popular song-writing, was now working in partnership with the playwright Guy Bolton, another expatriate.

Broadway during the First World War was enjoying a golden age. There were between seventy and eighty theatres on the Great White Way, supplying popular entertainment to a public whose appetite for musicals with their *mélange* of vaudeville, dance spectacular and hit songs was seemingly insatiable. Wodehouse, the veteran of the Strand and the West End, renowned for turning out clever lyrics to order, was not content just to watch and criticize from the stalls. Unusually, he was on both sides of the footlights. In the spring of 1915 he probably contributed part of the Herbert Reynolds song 'A Packet of Seeds' to *90 in the Shade*, a show that flopped. Its failure did not prevent Bolton and Kern getting a commission for another 'farce comedy in two acts', *Nobody Home*, which opened at the Princess Theater in the middle of April 1915. Wodehouse, meanwhile, was working hard to finish *Uneasy Money*, and did so at the beginning of May while Ethel was away in England. She was collecting Leonora from school, preparing her eleven-year-old daughter to meet her new stepfather.

Uneasy Money has another Anglo-American plot, like *Something Fresh*. When William, Lord Dawlish ('Bill') hears he has been left a million pounds by an eccentric American, he crosses the Atlantic under an assumed name and, after some romantic complications, finds himself being steered towards the altar by Elizabeth Boyd, an American woman who knows what she is after. She tells Dawlish:

When we get to New York, I first borrow the money from you to buy a hat, and then we walk to the City Hall, where you go to the window marked

'Marriage Licences', and buy one . . . after we've done that we shall go to the only church that anybody could possibly be married in. It's on Twenty-ninth Street, just around the corner from Fifth Avenue. It's got a fountain playing in front of it, and it's a little bit of heaven.

Wodehouse had written *Uneasy Money* with Lorimer in mind, and when it was completed gave it to him during a weekend visit in May. On the Sunday, Lorimer curled up on a sofa and started to read the script. Wodehouse sat there, pretending to be absorbed in a bound volume of the *Post*, but listening in anguish in the hope of hearing him laugh. After about half an hour, Lorimer looked up and said, 'I like this one better than the other.' Wodehouse told Townend that 'I have never heard such beautiful words in my life'.

Uneasy Money shows many traces of its author's recent experiences on Long Island, and describes the ideal girl as 'plucky, cheerfully valiant, a fighter [who] would not admit the existence of hard luck'. Tellingly, it contains not a single allusion to the war, even though, during the months in which Wodehouse was writing it, the war in France was beginning to have an impact on American life. On 7 May 1915 the *Lusitania* was sunk off the coast of Ireland with the loss of 1,200 lives. The disaster shocked America as much as the sinking of the *Titanic* and sent shudders through New York's artistic community. Jerome Kern, indeed, was supposed to have been on board; and the dead included Kern's celebrated producer, Charles Frohman, who was on his annual talent-spotting trip to London. In Europe, the war was entering a desperate phase. But in America the years 1915 and 1916 were good to Wodehouse. It was during a blissful summer in Bellport that, still on a surge of creativity, he completed the story, entitled 'Extricating Young Gussie', in which Jeeves makes his first appearance.

Years later, when he came to write the introduction to *The World of Jeeves*, Wodehouse addressed the vital question of Jeeves's debut:

I find it curious, now that I have written so much about him, to recall how softly and undramatically Jeeves first entered my little world. On that occasion, he spoke just two lines. The first was: 'Mrs Gregson to see you, sir.' The second: 'Very good, sir. Which suit will you wear?' That was in a story in a volume entitled *The Man with Two Left Feet*. It was only some time later . . . that the man's qualities dawned upon me.

'I blush to think', he concluded, 'of the offhand way I treated him at our first encounter.' The *Saturday Evening Post* published this first Jeeves story on 18 September 1916; it would appear between hard covers for the first time the following March, when Methuen published *The Man with Two Left Feet*, a new collection of stories, in London. So Jeeves glides into fiction much as his creator liked to do in real life, unobtrusively.

Jeeves takes his name from a Warwickshire county cricketer, the medium-pace bowler Percy Jeeves, who was killed on the Somme on 22 July 1916. As a gentleman's gentleman, Jeeves could hardly be further removed from the mud and slaughter of Flanders, but he was deeply Edwardian from the first. Wodehouse had been exploring the lineaments of the perfect servant for some years. There was the valet Barlow in *After the Show*; there was the butler in 'The Good Angel', a story published in *The Man Upstairs*; while, in a *Strand* story, 'Creatures of Impulse', published in October 1914, there was Jevons, another butler. A gentleman's personal gentleman is, of course, not a butler, but he is more than a mere valet; Jeeves is above and beyond such creatures. He is nothing if not unique. Jeeves is the nonpareil. Bertie Wooster tells his readers that 'Jeeves stands alone', and so he does. 'There is', says Bertie, 'none like you, none.'

Jeeves is a model in so many ways. There is his absolute discretion: 'It was the soft cough of Jeeves's which always reminds me of a very old sheep clearing its throat on a distant mountain top.' There is his mysterious gift of movement. Jeeves never walks. He 'floats', or 'filters', or 'oozes softly' into Bertie's presence: 'Jeeves entered – or perhaps I should say shimmered – into the room.' Finally, there is his benign calm: 'Jeeves doesn't exactly smile on these occasions, because he never does, but the lips twitch slightly at the corners and the eye is benevolent.'

The quest for Jeeves models has taken Wodehouse scholars into some remote literary pastures. Some have detected the influence of J. M. Barrie's sinister, 'puma-footed' personal servant Frank Thurston. Others point to the inscrutable character of Austin in Conan Doyle's *The Poison Belt*. Wodehouse himself told Richard Usborne that he got the idea for Jeeves after reading Harry Leon Wilson's *Ruggles of Red Gap* (published in magazine and book form in 1914 and 1915) which, he said, 'made a great impression on me and . . . may have been the motivating force behind the creation of Jeeves'. All of this overlooks the obvious point that the cunning servant–foolish master has been a staple of comedy since classical times, and Wodehouse certainly knew his Plautus and his Terence. Wodehouse himself was always severely practical about the genesis of Jeeves. He told Lawrence Durrell it never occurred to him that Jeeves 'would ever do anything except open doors and announce people'. But then, he explained in 1948, having got one of Bertie's friends into a bad tangle,

I saw how to solve the problem but my artistic soul revolted at the idea of having Bertie suggest the solution. It would have been absolutely out of character. Then who? For a long time I was baffled, and then I suddenly thought, 'Why not make Jeeves a man of brains and ingenuity and have him do it?' After that, of course, it was all simple.

In the early Jeeves stories, Wodehouse worked hard to establish a dramatis personae which could sustain a magazine series. Lorimer's *Post* liked to publish stories about characters its readers could follow from season to season and who could become part of American middle-class culture, from G. K. Chesterton's Father Brown to Irvin S. Cobb's Judge Priest. Conan Doyle had pioneered this technique with Sherlock Holmes; Wodehouse had grown up with and admired the Holmes and Watson stories. Now that he was established at the *Post*, Wodehouse was following his deepest instincts. Ever since he started writing, he once admitted to Townend, he had said to himself every day, 'I must get a character for a series.' He had attempted this first with Ukridge, then with Mike and Psmith, and had been frustrated by their limitations. Ukridge was too unattractive; Mike too public-school; and Psmith too Edwardian. Jeeves, as he evolved throughout the coming decade, was ideal. And so was his young master, the 'mentally negligible' Bertie Wooster who is nonetheless so cunningly constructed that he can sustain a complex and compelling narration while apparently missing large parts of what is going on around him.

Shortly before the *Post*'s publication of 'Extricating Young Gussie', Wodehouse's publishers in London had launched the first Blandings Castle novel, *Something Fresh*, featuring, among others, a certain Algernon Wooster, a minor character with only the most distant family connection with the infinitely more famous Bertie. There is no doubt that during the latter part of 1915 Wodehouse was returning to the idea of writing about what he called 'an English stage dude'. There was, as he later explained to his friend Denis Mackail, in language that reflects his Broadway experience, a practical reason for this: 'I started writing about Bertie Wooster and comic earls because I was in America and couldn't write American stories and the only English characters the American public would read about were exaggerated dudes. It's as simple as that.' Bertie, of course, is no ordinary 'dude', but one of literature's great innocents. He may be a chump; he may be a 'perfect ass', but he is, unwittingly, a narrator of genius. This is the sleight of hand that Wodehouse executes in his Jeeves and Wooster stories – the idiotic scrapes of a 'vapid wastrel' (Aunt Agatha's description) transformed into art.

Before this, however, Wodehouse was yet again distracted from his fiction by his passion for musicals. Throughout the autumn of 1915, he had covered Broadway's first nights. On 23 December, an evening he would later mythologize, he went to the Princess Theater on 39th Street, as *Vanity Fair*'s drama critic, to see *Very Good Eddie*, another new production Jerome Kern had developed with Guy Bolton. The Princess Theater had been opened by the ambitious Shubert brothers in 1913 and fitted out with just 299 seats to avoid the fire regulations that applied to theatres seating 300 or more. It was run by 'dear, kindly, voluminous Bessie Marbury', and Ray Comstock, a boyish hustler, who were struggling to find shows 'devoid of all vulgarity and coarseness', as Marbury put it, that would work on the Princess's tiny stage. They had commissioned *Nobody Home* from Bolton and Kern, and when that went well had commissioned *Very Good Eddie* for the Christmas season. Bolton and Kern's musical comedy about the romantic misadventures of two newly wed couples on a honeymoon cruise was judged a success, but they needed a lyricist who could bring a touch of magic to Bolton's book and who could respond to Kern's music. As it happened, the man they needed was already sitting in the stalls, no doubt relishing the prospect of watching his friend Alice Dovey playing the female lead. Wodehouse could see the deficiencies of the lyrics for himself. He was about to fulfil his boyhood dream and embark on a collaboration which would be a turning point in the history of the American musical.

8. 'Musical comedy was my dish'
(1916-1918)

Even at the tender age of twelve, the music hall appealed to the artist
in me . . . it was my earliest ambition to become a comedian on the
halls . . . It was because a music-hall comedian required vim, pep, *espiè-*
glerie, a good singing voice, and a sort of indefinable *je-ne-sais-quoi* –
none of which qualities I appeared to possess – that I abandoned my
ambitions and became a writer. (*Louder and Funnier*)

Later, when they looked back over their triumphant collaboration with
Kern, the two survivors, Bolton and Wodehouse, could not resist embel-
lishing the story of their beginnings. They liked to tell the story of
their chance first meeting in Kern's apartment on West 68th Street at
the opening-night party for *Very Good Eddie*. Bolton's journal is said to
have contained this entry: 'To Kern's for supper. Talked with P. G.
Wodehouse, apparently known as Plum. Never heard of him, but Jerry
says he writes lyrics, so, being slightly tight, suggested we might team
up.' Wodehouse, similarly, claimed to have noted their first meeting as
follows: 'Went to opening of *Very Good Eddie*. Enjoyed it in spite of
lamentable lyrics. Bolton, evidently conscious of this weakness, offered
partnership . . . his eagerness so pathetic that [I] consented.'

The circumstantial evidence suggests, however, that this record is as
artful as many of their recollections. Both men never scrupled to subordinate the facts to the satisfactions of a good story. 'We shall have to
let truth go to the wall,' Wodehouse once wrote to Bolton, 'if it interferes with entertainment.' In 1915, Wodehouse already knew Kern, and
may already have contributed to *90 in the Shade* in January. It is highly
improbable that he had not run into Bolton before 23 December.
Whatever the truth about the coming together of Wodehouse, Bolton
and Kern, there is no doubt that the timing of the match was perfect.

By 1916, the American musical, which had traditionally depended
on a range of European imports, from Viennese operettas like Lehár's
The Merry Widow to anything by Gilbert and Sullivan, was beginning

to develop a distinctively American voice, with characters who spoke American English and sang in an American rhythm. In the family of American music at the beginning of the new century, the musical was still in its infancy, with links to vaudeville, burlesque and black minstrel shows, but it was beginning to grope its way towards a mature and distinctive identity. When the popular song, which expressed for a mass audience the American belief in, and quest for, romantic happiness, turned away from the stately world of nineteenth-century European light music and became swept up in the syncopated rhythms of ragtime, it began to discover hitherto undreamed-of opportunities for wordplay. The First World War was a classic era of songwriting that produced, among others, Irving Berlin's 'A Pretty Girl Is Like a Melody', the best works of George Gershwin and Irving Caesar's 'Swanee'.

Kern, 'the American Schubert', was the catalyst in this explosion. Since his early days in Edwardian London, working for Frohman and Hicks, he had developed into a composer of genius with hugely successful songs like 'They Didn't Believe Me' (for the 1914 show *The Girl from Utah*), whose simple melodic line emphasized the natural self-expression of ordinary people. For Kern and his generation, the Ruritanian fantasies that had dominated the *fin-de-siècle* musical stage were no longer meaningful. Those earlier shows, with their massive choruses and lush forty-piece orchestras, had depended on cavernous, 1,000-seat theatres in which the proscenium arch emphasized the gulf between the performers and the audience and heightened the impossible glamour of the occasion. Now the mood was for a romantic entertainment related to everyday life. American theatre, under Eugene O'Neill's influence, was exploring a new, more realistic kind of drama. As Kern's work moved towards something less cluttered, the attractions of the big Broadway venues diminished. *Nobody Home* had shown Kern the potential of a smaller venue; the success of *Very Good Eddie* confirmed it.

By a happy coincidence, the moment at which Kern was becoming intrigued by the possibilities of a more modern kind of musical was the same moment at which Bessie Marbury and Ray Comstock were grappling with the commercial conundrum presented by the Princess Theater's tiny auditorium, narrow stage and cramped orchestra pit. Confronted with the question of how to make money out of a midget theatre, Marbury and Comstock realized that they had to produce chamber musicals that could be performed on one set per act by an eleven-piece orchestra. Where a big Broadway production at a theatre like the Amsterdam could cost between $50,000 and $75,000, Marbury and Comstock could spend no more than $7,500. Each production, including score, book and lyrics, had to be stripped to its essentials. So, as much by luck as by design, the Princess Theater became home to a radical theatrical experiment: light music with bright, contemporary lyrics in an American idiom.

Jerome Kern was ideally suited to this challenge. Small, wiry and irritable, he was a brilliant popular composer, a non-stop worker, and a tireless perfectionist. In Guy Bolton, he had found a conscientous playwriting partner with a good grasp of comedy but no gift for lyrics. For *Very Good Eddie* they had been forced to depend on the contributions of Schuyler Greene, whose idea of a first act closer was to rely on absurd lyrics like:

> This world's all right when someone loves you.
> 'Tis our delight to do as doves do.
> From morn to night we coo as doves coo,
> Pidgy woo, pidgy woo, pidgy woo.

In the Princess, this was untenable. There was no room for a dull score, a bad plot or a dud lyric. Cast and audience were cheek by jowl. Weaknesses that in a larger venue could be disguised by theatrical effects would never go unnoticed. The music had to sparkle, the comedy had to move like clockwork, and the lyrics had to fit into the very tight place between the book and the score. So the lyrics had to keep the narrative moving, express the personalities of the characters who sang them, and do this in a literate and witty way that complemented Kern's melodies. In December 1915, Bolton and Kern, smarting from reviews that singled out Greene's lyrics for particular scorn, were agreed on one thing: if there was one lyricist who could achieve all this while simultaneously providing an effortless transition from Bolton's dialogue to Kern's music, it was P. G. Wodehouse, whom they recognized as one of the first either on Broadway or in Tin Pan Alley to understand that a song lyric could be more than just a collage of mawkish cliché and trite similes.

Wodehouse, who physically towered over his new partners, did not take much convincing to join Bolton and Kern. *Very Good Eddie* was doing excellent business down on 39th Street; besides, he never said 'no' to a promising commission. He already respected Kern from their days with Seymour Hicks, and would soon discover a wealth of common ground with Guy Bolton. They were both expatriates, born just over a year apart, and were both in the process of establishing careers in wartime Manhattan. Bolton had trained as an architect but had begun to make his way as a writer, contributing to the same magazines that Wodehouse had written for in the 1900s. Unlike Wodehouse, Bolton had grown up in the comfort and security of his American father's home in Washington Heights, and, unlike Wodehouse, he was sexually confident, and had matured into a dapper ladies' man who, having divorced his first wife, became ensnared in a succession of romantic entanglements with chorus girls and singers. Bolton had stumbled into playwriting after an unlikely success in 1911 with a comedy, *The Drone*, had persuaded him to give up architecture for the stage.

Wodehouse was dazzled and liberated by Bolton's quick-witted, worldly sophistication and racy manner. He had experienced this kind of fascination before, with Herbert Westbrook, but Bolton was far more talented, and no slacker. They became lifelong friends. Next to Bill Townend, but in a less inhibited way, Bolton became Wodehouse's greatest confidant. 'Guy and I clicked from the start like Damon and Pythias,' he told Townend. 'We love working together. Never a harsh word or a dirty look. He is one of the nicest chaps I ever met and the supreme worker of all time.' This last quality was the clincher with Wodehouse, but it was Kern's music that would make the difference. 'I help [Bolton] as much as I can with the "book" end of things, but he really does the whole job and I just do the lyrics, which are easy when one has Jerry to work with.'

Wodehouse's retrospective assertion of ease was a typically English and typically Wodehousian gloss. Jerome Kern was *not* easy to work with. He was prickly and exacting, given to abrupt, impatient phone calls, often in the middle of the night. Wodehouse later admitted that their collaboration was conducted mostly over the telephone. More than that, Kern liked to write the music first and give his lyricist a 'dummy' on which to pattern his words. The versatile and accommodating Wodehouse, veteran of *Punch*, 'By the Way', and the Edwardian musical theatre, was not troubled by this requirement, but it was unusual. W. S. Gilbert had always said that a lyricist could not do his best work that way. But Wodehouse was a natural collaborator, and he loved to write lyrics. As he put it later:

I think you get the best results by giving the composer his head and having the lyricist follow him. For instance, the refrain of one of the songs in *Oh, Boy!* began 'If every day you bring her diamonds and pearls on a string'. I couldn't have thought of that, if I had done the lyric first, in a million years . . . it doesn't scan. But Jerry's melody started off with a lot of twiddly little notes, the first thing being emphasised being the 'di' of 'diamonds', and I just tagged along with him.

Wodehouse found another advantage to following Kern. 'When you have the melody,' he said, 'you can see which are the musical high-spots in it and can fit the high-spots of the lyric to them. Anyway, that's how I like working, and to hell with anyone who says I oughtn't to.' Kern established the mood. Wodehouse, temperamentally more formal and less tender, simply followed his lead.

For Wodehouse, this new world of musical theatre, which he would later conjure up with Guy Bolton in *Bring on the Girls*, was to be found between 39th Street and the brightly lit green rooms of echoing Gaiety Theaters in Trenton, Rochester, Schenectady and Buffalo. The transient cast passing across this scene included producers like Florenz Ziegfeld, with a fat cigar; Ray Comstock, with a bevy of 'Honeys'; Colonel Henry Savage, with a limp; actresses like Vivienne Segal; and a walk-on army of chauffeurs, bellhops and wardrobe mistresses, accompanied by theatrical props: orchids and American Beauty roses, champagne flutes, quails in aspic, black silk stockings and pearl bracelets. It was a world of one-night stands. Even Wodehouse's repressed sexuality flickered briefly when he became romantically involved – to Ethel's fury – with a chorus girl named Fleur Marsden, an admirer of his novels to whom he rashly gave a birthday trinket. When confronted by Ethel with the evidence (a receipt from Tiffany's) of what Guy Bolton loved to call 'Plum's one wild oat', the innocent philanderer is reported to have asked, 'How did you find out?' It says a lot about the Wodehouses' marriage that, though this episode inspired a lifelong coolness between Ethel Wodehouse and Bolton, who was blamed for leading Wodehouse astray, the errant husband, whose innocence of character was renowned, emerged unscathed.

In old age, nostalgic for Broadway days, Wodehouse wrote: 'Musical comedy was my dish, the musical comedy theatre my spiritual home. I would rather have written *Oklahoma!* than *Hamlet* . . . For years scarcely a day passed whose low descending sun did not see me at my desk trying to find some lyric for "June" that would not be "soon", "moon", "tune" or "spoon".' He was blessed with a perfect ear for rhythm. His stepdaughter Leonora once wrote that he was 'not a bit interested in music and can't play a note . . . But in spite of this, at the back of his mind the tune is there; with no knowledge of music he recognises the rhythm, the short beats and the long beats.' She recalled that on one occasion a composer had put the telephone on the piano, and played the tune to him just three or four times. When Wodehouse completed his lyric the same day, it fitted the tune perfectly.

Wodehouse, Bolton and Kern were committed to commercial inno-vation, and had ideas for artistic improvements, too. In the creaky stage musicals of 1915, it was customary to stop the plot of the show at an arbitrary point and 'interpolate' an unconnected song, in the hope that it might become a hit that would sell the show. Kern had begun his career in such shows, and, having done countless interpolations, had come to loathe the custom. Wodehouse, too, could be satirical about Broadway theatrical practice, as in this passage from *Jill the Reckless*:

Here, a composer who had not got an interpolated number in the show was explaining to another composer who had not got an interpolated number in the show the exact source from which a third composer, who had got an interpolated number in the show, had stolen the number which he had got interpolated.

Artistically speaking, Wodehouse and Kern agreed that there was no room any more for such conventions. The idea was to come up with an 'inte-grated' show in which each of the three elements – music, book, lyrics – played its part in a harmonious and, they hoped, successful production.

News of Wodehouse's association with Bolton and Kern soon got around the close-knit, gossipy world of Broadway. Before the new team could get started on a wholly original piece for Comstock and Marbury, they found themselves opportunistically signed up by one of the Shubert brothers' bitterest producer rivals, the much-feared Klaw & Erlanger, to rework a piece called *Pom-Pom*. Shortly after that, there was an approach from Erlanger himself – a mesmerizing impresario described as a cross between a toad and a czar of the American theatre – to collaborate with Emmerich (Imre) Kálmán, the folksy Hungarian, on his operetta *Fräulein Susi* (*Zsuzsi kisasszony*), provisionally titled 'Little Miss Springtime'. Now that Frohman was dead, Erlanger's syndicate was at war with the Shubert brothers in a battle for the control of Broadway.

Abraham Lincoln Erlanger was small, and had the small man's obsession with size. His massive office is said to have contained a desk as big as a pool table, where he kept a loaded revolver, a barber's chair in which he would be shaved during meetings, a punchbag, and a library of books about Napoleon, with whom the producer liked to identify. One of his many eccentricities was employing a twelve-year-old boy to second-guess his creative judgement, on the grounds that this was the mental age of the average Broadway audience. He was famous, too, for racing round rehearsals, dressed in a cap and sweater, ranting at everyone and everything. A fictionally diminished Abe Erlanger becomes, in a Jeeves story like 'Episode of the Dog McIntosh', the bullying and ridiculous producer Blumenfeld, whose voice is 'strengthened by a lifetime of ticking actors off at dress-rehearsals from the back of the theatre', and who defers to the instincts of his repellent twelve-year-old son.

Under Erlanger's dictatorial guidance, *Miss Springtime* (the 'Little' was excised after he reportedly said, 'We don't have nothing little at the New Amsterdam Theater'), became the hit of September 1916. Wodehouse claimed that he had not been greatly stretched by his contributions to the production, but a song like 'My Castle in the Air', a wistful, nostalgic number, expressing rather more private emotion than he allowed himself in his fiction, showed his mastery of the genre:

> I've a wondrous castle that I've never lived in yet
> Built so many years ago in days that I forget.
> It has no stone battlements and
> Great big wooden beams.
> Its walls and its bars are the dust of the stars,
> And its gate the gate of dreams.
>
> Come out there for a visit;
> I've lots of room for friends.
> And if you ask where is it,
> It's where the rainbow ends.

It's somewhere there in Fairyland,
Where there's never cloud or care.
We'll have joy and laughter, mirth and song,
And we'll all be happy as the day is long
In the shelter of my castle
Of my castle in the air.

In a world in which conflicts of interest hardly arose, Wodehouse himself reviewed the show for *Vanity Fair*. He cheerfully boosted Guy Bolton who, he claimed, had revolutionized musical comedy, admitted his own involvement, 'just a few trifles . . . dashed off in the intervals of more serious work', and added that candour compelled him to say that '*Miss Springtime* is a corker. It is the best musical play in years.' He was, he confessed in his column, drawing a royalty from the show which had already caused the wolf to move up a few parasangs – a parasang is an ancient Persian measurement of distance – from the Wodehouse doorstep.

He and Ethel had spent the summer of 1916 in Bellport, taking a larger bungalow to accommodate Leonora, who was in America for the holidays. The Wodehouses' summer retreat was a solitary old house set among salt marshes, overlooking a deserted canal in which Wodehouse loved to swim. In his study, according to Guy Bolton, he had linked his massive Monarch typewriter to a bolt of paper whose continuous feed enabled him to type uninterrupted as inspiration flowed. In undulating waves around the walls, Wodehouse tacked up pages of his work in progress, with gaps to indicate where more work was needed. The higher the page up the wall, the closer it was to its final draft. He was not just writing lyrics, he was also putting the finishing touches to three more Jeeves stories and a new novel entitled *Piccadilly Jim*, which he would dedicate to Leonora, now aged twelve, 'the most wonderful child on earth'.

When Leonora returned to school, Wodehouse and Ethel moved back to the city to a new apartment in Manhattan. Bellport was too remote for the impromptu script conferences favoured by Kern, though on one hair-raising occasion Kern, an appalling driver, had insisted on racing out there in the small hours from his home in Bronxville. After months of discussion and distraction, there was a lot of work in prospect with Bolton and Kern, and the partnership was ready to start work on *Oh, Boy!*, their first original production for the Princess. It was a hectic time. Simultaneously with *Oh, Boy!*, they were cutting their creative teeth as a trio on another show, *Have a Heart*, a sophisticated divorce comedy, which opened a five-month run at the Liberty Theater in January 1917.

Oh, Boy! starred two ditzy, breathtakingly glamorous, eighteen-year-old blonde actresses: Justine Johnstone, who was winding up an affair with Bolton, and Marion Davies, shortly to become the mistress of William Randolph Hearst. Anita Loos would later model Lorelei and Dorothy in *Gentlemen Prefer Blondes* on these temperamental starlets, who dazzled and exasperated their producers during several weeks of out-of-town previews. As in all the Princess shows, the theme of *Oh, Boy!* was the mating game. A wedding-night comedy buzzing with mistaken identities and amorous misunderstandings, it brought to the musical stage many of the settings and characters that were beginning to appear in Wodehouse's stories and novels: an upstate country club, a rich playboy, a newly wed wife, and a maiden aunt. Jim Marvin, the polo-playing friend of the romantic lead, George Budd, has a conversational tic that will eventually become part of Bertie Wooster's internal monologue. 'Don't be ridic.', says Jim at one point. 'Come and join the party and be a little ray of sunsh.' When asked, 'Why do you always abbreviate your words?' he replies, 'Oh, just a hab.'

Wodehouse matched Bolton's breezy, punning script and Kern's sunny score with lyrics whose warmth and charm steered effortlessly between sentiment and nostalgia and suffused the show with the wholesome and exhilarating romantic atmosphere that was the hallmark of what became known as 'the Princess shows'. As Kern and Wodehouse had planned, the songs, like 'Till the Clouds Roll by', grew naturally out of the situation and the dialogue, occurring only when, to paraphrase Oscar Hammerstein, the emotions became so intense that words alone were inadequate to convey the feeling. There was nothing, wrote the American critic Gilbert Seldes, that Wodehouse wanted to say that he could not say to music. The things he did *not* want to express – sexual innuendo; outrageous double entendres – would later be exploited, to the hilt, by Cole Porter. As the musicologist Steven Blier has noted, it was not so much that Wodehouse's lyrics were free of the frustrations of sex, more that they were essentially Victorian in sentiment, originating in the drawing room rather than the men's room. 'Rolled into One', for instance, is justly celebrated as a masterpiece of saucy rhythmic invention and deft characterization:

Though men think it strange
Girls should need a change
From their manly fascinations,
The fact is, this act is a thing we're driven to.
You don't have much fun,
If you stick to one;
Men have all such limitations.
Look round you: I'm bound you
Will find that is true.

At the op'ra I like to be with Freddie
To a musical show
I go with Joe.
I like to dance with Ted, and golf with Dick or Ned . . .

Oh, Boy! opened on 20 February and was the spring hit of 1917.
George S. Kaufman, later an acclaimed playwright and a friend of
Wodehouse, but then a reviewer for the *New York Tribune*, with a nice
line in nice lines ('I saw the show under unfortunate circumstances,' he
wrote of one hapless production; 'the curtain was up'), was ecstatic:
'The excellence of *Miss Springtime* and *Oh Boy!* has elevated [Bolton
and Wodehouse] in a single season to the enviable position of being
the most sought after musical comedy authors in the land,' he wrote.
The *New York Times* wrote: 'You might call this a musical comedy that
is as good as they make them, if it were not palpably so much better.'
The Princess sold out within a week. By the autumn of 1917, there
were no fewer than five out-of-town companies touring with *Oh, Boy!*

The success of *Oh, Boy!*, which would lead to the climactic production of the Princess years, *Oh, Lady! Lady!!*, and secure Wodehouse's
place as one of the founding fathers of the American musical, was a
watershed in his long career, in a variety of ways. Most importantly, it
brought him to the eager attention of all the top Broadway producers,
Florenz Ziegfeld, Charles Dillingham, Henry Savage and David Belasco,
a cast of personalities to rival the Napoleonic Abe Erlanger. Next, his
experience on Broadway began to contribute a new assurance to his
stories and novels, and to give him a taste for commercial success and
a popular audience: amid the business of finding new rhymes for 'June',
he managed to complete two new Jeeves stories, and began slowly to

recognize the potential of the series. This was also the year he published *Piccadilly Jim* and *The Man with Two Left Feet* and made the move to the St James's publishers Herbert Jenkins in London, with whom his name would be associated for the rest of his life. Finally, the money he earned from the Princess Theater enabled a change of lifestyle, a move to an unaccustomed level of luxury in Great Neck, Long Island.

While he was flavour of the month, in the first nine months of 1917, Wodehouse wrote lyrics for a succession of musical shows. It was the kind of work he both loved and hated. 'The fellow who does the words of the songs for a musical comedy', he wrote, 'is practically a one-man chain-gang.' Yet he could never refuse a new commission. He explained his addiction to Broadway in a revealing article for *Vanity Fair.* 'Every time I meet Guy Bolton, we vow that we will go on the musical comedy wagon,' he said, 'but our resolutions never come to anything.'

Somehow [he went on] we find ourselves in Mr Dillingham's office, and there is the box of cigars on the table and Mr Ziegfeld in his chair by the window and everything jolly and homelike and innocent; and then Mr Dillingham says casually 'Wouldn't it be fun if we were to get up some theatricals just for a lark?', and Mr Ziegfeld says 'Yes, wouldn't it', and Mr Dillingham says he knows a place round the corner which he could hire for an evening or two, and Mr Ziegfeld says that there's nothing like getting something to do in your spare time, as it keeps you out of the saloons and bowling alleys; and you get the general impression that you're all going to dress up and act charades for the children some evening later on; and then a voice through the smoke coos 'Sign here, boys!'; and you wake up on Broadway and find that you're going to do the next show for the Century.

Between 1916 and 1919, Wodehouse was involved with some fourteen productions. He would later boast that he and Bolton had had no fewer than five shows running simultaneously on Broadway in 1917 (*Oh, Boy! Leave It to Jane*, *The Riviera Girl*, *Miss 1917* and *The Rose of China*). This is slightly misleading. *Miss 1917* (notable for the presence at rehearsals of the young George Gershwin), *The Riviera Girl* and *The Rose of China*, described as 'a dead and gone turkey', were all flops. Only *Leave It to Jane* (an adaptation of a George Ade farce, *The College Widow*) was a genuine hit, establishing a genre – the college sports musical – that would become exceptionally popular in America during the inter-war years. *Leave It to Jane* is remembered for its cabaret-style song 'Cleopatterer', concerning the activities of the legendary queen:

> At dancing, Cleopatterer
> Was always on the spot.
> She gave those poor Egyptian ginks
> Something else to watch besides the sphinx.
> Mark Anthony admitted
> That what first made him skid
> Was the wibbly, wobbly, wiggly dance
> That Cleopatterer did.

The other, less successful shows, while allowing Wodehouse to practise his lyric skills, led to a falling-out with Kern over money – an Achilles heel for both men – that briefly soured their partnership, and would leave their mark on Wodehouse novels with chorus-girl heroines like *Jill the Reckless* and *The Adventures of Sally*.

For all its hectic glamour, Wodehouse's American life during the war was not as influential on his fiction as Edwardian London had been. He was older and less impressionable. American theatrical society was too exotic and foreign to become integral to his creative consciousness. However, his work begins to bear the unmistakable mark of his stage experience, as in the scene where Bertie plots a denouement with Jeeves:

This is the way I see it. We lay the scene in this room. Child, centre. Girl, l.c. Freddie, up stage, playing the piano. No, that won't do. He can only play a little of 'The Rosary' with one finger, so we'll have to cut out the soft music . . . Start with dialogue leading up to child's line. Child speaks line, let us say, 'Boofer lady, does 'oo love dadda?' Business of outstretched hands. Hold picture for a moment. Freddie crosses l. Takes girl's hand. Business of swallowing lump in throat. Then big speech: 'Ah, Elizabeth, has not this misunderstanding of ours gone on too long? See! A little child rebukes us.' And so on.

Similarly, he would borrow plots and characters from Broadway, and structure snippets of conversations like playscripts, as in this exchange from *Right Ho, Jeeves*:

As I recall, the dialogue ran something as follows:
SELF: Well, Jeeves, here we are, what?
JEEVES: Yes, sir.
SELF: I mean to say, home again.
JEEVES: Precisely, sir.
SELF: Seems ages since I went away.
JEEVES: Yes, sir.

Such frequent references to the stage and stage conventions are not, however, as completely assimilated as his other allusions. He would always transplant such borrowings to transatlantic liners or country houses, to a Wodehousian mid-Atlantic or English setting. These were now more prosperous and secure than hitherto. The shabby bank clerks and struggling writers who had populated the worlds of Ukridge and Psmith gave way to millionaires, playboys and eventually the Eggs, Beans and Crumpets of the Drones Club, silly young men with too much money in their pockets and too much time on their hands.

His next novel, published in February 1917, signals the slow transition from the pre-war to the post-war Wodehouse. *Piccadilly Jim*, which had already been serialized in the *Saturday Evening Post*, appeared in New York shortly after the first night of *Oh, Boy!*, and features Jimmy Crocker, who, like Jimmy Pitt in *A Gentleman of Leisure*, is an ex-newspaperman. He is also a full-time playboy, the subject of gossip columns on both sides of the Atlantic. When Crocker falls in love, he decides he must reform his character, but, to win the girl of his dreams, he must pretend to be 'Piccadilly Jim', that is, himself. Wodehouse always revelled in story-construction. On this occasion, his devilish plotting owed something to his new friendship with Guy Bolton. His prose certainly shows signs of his exposure to New York ('everything is as rocky and ding-blasted as stig tossed full of doodle-gammon'), but there is also the familiar figure of a ghastly literary aunt, Mrs Pett, who has 'filled her house with poets'. Wodehouse's years in America had not dulled his eye for the absurdities of cultural fashion:

At different spots in the room stood six resident geniuses . . . the air was clamorous with the hoarse cries of futurist painters, esoteric Buddhists, *vers libre* poets, interior decorators and stage reformers, sifted in among the more conventional members of society who had come to listen to them. Men with new religions drank tea with women with new hats. Apostles of free love expounded their doctrines to persons who had been practising them for years without realising it. All over the room throats were being strained and minds broadened.

Wodehouse had published eleven novels, and had built up a modest, but devoted, readership. Yet, within weeks of *Oh, Boy!*'s success, *Piccadilly Jim* was an unexpected hit. In England, it was sold to Herbert Jenkins who, for the first time in Wodehouse's literary career, achieved a sale of more than 2,000 copies. Thereafter, the novel went from strength to strength while Wodehouse, trapped in the torture chamber of writing lyrics for *Miss 1917*, reflected that at least with a novel the author was in sole charge of the show. Writing for the Princess had been relatively easy. By contrast, a lyric for a Ziegfeld revue was 'a monstrous freak with one verse and twelve refrains, each introducing a separate girl'. This, he observed, was the 'phase of the matter that finally whitens the author's hair. The stoutest admirer of feminine beauty would become a trifle soured on the sex if every woman he met for eight weeks backed him into a corner and asked him for lines . . . one takes to whizzing about the theatre like a hunted fawn.' Despite these trials, as the landmark year of 1917 ended, Wodehouse, Bolton and Kern were hard at work on *Say When*, subsequently modified to become *Oh, Lady! Lady!!*, also named after a popular vaudeville catchphrase. It would be their last show at the Princess. The plot was another mating-game variation on *Oh, Boy!* and Wodehouse would recycle it in his novel *The Small Bachelor*. Two lovers who want to get married have to contend with a mother's opposition and the comic complications presented by a couple of crooks, Spike and Fanny, whose contribution to the show is 'Our Little Nest':

> Our home will look so bright and cheery
> That you will bless your burglar-boy
> I got some nifty silver, dearie,
> When I cracked that crib at Troy;
> I lifted stuff enough in Yonkers
> To fill a good-sized chest;
> And, at a house in Mineola
> I got away with their Victrola
> So we'll have music in the evenings
> When we are in our little nest.

After many vicissitudes, the curtain falls with the lovers united. *Oh, Lady! Lady!!* was Wodehouse's favourite Princess show, even though 'Bill', the lyric for which Wodehouse is still remembered in stage-musical circles, was dropped during rehearsals. When *Oh, Lady! Lady!!* opened at the Princess on 1 February 1918, the critics turned a blind eye to the formulaic awkwardness of Bolton's book, and celebrated instead the pleasures of the music and lyrics. In the *New York Times*, George S. Kaufman laid aside his critic's scalpel and burst enthusiastically into verse:

> This is the trio of musical fame,
> Bolton and Wodehouse and Kern:
> Better than anyone else you can name,
> Bolton and Wodehouse and Kern.

A sterner critic, Dorothy Parker, demure and often devastating, gave her verdict in *Vanity Fair*. She had just succeeded Wodehouse, who had tired of newspaper criticism, as the resident drama critic, and was beginning to make a name for herself:

Well, Wodehouse and Bolton and Kern have done it again . . . I was completely sold on [*Oh, Lady! Lady!!*]. Not even the presence in the first night audience of Mr William Randolph Hearst could spoil my evening. But then Wodehouse and Bolton and Kern are my favourite indoor sport, anyway. I like the way they go about a musical comedy . . . I like the way the action slides casually into the songs . . . I like the deft rhyming of the song that is always sung in the last act . . . And oh, how I do like Jerome Kern's music.

Oh, Lady! Lady!! did not do as well as *Oh, Boy!* but it ran for a respectable 219 performances, and was even staged by an all-convict cast at Sing-Sing prison, in upstate New York.

When Wodehouse celebrated his success by moving away from Bellport to Arrandale Avenue, just outside the village of Great Neck and within easy reach of Manhattan, his metropolitan reputation gave him a natural entrée into a community of writers, actors and producers. His circle included W. C. Fields, the actors Ed Wynn and Gene Buck, the humorist Ring Lardner, and, later, F. Scott Fitzgerald, who would capture the post-war atmosphere of Great Neck in *The Great Gatsby*.

A well-heeled suburban arcadia of the kind that Wodehouse always favoured, Great Neck offered long country walks, peace and quiet, and congenial company. The great Ziegfeld had property here; Guy Bolton and his new wife Marguerite had moved out there during 1917. Wodehouse, who wanted to be near his friend and collaborator, rented the guest house on the Grace family estate, a fine, secluded residence with an English-style interior. 'I find I can do a lot of work here,' he told Lily Barnett, 'as it is so quiet, and there are no distractions. I go about all day in flannels, just like at Emsworth.' True to form, the Wodehouses had acquired three dogs, two parrots and a canary. He took up golf and would go out on the links at the Sound View Golf Club with actors like Ray Barnes, Donald Brain and Ernest Truex. Wodehouse was a poor golfer, but said he never minded losing because walking round the holes was such good exercise. 'If only I'd taken up golf immediately after I left school,' he confided to David Jasen, 'instead of playing cricket.' Despite his years in the thick of the hedonistic world of Broadway, he was still a Dulwich boy at heart. Frank Crowninshield, his editor at *Vanity Fair*, was to remember him, unkindly, as 'a stodgy and colourless Englishman; silent, careful with his money, self-effacing, slow-witted and matter of fact . . . I never heard him utter a clever, let alone brilliant, remark.'

There was no shortage of brilliance around him. Wodehouse became friends with F. Scott Fitzgerald, and, when the Boltons kept open house on Sundays at Great Neck, he and Ethel found themselves caught up in a brittle, boisterous theatrical and musical circle. Enrico Caruso, clowning in the kitchen, cooked spaghetti; Isadora Duncan and Rudolph Valentino dropped by; and Ethel flirted with the young men from Broadway. Wodehouse shut himself away indoors with a book, or a notepad and pencil, jotting down ideas for stories and rhymes for 'spoon' and 'June'.

Wodehouse's lyrics, now largely forgotten, were a holiday from his fiction, and show him in a mood that is more personal, more playful, relaxed and carefree. In his stories, Wodehouse is the laureate of repression, but in the lightness of verse he could begin to articulate hidden feelings. His versatility is remarkable. He wrote ballads, dance songs, comic Gilbertian historical numbers, innocent celebrations of bliss, and wistful, sentimental love songs. Then there are the numbers that express his ever-present longing for a fantasy world to which he could escape, for example 'The Land Where the Good Songs Go'. This was his deeply felt expression of the Wodehousian paradise:

> It's a land of flowers
> And April showers
> With sunshine in between
> With roses blowing and rivers flowing –
> 'Mid rushes growing green;
> Where no one hurries
> And no one worries
> And life runs calm and slow
> And I wish some day I could find my way
> To the land where the good songs go.

After *Oh, Lady! Lady!!*, Comstock and his 'trio of musical fame' could not agree on their next production, and the steam went out of the partnership. Both Bolton and Kern were becoming distracted by new projects with other producers and ambitious for their own careers in the theatre. From time to time during the next ten years they would collaborate separately with Wodehouse on other projects, but the three men would never recapture the magic of the Princess shows, one of those tantalizingly brief high spots in American popular culture. A succession of lyricists, from Ira Gershwin, Cole Porter and Howard Dietz to Oscar Hammerstein II and Richard Rodgers, would later pay tribute to their mentor, Wodehouse, and acknowledge his contribution as a turning point in the development of the American musical. Alan Jay Lerner wrote that Wodehouse was 'the pathfinder for Larry Hart, Cole Porter, Ira Gershwin and everyone else who followed'. Wodehouse was especially influential on Ira Gershwin. They shared a sensibility, a passion for light verse, a connection to operetta, especially Gilbert and Sullivan, and a certain fundamental innocence. They also collaborated on some lyrics. Indeed, if Wodehouse had not, subsequently, been acclaimed as a comic writer of genius, Wodehouse the lyricist might have had a wider, more general recognition.

At the time, in the autumn of 1918, Wodehouse and Bolton were such a hot property that producers would take almost anything that carried their names. When they could not agree on a project with Kern, they settled on a collaboration with veteran Broadway composer

Louis A. Hirsch. The result of this shotgun wedding was *Ask Dad*, a helter-skelter health-farm comedy with a witchy wife, a hapless philanderer and a dizzy plot (after an uneasy out-of-town first night, the title was changed to *Oh, My Dear!* for the opening at the Princess). It was notable as the first show ever to feature a psychiatrist, but was otherwise undistinguished. Dorothy Parker wrote that Hirsch's music was 'so reminiscent that the score rather resembles a medley of last season's popular songs, but it really doesn't make any difference – Mr Wodehouse's lyrics would make anything go'. The lyricist himself described the show as 'our *Ruddigore*', a reference to Gilbert and Sullivan's least-popular collaboration, and he plundered the original title *Ask Dad* for comic effect in his story 'Jeeves and the Chump Cyril'.

The war in Europe was now over. The defeated Kaiser went into exile in Holland. There, it is said that he discovered the works of P. G. Wodehouse and would read them aloud to his mystified staff, chuckling over and rereading the best bits. On 4 December, shortly after the opening of *Oh, My Dear!*, the *George Washington* sailed to Europe with Woodrow Wilson and the American delegation to the Paris Peace Conference on board, carrying an impossible burden of expectations. The watching crowds in Battery Park cheered; tugs' horns hooted and Robert Lansing, the Secretary of State, released carrier pigeons with messages of hope for a lasting peace. It was the first time a sitting President had travelled to Europe. Perhaps Wodehouse, too, sensed a shift in public taste. The hero of his next novel, *A Damsel in Distress*, for which the *Saturday Evening Post* paid a colossal $10,000, is George Bevan, an American composer, but the action is set in an English country house, Belpher Castle, the ancestral home of an English peer who loves his garden, is bossed by his sister, and has not only a half-witted son but also a butler who looks like a bishop. Not content with setting his work in England again, in a place highly reminiscent of Emsworth, Wodehouse was about to transfer his household to London and arranging to collect his recently unpublished stories in a volume entitled *My Man Jeeves*. Wodehouse was coming home.

9. 'A bloke called Bertie Wooster'
(1918-1923)

'You will find Mr Wooster . . . an exceedingly pleasant and amiable young gentleman, but not intelligent. By no means intelligent. Mentally he is negligible – quite negligible.' (*The Inimitable Jeeves*)

Ethel had found 16 Walton Street, a pretty neo-Georgian town house near Harrods. This became the Wodehouses' London base for the first year of peace, 1919, the beginning of a decade of non-stop work in which Wodehouse would compose the lyrics for some twelve musicals, write or adapt four plays and publish twenty books in London and New York. He was approaching forty now, had lost most of his hair and was on the brink of international literary fame. Critics, he noted with pride, were beginning to refer to 'the P. G. Wodehouse manner'; and he boasted to Leonora that he was becoming 'rather a blood these days'. This was also the time when, having read about Walter Camp's exercise regime in *Collier's*, he added a sequence of pre-breakfast stretching and toe-touching, the 'daily dozen', to his routine, never missing a day. Success, marriage and his years in America had left him strikingly unmarked. A contemporary *Strand* profile described Wodehouse 'watching humanity at work and play, rather like a curious and intelligent boy who has just left school and has not yet had time to lose hope and interest'. This was a characterization with which the subject might have concurred. 'I am much the same,' he insisted to Bill Townend, 'except that the trousers I was wearing [in 1914] have at last given out.' Joking aside, he knew that his wartime absence in America could be misconstrued. He told Townend he hoped that 'I'm not arrested and shoved in chokey for not helping to slug Honble Kaiser'.

There was, of course, no question of prosecution, but Wodehouse returned to a country much changed from his last visit in 1914. The war had blown Edwardian England to pieces. It was a society in shock. The old confidence, certainty and wealth had been replaced by doubt, anxiety and debt. Three-quarters of a million men had been killed.

Scarcely a family in Britain had not known that awful moment when the War Office telegram announced the death in battle of a husband or a brother. In literary London, Kipling and Conan Doyle both lost sons. The former would spend the rest of his life in an agonizing, obsessive and ultimately futile search for the truth about his son John's last moments; the latter turned to spiritualism. In this gloomy, neurotic atmosphere, Wodehouse's light-hearted country-house comedies were both a tonic for bereaved and depressed survivors, and a kind of lunatic elegy for a lost world.

Wodehouse was still exploring the characters and setting for which, ultimately, he would be renowned. Two of the books he published in 1919 – *My Man Jeeves*, a volume of Jeeves and Reggie Pepper stories, and *A Damsel in Distress* – are sketches for greater work to come. A third, *The Coming of Bill*, was a throwback to the bad old days of writing a Bob Davis *Munsey's* plot for hire. As well as the books, throughout 1919 Wodehouse maintained his presence on Broadway, while successfully establishing himself in the West End: in January 1919, *Oh, Boy!* opened at the Kingsway Theatre, renamed *Oh, Joy!* and starring Tom Powers and a young Beatrice Lillie. Shortly afterwards, in May, *The Girl behind the Gun*, a Bolton–Wodehouse Broadway collaboration with 'Fabulous Felix', the Belgian composer Ivan Caryll, retitled *Kissing Time* to catch the mood of the peace, opened at the Winter Garden, starring Leslie Henson and Stanley Holloway, and was a huge hit.

Whenever Wodehouse was over in America, to which he still travelled at least once a year, he was immersed in the ritzy world of postwar American plutocracy. As the year closed, he, Ethel and Guy Bolton took off for a Christmas holiday in Palm Beach, the winter playground for wealthy New Yorkers and, during the European war, a safe place for the very rich to gamble and frolic irresponsibly in the sunshine. Flo Ziegfeld was there and immediately invited them for a cruise on his yacht, *The Wench*, 'a real dream boat with a cocktail shaker for every port-hole'. The party included a newspaper proprietor, a theatrical manager, various *Ziegfeld Follies* girls, Walter Chrysler, the automobile tycoon, and a now forgotten American novelist and playwright, Arthur Somers Roche, together with his new wife, Ethel Pettit, a Broadway star. As the cruise ended in the Florida sunset, Pettit stood by the piano and sang 'Bill' so affectingly that Ziegfeld was inspired to start planning a new Bolton–Wodehouse–Kern collaboration, a rags-to-riches show eventually called *Sally*. Wodehouse thought he knew all about Ziegfeld's enthusiasms, paid no attention, and sailed back to England on the *Majestic* in the new year of 1920 to continue catching up with his pre-war life.

There, renewing his friendship with Bill Townend after a long absence, he now described his theatre work as the big source of his income. He also mentioned that he had managed to write a number of short stories for the *Saturday Evening Post* 'about a bloke called Bertie Wooster and his valet'. This sentence is absent from the original letter, and was interpolated by Wodehouse in the published version, with the benefit of hindsight. At the end of this first post-war year, Wodehouse had not yet fully detected the priceless comic potential of Bertie Wooster, and was concentrating on creating another lightweight Englishman, a chump named Archie. This, he decided, was his forte. As he wrote to Leonora, 'without a dude character where am I?'

Archibald Moffam, pronounced Moom ('to rhyme with Bluffinghame', he says), is a well-meaning young Englishman of 'no occupation and no private means'. As the protagonist of a neglected collection of stories, *Indiscretions of Archie*, Archie demonstrates Wodehouse adjusting to the changed social circumstances by placing another 'English stage dude' in a plausible post-war setting. Archie has just married Lucille, the only daughter of the hotel proprietor Daniel Brewster, head of a long line of intimidating Americans. 'Directly I was demobbed,' Archie tells his father-in-law, 'the family started talking about the Land of Opportunity and shot me on to a liner.' Cigar-chewing Brewster is appalled by his nincompoop son-in-law. Archie's attempts to melt Brewster's heart by finding a job is the joke that animates a series of stories set in New York during the early days of Prohibition. Archie, 'a friendly soul, a mixer', moves in a milieu similar to Jimmy Pitt and Jimmy Crocker, but is a hopeless incompetent whose madcap 'indiscretions' invariably land him in what he calls 'the gumbo'. Like his Edwardian predecessors, Ukridge and Psmith, and like almost all the Drones, Archie is on the look-out for entertainment: 'It seemed to him as though New York had simply been waiting for him to arrive before giving the word to let the revels commence.' If ever a city was equipped for revels, it was jazz age New York in the 1920s.

Archie is, however, 'no poltroon'; he has been away to war. When a highly strung actress, Miss Vera Silverton, points a loaded gun at him, he coolly invites her to go ahead and pull the trigger, observing that 'in the recent unpleasantness in France I had chappies popping off things like that at me all day and every day for close on five years'. Toughened by experience, he also comes from hardy English stock: 'the blood of generations of Moffams, many of whom had swung a wicked axe in . . . the Middle Ages, boiled within him.' This gives him consanguinity with Bertram Wilberforce Wooster, but unlike Bertie he is, in his limited way, in touch with reality. When his wife Lucille asks if he knows 'any really good swear words', Archie's reply places him firmly in post-war civilization:

I did pick up a few tolerably ripe and breezy expressions out in France. All through my military career there was something about me . . . I remember one brass-hat addressing me for quite ten minutes, saying something new all the time. And even then he seemed to think he had only touched the fringe of the subject.

Archie's adventures in New York take in the speakeasy, the stage, rooftop restaurants in Greenwich Village, and the faultless grandeur of the Cosmopolitan Hotel, echoing in fiction many aspects of Wodehouse's own recent American life. But there are some important points of difference. Wodehouse preferred his heroes to be bachelors – as Bertie is, and remains, despite the designs of some twenty fiancées. But Archie is not only married, he also is a father-to-be. Indeed, Archie Moffam's future as a magazine character is abruptly terminated when, to Mr Brewster's delight, Lucille announces that she is expecting a baby.

Wodehouse would never be a father – the mumps he suffered in 1901 may have left him sterile – but once he was re-established in London his paternal relationship with his stepdaughter Leonora, now fifteen, blossomed. His 'queen of all possible Snorkles' became the recipient of Dulwich sporting news ('The Haileybury match was a disaster, darn it') and his 'confidential secretary and adviser' to whom he showed his work-in-progress. Leonora was growing into an exceptional young woman, increasingly at odds with Ethel. Wodehouse found himself having to intercede in the inevitable teenage battles between mother and daughter. 'Oh, by the way,' he wrote in one postscript, 'you must stop borrowing Mummie's clothes. It worries her frightfully, and you know how nervous she is.' Once the family was settled in Walton Street, Leonora was moved from her boarding school in Felixstowe and sent to the Old Palace, a girls' boarding school at Bromley.

This was not just to give Wodehouse time to write. In her own way, Ethel was revelling in the return to England, and was quite in tune with the hysterical, rather desperate, pleasure-seeking spirit of the times. She took up golf, went shopping, to parties and to the races, and eventually bought a horse, a steeplechaser named Front Line. The picture of their marriage that emerges from his correspondence is of Wodehouse working all hours on his own, often staying at his club in Northumberland Avenue, while Ethel dashed about the place, spending his money, now at the Chingford races, now staying overnight in Folkestone, anon visiting friends in the country. Wodehouse liked her independence; it suited him, too. He was just as capable of taking off at a moment's notice to shut himself away in a favourite hotel with his pipe, his Monarch and a stack of foolscap paper. Even when they were under the same roof, they lived parallel lives in which they would be brought together by moments of domestic drama, as Wodehouse described to Leonora: 'Great excitement last night. Mummie came into my room at half-past two and woke me out of the dreamless to say that mice had been snootering her. She said one had run across her bed.' To soothe his excitable wife, Wodehouse added, he went to her room to spend the rest of the night, plainly an exceptional situation. 'We had hardly turned off the light when – zip! – one ran right across the pillow!!!' After this, they 'hoofed it' back to his bedroom, but the bed was too small. 'So I gave up my room to Mummie and went back to the mice room. And for some reason or other Mister Mouse made no further demonstration . . . the result is that we are both very sleepy today. I have been trying to work, but can't rouse the old bean.'

As 1920 drew to a close, Wodehouse was busy moulding the Archie stories into a book, *Indiscretions of Archie*, for publication in the coming spring. He was also starting work on a new Broadway novel, *The Adventures of Sally*, another Anglo-American love story. His attention was focused on his fiction that year; and the row he had with Kern in November 1920 about the production of the musical *Sally* illustrates how detached he had become from the day-to-day Broadway business that had so recently been his obsession during the war. After the trip to Palm Beach, and during Wodehouse's absence in London, Ziegfeld had hired first one and then a second new lyricist. Wodehouse, who

had already put in a lot of work on the show, in a fit of pique cabled
Kern: 'Cancel permission to use lyrics'. Then Kern put his lawyers onto
Wodehouse, who told Leonora that 'I don't suppose the action will ever
come to anything, but doesn't it show how blighted some blighters can
be when they decide to be blighters?'

   In addition to the stresses of simultaneous work in different genres,
there was a new worry, one that would increasingly trouble him
throughout these years and ultimately contribute to his downfall: income
tax, the complications of which were compounded by his constant
movement between Britain and America. As he confided to Townend
in February 1921,

I'm off tomorrow to Paris, en route for Biarritz. I find if I stay longer than
six months in this country I am liable to pay income tax on everything I
make in America as well as England. This is no good to Pelham, so I am skip-
ping . . . I simply must get on with this dam [*sic*] novel.

He and Ethel had just taken a pretty new house in Launceston Place,
Kensington, a short cab ride from Walton Street, but he needed more
seclusion. So Wodehouse returned to Emsworth to concentrate in a
familiar atmosphere of calm and contentment. He was writing at a
furious pace. 'On a novel', he told Townend, 'I generally do eight pages
a day, i.e. about 2,500 words. As a rule I like to start work in the
mornings, knock off for a breather, and then do a bit more before
dinner. I never work after dinner. Yet in the old days that was my best
time. Odd.'

   As well as writing, he was always reading, and always turning over
ideas for stories. It was during these months that he read *What Next?*,
a first novel with an ingenious plot about a clever butler by a young
British writer named Denis Mackail. Wodehouse, who was about to start
on a new burst of Jeeves stories, wrote the delighted Mackail a fan letter,
following up with an invitation to dinner. Mackail, who became a lifelong friend and devoted correspondent, sharing Wodehouse's love of
Pekinese, has left a good picture of the literary Wodehouse in action at
the Savoy Grill: 'he provided a considerable banquet and immediately
started talking about writing, without delay. For this – apart from Pekes,
and cricket and football matches at his old school, with which he also
seemed obsessed – was his one great, unending topic.' Mackail reports

that he could not remember Wodehouse ever lingering, for more than a few seconds, on any other subject. Denis and his wife Diana became part of a cosy London literary circle that included A. A. Milne and his wife Daphne, Ethel and Wodehouse.

Life with Wodehouse was comfortable but dull, an affirmation of Flaubert's dictum that a mundane routine is essential to good writing. Ethel's affectionate formula was that 'Plummie lives in the moon', but her loneliness in the relationship inspired a quest for entertainment at home as well as in the world at large. The house was always open to people she met at parties, and it was during these months that she introduced into the Wodehouse ménage a charming, recently demobbed, US army captain, R. J. B. 'Bobby' Denby, whose role in their lives, until he vanished from view during the 1930s, has never been fully explained. An inveterate ladies' man, Denby certainly became an acknowledged part of the household for the next few years, in Britain and in America (Wodehouse often refers to him in letters), was well known to Leonora, and later conducted literary business for Wodehouse in New York. If Denby had a relationship with Ethel, it was discreet, and one to which Wodehouse, working hard at his typewriter, turned a blind eye.

On his most recent trip to America, in March 1921, Wodehouse terminated the lease on the house in Great Neck, closing a chapter. At the same time, he was focusing his attention on some new Jeeves stories and, when he was not sweating over a new Ivor Novello musical, *The Golden Moth*, devoted much of 1921 to 'Jeeves in the Springtime', 'Scoring off Jeeves', 'Sir Roderick Comes to Lunch', 'Comrade Bingo' and 'The Great Sermon Handicap'. As Christmas drew near, he told Leonora he had had 'a great rush of ideas for a new novel . . . on the lines of *Something New* and *Piccadilly Jim*' (this would become *Leave It to Psmith*, partly written to please Leonora), and then in the new year (1922) he announced that he had 'got out the plot of a new Jeeves story where Bertie visits a girls' school and is very shy and snootered by the girls and the headmistress'. This was inspired by his experience of Leonora's headmistress, a severe, thin-faced woman named Miss Starbuck. Wodehouse was apparently so frightened of her that, when he took Leonora out from school, appearing on a bicycle with a knotted handkerchief covering his great bald head against the sun, he would hide in the shrubbery of the school drive and collect his stepdaughter at a safe distance from the premises.

The Bertie Wooster who appears in this second sequence of Jeeves and Wooster stories is, as the critic Kristin Thompson has pointed out, rather different from the Bertie who made his debut in the first series, 1916–17. In those days, Bertie was a frivolous young man, under the thumb of an aunt or uncle. Defying these relatives, with Jeeves's assistance, Bertie is enabled to retain his independence. He is a heavy drinker, never at his best in the early morning, who fritters away his time in clubs and bars. The cast of those early stories is confined to Jeeves, Bertie, various silly young men with names like Corky, Rocky and Motty, and a few oppressive relatives like the notorious Aunt Agatha, who 'wears barbed wire next to the skin'. In these stories, Jeeves is not the supreme deity who comes to preside over the action of the later work.

On their second appearance, in 1921–2, Bertie and Jeeves have both grown up a bit. The experience of writing about Archie's adventures has left its mark. Bertie still owes a lot to the Edwardian knut and the bachelor playboy whom Wodehouse had been writing about for years, but he has floated free into the idyllic world of the author's imagination. Wodehouse was more than ever alive to the importance of Bertie's wonderful innocence. But although he is still approximately twenty-four and a young-man-about-town, Bertie is no longer a brainless, drunken ne'er-do-well. In crises, he still deploys the classic adolescent defence (ignorance, then denial, followed by untruth), but he is marginally more intelligent, and the main sign of his growing complexity as a character lies in his ability to defy his valet. When Jeeves carelessly describes him as 'mentally negligible', his pride is so injured he strikes out on his own, refusing to ask for help, even though he faces the ghastly prospect of marriage to Honoria Glossop, 'one of those dashed large, brainy, strenuous girls you see so many of these days'. His defiance of Jeeves is almost gloating:

'Jeeves,' I said, 'I'm in a bit of difficulty.'

'I'm sorry to hear that, sir.'

'Yes, quite a bad hole. In fact, you might say on the brink of a precipice, faced by an awful doom.'

'If I could be of any assistance, sir –'

'Oh, no. No, no. Thanks very much, but no, no. I won't trouble you. I've no doubt I shall be able to get out of it by myself.'

'Very good, sir.'

So that was that. I'm bound to say I'd have welcomed a bit more curiosity from the fellow, but that is Jeeves all over. Cloaks his emotions, if you know what I mean.

These stories, published almost simultaneously in the *Strand* and *Cosmopolitan* during 1922, mark the beginning of Wodehouse's golden years. They would be collected into one of his most successful books, *The Inimitable Jeeves*, which, published in Britain in May 1923, is one of his undisputed classics, selling at least three million copies before the Second World War. Wodehouse knew that his writing had reached a new height, and he linked this explicitly to his Broadway years. 'I've found that writing musical comedy has taught me a lot,' he told Townend. 'In musical comedy you gain so tremendously in Act One if you can give your principal characters a *dramatic* entrance instead of just walking them on.'

Even now, with Jeeves and Wooster taking on their familiar outlines, Wodehouse could not resist exploring the potential of other series characters, like Ukridge, for the magazines that paid him so handsomely. Herbert Jenkins had just republished his Ukridge novel *Love among the Chickens* of 1906 in a new edition. Despite having Bertie in the wings, Wodehouse was still grooming Stanley Featherstonehaugh Ukridge for stardom. 'I think I'll do a series about Ukridge,' he told Townend, soliciting plots as usual. He pictured Ukridge, who on first appearance had been married to a cipher named Millie, as 'still unmarried', which meant he could make him 'always in love with girls, like Bingo, if necessary'. Short stories, written in hotels or on liners, were exactly suited to Wodehouse's nomadic lifestyle, and a Ukridge short story was especially portable. 'The beauty of this [Ukridge] series', he told Townend, 'will be that I can lay the scenes anywhere, Ukridge having travelled all over the world. So if you get a good idea for a Ukridge story laid in Buenos Aires, shoot it along.'

The numerous illustrated magazines, headed by the *Saturday Evening Post* and the *Strand*, which paid good money for humorous stories, were an essential part of the creative landscape in which Wodehouse flourished during these inter-war years – as important to him as the transatlantic liners, the Broadway producers' offices or the London clubs that inspired the Drones. In the world of the magazine story, Wodehouse was king: he had mastered the mechanics of a well-crafted plot; for the tone of such stories, he had perfect pitch; all he needed were suitable subjects on which he could display the brilliance of his light prose. Soon after he took up playing golf at the Sound View Golf Club, and because nothing in his life was ever allowed to go to waste, he began to write golfing stories.

The first volume of these, *The Clicking of Cuthbert*, was published in February 1921, and marked 'an epoch in my literary career. It is written in blood,' he wrote in a witty and self-mocking preface.

Two years ago, I admit, I was a shallow farceur. My work lacked depth. I wrote flippantly simply because I was having a thoroughly good time. Then I took up golf, and now I can smile through the tears and laugh, like Figaro, that I may not weep, and generally hold my head up and feel I am entitled to respect.

Golf links, especially the Sound View, provide the setting for these stories, but their subjects range from the title story, describing the triumph in love of Cuthbert Banks, a champion golfer, over Raymond Parsloe Devine, a Bloomsbury novelist, to 'The Coming of Gowf', described by Wodehouse as 'the best golf-story I have ever done'. The Oldest Member, or 'the sage', the resident club bore who often narrates these stories, is the precursor of Mr Mulliner: wise, conservative, misogynist and a stickler for convention. Some of Wodehouse's sharpest comic writing is to be found in these golfing stories, and they added another string to his bow. A second volume, *The Heart of a Goof*, followed in the mid-1920s.

Throughout the summer of 1922, Wodehouse was absorbed in rehearsals for *The Cabaret Girl*, another collaboration with Jerome Kern, starring George Grossmith the younger, son of the co-author of *Diary of a Nobody*, and a brilliant, hugely popular, light entertainer. Grossmith, who crossed the Atlantic with Wodehouse, has left a telling portrait of him mumbling through his latest work at a 'ship's concert', the kind of charitable occasion Wodehouse loathed, on the *Aquitania*:

Plummie, quite oblivious to any restlessness among his hearers, was enjoying himself immensely. Although the text proper escaped me, I caught several interjections that [Wodehouse] made from time to time: mm-m-er-z-z-z-mumble-z-z-z . . . by Jove that's good! I'd no idea . . . mm-z-zzz-mm-mmm . . . devilish funny, I'd forgotten that bit . . . mmm-z-z-mumble . . .

The Cabaret Girl was the first musical to deal with the fashionable phenomenon of the Roaring Twenties, and was greeted with acclaim in London at the Winter Garden in September. Wodehouse described the opening night to Leonora with his usual hyperbole: 'Honestly, old egg, you never saw such a first night. The audience . . . never stopped applauding during the cabaret scene.' The first-night party at the Metropole, with oysters, lobster and grouse, went on into the small hours; the Wodehouses did not get to bed until six, which was not unusual for Ethel, who was a night bird, but left Wodehouse feeling out of sorts.

Although Wodehouse regretted that 'this year I seem to have been separated from you [Leonora] all the time', in response to an urgent cable from New York he was soon back on the boat for yet another burst of work with Guy Bolton, staying with him in Great Neck while working on a Ziegfeld musical, a Cinderella story called *Pat*, and another show, provisionally titled *Sitting Pretty*, for the latest vaudeville sensation, the Duncan sisters. These extraordinary twins, Rosetta and Vivian Duncan, known to their intimates as 'Heim and Jake', were tough customers who had somehow convinced the young Irving Berlin to write a score for their next production, a promise, as it turned out, that he would never fulfil. Their forte was the close-harmony number. When Wodehouse had met them for the first time, backstage at the Royalty Theater, they looked, he said, 'like something left over from a defunct kindergarten'.

Wodehouse was happy to be associated with a potential box-office success, and in the tranquillity of Great Neck, he could at least get down to some serious work on his new Blandings Castle novel, *Leave It to Psmith*, which had been giving him a lot of trouble, but which now suddenly began to flow. He wrote 40,000 words in three weeks and sold it to the *Saturday Evening Post* for a record $18,000. Not everything was rosy. 'I am weeping tears of blood over the ghastly exhibition the boys of the old school have been making of themselves,' he complained to Townend. 'Just imagine scoring 18 points against Sherborne and not been [sic] able to win.'

Leave It to Psmith, 'a straightforward narrative of the simple home life of the English upper classes', is a novel that marks Wodehouse's steady creative transition towards a post-war sensibility. Although Psmith's urbane presence reminds the reader of Wrykyn days, Mike Jackson is now married to Phyllis and, as such, has reached the end of the road as a Wodehouse protagonist. Similarly, Psmith, as suave and amoral as ever, is in love with Eve Halliday, and when he marries her will find his career in the Wodehouse canon abruptly terminated. But, looking forward, Lord Emsworth, 'that amiable and boneheaded peer', is beginning to grow into a great comic character. The Empress of Blandings, the immortal pig, does not appear, but she will soon make her debut. As usual, the castle is full of impostors and crooks, united in pursuit of a diamond necklace. Lord Emsworth's secretary, Rupert Baxter, gets locked out of the castle in his pyjamas, throws flowerpots at Emsworth's window, and is sacked, thus setting up the opening of *Summer Lightning* and its brilliant sequel, *Heavy Weather*. Wodehouse took a lot of trouble with *Leave It to Psmith*, and the significant variations in the text between magazine and book versions also illustrate the role of the transatlantic market in Wodehouse's work.

Pat, the Ziegfeld musical, meanwhile made little progress, and *Sitting Pretty*, the Duncan sisters' project, was not helped by Irving Berlin breaking a succession of appointments with his lyricist. Wodehouse and Ethel headed south to spend the winter in South Carolina, at the golfing resort of Aiken where, by playing eighteen holes a day, he told Mackail, 'I have improved my golf beyond my wildest dreams.' It was here that he won an umbrella, his first and only golfing trophy. 'Playing to a handicap of sixteen,' he recalled, 'I went through a field consisting of some of the fattest retired business-men in America like a devouring flame.'

When, by late spring 1923, both the Ziegfeld show and the Duncan sisters' project seemed hopelessly stalled, Wodehouse began working again with George Grossmith on *The Beauty Prize*, a calculated attempt to cash in on the success of *The Cabaret Girl*. The Wodehouses took the train north to Long Island, where they rented a furnished house on the shore in East Hampton for the summer. Leonora, who was due to go to finishing school in France, came out for the holidays. The family was also joined by Bobby Denby and later by some friends of Grossmith's, Lord and Lady Ilchester. Wodehouse later revealed that Lady Ilchester, a bluff, red-faced woman with a loud voice, was often at the back of his mind when he was writing about Bertie Wooster's Aunt Dahlia.

Wodehouse had hardly installed himself at his typewriter when news reached him that his publisher, Herbert Jenkins, 'one of those fellows who look transparent and seem always tired', had died suddenly. Wodehouse, who set great store by regular meals and daily exercise, put this down to Jenkins's workaholic lifestyle. He had anticipated trouble, however, by having a clause in his contract whereby rights reverted to himself in such an eventuality. In fact, Herbert Jenkins Ltd. weathered its founder's passing and Wodehouse, after a year or two of dissatisfaction, stayed with it, becoming its *raison d'être*, and establishing a lifelong friendship with its new managing director, John Grimsdick. The reality of death, however, was making one of its rare appearances in a life which, until this time, had seemed otherwise utterly charmed. It was during Leonora's visit to East Hampton that Wodehouse was knocked down by a car on one of Long Island's wide new roads.

It was a close shave. 'If I had been a trifle less fit,' he wrote to Townend, 'I should have got the entire car in the wishbone.' It was quite in character for Wodehouse to make light of a bad experience, and the episode illustrates his instinctive determination to transform personal trouble into comedy. He had left the house for a walk in hopes of meeting Leonora, who had taken the family Buick to the railway station. When she spotted her stepfather coming towards her she had pulled over and Wodehouse crossed over to greet her, noticing too late that she was being followed by a Ford, which swerved to avoid the Buick. To his horror, he found the Ford coming towards him on the wrong side of the road. Wodehouse gave a gazelle-like spring sideways, but was caught in the leg. 'I thought the world had ended. I took the most awful toss and came down on the side of my face . . . my god, doesn't it just show that we are here today and gone tomorrow.'

The accident shook him up badly, and sent him into one of his periodical fits of depression about his work. When he sailed across to London on his own for the rehearsals of *The Beauty Prize* he found himself

in a perfect agony of boredom. What *is* the matter with London and England generally? . . . I am counting the days till I can get away and have decided from now on to live in America . . . there seems something dead and depressing about London, I don't know what it is . . . all I want to do is to get back and hear the American language again.

He was missing Ethel and Leonora; he was missing Townend; worst of all, he could not work – 'the old bean is in a state of absolute stagnation' – and he had to concede that the experiment of trying to turn Ukridge into a new series character had not prospered. 'I'm darned if I can think of anything for him to do,' he wrote.

Wodehouse's complaint about 'something dead and depressing about London' was widely shared among English writers of the 1920s and 1930s. The British literary diaspora, what the critic Paul Fussell has called a 'flight from a real or fancied narrowing of horizons', took Robert Graves to Majorca, Somerset Maugham to the South of France, Aldous Huxley to California and several lesser figures anywhere, from Beijing to Tenerife. Wodehouse, who would shortly experiment with living on the Riviera and then in Hollywood, and eventually settled in Le Touquet, was a popular writer who enjoyed poking fun at the Bloomsbury Group and literary modernism, but in this behaviour he was at one with his generation.

During his stay in London, Wodehouse took his new friend Denis Mackail to the Winter Garden for the dress rehearsal of *The Beauty Prize*. Conceding that it was 'a rotten piece', though, he soon after set sail for America to work with Kern and Bolton on *Sitting Pretty* in the hope that the old team could put together a successful new show. He also began to write his next novel, *Bill the Conqueror*, using what he called a 'new system'. Instead of making a few rough notes and then working the plot and characters into shape during the process of composition, he was now completing a 30,000-word 'scenario' before getting down to the business of the novel itself. This, he described to Mackail, was 'The dickens of a sweat, of course, but it ought to mean that I shall be able to write the novel in about a month. It is one of those full-of-action stories – you know – not a dull page from start to finish.' In the 1930s and 1940s Wodehouse would always write tens of thousands of words in scenario form before arriving at a final draft.

Back in America, staying with Bolton, he found himself caught up in the mad days of Prohibition, a law that had the electrifying effect of stimulating the quest for illicit pleasures. Shy, thoughtful and averse to self-publicity, he was a watchful bystander in a city described by the newly established *New Yorker* as a 'gymnasium of celebrities'. Great Neck was a haven from the bright lights, and his artistic circle included the humorist Robert Benchley of the Algonquin Round Table, and F. Scott Fitzgerald, now at the peak of his fame. 'I believe those stories . . . about his drinking are exaggerated,' he told Leonora, who was now at school in France. 'He seems quite normal, and is a very nice chap indeed . . . the only thing is, he goes into New York with a scrubby chin, looking perfectly foul.' He noted regretfully: 'I suppose he gets a shave when he arrives there, but it doesn't show him at his best in Great Neck,' and concluded, 'I would like to see more of him.' Wodehouse was still in Great Neck when *Leave It to Psmith*, dedicated to 'my daughter Leonora, queen of her species', was published in Britain. He told her he was missing her comments on his work-in-progress (Leonora was always shown his early drafts) and, prompted by Ethel, expressed a fatherly hope that she would watch her drinking. Meanwhile, *Sitting Pretty* and the musical show called *Pat* were both 'fizzing', and he had just completed a lyric for the former which, echoing 'Pack up your troubles', the anthem of trench warfare, is the perfect expression of the Wodehouse credo:

> Put all your troubles in a great big box,
>   As big as any box can be:
> Put all your troubles in a great big box
>   And lock it with a great big key:
> Crying never yet got anybody anywhere,
>   So just stick out your chin
> AND
> Jam all your troubles in a great big box
>   And sit on the lid and grin.

His recent months in New York had convinced him to give up any idea of settling in America. Now that Leonora was at finishing school in France, he told Townend, 'America is only for visits. New York is appalling. All noise and smell.' He and Ethel planned to live in Paris and learn French. As usual with him, when a new novel was going well – he was now halfway through *Bill the Conqueror* – he felt buoyant and optimistic. The recent Ukridge series was, on reflection, 'easily the best stuff I have done', and he wished he could get another idea for a series.

In fact, he would return to Bertie Wooster and Jeeves, briefly, in 1924, but would not publish *Carry On, Jeeves* until 1925 and would not work on a new series until the late 1920s. For the moment, with the prospect of an imminent move to Europe, he was looking forward with the usual mixture of hope and anxiety to the opening of *Sitting Pretty*, the long-awaited reunion of 'the trio of musical fame'.

The show had been dogged with troubles throughout its long gestation. When the opening night was postponed, the Duncan sisters had contracted to fill in with a little West Coast show during the summer of 1923. This, according to Wodehouse, was 'a sort of comic *Uncle Tom's Cabin*'. Against all expectations, this became such a hit that 'Heim and Jake' pulled out of *Sitting Pretty*; Irving Berlin lost interest; and the management had to persuade Kern to step in. As Wodehouse presciently observed, it remained to be seen if a show that had been written as a star vehicle for the two sisters would succeed with a more conventional cast.

Still, there was the old Wodehouse–Bolton–Kern magic to fall back on. The three men gathered at Kern's home in Bronxville and set about putting *Sitting Pretty* – a crooks' caper musical – into shape. Some of Wodehouse's lyrics have a cabaret mood that T. S. Eliot would shortly echo in 'Fragment of an Agon'. In 'Bongo on the Congo', a nonsense variation on 'The Land Where the Good Songs Go', three friends – Horace, Judson and Uncle Jo – reminisce about the things they've never done and the places they've never been:

HORACE: Beneath the silver Afric moon,
                           A few miles south of Cameroon

JUDSON: There lies the haven which you ought to seek.
                    Where cassowaries take their ease
                        Up in the Coca-Cola trees
                While crocodiles sit crocking in the creek

HORACE: Though on some nearby barren height
                     The heat's two hundred Fahrenheit
                 Down in the valley it is nice and cool.

UNCLE JO: And yet I don't know why it is

> The girls of all varieties
> Wear little but a freckle as a rule.

ALL: In Bongo! It's on the Congo!
> And oh boy, what a spot!
> Quite full of things delightful
> And few that are not . . .

The seventh of the Princess shows, *Sitting Pretty* was a clever musical, with a fine score, delightful lyrics, ahead of its time, which got rave reviews – and flopped. The mood of the mid-1920s was against it. Wodehouse, Bolton and Kern would never collaborate again. Wodehouse sailed thankfully home to London, travelling via Paris to visit Leonora. There would be other plays, and even other musicals, but from now on his real future lay with comic fiction.

10. 'All dizzy with work'
(1924-1927)

Life is like some crazy machine that is always going either too slow or too fast. From the cradle to the grave we alternate between the Sargasso Sea and the rapids – forever either becalmed or storm-tossed. (*A Damsel in Distress*)

Just before *Sitting Pretty* closed, another tragedy struck. Bert French, the director of *Pat*, the on-again, off-again Ziegfeld musical, died suddenly during rehearsals, taking the show with him into oblivion. Wodehouse was badly shaken by this news, but nothing could stop his writing. 'I am all dizzy with work these days,' he told Townend, describing how, having written 55,000 words of *Bill the Conqueror* in a month, he had just sent the first 70,000 words to the typist for a clean copy. He felt he had never worked so well on a novel before; to Leonora, he confided, 'This is certainly one swell story, as good as the old man has ever done, and, thank God, I have been able to work in that line about "I know it's paraffin, but what have they put in it?"' He added that 'Flick, the heroine, is so like you that the cognoscenti cannot help but be charmed'. While Wodehouse hammered at his typewriter, Ethel was getting herself into shape with so much regular exercise that she was now 'simply sylph-like'. Bobby Denby was also in New York, training to become a lawyer and staying at the Royalton Hotel, apparently at Wodehouse's expense. When Ethel and Wodehouse eventually sailed back to London in April, Denby stayed on in America to execute scraps of literary business, a role in which he would shortly be decisive.

Wodehouse's departure from the United States in the spring of 1924, and the failure of *Sitting Pretty*, marked the beginning of a new phase in which the English side of his life became as nomadic as the American had been. For the next three years, his incessant magazine and theatre work, and his colossal earnings in both genres, inspired a state of constant activity. Non-stop work had become such a habitual part of his nature, and so essential to his well-being, that Wodehouse had no knowledge of what life without constant deadline pressure might be like. He would often say that he hankered for solitude and tranquillity, but his daemon expressed itself in the opposite. Wodehouse's travel, mirroring his un-settled childhood, was also vital to Ethel, and gratified her need for entertainment. Rich, restless and celebrated, Wodehouse became a quintessential 1920s personality, photographed boarding transatlantic liners or on the steps of Pullman cars, often flanked by the glamorous and well-dressed figures of Leonora and Ethel, his schoolboy smile radi-ating his usual air of detached innocence. Even in Paris, where Ethel was buying new clothes, there was no respite. 'Our whole time since we got here has been spent in lunching and dining with Americans,' he moaned to Townend. 'This place is exactly like New York.' It partic-ularly bothered him that he had not had a story idea for three months. If Wodehouse's output during these golden years had not been so exhil-arating, it might be hard to escape the conclusion that there was some-thing rather joyless about his incessant cycle of work and restless travel. True, he loved to write. He often said it was all he wanted to do. But for those in his entourage, like Ethel and Leonora, supported by an ever-growing staff, there were moments when his solitary bread-winning was a nearly intolerable burden, and one which inspired the quest for distraction.

To satisfy their joint needs, Wodehouse and his wife had to find a place that guaranteed him peace and quiet while offering her sufficient luxury and entertainment. Within a few weeks, after a dutiful visit to his parents, who had now retired to Bexhill-on-Sea, they found what they were looking for in Le Touquet, a French seaside resort popular with the rich in the inter-war years, with gambling and dancing (for her) and golf, umbrageous pine woods, and seclusion (for him). Writing from the Golf Hotel, Wodehouse told Townend that 'We have practi-cally decided to build a house here', noting with approval that it would be extremely handy for England and Paris. On this occasion they could not find a suitable house to buy and the plan to build one became submerged in other ideas; but Le Touquet became lodged in both their minds as a convenient and agreeable alternative to England, and one, crucially, that imposed no quarantine on their dogs. They eventually returned here, with terrible consequences, in the 1930s.

The fallow period that usually followed the completion of a new novel ended as the autumn of 1924 drew on. Wearying of France, and with workmen still occupying their latest London address, Wodehouse and Ethel settled into the Grand Hotel, Harrogate. While he plugged away at the scenario of a new 'Valley Fields' novel, provisionally entitled *Sam in the Suburbs*, and played an occasional round of golf, Ethel took the waters and amused herself with the other guests. 'Mummie is the belle of the hotel,' Wodehouse reported to Leonora, 'and dances like a breeze.' Shortly after this, Ethel returned to London. She had taken 23 Gilbert Street, a luxurious new house, just off Grosvenor Square, complete with butler, and wanted to prepare it for her husband's return. Alone in Harrogate, Wodehouse found himself miserable without Ethel, but consoled himself with the thought that it was an ideal place to write. He was working on 'Honeysuckle Cottage' which was, he felt, 'the damned funniest idea I've ever had', a much-admired short story about a writer of hard-boiled detective fiction who inherits from a literary aunt a house so haunted by 'a sort of miasma of sentimentalism' that it begins to affect his prose, and finally his emotional life. 'Honeysuckle Cottage' is notable for its brilliant parody of the popular novelette and for the light it casts on Wodehouse's interest in the occult.

During the inter-war years, contacting the spirits of the dead was popular, even respectable. Fashionable mediums could fill the Albert Hall; 'Madame Sosostris', T. S. Eliot's 'famous clairvoyante', captured the contemporary fascination with the supernatural. In less exalted literary circles, Conan Doyle's passionate advocacy of spiritualism attracted a lot of attention, and Wodehouse, who knew Doyle and lunched with him from time to time, was impressed. After all, his brother Armine was a theosophist; it was a Wodehouse family subject. In 1924, he accepted an invitation to attend a seance at the Kingston home of H. Dennis Bradley, author of *Towards the Stars*, a popular guide to contemporary spiritualism. The occasion was a fashionable social event. Wodehouse's fellow guests included the editor of *Tatler*, two actors, and the journalist Hannen Swaffer. According to Bradley, a disembodied voice did speak to Wodehouse, but it was 'so faint that no recognition could be claimed'. Wodehouse became sufficiently intrigued to attend another seance in January 1925, and on this occasion he took Leonora. At a third seance in April he was addressed by a distant cousin, Ernest Wodehouse, and Leonora heard a voice say 'Loretta Wodehouse', which both she and her stepfather found spooky when they recalled that one of Leonora's childhood friends in Great Neck had been a little girl named Loretta.

Wodehouse told Armine that he did not know what to make of these seances, but his attendance at these sessions was proudly recorded in H. Dennis Bradley's spiritualist best-seller, *The Wisdom of the Gods*. He told Bill Townend that he wanted urgently to discuss the topic at their next meeting. 'I think it's the goods,' he wrote. Wodehouse's interest in mystical concerns lasted throughout his life. Some sixty-one titles on spiritualism and related subjects were found in his library after his death. It is not clear what he really thought about these questions (he was generally agnostic towards matters of faith), but in the 1920s his work exhibits an amused scepticism towards astral matters, combined with some mild teasing of Armine, as in this description of Jeeves's movements:

He's like one of those weird birds in India who dissolve themselves into thin air and nip through space in a sort of disembodied way and assemble the parts again just where they want them. I've got a cousin who's what they call a Theosophist, and he says he's often nearly worked the thing himself.

Wodehouse returned from Harrogate to his luxurious new home in Belgravia refreshed and invigorated. Ethel had organized the house so that he had his own den, and it was here that he now began to work in earnest on the novel that became *Sam the Sudden*. As usual, he found getting started difficult and warmed up by firing off lists of research questions to Townend about the realities of life aboard a tramp steamer. As Townend noted subsequently, the upshot of this research was the inclusion in the published version of a single sentence: 'He had dined well, having as his guest his old friend Hash Todhunter.'

Part of Wodehouse's trouble in getting the new novel underway was the ever-present distraction of metropolitan literary life. He envied Townend his cottage in the country: 'even if the windows leak,' he wrote, 'you can get some work done. I find it the hardest job to get at the stuff here. We have damned dinners and lunches which just eat up the time. I find that having a lunch hanging over me kills my morning's work, and dinner isn't much better.' He could tolerate a broken routine when he was writing short stories, but a novel was different: 'You have to live with a novel. I'm at the stage now where, if I drop my characters, they go cold and I forget what they are like.' Not all these distractions can be attributed to Ethel's gregarious nature. For a shy, private man who had difficulty with small-talk, Wodehouse was surprisingly clubbable. As well as his old favourite, the Constitutional, just off Trafalgar Square, he was also a member of the Garrick (actors, lawyers, journalists and publishers), the Savage (writers and artists), and the Beefsteak (actors and writers). It was in such clubs that he would meet friends like Mackail, professional associates like Grossmith, and fellow writers like Milne and Conan Doyle. To limit the intrusion of such situations on his imaginative freedom, he developed a Macavity-like capacity for disappearing, known in his family as 'The Wodehouse Glide', and described by Mackail:

At about half-past ten – for we always dined early – we suddenly started rushing through the streets, at Plum's prodigious pace, until a point where, just as suddenly, he had vanished and gone. No lingering farewells from that quarter. I *might* hear him saying Good-night, from the middle of the traffic; I *might* catch a glimpse of his rain-coat swinging across the road. But the general effect was that he had just switched himself off.

Nothing, however, could long keep him from a Dulwich rugby foot-ball match. There was a ritual to these occasions: a suburban train from Victoria to West Dulwich; a pint of beer and a cheese-and-pickle sand-wich at the Alleyn's Head before the kick-off; followed by a foggy after-noon of stomping up and down the touchline. 'That was the game of a lifetime,' he exulted to Townend, 'we won 11–5. I nearly got heart failure. We were on the Haileybury line half the time and the rest they were on our line. You never saw such a game, it just swept up and down the field. Our tackling was great.' Sometimes, if he was particu-larly exhilarated by the result, he would simply walk the seven miles back to Belgravia in a blur. Walking was always his best therapy, and he is remembered for the single-minded way in which he directed his steps towards his destination, looking neither to left nor right. The publication of *Bill the Conqueror* in November 1924, six months after *Ukridge*, a collection of his previously published Ukridge stories, confirmed his position as England's premier comic writer, selling 10,000 copies on the day of publication. Success came at a price, of course. There were bad reviews in *The Times* and the *Times Literary Supplement*. He confessed to Mackail that 'I feel as if someone had flung an egg at me from a bomb-proof shelter'.

He was relieved to get away from London at Christmas to stay in Norfolk at Hunstanton Hall, as the guest of Charles Le Strange, a distant cousin, and kinsman of the Kimberley branch of the family. Wodehouse described him as 'a weird bird'. The flamboyantly homosexual Le Strange, who is still remembered locally for wearing yellow kid gloves to church on Sunday, owned a crumbling pebble-and-red-brick Tudor country house with a fine moat on the north-east coast of Norfolk, a few miles inland from the sea, overlooking the Wash, with a nearby golf course. After this first Christmas holiday, the Wodehouses became friendly with Le Strange and paid frequent visits, staying at the Hall in the summers of 1926, 1927, 1929 and 1933. Wodehouse absorbed some of its rambling, ivy-clad features into the topography of Blandings Castle and also Aunt Agatha's house at Woollam Chersey. He also incorporated Le Strange's hobby of training prize Jersey cows for agricultural shows into his portrait of Lord Emsworth. The Hunstanton Hall visitors' book shows that Wodehouse and his wife often stayed there independently. Wodehouse was especially fond of the moat, loved to observe the ducks' quack 'that sound like a man with an unpleasant voice saying nasty things in an undertone', and would spend hours alone on a punt named *Plum* with his typewriter perched precariously 'on a bed-table balanced on one of the seats'. He wrote *Money for Nothing* here and also dedicated his next collection of Bertie Wooster stories, *Carry On, Jeeves*, to Bernard Le Strange, Charles's brother.

The years of plenty in America had given Wodehouse and Ethel a taste for winter sunshine in Florida or South Carolina, and now that they were back in London they were keen, on their return from Norfolk in the new year, to flee the dreary bleakness of the English winter. Accordingly, in February 1925, Wodehouse set off with Ethel for the Riviera, taking with him the nearly complete typescript of *Sam the Sudden*. The trip to the South of France was not a success. Wodehouse could always work anywhere, but Ethel's choices were limited to sitting downstairs in the lounge of the Gallia Hotel, walking along La Croisette, or spending money in the casino. This was not her idea of diversion and when, as a result, she fell into a strange, unnerving silence, Wodehouse's own mood darkened.

'Of all the poisonous, foul, ghastly places,' he wrote to Leonora, 'Cannes takes the biscuit with absurd ease . . . Mummie and I have come to the conclusion that we loathe foreign countries. We hate their ways, their architecture, their looks, their language and their food.' If there was any pleasure to be found at the hotel it was in the garden which, to his delight, had an ornamental pond with ducks and water rats. But that was not enough for Ethel, and the discussion soon turned to the possibility of getting a flat in Paris, with a house in the country for Leonora. Although he was working hard to finish *Sam the Sudden*, he had also begun to sketch ideas for a new novel, notes that came to nothing. In the end he had to scramble to finish *Sam the Sudden* to meet the *Post*'s deadline, and returned home with relief. London, however, was loathsome in a different way. 'What rot all this social stuff is,' he complained to Townend, regretting his incessant travelling. 'Never again, after this year. For me, at least. It kills my work.' The implied suggestion that he was in future going to let Ethel go her own way conflicts with the evidence of his easygoing responsiveness to her need for entertainment. Writing to praise Denis Mackail's new novel *Greenery Street*, he describes going with her to Ascot in a grey top hat and white spats, a special torture for a man who was always happiest in flannel trousers and an old sweater.

An essential part of Wodehouse's nature was to want to please others and to accommodate their desires. Now that he could afford to do whatever he wanted, much of his restless activity can only be explained in this light. He had, for instance, planned to spend the summer of 1925 at Hunstanton Hall, but when a new commission for *The Nightingale*, a musical about the life of Jenny Lind, the sensational Victorian diva, arrived from the Shubert brothers in New York, he interrupted his holiday and once again set sail from Southampton at the end of July. Possibly he justified his trip to New York on the grounds that he had two books scheduled for publication there: *Carry On, Jeeves* in October, and *Sam in the Suburbs* in November.

But he was still not happy. 'What a ghastly time since I wrote to you,' he exclaimed to Townend in November, announcing that he and Ethel had settled temporarily at the Hotel Marguery on 47th Street and Park Avenue in Manhattan. Part of this ghastly time was to do with Bobby Denby and a huge upheaval in Wodehouse's professional life: his decision to take his next serial away from the *Saturday Evening Post* and sell it to a rival magazine, *Liberty*. The precise details of this rupture, described to Townend as 'one of the few occasions in my life when I deliberately did the dirty', are now lost, but the outcome is not.

Wodehouse came away from a fraught negotiation with a contract for twelve new short stories (at $3,500 apiece) and two serial novels (for $30,000 and $35,000), described with more than a hint of self-justification as 'the sort of contract you generally get only in dreams'. Lorimer was very angry at this betrayal but later told Reynolds that he would eventually take him back, and expressed the hope that the *Liberty* contract would not be renewed. For a writer as basically loyal as Wodehouse (he did, after all, stick with the *Strand* and Herbert Jenkins throughout these years), and as fundamentally conservative, his departure from the *Post* was an extraordinary move (*Liberty*, a five-cent weekly, was inferior in almost every way to the *Post*) and can only be explained by the presence in his life of Bobby Denby, who, after failing to qualify as a lawyer, had landed an editorial job at *Liberty*. Eager to prove his worth, Denby then persuaded his bosses, for whom money was no object in the cut-throat magazine circulation war then raging, that he could exploit his relationship with Ethel and poach Wodehouse from the *Post*. What exactly this relationship amounted to is unclear, but Wodehouse undoubtedly went along with the deal to keep Ethel happy, to keep Denby happy and, not coincidentally, to make more money. The experience seems to have soured him on New York yet again. For a generally affable man, who purported to be relaxed, he was in private remarkably dissatisfied for much of these, his best years, comparing life in New York to St Vitus's dance, in which the good-time crowd of the 1920s suffered a kind of *delirium tremens*.

The 1920s was one of the great alcoholic decades of the twentieth century, and almost none of Wodehouse's characters is indifferent to the temptations of a quiet snort. Just as Edmund Wilson recorded more than one hundred synonyms for 'drunk' in his *Lexicon of Prohibition* (1927), including 'owled', 'spifflicated' and 'wasped down', so Wodehouse's Drones, who made their debut during these years (Freddie Widgeon, Barmy Fotheringay-Phipps, Gussie Fink-Nottle and assorted Eggs, Beans and Crumpets), will make for the bar like buffalo for a watering-hole. The Drones' terms for hangover include 'the Broken Compass, the Sewing Machine, the Comet, the Atomic, the Cement Mixer and the Gremlin Boogie' and their lexicon of euphemisms for 'inebriated' includes: 'awash', 'boiled', 'fried to the tonsils', 'full to the back teeth', 'hooched', 'illuminated' or 'lit up', 'lathered', 'off colour', 'oiled', 'ossified', 'pie-eyed', 'polluted', 'primed', 'scrooched', 'squiffy', 'stewed to the gills', 'stinko', 'tanked', 'tight as an owl', 'under the sauce', 'whiffled' and 'woozled'. Any Drone, identified by one of these adjectives, is deeply affiliated to the Pickwick Club, to Falstaff, Master Justice Shallow and inhabitants of the Boar's Head Tavern, and, further back, the lost pastoral society of Robin Hood and his Merrie Men. Appropriately, it is Bertie Wooster, Drone-in-chief, who has the perfect antidote to alcoholic after-effects in Jeeves's famous pick-me-up:

For perhaps the split part of a second nothing happens. It is as though all Nature waited breathless. Then, suddenly, it is as if the Last Trump has sounded and Judgement Day set in with unusual severity.

Bonfires burst out in all parts of the frame. The abdomen becomes heavily charged with molten lava. A great wind seems to blow through the world, and the subject is aware of something resembling a steam hammer striking the back of the head . . .

And then, just as you are feeling that you ought to ring up your lawyer and see that your affairs are in order before it is too late, the whole situation seems to clarify. The wind drops. The ears cease to ring. Birds twitter. Brass bands start playing. The sun comes up over the horizon with a jerk.

And a moment later all you are conscious of is a great peace.

The Drones Club code is boisterous, but harmless, an adult (but not grown-up) version of public-school behaviour:

A crusty roll, whizzing like a meteor out of the unknown, shot past the Crumpet and the elderly relative whom he was entertaining to luncheon, and shattered itself against the wall. Noting that his guest had risen some eighteen inches into the air, the Crumpet begged him not to give the thing another thought. 'Just someone being civil,' he explained.

The world of the clubs was one that Wodehouse now watched with typical ambivalence. He wanted a quiet life, and told Townend that he was now planning to buy a house in London, to put down roots once and for all, but he could never refuse an offer of work. Before he could settle down again, he found himself up to his eyes 'in the biggest bout of work I have ever done' – four short stories and a musical comedy.

This was not strictly true. He had been working full-on for years. However, 1926 would prove to be one of his busiest and most successful inter-war years, at least in the theatre. It was also exceptional for Wodehouse in his prime in having no new novel published. But there was always something in the pipeline, and April saw the publication of his second collection of golf stories, *The Heart of a Goof*, with its well-known dedication 'To my daughter Leonora without whose never-failing sympathy and encouragement this book would have been finished in half the time'. The musical comedy, another slightly misleading description, was a show on which he had contracted to collaborate with the fashionable Russian designer-director Theodore Komisarjevsky. Wodehouse's job was to adapt *The Orlov*, a Russian 'musical play' by Ernst Marischka and Bruno Granichstadten, which he did under the title *Hearts and Diamonds*.

Wodehouse, who never quite fulfilled his ambition to write a successful straight play, next contracted to adapt the Hungarian Ferenc Molnár's *Spiel im Schloss* as *The Play's the Thing*. This was a serious play, 'a hell of a job'. As he explained to Townend:

I was talking to Gilbert Miller [the producer of *The Play's the Thing*] and Al Wood [another New York producer] was there and I said to G.M. 'I wish you'd give me Molnár's next play to adapt'. He said 'You couldn't do it. It's not in your line. It's a serious play.' I said, 'Boy, I can write *anything*!' and Al Wood said, 'Well, I've got a serious play from the German' and I said 'Gimme', purely with the intention of scoring off Miller by showing him I could do the heavy dramatic stuff too.

That awkward mixture of pride and humility always lurks just below the surface with Wodehouse. The great advantage of an adaptation, based on a literal translation, was that the donkey-work of getting the plot straight was, in theory, already taken care of. But Wodehouse, for whom writing the dialogue was not taxing, worked hard to construct a satisfying commercial stage version and was rewarded, when it opened in New York in November, with a show that ran for 326 performances before transferring to London. *The Play's the Thing* was his biggest success in the straight theatre, but it always rankled with him that it was merely an adaptation.

The bulk of his energy in the second half of 1926, however, was directed towards America again and *Oh, Kay!*, a musical comedy about bootleggers. As so often in their collaborations, the idea had begun with

Guy Bolton. He had spotted the young Gertrude Lawrence in a 1923 London review and had determined to find a show for her talents, which rendered him slightly star-struck. 'She had everything,' he wrote. 'She could play sophisticated comedy, low comedy, sing every possible type of song, and she looked enchanting.' Bolton persuaded George and Ira Gershwin to do the score and lyrics. To come up with a libretto that could star a British heroine in a contemporary American setting, Bolton naturally turned to Wodehouse. The plot of the show then known as 'Mayfair', or 'Miss Mayfair', was a light-hearted Prohibition frolic, with an eligible bachelor, two musical comedy crooks, and a rum-running English duke, set in Southampton, Long Island. Once again, Wodehouse was summoned to work with Bolton. 'I am trembling on the verge of making another trip to America,' he told Townend, and was feeling 'torn between a loathing of leaving Ethel for a couple of months and a desire not to let a good thing get by me'. He sailed on 24 July.

Wodehouse went straight to Bolton's house in Kensington, Great Neck, where they worked through a summer heatwave to fashion 'Miss Mayfair' into something the Gershwins could work on. The summer of 1926, Wodehouse recalled, 'was considerably hotter than blazes . . . I played like one of those fountains at Versailles, taking off some four-teen pounds in weight.' As the work progressed, 'Miss Mayfair' became 'Cheerio!!' and finally *Oh, Kay!* Wodehouse had imagined that, since George and Ira Gershwin were a composer–lyricist team, he would simply help Bolton with the book. When Ira was taken ill with appen-dicitis – and because Ira looked up to Wodehouse as a mentor – Wodehouse played a larger part in the making of *Oh, Kay!* than his credit as co-librettist suggests.

Oh, Kay! premiered at the Imperial Theater in New York on 8 November. The Gershwin hits that especially delighted the critics included 'Someone to Watch Over Me', 'Do, Do, Do', 'Fidgety Feet', 'Maybe' and 'Heaven on Earth'. The all-powerful *New York Times* judged that 'usually it is sufficient to credit as sponsors only the authors and the composer. But the distinction of *Oh, Kay!* is its excellent blending of all the creative arts of musical entertainment.' The show sent Gertrude Lawrence's American career onto a new plane, confirmed Wodehouse's reputation on Broadway, and would run for nearly five hundred perform-ances in New York and London. Wodehouse had been doing pretty well for some years, but now, with the successful publication of *Carry On, Jeeves* and two American theatrical hits, with the prospect of London openings to come, his work had made him seriously rich. 'Gosh,' he exclaimed to Townend, 'it's amazing how money has been pouring in.' Wodehouse's earnings at this time were colossal. At current prices, he was certainly a millionaire from his writing, throughout the 1920s and 1930s. At the beginning of 1927, he and Ethel began negotiations to buy a palatial sixteen-room mansion in Mayfair, run by a staff of eleven.

11. 'I am planning a vast campaign'
(1927-1929)

Marriage had always appalled him, but there was this to be said for it,
that married people had daughters. He had always wanted a daughter, a
smart girl he could take out and be proud of; and fate had given him
Jill at precisely the right age. (*Jill the Reckless*)

Wodehouse himself judged his swanky new London address, 17 Norfolk
Street, just off Park Lane in the heart of fashionable Mayfair, to be 'the
gol-darnedest house you ever saw'. There was Pavey the butler, Mrs
Bostock the cook, parlourmaids, footmen in green uniforms with silver
buttons, two secretaries (for Ethel) and a chauffeur to drive the
Wodehouse Rolls-Royce, whose doors were decorated with the
Wodehouse crest, a heraldic detail that suggests he had inherited something of his Deane grandfather's taste for genealogy. As well as the
dogs, there was also a canary, which flitted freely about the opulent
interior.

'My library', Wodehouse told Townend, 'is magnificent, if a bit too
much like "Mr Wodehouse among his books".' These, he confessed,
were just 'book furniture', for show. 'To think', he wailed, 'that I should
have sunk to this!' The absurd luxury was Ethel's choice: secretly, he
rather enjoyed it and, passive in the marriage as usual, acquiesced in
her taste. His own mild rebellion against the ostentation was to install
a second Monarch typewriter and a plain deal table upstairs in his
bedroom. It was in this room that he talked and relaxed, and polished
his spectacles, and beamed, and was covered with Pekes. Denis Mackail
remembered him taking up the conversation: 'I can still hear him, "I
say, with regard to this business of plots".' Wodehouse, who abhorred
vanity, was always ambivalent about luxury, preferring simplicity. This
now extended to his friendships. 'Isn't it curious', he wrote to Townend,
'how few people there are in the world one wants to see. Yesterday, I
looked in at the Garrick at lunchtime, took one glance of loathing at
the mob, and went off to lunch by myself at the Cheshire Cheese.'

His return to London in the spring of 1927 was timely. During the inter-war decades, in which his work achieved an enviable marriage of literary accomplishment and wide popular acclaim, the years 1927–30 were pivotal. Jeeves finally became fixed in the mind of the reading public as one of English literature's immortals, and Wodehouse, recognizing what he had created, published some of his most memorable Bertie Wooster stories. In *Summer Lightning*, Blandings Castle consolidated its position at the heart of the Wodehousian paradise and the Empress of Blandings made her starring debut in a short story, 'Pig-hoo-o-o-o-ey!', while Wodehouse also completed 'Lord Emsworth and the Girl Friend', one of his finest stories, notable for its innocent admission of strong feelings. When Lord Emsworth, the character with whom Wodehouse identified most readily, has a girlfriend, she is Gladys, aged five. The moment in 'Lord Emsworth and the Girl Friend' when Gladys takes the dreamy peer's hand is one of the very rare, and lyrical, expressions of unfettered emotion in Wodehouse's work:

A welcome coolness had crept into the evening air by the time Lord Emsworth and his guest came out of the great door of the castle. Gladys, holding her host's hand and clutching the parcel [of food], sighed contentedly. She had done herself well at the tea-table. Life seemed to have nothing more to offer.

Shortly after this, now quite at ease, Gladys hides from McAllister behind Lord Emsworth, clutching the tails of his morning coat, and 'something happened':

It was, in itself, quite a trivial thing, but it had an astoundingly stimulating effect on Lord Emsworth's morale. What happened was that Gladys, seeking further protection, slipped at this moment a small, hot hand into his.

This 'mute vote of confidence' is, in Wodehouse, a unique, moving, and highly revealing expression of intimacy. According to Kipling, 'Lord Emsworth and the Girl Friend' was one of the most perfect short stories he had ever read. Now, with Wodehouse in his prime, another quintessential inter-war character, Mr Mulliner, appeared between hard covers for the first time with his wonderful elixir, Buck-U-Uppo, and Wodehouse's style, subtly maturing throughout the 1920s under the influence of the stage, the speakeasy and the popular song, became a kind of comic ragtime, so light and innocent that the underpinning plots, miracles of ingenuity, seem spun from nothing.

Wodehouse's popularity came at a singular moment in British social history. For the first time, the nation was almost universally literate, a fact which gave special significance to the printed word in magazines and newspapers. Simultaneously, in the 1920s and 1930s, a great age of class distinction, the universities were more than ever selective. While there were five and a half million children in elementary schools, there were just under 30,000 students at university. Wodehouse's polished and seemingly effortless combination of the suburban and the classical, matching compulsive popular storytelling with brilliantly allusive prose was, by chance, peculiarly well suited to a mass audience and the elite Oxbridge readership within it. Newspaper critics loved him. Writing in the *Observer*, Gerald Gould expressed a widespread opinion: 'In the most serious and exact sense of the word, [Wodehouse] is a great artist. He has founded a school, a tradition. He has made a language . . . He has explained a generation.'

Coincidentally, the international picture was steadily darkening. At this moment of Wodehouse's career, it is tempting to find in his astonishing popularity a yearning for escape into an innocent world far removed from events like the General Strike of 1926, the Wall Street crash of 1929, and the rise of the great dictators – a world in which there is no greater threat than a punctured hot-water bottle, a flying flowerpot or Bertie's Luminous Rabbit; in short, Wodehouse's Edwardian Elysium. 'Reconstruction, Restoration, Recovery were the key words of the twenties,' writes the historian A. J. P. Taylor, 'words of return. Nineteen-fourteen was the standard by which everything was judged.' Wodehouse in his prime was both a creature of his time, and an antidote to it, but also, like the greatest writers, superior to its vexations. Although the sales of his books were rarely spectacular in their first editions, he was earning big money from theatre and magazine work.

This money would shortly cause its own troubles. It was already exacting a price. As well as the distraction of workmen finishing off 17 Norfolk Street, there were incessant demands on Wodehouse's time: radio appearances, requests for stories from numerous magazines, invitations to lunch with his American publisher, his agent, and eager platoons of British booksellers. He had already finished *The Small Bachelor* for its autumn 1926 serialization in *Liberty*. Now he was bracing himself to start another new novel, and, finding no privacy in his grand new house, he retreated to one of his favourite hotels, the Impney at Droitwich. Returning to Norfolk Street, he found that it was 'awfully nice [to have] a home at last', but he could never settle for long, and was soon dashing back to the Hotel Impney and then, as summer came, to Hunstanton Hall where, 'sweating blood', he finished 53,000 words of *Money for Nothing*, one of his least distinguished inter-war light novels. At the same time, he was anglicizing *Oh, Kay!* for its London opening, working on *The Three Musketeers*, a new musical comedy for Ziegfeld, and looking forward to the publication of *Meet Mr Mulliner*, the first collection of Mulliner stories. This was dedicated to Herbert Asquith, who had let it be known that he had consoled himself after his general election defeat in 1924 by reading *Jill the Reckless*.

The Three Musketeers was a Ziegfeld commission for another collaboration with George Grossmith. Ziegfeld was a megalomaniac who liked to have his librettists on hand, obedient to his whim, during casting and rehearsals. So Wodehouse and Grossmith embarked once more on the old transatlantic crossing, redrafting their script en route. Arriving in New York, which he found noisier than ever, Wodehouse was caught up in not just *The Three Musketeers*, but also a second Ziegfeld production, *Rosalie*, starring Marilyn Miller, Ziegfeld's former mistress, and Jack Donahue, another big Broadway name. Ziegfeld had just fired the lyricist and composer of this Ruritanian romance and wanted Wodehouse to work with the Gershwin brothers on a new score and lyrics, while putting the finishing touches to *The Three Musketeers*. Wodehouse took a suite at an apartment-hotel on East 60th Street, just off Central Park, but the frenzy of the city in this late-1920s boom year did not agree with him. Looking for peace, and a quiet place to work, he found rooms at the Sound View Golf Club, and embarked on a reverse commute to Great Neck, writing lyrics for Ziegfeld there every afternoon, before returning to New York in the evening, while complaining that theatrical work was sapping his energy. At some point in the autumn, he was joined in East 60th Street by Ethel, and also by Leonora who, in her role as 'confidential secretary and adviser', was beginning to accompany him on his American trips.

The presence in his life of Leonora, who had grown into a fascinating and glamorous young woman of twenty-three, certainly accounts for a marked new sophistication in his stories and novels. Leonora was courted by many hopeful young men, including the young Godfrey Wynn. While no one should read Wodehouse's fiction for special insight into the relations between the sexes, his writing now begins to show a far greater emotional range. The women become less doll-like, and more complex. On the evidence of his correspondence, however, his own interests remained unvarying: books, dogs and Dulwich. Although, in November, 'Hell's foundations have been quivering like a jelly' from Ziegfeld's tantrums, he still found time, in correspondence with Townend, to celebrate Dulwich's excellent performance: '[we] seem to be doing jolly well this year. I thought we were going to have a bad season, with only two old colours left . . . I do wish we could beat Bedford again.' Even now, in his mid-forties, sport continued to give Wodehouse a code for the expression of real emotion. In *Money for Nothing*, the hero John Carroll expresses his feelings on an unexpected meeting with the girl he loves in a sustained classical metaphor inspired by Wodehouse's education:

Only once in his life before could he remember having felt as he felt now, and that was one raw November evening at school at the close of a football match against Marlborough when, after battling wearily through a long half-hour to preserve the slenderest of all possible leads, he had heard the referee's whistle sound through the mist and had stood up, bruised and battered and covered in mud, to the realisation that the game was over and won.

Rehearsals for *Rosalie* and *The Three Musketeers* kept Wodehouse in New York throughout the autumn of 1927. As Christmas approached, however, there was a new reason to stay on. Jerome Kern and Oscar Hammerstein were about to launch *Show Boat*, a landmark in American musical theatre that drew on the innovations of the Princess shows. Wodehouse's interest in *Show Boat* was doubtless piqued by the news that, after many vicissitudes, Kern had finally found a place in his latest show for 'Bill', the haunting, offbeat love song that Wodehouse had first written in 1918:

> I used to dream that I would discover
> The perfect lover some day.
> I knew I'd recognise him,
> If ever he came round my way . . .

He would draw a royalty on the song for the rest of his life, but what-ever the satisfactions of seeing his lyric find a place in a smash hit, he was approaching fifty, and he longed to be home with Ethel and the dogs. He sailed for England before the opening of both *Rosalie* and *The Three Musketeers*, travelling home with notes for a new Blandings Castle novel, entitled *Summer Lightning*.

Wodehouse was exhausted and dissatisfied on his return from America. New York had not lived up to expectations, and London also seemed 'a pretty rotten place'. A quiet long weekend at the Hotel Impney near the healing waters of Droitwich offered the perfect release from the hustle of New York and the interruptions of London life. Wodehouse revelled in the combination of peace and quiet with unin-terrupted composition. 'I am having a great time out here,' he wrote to Mackail during a second visit to Droitwich. 'Brine baths, quiet work on my Art, and riding about the country on a push-bike.' As well as resolving some tricky moments in the plot of *Summer Lightning*, he had also begun to write another Emsworth story, 'Company for Gertrude', and began to relax again after New York.

Wodehouse always loved the English countryside, and if Leonora had not been such a metropolitan daughter he might have lived there perma-nently. He never missed an opportunity to bring his work out to his favourite parts. That summer of 1928, he and Ethel took Rogate Lodge, near Petersfield, an estate of some 1,000 acres, including woods and gardens, some twelve miles across the Downs from Emsworth. Wodehouse transferred the Rolls-Royce, the entire Norfolk Street staff, and his daily writing routine to the edge of the South Downs. By July, he had the plot of *Summer Lightning* fully mapped out, and had written 10,000 words. In between his writing, he was living the life of a country gentleman with literary friends. There were house parties at the weekends; Leonora would drop in, often at the wheel of her two-seater Chrysler sports car. Later in life, Wodehouse would often say that he had met just about anyone who was anyone – once. John Galsworthy came to lunch. The playwright Ian Hay was an overnight guest. Hay and Wodehouse were working together on an adaptation of *A Damsel in Distress*. It was a merry collaboration: they would shut themselves away every morning and, Leonora reported, 'shouts of laughter keep coming from the library'. And when he was not writing, Wodehouse dabbled in theatrical business.

Progress on *Summer Lightning* was slow. He had spent all summer writing and rewriting the first 30,000 words, and calculated that he 'must have done about a hundred thousand' in total. As autumn drew on, he decided to shelve the novel for a while in favour of some more short stories, a genre he loved to work in. 'I am planning a vast campaign,' he informed Townend. 'I want to write six short stories simultaneously. I have three plots to begin with and want three more.' He was also devoting considerable energy to Bill Townend's faltering literary career, contributing an amusing foreword, entitled 'Old Bill Townend', to his friend's latest book *The Ship in the Swamp*, and badgering literary acquaintances like Kipling, Conan Doyle, Arnold Bennett and Owen Seaman at *Punch* for good reviews. His loyalty to Townend was mixed with his loyalty to the Alma Mater. 'Dulwich have got a red-hot team this year,' he informed Townend. 'Nine old colours from last year's side, which lost only to Bedford . . . You must come up and see at least one game.'

In December, *Collier's* began agitating for a sight of their latest Wodehouse serial, and he had to put the 'vast campaign' on hold while he met the deadline. By 1 January 1929, however, he had completed *Summer Lightning*, writing the final draft of about 80,000 words at his usual speed. He told his American agent that it was one of the best plots he had ever devised, and felt it had 'come out marvellously', but the strain had taken its toll and he collapsed with a serious bout of influenza, which left him ten pounds lighter and rather weak. Emerging from his sickbed, he was confronted with a new problem. According to Reynolds, the title *Summer Lightning* had already been used by the thriller writer George F. Hummel. This technical difficulty – which Wodehouse blithely ignored – inspired a witty and flippant preface to the novel in which Wodehouse said he hoped that 'this story will be considered worthy of inclusion in the list of Hundred Best Books Called *Summer Lightning*'. (In America the novel was published as *Fish Preferred*.) Looking back on what he had just done, he described the novel, with ironic detachment, as 'a sort of Old Home Week for my. . . puppets', acknowledging his role as master of ceremonies in an enchanted comic circus.

By the end of the 1920s, Wodehouse was artistically quite at home with both his characters and his setting, in a luminous world of pastoral romance where lovers disport themselves as innocently as shepherds and milkmaids. 'The fact is I cannot keep away from Blandings Castle,' he wrote. 'The place exercises a sort of spell over me.' It was a spell (a mixture of elegy, celebration and old farce) that would inspire some of his best work, including *Heavy Weather*, *Uncle Fred in the Springtime*, *Pigs Have Wings* and *Service with a Smile*, and sustain its grip right up to the end. The manuscript of his unfinished *Sunset at Blandings* was found at his bedside after his death. He often said that Lord Emsworth was the character with whom he most identified. He understood Emsworth's desire to be left alone with his pig; he certainly shared the woolly peer's dislike of formal clothing and speech-making, and he sympathized completely with Emsworth's penchant for quiet evenings with a favourite book. He also exhibited masterly tactical vagueness when confronted by the organizational demands of the women in his life. (Lady Constance Keeble certainly owes something to Ethel.) It is not difficult to find, in Emsworth's paradise of Blandings, an analogy with Wodehouse's private fantasy world.

Many of the most brilliant effects in *Summer Lightning* are so deft and apparently spontaneous that the narrative shimmers beyond analysis. However, there are several familiar elements: a young man hopelessly in love with an unsuitable girl; characters with shady secrets; comic crooks leading double lives; and, of course, a stolen pig. The story cleverly mingles *belle époque* misdemeanours with the brittle post-war raciness of the Bright Young Things. Evelyn Waugh recognized this when he described his *Vile Bodies* as 'rather like a P. G. Wodehouse novel, all about bright young people'. But in Wodehouse's world there is only innocence and none of Waugh's black satire. Ronnie Fish has just failed as the proprietor of the Hot Spot nightclub and is desperate to prevail on his trustee, Lord Emsworth, for the money to marry Sue Brown, a chorus girl whose mother had been one of Galahad Threepwood's *amours* back in the Naughty Nineties. As the comic engine of the novel begins to hum, Uncle Gally, Lord Emsworth's reprobate brother, who has a soft spot for Sue Brown, finds he is in no position to plead her cause, being *persona non grata* with Lady Constance Keeble, his fearsome sister, for presuming to commit the details of his disgraceful youth to paper in a volume of scandalous memoirs. (The fate of this sensational manuscript will animate the plot of the sequel, *Heavy Weather*, where it will eventually be eaten by the Empress in her sty, to almost universal relief.) Beneath the top line of the plot – Ronnie Fish's quest for Sue Brown's hand in marriage – are various interlocking sub-themes, notably the theft of the Empress, the false accusation of Sir Gregory Parsloe-Parsloe's complicity in the deed, and the appearance at the castle of several impostors on a variety of dotty missions. All ends happily when

Eleanor Wodehouse

Wodehouse, aged seven

Ernest Wodehouse (seated third from left) as a magistrate in Hong Kong

The three eldest Wodehouse brothers, from left to right: Peveril, Armine and PGW, *c.* 1898

A Wodehouse family portrait

Dulwich College

In cricket whites on
the playing field at
Dulwich College

A performance
of *The Frogs* at
Dulwich College.
(PGW is seated
in the middle
row, holding a
frog's head, at the
far right of the
picture.)

In the Hongkong and Shanghai Bank football team, *c.* 1901. (PGW is
seated in the middle row, second from the right.)

Wodehouse in 1917

Leonora, aged twelve

Bill Townend

Denis Mackail

The Trio of Musical
Fame: Guy Bolton,
P. G. Wodehouse and
Jerome Kern

Guy Bolton

With Ethel and Leonora,
at Le Touquet Golf Links,
1924

With Gertrude Lawrence
during rehearsals for *Oh,
Kay!,* 1927

At Great Neck with Broadway actors, 1924

Maureen O'Sullivan, mid-1930s

With Leonora at Hunstanton Hall, *c.* 1927

With Leonora and Ethel at Waterloo Station, on their way to America, *c.* 1930

Los Angele

SUNDAY MORNING, JUN

Funny! No Field for Him in Films

WODEHOUSE OUT AND STILL DAZED

England's Famous Humorist Ends Film Contract

After Year He Still Wonders Why He Was Engaged

Studios Nice But P.G. Feels They Were Cheated

BY ALMA WHITAKER

P. G. Wodehouse, England's most famous humorist, has just concluded his year's contract with M-G-M.

"They paid me $2000 a week—$104,000—and I cannot see what hey engaged me for," he said wonderingly, as we sat beneath the cocoanut palms beside his glistening swimming pool in Benedict Canyon. "The motion-picture business dazes me. They were extremely nice to me—oh, extremely—but I feel as if I have cheated them. It's all so unreasonable.

"You see, I understood that I was engaged to write stories for the screen. After all I have twenty novels, a score of successful plays, and countless magazine stories to my credit.

"Yet apparently they had the greatest difficulty in finding anything for me to do. Twice during that year they brought completed scenarios of other people's stories to me and asked me to do some dialogue. Fifteen or sixteen people had tinkered with those stories. The dialogue was really quite adequate when the script came to me. All I did was to touch it up here and there — very slight improvements....

NO HURRY INVOLVED

"Then they set me to work on a story called 'Rosalie,' which was to have some musical numbers. No, it wasn't my story. But it was a pleasant light little thing, and I put three months on it. No one wanted me to hurry. When it was finished they thanked me politely and remarked that as musicals didn't seem to be going so well,

P. G. Wodehouse, Who Loafed and Got Paid

SCREEN CASUALTIES HEAVY

Hordes of Players With Vaudeville and Musical Comedy Experience Among Those Missing

BY JOHN SCOTT

Hollywood's theme song should be "Where Have They Gone?" During the past year or two more players with vaudeville and musical comedy reputations have stormed the movies than at any time in film history. The changes in studio pay rolls have been several and often. Some of the transients stayed and found success, others returned to New York shows and many have apparently disappeared from the picture altogether. Take for instance, a year ago, Stanley Smith, familiar screen

Wodehouse reveals his views of Hollywood in the *Los Angeles Times*, 1931

'Bill': from the score for the film of *Show Boat*

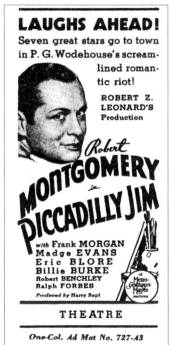

MGM's lobby advertisement for the film of *Piccadilly Jim*

Receiving an honorary doctorate, 1939

Uncle Gally, in a concluding masterstroke, ensures that Ronnie Fish gets the cheque with which he can go off and marry Sue Brown.

The sunlit mood of the novel contrasts strongly with the chilly spring setting of *Something Fresh*. Henceforth, Blandings Castle stories would always take place in high summer when roses, hollyhocks and rhododendrons are in bloom (Wodehouse is casual about the timing of these horticultural details), when tea can be served on the lawn, when the days are long and languorous and the nights short and balmy. Scholarly argument will for ever rage about the English country house models for the castle, but many details – its musty bedrooms, echoing corridors, ticking clocks and clapped-out Hispano-Suiza – certainly derived inspiration from 'the air of romantic decay' Wodehouse found during his successive summers at Hunstanton Hall. This, he wrote to Townend, was 'a gorgeous place' where he spent as much time as possible on the moat. Tom Mott, the chauffeur's son, who was a small boy of nine, remembers the clack-clack-clack of the typewriter as Wodehouse, in Oxford bags and an open shirt, worked in the punt for hours on end.

Once *Summer Lightning* began its American serialization in *Collier's* in April, and as his energy began to come back, Wodehouse returned to his 'vast campaign' of short story writing, trying to work up some new Jeeves plots. For the rest of the spring and summer he would focus his attention on the magazine versions of the Jeeves stories that would subsequently be published in *Very Good, Jeeves*. These late-period Jeeves stories show the continued development of the relationship between master and servant. Kristin Thompson has shown how Wodehouse reduces his plots to the demands of the aunts (Agatha and Dahlia), the plight of old pals (especially Bingo Little and Tuppy Glossop) and the influences of women whom Bertie thinks he wants to marry (Bobbie Wickham, Gwladys Pendlebury *et al.*). Bertie is more than ever inclined to defy Jeeves; and Jeeves, for all his erudite superiority, has come to seem more like Bertie's friend and equal, often with a personal stake in resolving Bertie's problems, sometimes a longed-for trip abroad, to somewhere like Monte Carlo. With a Jeeves story, once Wodehouse had got the plot straight in his mind, the prose flowed. He could complete a first draft in three or four days but would then be so exhausted that he could neither write nor see his work clearly, and would need to leave it for a week, 'to let it cool'.

He had intended to stay at Hunstanton until June, but on 27 May the news reached him that Ernest Wodehouse had died, aged eighty-four, and he returned to London. Wodehouse always said he loved his father, but his extraordinary childhood had left its mark on his emotions: there is not a single reference to this psychologically important event in any of his surviving correspondence. We can only guess at the comfort he offered his mother. For Wodehouse, in difficult moments, the surest balm was always work. Ernest's funeral was scarcely over before his son was reporting to Townend the completion of two new Jeeves stories and announcing the birth-pangs of a new novel: 'I am now in agonies trying to get out the plot of a novel which is not set in a country house atmosphere and contains no crooks!' The agonies of composition are a constant refrain with Wodehouse. However experienced he became, he always had to wrestle every piece of new work to the ground, and would usually fill some four hundred pages with notes towards a scenario before he could get started. 'There always comes a moment in the composition of a scenario,' he once wrote, 'when I pause and say to myself, "Oh, what a noble mind is here o'erthrown".' For Wodehouse, planning a story out and actually writing it were two different things. To achieve the all-important scenario in detail, Wodehouse was ruthless. One scribbled note reads: 'Pinch that scene from Elizabeth Bowen's *The Hotel* where man takes bath in private bathroom. Make it the solution of a Jeeves story.' His files are full of instructions to himself, often sign-posted 'Try this':

Father an actor? This might lead to something.

or,

Can I work it so that somebody – who? – has told her father that she is working as a cook

or,

Problems

Who is Girl B?
How do she and American get together?
How is cow-creamer restored to Amer's aunt?

It was only once Wodehouse had thought out his plots that the agony began to abate and his prose could play at liberty in the fields of his imagination. This, especially the endless rewriting, was the part he enjoyed. From his earliest years, Wodehouse had learned to write anywhere.

Back in Hunstanton in late July, he continued to plug away at another new Jeeves story for *Cosmopolitan* and to brood over the half-formed plots of no fewer than five future novels. In one of many insights into his creative thinking, he wrote that 'the actual core of a story must be intelligible to the reader', telling Townend that 'even in my stuff the basis has to be solid. That is why *Leave It to Psmith*, where there was a necklace at stake, was so much easier to write than *Summer Lightning*, where I had to convince the reader that a man could get all worked up about a pig.'

In the middle of his work on 'Jeeves and the Spot of Art', a cable arrived from Flo Ziegfeld requesting that he come back to Broadway to do the lyrics for a new musical comedy, *East is West*, a proposed revival of a 1918 show that was never to be produced. As usual, Wodehouse complained about leaving England, but he justified the trip as a chance to see the premiere of *Candle-Light*, his adaptation of Siegfried Geyer's *Kleine Komödie*, starring Gertrude Lawrence and Leslie Howard, while giving him an opportunity to 'brush up my American slang', and also to introduce Leonora, who would travel with him, to some New York editors as a way to further her fledgling career. 'I think with a bit of encouragement', he wrote to Townend, 'she might take up writing seriously.'

Leonora did eventually write some magazine pieces and had indeed already contributed to the *Strand* an affectionate, and quite revealing, portrait of her stepfather at the beginning of 1929. 'Plum is really the hardest of workers . . .' she wrote; 'when [he] is writing a novel or short story, the procedure is very much the same. He works in the morning and "broods" in the afternoon . . . After tea, if we're in London, he usually goes for a long walk, or in the country plays golf. His tastes are simple: books, pipes, football matches — he adores them all.' Part of Leonora's portrait is quite misleading, notably the claim that her step-father had 'no real sense of money' and her assertion that 'Mummie looks after all his interests and is very clever about it'. But many other details coincide with the picture derived from Wodehouse's letters. 'Mummie and I always arrange what our lives are to be, and where, because he hates making plans and is always perfectly happy whatever happens,' she wrote. To his stepdaughter, Wodehouse was someone with a big personal investment in continuity, combined with an inability to enjoy it: 'he never seems to like a steady diet of any one thing or person [and] has an overwhelming horror of being bored.' This, combined with his 'overpowering hatred of hurting people', made him vulnerable to the whims of others, and inspired his constant need to escape quotidian pressures. Nothing else can explain his extraordinary restlessness, except perhaps the deep, inner wound of his childhood. To friends and acquaintances, Leonora wrote (and it is a picture that does not change), he was 'someone to be rather fond of'. That 'rather' is telling. Wodehouse was a man that people generally liked, but rarely loved. He found it difficult to reciprocate the emotion involved in 'love'. Nevertheless, he had, Leonora concluded, 'that quality not many people seem to have, a quality of sweetness'. This quality, it seems, was something he passively conveyed but did not actively express. 'Without one sign of sympathy from him you get a great expression of it; without one word of kindliness from him, kindliness is your first and last impression of him.'

Leonora's portrait of Wodehouse is the work of a loving daughter, but the extent to which it misrepresents the larger picture can be seen in the fierce row Wodehouse had just concluded with Bobby Denby, Ethel's protégé and the couple's erstwhile family friend. Throughout the 1920s, Denby had managed to eke out a living in New York, attempting to become a lawyer, then working briefly for the magazine *Liberty*, and eventually becoming a senior member of the literary agency Hughes Massie. For some years, he also made ends meet by ghost-writing for the best-selling mystery author Rex Beach. As part of the Wodehouse family entourage he would occasionally conduct odds and ends of business thrown up by Wodehouse's incessant theatrical and magazine work. One such negotiation, which involved the cancellation of a movie contract with the Famous Players, a film production company, achieved a windfall payment of $5,500. When, subsequently, Wodehouse discovered that the Famous Players had actually refunded $7,500 and that Denby had pocketed $2,000 as commission, the temperature between them, never more than cordial, became positively arctic. Wodehouse, for whom this recalled his past troubles with crooked literary agents, 'the brave old days of Seth Moyle and Abe Baerman', instructed Reynolds to 'keep a sharp eye on [Denby] and don't let him have the handling of the money'. Denby, frantically trying to justify his behaviour and regain Wodehouse's favour, repaid the $2,000, but the episode shows that it was Wodehouse, not Ethel, who oversaw their finances and that, vague and impractical though he might be, he was neither too distracted by work nor too far removed from reality to miss being made a fool of. His confidential dealings with Reynolds confirm his tight grip on personal transactions. In November, writing to advise Reynolds that Ethel had been 'badly caught in the slump' (the Wall Street crash of October 1929), he asked for his agent's help in slipping $5,000 to Bill Townend 'without anyone knowing'. These are hardly the letters of a man who 'has no real sense of money'.

The trip to America did not begin well. The one bright spot was the first night of *Candle-Light* which opened on 30 September to excellent reviews, promising a long run. Otherwise, Wodehouse found himself caught in the usual Ziegfeld nightmare. After six weeks, nothing seemed to be happening, so, to make the most of his time, and perhaps to show the dyspeptic Ziegfeld who was boss, Wodehouse did one of his vanishing acts. Leaving no forwarding address, he simply boarded the *Chief* in Chicago, and took Leonora, amid the splendid luxury of a great transcontinental railroad, to Hollywood, a community in ferment in the aftermath of *The Jazz Singer*, the first talking picture. According to George Cukor, the premiere, on the night of 27 December 1928, had been 'the most important event in cultural history since Martin Luther nailed his theses on the church door', and Wodehouse, who had never been out west before, was curious about the opportunities of the new medium.

The Jazz Singer had certainly been a turning point. By the Christmas season of 1928/9, almost every major film company was in the process of acquiring sound, and the 4,000 principals of the Hollywood movie colony were waiting nervously to see if their voices would survive the nerve-racking and technologically mysterious transition to the new medium. Clara Bow, famously, went into oblivion. Only Chaplin sustained his stardom without uttering a word. The studios also had to change. It was not sufficient just to add sound. Producing and directing the new talkies required new skills. Scripts were different now. From 1927 to 1929, Hollywood wrestled with a huge creative adjustment. New faces appeared on the scene. Howard Hughes, aged just twenty-three, began to dabble in movies. William Fox built his new studios between Beverly Hills and Culver City. RKO was launched. Famous

Players Lasky, with whom Wodehouse had done much business, became Paramount Pictures. In 1929 Sam Goldwyn moved into new offices on the former United Artists lot, a modest site often referred to as 'Doug and Mary's' (Fairbanks and Pickford's) and absorbed the company into Metro-Goldwyn-Mayer.

Goldwyn, one of the first to see that the move from the silents had shifted the creative centre of gravity away from the producer towards the writer, set about acquiring a slate of artistically solid projects that would also be commercial. First, he tried George Bernard Shaw, but got the brush-off; then he signed up Sidney Howard, one of Broadway's hottest playwrights. Next, still looking to the Old World, he acquired Sapper's *Bulldog Drummond* and, when this became a hit, also E. W. Hornung's *Raffles*. It was only a matter of time before his English talent scouts would direct him towards P. G. Wodehouse, especially after he had signed up Frederick Lonsdale, one of London's most successful matinée playwrights, whom Wodehouse knew. Goldwyn nearly missed his chance. The author of *Jeeves* and *Oh, Kay!* and *Candle-Light* was being wooed by several studios, especially Fox, but was in no hurry to commit. He told Townend that he 'wanted to see what [Hollywood] was like before committing myself to it for an extended period'. After his trip out west, he said he liked what he found, and was soon planning to return there in the coming summer to do a picture.

Wodehouse was not alone in flirting with the studios. The talkies had triggered a new gold rush, anticipated by Herman Mankiewicz when in 1925, after a visit to the West Coast, he had cabled his friend Ben Hecht saying: 'Millions are to be grabbed out here and your only competition is idiots. Don't let this get around.' Post-war Hollywood was challenging New York, where the first big studios had been based. The movie-makers' desperate need for Broadway talent, people who could supply dialogue and scenarios, inspired a westward stampede of playwrights and short-story writers. The exodus from the East was, Wodehouse wrote later, 'like one of those great race movements of the middle ages'. As a big name on Broadway and one of the kings of the American magazine market, Wodehouse's services were at a premium. Many of his show-business friends and associates were heading west, too. On the musical side, Jerome Kern, George Gershwin and Irving Berlin would all come to live and work in Beverly Hills. From the stage, W. C. Fields, John Barrymore, Fred Astaire and Leslie Howard were just some of the New York stars he knew whose names would light up Hollywood in the 1930s.

Wodehouse's ten-day stay in California happened by chance to co-incide with a visit by Winston Churchill who, having been abruptly removed from power after the defeat of the Conservative government in which he had been Chancellor of the Exchequer, was licking his wounds on a visit to William Randolph Hearst. Travelling with his paintbrushes and his son Randolph, Churchill was given the obligatory tour of Hearst's spectacular property at San Simeon before being taken back to Los Angeles. Hearst hosted a lunch in his honour in the gardens of Marion Davies's palatial 'bungalow' in the oceanside paradise of Santa Monica, a fashionable community popular with British visitors. Local residents included Harold Lloyd, Douglas Fairbanks and Mae West. It was a glittering occasion attended by the heads of all the studios, two hundred guests, and a twenty-piece orchestra, with extravagant enter-tainment provided by a posse of chorus girls. The movie moguls managed to impress their celebrated visitor by demonstrating the wonders of recorded sound. After Churchill's postprandial remarks, Louis B. Mayer stood up and said, 'That was a very good speech. I think we would all like to hear it again,' and, to Churchill's amazement, had it played back to the throng from an apparatus concealed in a flower arrangement.

Marion Davies, who had been friendly with Wodehouse from Princess Theater days, smuggled him onto the guest list and in due course the two famous Englishmen were introduced. Amid the crush of Hollywood stars and the astonishing glamour of the moment, Churchill did not recognize Wodehouse, a fellow member of the Beefsteak Club, who commented wryly to Townend that 'I have reluc-tantly come to the conclusion that I must have one of those mean-ingless faces which make no impression whatever on the beholder. This was – I think – the seventh time I have been introduced to Churchill, and I could see that I came upon him as a complete surprise once more.'

Apart from this one moment of excitement, the trip was uneventful and Wodehouse returned to New York, to a frosty Gertrude Lawrence and Flo Ziegfeld, both incensed by his unexplained disappearance. Between the studios and his various agents there was all kinds of movie discussion, none of it amounting to much in the long term. There was speculation about a picture with Evelyn Laye, whose starring performance in Noel Coward's *Bitter Sweet* was the talk of the town; MGM's 'boy wonder' Irving Thalberg wanted to film *Rosalie* with Marion Davies; and on top of all this talk the money that was being dangled in front of him – seemingly incredible offers of $2,000 a week – came as a welcome relief to the Wodehouse exchequer, which had been severely battered by Ethel's losses in the stock market crash. Movie money, however, is rarely without complications and by late October, with nothing settled, and the Ziegfeld project going nowhere, Wodehouse and Leonora sailed on the *Homeric* for London where, hardly missing a beat, he settled down to write a new Jeeves story, 'The Ordeal of Young Tuppy', whose central rugby football scene was causing trouble. 'I suppose it will come,' he confessed to Townend. 'These things always do. But it isn't easy to get comic high spots.' He was also now hard at work on *Big Money*, which was coming out so well he wanted no distractions during its completion.

Then, as always with Wodehouse once things were set fair and a goal had been achieved, his appetite for something new quickly got the better of him, and Ethel was dispatched to New York and Hollywood to check out his next move. Ethel always claimed to have handled her husband's contract with MGM, but Wodehouse himself seems to have played an important part in the business, conducting some nerve-racking negotiations with Sam Goldwyn, who at first would not meet his terms. Wodehouse, defiantly, reported that he did not want to go to Hollywood and wanted to be left alone to finish *Big Money*, but perhaps this was part of his negotiating stance. Whoever did the deal, the upshot was princely. Metro-Goldwyn-Mayer would pay Wodehouse $2,500 a week for six months, with an option for a further six. Approaching fifty, world-famous and on top of his form, Wodehouse was about to translate himself to yet another earthly paradise. He was, as he put it later, finally 'in the chips'.

PART THREE

In the Chips

(1930-1939)

12. 'I altered all the characters to Earls and butlers'

(1930-1931)

'It's the system that's wrong,' said George. 'I blame the studio heads.'

'The Moguls,' said Eddie.

'The Mandarins,' said Fred.

'The Hitlers and Mussolinis of the picture world,' said George. 'What do they do? They ship these assortments of New York playwrights and English novelists out here and leave it all to them. Outside talent don't get a chance.' (*Laughing Gas*)

Wodehouse arrived in Hollywood, with Leonora, on 8 May 1930, stepping off the *Chief* into the Californian sunshine at the Santa Fe depot. This was the movie stars' stop, and a destination with which he was becoming quite familiar. While suitcases, golf-bags and his unwieldy Monarch typewriter were handed down by the porters, the dazzled visitors looked out at the strange new land that was to be their home, a scene Wodehouse was to describe in his theatrical memoirs, *Bring on the Girls*: 'Tall eucalyptus, blue-flowered jacarandas, feathery pepper trees dotted with red, and what looked like a thousand new cars.' Hollywood in 1930 was remote, fabulous, and rolling in hot money, 'a combination of Santa Claus and Good-Time Charlie', as Wodehouse put it. His movements were gossip now, and there were reporters to greet him. 'I've always wanted to spend more time in California,' the 'world's highest paid short story writer' told the *Los Angeles Examiner*. 'Yes sir, we are going to rent a home and buy an automobile or two . . . and settle down as real residents.' He and Leonora moved into the house they had taken, 724 Linden Drive, Beverly Hills, formerly the property of Norma Shearer but now owned by the actress Elsie Janis, who was well known to Wodehouse from her roles in *Miss 1917* and *Oh, Kay!*

California had long been a gold-rush state. Now, it seemed, the bonanza had become institutionalized by the studios who, to make the party go with a swing, had also imported plenty of drink, drugs and beautiful people, stars in the making. 'The slogan was come one, come all and the more the merrier,' Wodehouse later recalled. 'It was an era when only a man of exceptional ability and determination could keep from getting signed up by a studio in some capacity or other. I happened to be engaged as a writer.' But it was not writing as he understood it; and now that he was actually in this fabled milieu, Wodehouse soon discovered how ill-suited he was to the demands of the screen. Lines which sang on the page of a story could fall flat in front of the camera.

Although he was new to Hollywood itself, Wodehouse had sold the film rights in *The Man Upstairs* in 1914; *A Gentleman of Leisure* had been made into a silent movie by Cecil B. De Mille in 1915. His early work was littered with affectionate references to the genre. *Psmith Journalist* alludes to William Collier's performance in *The Man from Mexico*. In 'Ukridge's Accident Syndicate', one of the impoverished freelancers in 'Corky' Corcoran's exigent circle is Bertram Fox, described as 'the author of *Ashes of Remorse*, and other unproduced motion-picture scenarios'. Later, in 'The Passing of Ambrose', it is the hero's duty to take two small boys to a movie, a scene that Wodehouse milks for all it is worth:

Hollywood had done all that Art and Money could effect. Based on Wordsworth's well-known poem 'We are Seven', it was entitled 'Where Passion Lurks' and offered such notable favourites of the silver screen as Laurette Byng, G. Cecil Terwilliger, Baby Bella, Oscar the Wonder-Poodle and Professor Pond's Educated Sea-Lions. And yet it left Ambrose cold . . . nor could he get the slightest thrill out of the Babylonian Banquet scene which had cost five hundred thousand dollars.

Wodehouse had wisely never adapted his own work for the screen, but, as the popular medium boomed, it had become the automatic object of film-makers' attention in Britain and the United States. Several novels had been made into full-length silent films in America before Wodehouse's first visit to Hollywood, while a number of comedy shorts had also been made in England. Success on Broadway had only increased his reputation among film producers. His work in the theatre – notably *Oh, Boy!* and *Oh, Lady! Lady!!* – had been adapted for the silent screen in 1919 and 1920 respectively. And in 1929 there had been a talking-picture version of *Her Cardboard Lover*. As the latest recruit from

Broadway, Wodehouse was among friends, and was soon caught up in the affairs of MGM, or Metro as it was known. He worked for Sam Marx, the story editor, and, ultimately, for Irving Thalberg, Goldwyn's famous producer, the model for F. Scott Fitzgerald's 'last tycoon', Monroe Stahr. The studios treated less exalted contract writers as wage-slaves, who clocked on and off like factory workers, but Wodehouse was exempt from this indignity. Nonetheless, he was immediately set to work by Thalberg on script revisions to *Those Three French Girls*, an undistinguished farce partly set in a French chateau, starring a silly young Englishman in romantic difficulties, that would give him his first proper screen credit for 'dialogue', which was presumed to be his speciality.

Wodehouse arranged with the studio to work from home and quickly established a Californianized version of his lifelong routine. 'I get up, swim, breakfast, work till two, swim again, work till seven, swim for the third time, then dinner and the day is over,' he wrote to Mackail. After a bad bout of neuritis (an inflammation of the nerves) on the voyage over, he had given up alcohol. This, he boasted, had made him 'a lean-jawed, keen-eyed exhibit, like something out of Sapper'. His English walking habits excited some local comment, and gave him a reputation for eccentricity, but when he was summoned by the studio for meetings, he drove: 'I motor over there, stay there a couple of hours and come back. Add incessant sunshine, and it's really rather jolly.' 'This place is great,' Wodehouse exulted to Reynolds. 'I don't have to go to the studio, except occasionally for a conference and I pouch $1700 every Saturday.' The only sadness in his life ('like losing part of oneself') was the sudden death in London, during a walk in the park, of his beloved Pekinese, Susan. Professionally speaking, he was on top form. To a writer of his experience and discipline, screenwriting did not seem taxing. 'The actual work is negligible,' he boasted to Mackail, describing his contribution to *Those Three French Girls*.

I altered all the characters to Earls and butlers, with such success that, when I had finished, they called a conference and changed the entire plot, starring the earl and the butler. So I am still working on it. So far I have had eight collaborators. The system is that A. gets the original idea, B. comes in to work with him on it, C. makes a scenario, D. does preliminary dialogue, and then they send for me to insert Class and what-not. Then E. and F., scenario writers, alter the plot and off we go again. I could have done my part of it in a morning, but they took it for granted I should need six weeks.

While he was assigned to *Those Three French Girls*, he could devote his real energies to his own writing, which was in a ferment. 'There is something about this place that breeds work,' he told Townend. 'I have got a new plot for a short story every day for a week!' But once the job was done and film production began, he was once again vulnerable to new demands from Thalberg. 'I fear I shall not be able to string out the dear old picture I've been tied up with ever since I arrived much longer,' he told Guy Bolton. 'They really do seem to be starting the shooting on Monday, and they may give me something tougher to do next time.'

That 'something tougher' was a film version of the Ziegfeld musical *Rosalie* that Wodehouse had worked on in 1928. Thalberg had mistakenly believed that talking pictures were a passing fad. In the panic reaction to *The Jazz Singer*, much of MGM's interest in Wodehouse was as the author of several Broadway hits: in the first years of the talkies, the studios simply copied New York theatre. But if Thalberg had counted on having the author to hand, he reckoned without his star writer's elusive ways. Wodehouse, working on his own, kept aloof from studio life, and utterly detached from its politics. MGM's Sam Marx later remembered that, on the one occasion his staff tried to track him to his home, Wodehouse was nowhere to be found. When he did venture out socially, he often took Leonora, who was almost as gregarious as her mother, to shield him from bores, but mostly he kept to his own circle. 'I don't see much of the movie world,' he wrote to Townend. 'If I ever drive out or go to parties, it is with other exiles – New York writers etc. Most of my New York theatre friends are here.'

The tempo and complexity of life at home increased when Ethel arrived from New York. 'Bunny', as Wodehouse called her, was always responsible for the domestic arrangements and, as the Denby episode had shown, she did not hesitate to introduce her own gentlemen friends into the household. Wodehouse seems to have realized what was going on, and taken charge in his own feline way. Shortly after arriving in Hollywood, Ethel invited Gerard Fairlie, one of the writers of the 'Bulldog Drummond' series, to stay. In a pre-emptive move, Wodehouse visited Fairlie at his hotel and asked him to dinner. Fairlie, puzzled but grateful, accepted. As the evening drew to a close, Wodehouse smoothly suggested that their guest should stay on with them at Linden Drive while he acclimatized to the Hollywood scene. Fairlie, in some embarrassment, asked when he might commence his residence. 'You have already arrived,' replied Wodehouse. 'I had all your things brought to the house some time ago.' Wodehouse might be a complaisant husband, but he also wanted the steady running of his work to be disturbed as little as possible by the distractions of Ethel's life. The only exception to this rule was dogs. To Wodehouse's delight, Ethel had celebrated her arrival from New York with a new Pekinese puppy, Miss Winks, also known as Winky or Winks.

In October, once MGM had renewed Wodehouse's contract for a further six months, Thalberg, who had acquired the rights to *Rosalie* as a vehicle for Marion Davies, tried to inject some new life into the script. The project had been languishing, bogged down in creative disagreements. Now, trying to break the deadlock, Thalberg held a 'story conference' at which, in the manner for which he was famous, he ad-libbed a new scenario, sending a copy to Wodehouse as a memorandum immediately afterwards. Sadly, the memorandum in the studio's archive contradicts Wodehouse's engaging, retrospective account:

When he had finished, [Thalberg] leaned back and mopped his brow, and asked me if I wanted to have it read over to me. I was about to say Yes (just to make the party go), when I suddenly caught the stenographer's eye and was startled to see a look of agonized entreaty in it. I couldn't imagine what was wrong, but I gathered that for some reason she wanted me to say No, so I said No. When we were driving home, she told me that she had had a lateish night the night before and had fallen asleep at the outset of the proceedings and slept peacefully throughout, not having heard or taken down a word.

Thalberg, a pale, elfin workaholic who was married to Norma Shearer, one of Hollywood's biggest stars, operated out of a chic beaverboard sanctum at the MGM executive offices in Culver City. He and Wodehouse liked each other, and although Wodehouse would later have fictional fun at the expense of big Hollywood producers, vultures 'who had done [themselves] rather too well on the corpses', he respected Thalberg and always spoke affectionately of him. Thalberg knew how to handle writers. He told Wodehouse that *Leave It to Psmith* was his favourite book, though when challenged by the bashful author to acquire the film rights he 'smiled sheepishly and the matter dropped'. MGM's plans to make a Jeeves film also went into limbo when Thalberg discovered, disastrously, that his chauffeur thought 'Jeeves' was the name of his wife's butcher. Later, Twentieth Century–Fox would make two dreadful 'Jeeves' movies during the 1930s, one loosely based on *Thank You, Jeeves*, the other using the character of Jeeves, but none of his plots.

Thalberg recognized that Wodehouse had not yet made the difficult transition from stage to movie dialogue (his notable contribution to *Those Three French Girls*, for instance, was to add 'What ho!' to the English milord's first line) or really grasped the essence of screenwriting. So now he commissioned him to write *Rosalie* as a short novelization (45,000 words), from scratch. Wodehouse jibbed a bit, telling Townend that it would be 'about eight times as much sweat as just doing dialogue and [will be] a ghastly fag'. Once he had buckled down to it, he set about extracting maximum advantage from his efforts, asking Reynolds to acquire the story rights from the musical's co-librettists, Bill McGuire and Guy Bolton, and to sell it as a serial. In a covert literary manoeuvre, he instructed Reynolds not to send telegrams c/o MGM, as it was studio practice to have them opened 'and read to me over the phone, and I don't want them to know anything about it'. In the end, however, having completed the text, Wodehouse rightly decided that it was inferior work and the idea of selling *Rosalie* as his latest serial lapsed. After some preliminary shooting, the movie was eventually cancelled when Thalberg judged that the audience's appetite for musicals was in decline.

Wodehouse's attitude towards Hollywood was generally as ambivalent as his feelings about the projects to which he was attached. At times, it was 'the abode of the damned'; at other times, he tried hard to persuade Bill Townend, who had knocked about the American West as a young man, to come and join him as a scriptwriter: 'If you came over here and settled down, I think I would spend at least six months in every year here. I like the place.' But in the same letter he also wrote, 'I think Californian scenery is the most loathsome on earth – a cross between Coney Island and the Riviera, but by staying in one's garden and shutting one's eyes when one goes out, it's possible to get by,' concluding philosophically that 'as life goes by, don't you find that all you need is about two real friends, a regular supply of books, and a Peke?'

Dogs, especially Pekinese, and their foibles are a constant theme in Wodehouse's letters to Leonora, Townend and Mackail, partly because their dogs were often related. When the Wodehouse Pekinese, Susan, had puppies, Ethel arranged for one of them to go to Townend and his wife Rene, thus providing a constant source of doggy gossip. Townend himself noted that it was 'almost impossible to think of Plum without a Peke as a companion', and Wodehouse had refused to sign the MGM contract until he was certain he could take his dogs to California. After dogs, there was always sport. Like many English ex-public schoolboys far from home, Wodehouse could not resist an opportunity to spread the gospel of cricket in the new world. When he discovered that Charles Aubrey Smith, a famous cricketer, and a friend from the long-lost days of Actors vs. Authors cricket matches, had established himself in the film community as the archetypal stiff-upper-lip Englishman, Wodehouse joined forces with him to found the Hollywood Cricket Club. Thanks especially to Aubrey Smith, the club became a central part of the British Hollywood community, and an important element in Wodehouse's social life.

Aside from mixing with fellow expatriates, the Wodehouses were now well established in Hollywood proper. Their circle included Norma Shearer, Edward G. Robinson, Maureen O'Sullivan, W. C. Fields (whom Wodehouse described as 'a louse'), and several former members of the New York theatrical community. It is a measure of their new confidence in Hollywood life that, during the autumn, they moved north of Sunset Boulevard to 1005 Benedict Canyon Drive, a one-storey Spanish-style house with a lovely garden, swimming pool and tennis court. Ethel got into her stride as a Hollywood party-goer; Leonora was taken onto the MGM payroll as an assistant, and began working on 'quite a good picture'. Wodehouse was still swimming three times a day, although the water was much colder than it had been in the summer. 'The swim I enjoy most is before dinner,' he confided to Townend. 'I have a red hot bath and get absolutely boiled, and then race down the back stairs with nothing on and plunge in.'

Those Three French Girls was released in mid-October, to mixed reviews. The *American Spectator* judged, perceptively, that Metro had made 'the mistake of thinking that Wodehouse dialogue, if animated, would make acceptable screen entertainment', while the *New York Times* observed that it was a production 'spoiled by too many cooks'. Wodehouse would later claim that he had been underemployed by Hollywood, but the studios were plainly at a loss how best to exploit his talents. By his own prodigious standards he may have been loafing, but it can hardly be said that MGM did not try to get their money's worth. While he was finishing the novelization of *Rosalie*, he was assigned to write the dialogue on a screen adaptation of the Vincent Laurence play *Among the Married*, renamed *Men Call It Love*. A risqué comedy about adultery, the film was not an ideal subject for Wodehouse's gifts. Shortly after this, he was commissioned to do 'additional dialogue' for an adaptation of H. M. Harwood's play *The Man in Possession*, a comedy about two brothers in the women's underwear business, a theme that Wodehouse would later appropriate, to brilliant comic effect, in *The Code of the Woosters*. Writing 'additional dialogue' was the kind of job he later described as 'just above the man who works the wind machine', and almost none of his lines survived to the final cut.

Both these scripts suggest that MGM was having the greatest difficulty in finding suitable projects for their star recruit to work on. But towards the end of 1930 it seemed as though Wodehouse would find his niche at last when MGM acquired the rights to *Candle-Light*, Wodehouse's own adaptation of Siegfried Geyer's play *Kleine Komödie*. The plot of *Candle-Light* was never one of his favourites, being a racy European seduction drama whose only Wodehousian element is the mutual entanglement of a master and his servant in each other's affairs, but at least it was a project he was familiar with. Once again, though, he found script work unsatisfactory and told Townend that he fully expected the film to be shelved. Although Wodehouse had continuous, albeit frustrating, commitments with the studio from October 1930 to April 1931, he directed his energies elsewhere while he worked at his usual pace on his own writing. *Big Money* had been serialized in the autumn of 1930, and would be published as a novel in January 1931. By the end of December, he had completed yet another magazine serial, *If I Were You*, a hasty fictional reworking of an English country house play, while clearing the decks for a new full-length novel, provisionally entitled *Hot Water*. Simultaneously, he was dashing off a new version of *The Prince and Betty*, a novella entitled *A Prince for Hire*, selling it to *Illustrated Love Magazine* for a five-part serialization from April to August 1931.

Even in the laid-back atmosphere of California, Wodehouse could not allow himself a break from his self-imposed schedule, describing to Townend 'a tremendous rush of work' in the new year of 1931. First, there was a filmscript from Walter Hackett's play *The Way to Treat a*

Woman; and then two further interruptions, 'a ghastly job at the studio which will take up all my time for weeks' (probably *The Man in Possession*). This was followed by a week-long excursion up the coast to William Randolph Hearst's estate at San Simeon, a property of some 440,000 acres, north of San Luis Obispo, to which Wodehouse, Ethel and Miss Winks (who was 'a great hit') were invited in February. Wodehouse, an old friend of Marion Davies from Broadway days, joined a crowd of about fifty guests at Hearst's fantasy castle with its private zoo. 'You're apt to meet a bear or two before you get to the house,' Wodehouse told Townend. In the published version of this letter, he worked up the visit into a memorable comic anecdote, told against himself:

Meals are in an enormous room . . . served at a long table . . . The longer you are there, the further you get from the middle. I sat on Marion's [Davies] right on the first night, then found myself being edged further and further away till I got to the extreme end, when I thought it time to leave. Another day, and I should have been feeding on the floor.

A retrospective improvement on the original, this conveys quite neatly Wodehouse's declared sense of disaffection with Hollywood. On the other hand, Ethel, who liked to throw parties as much as attend them, was in her element. When Leonora returned to Benedict Canyon Drive in the spring of 1931 after five months of gallivanting about New York, the Wodehouse home was soon *en fête*. Wodehouse described Ethel the hostess to Mackail:

She starts by asking two people to lunch, then 'Who can we get to meet them?' This gets it up to four. Then come all the people who would be hurt at being left out, and eventually the thing becomes a Hollywood orgy. This afternoon we had fifty people to lunch! It's not as bad as it sounds, because in this lovely climate you feed out of doors. We had bridge tables spotted about the garden and the patio and a large table with cold food in the dining room, so that people simply helped themselves. As usual, Ethel feels it was a frost, but it wasn't really. It went off splendidly.

Wodehouse was not a natural host. He was quite capable of breaking away from his guests, and disappearing to work in his study if the mood took him. During the final months of his MGM contract, in the first half of 1931, he was preoccupied with *Hot Water*, which he dedicated to Maureen O'Sullivan, a young MGM contract star newly arrived from Ireland.

O'Sullivan, a friend of Leonora's, recalled that the first time she met Ethel, over English-style afternoon tea in Benedict Canyon Drive, Mrs Wodehouse had given her some blunt and sensible advice on a stormy romance she was going through. Afterwards, 'Plummie came out,' she remembered, 'blinking vaguely in the sunlight.' Like many young women, Maureen O'Sullivan found it impossible to feel shy with Wodehouse. 'He was large and affable, very English and rather vague, quietly amusing rather than frighteningly witty,' she said. As often happened with Leonora's friends, O'Sullivan, who also had a movie star's dog, a one-eyed Peke bitch named John-John, became closer to Wodehouse than to his wife. 'We walked all over Beverly Hills gossiping and telling each other our thoughts and feelings, as if we were the oldest of friends,' she recalled. Wodehouse liked younger women and was always most comfortable in a quasi-paternal role. Theirs became a great and lasting friendship in which Wodehouse was able to relax and be himself, although O'Sullivan makes it clear that it was always up to him to open the conversation. 'I can still picture him,' she recalled, 'floating motionless and happy in the pool, looking at his toes or at the deep blue Californian sky, while presumably working out the next bit of writing complexity.'

The plot-making was always the part he revelled in. *Hot Water*, written in the last months of his Hollywood year, has an ebullient and almost devilish complexity. He suggested to Townend that it is 'really a sort of carbon copy of *Leave It to Psmith*', but in fact the novel is a French farce, set in an idyllic fictional seaside town on the north coast of France, imaginatively close to Roville-sur-Mer, scene of many Bertie Wooster escapades. It features yet another country house, the Château Blissac, inhabited by Mr and Mrs J. Wellington Gedge, brash Prohibition-era American plutocrats. A fairly typical Wodehouse woman, Mrs Gedge is large, ambitious and domineering, with only one aim in life – to place her small, unfortunate husband in a French ambassadorial position. The success of her plans rests with another typical Wodehouse character from the 1920s, Senator Ambrose Opal, the 'great Dry legislator', a formidable American bully with an Achilles heel. Mrs Gedge's optimism that she can persuade Senator Opal to exert his influence on her husband's behalf is well founded: she has in her possession an injudicious letter from the drier-than-dry Mr Opal to his bootlegger which, if it were ever to be made public, would for ever cook the senator's political goose.

Into this fraught scenario comes another American, the former Princeton football star Packy Franklin; the 'Veek', his hell-raising Old Etonian friend, the Vicomte de Blissac; and two low-life crooks from Chicago, Soup Slattery and Oily Carlisle. And such is the way of fate in the Wodehouse universe that Packy Franklin, engaged to the formidable Lady Beatrice Bracken, finds himself falling in love with the Senator's charming daughter, Jane, herself nominally attached to Blair Eggleston, the rising young novelist. Eggleston is the author of *Worm i' the Root*, a 'side-whiskered bird' with a smudgy moustache who reflects Wodehouse's disdain for the 'Bloomsbury novelist':

On paper, Blair Eggleston was bold, cold and ruthless. Like so many of our younger novelists, his whole tone was that of a disillusioned, sardonic philanderer who had drunk the wine-cup of illicit love to its dregs . . . There were passages in some of his books . . . which simply made you shiver, so stark was their cynicism, so brutal the force with which they tore away the veils and revealed Woman as she is.

Hot Water, written just after Prohibition had been lifted, was an escape from the pressure, such as it was, of the studio. Despite Wodehouse's evasion strategies, MGM was now a real presence in his life. 'Oddly enough, Hollywood hasn't inspired me in the least. I feel as if everything that could be written about it has already been done,' Wodehouse had written to Townend on first arrival. 'What it was like in the early days, I don't know but nowadays the studio life is all perfectly normal, not a bit crazy,' he went on. 'I don't believe I shall get a single story out of my stay here.' But by the time his contract came up for renewal again in May 1931, and whatever the frustrations, he wanted to stay on, and confided to Mackail that he was 'doing a lot of hearty sucking up to the bosses to try to get it renewed'. Against all expectations, he was beginning rather to like the life, even, grudgingly, its loathsome social aspects. 'I've never been able to stay more than a few months in one place before,' he told Mackail, 'let alone a year. And the people here are quite fun. I find I enjoy going out to dinner.' Creatively, too, he was at last beginning to glimpse the literary potential in his recent experience. 'I haven't been able to get much out of Hollywood so far,' he admitted to Mackail, 'but then I have been restraining myself from satire out of love and loyalty for dear old M–G–M.'

Nevertheless, when on 9 May 1931 the studio lived down to his expectations by *not* renewing his contract, he felt a curious sense of release. 'I was lucky to get mine while the going was good,' he wrote. Having restrained himself thus far, creatively, he was now unmuzzled. The next three years saw a stream of Hollywood stories which, collectively, amount to a more closely observed, satirical assault on an institution than anything he had written since *Psmith in the City*. 'The Rise of Minna Nordstrom', for example, is an accurate but farcical rendering of the 1924 merger that resulted in Metro-Goldwyn-Mayer. 'The Castaways', with its blistering account of the imaginary production of *Scented Sinners*, with its ten scriptwriters and endless rewrites, owes something to his experience on the script of *Those Three French Girls*. The story ends with a scene of rare black comedy:

A bonfire had been started, and Mr Doakes, Mr Noakes, Miss Faversham, Miss Wilson, Mr Fotheringay, Mr Mendelsohn, Mr Markey and the others were feeding it with their scripts of *Scented Sinners*.

In the Front Office, Mr Schnellenhammer and Mr Levitsky, suspending their seven hundred and forty-first conference for an instant, listened to the tumult.

'Makes you feel like Lincoln, doesn't it?' said Mr Levitsky.

'Ah,' said Mr Schnellenhammer.

They smiled indulgently. They were kindly men at heart and they liked the boys and girls to be happy.

In 'The Nodder', Wodehouse addresses the studio hierarchy with forensic comic precision:

It is not easy to explain to the lay mind the extremely intricate ramification of the personnel of a Hollywood motion-picture organisation . . . a Nodder is something like a Yes-Man, only lower in the social scale. A Yes-Man's duty is to attend conferences and say 'Yes'. A Nodder's, as the name implies, is to nod. The chief executive throws out some statement of opinion . . . This is the cue for the senior Yes-Man to say yes . . . Only when all the Yes-Men have yessed, do the Nodders begin to function. They nod.

These stories express Wodehouse's divided feelings about the film community: an understandable contempt for Hollywood combined with an amused affection for its foibles. It was his nature to find comic potential in the most infernal experience, and Hollywood in the 1930s was far from wretched as, in his better moments, he would admit. In Wodehouse's vision of 'God's Back Garden', the place he christened 'Dottyville-on-the-Pacific', Metro-Goldwyn-Mayer becomes Medulla-Oblongata-Glutz or Ne Plus Ultra-Zizzbaum; the screenwriters' life is compared to a prison sentence; the writers' buildings at Perfecto-Zizzbaum Studios are known as the Leper Colony and the Ohio State Penitentiary; and his all-purpose studio executive, Jacob Z. Schnellenhamer, is an ugly, tyrannical dimwit, modelled on Louis B. Mayer:

At his desk, Mr Schnellenhamer had paused for a moment in his writing. He was trying to remember if the word he wanted was spelled 'clorse' or 'clorze'.

Later, in *The Luck of the Bodkins*, Wodehouse cheerfully anatomizes the character of another mogul, the boss of Superba-Llewelyn:

'He hasn't a heart.'
  'I see.'
  'I'd like to wring his neck.'
  'But he hasn't a neck either.'
  They fell into a moody silence again, musing on Ivor Llewelyn. The man seemed armed at all points.

He also took several swipes at the screenwriting community, observing that 'if you make a noise like a mutton chop anywhere within a radius of ten miles of Hollywood Boulevard, authors come bounding out of every nook and cranny, howling like wolves'.

Before Wodehouse's feelings about his year in the sun found their way into fiction, he was to fire a more explicit parting shot at his erstwhile employers, in a newspaper interview which he himself later cited as an example of his innocent propensity for inadvertently landing himself in the soup. In the course of an interview at Benedict Canyon Drive, Wodehouse told Alma Whitaker of the *Los Angeles Times* that he had been paid '$104,000 for loafing', adding mischievously, 'I cannot see what they paid me for. The motion picture business dazes me. They were extremely nice to me – oh, extremely – but I feel as if I have cheated them.'

Wodehouse could not have known that his conversation with Alma Whitaker would find its way onto the front page of the Sunday edition, but he was a former journalist who had spent the previous decade giving press interviews. He must have realized the newspaper value of his words. The context in which Wodehouse spoke to the *Los Angeles Times* certainly made his comments more newsworthy, too. The film industry was also undergoing one of its periodic crises. The Wall Street crash of 1929 had been followed by a drop in movie attendance, and though the public would always look to stars to brighten their lives in dark times, Hollywood seemed to be on the skids. MGM's profits halved; RKO's stock plummeted; Fox nearly went out of business; Warner Brothers barely scraped through; and Paramount went into receivership. As well as the timing of his remarks, the studied reasonableness of his tone, which Whitaker was at pains to stress, suggests an ulterior motive. He was settling a score, and at the same time mythologizing his Hollywood indolence. This version of his experience – as so often with Wodehouse – does not really square with the facts.

They set me to work on a story called 'Rosalie' [he told the *Los Angeles Times*]. No, it wasn't my story. But it was a pleasant light little thing, and I put three months on it. No one wanted me to hurry. When it was finished they thanked me politely and remarked that as musicals didn't seem to be going so well they guessed they would not use it. That about sums up what I was called upon to do for my $104,000. Isn't it amazing? If it is only 'names' they want, it seems such an expensive way to get them, doesn't it?

In his light-footed way, Wodehouse launched several lines of attack in this piece. But while he maintained to Townend and others that this interview had 'the effect [in Hollywood] of the late assassination at Sarajevo', prompting an immediate reappraisal of the studios' spendthrift habits by their East Coast bankers (a judgement that Townend loyally corroborated in his notes to *Performing Flea*), the contemporary American press does not bear out this analysis. The *New York Times* and the *New York Herald Tribune* both picked up the story, but the trade papers (*Variety*, *Motion Picture Herald*, *Film Daily*) hardly noticed it. Wodehouse's New York agent did write, drily noting that, from what he had read in the press, 'I judge that your arrangement with the motion picture people is at an end'; otherwise there was rather less *Sturm und Drang* than Wodehouse described to his friends.

Wodehouse, for his part, perpetuated the myth of his Hollywood year, later claiming that he had been required to do so little work that he was able 'to write a novel and nine short stories, besides brushing up my golf, getting an attractive sun-tan and perfecting my Australian crawl'. Similarly, in old age, he portrayed Hollywood as a kind of penal colony in a manner at odds with his actual enjoyment of the place: 'I got away from Hollywood at the end of the year', he wrote, 'because the gaoler's daughter smuggled me a file in a meat pie, but I was there long enough to realise what a terribly demoralising place it is. The whole atmosphere is one of insidious deceit and subterfuge.' In one sense at least, Wodehouse's account of the *Los Angeles Times* affair is accurate. Locally in Hollywood, an industry town, Wodehouse's candour did give offence. In the aftermath of his *Los Angeles Times* interview, there was, according to Maureen O'Sullivan, a lot of resentment against Wodehouse. But he was unconcerned, almost boastful, about his pariah status. 'My career as a movie-writer has been killed dead by that interview. I am a sort of Ogre to the studios now,' he told Townend. 'I don't care personally, as I don't think I could do picture writing. It needs a definitely unoriginal mind.' It was typical of his *Boy's Own* character that he should be hurt, but disdainful: exactly ten years later, he would respond to a controversy of far greater significance in an almost identical way.

Detached and unruffled, he was soon lost once more in the world of his imagination, happily completing *Hot Water* in a fourteen-week burst of inspiration. 'Honestly, this story is a corker,' Wodehouse advised Reynolds. 'There isn't an incident in it that doesn't act as a delayed bomb and lead to an explosion later.' When he did discuss movie matters he was, like many commentators at the time, exceedingly pessimistic about the future of the business. The summer of 1931 was particularly hot, and when he was not writing, he would spend hours in the pool, and also took up tennis. His relations with MGM were still sufficiently cordial that he continued to make the six-mile walk to the studio in

Culver City to collect his mail. But now that his contract was up, there was really nothing to keep him in California and, spurred on by Ethel, his old restlessness began to return. 'We are toying with a scheme for going round the world in December on the *Empress of Britain*,' he confessed to Townend, and Ethel excitedly told the Mackails that they were planning to stay with a Maharajah in India, 'so you can imagine Plum riding camels and elephants, and taking pot shots at anything he may see'. Wodehouse would always accommodate his wife, up to a point. But, he asked rhetorically, did he really want to see the world?

I'm darned if I know [he wrote]. I have never seen any spectacular spot yet that didn't disappoint me. Notably the Grand Canyon. Personally, I've always liked wandering around in the background. I mean, I get much more of a kick out of a place like Droitwich, which had no real merits, than out of something like the Taj Mahal.

He decided that 'one really likes the places which appeal to one as having possibilities in the way of locations for stories', and hoped that he 'might get a novel out of the cruise', though Ethel and Leonora were concerned about being cooped up with the same passengers for months at a stretch. Eventually, the plan for a world cruise was quietly shelved, to Wodehouse's relief.

Meanwhile, he had finished *Hot Water*. Reynolds was enthusiastic, reporting that he thought *Collier's* would snap it up. As usual, on completing a new novel, Wodehouse found himself creatively in the doldrums. He told Townend that 'my brain doesn't seem to work properly . . . I feel now as if I couldn't write at all.' In the past, he had always got himself back to form by writing short stories, but his contract with *American Magazine* was proving troublesome. The magazine market was undergoing one of its periodic downturns, and the editor, Sumner Blossom, having bought the serial rights to *If I Were You*, now requested that Wodehouse's new stories should contain some American characters, to which Wodehouse objected. 'Americans aren't funny,' he wrote. 'If they were, there would be more than about three American humorous writers.' He complained to Townend that he had 'a darned good mind to tell [Blossom] that if he insists on non-Wodehouse stuff', he would do it, though he would not guarantee it would be funny. Prudently, he added that it was not a good idea to alienate a magazine editor. The 'Mulliners of Hollywood' stories he wrote in the coming months were partly shaped by the requirement to come up with American characters.

If I Were You was published on 3 September. Simultaneously, *Hot Water* was being sold to *Collier's*. Wodehouse and Ethel began to think seriously about returning home. But the news from England was depressing. Forced by rising costs, Charles Le Strange had given up Hunstanton Hall, to Wodehouse's dismay. 'I don't know how I shall get on without Hunstanton to go to,' he lamented to Townend. 'It was the most wonderful place of refuge.' Wodehouse, who had just celebrated his fiftieth birthday, was in need of a new haven, and not just to write. As the year drew to a close, the tax difficulties with which his lawyers had been battling since 1930 began to threaten in the most alarming way.

13. 'My worst year since I started writing' (1932–1934)

Handsome, like all the Mulliners, he possessed in addition to good looks the inestimable blessings of perfect health, a cheerful disposition, and so much money that Income-Tax assessors screamed with joy when forwarding Schedule D to his address. ('The Ordeal of Osbert Mulliner')

Tax had been an issue between Wodehouse and the authorities almost from the beginning of his writing life, and the self-inflicted muddle in which he now found himself was one that would eventually play a decisive part in his wartime downfall. During these inter-war years, he was doubly vulnerable, both as an inveterate traveller, and as an increasingly high earner. As a successful freelance writer, from 1909 he had been first a transatlantic and then a transcontinental commuter; for the past ten years he had shuttled almost non-stop between London and New York. Before the Second World War, such travellers, with varied sources of foreign income, were exceedingly vulnerable to the world's revenue authorities. Incredibly, it was normal, in those days, for income tax to be charged, on the same income, both in the payee's country of residence and in the country from which the income was derived. Before the post-war introduction of tax credits eliminated such double taxation, the tax bill for someone like Wodehouse could be punitive. Worse still, from his point of view, in the 1920s there was not much guidance on the interpretation of tax law, and extraordinarily few competent income tax advisers.

Income tax had been introduced to Britain by William Pitt the Younger in 1799, to raise money for war with France, but not until the First World War, when the rate was raised to five, then six, shillings in the pound, did the state's exactions begin to excite serious protest. Once peace was restored, the burden was reduced, but not soon enough to erase the bitterness of those, like Evelyn Waugh for instance, who regarded the wartime rates as a kind of state-sponsored theft. Wodehouse, in tune with his generation, consistently made humorous references to taxation throughout his work, from the 'Parrot' poems to *Oh, Lady! Lady!!*

Wodehouse had always, for understandable psychological reasons, been exceptionally interested in money. Even in 1907, income tax started at a level of £130, a threshold which gave him familiarity with tax matters. As early as 1921, he had tried to reduce his tax liability by spending less than six months a year in England. Much of his incessant travel in the 1920s, when he was earning a fortune on Broadway, can be attributed, at least in part, to a continuing anxiety about income tax. Money, more generally, is a constant theme in his writing: finding, earning, inheriting, marrying, winning, borrowing, stealing, gambling with, and losing it. Once his modest personal needs had been met, he was a generous man, and the apparent indifference to money reported by some observers was the indifference of a man who knew he was extremely well-off. At the same time as he was banking hundreds of thousands of dollars from his writing, he was also discreetly disbursing much smaller sums to a string of dependants, first and foremost to Bill Townend, but also to Leonora, to his parents, and even to the Dulwich football team. He knew the potential of a tax joke and his work is littered with jocular and not-so-jocular references to the taxman. In *Bill the Conqueror*, Judson Coker describes how he advised Roderick Pyke to make the most of his father's generosity:

Some time ago, in order to do down the income tax people, old Pyke had transferred a large mass of wealth to this bird's account, the understanding being that Roddy . . . was to return it in due season. 'Be a man,' I said. 'Collar the cash, send a few wires of farewell and leg it for foreign parts.' He burst into tears, clasped my hand and said that I was one of the master-minds of the age.

The first serious tax problems Wodehouse faced began in 1924, when he placed his American tax affairs in the hands of John Rumsey, a 'play-broker' with the American Play Company. Rumsey's initial move was to set up a company, Jeeves Dramatics Inc. He seems to have believed that his responsibilities ended there because, when Rumsey resigned from the company in 1929, Wodehouse discovered that Jeeves Dramatics Inc. had not filed a single tax return for 1926, 1927 or 1928. Reynolds, who was temporarily dragged into this crisis, told Wodehouse that Jeeves

Dramatics had been atrociously handled from the first. Having consulted his own lawyer from the New York firm, Perkins, Malone and Washburn, Reynolds advised Wodehouse that he faced the prospect of substantial back taxes and a penalty payment. Preliminary calculations suggested that Wodehouse owed a hefty $32,753.56.

Reynolds's advice, when confronted with a dire situation, was sensible. He wrote to Wodehouse, 'The only way seems to be to face it and have done with it.' For some reason, perhaps associated with Ethel's involvement in this crisis, and possibly because Wodehouse did not want to put all his eggs in one basket, he did not let Reynolds – a highly competent and experienced administrator who actually offered to arrange things so that 'such a situation can never arise again' – take care of the matter. Instead, Wodehouse made the questionable decision to leave the handling of the case to Margaret Matusch, his secretary in London, and then to transfer the responsibility for Jeeves Dramatics Inc.'s tax liability to Bobby Denby, who had recently been restored to favour after the Famous Players Lasky row.

Denby was a flimsy character at the best of times. His track record during previous Wodehouse negotiations showed him to be highly irresponsible in financial matters. Denby had already become involved in Jeeves Dramatics Inc. when Rumsey resigned but, according to Reynolds's son, a junior in the office, had been afraid to bring up the tax problem because he thought that to do so would anger Wodehouse. So Denby had done absolutely nothing about the problem and now, formally handed the task of sorting out Jeeves Dramatics Inc., reacted by falling so dramatically ill with erysipelas (a skin disease sometimes known as 'St Anthony's Fire' or 'The Rose') that the year 1930 passed without any settlement being negotiated. True, Ethel did sail across to New York armed with power of attorney, but, after some parties and nights at the theatre, returned home without having accomplished anything significant. When a restored Denby returned to action in the summer of 1931, his first move was to retain the Manhattan tax experts Freeman and Greenberg, and to adopt a delaying strategy which would turn out to be highly dangerous. 'We shall be able', Denby blithely told Wodehouse, 'to make a settlement more favourable to us if we wear the tax people down a bit.' Uncharacteristically, Wodehouse took an instant dislike to Freeman and Greenberg and returned briefly to England from California. But Norfolk Street had been sub-let, and he found London uninspiring, cold and gloomy. Perhaps sensing that it was prudent to be out of the country for a while, he now took a year's lease on a house in Auribeau, France, in the hills outside Cannes.

Domaine de la Fréyère, a Provençal country estate, twenty minutes by car from Cannes, occupied a hundred acres in the Alpes Maritimes, and came with a large swimming pool and a considerable staff, 'a German butler, an Alsatian footman, a Serbian cook, a French chauffeur, an Italian maid, and an English odd-job man'. In summertime, it was supposed to be a good alternative to the pleasures of Benedict Canyon Drive, but when Wodehouse arrived in March he found it bleak. As usual, until he had acclimatized Wodehouse was unhappy with his new surroundings. He informed Townend that he considered 'the moral ethos of the Riviera' to be 'very unhealthy'. But not for long. 'We dined at the Casino last night,' he told Townend, shortly after reaching Cannes. 'I played chemmy [*chemin de fer*] after dinner, won four thousand francs, and legged it home with the loot at half past one.' He was deep into his first Jeeves novel (*Thank You, Jeeves*) and disliked jeopardizing his morning routine. 'Ethel stayed on till 8 a.m. and lost about as much!!' Although the Denby and Fairlie cases show him to be no fool in important marital matters, he evinced a detached puzzlement at the ways of the opposite sex. 'I can't understand women,' he wrote to Townend. 'I mean, their vitality. Ethel is always complaining of not being fit, but she can stay up all night without suffering for it. I collapse hours before she has begun to feel tired.' The Wodehouse marriage was unusual, but it was strong enough, during the coming ten years, to weather a succession of interconnected disasters, the first of which was about to irrupt into his life.

For the moment, confident that his tax affairs were in the hands of experts, Wodehouse was installed in Domaine de la Fréyère, reading voraciously as always, tut-tutting over Aldous Huxley's *Brave New World*, learning French at the local Berlitz school, lunching with visiting literary friends and neighbours like H. G. Wells, Michael Arlen and E. Phillips Oppenheim, and corresponding with Faber & Faber about its publication of his essays, *Louder and Funnier*. This was a collection of reworked *Vanity Fair* articles which, as Wodehouse perceptively observed, was notable for its Rex Whistler jacket illustration. His tax troubles seemed to stimulate his creative imagination, and he now wrote 64 pages of *Thank You, Jeeves* in seventeen days flat, a personal best to which he would often refer with nostalgia in later life. He would have done more, but he 'went off the rails, and had to rewrite all this three times. That is the curse of my type of story,' he confided to Townend. 'Unless I get the construction absolutely smooth, it bores the reader.' To Reynolds, he boasted, 'I find this a great place to work, and I have written the first 50 pages of the novel, always the hardest part, in ten days. This includes rewriting every scene about three times . . . I always find that my only way of writing the first third of a novel is to put something down and alter it and then keep on altering it till it is right.' He told Mackail that *Thank You, Jeeves* 'ought to be easy to write, but so far has proved a ghastly fag. That first person stuff cuts both ways. It gives you speed, but you're up against the fact that nothing can happen except through the eyes of the hero.'

Thank You, Jeeves develops the theme of Bertie's growing independence from Jeeves that Wodehouse had been exploring in the stories collected in *Very Good, Jeeves*. The plot is constructed like a classical romance in which a couple quarrel, separate and are finally reunited. When the action begins, the cause of the rift is Bertie's banjo. Jeeves, faced with the intolerable prospect of sharing a country cottage with his 'mentally negligible' young master and this objectionably frivolous instrument, hands in his notice, and Bertie accepts his resignation:

The Wooster blood boiled over. Circumstances of recent years have so shaped themselves as to place this blighter in a position which you might describe as that of a domestic Mussolini: but forgetting this and sticking simply to cold fact, what *is* Jeeves, after all? A valet. A salaried attendant. And a fellow simply can't go on truckling – do I mean truckling? I know it begins with a 't' – to his valet for ever. There comes a moment when he must remember that his ancestors did dashed well at the Battle of Crécy and put the old foot down. This moment had now arrived.

The second line of the plot now comes into play. The country cottage to which Bertie then repairs, banjo in hand, is the property of the 5th Baron Chufnell, 'Chuffy', who is in love with Bertie's former American fiancée, Pauline Stoker. As Chuffy's guest, Bertie finds himself thrown together with Pauline in progressively more embarrassing circumstances, culminating in her appearance in Bertie's bed wearing his 'heliotrope pyjamas with the old gold stripe', a move which elicits this response from their owner:

The attitude of fellows towards finding girls in their bedroom shortly after midnight varies. Some like it. Some don't. I didn't. I suppose it's some old Puritan strain in the Wooster blood.

The climax of the comedy comes when Bertie, disguised as a black-face minstrel, and seeking to escape the designs of Pauline's bullying millionaire father to ensnare him as a son-in-law, is forced to roam the neighbourhood of Chuffy's country seat during the course of a short summer night, looking for butter to clean his face, pursued by two incompetent rural policemen. By chance, the nerve specialist Sir Roderick Glossop, absurdly in love with Chuffy's Aunt Myrtle, is in the same predicament. Farce of a high order ensues during which Bertie's cottage (including the banjo) is burned to the ground, Sir Roderick is arrested, Pauline and Chuffy become betrothed, and Bertie and Jeeves are reconciled.

Thank You, Jeeves unites the levity and verve of a comic song with the intricacy of a great short story, combined with all kinds of borrowings from Wodehouse's experience in musical theatre. Wodehouse's mature prose is at its most scintillating, and the airiest of plots, as usual, is a brilliantly constructed maze. The policemen, Dobson and Voules, allusively connect some of the farce to Dogberry and Verges in *Much Ado about Nothing* and Constable Dull in *Love's Labour's Lost*, Wodehouse's favourite play. The way in which Jeeves and Bertie narrate a series of offstage set pieces owes everything to the conventions of classical Greek theatre, a form with which Wodehouse was fluently familiar. And almost every page is seasoned with felicitous allusions to, and quotations from, the English classics.

By the end of May 1932, *Thank You, Jeeves* was complete, and Reynolds then sold serial rights to *Cosmopolitan* for a record $50,000. Wodehouse had his usual 'brain blank' after a sustained burst of work. Alarmingly, too, the publication of *Hot Water* in August, and the attendant mixed reviews, provoked a rare attack of literary self-doubt. J. B. Priestley, writing in the *Evening Standard*, got under Wodehouse's skin: 'Priestley was the worst of all, because he . . . called attention to the thing I try to hush up, – viz. that I have only got one plot and produce it once a year with variations.' Behind the joking, there was a real anxiety that he had written himself out. He told Townend he couldn't write a story 'unless it seems real . . . that's why I do so much country house stuff.

Anything in a country house seems real to me, however fantastic, – I suppose because the atmosphere is so definite. I don't believe I could ever write a Cannes story or a real Hollywood story, because the two places simply don't exist.' This bout of introspection, though, seems to have galvanized Wodehouse's imagination because, as autumn drew on, he began work on a sequel to *Summer Lightning*.

Heavy Weather is one of Wodehouse's most exhilarating inter-war masterpieces, a book in which Blandings Castle becomes, in the words of the critic Anthony Lane, a 'blend of the fortress and the funhouse'. As he wrote it, though, the author was doubtful about its qualities. 'I can't kid myself', he wrote 'that it's as good as *S.L.* [*Summer Lightning*] – principally because the hero and heroine are already engaged, which deprives me of the good old light comedy love scenes.' He was also wrestling with 'a decent part for Galahad' and concluded 'this one will want a lot of thinking over'. The Riviera out of season was a perfect place to think out a novel, his favourite activity. Cannes was deserted; Ethel had dismissed almost all the staff. Even a visit from his brother Armine, chatting and chain-smoking as usual, could not put him off. Wodehouse's flattering letters to Denis Mackail illustrate the way his imagination was becoming absorbed in plotting the action of *Heavy Weather*: 'I always envy you being able to hold the reader with real life stuff,' he wrote. 'I have to have jewels, comic lovers and about a dozen American crooks before I can move.' Wodehouse's false modesty is in play, as usual, but, to a friend and fellow novelist like Mackail, there is candour too: 'My great trouble', he went on, echoing the complaints of all novelists writing for magazines, 'is that I have to have rapid action for serial purposes, and how can one get rapid action without there being something [that] at least half the characters want to steal[?]'

With *Heavy Weather* that 'something' is Galahad Threepwood's scandalous memoirs. The novel opens ten days after the end of *Summer Lightning*. Ronnie Fish is now firmly engaged to the chorus girl Sue Brown, but his mother, Lady Julia – Lord Emsworth's sister – is determined to stop him. Throw in newspaper magnate Lord Tilbury's determination to acquire Galahad Threepwood's manuscript for the Mammoth Publishing Company, and also to steal the Empress of Blandings, combined with the appearance at Blandings Castle of the impostors Monty Bodkin and Percy Pilbeam, and you have the essentials of one of Wodehouse's best plots, narrated at exhilarating speed and with masterful comic brio. Exactly how Wodehouse achieves his effects, knitting together the madcap complications of his narrative, is one of the pleasurable mysteries of his later work. All the reader can say with certainty is that Galahad's memoirs are finally consumed by the pig, that Sue and Ronnie drive off into the summer night with a cheque from Lord Emsworth for honeymoon expenses, and that the Empress is happily secure in her sty, contemplating the prospect of 'cabbage leaves in the morning'. In retrospect, both the book and its subject would seem like an idyllic interlude before the cyclone of tax trouble that was about to engulf Wodehouse.

Part of the satisfaction of this season also derived from Leonora's sudden engagement and subsequent marriage to Peter Cazalet, the youngest son of an influential landowning family, with a thousand-acre estate, Fairlawne, just outside Tonbridge in Kent. 'I'm so happy about it that I want to tell everyone I meet,' Wodehouse wrote to his step-daughter when she broke the news. 'Boo and Winks must be brides-maids, carrying your train in their mouths.' In correspondence with Townend, he expressed particular satisfaction with the wealth of Leonora's future father-in-law William Cazalet, noting that 'Snorky will be pretty rich'. It was, however, the end of an era. Leonora would set up home in a large house, The Grange, at Shipbourne on the Cazalet estate; quickly produce two children, Sheran and Edward; and become absorbed in the life of her young family. As proud grandparents, Wodehouse and Ethel were frequent visitors to The Grange, sometimes staying over several weeks, but he missed his 'confidential secretary and adviser' and, later, the loss of Leonora's practical wisdom in matters of everyday life was another small but contributory factor in his down-fall. For the moment, however, he was delighted. The wedding took place on 14 December, near the Cazalet family home, and he was espe-cially pleased that, in 'this beastly era of young Bloomsbury novelists', the groom was not a literary man, but a first-class games player and exceptional amateur jockey, with whom he could talk horses and cricket. Leonora had met her future husband through her friendship with his sister Thelma, a redoubtable woman who played an important role in Wodehouse's post-war career; in a world of finely tuned social antennae the Cazalet family was the equal of Wodehouse's.

Apart from this happy interlude, the early 1930s, the 'low, dishonest decade', were a dark time for Wodehouse. The England he had grown up in and would always write about was declining. Artistically, he was completely out of sympathy with the new generation of writers, men like Auden, Isherwood and Greene who espoused communism, wrestled with the dilemmas of religion, and seemed to conduct lives of sensual self-gratification. As a young man, he had always looked up to older writers, men like Kipling and Conan Doyle. Now he was a senior figure himself, but there was almost no one following in his footsteps whose work he could identify with, or who, conversely, seemed at all interested in his work. Writers like his friends Milne and Mackail were out of fashion. Graham Greene, writing in the *Spectator*, identified such '*Punch* contributors' as 'peculiarly dismal', a swipe that provoked Milne into a fierce riposte. Wodehouse, who was referred to in the row, wisely kept his head down, and remained unshakeable in his allegiance to his Edwardian mentors. The death of Kipling in January 1936 left him with 'a sort of stunned feeling'.

The wasteland of the 1920s had given way to the rise of fascism and the threat of war. Politically, Wodehouse was conservative, not a wholehearted appeaser, but with some sympathy for those who wanted to promote peace. He had been in California when the National Government was formed, and was dismayed, on returning home, to find British politics so bereft of leadership. The frivolity of the jazz age, to which he had contributed, and in which he had been at ease, was now followed by the bleak desperation of the British hunger marches, mass unemployment in America and, in Germany, the rise of Adolf Hitler. Wodehouse often made light-hearted references in his work to Mussolini, who was harder to take seriously, but the European picture was inescapably grim, and even in the south of France he could scarcely avoid it, although he did his best.

He had continued to work on *Heavy Weather*, drafting the all-important scenario during September, while being aware that huge tax bills were looming on both sides of the Atlantic. The blow, when it fell, was far worse than he expected. 'Hell's foundations have been quivering,' he told Townend in December, reporting a tax claim of some $187,000, a terrible shock when added to his and Ethel's losses in the Wall Street crash. All told, he estimated that 'when the smoke has cleared away, I shall have lost around a hundred and fifty thousand quid since 1929'. Reflecting on the actual situation, which would become progressively worse during the coming year, he decided that, his lavish lifestyle notwithstanding, 'the actual things you really want cost about two hundred a year. I have examined my soul, and I find that my needs are a Times Library subscription, and tobacco money, plus a bit extra for holidays.' Now that he was back in Europe and more keenly aware of how poorly Townend's literary career was going, he felt responsible for that, too. 'If only you [Townend] were making a couple of thousand a year steady, I shouldn't have a worry in the world.'

Wodehouse at fifty was not a carefree figure. The writer Claud Cockburn has repeated the story of his 'middle-aged cousin' who, stopping for lunch in a Cotswold hotel, came upon a lunch party for six in the dining room convulsed by a story so infectiously funny that 'they were all laughing and laughing until the tears ran down their cheeks'. Cockburn's cousin said that it was not just the humour of the story that was so hilarious, 'it was the wonderfully amusing way' it was told. When his cousin asked about the humorist's identity, he was told, 'P. G. Wodehouse'. Sadly, this apocryphal tale finds few echoes in any other reminiscences. To people who did not know him well, the middle-aged Wodehouse was not funny in person, but grave and withdrawn. Gerard Fairlie wrote that Wodehouse 'is not a particularly funny man . . . he talks gently, not a great deal, and rather seriously . . . he does not give you the impression of being very interested in his fellow men. He is curiously detached and impersonal.' Fans who contrived to meet him for drinks or dinner waited in vain for the flow of witty anecdote and priceless comic observation to begin. Wodehouse saved his humour for his typewriter, and his comedy was rarely spontaneous but worked up through countless drafts. Beverly Nichols, a literary young-man-about-town in the 1920s and 1930s, published a volume of contemporary pen-portraits, *Are They the Same at Home?*, in which he described the experience of being with Wodehouse:

When I first met him, we were both lunching at the House of Commons, and I noted that whenever he opened his mouth the faces of the politicians seated round him prepared to twitch up into set smiles. They were saying to themselves, '*Now* he's going to begin'. And when he did not begin, and behaved like an ordinary human being . . . they were quite disappointed . . . I fail to see why. After all, even if he does not make jokes, he is excellent company and he radiates charm. Best of all, he never talks about himself.

Nichols noted that the key to Wodehouse's character was 'a loathing for display', while the key to his public personality was 'his almost uncanny capacity for disappearances . . . At one moment he is there. At the next moment he is gone.' Like Jeeves, Wodehouse had perfected the art of disassembling himself in the course of everyday life. Those few who understood him best, like Ethel or Leonora, knew that these vanishing acts had only one purpose: a solitary rendezvous with the imaginative world at the keys of his typewriter, the place he was always happiest. A mystery to others, he was also a mystery to himself, and perhaps the conundrum of his existence only became bearable when reinterpreted through the antics of Drones, pig-men, peers and moon-struck lovers at large in the English countryside. It was in the pages of these great comedies that he could encrypt his art: the constant theme of the novels he completed during these difficult years – especially *Heavy Weather* and *Right Ho, Jeeves* – is the comic plight of silly young men blundering about in search of love.

Existential matters apart, there was, at this high point of his fame, still an almost overwhelming burden of revenue trouble which had not been laid to rest by the earlier payment. Briefly returning to London for Leonora's wedding, Wodehouse found himself spending hours trapped in meetings talking figures to the American tax expert Greenberg, whose honesty he doubted. In a vain attempt to straighten out the American end of things he now dispatched an English revenue expert, H. E. Wiltshire, to New York, while he himself retreated to Domaine de la Fréyère. Concluding these first skirmishes in his long battle with the British and American tax authorities, he told Townend philosophically that 'in many ways, I am not sorry this income tax business has happened. Everything was so easy for me before I was getting a bit bored. I now can spit on my hands and start sweating again, feeling that it really matters when I make a bit of money.'

In France, where he plunged back into *Heavy Weather*, he told Townend that he was 'getting on splendidly with the new novel . . . The first chapters were terribly hard to write, because I had to be careful not to assume that people had read [*Summer Lightning*] and at the same time not put in yards of explanation which would bore those who had.' He did not disguise the effort he invested in his writing. 'In order to get a hundred pages of o.k. stuff, I must have written nearly a hundred thousand words. Still, it pays. The result is fine.' But the strain of his tax troubles, combined with the work on *Heavy Weather*, left him prostrate with influenza, and put him out of sorts with the Riviera again. He told his regular correspondents that he was tired of Domaine de la Fréyère; that Cannes was too far from the centre of things; and that he disliked 'the constant temptation of the casino'. Nonetheless, he still spent many evenings gambling with Ethel in a distracted sort of way. His friend and neighbour E. Phillips Oppenheim, a best-selling mystery writer, has left a portrait of Wodehouse the unorthodox gambler: 'Tall, broad-shouldered and with a kind of hidden smile, looking more like an Oxford professor than a writer of humorous stories.' It was part of Wodehouse's system to devote his gambling winnings to Townend's welfare, and despite his tax troubles he seems never to have deviated from this plan. 'My idea', he wrote to Townend, 'is to guarantee an overdraft, so that you will feel safe.' This guaranteed overdraft, he added, should be 'a dead secret between us and the good old bank manager' (many of his letters to Townend close with cryptic references to similar covert subventions).

Disillusioned with France, he decided that London was 'the best spot, all round'. But now there were two difficulties about living in England: first, the tax liabilities of permanent residency; and second, the quarantine difficulties encountered by his dogs, with whom he and Ethel insisted on travelling. If they were to be brought back to England, they would have to spend six months of quarantine in kennels. He joked to Mackail that he was planning to smuggle them back, disguised as cats. In the back of his mind, then, as another difficult year unfolded, was the thought that he could eke out a solution by living in a part of France – Le Touquet for instance – that was sufficiently near London to facilitate lightning trips to Dulwich football matches and to Leonora. Throughout his life he had been drawn to seaside resorts – Emsworth, Bellport and Hunstanton were all part of that pattern.

In fact, he returned to Hunstanton, in the summer of 1933, having 'thought out' a new Jeeves novel, *Right Ho, Jeeves*, and wrote it in a matter of a few weeks. Throughout his career, Wodehouse's creativity had been intimately, even psychologically, linked to his financial situation. As a young man, he had written his way to freedom from the bank. As an expatriate in America, he had provided for himself and his new wife by selling his work on Broadway, and also to the great magazines like *Collier's* and the *Post*. Now, confronted with the demands of the taxman, he was inspired to produce one of the novels that has guaranteed his immortality. As soon as he finished *Right Ho, Jeeves*, he retyped it from start to finish, noting that this greatly improved what he had done. 'I find that when the labour of the first draft is off one's mind, one is able to concentrate on small improvements,' he told Townend. To Mackail, he was boastful about his recent productivity: 'three novels and 10 short stories which, as *Variety* would say, is nice sugar'. In November, he dispatched the manuscript to Reynolds, who noted drily that it was 'as good as Wodehouse's recent stories, in fact rather better'.

Right Ho, Jeeves has a three-act structure similar to *Thank You, Jeeves*. It is probably the Wodehouse novel that many readers know best. The climactic comic set piece – newt-fancying teetotaller Gussie Fink-Nottle giving away the prizes to the boys of Market Snodsbury Grammar School – is one of the most anthologized in the Wodehouse canon. When the action of the novel begins, Gussie is discovered roaming London in fancy dress, disguised as Mephistopheles, and in love with Madeline Bassett, to whom Bertie had been engaged, and who (according to Bertie) believes that the stars are 'God's daisy chain'. Gussie is in town to consult Jeeves on how best to pluck up the courage to propose to Miss Bassett. The quest for love soon carries both Gussie and Bertie to Brinkley Court, Worcestershire, home of Dahlia Travers, Bertie's favourite aunt and the editor of *Milady's Boudoir*, a magazine for gentlewomen to which Bertie had once contributed a piece entitled 'What the Well-dressed Man is Wearing'. Clothes, once again, play a decisive role in the plot. Bertie has returned from France with a fashionable white mess-jacket, and Jeeves does not approve ('I fear that you inadvertently left Cannes in the possession of a coat belonging to some other gentleman, sir . . . surely you are not proposing to wear it in England, sir'). A temporary coolness between master and valet ensues, and Bertie must try to resolve the complications of Gussie's wooing without the full benefit of Jeeves's omniscience. In the process, he manages to infuriate Aunt Dahlia's chef, Anatole, who responds with a memorable tirade of franglais inspired by Wodehouse's recent stay at Domaine de la Fréyère:

The hell you say it's all right? Of what use to pull stuff like that? Wait one half-moment. Not yet quite so quick, my old sport . . . It is some very different dishes of fish. I can take a few smooths with a rough, it is true, but I do not find it agreeable when one play larks against me on my windows . . . I buzz off and do not stay planted.

But all ends happily ever after. Anatole does not quit. During a triumphant nocturnal finale in the grounds of Brinkley Court, sundered hearts are reunited. Gussie's engagement to La Bassett is secured. As Bertie puts it, 'looking at the thing from every angle, I saw that Jeeves had done well'. Reynolds immediately sold the new novel to *Cosmopolitan*, giving Wodehouse the satisfaction of knowing that, even if the taxman was after his assets, he was still able to earn money from his typewriter at something like his regular rate.

But still the tax saga dragged on in America. Wodehouse believed that Wiltshire had met the authorities in conjunction with Reynolds's lawyer, Washburn, and that everyone was now working towards a settlement. This was always his way with things he didn't want to be troubled with: he would remain happily detached while others sorted out the difficulties. Reynolds's observation was that 'he [Wodehouse] is quite impractical and not at all interested in business matters. I am quite certain that he never handled the bulk of his own money . . . [when] I lunched or dined with him and endeavoured to discuss various contracts for his writings, his invariable retort was "Oh, Reynolds, you take care of that . . . I don't want to be bothered with details."' His literary agent was in an awkward position. His very valuable client was becoming increasingly irritable over the progress of the negotiations with the Washington authorities, but at the same time refusing to take full responsibility. Somehow he had to force Wodehouse to pay attention to the gravity of the problem without alienating him irretrievably. On 26 April 1933 he reminded Wodehouse that he would not be able to settle the matter unless Wodehouse agreed to pay his lawyer in America:

You have Mr Malone now refusing to act until you pay him . . . and you have no lawyer to represent you [in Washington] . . . you are running the risk of having to pay a tremendous amount, and, if an arrangement isn't made for payment of the taxes, the government . . . will simply prevent your getting any money from America.

Once the firm of Perkins, Malone and Washburn was formally retained, and paid, and Wiltshire, who had proved incompetent, had been removed from the case, at least the American end of the trouble was coming under control. But, in the absence of a clear law, there was still the unresolved question: Where should the bulk of Wodehouse's earnings be taxed – in Britain or in America? His advisers were divided on this matter, and the anxiety surrounding it, Wodehouse complained to Reynolds, 'is playing the devil with my work. I write a few pages, and then along comes another letter from Washburn, full of disturbing stuff, and I find it impossible to go on with my story.' This was special pleading. The evidence of his work in 1933 suggests the opposite: that adversity was bringing out the best in him, as it always had. Nonetheless, it was his deepest wish, a not unreasonable one in the circumstances, that these experts should come to an arrangement that would allow him to go on with his writing uninterrupted. 'If they would agree to a fixed sum,' he wrote to Reynolds, 'then we on our side would agree to drop all haggling about expenses and losses and so on. I can't see why this isn't possible.' Just as the American dimension of his troubles seemed to be under control, the English tax authorities, 'out of a clear blue sky', decided to pursue non-payment of tax on his American earnings, an initial assessment of £40,000, for the years 1927–33. Wodehouse decided to appeal, basing his case on the claim that he was 'out of the country all the time' from 1930 to 1933 (which was not strictly true). 'Our accountants seem to think the actual sum required will be a couple of thousand,' Wodehouse advised Townend, who had an acute personal interest in the outcome of the case.

The appeal was heard on 19 January 1934. Wodehouse was represented by Raymond Needham KC, a leading silk. After legal argument, the appeal commissioners found that Wodehouse had been resident in Britain for only two of the years from 1927 to 1933, and also that he *was* entitled legally to assign his contracts to Jeeves Dramatics Inc., a previously disputed point. The tax inspector, who had been pursuing this case for months, was reportedly furious that Needham had won, and perhaps all the more so in the knowledge that, in arguing his case, he had made a silly technical mistake that Needham had ruthlessly exploited. The furious tax inspector threatened an appeal against the decision, to which Needham replied, 'Well, anyway, come and have lunch with us now.' 'Us?' replied the inspector. 'Who else?' 'My client, P. G. Wodehouse,' said Needham. 'The Savoy Grill at one.'

So the three men went down the Strand to the Savoy and, in the course of the lunch, the tax inspector, a Bedford man, discovered that he and Wodehouse had been on opposing rugby football teams in the

1890s, and became reconciled to the appeal commissioners' decision. Afterwards, Wodehouse wanted to dedicate *Right Ho, Jeeves* 'To Raymond Needham KC, who put the tax-gatherers to flight when they had their feet on my neck and their hands on my wallet'; but not wishing to stir up old antagonisms with the revenue, he settled for 'To Raymond Needham KC, with affection and admiration.' Wodehouse immediately expressed his relief at the outcome to Reynolds. To Leonora he acknowledged the effectiveness of Needham's advocacy in the face of what, exaggerating as usual, he conceded had been a bold assertion at the heart of his case. 'Even now, I can't see how he worked the thing . . . I see him proving us non-residents for years when – I should have said – we were out of England for about three days.'

The upshot of two difficult months was a renewed appreciation of living abroad. On 10 March Wodehouse wrote to Townend that 'my income tax experts tell me I have got to leave England, if only for a short spell, before April 5th. Otherwise I shall get chalked up as a resident.' To Reynolds, he said his plans were as uncertain as ever. He was anxious to be in a position to go to America again ('my wife and I both want to make it our headquarters'), and he had had enough of England, except for visits. He concluded that he would 'like to settle in America and visit the South of France from there in the Summer'. But, while the tax case dragged on in Washington, America was still a difficult prospect. Wodehouse found himself in low spirits once again, complaining to Townend about 'the foulest week of my career' – afflicted by toothache; a bad head cold; a 'ghastly function'; an American interviewer; a 'snack luncheon to celebrate a young author's new book'; and finally the shifting of fifteen trunks, twenty suitcases and two Pekinese dogs (Miss Winks and a new arrival, Boo) into the Dorchester. 'It's costing the earth,' he confessed to Townend, 'but I have a little suite on the eighth floor and Ethel another further down the passage.'

Work was always his most reliable comfort. Now that *Right Ho, Jeeves* had appeared in the *Saturday Evening Post*, and *Thank You, Jeeves* was about to be published in book form, he could focus all his efforts on the scenario for his next novel, eventually called *The Luck of the Bodkins*, a marriage of some recent Blandings characters with his Hollywood experience. Meanwhile, in New York, Washburn was establishing a Swiss tax shelter, Siva Aktiengesellschaft (Siva). For the next four years all Wodehouse's contracts would be made with this company. Then, just as clarity and reason began to return to his professional life, his accountant, Weinbren, was dispatched to New York to try to bring the ongoing American tax negotiations to a resolution. The visit was a failure, and was followed by the US authorities issuing a lien, freezing all Wodehouse's American assets and prohibiting payment of any moneys in his name. The lien claimed a debt totalling $250,703.59, another staggering sum.

Wodehouse later told Townend that this had been 'my worst year since I started writing', but his first response to this potentially ruinous move by the US tax authorities was to look on the bright side. 'Things are not so bad as they seem,' he wrote. 'I have between ninety and a hundred thousand quid salted away in England and have always earned in England hitherto about eight or nine thousand [pounds] a year. So I propose to sit tight and do nothing.' He admitted that Ethel was worried by the turn of events, but was cheerful for himself, and speculated about developing a *nom de plume*. 'I feel as if I am starting a new life. I can now send stuff to America without having to make it exactly like all my other stories. It will be fun seeing if I can build up another name.'

If these were grounds for optimism, in the wider world it was the guarantee of the Wodehouse name that brought people to his door: in the spring of 1934, the *Oh, Kay!* producer Vinton Freedley proposed that Wodehouse should collaborate with Guy Bolton on the book for a new Cole Porter musical. It was also the Wodehouse name that ensured widespread British and American newspaper coverage of his tax troubles. In the short term, it was these troubles that sent him abroad to France, and within a decade set in motion the chain of events that would prove his undoing. When he was on the ropes, a vindictive misrepresentation of these difficulties would be used to blacken his name further. But the fateful move was the decision to go to France. In a real sense, Wodehouse's subsequent troubles can be said to have begun in this, his 'worst year', although of course the worst was yet to come.

14. 'The one ideal spot in the world'
(1934–1936)

It was the Drones Club week-end at Le Touquet. The thought of the girl I loved being surrounded by about eighty-seven members of the Drones in the lax atmosphere of a foreign pleasure resort . . . was like a knife in my heart. (*Uncle Fred in the Springtime*)

Wodehouse was en route for Cannes, exploring the boundaries of his new life as a tax exile, when the producers Alex Aarons and Vinton Freedley first approached him with the commission for a new musical with Bolton and Cole Porter. Their recent Gershwin show, *Pardon My English*, had just flopped, and they were looking for a cast-iron hit. It was nearly a decade since Wodehouse's name had been up in lights on Broadway, and he had vowed to resist such offers, but he was intrigued to work with Porter and tempted by the producers' financial inducements, their brash promises, and their talk of big stars. He told Reynolds that it was 'one of those big musical comedies which mean a lot of money'. Although he did not want to be distracted from his new novel, which was set on a transatlantic liner, the Aarons–Freedley proposal was, by chance, also for a shipboard caper. Another attraction was the opportunity of working with Guy Bolton again. Besides, Cole Porter was famous as a lyric-writing composer, so the only call on Wodehouse would be for his contribution to the book. Soon, Wodehouse and Bolton (with Cole Porter on the long-distance telephone) were deep in discussion about a show provisionally entitled 'Crazy Week', initially conceived as a story about the shipwreck of a pleasure liner.

There was only one, possibly deal-breaking, snag. Wodehouse was now in Paris, working all hours in a suite in the Hôtel Prince de Galles on the Avenue George V, and Bolton loathed Paris. He simply would not work there. So he and Wodehouse compromised on Le Touquet, just across the Channel from Bolton's Sussex cottage and familiar to Wodehouse and Ethel from their visit in the summer of 1924. Partly thanks to the patronage of the Prince of Wales and his circle, the resort had become a recognized inter-war playground for the fashionable rich. The two old friends installed themselves in the Royal Picardy Hotel and by July, punctuating their work with occasional rounds of golf, had completed a first draft of the script. Towards the end of his life, Wodehouse published an account of the day when Porter, who had been gadding about Europe, arrived with his music. The three men, lacking a piano, repaired to the casino, where Porter ran through the numbers he had completed, including 'You're the Top', and 'Blow, Gabriel, Blow', at a keyboard in the corridor leading to the gaming tables. Their meeting was interrupted by a pleasantly intoxicated young American socialite who, mistaking Porter for the casino's entertainer, asked him to play 'I Wonder Where My Baby Is Tonight'. When Porter laid aside the score and obliged without protest, the young man began to cry. 'That song hits me right here . . . Just been divorced, so can you blame me for wondering?'

We made sympathetic noises [Wodehouse continued], and Cole played 'You're the Top'. The intruder came weaving back through the door. 'Forget that stuff,' he said. 'Do you know a number called "The Horse with the Lavender Eyes"? It drove us down from the Plaza to the church. Dawn said the horse had lavender eyes,' he continued brokenly, 'so we sang the song all the way down the avenue. Dawn O'Day, that was her stage name. Pretty, isn't it?' He rose and laid a small column of 100-franc chips on top of the piano. 'What's that for?' we asked. 'For him,' he said, indicating Cole. 'He plays okay, but he picks out rotten numbers.'

It is not clear how close Wodehouse was to Cole Porter. He later claimed that his role in the show was confined 'to lending moral support', but the composer's intermittent presence in his life during this year brought him to the threshold of a world he had known, as a bystander, throughout his Broadway days. Porter was in every way the opposite of Wodehouse. The outstanding composer and lyricist of his genera-tion, who first made a hit with 'Let's Do It, Let's Fall in Love', he was a phenomenon: rich, brilliant, and glamorous, a celebrity with a charming and dangerous edge. Wodehouse admired Cole Porter, and knew he was lucky to be working with him, but as the summer passed, he complained that it was hard to work with the globe-trotting composer, who was even more elusive than himself, and who seemed at times to conduct himself as a dilettante. Porter was married to Linda, a wealthy Southern belle, and famous to the public as an exotic showbiz creature with a penchant for outré costume balls and elaborate parties. For instance, he had been a prominent guest at Elsa Maxwell's 'Barnyard Frolic' on the Starlight roof of the Waldorf-Astoria, to which the New York society guests like Mrs Vincent Astor and Mr and Mrs Douglas Fairbanks senior came dressed as peasants, emulating the court of Louis XVI and Marie-Antoinette. On that occasion, Cole Porter arrived in a cowboy outfit with rhinestone boots and amused fellow guests with lasso tricks. Ethel Merman, whose career took off after *Anything Goes*, later commented that 'Cole had a reputation as a sophisticate and a hedonist . . . No other Broadway tunesmith enjoyed a similar image.' Wodehouse, who was clever and easygoing but neither sophisticated nor hedonistic, met Cole Porter as a fellow artist. To what extent he was aware of Porter's homosexuality is uncertain. He hardly ever referred to him in his letters, and certainly never to the duality in the composer's life.

Extravagant exhibitionism was the racy public face of Cole Porter. Privately, often apart from his wife, he was a lonely thrill-seeker who would cruise the 'houses' of Harlem for marijuana and male prostitutes. Homosexuality, which was still a serious crime, operated on two levels in the America of the 1930s. Publicly, it was held in contempt and spoken of with horrified loathing. Behind closed doors, it flourished as an exclusive secret society made up of men like Somerset Maugham, Noel Coward and Lorenz Hart. According to Leonard Spigelglass, a homosexual New Yorker with memories of the gay *demi-monde* in pre-war New York, this was 'a club you couldn't get into. . . . I remember those houses on 55th St, with butlers, and the carrying on.' Overtly disdained, covertly it flourished. 'On the one hand,' Spigelglass recalls, 'if you said, "They're homosexual", [then] "Oh my, isn't that terrible" was the reaction. On the other hand, if you said, "the other night I was at dinner with Cole Porter", the immediate reaction was "what did he have on?", "what did he say?", "were *you* at the party?" You had this awful ambivalence.'

Neither a social nor a sexual animal, Wodehouse had always preferred to work alone at his typewriter, have a quiet supper, retire to bed with a detective story, and let Ethel go to the parties and balls. But there was a side of Wodehouse that took pleasure in worldly pursuits; many of his friends and professional associates from New York and Hollywood enjoyed a louche, cosmopolitan lifestyle, and in Le Touquet he once more entered into a life of well-heeled pleasure that is only in part attributable to Ethel's unquenchable capacity for living life to the full. Besides, after the incessant wandering of recent years, Wodehouse could console himself with the thought that, having at first disliked Le Touquet, he was beginning to find his new home 'the one ideal spot in the world': within easy reach of England (Leonora, Dulwich and Townend); only two and a half hours from Paris (Ethel's shopping); and within motoring distance of Cherbourg (transatlantic embarkation once his tax troubles were settled). In addition, Le Touquet had both a golf course and a casino. By chance, Low Wood, the house that he and Ethel had looked at to buy ten years before, was available, and they quickly leased it. Ethel, ever restless, wanted to modernize and redecorate it, and they planned to move in during the spring of 1935.

Meanwhile, he was having 'a devil of a time with this musical comedy'. At first, Bolton was absent across the Channel on other theatrical business, then he blamed his troubles with the 'book' on a serious illness, while 'what has become of [Cole Porter], heaven knows. Last heard of at Heidelberg and probably one of the unnamed three hundred shot by Hitler.' It is often said that Wodehouse was remote from the realities of the wider political world, but when Hitler interfered in Austrian politics on 25 July, encouraging local Nazis to murder the Austrian Chancellor, Engelbert Dollfuss, in defiance of international opinion, it is clear that, naive though his response was, Wodehouse was abreast of the situation. He approved of the ostrich-like way in which Europe's leaders were ignoring the gathering storm. He wrote to Townend:

Bill, do you realise that in 1914 just about a tenth of what has been happening in Austria would have caused a world war? I think the world's reaction to the Dolfuss [*sic*] thing is a very healthy sign. It seems quite evident that nobody wants war nowadays. I would much rather have all this modern unrest than that sort of feeling of swollen simmering of 1914. The great thing nowadays is that you can't just say to the populace 'Hoy! The Peruvians have invaded Antigua. Pitch in and attack France.' They have to be told exactly what is in it for them before they start.

Predictably, this analysis was subordinate in his mind to the news that Ethel had smuggled Leonora's Pekinese, Boo, into the house, as a companion for the other Wodehouse Peke, Winky. He told his regular correspondents that 'two pekes . . . is the right number', and his letters at the time are full of affectionately observed doggy scenes.

Progress on 'Crazy Week' (now 'Hard to Get') was set back by two problems: Guy Bolton's illness apparently worsened, and there was a transatlantic liner disaster off the coast of New Jersey, a fire on board the *Morro Castle*, with the loss of 134 lives. All at once, Wodehouse was working 'almost single-handed' on a light-hearted shipboard frolic that now seemed distinctly inappropriate. As usual, when work was going badly, Wodehouse became melancholy and introspective. 'My particular trouble', he confessed to Townend, 'is that what I feel I should really like is to vegetate in one place all my life, and [yet] I spend my whole time whizzing about.' He also had to work on the musical up against a rehearsal deadline while Guy Bolton played truant in Sussex. Once the first draft had been dispatched to Aarons and Freedley in August, Wodehouse could relax. Bill and Rene Townend crossed over from Folkestone on a day trip, lunched with the Wodehouses at the Royal Picardy, inspected Low Wood and went for a walk in the afternoon sunshine among sand dunes and pine trees. Increasingly, this would be the tenor of life in Wodehouse's middle age.

Professionally, meanwhile, *Anything Goes*, whose title dropped into place during rehearsals, was turning out to be every bit as stressful as any previous Broadway production. The first Wodehouse–Bolton script of the show was what Lee Davis, the musical theatre historian, has called 'an antic Hollywood satire'. Both Wodehouse and Bolton were fresh from the inanities of Hollywood. In their first draft they could not resist making the smalltime gangster 'Moonface' McGhee (later, Moonface Martin) Public Enemy Number 13, a former scenario writer who introduces himself with 'I'm a fugitive from a chain gang', a line that could have been lifted from 'The Mulliners of Hollywood'. The broad and crazy outlines of the mad-cap plot – a young man named Billy, fired for buying the wrong stocks for his boss, who happens to be the father of Hope, the girl he is in love with (who is also sailing to Europe to marry an English peer), stows away on a transatlantic liner and becomes goofily involved with Reno Sweeney, a hardbitten nightclub singer, but after numerous alarums and excursions is united with his sweetheart – survived every subsequent revision, and remain unmistakably Wodehousian. This is remarkable because Freedley's first reaction to the script was outright dismay. The producer's telegram came as a shock. Wodehouse told Leonora that he and Bolton had 'had a ghastly cable from Freedley saying that our version was hopeless and that it was being rewritten by hirelings'. Subsequently, he always maintained that 'Howard Lindsay [the director] meant all along to swipe the piece, and he poisoned the minds of Vinton [Freedley] and the stars'. The situation at rehearsals in America was hardly helped by the co-writers' absence. Bolton's prolonged 'convalescence' and Wodehouse's unresolved tax difficulties prevented either from crossing the Atlantic in the autumn. Aarons and Freedley, unhappy with the script, with rehearsals looming, simply turned to the show's director, Howard Lindsay, and to his newly recruited associate, Russel ('Buck') Crouse, and asked them to rewrite the book, thus launching the career of one of the most successful 1930s show-business partnerships.

Wodehouse later claimed that only two lines of his original dialogue survived, but the producers decided to leave Bolton's and Wodehouse's names on the marquee. *Anything Goes*, starring Ethel Merman as 'Reno', Victor Moore as 'Moonface', and William Gaxton as 'Billy', opened on 21 November at the Alvin Theater, New York, and was instantly acclaimed a hit. Cole Porter described the show as 'perfect', one that required no tinkering after the opening night. Charles Cochran snapped up the rights to a London production, which would open the following June at the Palace Theatre. Wodehouse, who was on 2 per cent of the gross, a royalty that was not affected by the Lindsay–Crouse rewrite, found himself with a windfall to lift his spirits during his tax battles.

Anything Goes, which owes most of its popularity to Cole Porter's score, is rightly taken as an exuberant celebration of inter-war liberation. Porter was celebrating the fact that 'Times have changed' (the world, says the song, is full of fast cars, low bars, bare limbs and four-letter words). By contrast, when it came to Wodehouse's additions for the London run, he was uttering a heartfelt, if humorous, lament in key with his mood at the time:

> When maiden Aunts can freely chuckle
> At tales much too near the knuckle
> The facts disclose
> Anything goes.

When in the House our legislators
Are calling each other 'Traitors'
and 'So and so's'
Anything goes.
The world's in a state today
Like Billingsgate today
We are each today for free speech today
Nothing's blue today or taboo today
Or meets with scandalised 'Ohs'
But while we hope for days more sunny
The Government gets our money
'Cause Neville knows
Anything goes.

Wodehouse had admitted to Townend that he was 'in melancholy mood', though he never allowed this to interfere with work. Marooned in France during the autumn, he toyed with writing some new stories under an assumed name, speculated about adopting 'Eustace Trevelyan', and explored the possibility of reworking some of Townend's rejected material into his own fiction. Shortly after this, desperate for something to write, he had accepted a $10,000 commission for 'a novelette' from the *New York Herald Tribune*. The toing and froing on *Anything Goes* had not helped his struggle with the final chapters of his current novel, *The Luck of the Bodkins*. 'Usually,' he told Townend, 'when I get to the last fifty pages of a story, it begins to write itself. But this time everything went wrong and I had to grope my way through it at the rate of two pages a day.' There was a power cut as he approached the end, but he had somehow managed to finish it the next day (30 November), and though it was far too long, he was pleased. As the autumn drew to a close, and with Ethel away in London, he was becoming determined to settle in Le Touquet for good.

First, the beach was an ideal place to exercise Winky and Boo. There were adult advantages, too: the front at Paris-Plage was dotted with many attractively simple restaurants and hotels where, after a long seaside walk, Wodehouse and Ethel could enjoy lunch together before heading home to Low Wood for afternoon tea, and the evening's first cocktail. They were perfectly content in Le Touquet. 'I don't see a soul except Ethel,' he told Mackail, exaggerating as usual. Wodehouse's account of

Le Touquet life to his stepdaughter gives a more accurate picture of the couple in middle age:

The other night [he wrote to Leonora] I went to the Casino, had a shot at Roulette, won three *mille* in two minutes and came home. At seven a.m. Winky was restless, so I took her out, and we had been out about ten minutes when Mummie arrived, having been at the Casino all night and lost three *mille*. So we took the dogs for a walk and went in and had breakfast.

As much as ever, Wodehouse was walking everywhere – four miles to get the newspapers every day, and sometimes six miles and more with the dogs, making a weekly total of at least fifty miles. He was, he reported on his fifty-third birthday, 'most extraordinarily fit', and proudly noted that he was now older than Shakespeare. The sea air was wonderful and made him feel 'like a giant', and he was getting a lot of work done, which always improved his mood. Once, however, he had finished *The Luck of the Bodkins*, the blues returned. After 'eight months of terrific strain' he told Townend that he was feeling 'very let down and at a loose end'. He would be glad when April arrived and he could return to England once more.

The habit of incessant work never left him and he was encouraged by the settled routine of life at Low Wood. Once Christmas, a festival he always disliked for its bad memories of childhood, was over and it was the new year of 1935, he sent Leonora a freshly typed copy of *The Luck of the Bodkins* and began work on a stage farce, based on *Hot Water*, entitled *The Inside Stand* and commissioned by the actor Ralph Lynn. It was always his desire to write a really successful play, something Ethel also wanted him to do, and he approached the task with anxiety, telling Townend that it was 'a ghastly sweat' that would 'teach one a tremendous lot about construction'. He was always willing to learn, never took writing for granted, and never failed to approach his work in a spirit of self-critical honesty. In a letter addressed to Leonora at this time, discussing H. G. Wells's autobiography, he wrote that 'what kills an author is complacency. I've watched Wells getting more and more complacent for years and going all to pieces as a writer.' Although Leonora was now married, Wodehouse still took comfort from her role as confidante:

It's a relief to me to know that I've got you to tell me if I am going cuckoo in my work . . . the only way a writer can keep himself up to the mark is by examining each story quite coldly before he starts writing it and asking himself if it is all right *as a story*. I mean once you start saying to yourself, 'This is a pretty weak plot as it stands, but I'm such a hell of a writer that my magic touch will make it all right,' I believe you're done.

He did not need to worry: when it came to his own work, he knew his limitations, telling Townend at this time, 'I believe there are two ways of writing successful novels. One is mine, making the thing frankly a fairy story and ignoring real life altogether; the other is going right deep down into life and not caring a damn.'

Wodehouse's introspective mood during this first year in Low Wood coincided with several important developments in his professional life. After twenty-two years, Ella King-Hall (Mrs Westbrook) was forced to close her agency through ill-health, and Wodehouse transferred his British contracts to the London literary agency, A. P. Watt. At the same time, the *Saturday Evening Post*, which had been his mainstay for two decades, rejected *The Luck of the Bodkins*, a verdict with which, upon rereading the typescript, he concurred. He could now see that it was too long. After a month of anxiety, Reynolds sold it to the Chicago magazine *Red Book* for $27,500. Shortly after this good news, Raymond Needham wrote to say that the English tax authorities had decided not to pursue the case against him. By April, too, he had finished his play, *The Inside Stand*, and was celebrating Herbert Jenkins's publication of *Blandings Castle and Elsewhere*, a collection of short stories that included 'The Mulliners of Hollywood', the stories inspired by his MGM year.

Mr Mulliner, who had made his debut in 1926, was a character in tune with the times, with whom the middle-aged Wodehouse was very comfortable. He sits in the bar-parlour of the Angler's Rest, sipping his hot scotch and lemon, attended by the barmaid, Miss Postlethwaite. Like that other regular Wodehouse narrator, the Oldest Member, Mr Mulliner views a changing world and its human comedy with a philo-sophical, faintly misogynistic, equanimity, and tells stories, usually about his nephews, on a range of subjects dear to Wodehouse's heart. Mulliner's themes – the Church, Hollywood, golf, the literary life and affairs of the heart – cover a wide range of human experience.

Many of his stories speak to some of Wodehouse's nearest concerns:

Chance ('How true it is that in this world we can never tell behind what corner Fate may not be lurking with the brass knuckles'); marriage ('he had never contemplated matrimony, except with that shrinking horror which all middle-aged bachelors feel when the thought of it comes into their minds'); the stiff upper lip ('Well-bred and highly civilised, he knew how to wear the mask'); mothers ('Bobbie's mater might . . . be awfully glad to see him, but she did not look like it'); nannies ('a blend of Lucretia Borgia and a Prussian sergeant major'); transatlantic crossings ('you must have noticed the peculiar attitude towards the opposite sex induced by the salt air'); women ('the march of civilisation has done much to curb the natural ebullience of women'); headmasters ('you are suffering from the well-known Headmaster fixation or phobia'); and, of course, the Norman Conquest ('I come of a fighting line . . . My ancestor, Bishop Odo, was famous in William the Conqueror's day for his work with the battle-axe. So I biffed this bird'). Concealed among the roster of Mr Mulliner's preoccupations is Wodehouse's profound distaste for literary modernism. 'Came the Dawn', the story of Mulliner's nephew Lancelot Mulliner's career as a poet and how he became ensnared by Hollywood, contains a parody of T. S. Eliot, 'Darkling, a threnody', which reflects Wodehouse's loathing of the modern movement:

> Black branches,
> Like a corpse's withered hands,
> Waving against a blacker sky:
> Chill winds,
> Bitter, like the tang of half-remembered sins;
> Bats wheeling mournfully through the air,
> And on the ground
> Worms,
> Toads,
> Frogs,
> And nameless creeping things;
> And all around
> Desolation,
> Doom,
> Dyspepsia,
> and Despair.

> I am a bat that wheels through the air of Fate;
> I am a worm that wriggles in a swamp of Disillusionment;
> I am a despairing toad;
> I have got dyspepsia.

Mr Mulliner is not as memorable as Lord Emsworth or Bertie Wooster, but is Wodehouse's truly inter-war character, a self-satisfied, slightly pompous, well-fed creature of the weekly magazines, the wireless by the fire, and the long weekend in the country. Mr Mulliner is the kind of Englishman who goes to the pub after evensong, watches rugby football at Twickenham, and questions the monarchy only when it seems to be letting the side down. His idea of poetry is found in the work of his niece Charlotte whose 'Good Gnus' begins:

> When cares attack and life seems black,
> How sweet it is to pot a yak,
> Or puncture hares or grizzly bears,
> And others I could mention:
> But in my Animals 'Who's who'
> No name stand higher than the Gnu . . .

Mulliner reflects the mood of his author's middle age. In England, he spoke to Wodehouse's now substantial readership – devoted, middle class and conservative – and, as his author's spokesman, he was allowed to borrow his favourite minor characters, on leave from duty in Jeeves and Wooster's Mayfair or Blandings Castle: Roberta 'Bobbie' Wickham, Freddie Widgeon, and Barmy Fotheringay-Phipps.

The next step in Wodehouse's steady retreat from 'whizzing about' took place in June. 'Sensational news,' he wrote to Leonora. 'Yesterday we bought Low Wood!!!' He and Ethel had been in a fever of indecision, but Ethel, impetuous as usual, had closed the sale and he was pleased. 'I must say I am delighted,' he wrote to Leonora. 'I have grown fond of the house, and with the alterations we are going to make it will be fine. We came to the conclusion that we wanted to live in Le Touquet and that Low Wood was the best bet on account of the position.' Le Touquet, which he later described tongue-in-cheek as 'the safest place in Europe', was certainly ideal for the kind of lightning raids across the Channel that Wodehouse preferred. Soon after the house was purchased, taking Armine for moral support, he made one of his extremely rare visits to his mother in Bexhill, and found her 'frail, but not too bad'. Rich, famous and successful, Wodehouse was still intimidated by his mother, who did not die until 1941.

Now that *The Inside Stand* was with Ralph Lynn and the producers, and having no novel in view, Wodehouse was afflicted – not for the first, or last, time – with the feeling that he had 'used up all the plots'. In this condition, he was always receptive towards new offers of work. So when Cecil Hunt, the literary editor of the *Daily Mail*, wrote asking for an article on any subject of his choice, he responded at once with his customary eye on the American market. 'I won't write what isn't good enough to appear simultaneously in the *New Yorker* . . .' he told his new agent, A. P. Watt. 'If I can't get something which New York calls a "smacko" I would prefer to remain in dignified silence.' Dignity aside, by August he was contributing a piece about the Ideal Marriage Certificate, published as 'Woman, Come Clean', and was also in correspondence with Cecil Hunt about an article on haggis. 'I find the taste for these Daily Mail articles growing on me!' he confided to Watt. 'Has Hunt any more ideas? I am willing to tackle almost anything. I am at present in the throes of trying to think out a novel, and it is a relief to have a short bit of writing to do at intervals.' At the same time, he was 'sweating like blazes' on a production that was later dropped. But there were compensations in the progress of *The Inside Stand*. Wodehouse persuaded his son-in-law Peter Cazalet to put up £500 (half of the money required) to get the play produced out of town, and the first signs were encouraging. Wodehouse, who travelled to Glasgow for the first night, reported to Watt that 'the show looks v.g. Laughter all the time and business jumping £40 a night.' *The Inside Stand*, starring Ralph Lynn, opened in London on 21 November at the Saville Theatre, but closed after fifty performances. So his hopes for a hit play continued to be frustrated.

Nineteen thirty-five was a slow year, creatively, for Wodehouse, but in July he published one of his finest short stories, 'Uncle Fred Flits By', the tale of Lord Ickenham's visit to Mitching Hill, and was so pleased with this new character that, brooding on his next novel, he informed Townend 'in Uncle Fred I'm sure I have got a great character'. While he puzzled over an appropriate plot, he picked up the 'novelette' he had written the previous year for the *New York Herald Tribune* and began to consider its potential as a full-length novel. Privately, he knew that it was 'a shameless crib' of a late-Victorian boys' classic, F. Anstey's *Vice Versa*, but he hoped that no one would notice.

Laughing Gas, which reflects Wodehouse's lifelong interest in astral matters, is set in Beverly Hills, and tells the story of an Englishman, Reggie, the 3rd Earl of Havershot, and the Hollywood child star Joey Cooley, who exchange identities while under the ether in a dentist's chair. The novel is narrated by Havershot, who also provides the 'love interest' in his contrasting relationships with the star April June and the studio publicist Ann Bannister. Havershot is trapped for most of the action in Cooley's pampered, juvenile frame. This gives Wodehouse the opportunity to make several cracks against the absurdities of the Hollywood system, notably the deference paid to an English accent:

you can't heave a brick in Hollywood without beaning an English elocution teacher. The place is full of Britons on the make, and if they can't get jobs on the screen, they work the elocution-teaching racket . . . there are English elocution teachers making good money in Hollywood who haven't even got roofs to their mouths.

He is also satirical about the desperate measures adopted by out-of-work actors hoping to be noticed by the studio boss T. P. Brinkmeyer, providing a Californian variation on his lifelong observation of the servant class, in this instance a Filipino footman:

'Sure,' he said, in faultless American. 'You got me right, brother . . . One of these days, if I can catch the old buzzard alone and he can't duck, I'm going to uncork a rapid-fire dialect monologue with the tear behind the smile that'll make Mr Brinkmeyer sign on the dotted line . . . We're most of us in the profesh downstairs.'

No one, in Wodehouse's version of Hollywood, is quite as they seem. Even the butler has missed his vocation:

'Ah Hollywood, Hollywood . . . Bright city of sorrows, where fame deceives and temptation lurks, where souls are shrivelled in the furnace of desire, whose streets are bathed with the shamed tears of betrayed maidens.'
  'Keep it clean.'
  'Hollywood! Home of mean glories and spangled wretchedness . . .'

Wodehouse's joke against screenwriters takes off when Cooley/ Havershot is kidnapped by aspiring screenwriters angry at the studio moguls' importation of British and New York literary talent. The two protagonists return to their own bodies only after a bicycle collision that briefly knocks them unconscious. The novel – a unique part of Wodehouse's output – faithfully reflects many aspects of his experience, including a fictionalized version of his *Los Angeles Times* interview: 'I hold strong views on the films . . . I told her what I thought was wrong with the pictures, threw out a few personal criticisms of the leading stars . . . Miss Wycherley got up and said it had all been most interesting and she was sure she had got some excellent material for tomorrow's paper.'

The perfect opportunity to revise and expand *Laughing Gas* came in the new year of 1936. Low Wood was again in the hands of the builders. Wodehouse and Ethel took off for a six-week stay in St Moritz, another spot he hated, pronouncing it to be a 'White Hell'. His solution to the unbearable social side of a ski resort was to work in his room till lunchtime, take an hour-long walk in the sunshine, and then retreat back to his room until bedtime.

The Wodehouses returned to Low Wood in the spring. There were good reasons to be near England again. Leonora was about to give birth to her second child, and Ethel was suffering from a mysterious but quite serious ailment, on top of persistent rheumatism, which would shortly require a 'cure' in London, and then major surgery. Wodehouse detested the intrusion of pain and suffering in his life and, when it involved those close to him, he was either (as with Ethel) laconic or (as with Leonora) agitated. 'This is just a line to tell you how much I love you,' he wrote as his stepdaughter's pregnancy advanced, 'and how much I am thinking of you. I am praying that you won't have too bad a time, because you're very precious to me. . . . I can't bear the thought of you being in pain. . . . tonight I shall take out all your old letters and read them.'

When Leonora's son, Edward, was safely born, the delighted grandfather made one of his cross-Channel dashes, and then returned to Le Touquet. The refurbishment of Low Wood was not yet complete, and Ethel had taken another house nearby. Alone with Winky and Boo, he found the dogs much less inclined to fight. 'My belief is that Ethel is the disturbing influence,' he told Townend. 'This peacefulness started

when she left.' Such disclosures, even to Townend, are almost unprecedented. Even with his closest friend, he was extraordinarily discreet, at
least on paper. So when, in June 1936, Townend, whose literary career
had faltered into virtually nothing, proposed collecting their thirty-year
correspondence into a sort of joint autobiography, Wodehouse's reaction
was guarded. 'A thing we've got to remember about the letters', he
warned, 'is that they were written very quick and with no idea of
publication.' Then there was the problem of mutual friends. One of the
letters Townend had forwarded to his friend to help make the case for
the book had contained some sentences about Denis Mackail which
had given Wodehouse pause. 'I don't want this book to make me any
enemies. But I can fix all that all right.' Much more alarming, from
Wodehouse's point of view, was what he considered to be the raw
directness of the material. After, for him, a long delay of nearly a month,
while he worked at the troublesome first chapter of *Summer Moonshine*,
he set out his real reservations to Townend:

I'll tell you what I feel about the letters book . . . the stuff is too private and
intimate. I don't believe it would interest the general reader. There is too much
about Pekes and Dulwich. In short, the letters are what they were intended
to be – of interest to you personally. What I feel is that we must fake them
a lot. They must be rewritten with an eye to the public.

Six months later, he returned to the subject, with the remarkable admission that while he found the correspondence absorbing, the letters
seemed, to him, 'so infernally intimate. I pour out my heart to you,
without stopping to weigh what I am writing.' Townend got the message.
When the 'letters book' idea resurfaced in the 1950s, Wodehouse had
both more and less to hide, but an even bigger reason for re-presenting
himself to the public. For the moment ('You can imagine the relief'),
the good news from America was that the tax authorities in Washington
had finally settled his case. Now he was free at last to visit America
again. Within three months, he was sailing to Hollywood on the
Normandie, under contract to MGM once more.

15. 'I am leading a very quiet life here'
(1936-1937)

Few who have not experienced it can realise the eerie solitude of a
motion-picture studio . . . The world seems very far away. Outside, the
sun beats down on the concrete, and occasionally you will see a man in
shirt sleeves driving a truck to a distant set . . . But for the most part a
forlorn silence prevails. ('The Castaways')

It was an odd decision, Wodehouse's return to California. When he left
Hollywood in the autumn of 1931, he had never expected to go back
and, in public at least, was loud in his expressions of disdain for the
place. 'The Mulliners of Hollywood' stories were intended as a final
goodbye, not an au revoir. 'Now that the pay envelope has ceased,' he
had written to Mackail, after MGM did not renew his contract, 'maybe
I shall be able to write some stuff knocking them good.' But, as with
his experience of the Hongkong and Shanghai Bank thirty years before,
his feelings about working for an institution were complicated, and
when, in June 1934, he received an offer from Paramount to go back
there at $1,500 a week, he was strangely pleased. On that occasion, his
tax difficulties meant he had to refuse 'as I am Public Enemy Number
One', but nonetheless he found the offer 'rather gratifying after the way
Hollywood took a solemn vow three years ago never to mention my
name again'.

Hollywood had done no such thing. Wodehouse exaggerated the
studios' response to his *Los Angeles Times* interview, and did not understand the film community's notoriously short institutional memory. In
the interim, the big studios had weathered the worst of the Depression.
MGM, Twentieth Century–Fox, Warner Brothers and Paramount were
all flourishing again. By 1936 they were once more on the look-out
for new screenwriting talent and new properties, with Wodehouse very
much in play as a writer. Fox, for instance, was already filming *Thank
You, Jeeves* with Arthur Treacher in the title role, and David Niven
playing Bertie Wooster. At MGM, despite the recent vicissitudes of the

business, Sam Goldwyn and Irving Thalberg were still the managerial and creative dynamo; the company was shooting films of *Piccadilly Jim* and *Anything Goes,* and Thalberg, who liked Wodehouse, had stubbornly not abandoned the idea of bringing *Rosalie,* the 1928 Ruritanian musical, to the screen. For Wodehouse, the MGM invitation came at exactly the right moment. His American tax troubles appeared to be behind him; the revised text of *Laughing Gas* was with the publishers; he had completed the vital preliminary work on *Summer Moonshine*; and he had not been to America for five years. Ethel celebrated by acquiring, just before they sailed, yet another Pekinese, a female puppy named Wonder.

The return journey to Hollywood was valedictory, and bittersweet. Reaching the East Coast, Wodehouse decided to pay a quick visit to Philadelphia to see George Lorimer at the *Saturday Evening Post.* Lorimer was due to retire in January, but Wodehouse was not just saying goodbye. In his mercenary way he was pursuing $2,000 he felt was owed to him for his story, 'The Crime Wave at Blandings'. Lorimer was not fazed by his star writer's debt-collecting mission but was, apparently, nonplussed at his massive, shiny scalp: 'he had not seen me since the days when I had thick black hair,' Wodehouse reported. Lorimer would be replaced by Wesley Stout, with whom Wodehouse had a less cordial relationship.

There was some bad news en route for Hollywood. Irving Thalberg, who was never in robust health, had died, aged thirty-seven. He had rehearsed a 'pageant' in heavy rain, while nursing a bad cold. On 13 September his strep throat was diagnosed as pneumonia. The next day he was dead. Thalberg's impressive funeral was national news. Clark Gable, Fredric March and Douglas Fairbanks were among the ushers. Wodehouse was uncomfortable with pain and loss and never referred to this tragedy in his correspondence, but he often said, later, how much he missed Thalberg. Life at MGM would not be the same, but there was, of course, no turning back. Soon he was heading west again, on the *Chief.*

'Well, here we are,' Wodehouse wrote to Townend, a month after arrival, 'settled in a house miles away up at the top of a mountain, surrounded by canyons in which I am told rattlesnakes abound.' Nothing speaks so eloquently about Wodehouse's mood of detachment from the movie world on his second Hollywood sojourn than the spectacular isolation of his new home, 1315 Angelo Drive. The house, which belonged to Gayelord Hauser, the best-selling diet guru and homosexual confidant of Greta Garbo, was a newly built, English-style mansion on the wild, unpopulated outskirts of Beverly Hills, with an astounding view of the city below and the ocean in the distance. The property was built into the hillside on different levels, had a superb swimming pool, and guaranteed privacy and seclusion. Their nearest neighbour, the actor Nelson Eddy, was several hundred yards away up the hill, and Wodehouse's cricket-loving friend, the actor Charles Aubrey Smith, had a house still further up Angelo Drive.

The Wodehouses lived here much more quietly than before – Leonora was not around to liven things up – but they soon renewed their friendship with Maureen O'Sullivan, who had recently married the Australian writer turned film director John Farrow. O'Sullivan picked up with 'Ethel and Plummie . . . as though no time at all had passed', and the Farrows soon became regular visitors to the house, taking a special delight in the new puppy. There was, however, none of the old social whirl of Benedict Canyon Drive and, in addition to the more sober mood, there was bad news from home.

Shortly after the Wodehouses arrived in California, at the beginning of October, the news reached them that Armine had died. His younger brother's response was typical. To Nella, Armine's widow, Wodehouse wrote that this was 'a stunning blow' that left him 'quite numbed by the shock of it'. Movingly, Wodehouse spoke of 'the gap in my life which can never be filled'. But the relationship between the two men was more complicated than that. Within the family, Armine had always described his brother's writing as 'beautiful rubbish'; Wodehouse for his part directed gentle teasing at Armine – jokes about the theosophists. Just before his death, Armine had written his brother a letter. Wodehouse claimed to have appreciated his brother's candour and graciously acknowledged to Nella 'how absolutely right [Armine] was in his criticisms of my work'. Plainly, some forty years after the inexplicable denial of that Oxford place, there were still things between the brothers that were unresolved. Now, having penned a conventional expression of grief, Wodehouse's actions made their own statement. While Ethel returned to England to join the mourners, comfort Nella and visit her daughter and grandchildren, Wodehouse stayed behind in California. He began to work, once again, on the *Rosalie* screenplay.

At first, the omens were promising. In 1931 the musical had been considered a hopeless commercial proposition, but now it was the original version of 1928 that was in favour. Bill McGuire, who had co-written the original book with Guy Bolton, had made a successful transition to Hollywood as a screenwriter and had a recent hit, *The Great Ziegfeld*, to recommend him to the bosses. 'Everything looks very bright,' Wodehouse reported to Leonora; 'anything [McGuire] approves of will go by with Sam Katz [the MGM producer in charge of the project].' He added, optimistically: 'I think I have got a good lay-out, and I have been working hard on it, having done half of it in three weeks.' Wodehouse's familiar insouciance towards screenwriting concealed a new note of anxiety. 'Have you ever done any picture work?' he asked his novelist friend Claude Houghton. 'It is quite interesting, but I hate having to condense my dialogue as one has to do. I can't seem to get used to writing a couple of lines for a scene between two characters, where in a novel you would be able to extend yourself to a page or so.' His work on *Rosalie* was not helped by the fact that he was, simultaneously, completing his new novel, *Summer Moonshine*.

His hopes for the movie were soon disappointed and by new year 1937 his participation in the production of *Rosalie* was turning sour. He was, he said, 'being quietly frozen out'. His 'old friend' Bill McGuire turned out to be nothing of the sort. Everything he turned in McGuire rewrote, keeping the substance of Wodehouse's work, but changing it enough so that he could tell his superiors that it was his own work. 'Eventually,' Wodehouse explained to Bolton, 'it got so that I couldn't make any progress.' At this point, MGM made it clear to Wodehouse that they had wanted McGuire to do the script by himself all along (he had, after all, been the co-author of the stage version) and that they would not be renewing Wodehouse's contract when it expired in April. 'There seems to be a curse over M-G-M, as far as I am concerned,' he complained to Townend, and turned his attention to the final pages of *Summer Moonshine*, which he swiftly sold to the *Saturday Evening Post* for $40,000. There was talk of more movie work with other producers, but a studio strike was looming and nothing was definite.

Even before Wodehouse's break with MGM, his tempo was more andante than allegro. 'I am leading a very quiet life here,' he told Townend. Unless there was a call from the studio, he would stay around the house all day, except for his regular one-hour afternoon walk. Occasionally there were visitors. Paul Reynolds's son, Revere, told Leonora that he had visited Hollywood and taken tea with her parents. Sometimes Wodehouse would have lunch with Leonora's friends, and send her bits of gossip about them. 'Helen Wills is getting a divorce!!' he wrote. 'I thought she would.' With Leonora, he could become quite uninhibited, for instance reporting a local scandal about the English actor Henry Daniell and his wife. 'Apparently', he told Leonora,

they go down to Los Angeles and either (a) indulge in or (b) witness orgies – probably both . . . there's something pleasantly domestic about a husband and wife sitting side by side with their eyes glued to peepholes, watching the baser element whoop it up. And what I want to know is – where are these orgies? I feel I've been missing something.

The fabulous wealth and many temptations of 1930s Hollywood attracted all kinds of louche characters who hoped to break into the movies. (One of these, an enigmatic young German called Werner Plack, who worked part-time as a wine-shipper, became acquainted with the Wodehouses and would later play a decisive role in their lives.) Meanwhile, up on Angelo Drive there was not much partying while Ethel convalesced after her operation, and in winter the pool was too cold for swimming. After dinner, Wodehouse and Ethel would retire to their rooms at half past eight, where they would read and listen to the radio. Wodehouse, enjoying a quiet life, took pleasure in describing to Townend the antics of the two dogs: 'My day starts when I hear the puppy [Wonder] bark in Ethel's room. I open the door, and she, the puppy, comes leaping out. Winky then pokes her head out of my bed, in which she has been sleeping, and I take them downstairs.'

Ethel had accumulated quite a staff to help her keep house and, at the beginning of 1937, the live-in couple who served meals and did the housework were joined by a fifty-cents-an-hour temp secretary, a young woman named Frances Mayer, who has provided a vivid picture of the domestic life of the Wodehouses in Angelo Drive. Miss Mayer (now Fran Ershler) was taken on to help Ethel catch up with paperwork after her operation. Ershler recalls that the only letter she typed for Wodehouse, who generally did his own typing and looked after his own correspondence, was to a champagne company, asking for a complimentary case in exchange for a mention in one of his *Post* stories. 'Miss Mayer' quite quickly seems to have taken the place in the household formerly occupied by Leonora, becoming, she says, 'almost one of the family'.

At first, her duties ended at four in the afternoon. Then, one day, Wodehouse, who obviously liked her, invited her to stay to tea, saying that if she would drive him to the English bakery in Beverly Hills to get a cake, he could return his library books. Soon this trip had become another fixed point in his daily routine. Frances, Wodehouse, Winky and Wonder would pile into her car, a roomy art deco saloon, the DeSoto Airflow, drive down the hill to the bakery, collect some buns, exchange books at the local library, and return for afternoon tea. They would sit in the magnificent picture window of 1315 Angelo Drive to watch the city lights come on in the twilight below. 'It was so comfortable, and he was always so charming,' Ershler remembers. As tea drew to a close, Ethel and Wodehouse, habitually dressed in khaki cotton trousers and short-sleeved shirts, would press her to stay for cocktails and then to dinner (usually meat and two veg, with a simple pudding). Gradually they established a postprandial ritual known as 'B & Bs' (benedictine and brandy) which made the twenty-year-old a little bit tipsy before her drive home down the hill.

Fran Ershler recalls that Wodehouse was always very relaxed and congenial, and 'very, very easy to talk to about anything', but that Ethel 'could be difficult to deal with', perhaps because she was in considerable dental pain. Despite this, Ethel 'took care of all the burdens of the house', and was also engaged in a tireless correspondence with Leonora about the refurbishment of Low Wood, exchanging swatches of potential fabric by post. Ershler remembers Wodehouse as perfectly content, but his letters to Townend tell a different story. 'I am getting very fed up with life here,' he complained in March 1937.

I don't find the people so attractive as last time. And there seems nowhere to go. I mean, when you have a let-down like one always gets after finishing a novel [*Summer Moonshine*], it seems impossible to get a real change . . . What I liked about Le Touquet was that in a few hours I could get to London and be in an entirely new atmosphere.

There were, however, some distractions to keep him interested. David Selznick wanted him to do 'a thing called *The Earl of Chicago*' (which came to nothing), and whizz-kid Walter Wanger, who had just signed a ten-year producing contract with United Artists, had an idea for a Hollywood satire, based on Clarence Buddington Kelland's *The Stand-In*, about the Wall Street takeover of a fictional 'Colossal Pictures', running into union trouble. 'I turned it down,' Wodehouse reported to Townend. 'I got myself in bad enough last time by criticising Hollywood, and didn't want to do a picture which would have been an indictment of the studios.' Next, he was put up to do comic dialogue for a Warner Brothers version of Robin Hood, but the idea fizzled out. There was also talk of a Grace Moore picture for Columbia. His chronic anxieties began to return. 'I'm not worth the money my agent insists on asking for me,' he told Townend. 'After all, my record here is eighteen months at a huge salary, with only small parts of pictures to show for it.' Only the completion of a new novel, he felt, would vindicate his stay.

As spring turned to summer, Wodehouse could interest himself in cricket again. The English test cricket captain, G. O. 'Gubby' Allen, whom he had recently met in Le Touquet, had stopped in Los Angeles on his way home from losing the latest Ashes series in Australia. Wodehouse saw a lot of him and heard all the cricket gossip. 'He told me the whole inside story of the Bodyline crisis,' he informed Townend. Wodehouse persuaded Allen to turn out for the Hollywood Cricket Club for a match against Pasadena, a game in which Allen scored 77 and a young David Niven, fresh from starring in *Thank You, Jeeves*, made 15. The club Wodehouse had founded in 1931 with Charles Aubrey Smith had become a flourishing part of the expat community in Hollywood and a fashionable feature on the scene. Its members now included some big stars: Boris Karloff, George Arliss and Errol Flynn. Wodehouse was an enthusiastic supporter, and served as a vice-president during his year at Angelo Drive. There is no record that he ever actually played.

Once he was released from his MGM contract, he could focus his attention on a new novel, and told Reynolds that he hoped to complete a new serial before he departed for England. A month later, he reported to Reynolds that he had 'got out a very good plot' for another Jeeves novel. 'The only catch', he added, was that 'I have got to do a picture first, which may take about six weeks.' RKO had just approached him to adapt *A Damsel in Distress*. This had already been filmed in 1919 with a Guy Bolton script and then successfully adapted for the stage by Ian Hay in 1928. Now the Gershwin brothers had persuaded Pandro S. Berman, an RKO producer celebrated for his Fred Astaire movies *The Gay Divorcee* and *Top Hat*, to reacquire the screen rights. George Gershwin had been friends with Wodehouse on and off ever since he had played the piano at the rehearsals of *Miss 1917*; he and his brother Ira had collaborated triumphantly with Wodehouse on *Oh, Kay!* and were now living not far away in Beverly Hills. Gershwin was convinced that the character of George Bevan, the American composer in the original novel, was based on him, and had already composed a number of songs, to Ira's lyrics, for interpolation in any future screenplay. In addition to the attraction of Gershwin's score (which had numbers like 'A Foggy Day', 'Nice Work if You Can Get It' and 'Stiff Upper Lip', an Ira Gershwin tribute to Wodehouse), the novel's romantic lead appealed to RKO as an ideal role for its contract star Fred Astaire, who was looking for a new picture.

Work started at once, and, as usual, Wodehouse set to in a blaze of optimism. 'I must say,' he enthused to Leonora, 'it is altogether different working at RKO on a picture based on my own novel from being on a salary at M-G-M and sweating away on *Rosalie*. I like my boss Pandro Berman very much. He is the first really intelligent man I have come across here – bar Thalberg, whom he rather resembles.' At first, Wodehouse was simply hired to polish a draft screenplay, but it bore no resemblance to the novel and, when it was discarded, after a script conference at Lucey's restaurant, Wodehouse was brought in to do a new version with Ernest Pagano, an easygoing Hollywood veteran who had been a gag-man in the days of silent movies. During his first Hollywood visit, Wodehouse's mood had swung wildly with the ups and downs of studio politics, and now he was having the same experience. 'What uncongenial work picture writing is,' Wodehouse moaned to Townend. 'It makes one feel as if one were working with one's hands tied.' However, in the middle of July, writing to Leonora, he was all optimism:

Everything is made very pleasant for me, and I like the man I am working with – a chap named Pagano. The way we work is, we map out a sequence together, then I go home and write the dialogue, merely indicating business, and he takes what I have done and puts it into screenplay shape. Thus relieving me of all that 'truck shot' 'wipe dissolve' stuff! It is also very pleasant to be working on something that you know is a real live production and not something that might be produced or may be put away in a drawer for years! As far as I can gather we are going to start shooting this picture in about a week.

In the midst of this came George Gershwin's sudden and unexpected death, on 11 July, from a brain tumour. Wodehouse reported the black comedy of the composer's fatal decline with unusual directness:

Everybody treated the thing so lightly. (I mean at first.) We had asked him to our party, and he couldn't come and Mrs Ira Gershwin said that it was 'simply something psychological' – in other words, rather suggesting that he had had a fit of temperament because Sam Goldwyn didn't like a couple of his songs. On the night of our party, too, Mrs Edward G. Robinson invited us to a party she was giving for George Gershwin on the night of July 14. I said we should love to come, but wasn't he supposed to be ill? She smiled in a sort of indulgent, knowing way and said 'Oh *he's* all right. He'll be there,' – again suggesting that he was doing a sort of prima donna act. Then last Sunday in the paper was the news that he had been operated on for a tumor in the brain, and a few hours later he was dead.

Gershwin's death cast a shadow over the production of *A Damsel in Distress*, and sent Wodehouse's spirits into a tailspin. Two weeks later he was exclaiming to Townend, 'Gosh, I'm sick of California! I can't think how I ever liked it. I feel as if I had been here all my life.' But there was no time to be downcast. Shooting on *A Damsel in Distress* commenced before the script was complete – Wodehouse signed off on 14 August – and continued until October. He was pleased to see his work actually translated to the screen. 'I have really come across with some good stuff, so that my name is big in the picture world,' he boasted to Leonora. 'Wodehouse, the man who gets paid $1500 a week for mere charm of manner has been supplanted by Wodehouse, the fellow who delivers the goods', adding that 'I think I have made a big hit in my work on this picture.' He reported that George Stevens, the director of *A Damsel in Distress*, had actually telephoned him at home to congratulate him on the script.

A Damsel in Distress starred Fred Astaire, but not Ginger Rogers, who wanted to pursue her own career as a straight actress and was currently filming *Stage Door*. Wodehouse's screenplay basically followed the plot of the novel, but merged or dropped many of its characters, so that the film bears only a passing resemblance to the original. George Bevan becomes Jerry Halliday (Astaire) whose romantic screen partner, in place of Rogers, was Joan Fontaine, a poor dancer who did not succeed as a star until *Rebecca* in 1940, and who later complained to Astaire that *A Damsel in Distress* 'put my career back four years'. Without Rogers, and to boost the appeal of the film, the comedians George Burns and Gracie Allen were drafted in to play Jerry Halliday's press agent and secretary, using their own names as usual. Wodehouse later told Hedda Hopper that he wished he had known Gracie Allen was going to be in the picture as 'she's one of the funniest women I've ever met', but it is clear from his notes that, originally conceived as 'a Vaudeville couple', Burns and Allen, a celebrated double-act, were part of his first scenario. Allen's presence in the picture would inspire two innovative dance routines, neither of which had much to do with the plot.

Not everyone was as impressed as Wodehouse with his contribution to *A Damsel in Distress*. The producer Pandro Berman, wary of the novelist as screenwriter, and unsure of Pagano's usefulness, had taken the precaution of assigning Allan Scott, one of the co-writers on the Fred Astaire–Ginger Rogers musicals, to babysit the production. Scott's recollections, possibly coloured by his political sympathies as an early advocate of the Screen Writers Guild, are not flattering:

When Wodehouse would occasionally show up for a conference, he would listen to what I proposed and would say, 'Amazing, my boy, keep it up!' Then he'd head off for lunch somewhere. He used to drive Berman crazy. Wodehouse was getting $6,000 a week. He would come in and sit in the first quadrangle on the bench and peruse a two-week-old copy of *The Times* of London. Pan [i.e. Pandro], exasperated, would watch him from his window. This went on for approximately ten weeks. When I had finished the script, he said once again, doubtless with his quiet irony, 'Amazing, old boy, simply amazing – what you did to my little story!' He said he would like to make changes, so I gave him the script and he took it home and came back. I searched through the script, and found one change he had made in red ink. I had written for someone to say, 'Well, I'm off.' He had re-written it to say, 'Pip, pip, I'm off, chaps.'

There was a new, politically aware generation emerging in Hollywood, screenwriters and directors with strong sympathies for the great European causes of the day such as the Spanish Civil War. In the politically committed climate of the mid-1930s, Allan Scott and his generation did not have much time for the 'mentally negligible', politically immature characters who flitted about Bertie Wooster's Mayfair and the well-appointed grounds of Blandings Castle – or for their author. Shortly after Wodehouse left the set of *A Damsel in Distress* he became embroiled in a row that is especially interesting for being political rather than artistic, and for the way it illuminates his conservative instincts, and his isolation from current affairs.

During the 1930s, after years of exploitation by the big producers like Zanuck, Goldwyn and Mayer, the screenwriters of Hollywood became militant. When they realized, in the unguarded words of one, that 'they were still the niggers of the studio system', they decided to form a union, the Screen Writers Guild (SWG) to press for better pay and conditions, especially in the vexed matter of screen credits. The studios, panicked by the screenwriters' new-found militancy, refused to recognize the SWG and branded its leaders, who included Dashiell Hammett and Lillian Hellman, left-wing communist agitators, an accusation that foreshadowed the 1950s McCarthyite assault on Hollywood. By no means everyone supported the SWG which like all new radical organizations had its noisy, hotheaded and intransigent elements. A rival, more moderate and conservative-minded organization, Screen Playwrights (SP) – founded in opposition to the SWG – was instantly recognized by the producers, causing much resentment within the community. Wodehouse was a prominent member of Screen Playwrights and when, in response to an appeal for support, he wrote to Philip Dunne, chairman of the membership committee of the SWG, disingenuously asking for a clarification of its role, he provoked the fiery young screenwriter to an intemperate diatribe which effectively accused Wodehouse of collaborating with the bosses. Wodehouse responded to Dunne's letter of 23 August by showing it to his SP associates, who decided it gave them the *casus belli* they had been looking for and sued the SWG for libel on Wodehouse's behalf, naming in the suit various SWG members like Hammett, Hellman, Donald Ogden Stewart and Dorothy Parker. This was industry news. *Variety* published Dunne's letter in full, and all hell broke loose.

At the time, Wodehouse, released from his duties on *A Damsel in Distress*, was working with an English director, Eddie Goulding, a friend from London days, on a film whose story he disliked. Now he was plunged into distasteful public controversy, just as he had been in 1931. This time, at least, the issue was confined to Hollywood and did not even make national headlines. When the libel suit came before a Los Angeles judge, a jovial Democrat named Robert W. Kenny, the case was dismissed on the grounds that, as it was a political matter, issues of libel could not apply. Wodehouse had been debating whether to stay on in California until the following spring. Now his mind was made up. He would sail for France as soon as possible, at the end of October. 'Bill, I hate this place!' he exclaimed to Townend, not mentioning the imminent lawsuit.

Not the place itself, mind you . . . but the people. If I don't have to go out to parties, it's fine. I work up to lunch, then go for a walk and have a swim, work till dinner, and up to my room at 8.30 to read and listen to the radio. I enjoy that. But I get so bored by the people I have to meet, especially at big parties. I would like to be an absolute hermit. . . . Of course part of the trouble is that I don't like doing pictures. The *Damsel in Distress* was great fun, because I was working under the best producer here and with a man I liked and on my own story, which they hardly altered at all. But as a rule pictures are a bore. And just now I am pining to get at a new novel, which I have all mapped out.

Wodehouse might have been out of sympathy with the politics of his times, but he was not completely out of touch. 'Our great excitement here is waiting for the ten o'clock news bulletin,' he reported to Townend. 'What a hell of a mess the world has got into!'

Two weeks later, after the usual frenzy of packing, he and Ethel were driven to the Pasadena railroad station by his West Coast agent, Bill Stevens, to begin the journey home to Le Touquet. Frances Mayer, who went along to say goodbye, remembers Wodehouse's sadness at departure, and Ethel's excitement at the journey and the prospect of seeing Leonora and her children.

16. 'I have become a biggish bug these days' (1937–1939)

'I wonder if you have noticed a rather rummy thing about it – viz. that it is everywhere. You can't get away from it. Love, I mean. Wherever you go, there it is, buzzing along in every class of life.' (*The Code of the Woosters*)

The world to which Wodehouse returned at the end of 1937 was indeed in a hell of a mess. Japan had invaded China. Europe was gripped by fascism, terror and the threat of war. In the Soviet Union, Stalin's latest purges were at their peak. The persecution of the Jews in Germany was driving refugees to London, New York and Los Angeles. In March 1938, Hitler marched into Vienna and annexed Austria. Churchill told the Commons that Europe was 'confronted with a programme of aggression, nicely calculated and timed, unfolding stage by stage'. In September, Britain almost went to war with Hitler when Germany occupied Czechoslovakia, a crisis averted by Chamberlain's disastrous 'peace with honour' at Munich. His climb-down rocked the government; many British conservative parliamentarians believed that Britain should have fought to defend the Czechs. Duff Cooper, First Lord of the Admiralty, resigned in protest. In less than a year, Britain would enter the war against Hitler that Chamberlain had struggled so earnestly to avoid.

The novel that Wodehouse wrote on the brink of world catastrophe, *The Code of the Woosters*, had already been mapped out in California. In some respects, 'The Silver Cow' (as it was originally called) is as sublimely detached from reality as *The Swoop!*, but it also bears the imprint of the times in which it was written. There are references to Mussolini, to 'a Dictator on the point of starting a purge', to 'Red propaganda'. And there is Roderick Spode – 'Big chap with a small moustache and the sort of eye that can open an oyster at sixty paces.' Spode, always referred to as 'the Dictator', is plainly modelled on Sir Oswald Mosley, the self-styled leader of the British Union of Fascists, or 'Blackshirts', based in London's East End. According to Bertie

Wooster, Spode is 'the founder and head of the Saviours of Britain, a Fascist organisation better known as the Black Shorts. His general idea, if he doesn't get knocked on the head with a bottle in one of the frequent brawls in which he and his followers indulge, is to make himself a Dictator.' While Wodehouse could escape from threatening reality into Wooster-shire, even he could not ignore it altogether. His devastating portrait of Spode is not only a clear indication of his political sympathies but also a characteristic use of humour to defuse a bad situation, and obliquely to suggest the virtues of tolerance through an infuriating tease.

The Code of the Woosters takes off from the point in *Right Ho, Jeeves* where Gussie Fink-Nottle's engagement to Madeline Bassett has been 'severed', as Jeeves puts it, after her fiancé has disgraced himself at Market Snodsbury Grammar School, and tells the story of Bertie Wooster's entanglement with Aunt Dahlia, Sir Watkyn Bassett, Roderick Spode and an elusive silver cow-creamer. The novel, one of his finest, is supremely demonstrative of Wodehouse's art, what he had called 'making the thing frankly a fairy story and ignoring real life altogether'. It begins *in medias res*, and at top speed:

I reached out a hand from under the blankets, and rang the bell for Jeeves.
    'Good evening, Jeeves.'
    'Good morning, sir.'
    This surprised me.
    'Is it morning?'
    'Yes, sir.'
    'Are you sure? It seems very dark outside.'
    'There is a fog, sir. If you will recollect, we are now in Autumn – season of mists and mellow fruitfulness.'
    'Season of what?'
    'Mists, sir, and mellow fruitfulness.'
    'Oh? Yes. Yes, I see. Well, be that as it may, get me one of those bracers of yours, will you?'
    'I have one in readiness, sir, in the ice-box.'

A masterpiece of narrative bravura, the action is largely concentrated into one long, hectic day and subsequent night. Even the preamble, some twenty pages, is crowded with incident and character, chiefly the introduction of Sir Watkyn Bassett CBE ('Slice him where you like, a hellhound is always a hellhound'), Roderick Spode and the cow-creamer. Wodehouse had always nurtured an admiration for Conan Doyle's detective stories and the plot of *The Code of the Woosters* is an oblique comic tribute to a former mentor: 'an imbroglio that would test the Wooster soul as it had seldom been tested before . . . the sinister affair of Gussie Fink-Nottle, Madeline Bassett, old Pop Bassett, Stiffy Byng, the Rev. H. P. ("Stinker") Pinker, the eighteenth-century cow-creamer and the small, brown, leather-covered notebook.' Wodehouse is proud of this one, and he tells the reader as much at the outset: '"Man and boy, Jeeves," I said, breaking a thoughtful silence . . . "I have been in some tough spots in my time, but this one wins the mottled oyster".' Wodehouse seems to revel in winding the plot up to a higher and higher pitch of complexity. 'Jeeves,' says Bertie, not yet one-third of the way through the narrative, 'stand by to counsel and advise. The plot has thickened.'

There are so many complications to come that the reader can scarcely imagine how Wodehouse is going to get himself out of the narrative straitjacket into which he has so cheerfully crammed himself. In the remaining nine chapters, Wodehouse will not only have 'Stinker' Pinker steal Constable Eustace Oates's helmet, and Aunt Dahlia threaten to trade her magnificent chef, Anatole, for Sir Watkyn Bassett's cow-creamer, but he will also have Bertie briefly propose marriage to Madeline Bassett (for ulterior purposes), Gussie Fink-Nottle break off his engagement to Miss Bassett yet again, and Jeeves expose Roderick Spode's terrible secret ('Eulalie') through the mysterious agency of the Junior Ganymede Club. All, however, will end well, with Jeeves triumphantly enabled to take his master on the round-the-world cruise on which he has set his heart, and which Bertie had, in best Wooster fashion, foolishly vetoed at the outset ('when two men of iron will live in close association with one another, there are bound to be occasional clashes').

But to summarize the plot of *The Code of the Woosters* is to concentrate on the well-oiled machinery of a beautifully constructed fictional timepiece to the exclusion of its style. As well as farce, *The Code of the Woosters* contains an extraordinary number of its author's most celebrated felicities:

He spoke with a certain what–is–it in his voice, and I could see that, if not actually disgruntled, he was far from being gruntled.

Or,

It is no use telling me that there are bad aunts and good aunts. At the core, they are all alike. Sooner or later, out pops the cloven hoof.

Or,

She was definitely the sort of girl who puts her hand over a husband's eyes, as he is crawling in to breakfast with a morning head, and says: 'Guess who!'

Or,

You see before you, Jeeves, a toad beneath the harrow.

The Code of the Woosters is a supreme example of Wodehouse's marriage of high farce with the inverted poetry of his mature comic style. The inspired lunacy of Bertie Wooster's triumph over Roderick Spode is perhaps all the more striking for the circumstances in which the novel was conceived and written. Fiction had always been an escape for Wodehouse, a blessing he had passed on to his devoted inter-war readership. Now, more than ever, the unhinged paradise of Totleigh Towers answered a universal need. But there is also a new maturity in Bertie Wooster. He continues to dread the snares of matrimony, and he does not mince words when referring to his romantic nemesis, Madeline Bassett – 'I call her a ghastly girl because she was a ghastly girl' – but he acknowledges that love is universal, that even bullies have their Achilles heel, and that even at the blackest moments the human spirit can find comfort in the loyal support of pals and relations.

The 'code' of the Woosters is a farceur's version of E. M. Forster's 'only connect'. None of this is explicit. As an Edwardian clubman with a flat in Mayfair, Bertie has a stuttering emotional vocabulary, and a stilted emotional life. He can refer to 'red-hot sparks of pash', but would not dream of elaborating the observation, nor of following through. He is, however, uniquely innocent, and wholly good, with an innate, if slightly antique, moral compass. When Stiffy Byng names her terms for handing over Gussie Fink-Nottle's scandalous leather-bound notebook with its excoriating portrait of Roderick Spode's asparagus-eating demeanour, Bertie says: 'I read her purpose, and shuddered. She was naming the Price of the Papers. In other words, after being blackmailed by an aunt at breakfast, I was now being blackmailed by a female crony before dinner. Pretty good going, even for this lax post-war world.' In his subsequent complaint to Jeeves, Bertie betrays not only Wodehouse's sentiments, but also his creator's Victorian origins. Wodehouse was, after all, approaching his sixtieth birthday:

The whole fact of the matter is that all this modern emancipation of women has resulted in them getting it up their noses and not giving a damn what they do. It was not like this in Queen Victoria's day. The Prince Consort would have had a word to say about a girl like Stiffy, what?

The Code of the Woosters, published simultaneously in Britain and America on 7 October 1938, also bears the unmistakable traces of Wodehouse's public school education at Dulwich and his Edwardian youth. When Bertie denounces Spode as a 'fat slob' – 'What the Voice of the People is saying is: "Look at that frightful ass Spode swanking about in footer bags! Did you ever in your puff see such a perfect perisher?"' – he is using the late-Victorian slang of the bank clerks and the Pooters, those lower-middle-class denizens of south London, land of laurels and semis. By the late 1930s, it was a language that, almost single-handedly, Wodehouse had forged into a universally recognized English style, a marriage of suburban vernacular with classical syntax. Seemingly effortless, it was always the product of constant revision.

Wodehouse had begun to work on the novel he was still calling 'The Silver Cow' the moment he came home to Low Wood. On 22 November 1937 he described to Townend how he had streamlined the opening by cutting a redundant scene with Aunt Dahlia ('isn't it ghastly to think that after earning one's living as a writer for thirty-seven years one can still make a blunder like that'). By the beginning of December he was still making good progress, and informed Reynolds that he had reached page 200 and hoped to finish soon, if there were no hidden snags: 'It is working out as quite one of the best I have done,' he wrote. After Christmas with Leonora and the family, which slowed his momentum, he returned to the manuscript, complaining that he lacked the drive and command of words that he used to possess. 'I imagine the trouble is that I have twice been stopped writing the book for long periods, and this has made me tired of it,' he speculated to Townend.

'Fortunately, the situations are so strong that I can't go off the rails.' By the beginning of February, however, the book was done. 'I thought it would never be finished,' Ethel told Reynolds, providing a rare insight into her husband's creative effort, 'he has worked so hard on it, and rewritten it so many times.' Reynolds acknowledged receipt of the type-script with the observation that it was one of his client's best, and promptly sold it to Wesley Stout at the *Saturday Evening Post* for $40,000.

After the frustrations of his year in California, Wodehouse found his return to the routine and tranquillity of Low Wood a stimulus to his creativity. *The Code of the Woosters* had scarcely been sold to the *Post* before he launched into his next book. This was the long-planned return of Lord Ickenham, *Uncle Fred in the Springtime*. Uncle Fred was an afterthought, a late-1930s addition to Wodehouse's world, an irre-pressible bounder of sixty-something whom Wodehouse saw as 'a sort of elderly Psmith' and whom his readers might be forgiven for confusing with Galahad Threepwood, Lord Emsworth's reprobate brother. On his debut in 'Uncle Fred Flits by', it is clear that Lord Ickenham has form. We never discover what exactly did happen at the dog races – 'they are letting a rather neurotic kind of man into the Force these days' – and no doubt a better type of magistrate would have been content with a reprimand, but it is clear that Uncle Fred is an Edwardian at heart, another representative of a brighter, breezier world. With his iron-grey hair, trim figure and zest for living life to the full, and armed with his great sponge Joyeuse, 'one of the hottest earls that ever donned a coronet' would be one of Wodehouse's most enduring heroes, later starring in *Uncle Dynamite* (1948), *Cocktail Time* (1958) and *Service with a Smile* (1962). But in *Uncle Fred in the Springtime*, he gets his name in the title, a sure indication of Wodehouse's delight in his company.

The new novel, written between May and September 1938, and containing an affectionate allusion to Low Wood, is ostensibly another tale of Blandings Castle, but Uncle Fred quickly establishes himself centre-stage. Alaric, the excitable Duke of Dunstable, for whom Lady Constance has a secret tendresse, has invited himself to the castle and installed himself in the Red Room. Worse, he has decided to take Lord Emsworth's domain in hand. Gardeners must not whistle 'Loch Lomond' outside his window; the vastly overweight Empress of Blandings should go on a diet; and so on. The idea that his idyllic home should be ration-alized by a half-mad peer is intolerable to Lord Emsworth, who decides to enlist Lord Ickenham's assistance in ridding his demi-paradise of this ducal menace. All seems set fair until, by a deft twist of the plot, Lord Ickenham arrives at the castle not as himself but as an impostor – and not any old impostor, either, but as Sir Roderick Glossop, the celebrated nerve-specialist. Others, like his long-suffering nephew Pongo Twistleton, who has been dragged along as his 'secretary', might quail at the prospect but Uncle Fred, like Wodehouse himself, relishes the complexity of the situation in which he has placed himself. Uncle Fred is the lord of misrule who scatters his opponents left and right, saves the Empress, smooths the path of true love and goes on his way, spreading sweetness and light.

Uncle Fred in the Springtime is more highly wrought and artificial than *The Code of the Woosters*. It shows Wodehouse enjoying the company of his favourite characters in his favourite English setting, demonstrating his utter mastery of the world he had created. Possibly it lacks the stylistic magic of a Jeeves novel, but – as in the moment when 'Mustard' Pott discovers that George, Viscount Bosham, Lord Emsworth's drivelling son, shares his passion for the game called 'Persian Monarchs' – it contains moments of comic joy rarely equalled in other books.

It is tempting, in hindsight, to see in these two novels of the late 1930s a kind of unconscious valediction. Wodehouse, unquestionably on top form, was in a reflective mood, and unusually self-aware. 'I go off the rails unless I stay all the time in a sort of artificial world of my own creation,' he confided to Townend. 'A real character in one of my books sticks out like a sore thumb.' Like his fiction, Wodehouse's private world was well insulated from the unwelcome interruptions of pain or anxiety. Occasionally, they were unavoidable. Towards the end of 1938, with *Uncle Fred in the Springtime* written, delivered to Reynolds and submitted to the *Post*, his beloved Pekinese Miss Winks died suddenly.

Wodehouse, who had been in Paris, shopping with Ethel, described the loss to Townend: 'I can hardly bear to write about it,' he reported. 'The usual thing – tick fever.' Wodehouse had taken her on the train to Paris, where she had seemed more than usually fit. 'On Tuesday morning,' he went on, 'Ethel took her and Wonder for a walk and told me Winkie had refused to run and seemed out of sorts. On Wednesday morning we took her to the vet and left her there. In the afternoon . . . We saw her in her cage and she was obviously dying,' he went on, with unprecedented candour, 'and that night the vet rang up and said it was all over.' They brought the body back to Low Wood and buried her in the garden, but Wodehouse found the empty house unbearable and crossed over to Kent to stay with Leonora and the family. In a life that ruthlessly suppresses the risks of strong feeling, it is only with the death of one of his dogs that the emotional side of Wodehouse's nature reveals itself. Soon after this tragedy, to Wodehouse's delight Ethel returned from a trip to London with a little black Peke puppy ('an absolute angel') concealed in the recesses of her fur coat. Wonder, meanwhile, now took pride of place in the home, as the top dog.

In this tense last year of peace, Wodehouse continued to lead the privileged life of an internationally renowned English writer – watching Dulwich rugby football matches, spending a snowy Christmas with his grandchildren in Kent, lunching with Randolph Churchill (a 'very good chap'), taking tea with old friends like Townend and Mackail, fending off new offers from Hollywood, working on a dramatization of *The Code of the Woosters* at a hotel in Cannes, writing to his regular correspondents, and beginning to mull over the plot of his next Jeeves novel, *Joy in the Morning*. In the wider world, the long slide to war had begun. On 28 April, Hitler repudiated the Anglo-German Naval Agreement of 1935. But Wodehouse seemed ignorant of the European crisis, strangely unworried by its implications, and shockingly wrong in his reading of the situation:

Do you know [he wrote], a feeling is gradually stealing over me that the world has never been farther from a war than it is at present. It has just dawned on the civilians of all countries that the good old days of seeing the boys off in the troop ship are over and that the elderly sportsmen who used to talk about giving sons to the country will now jolly well have to give themselves. I think if Hitler really thought there was any chance of a war, he would have nervous prostration.

Wodehouse is often described as 'naive' or 'innocent' in his political understanding, but neither of these descriptions quite captures the peculiar, even ironic, quality of his detachment. In so far as it is possible seriously to characterize Wodehouse's approach to international relations, it should be understood as essentially Victorian, in which great power politics were treated as a kind of game.

Incidentally [he went on], doesn't all this alliance-forming remind you of the form matches at school, when you used to say to yourself that the Upper Fifth had a couple of first fifteen forwards, but you'd got the fly half of the second, the full back of the third and three forwards who would get their colours before the season was over. I can't realise that all this is affecting millions of men. I think of Hitler and Mussolini as two halves, and Stalin as a useful wing forward.

Anyway, no war in our lifetime is my feeling. I don't think wars start with months of preparation in the way of slanging matches. When you get a sort of brooding peace, as in 1914, when a spark lights the p. magazine, that's when you get a war. Nowadays, I feel that the nations just take it out in blowing off steam. (I shall look silly if war starts on Saturday, after Hitler's speech!)

Shortly after this, Wodehouse received news from the Vice-Chancellor of Oxford University that, almost exactly forty years after being denied the opportunity to go to the 'Varsity', he was to be awarded an honorary doctorate of literature (D.Litt.) at the annual Encaenia, a special ceremony, on Wednesday, 21 June 1939.

Wodehouse was delighted with the news, which he could scarcely believe. 'I am rather stunned by this,' he told his publisher, 'as I had no notion that my knockabout comedy entitled me to rank with the nibs.' But he soon adjusted to the acclaim. 'Great excitement', he reported to Reynolds, acknowledging that the award was 'a biggish honor [*sic*]'. He was pleased to note that 'Mark Twain appears to be the only man who has got it, outside of dull, stodgy birds whose names are unknown to the public'. With a growing sense of mystified anticipation at the ordeal ahead, he wrote to his godson Billy Griffith that 'proceedings open at 11.20 with champagne and peaches at Magdalen and from then on until bedtime, as far as I can gather, it is one steady round of eating'. To Townend, he expressed quiet pride: 'I have become a biggish bug these days.' Meanwhile, the British press had got hold of the story and was conducting a lively analysis of the meaning and merits of Oxford's decision. *The Times*, summing up a national debate, pronounced that 'there is no question that in making P. G. Wodehouse a doctor of letters the University has done the right and proper thing. Everyone', the leader-writer went on, describing the shared values of a clubby, closely knit society whose day was almost over, 'knows at least some of his many works and has felt all the better for the gaiety of his wit and the freshness of his style.' Wodehouse probably shared the sense of puzzlement and, with his eye for a comic situation, would have enjoyed the process by which his nomination had gone forward.

In the spring of 1939, the University's Hebdomadal Council had met to discuss the proposed list of candidates for the great distinction of an Oxford honorary degree. The Vice-Chancellor, George Gordon, who was also president of Magdalen College, had already placed an impressive list of 'dull, stodgy birds' before the Council when he asked one of the committee – I. O. Griffith, a fellow of Brasenose College, and a mathematician with a well-known taste for the unconventional – to suggest another name. On the spur of the moment, Griffith, momentarily at a loss, had replied, 'Mr Vice-Chancellor, I should like to put forward the name of Mr P. G. Wodehouse.' In the stunned, incredulous silence that followed this intervention, Griffith found himself wishing that he had kept silent, but the Vice-Chancellor, a genial don with a sure command of his council, replied, 'Griff, I've always wanted to propose that name, but I've never had the courage to do it.' He paused. 'Well, there can't be any opposition to that, can there?' he said – and the proposal was carried with acclamation.

That was not the end of the matter for the dons of Oxford. When the Hebdomadal Council informed the University's Public Orator, Cyril Bailey, that one of the Encaenia's traditional Latin salutes would be addressed to the author of *Right Ho, Jeeves* and *Leave It to Psmith*, Bailey replied that he had never read a word of P. G. Wodehouse and could he have some help, please, from the proposer? Griffith asked his son John, a junior don who was also a Wodehouse fan, to prepare a Wodehouse reading list for the further education of the Public Orator. After consultation, the Griffiths, *père et fils*, decided that Bailey's citation should at least make reference to Gussie Fink-Nottle and the Empress of Blandings and they sent him their own copies of the appropriate works. The Griffith family had expected the Public Orator to come up with a speech in Latin prose listing Wodehouse's best known books. As it turned out, they got something special from a late convert to Wodehouse.

The ceremony was to be held on 21 June. Wodehouse arrived to stay with the Vice-Chancellor the day before. Dr Gordon's son, George, recalled that he had expected 'someone sophisticated and perhaps remote' but noticed that Wodehouse found the 'degree business rather embarrassing' and was evidently much happier in the company of the Gordon children and their dog, Simon. In the course of the afternoon, Hugh Walpole, a famous literary acquaintance who happened to be in Oxford to give a lecture, breezed grandly into the president's lodgings in Magdalen and took Wodehouse off for a walk, during which Walpole, with the professional anxiety of a popular writer obsessed with reviews, and alluding to the debate surrounding the University's controversial choice, brought up Hilaire Belloc's recently broadcast judgement that Wodehouse was the 'best writer of English now alive'. Wodehouse, who did not care much for Walpole, described the subsequent conversation:

He said to me: 'Did you see what Belloc said about you?' I said I had. 'I wonder why he said that.' 'I wonder,' I said. Long silence. 'I can't imagine why he said that,' said Hugh. I said I couldn't, either. Another long silence. 'It seems such an extraordinary thing to say!' 'Most extraordinary.' Long silence again. 'Ah, well,' said Hugh, having apparently found the solution, 'the old man's getting very old.'

The Encaenia was, reported the new Doctor of Literature, 'a terrific triumph'. The day started towards midday, at Magdalen, with the traditional peaches and champagne. Wodehouse, robed in a dove-grey and scarlet gown with a mortar board, joined his fellow honorands, who included Lord Lothian, the British ambassador to Washington, H. J. C. Grierson, the English critic and scholar, the lexicographer Sir Edmund Chambers, and the American Felix Frankfurter, a justice on the United States Supreme Court. In the procession through the Oxford streets to the Sheldonian Theatre, Wodehouse walked alongside Herbert Grierson but hardly said a word, perhaps because he was nonplussed by the boisterous undergraduate salutes along the route, and also because Grierson was plainly miffed by the acclaim for a popular comic novelist. There was more to follow. When it came to the ceremony, the other honorands were greeted with 'tepid applause' but Wodehouse (on his own account), 'had to stand for quite three minutes while thousands cheered'. Cyril Bailey, the Public Orator, who was due for retirement, rose to the occasion, presenting Wodehouse to the Vice-Chancellor with a brilliant and witty celebration of Wodehouse's gifts composed in faultless Latin hexameters after Horace. Having made ingenious reference to Bertie Wooster, Jeeves, Mr Mulliner, Lord Emsworth, the Empress of Blandings, Psmith and Gussie Fink-Nottle, Bailey concluded in prose that Wodehouse was 'our Petronius, or should I say, our Terence?' (*Petroniumne dicam an Terentium nostrum?*) a tribute that provoked more wild applause. The Vice-Chancellor then presented the degree, praising Wodehouse as a man who needed no testimonial, *Vir lepidissime, facetissime, venustissime, iocosissime, ridibundissime* (Wittiest of men, most humorous, most charming, most amusing, full of laughter).

'The only catch to the thing was that I kept being accosted by decrepit old gents with white beards who asked me if I remembered them at school,' Wodehouse confessed to Billy Griffith. 'As Uncle Fred said, it lowered the picture I had formed of myself as a sprightly young fellow on the threshold of life. Still it was a great day, culminating in a dinner at Christ Church of about four hundred, all in white ties and white waistcoats, which I attended in a dinner jacket.' Not only did Wodehouse signal his ignorance of Oxford's dress code, he remained imperturbably in character. As the dinner drew to a close, the undergraduates below the high table began to bang the tables, chanting 'We want Wode-house . . . we want Wode-house'. There were cries of 'Speech!' The new Oxford man, and the author of some of the funniest books in memory, rose awkwardly to his feet. If the guests were hoping for a comic tour de force, they were to be disappointed. Wodehouse simply mumbled, 'Thank you', and sat down in confusion.

The Oxford doctorate closed one chapter in Wodehouse's long life. A few weeks later, there was another farewell that would also turn out to be final. On a flying visit to London at the end of July, he and Bill Townend motored down to Dulwich together to see their old school play cricket against St Paul's. They sat in the pavilion together and met Alleynians they had known from years before. It should have been a happy occasion, but it was one of the dullest cricket matches either of them had ever watched. Townend, who had another appointment in town, said goodbye to Wodehouse at about four o'clock, and left him sitting in the pavilion, looking rather bored and disconsolate. They would never meet again.

Six weeks later, war was declared. Chamberlain's tense Edwardian voice came on the wireless to announce the expiration of Britain's ultimatum to Germany. Wodehouse was at Low Wood, putting the finishing touches to *Quick Service*, his latest novel. Earlier in the summer he had planned to do a new Uncle Fred story, but the plot had come to nothing and by the autumn he had a scenario for a new Jeeves novel ready instead. So stylized had his work now become, with the plots increasingly just a vehicle for his prose, that on this occasion he had completely subordinated the characters to the plot, telling Townend that 'now all I want is the names of the characters and what they look like!' and admitting that 'This is the first time I have ever planned a novel without knowing the name of a single character.'

At first, when war broke out, Wodehouse found himself paralysed with anxiety, and by the interruption of his routine. He was disinclined to write letters because he felt they would not reach their destinations; at night, there was the blackout, which was 'a nuisance'; and travel was restricted. 'Ethel was talking airily about running into Boulogne for a bite of lunch today,' he told Townend, but she had to give up the idea when she found they needed identity cards and several travel passes. 'I don't mind much,' he added, 'as I never do want to go anywhere.' Gradually, a weird kind of normality returned. The 'phoney war' began and, with the conflict seeming a long way off, he was happy. He was enjoying the new novel, and all the more so because, with the war on, he felt he could take his time over it. He had only a few qualms: the supply of typewriter ribbons and, looking ahead a bit, the shipping of the completed typescript to America. 'Qualm Three is the feeling what a blank it will leave in my life when I have finished the book,' he observed, anticipating his usual post-partum let-down in a rare fit of emotional self-analysis.

In the evening, after the day's work, he and Ethel would listen to the BBC. He approved of Churchill's broadcasts against the Nazis. 'Just what was needed, I thought,' he wrote to Townend. 'I can't help feeling that we're being a bit too gentlemanly. Someone ought to get up in Parliament and call Hitler a swine.' As well as listening to Churchill on the wireless, he was also reading his account of the First World War (a series entitled *The World Crisis*). 'Have you read them?' he asked Townend.

They are terrific. What strikes me most about them is what mugs the Germans were to take us on again. You would have thought they must have known that we should wipe them out at sea and that there never has been a war that hasn't been won by sea power. It's very curious to see how the same old thing is happening all over again, with the difference that we are avoiding all the mistakes we made last time.

Memories of the First World War were still fresh, and played an important part in conditioning his generation's response to the threat of
Nazism. Like many residents of Le Touquet, the Wodehouses believed
that they were safe behind the Maginot Line and that if hostilities broke
out, civilians would easily be able to remove themselves from the battle
zone and sit out the war in safety, somewhere else in France. Such was
Wodehouse's mood. Writing to his American friend Frank Sullivan in
the autumn of 1939, he reported that 'everything [is] very quiet and
peaceful here. I was just about to come over to America when all this
started, and now I suppose I shall have to wait till it's over.' He gave
the same message to Reynolds in New York, whose son acknowledged
the letter with words that would shortly seem richly ironic. 'I am glad
Le Touquet is so peaceful,' wrote Reynolds junior, 'and that you are
not being upset in your daily life by the war.' Wodehouse replied in
kind, calmly reporting that 'My new novel *Quick Service* is now being
typed in Paris . . . Everything is very quiet here. I wish I could get over
to America, but I think I will stay here till the Spring.'

PART FOUR

Disgrace

(1940-1947)

17. 'The *hors d'oeuvre* in Fate's banquet' (1940)

'Young men, starting out in life, have often asked me "How can I become an Internee?" Well, there are several methods. My own was to buy a villa in Le Touquet on the coast of France and stay there till the Germans came along. This is probably the best and simplest system. You buy the villa and the Germans do the rest.' (First Berlin broadcast, 28 June 1941)

The winter of 1940 was exceptionally bitter, one of the coldest of the century. The Wodehouses hibernated in Low Wood and dreamed of getting away to America. 'I think one has to get a permit to leave France,' Wodehouse wrote to Bolton. 'I suppose I could come by the Clipper, though I should have qualms!' In fact, Wodehouse never flew in an aeroplane, and he did not leave Europe until 1947. Out-of-season Le Touquet during the 'phoney war', which the French called the *drôle de guerre*, no longer had that 'desert island feeling' which Wodehouse had come to love. The town was occupied by units of the French army and, describing his contribution to the war effort, Wodehouse told Townend that he was 'running a doss house for French officers' – billeting two medical officers in the spare room. The English newspapers were now arriving a day late, but otherwise life was little changed. Ethel raced about in her blue Lancia; in March, she crashed the car into a bus on the icy road to Montreuil, but was unscathed. Her idea of morale boosting was to drive down to Paris-Plage with her secretary Jacqueline, the attractive daughter of the local golf pro, Arthur Grant, and invite likely looking young British servicemen to dinner. Ethel was always the star of her own show and thought nothing of accosting total strangers with these impromptu invitations. Rex King-Clark, a solitary young captain with the 2nd Manchesters, stationed on the Franco-Belgian border, was warming up in the White Star Café one winter afternoon, after gunnery practice in the dunes. Ethel, introducing herself as 'Mrs P. G. Wodehouse', pressed him to come to Low Wood. King-Clark soon discovered that he was not her only new friend. Young Hurricane pilots from RAF Squadron No. 85, stationed at Le Touquet, were in the habit of visiting the house for tea, cocktails and impromptu dancing, with perhaps a glimpse of young Miss Grant, who was susceptible to what she called 'a flutter', as an additional incentive. King-Clark remembered that 'I spent several happy evenings with the fighter pilots and Wodehouse friends', other English expatriates who had decided to stay in France and for whom Low Wood became an informal social centre, with entertainment orchestrated by Ethel. Jacqueline Grant recalls the gramophone playing 'My Heart Belongs to Daddy', and the carpet rolled up for dancing in the comfortable drawing room with its mullioned windows looking out over the garden and the links beyond. Wodehouse would poke his bespectacled bald head round the door. 'Is everybody happy?' he would ask with a smile. 'Yes, sir,' chorused the young people, 'won't you come and join us?' But he always made an excuse and went back to his study, a little room off the hallway. He was working on some new short stories and, oppressed by 'the weariness of war', took comfort in his routine. 'I work in the morning, take the dogs out before tea, do a bit of mild work after tea, and then read after dinner,' he told Townend. 'It is wonderful how the days pass.'

Despite his absorption in his work, he could be kind to the young soldiers who came to Low Wood. One day, Rex King-Clark recalled, 'I had tea with [Wodehouse] and his dog, alone in their lovely drawing-room. He was quiet and studious looking and I found it difficult to believe that I was talking to the creator of such splendidly eccentric characters as Psmith, Jeeves and Bertie Wooster. I remember that we talked about the war . . . and I left with the feeling that he was pessimistic about the outcome for the Allies.' Wodehouse told Townend that he derived comfort from Churchill's speeches, but in many respects his attitude to the European crisis echoed what George Orwell characterized as 'the mental world of the *Gem* and *Magnet*', the boys' magazines of Wodehouse's Dulwich schooldays:

There is a cosy fire in the study, and outside the wind is whistling. The ivy clusters thickly round the old grey stones. The King is on his throne and the pound is worth a pound. Over in Europe the comic foreigners are jabbering and gesticulating, but the grim grey battleships of the British fleet are steaming up the Channel . . . [and] we are settling down to a tremendous tea of sausages, sardines, crumpets, potted meat, jam and doughnuts . . . Everything is safe, solid and unquestionable. Everything will be the same for ever and ever.

If Wodehouse had a model of European conflict in mind, it was the First World War, which had scarcely disrupted French civilian life outside the combat zone.

In the spring of 1940, the Panzers of the Wehrmacht were massing on the Franco-Belgian border, some three hundred miles away, and Rommel was making final preparations for his blitzkrieg. Strangely, though, no one – not the RAF pilots, not the French officers, not the British consular officials in Boulogne – seemed remotely concerned about the dangers of invasion. Wodehouse, in common with his friends and neighbours, evinced only mild puzzlement at his circumstances. 'I can't think what is going to happen,' he wrote to Townend from Low Wood. 'Do you think everything will break loose in the spring? I don't see how it can, as surely by then we shall be too strong.' This view reflected the official British government line. In March 1940 Chamberlain described the British naval blockade as 'the main weapon' against Hitler. Wodehouse jokingly remarked that 'My only fear is that Germany will be able to go on for years on their present rations. Apparently a German is able to live on stinging nettles and wood fibre indefinitely.'

He did not repine. There were the dogs to fuss over, and plenty of literary business to conduct. Someone wanted to make *Hot Water* into a musical. Did he approve? Herbert Jenkins was releasing *Eggs, Beans and Crumpets*, a collection of Drones Club stories, on 26 April. How were sales holding up in wartime? The *Saturday Evening Post* was serializing *Quick Service*, one of his favourite novels, and *Life* wanted to commission a piece about his attitude to the war in Europe. Then there were the household pets. He was looking after a neighbour's parrot and seven dogs, while a stray cat had settled into the garage and produced a litter of kittens, which provoked fears about Wonder's likely reaction. Meanwhile, Wodehouse was plugging away at his new novel. This became *Joy in the Morning*, thought by a fervent minority to be his masterpiece. Although the manuscript was much on his mind, Wodehouse was still hoping somehow to get to America, and had begun vaguely to plan a transatlantic crossing from Genoa, whose port remained open. (It was closed on 10 June when Italy declared war on France.) 'It's such a business getting started,' he complained to Reynolds, '. . . so I am sitting tight and writing a new Jeeves novel [*Joy in the Morning*], of which I have finished the first four chapters.'

His work methods had hardly changed in forty years. As he explained to Reynolds, he was still hoarding comic set pieces:

I wrote a short story, a sequel to ['The Passing of Ambrose'], and it was a snorter. I was just going to send it to you, when it struck me that the blow out would make a fine solution to one of Bertie's problems, and as these are so terribly hard to get I decided to scrap the short story and think out a Jeeves plot culminating in this situation.

Looking forward to another of their lunches, but doubting if he would manage a trip to America until the autumn, he told Reynolds: 'I think [the novel] is going to be good, but it was agony to have to scrap the short story.' Europe was on the brink of catastrophe, but he was still planning his own campaign and badgering Townend about the plot of *Joy in the Morning*. 'Is it possible', he asked, 'for a hard-up young peer to become a *country* policeman? A London one, yes, but this must be country . . . (My chap has got to be a policeman, because Bertie pinches his uniform in order to go to a fancy dress dance.)'

So the weeks passed, and the war came closer, but the Wodehouses stayed put. On 9 April German troops overwhelmed Norway's defences, sweeping ashore out of a coastal snowstorm. The British response was a disaster, and ended ignominiously on 2 May with the complete withdrawal of all British forces, and afterwards with the resignation of Neville Chamberlain. On 9 May, after a backbench rebellion, Churchill became Prime Minister. He told the House of Commons: 'I have nothing to offer but blood, toil, tears and sweat . . . You ask, What is our aim? I can answer in one word: Victory – victory at all costs, victory in spite of all terror; victory, however long and hard the road may be.' This was a harsh, new and uncompromising note in British political discourse, perfectly suited to the life-and-death struggle with Nazi Germany, but it could scarcely have been further removed from the moral universe of the Eggs, Beans and Crumpets at the Drones Club, the world of preprandial snorts and young men in fancy dress killing time over billiards and 'Persian Monarchs'.

Churchill's promotion came not a moment too soon. Without

warning, and with unprecedented speed and firepower, the German army invaded Holland and Belgium in the early hours of 10 May. Within a week the Dutch army had capitulated. The Germans burst through the ill-defended Ardennes, overrunning the Maginot Line, and by 15 May Rommel and his Panzers were advancing so fast that he was actually overtaking the French army in retreat. In Paris, officials in the Quai d'Orsay began burning archives. Now, at last, Wodehouse was also getting nervous. Jacqueline Grant says that she and Ethel organized a bonfire of his 'anti-German' articles and notes on the terrace at Low Wood. There is no way of knowing what these might have been. Almost the only explicit Hitler satire Wodehouse ever wrote, apart from the opening lines of 'Buried Treasure', was a feeble *Punch* story, 'The Big Push', in which the narrator reports a meeting at the Wilhelmstrasse:

The front office was full, as any room would be that contained Field-Marshal Goering . . . A few minutes later the Fuehrer bustled in.

'Well, here we all are,' he said. 'Now, about getting this war started. Anybody any suggestions?'

'I was thinking –' said Ribbentrop.

'What with?' said Goering, who had a great gift for repartee.

'Now, boys, boys,' said the Fuehrer indulgently . . . 'Here's a thought that crossed my mind as I was coming here. Let's destroy Britain.'

Perhaps the burning of manuscripts was inspired by highly strung Ethel's concern that if her husband was captured there should be nothing, however slight, that could be used against him. The 'dreamlike trance' in which they had been living during these lovely spring weeks was rapidly becoming a nightmare.

Fifty miles to the north of Le Touquet, General Gort, the commander of the British Expeditionary Force, had begun retreating to Dunkirk on the coast, in a desperate effort to escape the encircling German forces. On Monday, 20 May, with nothing but bad news on all sides, the Wodehouses made the first of two belated attempts to escape southwards. Until now they had accepted official assurances that the German advance would be stopped, and had even made arrangements with the British vice-consul in Boulogne for an early warning about any German threat. As it happened, none of the British residents in Le Touquet received any warnings from British consular officials, mainly because no one – not even the BBC – knew what was happening. Ethel subsequently told Denis Mackail that they treated the BBC as 'our Bible at that time', and the BBC was issuing no warnings. Privately, across the Channel, Leonora was urging her parents to get out while they could; in Le Touquet the Wodehouses' friend Lady Dudley was begging them to leave. But they clung to the disastrous belief that the courageous English thing to do was to sit tight, have faith in the British army, protect their property and resist panic. Not for the last time in this story, the stiff upper lip exhibited by Wodehouse was completely inappropriate to the situation. Less gloriously, there were two practical arguments against returning to Britain, even at this eleventh hour: his dogs and his work-in-progress. If he crossed the Channel, he would have to quarantine Wonder, which he could not bear to do, and he would also have to take a break from his work on *Joy in the Morning*. That was equally unthinkable. Wodehouse was a writer whose first responsibility was to his art. Throughout the coming years, his inability to compromise that commitment would lead to his self-destruction.

In place of hard news there were rumours. It was said that hordes of French colonial troops were rolling back the advance; that great victories had been won inland; and that a gap in the line had been closed. Wodehouse later recalled 'the general feeling was that they [the Germans] would be repulsed before they reached Amiens', but when Amiens fell, the gravity of the situation became clear and the Wodehouses at last made plans to evacuate. On 20 May the German army's exact movements were still unknown but, from the occasional falling bomb and the sound of ack-ack fire from the direction of Arras, the situation was obviously deteriorating. Ethel Wodehouse drove across to the British military hospital at Étaples, a dilapidated relic of the First World War, and asked the Commanding Officer for the latest military intelligence. She was given the worst possible advice. The officer was so reassuring about the likely progress of the German advance that the Wodehouses and their neighbours decided, after fierce debate, to postpone their departure until the next day, 21 May. During the night the Wodehouses loaded their essential possessions into the family Lancia, buried some petrol in the garden, and gave a second, smaller car to the Swiss governess of their neighbour, Lady Furness. Then they went to bed, amid the chaos of last-minute packing, knowing that in the morning they would make their bid for freedom – a half-formed plan to head for Portugal, and then to sail for America – in the south.

Their flight was bungled from the start. When Ethel had crashed the Lancia in March it had been repaired badly. Now, it would only drive in second and third gear. After setting off in convoy through the pine woods of Le Touquet, two miles along the road towards Berck the car broke down irretrievably. Wodehouse, who was no mechanic, decided to abandon it and return in the second, smaller car to Low Wood. There, he and Ethel found Arthur Grant, his wife Ruth, and their daughter Jacqueline, also preparing to flee, together with another elderly expatriate, a Mr Lawry. The Grant party had two vehicles, a little Simca saloon and an old Red Cross Ford van belonging to another neighbour, Mr Kemp. After many farewells to the neighbours, who had agreed to look after the various dogs, the second convoy set off, the Wodehouses in front, followed by Jacqueline Grant in the Red Cross van, and her father bringing up the rear in his Simca. This second attempt – against the backdrop of the inexorable German advance – was as doomed as the first.

Le Touquet is approached by minor roads. When the Wodehouse convoy reached the coastal highway, it was confronted by an astounding scene of human chaos: cars with mattresses on the roof, vans, carts piled with furniture, bicycles, wheelbarrows; and all kinds of families trudging on foot in flight from the invaders. This extraordinary movement of population, dubbed the Exodus, was to become a characteristic twentieth-century scene, but it astonished contemporary observers. The French aviator Antoine de Saint-Exupéry wrote that from the air it looked as though a giant had kicked a massive anthill. The Exodus was not confined to the coast. Between six and ten million people fled the Nazi armies during the fall of France. Many would never forget the complete disintegration of social order.

In the midst of this sea of refugees, with the threat of strafing from the air adding terror to the disorientation, the Grants' Red Cross van broke down, and the Wodehouses became lost from view. By the time Jacqueline Grant had raised a mechanic from among her aviator friends at the local airfield, the afternoon was waning. The Wodehouses, who had waited in vain for the rest of the party to catch up, then reappeared with the news that the road south to Berck, Abbeville and safety was clogged with refugees and exposed to enemy fire. Wodehouse suggested they all go back to Low Wood and Ethel begged everyone to stay the night. When someone mentioned the dangers of bombing, she replied that they could all shelter in the drawing room and protect their heads with cushions. Not surprisingly, the Grants elected to make for their own home.

In fact, there was no bombing. Le Touquet was of no military significance. The victorious German army simply rolled on up the road towards Boulogne. 'The blazing sunshine softened into twilight, and the twilight into darkness, and still we waited and nothing happened,' Wodehouse wrote afterwards. 'Mingling with the call of the cuckoos, we could hear the distant thunder of the battle in Boulogne. A long, continuous roar, then silence.' But after 22 May the Wodehouses were trapped behind enemy lines. There was no possibility of escape. Across the Channel, Evelyn Waugh wrote in his diary, 'read P. G. Wodehouse (who has been lost along with the Channel ports) . . . and forgot the war'. Wodehouse might have welcomed the opportunity to do the same, but reality was now forcing itself upon him in the most uncongenial way.

'My own first meeting with the invaders took place in rather unfortunate circumstances,' Wodehouse wrote in his 'Apologia', an unpublished attempt to explain his wartime conduct. 'Embarrassing is the *mot-juste*. I did not actually get shot, but I was bathed in confusion.' This was his frightening encounter with the German foot-patrol (pp. 1–3, above). Within a few days, the streets of Paris-Plage were full of *feldgrau* uniforms. A nine o'clock curfew was established; sentries were posted; villas requisitioned. A German sergeant and three soldiers in heavy boots appeared at Low Wood to commandeer the Wodehouses' stores and later their cars and his bicycle. Wodehouse tried to remonstrate about the bicycle, but, lacking any command of German beyond '*Es ist schoenus Wetter*' (It is beautiful weather), failed miserably. It was hardly an ideal situation, and Ethel was predictably furious, but Wodehouse could still work on his novel, and gradually an odd kind of normality asserted itself. 'One's reactions on finding oneself suddenly surrounded by the armed strength of a hostile power are rather interesting,' he wrote.

The first time you see a German soldier in your garden, your impulse is to jump ten feet straight up into the air, and you do so. But this feeling of embarrassment soon passes. A week later you find that you are only jumping five feet. And in the end familiarity so breeds indifference that you are able to sustain without a tremor the spectacle of men in steel helmets riding round your lawn on bicycles and even the discovery that two or three of them have dropped in and are taking a bath in your bathroom.

All his life Wodehouse had accommodated himself to the vicissitudes of fate. Even now, he seemed unable to shake off a certain negligent detachment about the war. Publicly, like his hero Bertie Wooster, he 'wore the mask', and professed feelings of 'embarrassment'. Privately, he was incensed at the Germans' intrusion. Years later he protested to Townend that he had never, as some had suggested, '*invited* the blighters to come and scour their damned bodies in my bathroom'. What actually happened was that, after the second week of occupation, the house next door became full of German Labour Corps workers who just imposed themselves on the Wodehouses and their facilities. 'I chafed,' he wrote, 'and a fat lot of good chafing did me. They came again the next day and brought their friends.'

When the Germans first appeared, Wodehouse says he had feared internment and had worried about it, but as the 'weeks went by and nothing happened, optimism began to steal back'. Secretly, he sensed he was doomed: 'however jaunty the front I presented, there was always at my elbow a Spectre, mumbling of unpleasant things in store.' Wodehouse's uneasy forebodings were exacerbated by the appearance in Paris-Plage of a Kommandant with a glass eye to whom every ex-patriate male was obliged to report each morning at the Hôtel de Ville, a neo-Renaissance, fortress-like building built of red brick in the heart of Paris-Plage. Deprived of his bicycle, Wodehouse simply took the opportunity of getting some extra exercise, and made the two-mile walk across the heath to the Kommandantur part of his daily routine. In hindsight, the fearsome demeanour of the Kommandant was, as he put it, a mere preliminary, 'the *hors d'oeuvre* in Fate's banquet', but it seemed frightening enough at the time.

After the retreat from Dunkirk on 27 May had given the British new hope, and once the fall of France had become an accepted fact, Wodehouse's immediate circle swiftly adjusted to his new circumstances with sangfroid and efficiency. On 28 May, in response to a worried cable from Reynolds, Leonora replied 'Afraid no news but understand danger not great'. Emboldened by this, and responding like any good literary agent to the opportunity of a sale, Reynolds wrote to Low Wood, hoping that 'the whole experience hadn't been an unpleasant one' and asking if Wodehouse would write a magazine piece about his adventures. Two weeks later, Reynolds wrote to Ethel to inform her that 'a petition is being got up here addressed to the German ambassador asking him to use his influence to have Wodehouse released'. This would be the first in a series of American appeals on the writer's behalf during the early stages of the war, which would eventually alert the German authorities to the propaganda significance of their hostage. In the absence of more pressing literary business, Reynolds also asked Leonora to authorize the proposed musical production of *Hot Water*. Then the blow fell.

On the morning of Sunday, 21 July, a particularly lovely summer's day, Wodehouse came walking down the long straight road to the Kommandantur and found that his worst apprehensions had been fulfilled: 'The old stomach did a double buck-and-wing,' he wrote later in Broadway slang, 'and the heart started beating like a trap drum.' There, in front of him, was a local resident named Harold, *carrying a suitcase*. All Englishmen under the age of sixty were to be interned immediately. Describing this incident, Wodehouse later wrote in Woosterish tones that 'I shook from base to apex like a jelly in an earthquake', but it was an awful moment. It was, he admitted, 'the absolute finality of the thing that was so unnerving'. He was trapped. Finding the joke in a desperate situation as usual, he noted that this had happened to him only three times in his life before: leaving Dulwich for the bank; arriving in Hollywood in 1930; and putting on cap and gown for the D.Litt. ceremony.

Wodehouse was now escorted under guard back to Low Wood and given ten minutes to pack. Ethel was out in the garden with the dogs, oblivious to what was happening and unaware of Wodehouse's distress. He, meanwhile, had mastered himself sufficiently to decide to leave the manuscript of *Joy in the Morning* (complete except for the last four chapters) behind and instead to pack *The Complete Works* of Shakespeare, together with some tobacco, pencils, three scribbling pads, four pipes, a pair of shoes, a razor, some soap, shirts, socks, underwear, half a pound of tea – and Tennyson's poems. In the confusion, he forgot his passport, subsequently a source of immense trouble. Then Ethel appeared, in the nick of time, and contributed a cold mutton chop and a slab of chocolate. He said later, in an allusion to *Three Men in a Boat*, that she also offered a pound of butter but was dissuaded. Then he was taken back to the Kommandantur in Paris-Plage.

Here, after some delay, he and a dozen other Le Touquet internees, including some fellow golfers and Arthur Grant, were driven off in a bus to an unknown destination and an uncertain future. They were all frightened, but Algy, the retired clown of Algy's Bar, a popular Le Touquet establishment, kept their spirits up. After stops to pick up more internees at Étaples and Montreuil, where they were allowed to buy wine and cigarettes, the bus began an eight-hour drive to its destination – the city of Lille, about sixty miles away. It was after nine o'clock in the evening before they rolled through the gates of a grim-looking prison in Loos, a suburb of Lille, scene of some notable battles of the First World War. Wodehouse was registered as prisoner 'Widhorse' (crime: 'Anglais'), by an official who 'looked like something out of a film about Devil's Island'. Then he found himself in Cell 44 with Algy and Mr Cartmell, an elderly piano-tuner. The first phase of his internment had begun.

Wodehouse's experience as an 'enemy national' was typical of the Second World War. The Geneva Convention of 1929, governing the treatment of prisoners of war, did not cover the treatment of enemy civilians, and the ICRC (International Committee of the Red Cross) had to make agreements with the Axis countries that the Convention should be extended to civilians and merchant seamen. As a result, civilian internment camps were organized along the same lines as regular military camps. They were emphatically quite different from Nazi concentration camps, but in their own way severely scarred the lives of their often middle-aged inmates. It was some weeks, for instance, before it was definitively established that men over sixty (Wodehouse was nearly fifty-nine) had to be released; in the interim all kinds of wild rumours flourished among the prisoners. Uncertainty about the exact status of the civilian internees also bedevilled their treatment by the German authorities. Were they subject to civilian or military discipline? The situation was further confused by the fact that the cold, ill-clad internees appropriated discarded military uniforms on their travels, giving them the air of a ragged regiment.

Ethel, meanwhile, was having her own adventure. Later in the war her activities are sometimes mysterious but, at this early stage, her movements are well documented. When Wodehouse was taken away she said she was 'nearly insane'. It was impossible to stay on in Low Wood, which the Germans requisitioned, and after a couple of days she managed to get the address of a room with a Madame Bernard at a local trout farm, some thirty miles inland. A German soldier drove her – with a few suitcases, Coco the parrot, and Wonder the Pekinese – to 'a rather dreary house in a neglected field'. There, she was shown to a small back bedroom where she 'sat for an hour or so, wondering how I should keep up my courage and nearly out of my mind about Plummie'. Despite the Nazi seizure of power, life in occupied France continued to function surprisingly well. Ethel simply took Wonder for her daily walk, and waited for the postman. After about ten days, she told Denis Mackail, a card arrived 'from Plummie telling me not to worry, he was perfectly all right, and was at Lille'. Throughout the rest of a year-long separation, Wodehouse and his wife kept in touch by letter and post-card to a degree that now seems remarkable.

As a young man, practising his craft, Wodehouse had roamed the streets of London, looking for experience, recording it in his note-book. Now, in late middle age, with experience coming at him from all sides, he returned to his youthful habits and began to keep a frag-mentary diary, known as 'the camp notebook', which became the basis for a manuscript (now lost) about his wartime career that he some-times referred to as *Wodehouse in Wonderland*. These pencil notes make up virtually the only record of his life from July 1940 to June 1941. His journalistic instincts were galvanized by his sudden predicament. 'While this was a hell of a thing to have happened to a respectable old gentleman of declining years', he said later, 'it was all pretty darned interesting and I could hardly wait to see what the morrow would bring forth.'

Locked up in Loos prison, Wodehouse chivalrously yielded the only bed in Cell 44 to Cartmell, the senior man, and spent his first night in captivity on a thin straw mattress on the floor, lying under a rough blanket in his clothes. He found it impossible to sleep. The cell was scarcely big enough for three grown men; the notebook registers its starkness:

12 foot long by about 8 foot wide, whitewashed walls, bed in corner under window. Large window about 5 foot by 3, air quite fresh. Granite floor. Table and chair chained to it – toilet in corner near door. Door wooden with new

panels at bottom, where prisoners had kicked panels out during bombardment. One pane of window broken by shrapnel and shrapnel holes in walls
. . . Small basin in wall by toilet with tap, quite good running water. Overhead
two staples in wall . . . In corner by door, oak shelf, half broken off by prisoners
who beat in panels with it. One wooden hook.

The prisoners were roused at seven each morning and given breakfast
– watery soup in a tin bowl and a loaf of stale bread. At half past eight
they were taken to a cramped back yard for half an hour's exercise. The
rest of the day was spent locked up, with lunch ('vegetable soup') at
eleven o'clock and dinner ('vegetable soup but a bit thicker') at five.
Wodehouse experienced his incarceration as a mixture of uncertainty
and terrible monotony. There was also a dreadful stench from the drains
which was said by the Germans to be 'typically French'. With his
penchant for looking on the bright side, and the experience of Dulwich
to fall back on, Wodehouse noted that 'Prison brings out all that is best
in us all'. After three days, the internees protested to the Kommandant
who, upon discovering what the French prison staff had inflicted on
their English prisoners, threw a fit and liberalized the regime dramatically, allowing the internees to roam freely round the prison.

    Shortly afterwards, on 27 July, the Le Touquet contingent was trans-
ferred, by train, to a former Belgian army barracks in Liège. Wodehouse
had been 'Widhorse' throughout his stay, but as he was leaving on the
last day a German soldier came up and shook his hand with 'Thank
you for Jeeves!' Looking back, he found his regular voice to describe
his first week of internment:

Summing up my experience as a gaol-bird, I would say that a prison is all
right for a visit, but I wouldn't live there, if you gave me the place. On my
part, there was no moaning at the bar when I left Loos. I was glad to go. The
last I saw of the old Alma Mater was the warder closing the door of the van
and standing back with the French equivalent of 'Right away'. He said 'Au
revoir' to me – which I thought a little tactless.

At Lille station, with no food and drink except what they had bought
in town, some 800 English internees from the occupied territories were
crammed into windowless cattle trucks designed for 'Quarante Hommes,
Huit Chevaux'. After the usual delay, they were sent about a hundred

and five miles to Liège where they arrived at half past noon, after a 'pretty darned awful' twenty-four-hour journey. Wodehouse recovered his customary optimism to describe his arrival:

I was first to alight from train. Nice old German general asked me how old I was, felt my suitcase and said it was too heavy to carry and sent for truck – asked me if I had had anything to eat or drink. Very sympathetic and kindly. We walked through Liège, whistling 'Tipperary' and 'The Barrel', and up a long steep hill which tested some of us pretty severely. Then parade. Then hot soup. Lovely day, so arrival was not depressing.

Afterwards, Wodehouse was much less complimentary about the barracks in which he was now confined. 'We spent a week at Liège,' he wrote; 'looking back, I can hardly believe that our stay there lasted only a mere seven days. This is probably due to the fact there was practically nothing to do but stand around [on parade].' These roll-call parades became a farcical feature of the internees' daily life, highlighting their anomalous role as civilian prisoners under military discipline. Wodehouse added that these disgusting barracks, which were blood-stained and dirty, bore the same resemblance to a regular prison camp that a rough scenario does to a finished novel. Conditions were primitive and squalid. In the absence of proper mess tins, he was obliged to fashion a soup bowl from a discarded motor oil can, which, he joked, contributed something special to the flavour of his daily soup ration. He concluded that if he never saw anything Belgian again, it would be all right with him.

Meanwhile, in the outside world, probably because Ethel had no means of communicating with her daughter, Wodehouse's plight was still quite unknown. Leonora actually advised A. P. Watt that 'the latest news is that he is still in his house in Le Touquet and fairly comfortable'. In fact, on 3 August, the day after this note, Wodehouse and the other civilian internees of Liège were moved again, on an eighteen-mile journey to a new prison, the Citadel at Huy, a sleepy market town on a bend of the river Meuse.

'The Citadel of Huy', Wodehouse later wrote, in words intended to entertain, 'is one of those show places they charge you two francs to go into in times of peace . . . it is one of those places where, once you're in, you're in. Its walls are 14 feet thick, and the corridors are lighted by bays, in which are narrow slits of windows.' The Citadel, which was reached by a long, exhausting climb up steep stone steps, was built around an inner courtyard used for exercise and described by Wodehouse as 'a fairly roomy cuspidor'. Its cells were draughty and primitive: the internees were obliged to collect dirty straw and sleep on the floor. Despite its fearsome medieval appearance, this gloomy fortress-cum-prison had actually been built during the Napoleonic wars to defend a strategic point on the Meuse. To this day, even as a peacetime museum, it broods menacingly over the town of Huy. For the civilian internees in Nazi custody, their sojourn here was an experience they would never forget and in some cases never really recover from. In *Performing Flea*, his highly contrived 'self portrait in letters', it is not Loos or Liège, but his five weeks in Huy that Wodehouse chooses to describe, more than a month of exceptional hardship and privation that made a deep and lasting impression on him.

At Huy, still lost in the mass of internees, he was logged as 'Whitehouse', which, when shouted out in the evening, was occasionally confused with 'Lights out' – a mistake Wodehouse did nothing to correct. Displays of 'side' were taboo with Wodehouse, and he easily resisted the temptation to exploit his literary celebrity. On 21 August, however, writing on behalf of all 700 internees, he did break cover to appeal to the Red Cross in Brussels for the right 'to communicate with our families', in a letter that the Gestapo officer in charge of the citadel angrily tore up in front of him. Apart from this solitary act of leadership, Wodehouse made a point of being a regular internee. Among his mainly English fellows, however, it is clear that 'Whitehouse's' true identity was no secret. As Englishmen, they were reluctant to impose their knowledge of his work upon their famous room-mate. Towards the end of August, a 'ragged and down at heels' fellow internee approached him surreptitiously in one of the dingy, half-lighted stone corridors of the Citadel, asked 'how Ukridge would have liked this life', and revealed that he, too, was an ex-public schoolboy, from Merchant Taylors'. 'Another ragged man', Wodehouse noted, was 'Winchester and Oxford'.

The formative experiences of Dulwich certainly contributed to Wodehouse's stoical inner strength during these gruelling weeks. On 13 August, he noted that he had 'now been sleeping ten nights without a blanket . . . last night was bitterly cold', and gratefully acknowledged that his friend Algy had somehow come up with a thermos flask. 'I shall save some of the evening coffee, and drink it in the small hours,' Wodehouse confided to his notebook. Apart from the cold, he had no trouble coping with the dramatic loss of privacy in captivity and continued to do his 'daily dozen' unabashed. The first time he performed his exercises, 'a gaping multitude assembled', he said. 'Our crowd wear caps, scrubby beards and shiny coats and trousers and look like a football crowd up north.'

Public school also taught him to celebrate rare moments of unexpected happiness. The fourteenth of August, he recorded, was

A wonderful day! . . . suddenly, for no reason, I got a sort of exalted feeling – definitely happy, as if a cloud had rolled away . . . a man came up and paid back 5 francs which I had lent him a few days ago, he having no Belgian money. This touched me enormously . . . [and] made me feel how decent everybody is really.

In a spirit of camaraderie, he volunteered for a cleaning fatigue, potato-peeling duties and soup collection from the cookhouse. There were other powerful evocations of schooldays. 'It's extraordinary', he noted, 'how one's whole soul becomes obsessed with food . . . Sherrer went to town today (for canteen) and brought me a pound of sweets. Heaven!'

Rations were very short at Huy, and all the men went hungry. The supply of food was a hit-and-miss business: Huy was never intended to be a fully fledged internment camp, just a holding centre. When the meagre bread ration failed, as it often did, the internees were given small biscuits, like dog biscuits, a smear of butter which looked like 'a sort of pale axle grease', jam and minute pieces of cheese, if they were lucky. In some communal cells, the internees pooled their allowance of bread, jam, milk and sugar to make a kind of indigestible cake. Potatoes were a staple, and there was a regular supply of watery cabbage soup. When the supply of tobacco ran out, the men smoked tea leaves or old straw. Just as at boarding school, the internees learned to extract maximum advantage from the weaknesses in the system. Prisoners who were allowed down the hill to Huy for visits to the dentist or the oculist took the opportunity to smuggle luxuries. One man returned 'with a jam tart wrapped round his chest', and resourceful Algy 'came staggering back loaded with food'.

These were the brighter moments. Privately, Wodehouse's notes betray real distress. In his notebook, he writes of 'horror . . . lurking round the corner', of constant 'apprehension', and of 'the great fear' that the internees, who were becoming mutinous with hunger, would riot and be machine-gunned. One man developed a serious skin disease and a nickname – 'Scabies' – to go with it. 'At the back of one's mind', Wodehouse wrote, 'is always the thought – suppose an epidemic starts?' His well-protected emotions were becoming vulnerable. He worried incessantly 'about my poor Bunny' and, at least until letters began to get through, the absence of news about her safety 'stabs me like a knife sometimes'. Childhood training told him what to do in these difficult moments: 'one has deliberately to school oneself to think of something else quick.' Another way to cope with fear was to evoke literary comparisons. One of the youngest internees, a Belgian teenager, escaped by slipping through one of the stone window slits, and the Germans briefly introduced a reign of terror. 'Atmosphere like Dotheboys Hall after escape of Smike,' Wodehouse noted calmly.

The cruellest part of the incarceration in the Citadel at Huy was the tantalizing propinquity of everyday life. The internees could easily look down on the town below. Distraught wives would appear at the foot of the massive stone walls and shout up to their husbands. Looking back, Wodehouse made light of this ('Neither can see the other, and the whole thing is like something out of Il Trovatore'), but there were terrible scenes. For the first time in years, Wodehouse was forced to confront the harsh reality of painful emotion. On one occasion he was sitting in the canteen room when two men rushed in. 'Their wives are down below,' he wrote, 'hundreds of feet. They lie on broad window sill, looking down and shouting and we hear women's voices.' He went on: 'Finally we drag them in, afraid they may lose their heads and jump, and Algy, wonderfully gentle, makes them sit on bench. – They sit there with bowed heads, crying, and Algy talks to them like a mother, saying they know their wives are all right and we shall soon all be out etc.' Wodehouse's laconic 'etc.' comes from a deep well of unexpressed feelings, and is eloquent of a pain he can hardly bear to face.

Occasionally, there were rumours that the war was about to end, and that they would all be released, but generally there were few grounds for optimism, and change when it happened was sudden, dramatic and unnerving. On 8 September, Wodehouse and all 700 internees were transferred by train to a converted lunatic asylum in Tost, a small town in Upper Silesia, in the agricultural south-east of Greater Germany. 'Subita Germanorum sunt concilia [swift decisions are typical of the Germans],' noted Wodehouse, the classical scholar. He had just washed his clothes and had to pack them, still damp, for yet another unexpected journey. 'Fate's banquet' was still in progress.

18. 'Camp was really great fun'
(1940-1941)

Tost is no beauty spot. It lies in the heart of sugar-beet country . . .
There is a flat dullness about the countryside which has led many a
visitor to say, 'If this is Upper Silesia, what must Lower Silesia be like?'
(*Performing Flea*)

Wodehouse made the three-day journey to Internierungslager (Ilag)
Tost, through the heart of Nazi-occupied Europe, in the overcrowded
compartment of a civilian train. His rations were just a bowl of soup,
a loaf of bread and half a sausage; the trip was a grim combination of
hunger, sleep deprivation, and uncertainty, and left Wodehouse 'looking
like something the carrion crow had brought in'. Even he, who rarely
acknowledged the horrors of Nazi Germany, wrote in his diary that
the 'frightful thing about these journeys is that you have no means of
knowing how long they are'. Typically, he edited the experience,
presenting himself as stoical, good-humoured and ironically detached
throughout the ordeal. For others, it was terrifying. Bob Whitby, who
travelled with Wodehouse, remembers that when the train made a station
stop there were guards with fixed bayonets. 'Sometimes, somebody who
had the nerve [would ask] the German soldiers "Where are you taking
us?" The answer was always "Salt mines. To the salt mines". I was scared
to death of [going to] the salt mines.' But while some internees suffered
agonies of uncertainty, Wodehouse still found time to jot down an overheard joke: 'Some humorist on parade: "When the war is over, if I have
any money, I'm going to buy a German and keep him in the garden
and count him!"' The interminable journey to Tost had begun on 8
September. The day before, church bells had rung out across Britain as
the Home Guard prepared to resist what was believed (wrongly, as it
turned out) to be an 'imminent invasion'.

During the remaining ten months of Wodehouse's incarceration in
Nazi Germany, from September 1940 to June 1941, the war entered its
most desperate phase. The blitz of autumn 1940 was followed by the

Battle of the Atlantic, from March to July 1941. The combination of the air raids, the losses at sea and a succession of setbacks in the Allies' Mediterranean campaign put the British war effort on the defensive. America had yet to join the Allies. The crisis inspired a fiercely patriotic siege mentality that looked back with loathing on the shameful years of appeasement. Wodehouse, shut up in Tost, was oblivious to this.

His stepdaughter Leonora Cazalet, living in Kent, was fully exposed to the Battle of Britain. 'We have air battles overhead the whole day,' she informed Reynolds, writing to him about literary business on Wodehouse's behalf. Leonora also advised Reynolds that Ethel had been traced to the home of Madame Bernard, the trout farm in the Pas de Calais. She asked for $1,000 to be cabled, care of the American embassy in Paris. 'I have no news of Plummie,' Leonora told Reynolds, 'except that they were separated and we are trying to get his address.' In New York, Reynolds was also making strenuous efforts on his client's behalf. In September, knowing only that Wodehouse had been captured by the Germans, he had appealed to the Red Cross to intervene, and had been ignored. By mid-September he had discovered that Wodehouse 'is believed to be in a concentration camp [and that] it is impossible to communicate with him'. On 10 October, he learned from the American consul in Paris that 'Mr Wodehouse is stated to be held a prisoner at Huy Fortress, Belgium, near Liège'. This news was already a month out of date, as Reynolds soon discovered when, in late October, he received a thin, plain postcard written in pencilled block letters from 'Gefangennummer 796', breaking weeks of worrying silence:

Goodness knows when you will get this. Will you send me a five pound parcel one pound Prince Albert tobacco, the rest nut chocolate. Repeat monthly. Am quite happy here and have thought out new novel. Am hoping be able [*sic*] to write it. When I was interned, I had finished a Jeeves novel, all but four chapters, also two short stories.

'Am quite happy here and have thought out new novel'. This is the authentic voice of Wodehouse, expressing his lifelong preoccupation. It is easy to forget that, although he was a humorist with a mass audience, Wodehouse possessed in his diffident English way that precious inability to compromise that marks the true artist. Even *in extremis* his comic voice was never silenced. *Money in the Bank* is neither *Don Quixote* nor *Pilgrim's Progress* (both written in captivity), but it is irrefutably part of the Wodehousian vision. The novel was written, he explained to Townend, 'in a room with fifty other men playing darts and ping-pong', or with German guards looking over his shoulder. But it says a lot about his conduct during these war years. Although entirely composed in the worst possible circumstances, it carries very few traces of its author's gruelling experiences. It is as though the war has simply passed Wodehouse by. The world that was most real to him was the world of his imagination.

Money in the Bank is set partly in Wodehouse's London and partly in that English Arcadia in which men and women dress for dinner and where a green baize door separates servants from masters. Its hero, George, 6th Viscount Uffenham, a pear-shaped, balding giant of a man whose 'two huge unblinking eyes of the palest blue looked out from beneath rugged brows with a strange fixity', was recognizably based on Wodehouse's dormitory-mate, Max Enke. The novel describes how the viscount has rented his ancestral home, Shipley Hall, to a loud, rich, big-game-hunting widow, Mrs Cork, who has turned the place into a health farm. Unable to bear being parted from the Hall, not least because he has hidden a cache of diamonds somewhere and has forgotten where, Uffenham stays on, masquerading as the butler, Cakebread. Tangled up in this plot is one of Wodehouse's innocent love stories, Jeff Miller's pursuit of his love for Anne Benedick, and one of his regular crime stories, the scheming of three American crooks (Chimp Twist and the husband-and-wife team, Soapy and Dolly Molloy) to snaffle the diamonds for themselves. Whatever the nostalgic and sentimental similarities between Shipley and Fairlawne, Leonora Cazalet's home in Kent, the reader is firmly in Wodehouse's private universe. The novel describes an England that, by 1941, was already extinct, but, like all his work, it transforms experience into a farcical simulacrum of reality. Mrs Cork's health farm, whose clients long for a square meal and dream of steak-and-kidney pudding, is Wodehouse's representation of Tost. Not everything is done with his usual light touch. The directness of his exposure to camp life probably accounts for the un-Wodehousian use of 'fanny', and 'too bloody much', but in all other respects *Money in the Bank*, while not one of his best works, is strikingly free of wartime references, and looks back, not forward.

Wodehouse's oblique rendering of internment is all the more remarkable because, for most inmates, Ilag VIII was a life-changing experience. On the three-day journey across Germany, Wodehouse had complained of a 'lost feeling', evocative of his childhood, in which the sergeant escorting the internees was like 'a temperamental mother, in fact more like an aunt', but he had soon acclimatized. Despite its institutional exterior, his new home, a converted mental hospital and part of a network of Silesian prison-camp facilities, was so reminiscent of Dulwich that he soon found himself to be quite at ease in an all-male society that many other inmates found alien and stressful. 'The thing about Tost that particularly attracted me, was that it was evidently a going concern . . .,' he wrote later. 'For the first time, we were in a real camp, not a makeshift.' Once registered, searched, de-loused, vaccinated, and settled in camp, Wodehouse found the detail that would eventually give him the perfect opportunity for a joke: 'They [the Nazis] took a look at me . . . got the right idea at last [and sent] us off to the local lunatic asylum.' Flippancy aside, Silesia concealed the Third Reich's grimmest secret: Auschwitz (Oświęcim) was barely thirty miles from Tost, and Belsen-Birkenau less than a day's drive.

Tost's former asylum was a brooding, dark red-brick building, more like a school, or a prison, overlooking a small park. It was enclosed on one side by a high wall and separated from some adjacent farm buildings by rolls of barbed wire. From its barred windows the inmates could watch everyday life passing up and down the road outside. Three hundred yards across the park, which served as an exercise yard, was a second building, used as a dining hall, and a third, known as the White House, which became a hospital and a recreation centre where Wodehouse shared a writing room, formerly a padded cell, with a saxophonist. In the main building, which had space for about thirteen hundred, the men slept in dormitories. Wodehouse had sixty-four in his, room 309, 'the cream of the camp we think', he noted proudly. The dormitory scene he painted in his notebook is evocative of nothing so much as an English public-school house:

White frost on roofs. I am lying on my bed after breakfast, amusing to see different occupations of the men. – Arthur [Grant] sweeping floor under his bed, George Pickard darning sock, Scharny sewing vest, McCandless writing up diary, Smythe having back of his neck shaved by Rex Rainer, Tom Sarginson at table studying German, Enke and McKenzie playing chess, Brimble darning his boots, more sweeping going on in middle room. Tom Musgrove comes in from second floor with his daily rumour.

The camp routine, which Wodehouse said was governed by 'rumours and potatoes', began with reveille at 6 a.m., then breakfast from 7.00 to 8.30, followed by a roll-call. For the rest of the morning, until three sittings of lunch beginning at 12.30, the men were occupied with camp duties. Until February 1941, when Red Cross supplies began to flow regularly, rations were short and the men weak with hunger. Lunch was 'a slop of vegetables', made with swedes, turnips and carrots, or fish stew and boiled potatoes. There was plenty of tea and ersatz coffee. Food parcels were objects of suspicion: the Germans saw luxuries sent from Britain as a kind of propaganda, and were capricious about distributing them.

Tost life was bleak, but there were some improvements over Huy and Liège. For instance, men over fifty were not liable for 'fatigues'. Wodehouse later commented in one of his broadcasts that

At Liège and Huy, there had been no age limit. We had all pitched in together, reverend elders and beardless boys alike. . . . At Tost, the old dodderers like myself lived the life of Riley. For us, the arduous side of life was limited to making our beds . . . When there was man's work to be done, like hauling coal or shovelling snow, we just sat and looked on, swapping reminiscences of the Victorian Age, while the younger set snapped to it.

His private account of the experience was scarcely less enthusiastic. 'Camp was really great fun,' he told Townend. 'I really do think that there is nothing on earth to compare with the Englishman in the cloth cap and muffler. I had friends at Tost in every imaginable walk of life, from Calais dock touts upwards, and there wasn't one I didn't like.' In his diary he observed that 'without women . . . we relapse into boyhood – all our emotions are boyish'.

After lunch there was more leisure time. 'The great advantage [of Tost] is that the internee is left to himself,' he noted with approval. Supper was in three sittings from 4.30 p.m. This was followed by more free time, until the men were counted outside their dormitories at 8.00 p.m. Lights out was at 9.15 p.m. In his description of the running of the camp, Wodehouse naturally identified the parallels with Dulwich. The Kommandant, Kapitäns and Oberleutnants, like the headmaster and his staff, were not important in the day-to-day life of the inmates, and in fact he only saw the Kommandant on one occasion. 'The really important thing is the inner camp,' he explained later, echoing his youthful description of the public-school house. During his time there, Ilag Tost was 'presided over by a Lagerführer and four corporals', reminiscent of a housemaster and his prefects. Wodehouse's Lagerführer, whom he described as a 'nice chap', was a man named Buchelt who had been interned in England during the First World War. Just as in school, his corporals had nicknames: 'Pluto', 'Rosebud', 'Ginger' and 'Donald Duck'.

Lagerführer Buchelt, who would shortly play a decisive and much-discussed role in Wodehouse's downfall, was 'the answer to an internee's prayer', a liberal-minded man who 'was working all the time in our interests'. Wodehouse liked Buchelt for starting a library and a camp newspaper, and for organizing a typewriter and a place for him to work on his novel, the padded cell in the White House. In hindsight, the ease of his relations with the Lagerführer was fatal, though in character. Wodehouse had been friendly with many Germans in Hollywood, and the war made no difference to him. In Tost, he also became fond of two German interpreters, one of whom had worked in America and liked to show off with phrases like 'Have you got me, boys?' Wodehouse's relationship with these two men, whose names are not known, 'bears out what I have always said', as he confessed in his camp diary, 'that Germans are swell guys, and the only barrier between us is one of language. I have never met an English-speaking German I didn't like instantly.' Apart from this unexceptionable comment, there is not a single reference, either pro or anti, to the Nazi authorities administering Upper Silesia.

Ilag VIII housed a mixture of British and Dutch prisoners whose mood was intensely patriotic. Internees were required to salute German officers, but beyond this quasi-military formality, the prevailing attitude was defiant, verging on insubordinate. Although his literary celebrity set him apart from his fellows, many of whom were merchant seamen, or war graves gardeners like his friend Bert Haskins, Wodehouse's loyalty to the group was whole-hearted and instinctive. 'The morale of the men at Tost was wonderful,' he said later. 'I never met a more cheerful crowd, and I loved them like brothers.' And they respected him, standing behind his typewriter when he worked outside but rarely interrupting. His role in Tost was that of a much-admired senior boy – mediating with authority, adjudicating small disputes, calming contentious situations, a figure whom the internees treated with respect. Their sense of betrayal, on Wodehouse's premature departure, reportedly led to various internal protests. He was also a father figure of sorts to some of the teenagers in the camp. Bob Whitby, who looked younger than his eighteen years, now an elderly gentleman in his eighties, recalls that Wodehouse, whom he knew slightly, always inquired kindly after his welfare and repeated the internees' mantra, 'Home Before Christmas', to lift his spirits.

That was not to be, of course, and when the first snow came in October, the Silesian winter turned a just bearable experience into something much harsher. The wind from the east was especially bitter, the food was inadequate, and camp life was remorseless. Some men died; others had nervous breakdowns; there were a few suicides. Whitby recalls obsessive conversations among the inmates about food and sex, usually in the coarsest language. Then, as the second Christmas of the war approached, the outside world began to intrude on Wodehouse's enforced, but not unwelcome, solitude.

Throughout the autumn, Leonora and Reynolds had continued to campaign in Britain and America for Wodehouse's release, but there had been little media interest in his story, mainly because he was inaccessible to reporters. America was not yet at war with Germany, however, and there were several American journalists in Berlin, including Angus Thuermer, an Associated Press reporter. Thuermer had been working on a special report about prisoner-of-war and prison camp conditions when he stumbled on the fact that the novelist P. G. Wodehouse, or 'British Civilian prisoner no. 796', as he was known officially, was in Ilag VIII near Gleiwitz. Intrigued, Thuermer requested an interview, and was given controlled access.

Wodehouse spoke to Thuermer, in the presence of the Lagerführer and a Gestapo minder, as he always spoke to the press – courteously, openly, and without much thought for the consequences, imagining that any publicity would simply reassure his numerous readers that he was, despite the war, alive and well and in good spirits. He took the opportunity to do a bit of literary business, using Thuermer as a go-between with the *Saturday Evening Post*, which was interested in a light-hearted magazine piece about his experiences provisionally titled 'Whither Wodehouse?' Published as 'My War with Germany', this article would later give Wodehouse nothing but aggravation. Typically, he also drew Thuermer into a discussion about the title for his new novel. Thuermer advised that 'Money for Jam' would not make sense to readers in the American Midwest.

Thuermer's report went out on the AP wire over Christmas, and was published in the *New York Times* on 27 December 1940. It would have calamitous consequences, rapidly building up to the crisis that became the defining moment of Wodehouse's life. In the short term, there were three immediate consequences of Thuermer's visit. First, Thuermer's article inadvertently launched what might be called the 'myth' of Wodehouse's war. Although it was supremely factual and scrupulously free of editorial comment, the article focused on what Thuermer considered to be the remarkable fact that Wodehouse was explicitly *not* receiving special privileges and had even refused such favours as the private room offered to him by the authorities out of respect for his age and reputation. But the article was accompanied by headlines that inevitably raised issues of conduct in readers' minds: one of the sub-headings was 'He [Wodehouse] Declines Favors'. Ironically, it was Wodehouse's refusal to accept favours, together with his instinctive denial of the hardship he suffered, that would help to convict him of seeming light-hearted about the war.

Second, Thuermer's article was accompanied by a photograph of Wodehouse in a scarf and dressing gown in which he looked so old, sad and thin that his American friends, especially Guy and Virginia Bolton, became greatly alarmed. As a result of the *New York Times* story, the Boltons now began to organize a petition appealing for their friend's release, enlisting the support of Senator Warren Barbour, a Republican senator from New Jersey. Press reports of this petition, in turn, inspired well-intentioned letters of protest from various influential Americans, notably Dorothy, the wife of Demaree Bess, the European correspondent of the *Saturday Evening Post*, a friend of Ethel's who had been agitating on Wodehouse's behalf from as early as June 1940. Petitions were one thing; newspaper coverage was something else. Once Wodehouse's story was reported in the *New York Times*, the German authorities became aware, really for the first time, of the international publicity potential of prisoner no. 796. And then, thirdly, there was the article he was writing, 'Whither Wodehouse?' This was full of light-hearted lines about internees' beards and the correct etiquette for eating potatoes, but it unquestionably habituated Wodehouse to the idea of writing humorously about camp life and his experience of Nazi Germany, a subject that was no laughing matter.

For the moment, however, there seemed little prospect of Wodehouse's release, and his immediate family had come to terms with that. Shortly after the *New York Times* piece, Leonora wrote to Reynolds that 'Plum is in an internment camp in Germany . . . he has been interviewed there – I've also seen a report of the camp conditions which, consider-ing everything, are pretty good. Warmth. Plenty of clothes. Adequate food etc.' Leonora had this information from the British government, which, long before his release in June 1941, was following his case from afar. This was not privileged treatment, but part of a concerted oper-ation run from the Foreign Office in London. Throughout the war, Ilag, Oflag and Stalag camps were monitored by a combination of Red Cross and Swiss embassy representatives, who reported back to London.

The internees, moreover, were in regular contact with the outside world, following events with patriotic interest, and having a highly moti-vated attitude to self-improvement. Several younger internees sat, and passed, exams for British universities, including Oxford and Cambridge. There was an internees' newspaper, the *Tost Times*, for which Wodehouse abridged a story based on 'All's Well with Bingo', and a German-run paper, the *Camp*, that Wodehouse had nothing to do with, which printed a Jeeves and Wooster parody – with Bertie as a military man – signed 'P. G. Roadhouse'. The internees, who included Dutch university profes-sors, some professional musicians, elegant young lecturers and language school proprietors, also organized a variety of talks and concerts and ran an excellent library of books sent by overseas well-wishers. Ilag VIII was certainly a severe test of character, but this did not prevent some of the livelier spirits from organizing plays, concerts, and a pantomime at Christmas 1940, staged in the 'White House', and watched by an interpreter to guard against anti-Hitler jokes.

Up to that point, the moment of Angus Thuermer's interview, Wodehouse had been relatively anonymous and obscure, lost in the turmoil of wartime Europe. After the press furore of December 1940–January 1941, everything changed, and it is from this moment that his real troubles begin. In the new year of 1941, international curiosity about Wodehouse's internment and a dawning German recognition of the significance of 'Gefangennummer 796' quickly fused into a combustible mixture of personal publicity, Nazi propaganda and patriotic outrage. In America, especially, many fans now expressed support for Wodehouse, highlighting his anomalous quasi-American status. Reynolds unwittingly contributed to the excitement by authorizing the reproduction of Wodehouse's prison-camp postcards, and encouraging *Time* to remind its readers of his plight. Reynolds was now in regular contact with his client, sending tins of Prince Albert tobacco as requested. He also arranged for his client to receive money, which Wodehouse often shared with fellow internees.

Meanwhile, working steadily in Tost, Wodehouse was completing *Money in the Bank*, and had begun to draft a humorous account of camp life that he read to some of his fellow internees, who, he said, 'not only laughed, but applauded and cheered and cheered' at one of their regular entertainments during the spring of 1941. In a manner reminiscent of his early struggles at the bank, Wodehouse was exercising his considerable will-power to overcome adversity. Transforming his experience into humorous copy came naturally: it was what he always did. He did not think through the implications of what he was doing, and no one at Tost, it seems, ever questioned his motives. It was no secret that he was working on a magazine article. In the communal society of the camp, there was considerable interest in what the internationally renowned writer was going to say about the experience of internment.

Across Europe, now that his whereabouts and situation were known, Wodehouse became the subject of wild rumours in both the British and the international press, which was now much more attentive to the Wodehouse story than hitherto. Early in March, a *Saturday Evening Post* correspondent in Budapest picked up a report that Wodehouse had spirited his novel out of Germany, and a *Daily Express* journalist based in Geneva began sending him food parcels, possibly hoping for a scoop to rival Thuermer's. Many of the stories about the Wodehouses' living conditions were totally untrue. Even the usually reliable Reynolds, for instance, told Leonora there was 'a likelihood that [Ethel] has been interned'.

Ethel, in fact, had left the trout farm, taking the parrot with her, and secured a permit to go to Lille where, after a moment of near destitution, she spent three winter months in a bedsit. At first not even the British embassy had any news of her whereabouts, but eventually Leonora – with the improbable assistance of the Chinese embassy – established that Ethel was alive and well and living at 241 rue Nationale, Lille. Subsequently, she was taken into 'a charming house with a huge park' in Hesdin, a move confirmed on 14 May when the British embassy informed Reynolds that Mrs Wodehouse was now staying with a Madame de Rocquigny in the Pas de Calais. This would remain her base until July, when she was reunited with her husband. Coco, the parrot, meanwhile, had learned to sing 'God Save the King', and later became very popular with German soldiers quartered in the chateau. Leonora was often as much in the dark about her parents' situation as anyone, but she was not overly concerned. She confided to Reynolds that 'Mummie and Plum evidently get news of each other. Which explains why he hasn't made any enquiries about her in his postcards to you.'

In Ilag VIII, meanwhile, as a direct result of the *New York Times* interview, Lagerführer Buchelt launched an unexpected German charm offensive towards his famous prisoner. Buchelt had already arranged for Wodehouse to rent a typewriter, and was now taking a close interest in how his writing was going. Wodehouse, who always liked to please, responded by showing him an early copy of 'Whither Wodehouse?' When Buchelt discovered that, in addition to this journalism, Wodehouse had actually completed a new novel (*Money in the Bank*) he – or his superiors – suggested having it shipped to America, an offer Wodehouse gratefully accepted. This was done, in the best German manner, through the proper channels. Wodehouse, naturally, responded with enthusiasm to this attention. Leonora told Reynolds that her stepfather 'appears to be in terrific form loving everybody [and] says he has just finished the best novel of his life!!'

However, as Wodehouse had occasionally observed in his Bertie Wooster stories, Fate was always lurking round the corner. As he had written in 'Jeeves and the Unbidden Guest' as long ago as 1917:

I'm not absolutely certain of my facts, but I rather fancy it's Shakespeare – or, if not, it's some equally brainy bird – who says that it's always just when a fellow is feeling particularly braced with things in general that Fate sneaks up behind him with a bit of lead piping. And what I'm driving at is that the man is perfectly right.

In May 1941, the bit of lead piping was the conversation Wodehouse had with Lagerführer Buchelt. This was the conversation that would lead inexorably to his disgrace.

As he reported it later, to the British authorities, the exchange with Buchelt was informal, but on the Lagerführer's part it was plainly calculated and made on instructions from above. Wodehouse was summoned to his office on the pretext of discussing his continued use of the typewriter. Here, Buchelt revealed that he was about to be transferred to a new post, and suggested that this would be a good moment to turn in the machine. A copy of the *Saturday Evening Post* containing the serial version of Wodehouse's most recent novel, *Quick Service*, was lying on the table. Buchelt began smoothly, saying how much he had enjoyed 'Whither Wodehouse?', and went on to say, 'Why don't you do some broadcasts on similar lines for your American readers?'

Wodehouse's response to this enquiry was instinctive but horribly ill-judged: 'I said "I would love to" or "There's nothing I should like better" – or some similar phrase. These remarks were quite casual and made no impression on my mind,' he said later. With hindsight, Wodehouse claimed that 'The inference I draw from this episode is either (a) that he had been told to sound me out as to my willingness to broadcast, or (b) that having been informed by me that I was willing . . . he reported to Berlin'.

Wodehouse could not have foreseen the complexity of the situation into which he was being drawn. The whole conversation had, in fact, been stage-managed by the German Foreign Office which, having been made aware of Wodehouse's importance to the Americans, had decided to use him as part of its wider campaign to keep the United States out of the war. This foreign policy objective was all the more crucial in May and June 1941 because Hitler and his generals were now in the final stages of their preparations for Operation Barbarossa, the invasion of the Soviet Union. If Wodehouse had been more aware, he might have noticed the signs of exceptional military activity simmering in Poland during recent weeks. Other Tost internees, for instance, reported seeing columns of Nazi armour rumbling down the road outside the camp on their way to the front.

Back in Berlin, Paul Schmidt, a career diplomat and the head of the German Foreign Minister von Ribbentrop's private office, who had fielded the many appeals for Wodehouse's release since May 1940, had come to the view that the release of civilian prisoner 796 would be desirable on a number of counts. Most important, it would placate American public opinion and show that Germany was taking America's neutrality seriously. This act of humanity might also assist the German Foreign Office's campaign to keep America out of the war before the invasion of the Soviet Union. 'The release of Wodehouse', George Orwell wrote later, in a famous defence of Wodehouse, 'was a minor move, but it was not a bad sop to throw to the American isolationists.' More than that, it might score a propaganda triumph at home, a demonstration of the superiority of the Foreign Office over the Ministry of Propaganda across the Wilhelmstrasse. Von Ribbentrop and Goebbels loathed each other, and there was bitter competition between their respective ministries. The diplomats, typically, considered themselves to be superior civil servants, polished professionals, where the Nazi propagandists were crude, petit bourgeois fanatics. One of the features of the Reich that certainly contributed to Wodehouse's downfall was the ferocious inter-departmental feuding between the upstart Nazi ministries and the proud, long-established ministries of the former Prussian state. As Iain Sproat has written in *Wodehouse at War*, the value of Wodehouse to the professional diplomats 'was precisely that he was *not* a Nazi sympathiser nor a collaborator . . . it was essential [to the Foreign Office plan] that Wodehouse be seen to be released because of American pressure'. But now this carefully orchestrated exercise ran into trouble: the Gestapo would not approve Wodehouse's release.

It is at this point that the plot becomes almost Wodehousian in its complexity. The head of the Foreign Office department that handled American press relations was Hitler's English-language interpreter, confusingly also named Paul Schmidt, a stout, red-cheeked civil servant in his early thirties. By chance, Schmidt was an admirer of Wodehouse's work and had in his department a liaison officer with the propaganda ministry who not only shared his enthusiasm but had actually been on the fringes of the Wodehouses' circle during their California days: Werner Plack. To the Wodehouses, Plack had been a wine salesman and a would-be film actor. With his broken English, soft-spoken charm, fawn overcoats, longish hair, and puffy, boxer's features, Plack cuts a suspicious figure that conforms to the reality. American records show that, even in his Californian days, Werner Plack had been a German agent, working out of the consulate in Los Angeles; when he finally left the United States it was under suspicion of espionage. A born survivor, with a penchant for sleazy women and luxury living, he had then carved a niche for himself in the Wilhelmstrasse as the self-styled English-speaking go-between with foreigners the Nazis hoped to exploit for propaganda purposes.

Plack was assigned to the Wodehouse case by the interpreter and resident anglophile, Paul Schmidt. Unsavoury though Plack was, he liked and admired Wodehouse and later claimed to have done his best to protect him in the ruthless, competitive world of the Nazi propaganda machine. He also had a risk-taking, exhibitionist side that appealed to Ethel Wodehouse, who took a shine to him when she eventually joined her husband. According to Iain Sproat, Plack once walked with the Wodehouses through the streets of Berlin, dressed in a British army uniform picked up in Tobruk, wearing a helmet on which its former British owner had scrawled 'Down with Hitler'. The closeness of his relationship to Ethel in particular is borne out by the fact she became godmother to his son in 1948. In one of the very rare photographs from this episode in Wodehouse's life, Ethel and Plack are seen enjoying a joke outside a Berlin café while he watches from one side. The haunting expression of embarrassment, disgust and loathing on Wodehouse's face tells its own story.

Plack's role in Wodehouse's broadcasts is crucial, but obscure. It was alleged, for instance, that Plack visited Wodehouse in Tost to discuss the implications of his conversation with Lagerführer Buchelt and to finalize a deal. Wodehouse's circumstances during May and June are uncertain. The mystery of what happened during these weeks is not clarified by the line in Wodehouse's diary which reads: 'I have no entries between May 28 and June 20.' But the one thing on which the main participants in the affair are agreed is that Plack never went to Tost, though he could have spoken to Buchelt on the telephone.

If there was a plot, Wodehouse did not know about it. The idea of his broadcast did not come with strings attached, at least explicitly. As far as Wodehouse was concerned, there was no quid pro quo, a point he returned to repeatedly in all his later writings about his troubles. Nonetheless, unbeknown to him, his responsiveness to Lagerführer Buchelt's idea of a broadcast to America had the desired effect, from the point of view of the German Foreign Office. Once Buchelt reported that Wodehouse was willing to go to the microphone, the Gestapo withdrew its objection to his release. Wodehouse the plot-maker might have relished the complexity of his position; Wodehouse the political innocent was already a lost soul.

It is hard now to recapture the significance, in the 1930s and 1940s, of the political radio. In 1933 Goebbels, who was one of the first to grasp its propaganda potential, had transferred control of German radio to his newly created Ministry for Public Enlightenment and Propaganda, colloquially known as 'Promi'. Greater German radio never confined its activities to the Reich. Lord Haw-Haw, for example, was merely the most prominent in a Europe-wide series of radio Nazis. In February 1941 Goebbels had intensified his recruitment of foreign pro-Nazi broadcasters. One of these, an American, Frederick Wilhelm Kaltenbach, was known as 'Lord Hee-Haw'. By agreeing to use Nazi radio, even for what he considered the most innocuous talks, Wodehouse, an instinctive patriot, was unwittingly putting himself in bad company.

Worse still, the propaganda climate in which the manoeuvres leading up to Wodehouse's release were conducted was neither tranquil nor straightforward. On 10 May Rudolph Hess had made his bizarre solo flight to Scotland, to the Nazis' acute embarrassment. The news of such a senior Nazi freelancing a peace treaty with Britain was impossible to explain away or gloss over. Hitler was enraged; Goebbels was desperate. The Allies might be struggling militarily (Yugoslavia and Greece had just fallen to the Wehrmacht), but Britain seemed to be winning the propaganda war. In a widespread joke, Churchill was supposed to have summoned Hess. 'So you're the madman, are you?' demanded the Prime Minister. 'Oh no,' Hess was said to have replied, 'only his deputy.' Both sides were straining to extract every ounce of advantage from press and radio. Facetious broadcasts by a best-selling writer of comic novels might seem unimportant in the larger scheme of things, but in the context of the time, their significance was immense.

The object of all this manoeuvring was, meanwhile, sequestered in Ilag VIII but becoming more and more intrigued by the idea of writing humorously about his recent experiences. He was in good spirits and said later that he felt terrific and looked like Fred Astaire. The invitation to broadcast had come after several months of steadily growing public interest in what he had to say. His talks to fellow internees had gone down well. Lagerführer Buchelt had enjoyed his 'Whither Wodehouse?' and had sent it to Reynolds in New York, where it had arrived in early June, apparently uncensored. Nervous of readers' reaction,

Life had turned the piece down, but the faithful *Saturday Evening Post* bought it, on condition that they could publish it as 'My War with Germany', which is how it finally appeared in print in July 1941. Wodehouse's jocular proposal to broker a peace with Germany might have been amusing to the inhabitants of Tost, but when it was published internationally it seemed spectacularly misguided, exacerbating an already disastrous situation:

It should be simple to arrive at some settlement which would be satisfactory to both parties. The only concession I want from Germany is that she give me a loaf of bread, tell the gentlemen with the muskets at the main gate to look the other way and leave the rest to me. In return for this I am prepared to hand over India and an autographed set of my books.

All his working life, from the age of twenty-one, Wodehouse had been acutely responsive to his audience and his editors. He had rarely said 'no' to a commission, and he was always keen to keep in with his readers, whom he saw as his livelihood. As Major Cussen, his MI5 interrogator, would correctly observe, Wodehouse was now, for the first time in many years, placed in a position where, deprived of his usual advisers – Reynolds, Ethel, Leonora – he had to make decisions for himself. He was, moreover, missing his wife, and longing to see Wonder again. After a year of enforced silence, he was uniquely ill-equipped to handle this responsibility, but eager to reconnect with the outside world, entertain his audience, take on some new work, and be reunited with Ethel and his favourite Pekinese. The war might be raging, but to a writer whose first and deepest loyalty was to his craft, it seemed like a good opportunity to do what he had always done. George Orwell understood this when he wrote, '[his] main idea . . . was to keep in touch with his public and – the comedian's ruling passion – to get a laugh'. What Wodehouse did not know, and never fully grasped, was that the market for his comedy had changed completely. A tragic figure in his own fairy tale, he had become the jester whose jokes were no longer funny.

19. 'It was a loony thing to do'
(June 1941)

He was reviewing the recent scene and wishing that he had come better out of it. He was a vague man, but not so vague as to be unaware that he might have shown up in a more heroic light. ('The Crime Wave at Blandings')

Wodehouse was happily playing cricket, bowling leg-breaks on a dirt pitch in the park at Tost, when two Gestapo men arrived on the evening of 21 June to take him out of camp. He was in the middle of an over, but he was told to leave the game at once and given ten minutes to pack up his effects, leaving the unfinished manuscript of *Full Moon* behind. Then he and another man named Mackenzie were driven to the neighbouring town of Gleiwitz and put on the night train to Berlin.

It was all very sudden. Wodehouse had assumed, he wrote later, that he would not be leaving for another four months, when he turned sixty. As recently as 14 June he had written to Ethel mentioning that he had enough tobacco for the foreseeable future. But he also claimed not to be greatly surprised by the turn of events which he 'attributed . . . to the efforts of my American well-wishers'. He knew all about Senator Barbour's petition and he was familiar with Dorothy and Demaree Bess's pressure on his behalf. Dorothy Bess had been sending him progress reports throughout the spring, stressing the unpredictability of the Nazi regime. On 12 January she had written 'you may get the good news almost any day from some quarter'. On 9 February she had expressed 'every hope that your release can be arranged before much longer', and finally, on 20 February, had sent the best news of all: 'We have been assured that the Foreign Office is quite agreeable to your release, and it is only necessary to obtain the consent of the Army.' If, as he travelled to Berlin through the midsummer night of 21 June, he had wondered about the reasons for his unexpected deliverance, he would have found the explanation in this American campaign. When he arrived in Berlin, on the very day that Hitler launched Operation

Barbarossa, he soon discovered that his new-found freedom had come at a price.

The Gleiwitz train pulled into the Friedrichstrasse station at about seven in the morning. Wodehouse, Mackenzie and the two Gestapo stooges had 'a sketchy breakfast' at the station buffet and then set off down the Mittelstrasse to look for somewhere to stay. Wodehouse, in his threadbare camp clothes, cut a ragged figure on the street. In mid-1941, Berlin was buoyant with prosperity and optimism. Only the short-ages of chocolate and coffee and the rationing of cigarettes indicated that there was a war on. There were very few air raids, the restaurants and theatres were busy, and on this particular day there was a cup-final football match between Schalke 04 and Rapid Wien (Vienna was then part of Greater Germany). Berlin that morning was full of out-of-town fans and each of the five hotels the Gestapo men tried was fully booked. According to Wodehouse, his minders now decided to ask for a room at Berlin's most famous luxury hotel, the Adlon. The equal of the Ritz, this was an appropriate choice for a famous British writer, and it brought him to the heart of Nazi Berlin.

The festival atmosphere was misleading. Behind the desperate gaiety Nazi Berlin was a grim city. As the historian Alexandra Ritchie has written, the capital of the Third Reich 'was the pinnacle of a ruthlessly centralised Nazi state and housed the hundreds of ministries, depart-ments, offices and institutes filled with tens of thousands of willing employees who directed the most criminal aspects of the war ... Berlin [was] the oppressive administrator of Nazi terror.' The Adlon, which overlooked Unter den Linden, was on the same block as the Reich Chancellery and the Foreign Office; it was also a favourite rendezvous for members of the regime, and its staff were renowned as Nazi informers. If Wodehouse was free, he had landed in the worst possible environment and quickly became caught up in a succession of events that bear the hallmarks of a well-laid plan.

Once Wodehouse had checked into the Adlon, he was given time to have a wash and take a rest and then, later the same morning, was escorted down to the lobby by his minders and allowed to walk about in a courtyard at the back of the hotel. Here, apparently by chance, he found himself greeted by an old friend, an Americanized German stockbroker named Baron Raven von Barnikow, whom he had first met in New York in 1929 and with whom he had spent a lot of time

during his second Hollywood year at Angelo Drive, when von
Barnikow was living in San Francisco and was once engaged to the
movie star Kay Francis. At the outbreak of war, von Barnikow had
returned home to serve in the Luftwaffe, and was later sent to the
Eastern Front. Von Barnikow was an exceedingly handsome minor
Prussian aristocrat, and a First World War veteran of the Richthofen
squadron. Well connected in the German Foreign Office, he had been
trying to use his influence to get Wodehouse exchanged for a German
businessman interned in England. Von Barnikow turned out to be a
committed anti-Nazi, on the edge of the circle that carried out the
bomb plot of 20 July 1944. Wodehouse, who was still adjusting to his
new circumstances after a year of isolation, appears not to have found
anything strange in von Barnikow's fortuitous appearance at the Adlon
hotel. He was, besides, delighted to find an old friend so soon after
his release into a menacing new environment, and all the more so
because, fresh from camp, he had no money and only the clothes he
was wearing – a sports shirt, an old coat and a pair of grey flannels.
Von Barnikow loaned him five hundred marks and promised to come
up with a change of clothes.

While von Barnikow and Wodehouse were renewing old acquaintance, they were joined – again, apparently by chance – by Werner
Plack. The lobby of the Adlon was becoming the scene of quite a
Hollywood reunion. Plack, Wodehouse and von Barnikow were soon
chatting about life in Beverly Hills. It was probably an awkward conversation. Wodehouse always said that Plack's English was difficult to follow.
Eventually, in an obviously premeditated move, von Barnikow excused
himself to go back to his own hotel, the Bristol, to collect some clothes
for Wodehouse, and left him all alone to talk to Plack, whose opening
gambit was to say how much he had enjoyed the *Saturday Evening Post*
article, 'My War with Germany', which had been given to him to censor
before it was mailed to the United States. Plack, who knew Ethel from
Hollywood days, also implied that from his position in the Foreign
Office he could expedite her return to Wodehouse's side. 'It was during
this conversation', Wodehouse said, 'that the idea of broadcasting my
camp experiences to the United States came up.' In his own defence,
smarting from accusations of treason and collaboration, he later wrote
that he had been released from Tost '*before* this conversation took place'.
In his mind, this was 'a vital point [which] establishes beyond any

question that I could have had nothing to gain from the German government by agreeing to broadcast'. But what he could not have anticipated was the interpretation placed on his behaviour by the Nazis, or
the way they publicized it.

For Plack the Foreign Office representative, this conversation was
simply the natural extension of Lagerführer Buchelt's report in May
informing the German Foreign Office that Wodehouse was prepared
to broadcast. Plack's interest, on behalf of his boss, Paul Schmidt, was
to confirm Wodehouse's willingness to go along with the Foreign Office
plan. As Plack was leaving, to reinforce the point Lagerführer Buchelt,
dressed in civilian clothes, also appeared in the lobby of the Adlon and
congratulated Wodehouse on his release. A more politically astute man
than Wodehouse might, at this point, have smelt a rat, and refused point-
blank to co-operate further in any way. But such was not his nature.
Temperamentally eager to please, confused by the rush of events, relieved
to see his friends, and probably a little frightened by the atmosphere
of Nazi Berlin, he was ill-equipped to deal with the challenge
confronting him. Besides, after a year shut away from the outside world,
he behaved as he always did when confronted by difficult or complex
choices, which was to let others take care of the arrangements. There
is no question that the situation in which he had allowed himself to
be placed was both complex and severely testing, but the events of June
1941 hardly convict Wodehouse of anything worse than gross stupidity.
Robert Chalker, an American vice-consul with the embassy in Berlin,
who saw Wodehouse in the lobby of the Adlon on a number of occasions during this first week, reported to Washington that he did not
seem 'anxious to perform a service for the German propaganda agencies.
On the contrary, it appeared that the task was rather an unpleasant one,
and that he was making the best of a difficult situation.'

To answer the questions 'Why did Wodehouse make this blunder?'
or 'Why did he never understand his folly?', it is helpful to look at
Orwell's 'Defence', published shortly after the events described here.
Orwell, born in India in 1903, had a childhood like Wodehouse's, and
also an instinctive understanding of his fellow writer's predicament.
Orwell's observation of 'Wodehouse's complete lack . . . of political
awareness' has to be taken as seriously as his argument that Wodehouse's
'moral outlook has remained that of a public school boy'. Orwell, the
maverick English socialist, felt the nuances of Wodehouse's situation in

his bones. In politically alert circles, he wrote, 'to broadcast on Nazi radio, to have any truck with Nazis whatsoever, would have seemed just as shocking an action before the war as during it'. That, he pointed out, was a habit of mind that had been developed during nearly a decade of ideological struggle against fascism. But, like the majority of middle-class Englishmen, Wodehouse had been ideologically illiterate, and indifferent to the struggle against fascism, as his 1937 row in Los Angeles with the Screen Writers Guild illustrates. Wodehouse's cast of mind was conservative and highly detached. European dictators were ridiculous. European political violence, of the kind alluded to in 'The Clicking of Cuthbert', was a frivolous distraction from more important matters, a game of golf, for instance.

The moral test with which Wodehouse was confronted in June 1941 was one that was beyond him. In addition to his upbringing, there was his temperamental preference for finding the easiest way out of a tricky situation – and his obsessive commitment to his writing. It is these two factors that colour his actions with the taint of irresponsibility. Combined with his failure to understand the nature of Nazism, they proved fatal to his reputation. Wodehouse's innate lack of political awareness was also exacerbated by the peculiar timing of his internment. When he was taken prisoner, the 'phoney war' had just ended. When he was released, the war had reached a desperate phase, and it looked as though Germany might even win. Two years on, Wodehouse was still operating on 1939 terms. More than that, Wodehouse was at heart an Edwardian, born in the age of imperial adventure, gunboat diplomacy and great power squabbles. To his generation, war with Germany (or France or Russia) was, as he had written to Townend in 1939, a kind of away match.

Wodehouse was not wholly naive. In many ways, he was a very clever man who knew exactly how to navigate complexity, as his handling of his literary career shows. Jeevesian in his professional life, it was his fate to be Woosterish in Berlin. His character was exceptional: unusually good-natured, remarkably lacking in cynicism and in many ways always eager to please. Evelyn Waugh, who knew him, spoke of his 'humility' and 'beauty of character'. These were not qualities suited for dealing with the Nazis. Ironically, it was Wodehouse's best qualities that came into play after his disgrace. Even though he never fully grasped the true nature of his blunder, he freely acknowledged, as he wrote to Townend, that 'it was a loony thing to do', and refused to minimize his mistake. In a letter to the Foreign Office, written in 1942, he put it in more measured terms. 'I can now, of course, see that this was an insane thing to do.' In the heat of the moment, being in 'an emotional frame of mind', he had simply blundered. 'Isn't it the damnedest thing,' he wrote to Guy Bolton, 'how Fate lurks to sock you with the stuffed eelskin?'

The extent of the trouble towards which he was heading became clear within days of his release – phase one in the process of his disgrace. At first, the German Foreign Office's strategy seemed to be going according to plan. On the morning of Monday, 23 June, at the beginning of a hectic and fateful week, Wodehouse was escorted by the Gestapo down the Wilhelmstrasse to visit Werner Plack at the Foreign Office. There, he was introduced to the head of Plack's department, Hitler's interpreter, Paul Schmidt, who expressed his sincere admiration for Wodehouse's work, and his gratitude for the agreement to broadcast. Then, moving to the heart of the matter, Plack showed him how the proposed talks would be recorded on wax discs, and Wodehouse was sent back to the Adlon to prepare the first of his broadcasts. The next morning, Tuesday, 24 June, one of the Gestapo men returned Wodehouse's passport and disappeared, along with Mackenzie, who fades from view.

By now, to the numerous foreign correspondents in Berlin, especially the Americans, 'P. G. Wodehouse released from internment' was a first-class breaking story. No sooner was he installed at his typewriter in the Adlon, with the Foreign Office commission to complete, than Wodehouse was besieged with requests for comment and interviews from 'every country in the world'. When he tried to recall the sequence of events afterwards, he admitted, ruefully, that his recollection of an extraordinary week began 'to get blurred'. Once the media frenzy died down, the *New York Times* had a good story ('I told them I was going to broadcast'), CBS had secured an agreement to an interview, and the Hearst representative had the promise of a magazine article about camp life for *Cosmopolitan*. As he had done throughout his working life, Wodehouse was extracting the maximum value from his material. From the moment he reached Berlin, his attention had been entirely focused on his relationship with his public, and secondarily on being reunited with Ethel and Wonder. All his life, it was his practice to answer fan-mail himself, and now that he was at liberty, he wanted to catch up.

While in camp, 'I had received a great number of letters from American readers of my books,' he wrote later, 'and none of these had I been able to answer. . . These letters had been preying on my mind.'

For Wodehouse, his publicity campaign had two almost equally important objectives in America and Britain. To the Americans, he wanted to say 'thank you' for the countless letters and food-parcels he had been unable to acknowledge in Tost, and in all his subsequent self-justifications he returned obsessively to this theme. To the British, he wanted to demonstrate what he believed to be a typically English patriotism, his refusal to be downhearted or dismayed by his internment, that is, to exhibit the stiff upper lip; as he put it, to show 'how a little group of British people were keeping up their spirits in difficult conditions'. What he never grasped, to the end of his life, because it was beyond his understanding, was either the offensiveness of using Nazi radio, or the stupidity of placing himself, by association, in the company of genuine traitors like William Joyce. There is no doubt that his celebrity worked against him. Other British prisoners of war had been brought to the microphone, and had sometimes made comments at least as tactless as Wodehouse's, without attracting the same attention. As he put it later, 'My motive . . . in doing the talks was no more culpable than that of a hundred English prisoners of war who came to the German radio and sent messages home saying that they were in the pink.'

It is important to note that the text of what he said was not the main issue: Wodehouse was in difficulty before a single word of his talks had been broadcast, or even recorded. He had always been a quick worker, but the speed with which he completed his script and its assured narrative voice indicates that he based it on material he had already used in camp and on the notes he had begun to draft for *Wodehouse in Wonderland*. In other words, he saw these talks as a continuation of his various writings about camp life. At all events, the first talk was ready to be recorded on 25 June, and this was done. A cheery cable to Maureen O'Sullivan in Hollywood suggests he still had no inkling of the furore he was about to inspire; nor did his closest associates. When Wodehouse cabled Reynolds in New York with his latest plans, his agent blithely responded in language based on years of literary representation: 'Hope broadcasts will be of such nature as to promote value of the novel.' This is doubtful. The first talk was all about Wodehouse's enforced departure from Le Touquet and ended with the typical observation that 'we felt very far from our snug homes and not at all sure that we liked the shape of things to come', striking a note that was wrong from the start.

Wodehouse had not been in Berlin a week before his publicity campaign began to unravel disastrously. Scarcely had he recorded the first talk, 'How to Be an Internee', with Plack, than his relationship with the American press began to turn sour. First, the *New York Times* reported that he 'would broadcast once a week to the United States by arrangement with the German Foreign Office. He [Wodehouse] said the contents of his broadcast would be entirely about his personal experiences. There would be no politics.' Damagingly, the *New York Times* reported him as saying that 'I never was interested in politics. I'm quite unable to work up any kind of belligerent feeling. Just as I'm about to feel belligerent about some country I meet a decent sort of chap. We go out together and lose any fighting thoughts or feelings.' Later, Wodehouse vehemently denied making these comments, but at the time the reaction was hostile and instantaneous. In the week in which Hitler's armies were sweeping across the Soviet Union, such comments were astonishingly out of touch with Allied opinion. In July, after the broadcasts had gone out, and as patriotic outrage at his behaviour took hold across the English-speaking world, the phrase 'I'm quite unable to work up any kind of belligerent feeling' was repeatedly turned against Wodehouse as evidence of collaboration with the Nazis.

There was worse to come. Even before the five talks had been transmitted, it was his interview with Harry Flannery of CBS – the first time Wodehouse's voice was actually heard on the airwaves – that did the most immediate damage to his reputation. The CBS broadcast preceded his own talks by several days, but it became hopelessly confused with Wodehouse's script and contributed to the bad publicity he was now attracting every time he opened his mouth in Berlin. Once again, the damage was largely self-inflicted, and stemmed directly from his failure to understand the troubling political and moral implications of his new freedom, or the enormity of the Nazis' misdeeds. Fatally, too, he trusted Flannery and misread his interest. The CBS man, who had first visited Wodehouse in Tost at the beginning of 1941, in the aftermath of the Thuermer interview, was a committed anti-Nazi who saw the interview as an opportunity to extract maximum propaganda value from Wodehouse, whom he believed to be a mixture of dupe and collaborator. After Flannery had encountered Wodehouse in the press scrum at the Adlon, he cabled the news to CBS headquarters in New York, which ordered him to interview Wodehouse, live, on the radio. Wodehouse, ever obliging, still blindly thinking he could use the chance to thank his American audience, agreed.

This 'interview', following CBS custom, was scripted in advance by Flannery, shown to Wodehouse for his approval, and then performed by the two men in a live radio feed to New York. It is hard now, listening to the tape recording of this broadcast, not to be astounded at Wodehouse's folly in agreeing to co-operate with Flannery, and to follow the other man's script. One crucial exchange went as follows:

Flannery: I believe you wrote a book while you were in the internment camp.
Wodehouse: Yes, the only one in thirty years which I've written by hand and not on the typewriter . . . *Money in the Bank* I called it, and I've just heard that the script has been safely shipped to the United States . . . After I'd done that one, I wrote a hundred pages of another. I call it *Full Moon*, because my characters are more moonstruck in it even than usual.
Flannery: Do the books tell anything about the life of a prisoner of war, Mr Wodehouse?
Wodehouse: Good Lord, no, Mr Flannery. There are enough other people writing about the war . . . But I'll tell you something about the war and my work that's been bothering me a good deal. I'm wondering whether the kind of people and the kind of England I write about will live after the war — whether England wins or not, I mean.

The CBS 'interview' was sandwiched between foreign correspondents' reports of a world at war, in Russia, North Africa and the Far East, and sounded — as it does today — irredeemably frivolous. Although the full exchange lasted less than four minutes, it contained three scripted replies, each of which gave deep offence to a war-ravaged audience. First, at the opening of the conversation with Flannery, Wodehouse, who was described wearing a khaki sports shirt, light tan trousers, a brown tweed jacket and a paisley ascot, was heard to say, 'I'm living here at the Adlon — have a suite on the third floor, a very nice one, too — and can come and go as I please.' Secondly, in answer to a question about whether he minded internment, he replied: 'Not at all. As long as I have a typewriter and plenty of paper and a room to work in, I'm fine.' Thirdly, in addition to the phrase, already quoted, 'whether England wins or not', there was Wodehouse's claim that 'I've always thought of the United States as sort of my country'.

Taken together, these comments seemed to show Wodehouse living happily in a luxury hotel in the heart of Nazi Germany, eager to avoid the hardship of life in Britain, unconcerned about England's fate, and posing as an American. Combined with news reports that he was proposing to enlarge on his experience in some future broadcasts for the Nazis, the CBS interview had devastating results. In one of the darkest months of the war, when the British were up against it, Wodehouse came across as cowardly, disloyal and selfish. This negative perception was reinforced by the programme's producers. When the interview was over, Flannery returned the audience to the studio in New York, where the host of the show, Elmer Davis, who later published a vicious attack on Wodehouse in an American magazine, added his own commentary:

Mr Wodehouse's many friends here in the United States will be glad to know he is free and that he is apparently comfortable and happy . . . and, of course, he was only in an internment camp . . . People who get out of concentration camps, such as Dachau, for instance – well, in the first place, not a great many of them get out, and when they do, they are seldom able to broadcast.

Wodehouse heard this, sitting in the studio in Berlin, and unable to protest or interrupt. It was probably the first time since his release that he had any inkling of the way his behaviour was being received in the wider world. Flannery (an unreliable witness) claimed that, as they left the cramped recording studio, Wodehouse, lost in thought, said of Davis's concluding remarks, 'Nasty of him, wasn't it?' to which Flannery claimed he responded by trying to explain to Wodehouse the nature of his offence.

Friends of Wodehouse both in America and in Germany, on either side of the conflict, were now becoming equally alarmed by his comments, though for quite different reasons. In New York, Reynolds, having heard the interview and read the press reaction to it, urgently tried to telephone his client in Berlin and spell out to him the folly of his behaviour. Simultaneously, in Berlin, even Wodehouse's Foreign Office minders were becoming concerned at their star broadcaster's propensity for attracting bad publicity, and at the growing perception that he was a collaborator.

After his first week of freedom, the first of Wodehouse's talks had not even been transmitted to its intended audience, and already he was being denounced as a Nazi stooge. From the German Foreign Office point of view, this was disastrous. It was essential to its plan that Wodehouse's role as an independent voice, a *non-Nazi*, should be preserved. To this end, Plack and von Barnikow arranged for Wodehouse to be removed from Berlin. His new residence would be the home of von Barnikow's fiancée, Anga von Bodenhausen, in a place called Degenershausen on the edge of the Harz mountains. From 27 June this became Wodehouse's new base. It was from here that he was driven back to Berlin twice in the coming month to record what would be the last three broadcasts.

20. 'The global howl'
(July 1941)

> It was the being without advisers that made the situation so bleak. On these occasions when Fate, having biffed you in the eye, proceeds to kick you in the pants, you want to gather the boys about you and thresh things out, and there weren't any boys to gather. (*The Mating Season*)

Wodehouse's real disgrace began when the first of his prerecorded 'talks', as he always referred to them, was broadcast from Berlin on 28 June 1941, two days after Flannery's CBS interview. Wodehouse's mild, reedy, educated English tones were transmitted to America late at night, on the short wave. He was introduced by a German announcer as 'the father of the inimitable Jeeves' and, the announcer went on, 'we felt that his American readers would be interested to hear from Mr Wodehouse, so we have invited him to the microphone'. At this stage, only a very few British radio listeners who happened to be prowling the airwaves in the small hours would have heard Wodehouse's words, expressed in a voice redolent of a civilized tranquillity now lost in the horrors of world war. By chance, Denis Mackail was one of these: he was pleased his old friend sounded in good heart and relieved that he seemed to have come through internment unscathed. Like many who heard the broadcasts at the beginning, before the international furore began, Mackail was not indignant. 'He was being funny; I thought he was being remarkably courageous,' he wrote later; 'he seemed to be making a quiet and almost casual plea against intolerance.'

Indeed, reconsidered today, removed from the feverish atmosphere of wartime, and the desperate struggle between Hitler and Churchill, Wodehouse's text seems relatively harmless:

It is just possible that my listeners may seem to detect in this little talk of mine a slight goofiness . . . If so, the matter, as Bertie Wooster would say, is susceptible of a ready explanation. I have just emerged into the outer world after forty-nine weeks of Civil Internment in a German internment camp and

. . . I have not yet quite recovered that perfect mental balance for which in the past I was so admired by one and all.

This was followed by ten minutes of light, self-deprecating humour of the inconsequential kind at which Wodehouse had always excelled. His past year, he said,

had been in many ways quite an agreeable experience. There is a good deal to be said for internment. It keeps you out of the saloons and gives you time to catch up with your reading. You also get a lot of sleep. The chief drawback is that it means your being away from home a good deal.

Wodehouse could not resist fictionalizing some aspects of his story. For instance, his account of the German army's arrival in Le Touquet bore scant relation to the facts, as he knew them, and would be endlessly quoted against him in years to come as evidence of pro-Nazi sympathies:

All that happened, as far as I was concerned, was that I was strolling on the lawn with my wife one morning, when she lowered her voice and said 'Don't look now, but there comes the German army'. And there they were, a fine body of men, rather prettily dressed in green, carrying machine guns.

This first talk was permeated by Wodehouse's lifelong preference for looking on the bright side. After the Germans occupied Le Touquet 'a perfect atmosphere of peace and goodwill continued to prevail'. The sergeant in charge of the internees was 'a genial soul . . . infusing the whole thing [with] a pleasant atmosphere of the school treat'. The bus journey to Loos prison was 'practically a feast of reason and a flow of soul'. Wodehouse made no attempt to tailor his script to suit his audience. After all, he had read drafts of this material to a crowd of super-patriotic Englishmen in Tost and been applauded for it. 'I remember', he wrote later, 'being conscious of a slight smugness at the thought that I had it in me to treat internment lightly, a sort of complacent feeling that by not making heavy weather about it I was keeping my end up and proving myself worthy to associate with these fellow internees of mine.'

But in the world beyond Ilag VIII, his frivolous tone was doomed to fall flat. Outside Berlin, the friends and family who heard Wodehouse's words became alarmed and protective. Shortly after this first broadcast to the United States, while he was still settling into Degenershausen, Wodehouse received two quite explicit appeals from his immediate circle. The first was a telegram from the editor of the *Saturday Evening Post*, concerned to stop one of his top contributors from alienating future readers. 'Impossible you to realise American state of mind,' cabled Wesley Stout. 'Even Columbia [CBS] broadcast hostilely received.' The second, more frantic, came from Leonora on 4 July: 'At all costs to ourself [*sic*] my darling stop broadcasting.'

But there was nothing to be done. Broadcasts two and three had already been recorded. Wodehouse later said that he suffered 'a great deal of mental pain' when he realized his mistake, but the genie was out of the bottle and at large in the world, and his terrible blunder was becoming part of the official record. This British phase, essentially a national affair that fed off the international opprobrium, was inspired by the press. In late June, in the highly charged atmosphere of wartime Britain, the idea that such a popular and famous Englishman should be publicizing his intention to broadcast on Nazi radio inevitably caused an almost immediate outcry. The press assumption that Wodehouse had bought his freedom was first expressed in the *Daily Mirror* headline, 'The Price Is?' In the same edition, William Connor used Wodehouse's remark about being 'unable to work up any kind of belligerent feeling' against him in his regular 'Cassandra' column, beginning: 'P. G. Wodehouse . . . has been "browsing and sluicing" with the Nazis in Berlin's biggest and best hotel.' Connor went on to contrast this with the 'great acres of London, Coventry, Liverpool and other cities flattened by his Hunnish hosts'. This assault was followed on 1 July by a report in the *Daily Express* which reprinted, but distorted, extracts from the first broadcast to America to give the impression that Wodehouse had actually been giving a cocktail party in Low Wood when the Germans arrived to arrest him.

At the upper end of the newspaper market, particularly in the *Daily Telegraph*, there was a vehement correspondence about Wodehouse's conduct, to which several of his literary friends and acquaintances contributed. These letters set the tone for the bitter public debate that followed. The inventor of the clerihew, E. C. Bentley, wrote that there was 'only one opinion about Mr P. G. Wodehouse's bargain with the

German government', and urged Oxford to strip him of his D.Litt. Ian Hay, who had worked with Wodehouse on comedies like *Baa, Baa, Black Sheep*, wrote that he was 'horrified . . . No broadcast from Berlin by a world famous Englishman . . . can serve as anything but an advertise-ment for Hitler.' Sean O'Casey, the Irish playwright renowned for his anti-British views, wrote that he was amused 'to read the various wails about the villainy of Wodehouse . . . If England has any dignity left in the way of literature, she will forget for ever the pitiful antics of English Literature's performing flea' — a brilliant phrase that Wodehouse later turned to his advantage. Fellow popular novelists of the day, like Sax Rohmer, Dorothy L. Sayers, Storm Jameson and Gilbert Frankau, who tried to defend him, still had to concede his stupidity.

Most wounding of all, in the long term, was a chilling denunciation from A. A. Milne, who, consumed by envy of his old friend's literary success and frustrated in his own career, accused Wodehouse of shirking all civic obligations, even the responsibilities of fatherhood — a notably cruel jibe. 'He has encouraged in himself a natural lack of interest in "politics",' Milne wrote. 'Irresponsibility in what the papers call "a licensed humorist" can be carried too far; naïveté can be carried too far. Wodehouse has been given a good deal of licence in the past, but I fancy that now his licence will be withdrawn.' This last sentence was a coded allusion to Wodehouse's tax troubles of the 1930s, an insinua-tion explicitly stated by some of the *Telegraph*'s other correspondents. Lurking behind several of the more hostile reactions from erstwhile friends was the belief that Wodehouse had finally had his comeuppance for a lifetime of evading responsibility. Privately, even Bill Townend, who would later lead a belated campaign to clear his friend's name, concurred. 'The trouble with P. G.', he wrote to 'Slacker' Christison, the secretary of the Alleyn Club, 'is that he has always lived in a kind of unpractical dream, taking little interest in anything save what most people would regard as trivialities: his stories, his home, Dulwich, his dogs, his family, his plays, and — I have to add — his earnings.'

As the press campaign gathered momentum, official Britain began to react to the news from Berlin. In the all-important propaganda war, the enemy appeared to have achieved a coup. At first, there were noises of outrage from parliamentary patriots. On 9 July, in answer to a question in the House of Commons, Anthony Eden accused Wodehouse of having 'lent his services to the German war propaganda machine'. In the same debate a prominent Conservative, Quintin Hogg, in an intemperate speech, compared Wodehouse to the infamous Nazi propagandist Lord Haw-Haw, and called him (Wodehouse) a traitor. Even at this stage, only two broadcasts had been directed at the United States and very few Britons had actually heard them. With hindsight, Eden's comment was the preamble to the next phase of Wodehouse's disgrace, a government-led campaign against him that was about to become exceedingly ugly.

Between 2 July and 9 July, the day of Anthony Eden's official reaction to the case, there were frequent questions in the House of Commons, in which Wodehouse was often mentioned by name, about British subjects broadcasting under enemy auspices. The issue soon became a matter of government concern. The Minister of Information, Alfred Duff Cooper, had his own reasons to be incensed by the news of the broadcasts. He had recently returned from a long lecture tour of America, where he had campaigned vigorously, on Churchill's behalf, against the United States' isolationism, advocating war against Germany. Wodehouse's broadcasts obviously threatened these efforts in the most selfish and gratuitous way. Duff Cooper's belief that Wodehouse was behaving like a traitor at a time when Britain was fighting for survival was backed up by his parliamentary secretary, Harold Nicolson, who later wrote in his diary, 'I do not want to see Wodehouse shot on Tower Hill. But I resent the theory that "poor old P. G. is so innocent that he is not responsible". A man who has shown such ingenuity and resource in evading British and American income tax cannot be classed as unpractical.'

On 4 July, shortly after Wodehouse's arrival in Berlin, Duff Cooper, in his role as Minister of Information, had entertained a number of well-known journalists to a lunch at the Savoy. These included A. J. Cummings of the *News Chronicle*, Hannen Swaffer of the *Daily Express* and William Connor, 'Cassandra', of the *Daily Mirror*. Connor was a columnist whose vitriolic style had moved even Churchill to regret that 'so able a writer should show himself so dominated by malevolence'. According to Hugh Cudlipp, who was later editor of the *Daily Mirror*, Connor was like a one-man car crash: it was never a question of 'What Makes Connor Tick, but What Makes Connor Clang'. His presence at the table guaranteed controversy. Inevitably, the lunchtime conversation turned to the Wodehouse affair, with the minister being accused of 'doing nothing about P. G. Wodehouse'. The upshot of the discussion, which was fuelled with a vicious yellow vodka, was that Duff Cooper asked Connor, whose journalism he admired, to enlarge his Cassandra column on the Wodehouse affair and to write a 'postscript' to a BBC evening news bulletin. These editorial comments were often delivered by J. B. Priestley, and were a popular feature of BBC wartime broadcasting, with an estimated audience of more than ten million listeners. Connor's first reaction was to refuse, on the grounds that it was against his professional pride to submit to 'blue pencils, censors, the Ministry of Information and the iniquities of the BBC'. By 11 July, however, Connor had been squared, after Duff Cooper had undertaken personally to hand the script, uncensored, to the BBC. Accordingly, Connor's script was given by the minister to the Director of Talks who, appalled by what he had read, argued strongly against broadcasting it as a 'postscript'.

The BBC view, in outright defiance of Duff Cooper and ultimately of Churchill, was that Connor's text was 'quite clearly libellous and, if broadcast, slanderous as well'. Lawyers were called in to back up this position, and a bitter row erupted behind the scenes. Advised of the legal position, Duff Cooper angrily told A. P. Ryan of the BBC that it had 'nothing to do with you or the BBC'. The BBC's response was simply that 'Wodehouse has merely done something which is ill-advised'. Amid deteriorating relations between the government and Corporation, a regular feature of Britain at war, the minister then simply ordered the BBC to broadcast the 'postscript' on both the Home and the Empire service. The BBC replied by holding a special meeting of the board of governors on 14 July. This meeting instructed the Director General to ask Duff Cooper to reconsider his order, but the minister, complaining of a mutinous BBC, insisted that Connor go ahead. And so, at nine o'clock on the evening of 15 July, after a regular news bulletin, Cassandra made the broadcast that launched the penultimate phase of the Wodehouse affair.

Connor's script was breathtakingly intemperate, a polemic unique in the annals of the BBC.

I have come to tell you tonight [Connor began] of the story of a rich man trying to make his last and greatest sale – that of his own country. It is a sombre story of honour pawned to the Nazis for the price of a soft bed in a luxury hotel. It is the record of P. G. Wodehouse ending forty years of money-making fun with the worst joke he ever made in his life.

Warming to his theme, Connor cast Wodehouse as the craven pawn of the devilish cripple, Josef Goebbels: 'Wodehouse was stealthily groomed for stardom, the most disreputable stardom in the world, the limelight of Quislings.' He concluded with a rhetorical flourish:

Fifty thousand of our countrymen are enslaved in Germany. How many of them are in the Adlon Hotel tonight? Barbed wire is their pillow. They endure – but they do not give in. They suffer – but they do not sell out. Between the terrible choice of betrayal of one's country and the abominations of the Gestapo, they have only one answer. The gaols of Germany are crammed with men who have chosen without demur. But they have something that Wodehouse can never regain. Something that thirty pieces of silver could never buy.

This extraordinary broadcast had the instant effect of transforming a row confined to newspaper columns and parliamentary debates into a great national controversy. As the BBC had feared, the public reaction to Cassandra was swift and vehement. Protests came in from all over the country. Of the 166 letters, telephone calls and telegrams received by the BBC, 31 favoured Cassandra, but 133 were hostile to him, and felt that he had treated Wodehouse too harshly. The BBC duty log recorded a variety of complaints from members of the public: 'deplorable bad taste'; 'vulgar wartime passion'; 'we were shocked'; 'disgusting, irrelevant, unwise and unnecessary', and so on. In a private letter to the director of talks, the respected crime novelist and well-known broadcaster Dorothy L. Sayers wrote: 'I have never heard anything like this from the BBC; I hope I never shall again . . . It was as ugly a thing as ever was made in Germany.' Several letters to *The Times* between 18 and 23 July also expressed anti-Cassandra sentiments, and urged readers only to judge Wodehouse when 'all the facts and circumstances are known'. Orwell later wrote that it was Cassandra's 'postscript' which intensified popular feeling about Wodehouse and, as much as Wodehouse's alleged 'treachery', made the mud stick.

Emboldened by the public reaction, the BBC governors met again on 17 July, with Duff Cooper present. They urged him to take full responsibility for Connor's broadcast, and to make it known that he had overruled the BBC and had ordered them to run it. The row now entered that British establishment stratosphere that Wodehouse would have understood only too well but which, to outsiders, is virtually incomprehensible: the chairman of the BBC governors threatened to write a letter to *The Times* setting out the governors' position. In response to this arcane pressure, Duff Cooper drafted his own letter to *The Times* in which he made it plain that his

was the sole responsibility for the broadcast which last week distressed so many of your readers. The Governors indeed shared unanimously the view expressed in your columns that the broadcast in question was in execrable taste. *De gustibus non est disputandum.* Occasions, however, may arise in time of war when plain speaking is more desirable than good taste.

Duff Cooper also wrote a letter of thanks to Connor, closing with the intriguing information that, during the furore, his script had been shown to Churchill, who 'expressed the view that he could find no fault with it, except that the language seemed rather too mild'.

Across the country, the debate on the Wodehouse affair was conducted by the British reading public in various ways. In an extreme case, Southport Public Library withdrew some ninety Wodehouse volumes from its shelves and destroyed them. In Portadown, Northern Ireland, his books were banned outright, while other public libraries announced a ban on future acquisitions. The BBC declared it would in future broadcast neither Wodehouse stories nor lyrics (a decision that was rescinded after the war was over). The press position was that Wodehouse was at best a collaborator, at worst a traitor: 'a Goebbels' stooge' or 'a Nazi stooge'. The hostility to Wodehouse was derived partly from patriotic disgust, partly from ideological conviction. As George Orwell pointed out, Wodehouse became associated in the public mind with the wealthy, idle, aristocratic nincompoops he often wrote about, and made an ideal whipping boy for the left.

Cassandra's accusation that Wodehouse was Goebbels' puppet was polemically effective, but factually wrong. Wodehouse had been manipulated by the German Foreign Office, not the Ministry of Propaganda. However, in one of the many twists in this contorted story, it was during this phase, when Wodehouse was being denounced as a traitor, that Goebbels and the Ministry of Propaganda *did* become interested in exploiting Werner Plack's recordings. Where Wodehouse had first been commissioned as a benign, neutral voice by Germans at odds with the regime, now he was exploited, against his will, after the initial furore, as a *pro*-Nazi sympathizer. Ironically, when Cassandra had broadcast his 'postscript', only two talks had been transmitted, and only to the United States. The third, fourth and fifth talks were recorded while Wodehouse was staying at Degenershausen and were not actually broadcast until much later, on 23 and 30 July and 6 August. But the Ministry of Propaganda, which was now actively promoting the idea of Wodehouse the pro-Nazi, acquired the recordings and rebroadcast them to the United Kingdom on 9, 10, 11, 12 and 14 August. For most listeners, this was their first real opportunity to hear what he had actually said.

In this clever, and rather modern, manipulation of radio propaganda, Wodehouse was helpless. It was not in his nature to cause a scene; but he did exhibit a characteristic stubbornness about his work. In fact, he made only one attempt to set the record straight. In the retrospective preamble to the script of his fourth broadcast, he said: 'The Press and Public of England seem to have jumped to the conclusion that I have been in some way bribed or intimidated into making these broadcasts. This is not the case.' This belated and ineffectual self-justification was as ill-conceived as every other aspect of his conduct during these unhappy weeks, and completely failed to address the substance of the case against him. Rebutting the charge that he had made a bargain to secure his release, he simply asserted once more that his reason for broadcasting was to answer the letters of his American fans, and moved on to the parts of 'How to Be an Internee without Previous Training' that would, he said blithely, have 'entertainment value for listeners'. Because he did not comprehend the argument that he should never have used Nazi radio in the first place, he made no attempt to address it.

In later years, Wodehouse would take full responsibility for his actions, at least in private. Almost unnoticed among the mass of his papers left after his death, neither published nor ever properly analysed, is an extraordinary, but modest, 60-page document, simply titled 'Apologia'. A vital key to Wodehouse's thinking at this time, frank, painful and frustrating in equal parts, this typescript is probably a discarded section of *Wodehouse in Wonderland*:

I can honestly say [he wrote] that it never occurred to me that there could be any objection to my telling my American friends a few frivolous facts about life in an Ilag . . . I can see now, of course, how injudicious I was . . . As a genial Canadian newspaperman put it the other day when we were discussing the subject, I missed a damned good chance of keeping my mouth shut.

The terms of his 'Apologia', however, remain consistently nonchalant, and indicate what many have observed, that Wodehouse never quite understood the true gravity of his offence, and simply could not find a tone appropriate to his predicament:

I am not attempting to excuse myself. Nor am I complaining. The global howl that went up as a result of my indiscretion exceeded in volume and intensity anything I had experienced since the time in my boyhood when I broke the curate's umbrella and my aunts started writing to one another about it, but I felt from the first that it was entirely justified. It was inevitable that when it was announced that I was about to speak on German radio, it should be assumed that what I was going to speak would be German propaganda.

Those like Leonora who knew him best understood Wodehouse's behaviour to be exasperatingly in character. She wrote to Reynolds, 'I have heard records of all the broadcasts to date and in my own mind I am completely and utterly certain that he is completely unconscious of any wrongdoing.' She went on, coolly: 'However, it isn't exactly helping our war effort, so he is very naturally judged accordingly.' To Denis Mackail she wrote that she felt 'a bit like a mother with an idiot child that she anyway loves better than all the rest'. In America, where Wodehouse's offence was compounded by the *Post*'s publication of the egregiously flippant 'My War with Germany', public reaction had been almost as adverse as in Britain, and Reynolds in New York was battling on his client's behalf. Reynolds was dismayed by Wodehouse's actions, but wisely kept quiet. 'I did not make any statement about Plum over here,' he told Leonora. 'I was strongly advised not to as there was such an uproar about it all and *one* pro-letter seemed to produce 1000 anti-Plum.'

Even the loyal *Saturday Evening Post* expressed alarm. Wesley Stout, the editor, warned Reynolds on 21 July that

We must have Mr Wodehouse's express promise that he will not again broadcast from Berlin . . . the mail on last week's article has confirmed my fears that he would be a liability to the *Post* . . . if he again does anything which can be construed as condoning the Nazi regime or serving its ends. As it is, he already has alienated readers.

Reynolds had just received the typescript of *Money in the Bank* and nervously submitted it to Stout, who cabled Wodehouse in Germany, repeating his demand. '*Money in Bank* good. Eager to buy but can only on your explicit assurance you will not broadcast from Germany . . . or act publicly in manner which can be construed as serving Nazi ends. Your article strongly resented by many.'

To Reynolds, Stout was brutally frank. 'Our belief is that he traded himself out of prison camp with his eyes open,' he wrote on the same day. Reynolds continued to defend his client and made a private overture to Sumner Welles, the US Under Secretary of State, begging him to get a letter to Wodehouse explaining in the starkest possible terms 'why his broadcasts are folly'. As it happened, Reynolds did not need to worry. Help was at hand. The day before, on 27 July, Ethel had arrived in Berlin, spirited there by the faithful Plack. By 29 July, she was making the long car journey to Degenershausen. She, for one, was quite determined that 'Plummie' was going to have nothing more to do with publicity.

July 1941 was the worst month of Wodehouse's life, and the disgrace would never leave him, but Wodehouse took the hurt into himself and wore the mask. Even to friends like Townend he affected disdain: 'Those letters in the *Daily Telegraph* about my having found internment so awful that I bought my release by making a bargain with the German Government made me laugh,' he wrote. Afterwards, he rarely betrayed his feelings about the broadcasts, but he did concede 'a great deal of mental pain' in confidence to a British government interrogator. There is no doubt he was badly wounded. Rare hints of autobiography in his fiction do not unlock any secret chambers but they do open an anteroom of suggestion. A passage in *Full Moon*, the novel he was working on at this time, gives a glimpse of his inner feelings:

In every difficult situation, when the spirit has been placed upon the rack and peril seems to threaten from every quarter, there inevitably comes soon or late to the interested party at the centre of the proceedings a conviction that things are getting too hot. Stags at bay have this feeling. So have Red Indians at the stake. It came now to Bill.

Wodehouse's subsequent actions also provide a clue to his distress. Wodehouse wanted to go home to explain himself and protest his innocence: on three separate occasions he formally requested permission to leave. First, he proposed travelling overland to Palestine and then back to London, but the Ministry of Propaganda saw to it that the request was turned down. Next, he tried and failed to get authorization for a return to England via Lisbon, a neutral port. Finally, he asked to go to Sweden, where he was always popular, but in vain. The Nazis were determined to hang on to him. Wodehouse's response was predictable: he buried himself in work. Remaining in Germany was never collaboration, but it was coexistence, funded partly by the sale of Ethel's jewellery, loans from German friends, and the payment of substantial royalties on his books in translation, especially from Sweden and Spain, and also from his German publisher, Tauchnitz.

From among many wild accusations, there are two main charges levelled against Wodehouse about his activities during the Second World War. The first, that he betrayed his country, does not stand up. His behaviour was incredibly stupid, but it was not treacherous. The second charge – that he and Ethel enjoyed a life of civilian comfort and privilege in Nazi Berlin – is more complex and one that his British government interrogator, Major Cussen, wrestled with in his final report. Ethel's flamboyant behaviour was probably 'unwise', but, apart from a few anecdotes of high-spirited silliness, nothing on which a serious charge could be based. There is absolutely no evidence of collaboration on her part. Despite many allegations, one thing is certain: there was never any question of Wodehouse accepting money from the Nazis. He always paid his own way. Indeed, after July 1941, he became more scrupulous than ever about keeping a distance between himself and the regime.

Wodehouse was relieved to be taken out to the countryside. 'Being an enemy,' he once said flatly, 'I don't like staying in Berlin.' He was not alone in wanting to find for himself a refuge away from the Reich capital. Raven von Barnikow and Werner Plack, who had both been dismayed at the obloquy heaped on their friend, were eager to make amends. It was von Barnikow who arranged for Wodehouse to meet Anga von Bodenhausen, just as the storm was beginning to break at the end of June; and it was Baroness von Bodenhausen who took Wodehouse under her wing, gave him shelter in her country house – and kept the German Foreign Office at arm's length. She was an anglophile German who was delighted to offer sanctuary. Overnight, the creator of Blandings Castle now found himself in a German arcadia, a place which, after Huy and Tost, seemed like paradise.

21. 'Now I shall have nothing to worry about until 1944'
(1941–1943)

After the thing was over, when peril ceased to loom and happy endings had been distributed in heaping handfuls and we were driving home with our hats on the side of our heads, having shaken the dust of Steeple Bumpleigh from our tyres, I confessed to Jeeves that there had been moments during the recent proceedings when Bertram Wooster, though no weakling, had come very near to despair. (*Joy in the Morning*)

Degenershausen is a tiny village on the edge of the Harz mountains, some seventeen miles from Magdeburg in the province of Halle, the heart of old Germany. The war hardly reached here and, although people had to be careful what they said in front of one or two local Nazis, the spirit of the place was independent, rustic and happily out of touch. Here, amid the hayfields and cherry orchards of her estate, Anga von Bodenhausen, a beautiful widow, lived with her ten-year-old daughter and family retainers in a fine old eighteenth-century lodge, adjoining a modest farm and surrounded by some two and a half thousand acres of beautiful parkland, an arboretum stocked with trees and shrubs from all over the world: English yew, Scots plane, magnolia, tulip, wild apple, Spanish chestnut, goat willow, silver fir, quince, hazelnut, hawthorn, beech, linden, lime and acacia. For the next two years, from the summer of 1941 to the spring of 1943, Degenershausen would become Wodehouse's escape from Berlin, a haven in which he could follow his routine, write, read, ruminate, go for long walks, think out plots and try to put the nightmare of his release from Ilag VIII behind him. It was at Degenershausen that he completed *Joy in the Morning*, *Full Moon* and his account of camp life, *Wodehouse in Wonderland*, together with several short stories. These, he wrote to Townend, were now shuffling their feet nervously, 'wondering if they will ever get into print'.

The old house was perfectly suited to his needs. His hostess gave him a quiet, well-lit room on the ground floor, looking out over the park. The maid Rosemarie brought breakfast to his suite every morning at half past eight. He would do his 'daily dozen' on the wet grass outside, to the amusement of the staff, and then settle down at his typewriter, working all morning until, at about one o'clock, the gong sounded for lunch, which was served upstairs in the library. In the afternoon, Wodehouse usually took a long walk and then passed the time with Reinhild, Anga's daughter, and her school friend, Ortrud. He would join in the life of the farm, sweeping the stables, feeding the goats, and helping to milk the cows, until the day ended. After dinner, he and Anga would take a regular evening walk around an inner circuit of the park, followed by dogs and children, chatting about this and that – leeches, wild geese, fiction, spiritualism and Conan Doyle – while, on hot summer nights, glow-worms winked in the darkness under the trees. In notes written at the time, Anga observed that her distinguished guest was 'a very kind and light and large personality. He could never hurt, he could never be narrow or disturbing, [he is] soft, kind, unselfish . . . Plummie is as light as a feather in his attitude with other people; he never approaches anybody too near, he dislikes pathos; he never tries to be impressive or funny . . . Yes, Plummie lives in a dream world and he charmingly forgets all you have told him . . . and then he just says: "Oh no, really?" and polishes his eyeglasses.'

The baroness, like Raven von Barnikow, was anti-Nazi, and had been dismayed at the way in which Wodehouse had been manipulated. When Ethel arrived at Degenershausen at the end of July, the two women, who did not always see eye to eye, joined forces to make it clear to Wodehouse that on no account should he agree to any further requests from the Ministry of Propaganda. He had already given a written commitment to the *Saturday Evening Post* to this effect, to expedite the serial sale of *Money in the Bank*. Armed with this reassurance, Wesley Stout did agree to buy the new novel in mid-August for $40,000, though with many misgivings. He told Reynolds he had 'considerable doubt as to whether it is worth this much to us'. The *Post*'s acquisition of *Money in the Bank* was concluded just as the Ministry of Propaganda's transmission of the broadcasts to Britain was coming to an end. From then on, Wodehouse could concentrate on his writing and immerse himself in country life. In Degenershausen, the war seemed further from everyday life than ever; probably the only reminder of the

Reich was the sight of Charles and Yves, French prisoners of war, in black overalls working in the fields.

At first, there was some local suspicion of the resident Englishman, but the neighbourhood farmers soon realized that this 'Tommy' was quite unlike the ones with whom they were at war, and he was left to roam the countryside in peace. To Reinhild and her schoolfriend, Wodehouse became 'Oncle Plummie'. He scarcely spoke a word of German and the girls' English was severely limited, but they found a bond in a love of animals, especially Bwana, Reinhild's frisky white Maltese dog. Reinhild was impressed that Wodehouse did not patronize her. 'He treated me terribly respectfully,' she says, looking back, 'not like a little girl', and encouraged her to keep a diary. 'When you have problems and you write them down,' he told her, 'they shrink.' By October, Wodehouse had become one of the family. On his sixtieth birthday, the girls recited a poem in his honour and gave him home-made presents with posies of wild flowers from the park. Perhaps for the first time ever, Wodehouse saw what family life could be like, and he revelled in it, as far as he was able. Amateur film footage shows him playing in borrowed tartan plus fours with the girls in the park, but his body language suggests a man for whom physical intimacy did not come easily or naturally. Anga, whose sympathy and understanding helped to unbutton him, encouraged Wodehouse to participate in the girls' lives, saying goodnight to them when they were tucked up in bed after their evening baths, and reading bedtime stories. According to Reinhild, 'he would come and say prayers with us every evening', which is surprising because Wodehouse was never a religious man. He did, however, admit to Townend that he had become 'very religious in camp', and these prayers in Degenershausen were part of a new mood of self-reconciliation. Once the girls were in bed, and he was alone with his thoughts before dinner, Wodehouse would often go out and sit alone on the balcony overlooking the park at the gable end of the house. Wrestling internally with his international disgrace, he would take Werner Plack's record of the broadcasts and, in the stillness of the evening, play it obsessively on the gramophone, as if by repetition he could somehow find the key to his terrible blunder.

When Wodehouse first arrived at Degenershausen, he was, according to Anga von Bodenhausen, 'worried and uncertain', but as he grew more confident and at home he relaxed into his most delightful self.

'Yes,' she wrote, 'he is a child. At dinnertime, when we sat as usual at the fireside in the library, he . . . put his nose to Bwana's black little nose and exclaimed "Oh my God, his nose is quite warm. I hope he is not ill."' Anga's family had estates in Kenya and the house was full of stuffed animals. When Wodehouse passed one of these in the corridor he would pat it with a 'Hello, Mister Lion'. Anga added, 'There is not much else to write about Plummie, because he is very quiet, very kind and withdrawn in himself. I never met anyone who was so easy to be with . . . one feels his genial personality like the ticking of a clock in a room . . . [then] all of a sudden like a conjuror he is outside and you are left alone.' Anga's relations with 'Auntie Ethel' were less affectionate. Ethel was evidently bored by country life, and her loud, impatient and organizing manner did not appeal to Anga. On Wodehouse's later visits, Ethel stayed behind in Berlin.

During this strange idyll, Wodehouse was lost to the world, recuperating from his disgrace. 'Degenershausen is just like a dream,' he told Anga. Even here, he could not put the evil of the world out of mind. 'It grips you how wrong things are,' he told her one evening. At the beginning of October, Leonora fretted to Reynolds that 'I haven't heard from Plum for about two months', and asked him to find out where her stepfather was. When Reynolds tried to telephone Germany (the United States had not yet entered the war), the authorities refused to let the call through, although Wodehouse was now staying at the Adlon hotel again. He and Ethel had moved back there on 10 November 1941 when Anga closed the house for the winter due to prohibitive heating costs.

In Berlin, which was greyer and drabber, but still buzzing with a desperate gaiety, the regime could no longer conceal the worsening military situation or the intensification of the Allied bombing campaign. Wodehouse threw himself into literary business, anxiously monitoring the American public's response to his broadcasts. He badgered Reynolds for news of the *Post*'s serialization of *Money in the Bank* ('Hope well received') and wrote a long letter of self-justification to Stout, including the news that he had just completed '*the* supreme Jeeves novel of all time', *Joy in the Morning*.

'The super-sticky affair of Nobby Hopwood, Stilton Cheesewright, Florence Craye, my Uncle Percy . . .' is one that Bertie Wooster believes his biographers will refer to as 'the Steeple Bumpleigh Horror'. A more brilliant example of Wodehouse's literary escapism is hard to find. Not only does he weave together many of his best characters and themes around the plot of Florence Craye's matrimonial designs on Bertie ('she was one of those intellectual girls, steeped to the gills in serious purpose, who are unable to see a male soul without wanting to get behind it and shove'), it was also conceived and written during the 'phoney war', all but completed during the Nazi occupation of Le Touquet, and left behind with Ethel on Wodehouse's arrest. It is perhaps not too fanciful to see in Bertie's 'cold gesture' to Florence's boy scout brother Edwin ('a small boy with a face like a ferret') a sly allusion to the behaviour of Le Touquet's German garrison:

Now, I don't know how you would have made a cold gesture – no doubt people's methods vary – but the way I did it was by raising the right arm in a sort of salute and allowing it to fall to my side.

Joy in the Morning is an anthology of Wodehouse's favourite comic situations (a blazing cottage; a nocturnal confrontation; a fancy dress ball) and he achieves the perfect union of style and content when a running gag about 'the fretful porpentine' culminates with a 'hidden hand' concealing a hedgehog in Bertie's bed. Almost as satisfying, *Joy in the Morning* also has some of his best lines:

Like a man who, stooping to pluck a nosegay of wild flowers on a railway line, is unexpectedly struck in the small of the back by the Cornish Express.

and,

He spun round with a sort of guilty bound, like an adagio dancer surprised while watering the cat's milk.

The novel also conceals a subtle strand of oblique self-justification, teasing references to writers' inability to conduct their own lives:

I mean, it's all very well for a chap to plead that he's an author and expect on the strength of that to get away with conduct which would qualify the ordinary man for a one-way ticket to Colney Hatch, but even an author . . . ought to have had the sense . . .

'I doubt', says Bertie at one point, speaking of his literary co-conspirator, Boko Fittleworth, 'if you can ever trust an author not to make an ass of himself.'

Wodehouse brings the revels to a harmonious conclusion (Florence will marry 'Stilton' Cheesewright, not Bertie) in which, for once, Jeeves plays only a minor role. With the happy ending secure, Bertie and Jeeves, like their creator, make a sneaky getaway:

'How would it be,' I suggested, 'to zoom off immediately, without waiting to pack?'
   'I was about to suggest such a course myself, sir.'
   'It would enable one to avoid tedious explanations.'
   'Precisely, sir.'
   'Then shift ho, Jeeves,' I said.

As the pair motor happily back to the beloved metropolis, it is Jeeves, prompted by Bertie, who finds the quotation ('A wheeze. A gag') that sums the whole thing up, 'Joy cometh in the morning'. It is impossible to know if this line was inspired by the experience of Degenershausen, where the novel was completed, but it certainly captures Wodehouse's mood in his Harz mountain retreat.

'My Art is flourishing like the family of an Australian rabbit,' he boasted to Stout. Back in Berlin, Wodehouse's adaptability, once his working routine was secure, was as remarkable as ever. 'Life', he informed Anga von Bodenhausen just before Christmas, 'jogs along quite peacefully.' He was now working hard to finish *Full Moon*, punctuating the day with walks in the Tiergarten, accompanied by his beloved Wonder. In his plus fours and cloth cap, with the Pekinese snuffling around at his feet, he cut an eccentric figure in the heart of the wartime capital. The extent of his detachment from reality is illustrated by his curious encounter with Michael Vermehren, a young German journalist.

Vermehren, who was born in Lübeck in 1915, was the son of a prominent north German family, distantly related to the novelist Thomas Mann. His family were anglophiles and he grew up reading the English classics of the day, including Wodehouse. Vermehren had been educated at the London School of Economics, had worked briefly for Price Waterhouse and had read *The Inimitable Jeeves*, *Leave It to Psmith* and *Uncle Fred in the Springtime*. When war broke out in 1939, Vermehren was working for a press agency in Berlin as a translator. Towards the end of 1941, he received an approach out of the blue. 'A friend of mine rang me and said, "Michael, we have a curious chap here. He must be quite a well-known author. He wants to get in touch with a German barrister. Would you know any?" . . . I was flabbergasted, and I went straight over to the Adlon Hotel and asked the porter, "Could I talk to Mr Wodehouse in his room?" . . . He [Wodehouse] came down like a flash, and we sat in the hall, and I said, "What is your case?" He said, "You know that I write books?" I said, "Yes I do. You can consider me a fan."'

Wodehouse, who was dressed in a tweed jacket and grey flannel trousers, then described how he had been attacked by the English press, and – incredibly – how he wanted to sue for libel. Vermehren remembered him saying, 'I need a lawyer I can talk to here, who can then plead for me in England.' It was an impossible suggestion, and one that underlines Wodehouse's remoteness from the real world. Vermehren politely talked him out of this bizarre scheme. 'I said, "Mr Wodehouse, I do know such lawyers, but do you think it's likely that they would get a special permit to cross the war zone and the frontiers and go to England and plead your case?" Wodehouse replied, "Do you think that would be difficult?" I said: "Actually, I think it would be completely impossible."'

Eventually, after a long discussion about the circumstances of the broadcasts, which recapitulated all the justifications that Wodehouse would later repeat to the wider world, he accepted Vermehren's advice, and the matter was dropped. The two men, however, became friends. Vermehren, whose office was just a short distance from the Adlon hotel down Unter den Linden, used to make a point of dropping by to see him. His account confirms the sad and isolated life Wodehouse was leading in the city. 'When I was in Berlin,' Wodehouse told Townend later, 'I did nothing but write and take Wonder for walks . . . I lived the life of a hermit.' Vermehren, who is now an old man living in retirement in Spain, observes that 'I don't think he had any contact whatsoever with anybody. When he came down you had the feeling he'd just left his desk, and that when he went up again he would go back to his desk and continue writing.' Vermehren was so touched by the writer's plight that, unbeknown to Wodehouse, he went to the Swiss embassy to try to persuade the officials to let him leave Germany via neutral Switzerland. As he remembers it, 'I said "I have been in contact with Mr Wodehouse and I want to make it clear that I, after many conversations with him, have found him completely incapable of judging what goes on politically in the world."'

Vermehren's account casts invaluable light on the circumstances in which Wodehouse and Ethel found themselves in 1941 and 1942, and on their conduct during these years. To Vermehren, they were both, in their contrasting ways, extraordinary characters. 'One night we were on the underground, and the train stopped between stations [because of an air raid]. Mrs Wodehouse said in a loud voice, speaking in English, "Now what is this ridiculous nonsense. Why must we stand here? Why can't they move on another few hundred metres and let us out? . . ." I thought, Oh my God . . . The tube was full of exhausted German workers, but nobody stood up and said "Shut up, it's because of the British planes." Nobody. She was very elegant, in this beautiful fur coat, complaining about this incredible situation.'

Vermehren was later arrested, and imprisoned in a concentration camp. When he was released, the Wodehouses had moved to Paris, and then to the United States. He never saw or communicated with them again. Many of the Germans who befriended Wodehouse had the same post-war experience. He simply vanished from their lives, as though his time in Nazi Germany was something he wanted to put behind him. This ruthless suppression of the past caused Anya von Bodenhausen and her daughter much sadness when they tried to renew old acquaintance in the 1950s. Although Wodehouse was accused of having pro-German sympathies, he never acclimatized and the Vermehren episode illustrates how cut off he was. When Werner Plack managed to get him a radio, he could not use it because it was tuned to a Breslau frequency. Despite eighteen months in Germany, Wodehouse never acquired even a schoolboy knowledge of the language. It is probably the measure of his unworldliness that he was able to live a comparatively normal life surrounded by the Nazi state. As an inveterate traveller, he adorned his prose with zestful borrowings from American English and French, but German left no trace. 'I wish I could learn German,' he complained to Reinhild, admitting that he could only manage a few hotel terms like 'gemischte Gemüseplatte' (a plate of mixed vegetables), his habitual meal. It was as though he had been living somewhere else.

Wodehouse had always worked well in hotels, but the Adlon was neither relaxing nor congenial. In the dining room, he and Ethel were constantly accosted by enthusiastic fellow diners, and eventually found privacy by arranging to eat in their suite. Ethel, who rarely rose much before noon, never failed to attract attention in the Adlon; surrounded by handsome young men in uniform, she was in her element. On one occasion, when Plack joined the Wodehouses for lunch she summoned him to the table with 'Werner, will you please tell the head waiter that I have been waiting for an hour and a half. An hour and a half! What's more, this table wobbles!' So saying, she took a bread roll, a rationed luxury item, and jammed it under one of the table legs. Sproat, who was told this story by Plack himself, reports that the Germans in the dining room could scarcely believe their eyes and ears. This account of Ethel's behaviour is corroborated by Isabel Russel Guernsey, an American stranded in Berlin, who reported that Mrs Wodehouse would wrap scraps of food for Wonder in her napkin, while loudly protesting her ignorance of German.

Ethel could be outrageously flamboyant, indifferent to the sensitivities of a situation, but she was a survivor. A weaker woman might have been crushed by her wartime experiences, and her slightly hysterical toughness was the weapon she used to protect Wodehouse. He, for his part, would often say to Anga von Bodenhausen, 'I'm leaving the arrangements to Ethel.' It was Ethel, for example, who made sure that they were allowed – against hotel rules – to keep Wonder in their suite, a privilege not even granted to Admiral Doenitz, who was a regular hotel guest. The Nazi aspect of the Adlon, which was adjacent to the ministries of the Reich, was one of its least attractive features, and Wodehouse learned to turn a blind eye to the fact that the lobby was a meeting place for senior Nazis as well as the flotsam and jetsam of European fascism, men like William Joyce (Lord Haw-Haw) and Julian Amery. Pro-Nazi Americans of dubious reputation, like Edward Delaney (E. D. Ward) and Robert H. Best, also used the hotel as an informal club.

Wodehouse, scorched by the furore of the broadcasts, had no interest in this world, kept himself at a distance and, aside from his dealings with Plack, had no professional contact with any Nazi officials. His behaviour was correct, but it was not irreproachable. In *Wodehouse at War*, Sproat says that the Wodehouses never went to the theatre, opera or cinema, but Vermehren's testimony contradicts this, recalling the occasions on which he accompanied them on evenings out. It is important to stress that this was not exceptional. Rationing was relaxed in Berlin for Christmas 1941. People celebrated with lavish dinners surrounded by trees, lights, toys and presents, and the new year was launched in style, with all the clubs and restaurants doing good business. Even in 1942, before the news of Stalingrad changed everything, Berlin enjoyed a surprisingly normal city life. Wodehouse's writing schedule prohibited much socializing, and *Full Moon*, a regular Blandings Castle novel, underlines his remoteness from the war. His subsequent account of its inception, to Townend, confirms the extraordinary integrity of his imagination:

I find that the best way to get my type of story is to think of something very bizarre and then make it plausible. I remember in *Full Moon* I started with a picture in my mind of a man crawling along a ledge outside a house, seeing a man through the window and gesturing to him to let him in, and the man inside giving him a cold look and walking out of the room, leaving him on the ledge. I find that, given time, I can explain the weirdest situation.

But he was oblivious to the weirdness of his situation in Berlin, and the very quiet and regular life he described to Anga von Bodenhausen, in which he took walks in the snow, paid occasional visits to the Press Club, and feuded with the hotel manager over his habit of leaving breadcrumbs for the birds on the window sill of his suite, emphasizes his utter detachment from wartime reality. 'We have had quite a pleasant winter,' he informed Anga, when spring arrived, reporting the completion of *Joy in the Morning* and his hope that the American embassy would ship the typescripts of his new work to New York for him. His professionalism never left him. After the trials of 1941, he told Anga, he was relieved to have two new novels in the pipeline ready for publication. 'Now I shall have nothing to worry about until 1944,' he crowed. Money worries, always a preoccupation, especially in wartime, receded further when the Berliner Film Company paid a substantial sum for option rights to an original Wodehouse script of *Heavy Weather*.

When spring came, Wodehouse repaired to Degenershausen once more, well pleased with the winter's work. *Joy in the Morning* and *Full Moon*, he told Stout, were 'about as good as I have done. I took immense trouble over them.' With something of his former brio, he added that 'I can stand for all the horrors of war except the being deprived of *Saturday Evening Posts*'. Irony apart, even he could now see that the world had changed irrevocably. 'I am mulling over the plot of a new [novel],' he confided, 'but rather with the feeling of a man who plans a historical novel.' This was a line he would develop in the coming years, until it became a joke against himself, repeated in almost every newspaper, radio and television interview. Preserving the world he had made, rather than seriously attempting to update it, became an essential part of his celebrated 'timelessness'.

While Ethel, making the most of the Adlon, lingered on in Berlin with Wonder, out in the country Wodehouse threw himself into his role as 'Oncle Plummie' – adopting Reinhild and Ortrud as proxy-daughters, making Bwana his favourite, participating in pageants of childish make-believe, and befriending the farm's goat. 'The children are too sweet for words,' he wrote to Raven von Barnikow, who was away on the Eastern Front. 'They climb an enormous fir tree every day like monkeys, and were disappointed yesterday because they could not persuade me to come up after them.' His other recreation, as usual, was taking long walks, trying to think out a novel. To his great satisfaction, he had completed a draft of *Wodehouse in Wonderland*. 'It has come out very funny,' he boasted to von Barnikow, 'but I'm wondering if everybody won't be in too bad a temper after the war to like funny stuff.' In the wider world, beyond Degenershausen, there was plenty to remind him of the risks of making jokes about the Nazis. Harry Flannery's *Assignment to Berlin*, an opportunistic rehash of all the old fabrications, was being promoted in Britain. 'I'd like to murder Master Flannery,' Leonora wrote helplessly to Reynolds. Wodehouse gossip was everywhere. Over in New York, Reynolds picked up a rumour that his client was about to be allowed to leave, and offered to orchestrate the press relations, but it was a false alarm. Autumn drew on. The typescripts of *Joy in the Morning* and *Full Moon* arrived safely in New York. Robert Chalker, from the American embassy, reported both Wodehouse and Ethel to be 'in good health and spirits', but gave no details of their activities. Wodehouse was still out in the country where he celebrated 'the most wonderful birthday', fêted by Anga and Reinhild, and showered with gifts of pipe tobacco and an embroidered handkerchief. This, he said later to Anga von Bodenhausen in a telling admission, 'was the happiest time in all my life'.

The Degenershausen 'dream' could not last. Now, like a boy returning to boarding school after the summer holidays, Wodehouse prepared to go back to the Adlon. When the day of departure came, the taxi was waiting on the gravel outside the front door of the old house. 'Uncle Plummie's' bags and typewriter were packed and ready for the train, but he was nowhere to be found. Reinhild ran through the house, calling out his name. Eventually, Wodehouse appeared from the trees, walking inconsolably across the park towards his friends, his big round face flushed with tears.

Returning to Berlin, he was happy to be with Ethel again, and Wonder seemed pleased to see him, but the capital was 'very wet and sad', and what he called 'the usual Adlon life' – the pressure of fan-mail, well-wishers and overseas reporters – was incessant. 'Every time we sit down to a meal,' he complained to Anga, 'someone comes up and talks to us!' But his rustic sabbatical had worked wonders and after the upheavals of 1941 he had now regained enough equilibrium to answer letters with his old courtesy. He told a Swedish correspondent that he was glad 'people in Sweden don't think badly of me. The whole thing is a lesson to me not to yield to impulse!' He continued to rehearse his regular defence. 'I made the broadcasts in the most innocent spirit possible, meaning only to let my friends in America know how I had been getting on,' he wrote to one correspondent. Typically, he adver-tised his forthcoming work, reporting that he had 'mapped out the plot of another novel [probably *Spring Fever*] and have written five short stories', while joking that 'I shall have to publish them as historical stories and explain that there used to be a time when butlers existed!' Despite the gloom of Berlin, he was working steadily and told Anga that 'I feel quite happy these days', a new mood of confidence that expressed itself in renewed efforts to get out of Germany, which was becoming a very dangerous place to be.

After Stalingrad, at the end of January 1943, even Hitler acknow-ledged that Germany now faced a desperate struggle. The surrender of Field Marshal Paulus and the Sixth Army was marked by three days of national mourning, German radio stations played solemn music, and the mood in Berlin darkened. The city was suffering badly from the Allied bombing. Wodehouse and Ethel moved from the Adlon down Unter den Linden to the Bristol, possibly to get some peace and quiet and perhaps because Ethel's insistence on keeping Wonder in their suite was causing friction with the hotel manager. They had just relocated when, at the beginning of March, there was a very bad air raid. After the all-clear sounded, Wodehouse and Ethel went out onto Unter den Linden. It was, he wrote to Anga, 'an extraordinary sight. Large fires seemed to be blazing everywhere . . . then I discovered that the Bristol was on fire. So I rushed up to my room and threw half my things into a suitcase.' He then managed to get a room for the night at the Adlon and was pleased to report that 'Ethel took the raid splendidly, and did not seem a bit nervous . . . Wonder remained perfectly calm throughout.'

In the weeks after Stalingrad, Goebbels initiated a frenzy of new propaganda efforts, and now that Wodehouse was back at the Adlon, the Ministry of Propaganda renewed its interest in his services. But he had learned his lesson. At the beginning of April he was invited to join a press party to visit the site of the Katyn massacre or, as he put it, to 'look at the corpses of those unfortunate Polish soldiers who were murdered by the Bolsheviks in 1940', and though the journalist in him thought it would be 'a great experience', he knew he had to refuse, 'because of what would have been said in England'. Shortly after this, to get away from the bombing, and because he was finding Berlin 'terribly melancholy', he and Ethel went to stay as paying guests with some anglophile acquaintances, the Count and Countess von Wolkenstein in Lobris, Upper Silesia.

Wodehouse's latest refuge was another home from home, a country house built round an inner courtyard, with stone stairs, an embossed front door and even a disused moat. To his delight, the library was full of English books, and also five years' supply of *Punch*, the *Saturday Review*, the *Cornhill* and other magazines. 'I don't think I heard a word of German spoken all the time I was there,' he told Townend. The Wolkensteins' summer residence was situated in farming country that was the exact opposite of Degenershausen, 'practically no woods, just corn fields and beet fields', he wrote sadly to Anga. He had started to write *Spring Fever*, but was discouraged by the limbo in which he was working. He complained to Anga that 'it is trying to write a novel when you don't know if it will ever be published'. Especially in America, conditions were bad. The *Saturday Evening Post* was in trouble. Wesley Stout was no George Lorimer and he had alienated many readers by publishing an inflammatory article entitled 'The Case against the Jew' that cost the magazine dear in subscriptions and advertising revenue. Issues shrank; the cover price went from five to ten cents; Stout was replaced by Ben Hibbs, who was nervous of publishing Wodehouse's work in the aftermath of the broadcasts. Wodehouse was troubled. For thirty years he had relied on the *Post* for regular income. His new situation, he noted, was 'very different from the last war, which hardly touched the magazines. I had three serials in the *Saturday Evening Post* from 1915 to 1917 and they were all about peacetime England, and no one seemed to mind.'

To add to his anxiety, another old trouble reared its head. The American tax authorities, with whom he believed he had settled in 1934, suddenly came to life again on 15 June, issuing a punitive 'jeopardy assessment', demanding $21,328.82 together with penalties of $17,382.99. This curtain-raiser to another protracted bout of tax negotiations had only one consolation: it was confined to the United States. Whereas in the 1930s Wodehouse had contested such claims, on this occasion Reynolds not only took immediate steps to settle the claim from money he was holding in his client's account, but also launched a campaign in the press and with likely members of Congress on Wodehouse's behalf, protesting about 'the arbitrary seizure of property' from 'a British subject who has been . . . a prisoner of the Germans for more than three years'. In her stepfather's absence, Leonora became drawn into the controversy. 'How sickening about the jeopardy tax,' she wrote to Reynolds. 'I suppose there is absolutely nothing to be done at present except to see that all taxes etc are paid bang on time.'

While these new troubles gathered in America, the worsening situation in Germany was at last improving Wodehouse's own chances of leaving Berlin, which, as Ethel told Anga von Bodenhausen, had become 'a very dangerous spot at the moment!' As the summer passed, Wodehouse and Ethel began to make real progress in their latest attempt to get out of Germany. In June, Ethel told Anga that they had high hopes of getting permission to go to Sweden, Lisbon or Switzerland. Having adamantly refused to release them, the authorities were beginning to soften. By mid-August, Ethel was in correspondence with Paul Schmidt at the German Foreign Office about permission to go to France, to escape the bombing which had become terrifying. If the authorities would relent, the timing could scarcely be better. Wodehouse had just finished *Spring Fever* after a seventeen-week burst of writing and was ready for a change of scene. There was uncertainty to the last minute. 'If it is old Werner [Plack] to escort you,' wrote Anga, 'what shocks and thrills you will undergo until you reach the train!' But, in

Low Wood, Le Touquet, May 1940. PGW sits on the extreme left;
Ethel Wodehouse, centre.

In the Kommandant's
Office, Civil Internment
Camp, Tost, Boxing Day
1940

Camp group photograph, 1941. (PGW, in spectacles, stands in the third row back.)

2

500 francs, knives etc.

The cell 12 foot long by about 8 foot wide, whitewashed walls, bed in corner under window. Large window about 5 foot by 3, air quite fresh. Granite floor. Table & chair chained to it, — toilet in corner near door. Door wooden with new panels at bottom, where prisoners had kicked panels out during bombardment. One pane of window broken by shrapnel & shrapnel holes in walls. (Glass roof over main corridors badly smashed & occasional

A page from Wodehouse's camp notebook

With Ethel and Werner Plack, Berlin, 1941

With Werner Plack,
Berlin, 1941

Baroness Anga von Bodenhausen at Degenershausen, 1940

With Reinhild von Bodenhausen and Ortrud, a schoolfriend at
Degenershausen, 1941

Malcolm Muggeridge,
1949

J. D. Grimsdick

William Connor, alias 'Cassandra'

Returning to the United
States with Ethel after
the war

Still at work in his eighties

Walking down Basket Neck Lane with one of his manuscripts
ready for the post office

The 'daily dozen'

With Ethel at home in
Basket Neck Lane

Receiving his knighthood with a replica Japanese ceremonial sword, 1975

the event, everything went without a hitch, and on Tuesday, 7 September they left for Paris.

Werner Plack had organized a room in the five-star Hôtel Bristol on the rue Faubourg Saint-Honoré. As usual, Wodehouse was fussing about money. In a valedictory letter to 'Dearest Anga', he reported that 'I am [still] being published in Sweden, Spain, Hungary, Rumania and France, so I seem to be all right as far as the Continent is concerned.' He went on, 'I got a letter yesterday from a man who was translating one of my books into French, to say that he had made arrangements with a publisher and that he has three thousand francs to give me. That, as far as I can gather . . . will about buy us three lunches!' After all the vicissitudes of the past three years, and in one of his most bizarre glosses on reality, he felt, he said, 'terribly sad about leaving Germany and all our friends . . . I wonder if you are right in being so optimistic about peace coming soon. How marvellous it would be if it did.' Peace was still a remote prospect, and before hostilities ended Wodehouse and Ethel had yet one more terrible personal blow to endure.

22. 'I made an ass of myself, and must pay the penalty'
(1943–1947)

It has been well said of Bertram Wooster that though he may sink onto rustic benches and for a while give the impression of being licked to a custard, the old spirit will come surging back sooner or later. (*The Mating Season*)

Wodehouse was relieved to be back in a city he knew and loved, but his troubles were far from over. The years he and Ethel spent in Paris, from the autumn of 1943 to the spring of 1947, were more mundane but occasionally just as harrowing as his time in Nazi Berlin. The hysteria of 1941 had been replaced by the lingering taint of collaborationism. He was still under a cloud as 'Goebbels' stooge', and had to live with the unresolved accusations of treason in England for which, as he knew only too well, the sentence was the death penalty. Even now, he and Ethel could not shake off their association with the Third Reich. Paul Schmidt continued to write friendly letters, and Werner Plack was always coming and going on mysterious missions.

The new hotel was a poor choice. Wodehouse may have been oblivious to the fact (he certainly does not refer to it), but the Bristol was *the* Nazi hotel in occupied Paris. After December 1941, it had been given quasi-official status with visiting Germans and French, Dutch and Belgian 'collaborationists'. The hotel ran two dining rooms, a 'diplomatic' one for Germans and their friends, and a second, inferior one for regular guests. Through its dubious connections, informers and black-market racketeers, the Bristol managed to be nearly as well supplied with food and fuel as in peacetime. Wodehouse told Anga von Bodenhausen, 'The manager has been charming and given us splendid rooms at a nominal rate,' but, according to one clandestine American source, the Vichy management of the hotel was 'thoroughly bad'. In some ways, he and Ethel were as much prisoners of the regime as before. As Major Cussen, his MI5 interrogator, put it, 'I shall not be surprised if we receive complaints as to their [the Wodehouses'] conduct while in Paris . . . [arising] from the attention paid to them by German officers and officials. I think that Wodehouse may have been in rather a difficult position in this regard because it was not easy for him to ignore a German who might choose to speak to him.'

Wodehouse put the best face on his situation. He was, he wrote to Anga, 'having a very pleasant time in Paris', enjoying his walks down the eerily deserted streets, and trying to learn French with a private teacher. In contrast to his failure to master even the simplest German, he was making a determined effort, reading Colette and even translating his own last novel into French. His determination to find stability in daily life was as exceptional as ever. Paris in 1943–4 was chaotic, lawless and starving. The Nazi occupation was disintegrating and, until de Gaulle took control of the administration, there were often violent street battles between warring factions, exacerbated by the settling of scores with the dying Vichy regime. Suspected 'Collabos', like the dramatist Sacha Guitry, endured a brief witch-hunt as literary France purged its conscience. Céline fled abroad. Whatever Wodehouse's sangfroid, the atmosphere in Paris was vengeful, hysterical and frightening, made worse by the bitter cold and severe food shortages.

While Wodehouse stayed in his room with his books and typewriter, or roamed the hotel corridors in his slippers, attracting the suspicious attention of at least one informer, Ethel went out shopping, visiting galleries, and meeting old friends from Le Touquet. In her scatty way, Ethel was something of a liability. One night she was arrested for being without her papers, an unpleasant experience that ended happily when one of the five military policemen who brought her back to the Bristol turned out to be a Wodehouse fan. So perhaps his name was not as hopelessly ruined as he feared. At the same time, an American newspaper reported, to his joy, that his books were 'the favourite reading of Princess Elizabeth', which gave him a boost during the lonely and difficult transition to regular civilian life.

By the new year of 1944, it was clear that the days of the Nazis' occupation of Paris were numbered. As well as growing talk of Allied invasion, there was the constant reminder of approaching victory in the city's air-raid warnings. Allied bombers would fly over Paris twice a night, to and from German targets, and on each occasion the *alerte* sent

Wodehouse and Ethel down to the cellars in their pyjamas. Ethel, particularly, found it very stressful. Apart from the threat of bombing, the cost of living in Paris was beginning to worry Wodehouse, especially as Paul Schmidt in Berlin, who was ultimately responsible for administering his resources, had been badly hurt in a car accident and Wodehouse now had to depend on the unreliable assistance of Werner Plack to get his money transferred. This money has occasionally been the subject of controversy. Although it certainly did pass through German diplomatic channels, and the German Central Bank, it was *not* Nazi money but Wodehouse's legitimate earnings from his writing, boosted by a big new advance from his Spanish publisher.

Financial prudence, a desire to lie low, and devotion to his writing encouraged Wodehouse to lead a very quiet life, progressing with his French lessons, thinking out the plot of a new novel, *Uncle Dynamite*, and occasionally going to the theatre. Adrift in the Bristol, Wodehouse's mind went back wistfully to Degenershausen, that 'oasis of safety and happiness'. When the May sunshine came, and the chestnuts and lilacs blossomed in Paris, all he could think about was his favourite linden tree and 'Mister Bwana and Mrs Goat and the rest'. There was a sentimental side to Wodehouse that only a few people – usually women – were permitted to know. Anga von Bodenhausen was one. Leonora, whom he and Ethel were longing to see again, was another.

But Leonora was dead. On 16 May she had driven up to London, checked into the London Clinic for a routine gynaecological operation and had suffered an unexplained post-operative collapse during the night. Her husband Peter Cazalet immediately cabled Reynolds, and although it has often been said that this dreadful news was first broken to Wodehouse in September, it is inconceivable that he and Ethel were not informed, either via Berlin or, more probably, direct to Paris. No contemporary letters survive. Wodehouse never explored the really painful things in his life on paper. He simply told Townend, in a scribbled postcard, that 'We are quite crushed by the dreadful news about Leonora'. Coming on top of his wartime troubles – arrest, internment and disgrace – the death of his beloved stepdaughter at the age of forty was Fate's unkindest cut. In the next few years, he would obsessively rehearse the events of June and July 1941, but he hardly ever uttered a word about Leonora. The war had wrecked his career; now her death broke his spirit, and helped send him into permanent exile. For a man who never ceased to write letters, the silence that fell throughout the coming year is profoundly eloquent. There was nothing he wanted to say. 'Nothing much matters now,' he told Townend, sadly. Ethel was shattered, too. 'I shall never recover,' she confided to Denis Mackail.

While the Wodehouses nursed their grief, the war was entering its final, decisive phase. After the Normandy landings of 6 June, the Allies advanced steadily across occupied Europe. The Americans liberated Paris on 25 August. There was fierce fighting in the Latin Quarter, across the river from the Bristol, but the Parisians were typically unmoved. On the banks of the Seine, they continued to fish or paint while the battle raged around them. Then de Gaulle arrived in Paris; on 26 August, he led a victory parade down the Champs-Elysées, cheered by huge crowds. Wodehouse happened to be among them, exercising Wonder, when a fierce gun-battle broke out near the Marigny Theatre. Wodehouse said he was lucky not to be killed; he saw a girl shot dead, and in the mêlée Ethel disappeared. Wodehouse eventually found her safe and sound back at the Bristol. 'It was all very exciting,' he reported to Townend, 'but no good to me from a writing point of view.'

Wodehouse had been living in a kind of limbo, but now there was a rush of events. Once the Allies arrived, he knew what he had to do. Still numb from Leonora's death and in a mood of resigned fatalism, knowing he must turn himself in, he asked an American colonel to inform the British authorities of his whereabouts. On 29 August the news was relayed to the Security Services in London. The next day the Security Services informed the Home Office, who decided that they did not want Wodehouse brought to London but would interrogate him in Paris. On 5 September, therefore, Major Cussen of MI5, a barrister by profession, was flown to Paris to question him about his wartime behaviour.

In the interim, before the formal interrogation got under way, the Wodehouses, already on a list of 'British subjects in enemy occupied territory whose cases required special investigation', had been assigned to a young MI6 liaison officer attached to de Gaulle's *services spéciaux*. Malcolm Muggeridge was a former *Manchester Guardian* journalist whose Fabian socialist circle considered Wodehouse and his light-hearted comedies of upper-class life 'somewhat reprehensible'. Not only was Muggeridge initially disdainful of Wodehouse's work, he had also been too busy with the war in 1941 to pay much attention to the public frenzy about the broadcasts. So when, one evening at the end of August, he presented himself in uniform at the front desk of the Hôtel Bristol and was directed to Wodehouse's suite, he had no idea what to expect.

The lift was not working. Muggeridge climbed the stairs, reached Wodehouse's room and found himself shaking hands with 'a bald, amiable-looking large man . . . wearing grey flannel trousers and a loose sports jacket, and smoking a pipe; a sort of schoolmaster's rig'. At first, Muggeridge felt obliged to stress the gravity of Wodehouse's situation and rehearsed both the accusations against him and the terrible penalties if he was found guilty. Soon, however, he came under Wodehouse's benign spell, conceding that the row about the broadcasts was one that he, Muggeridge, 'personally considered ludicrous'. As always with Wodehouse, the conversation quickly turned to books and writers. Wodehouse wanted to know what new novels had been published and how they were selling; what plays had been put on, and how long they had run. 'Did clubs go on? And the *Times Literary Supplement*? And A. A. Milne? And *Punch*?' Ever hospitable, Wodehouse sent down for a bottle of wine and, as the two men went on talking, dusk fell. This twilight moment was an exquisite one for Muggeridge. Astonishingly, the young officer sent to initiate the interrogation of a notorious traitor found himself seduced into admiring complicity. 'I was happy to be sitting there with Wodehouse,' he recalled, 'and from that moment have always loved him.' As he wrote later, Muggeridge saw at once that Wodehouse was 'ill-fitted to live in an age of ideological conflict. He just does not react to human beings in that sort of way, and never seems to hate anyone . . . such a temperament unfits him to be a good citizen in the mid-twentieth century.' Even when he got to know him better, Muggeridge always found him elusive. 'An innate shyness, or perhaps timidity, restrains him from coming out in the open. His very humour provides a kind of camouflage . . . It is not that he is other-worldly, or unworldly, so much as that he is a-worldly; a born neutral.' He added, in words that must haunt all those who try to probe Wodehouse's character, 'Whether this benignity is no more than a brilliantly devised mask, with, deep down, another Wodehouse, it is impossible to know.'

So began a friendship, a rare piece of luck after a succession of misfortunes, that would make the difficult first months of the liberation tolerable for Wodehouse. It was an association that would flourish in a most important way in the 1950s and last until Wodehouse's death in 1975.

Muggeridge loved both the Wodehouses. Ethel, he found, was 'a spirited and energetic lady trying as hard to be worldly-wise as Wodehouse himself to be innocent . . . a mixture of Mistress Quickly and Florence Nightingale, with a touch of Lady Macbeth thrown in'. They, in their turn, came to rely on Ethel's 'Darling sweet adoreable [*sic*] Malcolm'. It was Malcolm whom they could call in a crisis, Malcolm who knew his way around the Allied bureaucracy, Malcolm who sent them food parcels, Malcolm who would drop by for tea and gossip about literary London, Malcolm who would run errands for them in London; and it was Malcolm to whom Wodehouse expressed his grief, on receiving from him, officially, the news of Leonora's death. 'I thought she was immortal,' he said, after a long silence, one of the most perfect lines he ever uttered. Both Wodehouses loved Muggeridge in their different ways, and struggled to express it. 'Plummie and I will *never never* forget what you have done for us,' wrote Ethel. For his part, Wodehouse displayed a rare side of himself. 'We miss you terribly, Malcolm,' he wrote after Muggeridge was transferred to London. 'We have tried at times to express all we feel about your wonderfulness to us, but we feel we made a poor job of it.'

Wodehouse was a reflective, deliberate man, who liked a timetable and preferred to take things one by one, but once the Allies were in Paris there was no time for reflection or deliberation, and suddenly a lot to worry about. On 8 September a letter came from Paul Reynolds junior in New York with the news that Reynolds senior had just died, shortly after his eightieth birthday. Wodehouse had been represented by Reynolds since the heady days of *Something Fresh*, and though they rarely met he had become close to him over three remarkable decades of literary association: it was the end of an era.

As if to make this point, on 9 September Major Cussen arrived at the Hôtel Bristol to begin his all-important interrogation. In his nonchalant, practised way, Wodehouse managed to turn a potentially dangerous encounter into a personal vindication. Ethel found the process 'tiresome', but Wodehouse was painfully frank and his account soon convinced his interrogator of his fundamental innocence. Cussen took Wodehouse, the alleged pro-Nazi, through everything: his career up to 1939; his life in Le Touquet before internment; his life in Tost; his 'frame of mind while in internment at Tost'; the first mention of broadcasting; his release from Tost; his life in Berlin and his activities in Germany after the broadcasts; his activities in Paris, and finally his finances. Cussen's interrogation continued on 10 and 11 September and concluded after a fourth day on 12 September. His report was delivered on 28 September, just one month after the liberation of Paris and while the war was still going on.

Cussen's fifteen-page report might have led to a prosecution. Indeed, though he exonerated Wodehouse, his analysis was no whitewash. Cussen doubted 'whether either Wodehouse or his wife . . . had any idea of the proper standard of conduct towards [the Germans] on such occasions', and observed that 'Wodehouse in particular [was] very susceptible to any form of flattery'. He was afraid 'that their behaviour [in Germany] has been unwise', a statement he did not elucidate further, and he considered that 'by lending his voice and personality to the German broadcasting station, Wodehouse did an act which was likely to assist the enemy'. His report also contained strong criticism of Ethel. 'From what I have seen of Mrs Wodehouse,' he wrote, 'I expect to learn that she conducted herself [in Germany] in a flamboyant manner and that she accepted all the attention which was no doubt paid to her by German officials.' Despite these negative comments, Cussen concluded that 'a jury would find difficulty in convicting him of an intention to assist the enemy'. After three years of the wildest speculation and misrepresentation, Cussen's interrogation was a vital first step in debunking some of the most scurrilous tales about Wodehouse and of establishing his innocence of the worst accusations levelled against him.

For Wodehouse the Cussen report had two important deficiencies. First, because Cussen completed his work long before VE Day, it contained no examination of German documents (now lost) or German witnesses (now dead). No one, for example, ever questioned Lagerführer Buchelt or spoke, officially, to Werner Plack. So the Cussen report left unanswered a number of questions that can never be resolved and which will, inevitably, continue to bedevil any discussion of the case. Second, although the Director of Public Prosecutions appended a note to the file saying that 'there is not sufficient evidence to justify a prosecution of this man', its findings were never revealed to Wodehouse and could not be made public until 1980, five years after Wodehouse's death. The cruellest feature of Wodehouse's long old age was that he never knew, definitively, that his case was closed.

Amid these ominous legal manoeuvres, there was a moment of near farce. When Duff Cooper, the newly appointed British ambassador to France, arrived with his wife, Diana, shortly after the liberation of Paris to find the embassy not yet ready, his staff naturally installed him in the luxury of the Hôtel Bristol. On his very first night there, the new ambassador, who was a keen Wodehouse reader, encountered the writer in the lift. There is no evidence that Wodehouse and his nemesis actually exchanged words, but Duff Cooper recorded the potential for embarrassment in his diary and noted that 'the press have already got hold of it'. By 3 October, thanks to Muggeridge, Wodehouse and Ethel had been discreetly moved to the Hôtel Lincoln on the rue Bayard, a much quieter establishment, better suited to his mood. Everyone commented on his low spirits. Leonora's sister-in-law, Thelma Cazalet-Keir, a Conservative MP, who was now the Cazalet family's self-appointed adviser to Wodehouse, told Reynolds that she had received a very sad message, but noted with satisfaction that the Wodehouses did not intend coming to Britain in the near future.

Now that Wodehouse was out of Germany and ostensibly a free man in liberated France, albeit under investigation by the authorities, there were two schools of thought about his appropriate conduct. The Cazalet family line, represented by Thelma, on advice from her political contacts, and with the intermittent support of Wodehouse's English literary agent, A. P. Watt, and publisher, Herbert Jenkins, was that he should lie low. He should suppress all reference to the broadcasts, do nothing to re-ignite controversy, and let his disgrace fade from public memory. There was even the suggestion that he should refrain from publishing *Money in the Bank*. Against this, at first, was Wodehouse's own determined conviction that he had a good case to make and many lies to expose, and that a true account should be published to exonerate him. After many behind-the-scenes battles, a compromise version of this approach prevailed. Wodehouse would not take issue with his critics or discuss the broadcasts (he never liked to do this, anyway), but equally he would not remain silent, in exile, as Thelma had advised. Moreover, he would of course continue to write and publish his novels. Work was the thing that gave his life its meaning, and one could never be sure when one's time would be over. His old friend, the composer Jerome Kern, after all, had recently suffered a stroke and died, on 11 November, in New York.

In Berlin, Wodehouse had resigned himself to being, in future, an outcast with few friends, but in fact the liberation brought all kinds of warm greetings from England which cheered him up and inspired the hope that 'eventually things will straighten themselves out'. It was, he complained, difficult to establish the true state of public opinion towards him. 'I meet English and American soldiers,' he told Townend, 'and when they discover who I am they are perfectly friendly . . . But I am afraid there is a long way to go before things can come right, but I haven't a twinge of self-pity. I made an ass of myself, and must pay the penalty.'

His life was still vulnerable to sudden irruptions of random wartime menace. On 21 November he and Ethel were arrested at one in the morning by two French *inspecteurs* with coat collars turned up 'exactly like a movie', and carted off to the Palais de Justice. According to Muggeridge, an unidentified English guest at a dinner party given by the Prefect of Paris had remarked on how scandalous it was that two such notorious traitors as the Wodehouses should be at large. Prefect Luizet, in a display of bravado, had given immediate orders that the Wodehouses be taken into custody. In desperation, Wodehouse scribbled a note to Muggeridge,

we are absolutely fainting with hunger, – Ethel is on the verge of collapse . . . There seems to be nothing against us except the five talks . . . This is absolute hell, old man. We have spent the day sitting on hard chairs in a draughty passage – nothing to eat, not even a glass of water to drink. I can't wash and my face is a foul mess of beard!

When Muggeridge traced them to a police station on the quai d'Orléans, no one seemed to know why Monsieur and Madame Wodenhorse (as they had been charged) were there, but the combination of Ethel's hysterical French and Wonder's short temper enabled Muggeridge to get Ethel released. Wodehouse himself was detained for a further four nerve-racking days, during which he distracted himself by working on *Uncle Dynamite*. At first, there was talk of sending him to a notorious prison at Nancy, but eventually, with some humanity, the French authorities decided that, although they could not release him at once, they could improve his conditions by declaring him unwell and placing him in hospital, under guard. It was, Wodehouse told Guy Bolton, with whom he was in correspondence again, 'a lot of phonus-bolonus'. More farce ensued. The only clinic available was a maternity home and there, for some weeks, with babies being born all around him, Wodehouse was sequestered. Although he found it 'pretty foul to be cooped up', he told Townend that he had his own room, 'quite good food, plenty of tobacco and drinks, and Ethel is allowed to come and see me'. (He would later joke that his war had begun in a lunatic asylum and ended in a maternity ward.) Wodehouse's arrest made new headlines in Britain, revived the old accusations, provoked more questions in the House of Commons, and finally prompted a short debate, led by Quintin Hogg, in which the definition of treason and the other complex and serious legal aspects of the case were thrashed out once more with the righteous indignation that the Wodehouse affair always inspired. And once again the government took the line that, technically, Wodehouse had broken no laws and so could face no charges.

It was only now, after the press coverage in *The Times* and the *Daily Mail*, and the questions in the House, that Churchill showed any interest in the Wodehouse case. He told the Foreign Secretary that the French were 'overdoing things about P. G. Wodehouse', adding that if Wodehouse was a British citizen 'we ought to know what he is accused of doing'. Churchill's note was forwarded to Duff Cooper, who replied that the press coverage was exaggerated, and that although there was no legal basis for the French detaining Wodehouse, neither the Home Office nor MI5, to whom he had been offered, wanted him either. Churchill responded by pointing out that public opinion was moving in Wodehouse's favour. He had no liking for Wodehouse, and he did not want the French authorities to increase sympathy for Wodehouse in Britain, telling his ambassador in Paris that 'if you are shy about making the enquiries which have been suggested and sending a report on the subject, I will telegraph de Gaulle myself'. Finally, in a further response to Duff Cooper's complaint that he had received no clear instructions about how to handle the Wodehouse case, Churchill fired off one of his inimitably brutal memoranda, closing the discussion, at least to his own satisfaction: 'We would prefer not ever to hear about him again . . .', he wrote. 'His name stinks here, but he would not be sent to prison. However, if there is no other resort, he should be sent over here and if there is no charge against him, he can live secluded in some place or go to hell as soon as there is a vacant passage.'

While the authorities wrangled off-stage, and until he was finally released from 'preventive detention' in mid-January 1945, Wodehouse, the old campaigner, simply adopted his habitual routine:

I generally wake up at four a.m., lie in bed till six, then get up and boil water on a boiler lent me by one of the doctors and have breakfast. The concierge arrives with the Paris *Daily Mail* at nine, and after my room has been cleaned, that is by half past nine, I start writing. Lunch at half past twelve. At four I get my walk in the garden with an inspector, the only time I am allowed out of doors. I walk up and down on the landing from six-thirty to eight, and then go to bed. Lights out at nine-thirty. The nurses and inspectors are very friendly, and I am improving my French. When I get visitors, they usually come at three. It isn't a bad sort of life at all, if you have a novel to write.

The novel in question was *Uncle Dynamite* – an 'Uncle Fred' novel which contains the line 'Don't kill him, Bill. He's my publisher!' – but the manuscript that was increasingly exercising his mind was *Wodehouse in Wonderland*, especially after the press and parliamentary comment stirred up by his latest arrest. The 'camp book', he told the faithful Townend, would be a comic book about his adventures at Tost. But the more he looked at it, the more unsure he felt about it. He was acutely aware that 'a humorous treatment', in his usual vein, of some very serious matters might go down very badly with his public and renew the old accusations of flippancy. But, as Muggeridge pointed out, he would be making a mistake if he tried 'to write differently'. On the other hand, he had to acknowledge how badly out of tune he was with English life. From childhood, Wodehouse had been taught never to 'stick on "side"', to eschew subjectivity, and instinctively to exhibit the stiff upper lip. His comic prose had celebrated these qualities in lunatic situations. Now, confronted with the pressing need to defend himself in print, on a subject of deadly seriousness, he was painfully coming to terms with the fact that his voice was inadequate to the task and had no place in a discordant post-war world. It would be at least another year before *Wodehouse in Wonderland* was definitively shelved, although parts of the manuscript continued to surface in other ways throughout the 1950s.

After his release from the maternity hospital, Wodehouse and Ethel took refuge at a deserted country hotel in Barbizon, some thirty miles outside Paris, but were forced to return to the Hôtel Lincoln when

SHAEF (Supreme Headquarters, Allied Expeditionary Force) moved into the village and requisitioned their rooms. Life was not easy. The winter of 1944/5 was bitterly cold. Living costs were high and food so scarce that the Wodehouses sometimes dined on bread and jam. When the Lincoln was also requisitioned, Wodehouse was forced to go and stay with a Danish friend in Neuilly, while Ethel lingered on in Paris, looking for a furnished flat, speculating in her neurotic way that she might end up sleeping in the Métro. These constant upheavals did not distract Wodehouse but, writing to Townend about his new interest in Shakespeare, he did consider the question of the relationship between life and art. 'Do you find that your private life affects your work?' he asked, adding in a typically opaque admission, 'I don't. I have never written funnier stuff than during these last years, when I certainly wasn't feeling exhilarated.' But he was beginning to feel his age. He completed *Uncle Dynamite* by the end of March, and complained to Denis Mackail that he was now 'relying on technique instead of exuberance'. The completion of a new novel, and the return of his old worry that he would never come up with another plot, rekindled his determination to revise 'the camp book' for publication, but how? Now that he was able to have some perspective on what had happened in Germany, he acknowledged that his fundamental difficulty was 'writing about unpleasant experiences . . . without having the sympathy of the audience'.

There were other anxieties to contend with, too. The latest American tax case was still rumbling on. From New York, Revere Reynolds broke the bad news that he had been unable to persuade any magazines to buy serial rights to any of the manuscripts so carefully shipped across in 1942. Young Reynolds, nervous of dealing with his father's old client, managed to combine an odd evasiveness with a slightly tactless candour. 'This was partly, or perhaps chiefly, due to feeling that was aroused,' he wrote to Wodehouse. 'There was also feeling . . . that your stories, which pre-supposed an England before the war or an England not at war, would seem unreal and hence not as funny.' Similar worries were expressed in London. When Herbert Jenkins, backing Thelma Cazalet-Keir, had questioned the need for the immediate publication of *Money in the Bank*, A. P. Watt had prudently solicited a rival bid from the publishers William Collins. This move concentrated the minds of the Jenkins executives, who suddenly discovered that they did, after all, badly want to publish the latest Wodehouse novel. Their long-standing author was glad to stay put, though he disliked the Herbert Jenkins book covers. 'I suppose you are apt to get a pretty foul jacket from a popular publisher,' he observed philosophically to Townend. 'God may have forgiven Herbert Jenkins Ltd for the jacket of *Meet Mr Mulliner*, but I never shall.'

Living hand-to-mouth in Paris, they had much to contend with. In the coldest weather, there was neither heating nor hot water. There were daily blackouts. The Wodehouses eked out their refugee existence with trips to the comfort of the American Library and warmed themselves with tots of gin and Italian vermouth. Accommodation was equally hard to come by, but Ethel somehow found a very snug apartment at 78 avenue Paul Doumer, a busy street in the sixteenth arrondissement. Wodehouse was delighted, telling Muggeridge that the apartment had that touch of slight dinginess which he preferred. The furniture was a little faded and there were tapestries on the walls. It was on the first floor, and got the afternoon sun. 'We are now safe and can't be moved or thrown into the street,' he wrote. 'If necessary, we can dig in and stay there for years.' Wodehouse resumed his daily five-mile walks, and began to write a play, frugally reworking his unpublished novel, *Spring Fever*. When summer came, his thoughts turned to Dulwich, as they always did during the cricket season, and, ignoring Thelma Cazalet-Keir, he arranged for a long letter of self-justification to appear in the *Alleynian* in July. At the same time, he was working 'desperately hard' on *Wodehouse in Wonderland*. By mid-September he had completed his latest draft. 'My trouble has been to get the right tone . . .', he admitted to Townend.

I go for a walk and work up a spirit of defiance and come back and write a belligerent page or two indicating that I don't give a damn whether the public takes a more favourable view or not, because all my friends have stuck to me and it's only my friends I care about. Then I sleep on it and wonder if this is quite judicious! Also comedy will keep creeping in at the most solemn moments.

To send his latest work to Watt in London, Wodehouse entrusted the typescript of 'the camp book' to H. D. Ziman, a visiting literary journalist introduced to him by Malcolm Muggeridge. Chatty, well-informed and judicious, Ziman, who was known as 'Zed', would later have a distinguished career as literary editor of the *Daily Telegraph*, but it is an indication of Wodehouse's isolation that he chose to solicit a self-assured stranger's opinion of the book. Ziman had two main criticisms. First, he observed that, although Wodehouse took on the critics of the broadcasts in a 'ding dong' chapter, he did not explain the cause of the furore and reprint the texts of the actual broadcasts themselves. Second, Ziman believed that Wodehouse had left out the most interesting part – 'what happened to you in Germany [after the broadcasts] and later in Paris' and 'what happened to your wife before she joined you and both of you later'. Ziman also pointed out the awkward facts that showed, he wrote, 'not that you were a Benedict Arnold but that you were remarkably out of touch with the sentiments of the British people'. Finally, he urged Wodehouse to admit candidly that he had made a mistake.

Wodehouse's response is revealing. To the first criticism, he replied that he was intending the text to be sold for serial publication, saving the broadcasts for subsequent book publication. To Ziman's second objection, he wrote:

as regards my life in Germany, there is so little to tell. Naturally everyone would suppose that an Englishman in Germany in wartime would have a thrilling tale to relate, but I am a creature of habit and as a result of forty years of incessant literary composition have become a mere writing machine. Wherever I am, I sit down and write, or, if I have nothing to write about, I walk up and down and think out plots.

His letter to Ziman corroborates the picture painted by Michael Vermehren:

When I was in Berlin [Wodehouse wrote] at the Adlon, this was my life day after day. Get up, do my Daily Dozen, bathe, shave, breakfast, take dog for saunter, start work. Work till lunch. After lunch, the exercise walk, resuming work at five. Work from five till eight. Go down to dinner back to my room to read or else walk round and round the corridors of my floor, thinking. Except when we went to lunch with an English or American friend, this programme never varied. I seldom spoke to a German.

Wodehouse agreed that he should admit his mistake, but said that 'what has hampered me is the difficulty of . . . "expressing contrition" without grovelling', and concluded this defiant note with the observation that 'I would much rather be thought a Benedict Arnold than a Uriah Heep'.

The summer spent addressing his critics had given him new zest and, as he told Bolton, 'things are beginning to stir faintly, like the blood beginning to circulate in a frozen Alpine traveller who has met a St Bernard dog and been given a shot from a brandy flask'. His English assets, restricted during the war, could now be transferred to France. He told Townend that he was enjoying life much more than the year before. It was in this brisk new mood that, shortly before sending 'the camp book' to Watt in London, and perhaps because he was irritated by the younger Reynolds's failure to champion his work as his father had done, he peremptorily fired him in a letter of brutal abruptness. 'I was a new personality whom he [Wodehouse] did not like,' Reynolds wrote later. The truth is that in important literary business Wodehouse was always clinically decisive.

Closer to home, the upshot of the prolonged and acrimonious debate among his advisers about what to do with *Wodehouse in Wonderland* was, he told Mackail at the beginning of November, that the consensus of opinion against publication was too strong. He had decided to withdraw the manuscript 'until this Belsen business has become a thing of the past'. This one reference to the Holocaust is Wodehouse's only acknowledgement of the horrors endured by the Jews during the Third Reich, but charges of anti-Semitism do not stick. Compared to that of other popular Edwardian writers of his generation, John Buchan for instance, his writing, published and unpublished, is strikingly free from either racist or anti-Semitic prejudice. On Broadway and in Hollywood, his close friendship with Jewish musicians such as Jerome Kern and the Gershwin brothers, especially Ira Gershwin, was a vital part of his professional life. A letter to Townend during the 'Exodus' affair of 1947 confirms both his hostility to British government policy towards the Jews and, once again, the innocence of his vision: 'Aren't the Jews extraordinary people,' he wrote. 'They seem to infuriate all nations, as nations, and yet almost every individual has a number of Jewish friends . . . apart from my real inner circle of friends (numbering about three) most of the men I like best are Jews – e.g. Scott Meredith, Ira Gershwin, Molnár, Oscar Hammerstein, Irving Berlin . . . and a lot more.'

Wodehouse would work with anyone who might serve his purpose.

His focus on his work was uncompromising. He was, at heart, a proud man who disliked to be bullied, especially about his writing. In the debate about *Wodehouse in Wonderland* he dispatched a copy to America for a second opinion from Bobby Denby, who was back in the Wodehouses' lives again. Wodehouse was also in contact with a young American named Scott Feldman, who had written to him out of the blue to announce his fervent support and to urge – in an implied criticism of Reynolds – a more robust campaign towards American public opinion. Feldman, who had been a successful short-story writer for the pulps in the 1930s, was about to change his name and make the transition to a distinguished career as the literary agent Scott Meredith. He claimed to have written no fewer than three hundred letters to newspapers and magazines on Wodehouse's behalf and this vigorous, unsolicited campaign made a big impression in Paris. Further encouragement came with more good news from London. Herbert Jenkins were now proposing to print an unprecedented 20,000 copies of *Money in the Bank*, and the first reactions from the book trade were reported to be promising. 'If I can get by with that one,' Wodehouse wrote, 'the others ought to be all right.' He was referring to his backlog of unpublished novels: *Joy in the Morning, Full Moon, Spring Fever* and *Uncle Dynamite*. 'I'm beginning to feel that it won't matter that they are about conditions and a life that has ceased to exist. I don't believe people care a damn, so long as the story is funny.'

To coincide with this upswing in his fortunes, he and Ethel had just moved to a superior apartment, reminiscent of New York, at 36 boulevard Suchet, two doors down from the Duke and Duchess of Windsor, and a short walk from the Bois de Boulogne. Wodehouse pronounced his new base, 'a tremendous success. It is like living in the country with all the advantages of town.' After years of deprivation and worry, it was quite like old times. Describing the move to Townend, he wrote, 'I go out into the Bois every morning before breakfast in a sweater and golf knickers and do my exercises, and wear golf clothes all day. The great merit of Paris is that nobody stares at you no matter what you do or wear.' In this new spirit of optimism, Wodehouse now wrote to Bolton that 'I have great hopes of the Spring, feeling that it will mark a turning-point in the world's history . . . when it gets a bit warmer I think things will mend.' A sure sign of his good spirits was the renewed flow of his letters and his animated discussion of his craft. 'I wish I could get a glimmering of an idea for a novel,' he wrote to Mackail just before Christmas; 'what the devil does one write about these days, if one is a specialist on country houses and butlers . . . ?' A few days later he added that he was happy to be classed as an early Edwardian. 'I look on myself as a historical novelist. I read a book about Dickens the other day which pointed out that D. was still writing gaily about stage coaches etc long after railways had come in. I don't believe it matters and intend to go on hewing to the butler line, let the chips fall where they may.'

In this ebullient mood, his ideas began to flow at last and in March 1946 he announced to Mackail that 'the day before yesterday, after four blank years, I suddenly started getting out the plot of a novel [*The Mating Season*] which I began to brood on in 1942 . . . As always, it treats of a world that no longer exists and will depend for its appeal entirely on nostalgia.' He was also becoming much more social. In the aftermath of the liberation, visitors began pouring into Paris and taking up all his time. Among his lunch companions was George Orwell, who was in Paris on assignment from the *Observer* and introduced to him by Muggeridge. They lunched at a dingy little restaurant down by Les Halles and Wodehouse later said that the Old Etonian Orwell struck him as 'one of those warped birds who have never recovered from an unhappy childhood and a miserable school life', but school was precisely what they shared and the two men got on very well. Both, for instance, habitually checked the performance of their school teams in the newspaper. Their subsequent correspondence led directly to Orwell's 'Defence' of Wodehouse, published in the spring of 1945, for which, at the time, Wodehouse was grateful. 'I don't think I have ever read a better bit of criticism. You were absolutely right in everything you said about my work. It was uncanny.' There was also a cheering letter from a New York theatrical manager who wanted to mount an adaptation of *Leave It to Psmith*, and talk about a revival of *Oh, Boy!* All he needed now was an American visa, but his application was tied up in bureaucracy.

These welcome reminders of his theatrical past conveyed the welcome implication that his name was no longer mud, as he had feared. Now the ideas were coming thick and fast. 'Listen,' he wrote to Bolton in the new year of 1946,

I've suddenly got the most terrific idea – a book of theatrical reminiscences by you and me to be called

BOOK AND LYRICS
by
GUY BOLTON and P. G. WODEHOUSE

. . . My idea would be to make it a sort of loose saga of our adventures in the theatre from 1915 onwards, studded with anecdotes. Think of all the stuff we could put into it!

The belief that America was where his future lay was confirmed when Doubleday decided to press ahead with the publication of *Joy in the Morning*. He began to lobby for a visa. On 8 May, as a preliminary to his return to New York, he drafted a self-explanatory letter to *Variety*, along the lines of his defence to the *Alleynian*, but aimed at American readers, including the hope that *Variety* might be able to print the text of the broadcasts so that everyone could see how harmless they were.

These expressions of support from Broadway, Feldman and his American publisher came in stark contrast to the situation in England. There, dealing directly with Watt, and not telling Wodehouse, Thelma Cazalet-Keir was using her political influence to get the publication of *Money in the Bank* postponed. A bitter battle ensued, but Wodehouse eventually forced the issue by telling Herbert Jenkins that they had a choice between publishing in May, as planned, or not publishing at all, an ultimatum that did the trick. Full of combative self-confidence, Wodehouse told Mackail, 'What the hell? If a section of the press gets up and howls it won't affect me, because I shan't read what is written.'

Authors who claim not to read reviews are usually being disingenuous, and Wodehouse was no exception. He monitored the sales and the reviews of *Money in the Bank* very carefully, noting 'a stinker in *The Observer*', and taking particular pleasure in a favourable review on the BBC from the distinguished and influential critic V. S. Pritchett. His grateful letter of appreciation says a lot about his attitude towards his wartime disgrace:

You can probably imagine how I felt when I heard of your talk, for it was not without diffidence that I agreed to the publication of the book. I saw myself rather in the position of a red-nosed comedian who has got the bird at the first house on Monday and is having the temerity to go on and do his stuff at the second house, outwardly breezy and cheerful but feeling inside as if he had swallowed a heaping tablespoonful of butterflies and with a wary eye out for demonstrations from the gallery. And now comes this applause from the stalls, thank God! Bless you.

Pritchett's review came shortly after Wodehouse received formal notification from the French government clearing him of the trumped-up charges on which he had been arrested, and announcing that he was no longer considered 'dangerous to the Republic'. In high spirits, he wrote to Bolton:

Up till now, of course, the Republic has been ducking into hallways when I came along, swallowing nervously and whispering 'Cheese it, boys! Here comes Wodehouse!' It's very gratifying. The way I look at it is that if France, the jumpiest country on earth, considers I'm all right, the other countries will have to fall into line.

Finally, in July, after protracted negotiations, the visa came through. For a mad moment, Wodehouse toyed with settling in Switzerland, but an overnight visit there convinced him against the idea. Now he announced that he was planning to fly to America on his first flight ever. But he dreaded the prospect, so he and Ethel decided to revert to their old ways and wait for a boat. Apart from wanting to be in New York for the production of *Leave It to Psmith*, which was eventually postponed, Wodehouse was in no hurry. 'My heart is in France,' he told his French translator. From late July, he was working hard on his new novel, *The Mating Season*, which he had virtually finished by the new year of 1947. 'I used to write a novel in three months,' he complained to Bolton, 'so I am exactly half as fast a worker as I used to be. Not that it matters if the stuff is all right, and I am very pleased with this one.' *The Mating Season* marked the high point of Wodehouse's wartime creativity. He would not complete a new novel until 1951; and the return to America would prove to be every bit as difficult as he had feared.

PART FIVE

Atonement

(1947-1975)

23. 'My world has been shot to pieces'
(1947–1951)

The world of which I have been writing ever since I was so high . . .
has gone with the wind, and is one with Nineveh and Tyre. In a word,
it has had it. (Preface to *Joy in the Morning*)

Wodehouse postponed his return to America several times. Inwardly,
he dreaded it. He was older, out of touch, and no longer sure of his
place in the world. The next five years would be a period of intense
frustration. There were so many uncertainties. His professional life in
New York, settled and prosperous for so many years, was in post-war
flux. Reynolds was dead. The great magazines, his mainstay, were cool
towards him or, like the *Saturday Evening Post*, in decline. The Broadway
of the 1920s and 1930s was long gone. Hollywood was in crisis; cinema
attendances were down. Also on his mind was the knowledge that his
American readers had been as divided by the broadcasts as his British.
He anxiously scanned the American reviews of *Joy in the Morning* for
signs of hostility. No wonder he and Ethel dithered over their plans.

Low Wood had been looted and badly damaged during the
Occupation. There was no question of Wodehouse's returning to Britain,
so perhaps they should repair the house and settle once more in Le
Touquet? Or should they spend the summer in New York and come
back to plant the garden in November? Ethel, characteristically, relieved
her anxieties about the future with a whirlwind of shopping in Paris
and London. Whatever her husband's problems, *she* could cross the
Channel. She took a suite at the Ritz, for a flying visit which may have
inspired the apocryphal story that Wodehouse himself made a secret
post-war return to Britain. As their transatlantic sailing date approached
things grew calmer. Wodehouse confided to Guy Bolton that he planned
to stay in America as long as the authorities would let him. If he wasn't
deported, he added nervously, he expected to be there at least a year.
He was eager to take up his old life ('we shall start in at the Savoy
Plaza') and now that he was 'in the chips again', from an unexpected

American government tax refund, he hoped to be able to cut a dash for a while. As well as this windfall which, he said, made him feel 'frightfully rich, as if I had just been left $19,000 by an uncle in Australia', he still had some £105,000 in Britain, and US bank deposits of about $100,000. Any uncertainties he felt, of course, had no impact on his writing life. He continued to work at the new Jeeves novel (*The Mating Season*), telling Townend that he would write the final chapter on the boat.

After a nerve-racking and exhausting delay, caused by fog in the Channel, the SS *America* (one of the most beautiful and luxurious of the American passenger liners, recently recommissioned after wartime transport service) steamed out of Cherbourg on 18 April 1947 carrying the Wodehouses, Wonder and almost a decade's worth of luggage. At the last minute, with Ethel neurotically packing and re-packing, the shipping line upgraded them to a stateroom with a private bath, more appropriate for the famous writer. As well as the unfinished typescript of *The Mating Season*, Wodehouse also took a new Ferenc Molnár comedy, *Arthur*, to adapt en route. It was almost like the good old days. But there was still the New York press to face, and the rough spring crossing seemed a poor omen. In a further twist of bad timing, Guy and Virginia Bolton would be absent from New York, crossing the Atlantic in the other direction for a prolonged European trip at the exact moment of their old friends' return.

However, once the *America* docked at the pier in Lower Manhattan, the Wodehouses' re-entry went better than they could have dared to hope. It was, as he put it with his usual hyperbole, 'a sensational triumph'. New York's reporters surged on board in pursuit of the big story, and found Wodehouse, chastened by his troubles in Berlin, now a master of media relations. He swiftly disarmed the yelling mob of newspaper-men, and even made such good friends with the journalist from *PM*, a left-leaning evening paper that Wodehouse had been convinced would tear him to pieces, that he found himself accepting its correspondent's invitation to dinner in Greenwich Village. Meanwhile, his publishers were anxious to publicize *Full Moon* and to promote sales of *Joy in the Morning*, so next day, more dauntingly, Wodehouse held a formal press conference at the Doubleday offices. But there was no acrimony. In sharp contrast to the British press, everyone in America, he noted with relief, 'was wonderfully cordial', and, now considerably relaxed, he followed up the press conference with a cocktail party for several literary journalists. Back in the American publicity groove, he next appeared on the popular syndicated radio show, 'Luncheon at Sardi's'. Here, he made no reference to the German broadcasts and confined himself to some prepared cracks about New York (returning to the city, he said, was 'like meeting an old sweetheart and finding she has put on a lot of weight'). Ethel, quivering with nervousness, monitored his interview from the control room. But he survived the ordeal, and reported gaily to Townend: 'Final Score – everything in the garden is lovely.'

Wodehouse's euphoria at finding the American press no longer hostile was enhanced by the exhilaration, after years of trouble, of being back in New York. The city he had last visited in 1936 was 'simply incredible. About five times larger than it was when I last saw it, and more bustling than ever,' he wrote to Townend. 'The prosperity stuns one after being in France so long. There is nothing in the way of food and drink you can't get here.' To cap it all, Doubleday's publication of *Full Moon* went off successfully, with good reviews in the *New York Times* and the *New York Sun*, and 'a terrific boost' in the *New York Herald Tribune*. 'Everything has gone marvellously well for me since I arrived,' he concluded. After shuttling between expensive hotels during these hectic first weeks, he and Ethel decided to take a penthouse apartment with an attractive roof garden at 53 East 66th Street.

The thrill of being back in America soon wore off, as most of Wodehouse's thrills generally did. After *The Mating Season*, he had no new novel to work on, and, for the first time in his career, no idea for one, either. Initially, he had expressed some optimism that he would shortly be taken up by the magazines again, but now he discovered that the serial market for his stories had evaporated. The truth about his situation took a while to sink in, chiefly because Scott Meredith, newly launched as his literary agent, was exerting himself in the manner customary to authors' representatives who have just acquired important new clients. Just as Seth Moyle had done in 1909, Meredith quickly struck gold, landing $3,000 contracts for two regular Wodehouse stories with *Cosmopolitan* and *This Week*. But once Wodehouse was no longer the topical sensation he had been on his return, the rejection letters started, and his spirits plummeted.

After just one month in the city, he and Ethel began to feel depressed again. He admitted to Townend that he was not enjoying life in the duplex; Ethel couldn't keep the maids she hired; he was suffering from a lack of ideas; and the change that had come over the theatre was preying on his nerves. He complained to Townend that he missed the old-time Broadway manager of the 1920s, who seemed to have completely disappeared. In the old days, he wrote, he could 'pop in on Flo Ziegfeld and find that he wanted lyrics for a new show, and then call on Dillingham and get a contract for a musical comedy'. That, he noted, was all over now: 'As far as I can make out, you have to write your show and then go about trying to interest people with money in it.' To Bolton he lamented, 'It's so damned difficult to write a show without knowing who you are writing it for . . . I feel lost without you.' He returned to this theme a month later, telling Townend that 'Oscar Hammerstein and Richard Rodgers gave *thirty-nine* auditions of "Oklahoma" before they raked in enough to start production. What a life, what!'

Nothing was going right. Ethel suffered an excruciating attack of shingles, 'an almost comic word to label a major illness'. New York was hot and dull. He had always preferred the hustle of Broadway, and disliked the moneyed indolence of the Upper East Side. Madison and Park were just crowded with shopping women. To Townend, he observed, tetchily: 'There are too many women in the world, Bill.' It irked him that Wonder was not welcome in the city's restaurants in the way she had been in France. Although he loved the roof of 53 East 66th Street, and could take Wonder over to Central Park for her daily exercise, there was nowhere to go for a really good long solitary walk, his passion. In desperation, he took a day trip to Great Neck, scene of so much past happiness, and wished they were living there. Cooped up in the apartment, New York's oppressive summer humidity was taking 'all the starch' out of him, and he could not muster 'the remotest flicker of an idea for any sort of story these days, long or short'.

Wodehouse's greatest problem lay with the old magazines like *Collier's* and the *Saturday Evening Post*. He had always enjoyed good professional relations with a succession of editors, from Bob Davis and George Lorimer to Sumner Blossom and Wesley Stout, adjusting his work to suit their tastes and rarely failing to trade on the fundamental Englishness of his material. To the new generation of editors in Truman's America, only too well aware that post-war Britain was a shattered, bankrupt society with a socialist government and severe food rationing, new

Wodehouse stories seemed redundant, out of tune with the mood of the times. The next generation of editors, men like Ben Hibbs of the *Post*, offered excuses, telling him, he reported, that 'they couldn't use comic stories of English life at a time when England was in the soup'. Privately, Hibbs described Wodehouse as 'dated and out of place'. Nothing could disguise the fact that, for the first time in his professional life, Wodehouse was being rejected all over town. Between 1947 and 1951, only seven of his stories were accepted for publication, and then only in relatively minor North American magazines. Philosophical to a fault, he told his French translator, Benoît de Fonscolombe, that he had rather expected his literary business to move slowly at first, doubting if he would make much out of the magazines. 'Their whole policy seems to have changed,' he wrote. 'They now want heavy, serious stuff about life in the swamps of Carolina and that sort of thing and won't look at my English dudes!' He said he believed he could get along quite well without the magazines, but despite his fighting words, Wodehouse was evidently disconcerted by this new indifference. He fretted to Townend about his creative difficulty in the hostile climate of post-war America. 'I am hopeless unless I'm creating fictional characters,' he wrote, with the revealing aside that, 'I never feel that real people *are* interesting. Even if they are, they never actually *do* funny things, at any rate in sufficient quantity to make an article.' On the positive side, the fears Wodehouse had that he might not be able to stay in New York proved groundless. America would now become his permanent home, and as time passed he became increasingly resigned to his exile from the country he loved. There was also the consolation that his books were still 'selling terrifically in England'. Despite his wartime troubles, his readership remained loyal.

Wodehouse's reaction to his predicament was in character: part philosophical ('it's a bit thick, of course, having one's whole background barred, but I can understand it'), and part dogged determination to find work – even if it had to be in another genre. Expressing 'a sort of loathing for short stories', he threw himself with vigour into his theatrical work, even though he was out of touch with that world, too. He finished adapting Molnár's *Arthur* (with talk of another Molnár adaptation, *Game of Hearts*) and was soon 'working like blazes' on *Summer Guest* with Melchior Lengyel, the popular Hungarian playwright best known as the screenwriter of the classic Ernst Lubitsch comedy, *To Be or Not to*

Be. Simultaneously, he was discussing what he described as a 'pretty rocky' proposal from another producer for a musical version of *Enter Madame*, a Broadway hit, which would be co-written with Ogden Nash. During the next five years, as he struggled to find his creative feet in post-war America, Wodehouse became involved with an eclectic catalogue of speculative showbiz ventures, few of which came to anything: a troubled production of *Leave It to Psmith*; a musical of the life of Puccini; shows with Dick Myers and Hans Bartsch; a revival of *The Waltz Dream*; a rewrite of a melodrama by E. P. Conkle; a revival of *Good Morning Bill*; and bits and pieces of script-doctoring. There were also endless pie-in-the-sky letters to and from Guy Bolton who, perhaps even more than Wodehouse, was wrestling with the changed artistic circumstances of post-war Broadway.

In short, Wodehouse behaved exactly as he had done in the past. But times had changed, and he was no longer a promising youngster in his twenties. Isolated, under-employed and creatively frustrated, he was counting the days until the return of Guy Bolton. 'I haven't really got going yet,' he wrote to his old friend, as the hot summer drew to a close, 'and I feel I shan't until you are here.' On their return, in September, Guy and Virginia Bolton saw immediately that Wodehouse needed a change of scene and took him off to their Long Island home, known to Wodehouse as 'Bolton Arms', for hearty walks along the beach, preprandial dry martinis and hours of happy theatrical reminiscence. Practically speaking, there was also work to discuss, in particular a revival of *Sally*. The original Broadway production in 1920 had been a celebrated hit, and Bolton spotted, in Wodehouse's return, an opportunity to revise the book and lyrics, add some new material, and cash in. Wodehouse also saw *Sally* as a meal ticket, a way to get back on Broadway with a bang. Success on the Great White Way would, he hoped, 'lead to all sorts of other work'. While the two old friends dreamed of new glory, Ethel stayed in New York. The lease on 53 East 66th Street was drawing to a close, and as always it was her job to find new accommodation.

On his return to the city, fresh from the psychological uplift of the weeks on Long Island, Wodehouse declared the new address, a seventeenth-floor apartment in the Hotel Adams, at 2 East 86th Street, a great success. As well as a terrace with a fine view of Central Park and the reservoir, Wodehouse noted with satisfaction that, although he had to work in his bedroom, 'I have at last got a decent sized desk, one of those where you have room for papers on each side of the type-writer'. Almost as important, for his daily walks with Wonder, they were just off Fifth Avenue, 'so I can nip across [and there] I am in the Park'. With the move came a new mood of resigned acceptance. As the un-settled year of 1947 drew to a close, Wodehouse's best hopes seemed to lie with Bolton, and he now distracted himself from the commer-cial and artistic difficulties of his fiction by immersing himself in the renewal of their old association. Nineteen forty-eight would be largely taken up with the new production of *Sally*, which had reached the casting stage. There was also a revival of *The Play's the Thing*, the Molnár hit comedy from 1926. As well as promoting *Sally*, Bolton had acquired the rights to *Don't Listen Ladies!* by Sacha Guitry, the French play-wright, a self-confessed Nazi collaborator whose dubious wartime record ended up causing the production a great deal of difficulty. Wodehouse's instinct was to ignore the critics, but it is a measure of his anxiety about his reputation with the public that he agreed to adopt a pseudonym, Stephen Powys, for the London production. He tried to reverse this decision in October 1948: 'Let's suppress Stephen Powys for New York and have the show "by Guy Bolton and P. G. Wodehouse". I am very anxious to get the old trade name working again.'

While the revival of *The Play's the Thing* was going through the inter-minable pre-production process, Wodehouse continued to fuss over his money. The Fifth Avenue apartment had seemed to bring ten years of wandering to an end, but his financial situation, never far from his thoughts, was 'maddening and tantalising'. He had plenty of money in England, but legally he could not touch it. In America, while another unresolved income tax case, initiated in 1943, was bogged down temporarily in the appeals court, he could not collect an estimated $40,000 owed to him by the authorities. In June he was in trouble again, this time over the transfer of money from a French to a British bank account as part of his investment in the London production. 'Oh, Architect of the Universe,' he exclaimed in a letter to Bolton, 'bring back the days when I could win a couple of hundred thousand francs at Monte Carlo and ship it straight over to my London account and then take it over to New York if I wanted to.'

Life in New York, meanwhile, had settled into the familiar routine of work in the morning, long afternoon walks in the park with Wonder, punctuated by occasional lunches and dinners with literary and theatrical

acquaintances. *Spring Fever* was published in May 1948, another milestone in the agonizingly slow process of Wodehouse's rehabilitation.
While Wodehouse reacquainted himself with his pre-war show-business
and movie-making cronies, he also did his best to break down the
hostility of the big magazine editors towards him. To this end, in June,
he hosted a dinner at the St Regis Hotel for the editor of *Cosmopolitan*.

Ethel, meanwhile, continued to shop. There was a moment of drama
in the spring when she was mugged at her dressmaker's on Madison
Avenue, but she was unharmed. Shortly afterwards, her old restlessness
returned and she sailed for England. Partly she wanted to see her grandchildren and some old friends; partly, Malcolm Muggeridge noted, when
he had dinner with her, she had not really acclimatized to Manhattan
life and was 'very weary of wandering about the world trying to find
somewhere to settle'. At first, Wodehouse said he would accompany
Ethel as far as France, but in the end he stayed put. There were, he
told Townend, too many 'things cooking', and though he wished he
were back in France he was reluctant to revisit the scene of former
troubles.

The psychology of the individual might be downcast, but physically
Wodehouse was in good shape, up to a point. 'I don't feel a bit older
than I did twenty years ago,' he crowed to Townend, 'except that my
eyes are definitely worse.' His tastes were ageing, too; he confessed that
'I can find practically nothing to read now'. His dislike of contemporary American culture is a refrain running through all his letters to
friends at this time. Wodehouse in post-war New York is a little like
a demobilized soldier, uncertain about his place in the world to which
he had returned, and at the same time just a grumpy, and nostalgic, old
man. The schoolboy sensibility of his letters to Townend, with their
obsessive analysis of the Dulwich team's prospects, emphasizes his alienation from post-war society.

When writers are out of sorts with themselves and their work they
often switch publishers, and it is symptomatic of Wodehouse's state of
mind that he decided to sell *Uncle Dynamite*, the next volume of his
wartime backlog, not to Doubleday but to a small, energetic but now
forgotten firm named Didier. He blamed the move on 'the Doubleday
organisation', which, he felt, was 'a huge factory' that did not care about
his books. He claimed that his defection had caused a tremendous stir
in the literary world, but this is improbable for a writer so out of favour

with publishers and magazines. He had written *Uncle Dynamite* in Paris, parts of it 'in the Inspecteur's room in the Palais de Justice, with the lads crowding round to see how the stuff was coming', and with its publication in October he now had to face the unpalatable truth that, once *The Mating Season* went to the printers, he had used up his wartime stock of fiction. In England, *Uncle Dynamite* sold as well as *Spring Fever*, but in America, despite Didier's efforts, sales were not enhanced; the future looked bleak. Aside from book publishers, he had given up on his initial optimism and had abandoned the magazines as hopeless. 'All I do now is sit in a tree like a vulture and watch them dying one by one,' he told Townend.

Against all the evidence, Wodehouse continued to believe that his future lay with the stage. Throughout the second half of 1948, with several other theatrical projects on the point of take-off, he worked away at successive drafts of a dramatic version of *Spring Fever*. As early as June he had rewritten it twice, and by 8 December the scenario, now in its fifth draft, had changed almost beyond recognition. But here was the rub: Wodehouse's name was no longer enough to raise the money for a production, so each version had to be shaped to appeal to one Broadway star or another. As each new draft missed its intended target, the script became increasingly removed from the source of its inspiration. In a moment of clarity, Wodehouse admitted to Bolton, 'it's crazy to spoil a play by trying to torture it into a star vehicle . . . It never works.' Finally, in the spring of 1949 Wodehouse showed it to an old friend, George S. Kaufman, the experienced author of *The Man Who Came to Dinner*. When Kaufman told him that it was 'too thin', Wodehouse resolved to put it aside. But he could not quite let it go, and continued to fiddle with it under various titles, including 'Phipps' and 'Kilroy Was Here', until 1953. Thereafter it fades from view, and has only been performed by amateurs, in Devon.

Meanwhile, on Broadway, *Sally* closed after thirty-six performances. This was followed by another disappointment. *Don't Listen Ladies!*, the Sacha Guitry adaptation, which had prospered in the West End in the autumn of 1948, flopped after fifteen performances at the Booth Theatre, done to death by the critics and the controversy surrounding Guitry's name as a Vichy collaborator. Shortly afterwards – 'a worse blow' – the touring production of *The Play's the Thing*, which had done good business both on Broadway and in the West End, also closed in the new year. So, flitting between genres, and trading his own material, as he had throughout his professional life, Wodehouse returned once more to fiction, but without much zest. Ever reluctant to waste good stuff, he embarked on making a novel out of the discarded playscript of *Spring Fever*, which he wittily entitled *The Old Reliable*. Amid these frustrations, there were occasional reminders of the world he had left behind. Evelyn Waugh, visiting New York on a commission from *Life* magazine to write about the Catholic Church in America, invited 'Dr Wodehouse', as he liked to call him, to lunch at his club. Waugh had written to Nancy Mitford about 'the awful flat dreariness of England under Welfare', and he shared Wodehouse's disenchantment with the post-war world. They had never met before, but Waugh was a fan, and Wodehouse liked him.

Evelyn left no record of the encounter, but his brother Alec later described the experience of lunching with 'Plum', either at his club, the Century, or Wodehouse's, the Lotos. Looking back, Alec Waugh remembered that the five or six times they met became blurred together. Wodehouse was so exactly the same person that each new meeting was simply another instalment of a conversation in which he would express his abiding interest in exactly the same things that had preoccupied him a quarter of a century before. Waugh, like many who met Wodehouse in his later years, found there was something comforting about his fascination with a bygone age, and in the utter consistency of his mindset. In his late sixties, he had become an ageless figure, benign, reserved and predictable; as Alec Waugh observed:

He looked exactly the same. He had not put on weight. He was always completely hairless. He was his familiar, massive, genial self. He had no peculiarities, of manner or expression. He was not funny. He never repeated jokes. There was no sparkle in his conversation. He did not indulge in reminiscences. There was a straightforward exchange of talk . . . 'It is an extraordinary thing,' he would say, 'Marlborough beat Tonbridge and Tonbridge beat Uppingham, but Uppingham beat Marlborough. What do you make of that?'

This does not sound like a flattering recollection but Alec Waugh, another lifelong public schoolboy, felt very comfortable with Wodehouse. 'Our talk moved smoothly from one subject to another. Yet the ease was such that I find I cannot recall the matter of the conversation, only the pleasure of his company.'

The man and the work were one. Evelyn Waugh later described Wodehouse's world as 'timeless', but it is also immutable. The comparative lack of development in his writing is one of its unique features: no other twentieth-century English writer of consequence evolves in his mature work as little as Wodehouse. He had created a world that was complete, self-sufficient and almost faultless. Close critical analysis reveals some small stylistic and narrative adjustments, but there are few innovations. The indifference of the post-war world only strengthened Wodehouse's determination to stick to the society he knew and to stay within his peculiar paradise. He would, as he put it, 'hew to the butler line'. In the short term, this would limit his audience and his sales; eventually, it would inspire veneration. In 1948 his greatest gift was also his greatest weakness, but it was of a piece with his character.

As the decade drew to a close, Wodehouse was becoming at home in New York. In the spring of 1949 he and Ethel moved apartments again, signing a five-year lease on a duplex at 1000 Park Avenue, between 84th and 85th streets, a comfortable address two blocks south of the Hotel Adams. Their new home was a spacious penthouse with two bedrooms, a big sitting room, and, best of all, 'an enormous roof about the size of a suburban garden' with an uninterrupted, panoramic view of Manhattan. This was the aspect of 1000 Park Avenue Wodehouse came to love, a place to eat meals and to sit reading on hot nights. The great advantage of the roof, which Ethel turfed and remodelled with shrubs and pot plants, was that it was an ideal place for Wonder and any other visiting dogs (Guy Bolton's Squeaky, for instance) to exercise during the day while he was working. His routine continued, unbroken: up at seven, the exercises on the roof, breakfast, work, lunch, the long walk, usually round the Central Park reservoir, more work, the stiff cocktail, dinner, light reading, bed. By mid-summer, he had turned the playscript of *Spring Fever* into a '25,000 word novelette' and Scott Meredith had embarked on the thankless task of trying to place it with a magazine. This time, though, his efforts paid off: after many rejections, *The Old Reliable* was sold to *Collier's* for $20,000 and was finally published in April 1951.

Publicly, Wodehouse betrayed no hint of inner turmoil, holding meetings with theatrical managements, dining with old acquaintances like

Moss Hart and George Kaufman, attending first nights and a few cocktail parties. Privately, his letters to Bolton, Townend and Mackail were
plangent with misanthropy and self-doubt: 'Don't you loathe journalists?' and again, 'Do you ever wonder if you are really a writer?' 'What
damned times these are,' he exclaimed, noting that Hollywood 'has
become a ghost town'. He went to *South Pacific* and hated it. 'I am
absolutely out of touch with the taste of the modern American public.'
As his sixty-eighth birthday approached, he confessed that, although he
could still manage a six-mile walk, 'the physical act of writing [is]
becoming more and more arduous . . . I used to write my stuff direct
on the machine, but now I find I have to make a lot of pencil notes
first.' In parallel with his psychological disaffection, he was also suffering
from occasional giddy spells but, with typical English stoicism, did not
mention these to his doctor.

An important reason for reticence about his medical condition was
the tedious process of upgrading his visitor's visa and getting accepted
for a 'quota visa', a prized document among overseas visitors. For
Wodehouse, this involved complex immigration formalities: a medical
examination on Ellis Island, followed by re-entry to the United States
at Niagara, on the Canadian border. 'To think,' he wrote to Townend,
'that in 1914 I came over here without a passport and stayed six years.'
However, as 1949, another difficult post-war year, drew to a close, at least
he was at peace with both the tax and the immigration authorities,
established on Park Avenue and relieved to discover, after all these trials,
that *The Mating Season* was enjoying good reviews and excellent sales.

The Mating Season marks the end of his wartime output. It is, as
Christopher Hitchens has written, 'perhaps the Wodehouse tale that is
most exclusively concerned with romance and its distractions'. From a
biographical point of view, the novel bears the faint but bitter traces of
its author's wartime troubles and post-war anxieties. When the story
opens, Bertie is not himself. He is masquerading as Gussie Fink-Nottle.
There are good, romantic reasons for this subterfuge, but the bulk of
the action concerns the preparations for a Saturday night concert in
the Hampshire village of Deverill. When Bertie is prevailed upon to
recite A. A. Milne's Christopher Robin poems (described as 'nauseous
productions'), Wodehouse has a lot of sarcastic fun with 'Christopher
Robin going hoppity-hoppity-hop (or, alternatively, saying his prayers)'.
There are also allusions to Ernie Bevin and Stafford Cripps, a dig at

'Alfred Duff Cooper', and a speech about the 'planned Americanisation' of England, seasoned as usual with some typical American slang, from 'brusheroo' to 'bum's rush'. Most notable of all, there are signs that Bertie and his inner circle are no longer carefree innocents. Their mood has changed. Fink-Nottle, for instance, reproaches Bertie's 'Dickensy' sentimentalism. Jeeves, wanly philosophical, quotes Marcus Aurelius; and Bertie's clubland friend, Claude Cattermole Pirbright, is 'low-spirited':

His brow was sicklied o'er with the pale cast of thought and his air that of a man who, if he had said 'Hallo, girls' would have said it like someone in a Russian drama announcing that Grandpapa had hanged himself in the barn.

The Mating Season lacks the comic brio of *Right Ho, Jeeves* or the artistry of *The Code of the Woosters* or even the joyous felicity of *Heavy Weather*, but it is still an essential part of the canon. Esmond Haddock, Bertie's host for the duration of the plot, is a new Wodehouse character, but he comes with a country house (Deverill Hall). There are also a 'surging sea of aunts' ('the Misses Charlotte, Emmeline, Harriet and Myrtle . . .') two old hands from Bertie's turbulent past (Fink-Nottle and Madeline Bassett), and the familiar figure of a 'rollicking' Drone, Claude Cattermole (aka 'Catsmeat') Pirbright, scion of a prominent theatrical family. The task imposed on Bertie by the fearsome Aunt Agatha, 'who chews broken bottles and kills rats with her teeth', is to ensure that Catsmeat's fiancée, Gertrude, does not succumb to the advances of Esmond Haddock, while at the same time promoting among the aunts of Deverill Hall the idea that Fink-Nottle would be a suitable husband for Madeline Bassett. Wodehouse's narrative is nearly flawless. When the story ends, there is, as Bertie puts it, 'Not a single loose end left over', and every sundered heart is happily reunited, with much of the credit going to Jeeves's unremitting efforts.

Real life did not provide happy endings. At the close of the year came news from England that Diana Mackail, the wife of Wodehouse's old friend Denis Mackail, had died from cancer, aged just fifty-three. Wodehouse's composure rarely failed; it did now. 'I wish to God I could be with you,' he wrote to Mackail.

I feel so utterly helpless all these miles away . . . I don't know how to go on. Words seem so futile and I am afraid that nothing I can say can be much good, but I do think it helps a little when you have had an awful blow to know that the people who love you are thinking of you. Ethel is upstairs writing to you now. She is heartbroken. She loved Diana as much as I did. You two were always our dearest friends.

For Wodehouse there was only one way to cope with pain. Resuming his correspondence with Mackail, he soon returned to the troubles of the writing life, becoming frank and confidential. 'I know those blank periods when the idea of writing seems just silly and you wonder why you ever started the thing . . . my trouble [is] a sort of scornful loathing for the reading public. One feels what's the use of strewing one's pearls before these swine?'

There was a rare piece of good news that spring of 1950: Wodehouse's English bank account was redesignated as an American account, unfreezing his accumulated royalties ('which tots up to quite a bit') and transforming his financial situation. Now, he told friends, he was 'on Easy Street'. Still, he could make no headway with a new novel. What he needed was a plot, and he returned to this old complaint, made more urgent by changed circumstances. While his lunatic celebration of an Edwardian twilight seemed redundant, he was struggling, as he explained to Townend:

There is the problem of whether to ignore the upheaval in English life and go on doing Blandings Castle and Jeeves stuff or try to do something modern. My sales have been so good in England with the out-of-date stuff that I am inclined to carry on on those lines. I believe people having a rotten time in England like reading of the days when there were butlers and so on. After all, if you can write about the Crusades, why not about 1920 or even 1913?

After another frustrating autumn of disappointments and dashed hopes, he reverted obsessively to this theme in a Christmas Day letter to his old friend: 'My only trouble', he wrote, 'is that I don't seem to get any ideas for stories, which I think is due to the fact that my world has been shot to pieces and I can't manufacture another one.' The news that the *Strand* was to close seemed to underline his predicament.

So desperate was Wodehouse for a plot – any plot – to which he could attach his prose that he decided to buy one off-the-peg, offering his friend, the playwright George Kaufman, $2,700 for the right to adapt his 1925 screwball comedy, 'The Butter and Egg Man'. Meanwhile, in the absence of new work, and to sustain a presence in the book-stores, he published a collection of magazine stories, *Nothing Serious*, in July, a volume which contained an uncharacteristically explicit assault on A. A. Milne in 'Rodney Has a Relapse', one of his most savage, even vindictive stories, a piece of out-and-out revenge for Milne's betrayal, and another indication of the pain the broadcasts still caused him.

During this creative drought, Wodehouse did what he could to keep himself busy. One of his projects for the theatre was a rewrite of an old repertory play, *The House on the Cliff*, whose first production had flopped. In July/August 1950, the management decided to take this show on tour on the 'straw hat' summer circuit, one-horse stops like Skowhegan, Maine, and Watkins Glen, New York State. Wodehouse gamely joined the company. 'If I'd known what I was letting myself in for,' he reported to Bolton, 'I'd have kept away.' After five weeks of gruelling twelve-hour drives in a station wagon round upstate New York, Wodehouse confided to Mackail that 'this has cured me of being stagestruck'. Ethel celebrated his return from the straw hat circuit at the end of August with the purchase of a new car, a Nash; Wodehouse's optimism returned. He boasted to Townend that he had 'never been in such form physically and mentally as now . . . I swear I'm fitter at 70 [he was actually 69] than I was when I was living in London in 1926 and used to have eggs and bacon for breakfast, four courses for lunch, tea and toast and cake at five and six courses with port to follow for dinner.' Wodehouse had always been proud of his fitness, believing, he told Townend, that he was 'a sort of freak whom age could not touch'.

But age, of course, was creeping up on him, and in the spring of 1951 there was a crisis. In February, after an exceedingly good lunch at his club ('two cocktails, dollops of Burgundy, about five cognacs and two fat cigars'), he was returning some books to the library, part of his routine, when he found himself *bouleversé* by a return of the dizzy spells he had suffered the year before. He described the episode to Townend: 'I started to walk down town to change my library books, and I had got to 82nd Street and Park Avenue when without any warning I suddenly felt giddy again. (At least, it's not exactly giddiness. The scenery doesn't get blurred or jump about. It's just that I lose control of my legs.)' Park Avenue was full of specialists. Wodehouse groped his way to the nearest one, B. H. Kean, by chance a celebrity doctor whose clients included Oscar Hammerstein and Gertrude Lawrence. Kean soon realized that the shabby old man who had stumbled into his office was neither a drunk nor a down-and-out, but an elderly Englishman who had probably suffered a small stroke. After consulting Hammerstein, Kean discovered that his anonymous patient was a writer whose work he greatly admired. Wodehouse was hospitalized for ten days. The preliminary diagnosis looked bleak: a brain tumour. Whatever his inward feelings, Wodehouse expressed no fear, but told Townend, in a familiar formula, that 'hell's foundations have been quivering'. But after seven doctors had administered a battery of tests, including a painful spinal tap, Wodehouse was given the all-clear. He himself attributed the scare to his failing eyesight (a new pair of glasses seemed to make all the difference), but it was a frightening experience, and a virus he picked up on leaving the hospital left him so weak that he could not take exercise, except for short strolls. This episode made Ethel, anticipating Wodehouse's retirement, more than ever determined to leave New York City. Ideally, they would move back to France and live outside Paris, but this was out of the question because it would mean giving up their precious 'quota visa'. From now on, Ethel was on the lookout for an alternative to city life.

Just before what he called his 'crack up', Wodehouse had reported wistfully that 'for the first time almost since I can remember, I haven't any definite job of work'. Now, during convalescence, he addressed himself in earnest to 'The Butter and Egg Man'. He knew it 'ought to be a Bertie and Jeeves story', but he was apprehensive about reviving the old double act. In the end, he settled on 'Wonderland', his term for the American theatrical world he knew so well, exposing the expatriate Drone, Cyril 'Barmy' Fotheringay (pronounced Fungy) Phipps, to the charms of 'Dinty' Moore, the secretary of Broadway producer Joe Lehman. After all the fretting and dithering, the writing went swimmingly. Perhaps because the agony of plotting had been largely taken care of, Wodehouse found he was no longer blocked. After three years of frustration, and much fretting about how to start the book, he completed it in two months flat, boasting that he had broken his own record and written 27 pages in a day (better than the 26 pages he had once written of *Thank You, Jeeves*). This, he noted with satisfaction, showed that 'there is life in the old dog yet'.

In hopes of a serial, he tailored the new book to the *Saturday Evening Post*'s preferred length, 60,000 words. But, in stark contrast to the good old days, the *Post* turned it down. Then *Collier's* said they wanted a 30,000-word version. But when he duly obliged, *Collier's* rejected that too. Exasperated, but calm and professional, Wodehouse reworked the text again, to a book-length 75,000 words. The revised text of the new novel went to Herbert Jenkins, who published it as *Barmy in Wonderland*. There was no allusion to Kaufman's original version and when one carping reviewer complained that P. G. Wodehouse was all very well, but had never learned to do American dialogue, Wodehouse was delighted to squash him, pointing out that the dialogue in the novel was all Kaufman's. 'I shan't bother again about serial publication,' he told Townend. Although his work continued to make sporadic appearances in magazines, including *Playboy*, this prediction proved accurate. Not one of Wodehouse's later novels was published in the grand serial form of the 1930s. Now, separated from the magazines, Wodehouse's fiction entered its final stage. Opinions vary, but few critics are as unequivocally praising of Wodehouse's late work as they are of the novels written in his prime.

The final days of writing on *Barmy in Wonderland* had been clouded by a domestic sadness. Wonder, who had survived so many of her master's vicissitudes since 1939, and been his constant companion during some of the darkest days of his war, became too ill to go on. Now fifteen and almost blind, suffering badly, 'she suddenly broke up,' Wodehouse wrote.

The vet said it was mental . . . We had to have her put away. I had always sworn that I would never do that to a dog, but even I could see that it was the only thing to be done. For one thing, it was killing Ethel, who never got any sleep night after night.

Another Peke, Squeaky, who had once belonged to the Boltons, was now top dog in the home, and Wodehouse transferred his affections with practised ease, finding her 'more lovable every day'.

Wodehouse's capacity for looking on the bright side of life was never more successfully employed than in this post-war period. For ten years now, he had sustained his career through sheer will-power and dedication to his craft. He had weathered 'the global howl', survived the hostility and indifference of the magazines and, after his unhappy flirtation with Didier, had returned to his former American publisher, Doubleday. Slowly recovering from writer's block, he was beginning to rehabilitate his most important characters, principally Lord Emsworth, Bertie Wooster and Jeeves. His work was once again selling well in Britain and steadily in America. But his wartime conduct and its aftermath made up the one blemish: the broadcasts still clouded his thoughts and coloured the public's perception of him, while the British authorities continued to equivocate, behind the scenes. This mark against his character continued to torment him like a classical curse.

24. 'Our slogan must be Entertainment' (1951–1954)

British Baronets, like British pig men, are resilient. They rise on step-ping stones of their dead selves to higher things and are quick to discern the silver lining in the clouds. (*Pigs Have Wings*)

Wodehouse celebrated his seventieth birthday modestly, remarking that he was now 'on the home stretch'. He had been strangely bucked by his recovery from the dizzy spells and now returned, with new enthu-siasm, to his beloved paradise, Blandings Castle. Four months later, he had completed *Pigs Have Wings*, the latest instalment in the series he had begun in 1915 with *Something Fresh*. Writing to Townend the day after his birthday, he was his old confident self again:

I have suddenly started to get what looks like being quite a good Blandings Castle plot. It is still in the chaotic state and when I read the notes I have jotted down, I think I must be going cuckoo. But this always happens with me. I find the only way I can get a plot is to shove down everything that comes into my mind. Then gradually it becomes coherent. I always find my best way is to think up some crazy situation and then manipulate the char-acters to fit it and make it plausible.

Pigs Have Wings is not just a new Blandings novel; it is a renewal of Wodehouse's lease on Eden. Nothing has changed. The Empress of Blandings, competing for a third successive trophy in the Fat Pigs class at the Shropshire Show, is as majestic as ever. Lord Emsworth, his brother Galahad and their bossy sister Constance are still dysfunctionally co-existing in their 'first-class ancestral home with gravel soil, rolling park-land and all the conveniences'. Trouble comes when the news breaks that Lord Emsworth's neighbourhood rival, Sir Gregory Parsloe-Parsloe, has not only lured Emsworth's pig man, George Cyril Wellbeloved, into his service with the promise of higher wages, but has also betrayed the pig-breeders' unwritten code by actually *buying* a super-fat sow,

the Queen of Matchingham, to challenge the Empress. After some preliminary skirmishing, a pig war breaks out in which Galahad master-
minds the theft of Parsloe's Queen at the very moment that Sir Gregory
and Wellbeloved are stealing the Empress. The plot reaches an exhilarating high point when, unbeknown to their owners, the prize pigs are
residing in each other's sties. Blandings has fewer impostors than before,
but is still offering unruffled hospitality to several house-guests, and
Wodehouse contrives to entangle their lives. Satisfyingly, Parsloe-Parsloe's
stratagems are foiled when the insatiable Queen of Matchingham guzzles
six bottles of Slimmo, a patent slimming medicine, and the Empress
wins the coveted silver medal for an unprecedented third time.

Once Blandings Castle was secure and the Empress supreme in her
class, Wodehouse addressed the issue that had been nagging away at the
back of his mind since his return to America: the mocking echoes of
'the global howl'. Wodehouse's response to the intractable problem of the
broadcasts had been instinctive. When he first got to America, he had
repressed all reference to his historic blunder. The broadcasts were almost
unmentionable, even among his immediate circle. Writing to friends, he
adopted a variety of euphemisms – 'my Berlin/German troubles', for
instance, and 'the broadcast stuff' – to describe the poisoned aftermath of
those fateful days in the summer of 1941. Bad news had always been taboo
with him; now he silently dropped anyone associated with his German
years. Friends like Anga von Bodenhausen and her daughter Reinhild,
who idolized her 'Oncle Plummie', were dismayed to discover the ease
with which he could glide away from the complexity of the recent past.

Repression was one strategy for coping. Stoicism was another. His
Dulwich education had trained him to believe in fate. He had written
in *Uneasy Money*, '"What is life but a series of sharp corners, round
each of which Fate lies in wait with a stuffed eel-skin?"' Wodehouse
knew from bitter childhood experience that the thing about fate was
that you had to accept its inscrutable workings. Publicly, his attitude
seems to have been that he should endure his situation as well as he
could, without complaint and with a minimum of soul-searching.
Privately, he puzzled over the nature of his offence, and slowly recognized that the questions raised by the broadcasts were not going to go
away.

Among his family and close friends, there had been, roughly, three
schools of thought about the best way to deal with 'the German

problem'. Ethel's reaction, first and most importantly, was that it had all been a ridiculous brouhaha in which her 'Plummie' had been cruelly misused, and she would protest his innocence to anyone who would listen. The Cazalet family line, led by the redoubtable Thelma Cazalet-Keir, by now an ex-MP, was that, in disgrace, Wodehouse should lie low and do nothing to rock the boat, in word or deed. This, too, he found intensely irritating. 'Thelma makes me sick,' he exclaimed to Denis Mackail. 'If I had taken her advice, I would now be living in Switzerland – she said I must not dream of going to America – and none of my last six books would have been published.' Finally, there were those friends, like Bill Townend and Scott Meredith, who believed in trying, constructively, to clear his name. Meredith had already attempted this in America, with very limited success, in 1944 and 1945. Now, nearly a decade later, it was Townend who revived the idea, first mooted in the 1930s, of publishing their lifelong correspondence, with the unspoken agenda of establishing Wodehouse's natural innocence in general and political 'innocence' in particular.

Bill Townend, who cuts a pathetic figure when compared with his infinitely more famous and successful Dulwich contemporary, appears to have broached the idea of 'the letter book', as he called it, from a variety of motives. There was his righteous indignation at the obloquy heaped on his old friend, together with his rather self-important belief that, if Wodehouse would not exert himself to clear his name, then – in a neat reversal of their roles – at least he could act as his champion. Townend felt indebted to his old room-mate. Ever since the publication of *Love among the Chickens*, Wodehouse had contrived, on the feeblest of pretexts, to share some of his earnings with Townend. For years, he had discreetly supported Townend and his wife Irene with food parcels, magazine subscriptions, and random but generous disbursements from his Hongkong and Shanghai Bank account, going to great lengths to conceal this surreptitious patronage from Ethel, who was suspicious of freeloaders, and who liked to keep the family's money in the family. Almost as important, from the 1920s he had acted as Townend's loyal and perceptive first reader on a succession of uncommercial, and almost unreadable, sub-Conradian novels of adventure with titles like *Tough Stuff* and *Fool's Gold*.

Townend had other motives, not quite so altruistic. By the late 1940s his literary fortunes, always precarious, had reached a crisis point. With his long-standing literary ally out of favour, Townend was facing rejection by his own publishers, Rich and Cowan, and had become a marginal, almost invisible, figure on the English literary scene. A book of literary correspondence, even with a disgraced Wodehouse, would put his name before the public and perhaps give his latest novel a lift. Out of this awkward tangle of good intentions, schoolboy loyalties and thwarted ambition, the 'letter book' emerged as a project on which the two men, who had last seen each other in the Dulwich cricket pavilion one afternoon in June 1939, could collaborate.

Wodehouse's first decisive move to grapple with the demons of the past occurred the day after his seventieth birthday; it was generous and unequivocal. 'I think the letters scheme is terrific,' he wrote to Townend. He was worried about stirring up old antagonisms, but in other respects the timing could not have been better. He was in a mood to look back on his long career. He and Guy Bolton had already begun to compile a selective and unreliable volume of Broadway memoirs, *Bring on the Girls*. The 'letter book' would solve the problem of what to do about the other parts of his life that were still unexplored. He had always wanted to write his autobiography, but felt too self-conscious. Wodehouse had his own kind of self-knowledge, but he was reluctant to write about himself, and was not, by temperament, a self-analytical writer who would relish, as he had once put it, 'going deep down into life, not caring a damn'. One of Wodehouse's most attractive qualities is his modesty. A conventional autobiography would have seemed to him unpardonably egotistical. Worse, it would run the risk of straying into an emotional minefield – childhood, family, marriage, Leonora – best left unexamined. An additional attraction of Townend's proposal was that, in the first instance, Townend would do the laborious work of transcribing, editing and annotating, submitting the completed typescript to Wodehouse for his approval. Wodehouse wasted no time in issuing instructions, and was quick to decide that the letter book should be a blank slate. 'The great thing', he reminded Townend, 'is not to feel ourselves confined to the actual letters . . . we can fake as much as we like.'

The project quickly focused on the broadcasts. Townend, typically, was more literal-minded. 'It should be clear to anyone', he wrote to Evelyn Waugh, 'that when he [Wodehouse] spoke over the German radio he had no idea that he was offending.' From its inception, there were two threads to the letter book, never quite harmonized. There was Townend's honest defence of his friend, essentially an annotated collage of favourable press comment, combined with a critique of those who had denounced Wodehouse in 1941. In parallel, there was Wodehouse's picture of himself as a harmless literary man, out of his depth in the big wide world. Over the next several years he would refine and perfect his portrait of the artist as a 'dumb brick' in a succession of newspaper interviews, articles and television appearances.

Townend's work proceeded apace, and once the first draft was delivered to Park Avenue, Wodehouse, the inveterate reviser, told him that 'my letters need a bit of polishing . . . Reading them, I get the impression of a rather conceited man who is always boasting about his prices.' No amount of revision, however, could explain away the broadcasts, as Wodehouse soon came to recognize:

The trouble is that I can't very well pose as a completely innocent injured person, because I did broadcast from Germany in time of war. True, a lot of fatheads jumped at the conclusion that it was anti-British propaganda and so made asses of themselves, but that does not make me blameless . . . one wants to be awfully careful.

One solution, which was Townend's idea, was to include the text of the broadcasts in the book, and let the public decide for themselves. This presented a new problem. Wodehouse no longer had a copy of the offending texts, but thought he could reconstruct them from the abandoned chapters of *Wodehouse in Wonderland*. In its earliest draft, the letter book became little more than a defence of the broadcasts. This version does not survive, but it seems to have been quite polemical. 'I found myself getting more and more angry when I was writing about Milne,' Townend vouchsafed to Wodehouse. 'You are a much more civilised being than I am.'

Wodehouse was putting the finishing touches to *Pigs Have Wings*, after a steady burst of sixteen weeks with hardly a day's respite, and during the early spring of 1952 he put the letter book onto the back-burner. Coming up for air, he reread the manuscript and began to worry about the image he was presenting. 'I want to edit the stuff about my Berlin troubles very carefully . . . I don't want to publish anything that will put me in the light of a man hoping for people's good opinion,' he wrote to Townend. 'I want to seem much more detached.' Townend continued to labour away in Folkestone and when the next draft, accommodating Wodehouse's suggestions, arrived in New York, it had swollen to 538 pages of typescript, some 145,000 words. Now Wodehouse set about it again with enthusiasm ('I am convinced we have got something big'), cutting 53,000 words, but adding a further 40,000 words of new material. He was quite explicit about what he saw, for both of them, as the public relations side of the exercise:

The two things I want to avoid are (a) the slightest hint that I was ever anxious or alarmed or wondering if I should have lost my public and (b) any suggestion that your books have not done so well lately as earlier ones did. As regards (a), I naturally poured out my hopes and fears to you, but I don't want the public to know that I ever had a doubt about my future . . . I want my attitude to be a rather amused aloofness. . . . I was a little anxious lest Ethel should think it a bad thing to rake up all the broadcast stuff and publish the broadcasts, but she is all for it. So that's a weight off my mind. I wonder what the effect will be in England. Will it revive a storm of indignation, or will it put me right?

The first answer to this question came from the Cazalet family who, getting wind of the book, tried hard to persuade Townend to abandon the project. Wodehouse, now determined to make his case, was adamant in support of his friend, telling him, 'This book is going through, no matter what anybody says.' Townend, in his quietly stubborn way, was just as determined to press on, writing with prescient self-awareness that 'My one hope of fame is . . . in getting the book about your letters published.' Once this family pressure had been resisted, the typescript went to Wodehouse's agent, A. P. Watt, and his editor, Derek Grimsdick, at Herbert Jenkins. Both were supportive, though the latter expressed doubts about his client's efforts to justify his wartime conduct and would later advise Wodehouse to forget about visiting the United Kingdom. Now that the text of the letter book was in circulation, Wodehouse had clarified his intentions, at least to Townend: 'I want the reader to say "Dear old Wodehouse. What a charming nature he must have! Here are all these people writing nasty things about him, and he remains urbane and humorous. Bless my soul, what a delightful fellow he must be!"' He was grateful to Townend. 'I would never have written a straight autobiography,' he confessed, once the book was with Herbert Jenkins, adding that, 'our slogan must be Entertainment . . . all that matters is that the stuff is entertaining.'

Wodehouse spent much of the spring of 1952 at Guy and Virginia Bolton's home in Remsenburg, Long Island, and his emphasis on 'entertainment' was partly inspired by the conversations he and Bolton were having about their new farce, *Come On, Jeeves*. Remsenburg, adjoining the Hamptons, takes its name from a Dutch settler driven from New York by the colonial British, and was a scattered oceanside township of potato fields and wooded seclusion, whose marshy reedbeds and creeks were reminiscent of Bellport, the scene of his and Ethel's early married life. Wodehouse was glad to be away from Manhattan, and happy to be beside the seaside, and Ethel could see that. Once again, it was she who made the decisive move, one that would shape the rest of their lives together.

In May 1952, the penultimate chapter in Wodehouse's long life began when he announced to Townend, 'Ethel has bought a house!!!' The new address, a modest suburban bungalow in Basket Neck Lane, was set in about four acres of grounds, including a wood that ran down to the water. One of its many virtues was that Guy Bolton was just two miles away, an easy walk. Here for the next twenty-five years the Wodehouses – 'Plummie' and 'Bunny' – would remain in discreet retirement, as reclusive and sedentary as they had once been so astonishingly sociable and peripatetic. Wodehouse was content in his new writing haven; Ethel's love for her husband had a late flowering in this considerable sacrifice: there was very little social life to be found in Remsenburg, and most of their neighbours were excruciatingly dull.

By July, Wodehouse and Bolton had completed their Jeeves farce (which Wodehouse promptly reworked as fiction in *Ring for Jeeves*) and now, in a lighter, more ebullient mood, he told a dismayed Townend that he had decided to cut the broadcasts out of the letter book. If Wodehouse could persuade the reading public that he was just an entertainer, he thought, perhaps he would be forgiven. He continued to fiddle with the letter book for another year, long after Townend had ceased to play any role. 'I have gone for entertainment,' he repeated, breaking the news that he had revised their book yet again. He was now dealing directly with Grimsdick at Herbert Jenkins, not Townend, and had taken sole charge of the book. 'We are calling the book *Performing*

Flea,' he informed his co-author at the beginning of 1953, hoping the changes would not upset him. The new title had an almost insolent irony, a deliberate reference to Sean O'Casey's disparaging characterization of Wodehouse, at the height of the row about the broadcasts. Now Wodehouse responded with an exquisite, slightly lethal, courtesy: 'With Sean O'Casey's statement . . . I scarcely know how to deal. Thinking it over, I believe he meant to be complimentary, for all the performing fleas I have met have impressed me with their sterling artistry and that indefinable something which makes the good trouper.' Along with a definitive title came a change of tone. 'I have tried to keep the whole thing airy and nonchalant . . . It's a mistake to make at this late date anything in the nature of a "defence". The note throughout should be casual and amused.' After this reconciliation of stoicism to indignation, there were a few more changes to come. At this late stage, *Performing Flea* still contained three chapters from *Wodehouse in Wonderland* and the broadcasts were back in. When the proofs arrived in July, however, Wodehouse found himself 'shuddering over some of the things I said in the broadcasts' and decided, once and for all, to cut them. This crucial decision marked the end of any attempt to incorporate Wodehouse's Berlin crisis into the larger narrative of his life. Henceforth, it remained an unmentionable subject, as if it had nothing to do with the rest of his work as a writer of comic novels.

While he was still fussing over *Performing Flea* Wodehouse found light relief in accepting a commission from the new editor of *Punch*, his old friend Malcolm Muggeridge, to write about America. The result, 'This Is New York', appeared in the July issue of the magazine, renewing a connection of almost half a century. At the same time, he was working with Guy Bolton at *Bring on the Girls*. Here, too, manipulation was all. 'I think we shall have to let truth go to the wall', he wrote, 'if it interferes with entertainment . . . 'WE MUST BE FUNNY !!!!!!' Wodehouse was well aware that co-authored reminiscences were likely to seem contrived. *Bring on the Girls* was mostly written by Bolton and is Wodehouse's least successful autobiographical volume; its air of complacent self-congratulation is grating, but nonetheless it conveys something of Broadway in the 1920s.

Wodehouse was feeling buoyant again, bolstered by the news that *Pigs Have Wings* had just sold 25,000 copies in England. When Doubleday tried to cut both the royalty and the advance on his next contract, he told them 'to go to blazes', breaking an on–off relationship that stretched back to 1928. Dutton was eager to take him on, but in the end Scott Meredith sold both *Ring for Jeeves* and *Bring on the Girls* to Peter Schwed at Simon & Schuster, establishing a congenial connection that would see Wodehouse through to the end. His agent had always been a fan of his; the addition of a new American editor to the team was an important brick in the wall of Wodehouse's post-war security as a writer.

The new relationship got off to a near-farcical start, though. When Wodehouse came to deliver his typescript to the Simon & Schuster offices, a miscommunication by the receptionist left him stranded for almost an hour in a dark corner of the foyer. According to Schwed, 'Plum, ever a courteous and philosophical man as well as a shy one, sat in his corner and puffed his pipe. And sat. And sat.' When, wondering what had happened to his distinguished new author, Schwed came out to look for him, Wodehouse advanced from the shadows, beaming, with one hand outstretched and a manuscript held in the other. Wodehouse, who was never one to make a fuss, shook off all Schwed's apologies. 'I've had plenty of practice,' he said, 'in doctors' waiting rooms.' Schwed became a devoted editor and friend, even giving one of his sons the initials P. G. He described editing Wodehouse as a 'painless job'. Actually, he played a much more dynamic role in the preparation of Wodehouse's last books for the press than many previous editors, coming up with American titles (*Bertie Wooster Sees It Through*, *The Cat-Nappers*, *No Nudes Is Good Nudes*) and in the case of *Much Obliged, Jeeves* not only changing the title to *Jeeves and the Tie That Binds*, but even redrafting the plot's resolution for the Simon & Schuster edition. Whatever Wodehouse's private feelings about this clumsy interference, he never complained and was generous in his praise of Schwed. From the publisher's point of view, he was a dream author, 'delivering a new and invariably wonderful book . . . virtually every year'. The sales of these late Wodehouse books were never huge, but they were steady, and no one at Simon & Schuster questioned the economics of publishing him.

For the moment, all Wodehouse's anxieties were focused on the publication, at last, of *Performing Flea*. Although, typically, he had given little away, the book marked the closing of a terribly painful period. As Townend remarked in answer to a letter from a reader of the book, with a rare flash of sympathetic insight, 'I think P. G. . . . had a much

worse time than the book would give one to suppose, [but] I think
that *Performing Flea* has helped him.' In the analysis of *Performing Flea*,
which is unquestionably a vital text in the Wodehouse canon, it is probably a mistake to dwell on the airbrushing of inconvenient facts or
opinions. For all its artifice, the book has its own authenticity.
Wodehouse's embroidering of his original letters is often revealing. Take,
for instance, the way in which he pastoralized his own experience, and
returned it to a state of innocence. On 15 July 1952 his letter to Townend
included the following passage:

I think I told you that the first day Ethel was down here a starving hound
dog (now named Bill) clocked [in] and got adopted . . . Two or three nights
ago Peggy our maid . . . said there was a wild animal in the garden . . . and
sure enough there was something crying in the dark . . . a kitten about three
inches long . . . So now we have Squeaky, Bill, the guinea hens and the kitten.

In the published version, this letter was relocated to 11 August 1952
and revised, in part, as follows:

. . . so the score now is one foxhound, two guinea hens, Squeaky, and two
kittens, and we are hourly expecting more cats and dogs to arrive. I think the
word must have gone round the animal kingdom that if you want a home,
just drop in at Basket Neck Lane, where the Wodehouses keep open house.

Although embellished and rewritten, this passage contains a kind of
deeper truth, expressive of Wodehouse's longing for a safe haven not
only for himself but also for his beloved animals.

   *Performing Flea: A Self-Portrait in Letters by P. G. Wodehouse, With an
Introduction and Additional Notes by W. Townend*, was published in London
on 9 October 1953, scarcely a week after the American publication of
Bring on the Girls. Wodehouse sat in Remsenburg waiting breathlessly
for the first reviews. There was no need for anxiety. The British press
was almost universally favourable, rolling out epithets of approval: from
'delicious entertainment', 'extremely funny' and 'witty', to 'delightful'
and 'full of laughs and insight'. *Performing Flea* sold 4,500 copies before
Christmas. It was a bumper year: Penguin had just reissued five backlist titles (*The Inimitable Jeeves, Right Ho, Jeeves, The Code of the Woosters,
Leave It to Psmith* and *Big Money*) in a combined print run of one

million copies, attracting a huge new readership of paperback buyers. Wodehouse was swamped with correspondence. As a popular writer with a mass audience, he had always had fan-mail. Now, in old age, dealing with his postbag became a significant feature of his routine, and part of each day would be devoted to answering every letter. He occasionally complained about this, but it was part of his continuing atonement. To those he trusted, he was quite explicit about having his eye on posterity. He told his publisher, 'I had better spend my last days strewing sweetness and light wherever possible. I don't want St Peter looking at me sharply as I arrive at the pearly gate.'

Performing Flea was a bravura demonstration of tact, evasion and wishful thinking. There was not a single mention of the Cazalet family, who had so opposed it, and snarky references to John Buchan, Charles Graves, Ian Hay and Howard Spring, scattered through the original letters, were excluded. It also offered a masterclass in literary technique, and remains one of the best books ever written on the craft of popular fiction. To what extent it purged the stain of the broadcasts or seriously improved the public perception of Wodehouse is a moot point, but, in one wholly unexpected way, it did help to heal old wounds.

Back in 1941, one of Cassandra's more bizarre slurs in his BBC postscript had been against the names 'Pelham' and 'Grenville'. In a deft afterword to *Performing Flea*, Wodehouse expressed the hope that William Connor's initials, which he mistakenly identified as W. D. (in fact, they were W. N.), stood for Walpurgis Diarmid, and that one day the columnist would 'have to admit this in public'. By chance, Connor was in New York on the publication of *Performing Flea* and wrote a joshing reply in his *Daily Mirror* column, correcting the mistake and saluting the invention of 'Walpurgis' as 'a corker'. Wodehouse saw his opportunity and, in a masterstroke of magnanimity, invited Connor to lunch.

In prospect, this occasion was an encounter fraught with anxiety, but Wodehouse carried it off, as he intended, with nonchalant ease. He glided into the restaurant in his habitual grey flannel trousers, smoothly denying any ill feelings; then, with teasing affability, addressed Connor as 'Walp', and proceeded, to Connor's consternation, to turn on his charm and likeability. He announced his triumph to Townend, saying that they had got on like a couple of sailors on shore leave. Thereafter, 'Walp' and 'Plum' became, in Wodehouse's words, 'bosom pals', corresponded warmly and always lunched together on Connor's visits to

Manhattan. Years later, Connor wrote in the *Daily Mirror* of his wish 'to bury the whole story and to forgive and, where necessary, to hope to be forgiven'.

Unofficially, then, Wodehouse could and did achieve a significant measure of private redemption. But the British establishment remained implacable. Despite clearing Wodehouse in his report, Major Cussen had advised him to stay 'out of the Jurisdiction'. In April 1947 the Attorney General, Hartley Shawcross, an Old Alleynian, had confirmed this advice, making it plain that if Wodehouse returned to England he would run the risk of prosecution. 'If he were prosecuted,' Shawcross wrote, coldly unforgiving, 'it would be for a Jury . . . to decide whether his conduct amounted to being no more than a silly ass.' In the spring of 1952, Thelma Cazalet-Keir, using her political influence, asked David Maxwell-Fyfe, the Home Secretary, about the government's attitude to the Wodehouse case and was told that, after consultation with the Attorney General, 'it would not be right . . . to give any undertakings in regard to possible proceedings . . . should he [Wodehouse] return home'. Wodehouse, piqued, told Townend 'I don't want to come to England', which was not really true, and he continued, discreetly, to explore ways of liberating himself from the official disapproval which haunted so many years of his long exile.

25. 'I keep plugging away at my Art'
(1955–1961)

If you search that portion of the state of New York known as Long Island with a sufficiently powerful magnifying glass, you will find, tucked away on the shore of the Great South Bay, the tiny village of Bensonburg. Its air is bracing, its scenery picturesque, its society mixed. (*French Leave*)

In old age, Wodehouse craved solitude as much as redemption. In a return to childhood habits, he wanted more than ever, he said, to be left alone with his characters. At first, the house in Basket Neck Lane was simply a summer retreat, a place of cooling ocean breezes, but gradually Remsenburg became the home that he preferred, ideal for afternoon walks with Guy Bolton, well suited to the Wodehouse menagerie, and close to the sea in a landscape that reminded him of Emsworth and Bellport. There was, he told friends with typical bravado, never a dull moment in the country, while the daily four-mile round-trip to the post office kept him very fit. In April 1955 the Wodehouses moved out of 1000 Park Avenue for good. During the next few years, Ethel, ever restless, remodelled their new home, installing a bar and a spacious sun room. She also established her bedroom and a small private sitting room at the top of the house, up a single flight of stairs, with a commanding view of what soon became a large and well-appointed twelve-acre estate. Wodehouse's sleeping and working quarters were on the ground floor, just as he liked them, with their own entrance into the garden, as in a drawing-room comedy.

For the past two years, as part of his drive for re-acceptance in England, he had continued to write regular pieces for *Punch*, contributing more than forty articles, mostly written in his seventies. It was a pleasure to write for Muggeridge, and to work to a deadline; it also gave him great satisfaction to return to his literary Alma Mater. Now, in the seclusion of the South Shore, he put the finishing touches to 'a sort of autobiography' dealing with his fifty years in America. This, he explained to Townend, would not be a tell-all memoir, just a peg on which to hang his *Punch* articles. Adopting the voice he had found so congenial in *Performing Flea*, Wodehouse continued, with ironic detachment, to explore and develop the idea that he was most fully at home in America. Today, Wodehouse is renowned for his English butlers, peers and Drones, but his world had always been infiltrated by American characters – gimlet-eyed senators, overweight movie moguls and shifty bootleggers – while the pure spirit of his prose was always hospitable to the zest of American idiom – 'rannygazoo', 'hotsy-totsy' and 'bum's rush'. No English writer of the twentieth century, with the possible exception of Raymond Chandler, was so successful at relating the two cultures to each other, and Wodehouse's American fans are still as passionate as his British.

The move to Remsenburg settled any lingering thought that the Wodehouses might resume their pre-war life somewhere in Europe. Their friends believed that if Leonora had lived, this exile would not have become so permanent. But America was unequivocally their home now, besides being the country that had given Wodehouse refuge after the war, the place where he was free from the fear of prosecution. Even after a decade of peace, he was still tormented by such worries. 'Till now,' he confided to Townend, 'I have always had the idea that there might be trouble if I went to England . . . but I imagine they would hardly dare to arrest an American citizen!' So, at Ethel's urging, Wodehouse began to follow the logic of their situation and consider taking American citizenship. Early in the morning of 16 December 1955, after months of agonizing, he was driven to the court house in Riverhead, Long Island, and underwent the formalities which, according to his friend, the *New Yorker* writer Frank Sullivan, 'makes up for our loss of T. S. Eliot and Henry James combined'. In grateful exhilaration, Wodehouse replied that, now he could vote, he anticipated a lot of changes. 'I see myself directing the destinies of this great country and making people sit up all over the place,' he joked. 'I may decide to abolish income tax.'

Wodehouse celebrated his naturalization with the publication of his 'sort of autobiography' in the spring of 1956. *America, I Like You* was, like *Performing Flea*, another offbeat slice of unreliable recollections, an unabashed reworking of old material. True to form, it tiptoed past any awkward personal difficulties and made no reference to his German troubles. Characteristically, he revised it again for the English market as

Over Seventy. Published in 1957, it was subtitled 'An Autobiography with Digressions', a masterpiece of contrivance, perpetuating the myth of 'Dear old Wodehouse', and advertising a mood of contentment: 'Do I prefer living in the country to living in New York? I do, definitely. I work better, look better and feel better. The cry goes round Remsenburg, "Wodehouse has found his niche".'

Out on Long Island, Wodehouse could almost forget the pain he had suffered in wartime, and by the mid-1950s he was fully habituated to life in the country. Compared with New York there were, of course, minor drawbacks, like no newspapers in the morning. But he could list some important advantages: 'Not having to take Bill the foxhound for his walk on a lead every afternoon. Being able to go out without ringing for the lift. Fresh air and no smuts.' The coolness of the air in summer and the joy of wrestling with the ocean waves on the nearby shore were additional pleasures that made Remsenburg the perfect haven, the last in a succession of retreats in which he had sequestered himself from the world. There were, as there had always been, occasional dramas with the servants, but once Lynn Kiegiel, a Polish girl, joined the staff, the household began to develop the routine that Wodehouse preferred. On first arriving in post-war America, he had loathed the television; now it became an integral part of his routine, ideal for boxing matches, baseball and daily soap operas like *Love of Life*. When Guy Bolton was at home, the two old friends would meet most days and walk a circuit that took in a view of the ocean and long conversations about Broadway.

Behind the rustic nonchalance expressed in *Over Seventy*, it is clear from letters to close friends that, throughout the 1950s, Wodehouse still found himself out of sorts with the culture of which he had been such a visible part, and at odds with the post-war world. After making allowances for his love of striking an attitude in his letters, and the inevitable hyperbole involved in letting off steam, there is no mistaking his persistent grouchiness. He was 'appalled at the state literature has got into these days'. Nancy Mitford's novels were 'dirty', or 'very dull'. Christopher Fry 'ought to be shot'. Kingsley Amis was 'pretty lousy'. On Broadway, *My Fair Lady* was 'the dullest lousiest show I had ever seen'. Drama critics were 'a loathsome sub-species'; other critics were 'lice'. To Townend, he wrote that Graham Greene was 'drivelling and crazy'. If the arts brought little joy, society seemed to be falling apart. He told Mackail that 'Homosexualism seems to be all the rage these days', and that the BBC was 'a loathsome institution'. Bert Haskins, a friend from Ilag VIII, continued to send him batches of newspapers including the *Daily Express* and the *Daily Mirror*, whose contents horrified him. 'I find myself shaking my head a bit over the England of today,' he wrote. Like Evelyn Waugh, he was happy to affect the role of the elderly curmudgeon, observing that 'my principal pleasure in this evening of my life is writing stinkers'. Unlike Waugh, though, he had little stomach for public rows and preferred to keep this side of his nature to himself, while working hard to present himself as a remote and affable old gentleman, 'Squire Wodehouse' of Remsenburg. Simultaneously, he continued to make discreet, but deliberate, attempts to exorcize the spectre of Berlin.

Shortly before the final move to Remsenburg, and after all the dithering over *Performing Flea*, Wodehouse accepted an invitation from the poet Stephen Spender, then editor of *Encounter*, to publish the script of the broadcasts. Once again, Malcolm Muggeridge was the go-between, picking up the manuscript on one of his frequent visits to America. Wodehouse had managed to reconstruct it from notes and memory and Muggeridge delivered it to Spender in London, who published the text in the October and November issues of *Encounter* in 1954.

This was a very big deal, but Wodehouse played down the significance of what he had done. In a prefatory comment, he wrote, airily, that 'the idea of finally seeing my five Berlin broadcasts in print appeals to me'. It might, he added in a tone of cool reasonableness, 'be as well to print the broadcasts just for the record'. As with many of his blandest statements, this is slightly misleading. The version published by *Encounter* differs in a number of significant ways from the texts held by the German Foreign Office, from which the broadcasts were actually made. This is explained partly by the re-use to which Wodehouse had privately put his original material in various unpublished manuscripts: *Wodehouse in Wonderland*, his 'Apologia', and also a self-exculpatory essay, 'Now That I Have Turned Both Cheeks'. It was always part of his craft as a writer to revise and improve on his work. But after his bitter experience of the pillory there was his determination to make the authorized version of the broadcasts as crisp, funny and above all as harmless as possible. For example, the original opening of the first Berlin broadcast had read as follows:

It is just possible that my listeners may seem to detect in this little talk of mine a slight goofiness, a certain disposition to ramble in my remarks. If so, the matter, as Bertie Wooster would say, is susceptible of a ready explanation. I have just emerged into the outer world after forty-nine weeks of Civil Internment in a German internment camp and the effects have not entirely worn off. I have not yet quite recovered that perfect mental balance for which in the past I was so admired by one and all.

It's coming back, mind you. Look me up in a couple of weeks and you'll be surprised. But just at the moment I fell [*sic*] slightly screwy and inclined to pause at intervals in order to cut out paper dolls and stick straws in my hair, – or such hair as I still have.

This, no doubt, is always the effect of prolonged internment, and since July the twenty-first, 1940, I have been spending my time in a series of Ilags. An Ilag must not be confused with an Offlag or Stalag. An Offlag is where captured officers go. A Stalag is reserved for the rank and file. The Civil Internee gets the Ilag – and how he loves it!

The *Encounter* version of the same passage reads:

If anyone listening to me seems to detect in my remarks a slight goofiness, the matter, as Bertie Wooster would say, is susceptible of a ready explanation. I have just emerged from forty-nine weeks' sojourn in a German prison camp for civil internees, what is technically known as an Ilag, and the old bean is not the bean it was.

He had also learned that to make light of his experience in Nazi Germany did not go down well with the public. So he cut out a paragraph which had described internment as 'quite an agreeable experience':

There is a good deal to be said for internment. It keeps you out of the saloons and gives you time to catch up with your reading. You also get a lot of sleep. The chief drawback is that it means your being away from home a good deal. It is not pleasant to think that by the time I see my Pekinese again, she will have completely forgotten me and will bite me to the bone – her invariable practice with strangers. And I feel that when I rejoin my wife, I had better take a letter of introduction, just to be on the safe side.

He had also taken a lot of flak in the British and American press for the finely turned sentence that had been alleged to express his admiration for the Wehrmacht: 'I was strolling on the lawn with my wife one morning, when she lowered her voice and said "Don't look now, but there comes the German army". And there they were, a fine body of men, rather prettily dressed in green, carrying machine guns.' This passage, too, was silently dropped from the *Encounter* text, along with a number of other troublesome sentences.

It was typical of Wodehouse that he should amend his own work without indicating that he had done so. After fifty years of literary activity, it was second nature for Wodehouse to revise his material before releasing it. And of course, his ulterior motive was to present himself in the best possible light. He still did not – and never would – grasp the historical dimensions of his offence. It would never have occurred to him to indicate how the version he was printing differed from what he had actually read out from a studio in Berlin. At the same time, he still nurtured a profoundly injured sense of innocence: the defiant act of printing the texts was testimony to that.

The measure of Wodehouse's satisfaction with the move from Park Avenue to Remsenburg and the renewal of his friendship with Guy Bolton can be seen in *French Leave*, a romantic comedy, based on a Bolton plot, and without any regular Wodehouse characters. The novel, a Franco-American mating-game entertainment, opens with an affectionate portrait of Remsenburg, alludes teasingly to *Love among the Chickens*, and comes to a climax in the French holiday resort of Roville-sur-Mer so often favoured by Bertie Wooster. For all its light-heartedness, it was, Wodehouse wrote, 'the longest and most difficult job I've ever had . . . Rather an experiment', and it attracted a vicious review in the *Observer*. But Evelyn Waugh came to its defence ('Years and years ago . . . I was one of the regular reviewers on the *Observer*. We were far from dedicated, but we had certain old-fashioned ideas of fair play. One of them was that you did not abuse a book unless you had read it'), inspiring a prolonged and bruising correspondence about the merits of Wodehouse the novelist, a debate which did nothing to hurt his sales. Nonetheless, the experience convinced Wodehouse to stick to what he knew. 'I shall certainly keep the flag flying as regards earls and butlers,' he told one correspondent, in words that are a kind of manifesto for his final years. Accordingly, his late work would renew the acquaintance of some old friends: *Jeeves in the Offing*, *Service with a Smile*, *Stiff Upper Lip, Jeeves* and *Galahad at Blandings*. In old age, Wodehouse was especially comfortable with characters he had written about for close-on fifty years, and also with ancient companions-in-arms like Guy Bolton.

When Bolton was travelling, as he often was, Wodehouse's chief recreation was the daily walk to the post office, accompanied by Bill the foxhound and any other residents who could be persuaded to make the trip. If errands stretched further afield, and there was driving to be done, Ethel would get behind the wheel of the Wodehouse saloon and navigate the wooded highways of rural Long Island, terrifying her passengers. The inhabitants of Remsenburg quickly came to understand that, while the Wodehouses were friendly, they were not sociable, and preferred to keep to themselves. 'Ethel and I never see a soul these days,' he informed Mackail, 'and thank goodness the neighbours have stopped inviting us to their binges. About three times a year I motor up to New York, lunch, buy books and return the same day. It's odd about living in the country, there always seems such a lot to do.'

Increasingly, Wodehouse's life in Remsenburg centred on animals. 'Dogs and cats – and of course Ethel – are the only people worth associating with,' Wodehouse wrote to Mackail. Wodehouse's life and work had always been replete with livestock: parrots, gnus, snakes, pigs, cats, and any number of Pekes, terriers, spaniels, poodles, Irish wolfhounds and assorted mongrels. Now, in Basket Neck Lane, it was as though the animal cast of his fiction was assembling for a grand finale. Visitors to the house found the celebrated author and his wife amid a sea of cats and dogs.

In fact, visitors from outside were few, although Leonora's children, Edward and Sheran, became regular summer guests as they grew up. Edward was careful not to disturb the routine of the house and was popular with his grandfather. Privately, they referred to Ethel as 'the Colonel', which says everything about her role in the household. Wodehouse had adored Leonora and some of that affection was passed on to her son and daughter. Even here, the past, and especially the broadcasts, were never far away. Edward Cazalet recalls that, as a young man, he brought up the subject while walking with his grandfather one day in the garden. 'Sometimes,' Wodehouse confided, 'I still can't see where I went wrong.' Later, Cazalet asked Wodehouse if he would write a memoir of his mother Leonora, but after several days of brooding on this, Wodehouse demurred, characteristically saying he felt it would be 'too difficult and too distressing'. Apart from the family, Wodehouse was at home to friends like Muggeridge and associates like Meredith and Schwed, who all paid occasional visits. From time to time, fans would make their way to Basket Neck Lane. If they managed to locate the Wodehouse residence, sequestered among the trees, and marked only by a doormat inscribed 'the Wodehouses', and to get past Ethel's defensive cordon, they would find 'dear old Wodehouse', a picture of rustic benevolence among the rose bushes, fussing over his animals.

One young Englishman, John Hughes, who happened to be visiting family friends on Long Island, negotiated his way to Basket Neck Lane, and found Ethel leaning out of her bedroom window, drying her hair. 'Plum', she reported, was out, walking the dogs, but she breezily invited Hughes to return the following afternoon, which he did, in some trepidation. Ethel offered tea, and eventually Wodehouse appeared, all apologies and affability, and after some small talk quizzed Hughes searchingly on the state of London theatre, especially its musicals. 'By now,' writes Hughes, 'it was cocktail time, and the martinis were mixed by Wodehouse the barman.' In answer to Hughes's deferential questions about working methods and work-in-progress, Wodehouse gave courteous but vague replies and, after an early dinner, as the evening drew to its close, Wodehouse signalled the young man's departure by presenting him with signed copies of *French Leave* and his latest collection of short stories, *A Few Quick Ones*. Hughes describes his host as an Englishman of the old school, never brusque or off-putting. Out of the fray, Wodehouse was always accommodating to his fans. In September 1958, shortly before Hughes's impromptu visit, an American admirer, David Jasen, appeared one afternoon, also unannounced. He happened to meet Wodehouse as he was setting out with the dogs, asked for an interview, and was invited to join the walk. Jasen also left with a signed copy and, when he wrote up his encounter in his college magazine, began a relationship with Wodehouse that would mature, throughout the 1960s, into *P. G. Wodehouse: Portrait of a Master*, the first authorized biography.

A less welcome but equally inevitable kind of visitor, the interviewing journalist, was also treated with hospitality, but not always with happy results, especially when the conversation turned to the broadcasts. The circumstances surrounding their transmission, and Wodehouse's attitude, were still a newspaper story. On one disastrous occasion, René McColl from the *Daily Express* secured an invitation to lunch at Basket Neck Lane by claiming friendship with Malcolm Muggeridge. McColl's account of the occasion, a feeble parody of Bertie Wooster, reported Ethel admitting that 'Plummie is terribly hurt', and described Wodehouse's 'melancholy' at being confronted with questions about the war. 'This settles it,' Wodehouse wrote to Townend, in a fury. 'Any news-papermen who want to interview me in future [will] get the Waugh treatment.' Waugh was in the middle of a celebrated public row with two *Express* journalists, which ended up in the libel courts, and in which Wodehouse joined with a set of comic verses, 'The Visitors', which harked back to his 'Parrot' poems. More usually, Wodehouse, the old-school Englishman, perfected a routine for himself, designed to neutralize the risks of sitting down with the press, in which he simply repeated, almost word for word, a succession of charming stories about his early life. His artful modesty, he knew, might consign him 'to the obscurity which is the fate of light writers', he said. 'Not that I mind it.'

More troubling, perhaps, was the fact that his life and work were beginning to attract scholarly interest in England. A freelance writer named Richard Usborne, in particular, was now well advanced on a study of Wodehouse's fiction. Usborne had already written *Clubland Heroes*, a study of the fiction of John Buchan, 'Sapper' and Dornford Yates. Wodehouse had admired the book and Usborne, encouraged by Grimsdick, had then proposed a literary critical volume. Wodehouse agreed, on the understanding that it should be about his work, not his life. Usborne had launched into his research with zeal. To explore the context of the novels and the stories, he had, perforce, to make dozens of biographical inquiries, and rapidly became an authority on his subject's fascinating, and much neglected, early life and work. Wodehouse found Usborne's questioning, which was conducted through the post, 'a pain in the neck', and complained to Mackail that he (Usborne) 'seems to think that I must have suffered greatly from tyrannical aunts in my childhood, having written so much about them'. In a defensive challenge to all future biographers and critics, he added, 'Why do these fellows always think there is something hidden and mysterious behind one's writing?' Eventually, when the final draft of *Wodehouse at Work* was submitted to Remsenburg for approval, it was discovered to contain –

horror of horrors – a 20,000-word chapter about his internment and the broadcasts. Wodehouse's reaction was ruthless and clinical. He simply destroyed the offending chapter and returned the typescript to Usborne without comment, rightly guessing that Usborne had not kept a copy and would be too intimidated to protest.

None of the interest aroused by Wodehouse the man was allowed to interrupt the flow of work from Wodehouse the writer. The 1950s saw the publication of several late-period Wodehouse works, set in familiar landscapes. He did not repeat the experiment of *French Leave*, and novels like *Jeeves and the Feudal Spirit*, *Something Fishy* and *Cocktail Time* were designed to reassure his fans that his world had survived more or less unscathed and that Jeeves and Bertie were still in harness. Thus, in *Jeeves and the Feudal Spirit*, Wodehouse deploys his usual cast with practised aplomb. Bertie, horrifyingly, has grown a moustache. As usual, Jeeves exacts a high price for sorting out a fiendish imbroglio involving Aunt Dahlia, her cook Anatole, Bertie's ex-fiancée Florence Craye and the future ownership of *Milady's Boudoir*. Bertie must shave off the offending whiskers. In *Something Fishy*, Wodehouse reverts to the American scene, New York before the Wall Street crash of 1929, combined with scenes from 'Valley Fields' in the summer of 1955. *Cocktail Time* returns to the world of Uncle Fred, Lord Ickenham and the Drones Club, and also features Sir Roderick Glossop and Peasemarch, the fatalistic ship's steward from *The Luck of the Bodkins*. This, in turn, was a curtain-raiser to a collection of short stories, *A Few Quick Ones*, four of them set in the Drones Club and all with happy endings.

Behind the apparent effortlessness of his composition, there was still the old agony, mixed with a new note of occasional self-doubt. 'The awful part of the writing game', he observed to Mackail, who had abandoned fiction after the death of his wife, 'is that you can never be sure the stuff is any good.' Two months later he admitted to Mackail that he was having 'a hell of a time with my novel . . . I wish I had retired, too.' From time to time, English critics expressed the same opinion in less charitable tones. After a wounding attack from John Gordon of the *Daily Express*, Wodehouse wrote broodingly to the new editor of *Punch* that '*Punch's* position is rather similar to mine. I have been doing the same sort of stuff for fifty years and more and the critics are always sniping at me for being Edwardian and making my heroines too pure . . . but I know from the sales that I write what the public want, so I don't lose my head and try to do something quite different.'

The adversity of changes in the market and a more difficult literary climate provided a challenge to which Wodehouse responded in the only way he knew. 'I keep plugging away at my Art,' he told Mackail, as the decade ended. He found comfort in the habits of a lifetime. He would go to sleep with the cats, Poona and Blackie, in his bed, and Bill the foxhound, now 'stone blind and completely deaf', on the floor. His working methods were unchanged, too. He was now openly speculating about re-using the plot of *Sam the Sudden*, his favourite 'Valley Fields' novel. As usual, he had doubts. 'I've just finished my new novel' (*Ice in the Bedroom*), he wrote to Mackail at the beginning of 1960. 'Fairly good, I think, but what does it *prove?*' He was only too aware that public taste had moved on. 'I sometimes wish I wrote that powerful stuff the reviewers like so much,' he joked, 'all about incest and homosexualism.' Was it, he wondered, 'about time to be calling it a day'?

And yet, as he approached eighty, Wodehouse's quest for rehabilitation had been so successful that, in America, Simon & Schuster began to prepare for the anniversary, announcing that it would publish a birthday collection, *The Most of P. G. Wodehouse*, a full year early. Wodehouse was rather discomfited by his great age: 'having my octogenarianism hurled at me like that shook me a bit,' he said. 'I consoled myself with the thought that I can still touch my toes fifty times every morning without a suspicion of bending the knees, which I bet not many octogenarians can.' When the *New Yorker* made the pilgrimage to Remsenburg to celebrate what turned out to be his seventy-ninth birthday, he repeated all the old stories, handed out martinis on the verandah, and presented his self-deprecating side. 'I suppose my work is pretty juvenile,' he said. 'When you've written about eighty books and they're always exactly the same Edwardian stuff, it's sometimes difficult to churn it out, but I love to write . . . I don't know what I'd do if I didn't write.' No one mentioned the war, and Simon & Schuster's premature celebrations, hastily revised to honour Wodehouse's '80th year' were made less comical by a newspaper advertisement in which some of the greatest English and American writers of the day – W. H. Auden, Ivy Compton-Burnett, Graham Greene, John Betjeman, Nancy Mitford, Aldous Huxley, Christopher Isherwood, Rebecca West, Ogden Nash, John Updike, Cole Porter, James Thurber, Lionel Trilling – paid tribute to 'an inimitable international institution and a master humorist'. Wodehouse, who never really understood his own greatness, was overwhelmed. But there was another, much bigger, birthday surprise to come.

On 15 July 1961, twenty years to the day since Cassandra had launched his BBC assault on 'Pelham Grenville Wodehouse', Evelyn Waugh broadcast a birthday salute, also on the BBC, 'an act of homage and reparation' to his friend. 'An old and lamentable quarrel must be finally and completely made up and forgotten . . .' he said, adding that 'there is a hideous vitality in calumny'. Waugh's remarks, which were published the next day in the *Sunday Times*, were a rebuke to the English establishment's treatment of Wodehouse, and fell into two parts, a rebuttal of Wodehouse's supposed treachery, followed by a celebration of his 'idyllic world'.

This broadcast was commissioned by a BBC producer, Christopher Sykes, who would later become Waugh's biographer. When Wodehouse got wind of it in May, he intervened to ask Waugh to refrain from attacking Cassandra, who, as William Connor, had become his newfound friend. Waugh obliged, and devoted the first half of his talk to an analysis of the broadcasts. Although he easily disposed of the charge of treason, he was unable to eradicate the accusation of collaboration. That, as scores of Wodehouse commentators have discovered, would prove impossible. Waugh's long concluding passage, a salute to his friend's genius, closed with a famous peroration that would set the tone for all the commentary in the remaining years of his life:

For Mr Wodehouse there has been no fall of Man; no 'aboriginal calamity'. His characters have never tasted the forbidden fruit. They are still in Eden. The gardens of Blandings Castle are that original garden from which we are all exiled. The chef Anatole prepares the ambrosia for the immortals of high Olympus. Mr Wodehouse's world can never stale. He will continue to release future generations from captivity that may be more irksome than our own. He has made a world for us to live in and delight in.

The years of atonement were drawing to a close.

26. 'The Grand Old Man of English Literature'
(1961-1975)

Unless I suddenly hit mid-season form in my eighties, humanity will remain a message short. (*Over Seventy*)

'At eighty things begin to get a bit serious,' Wodehouse told Frank Sullivan. Joking aside, he dreaded his imminent birthday, particularly when the news came that his old friend from Broadway days, Marion Davies, had died. 'I'm beginning to dislike very much the thought of being eighty,' he told Guy Bolton. But the big day turned out happily. Sheran Cazalet, who happened to be staying at the house, sat by the telephone and took down all the cables and telegrams from around the world. With his good-natured diffidence, Wodehouse was flattered and gratified by the attention. A procession of press, radio and television interviewers to Remsenburg was followed by several hundred column inches of worldwide newspaper coverage, in which Waugh's resounding 'act of homage and reparation' was widely quoted.

'I got a good press,' Wodehouse told Mackail. To Bolton, he boasted that 'I seem to have become the Grand Old Man of English Literature'. Herbert Jenkins marked the occasion with the publication of *Ice in the Bedroom*, Wodehouse's reworking of *Sam the Sudden*; in America, Simon & Schuster offered renewed birthday greetings with *Service with a Smile*, a new Uncle Fred and Blandings Castle novel. The well-received publication of Usborne's *Wodehouse at Work* simply confirmed his status as a writer to be taken seriously. In the past, he had suffered for his mass audience and a perceived lack of consequence. Now, he had become 'the Master', not just to Evelyn Waugh, but to admirers all over the world.

Alistair Cooke, reporting for the *Manchester Guardian*, was one of many journalists who made the pilgrimage to Basket Neck Lane to visit the newly sociable Hermit of Remsenburg. On a hot summer Saturday afternoon, with garden mowers droning in the background, he found 'a big, pink, shambling, bald-headed man with thick glasses', greeting him with 'How nice of you to come, where shall we go? I think it might be cooler in the house.' Cooke found Wodehouse's voice secure and genial, with a disarming air of wanting to help, a voice 'tuned entirely in C major'. Wodehouse, whose features were, he noted, as ripe and smooth as an apple, was dressed for the interview in a long linen coat over a check sports shirt, fawn trousers, and canvas shoes with thick soles the colour of almond icing. Well-practised in the art of presenting an image, Wodehouse turned in a vintage performance of a man delightfully blessed with sound mind, sound body, good spirits and good fortune. How was his health at eighty? 'A little hard of hearing in the left ear, that's all.' How did he like Long Island? 'I love it here and go to New York only two or three times a year.' Was he happily married? 'My goodness, it's been forty-seven years.' A steady income from his books? 'I get an awful lot of money out of Sweden, I can't think why.'

Wodehouse was always happiest talking about his work. 'It's the most *remarkable* thing. I don't believe there is a *single* language – wait now, I'm not sure about the Russians – that hasn't translated it. I get books in Burmese and Korean and Japanese, and I can't think what they are. You have to trace them like hieroglyphs and read them backwards. And all the time, you wrote them. It's *most* amazing. I can't think what *they* think they're reading!' Cooke reported that Wodehouse's bewilderment at his readership seemed 'completely genuine, and through all our talk there was the novel feeling that here was a hermit, a recluse, a sort of musical comedy [Albert] Schweitzer; who had honestly no idea that he'd ever been heard of, or read outside the dormitories of English public schools when the lights were out.' There was always an element of contrivance about these press interviews. Wodehouse's modesty about his achievements was genuine enough, but he was a lifelong professional who knew it was right to entertain good relations with his readers, through the press.

Once the television crews and reporters had departed Basket Neck Lane, Wodehouse gratefully went back to his old routine, a pattern of life that would persist until the day he died. On most days, he would get up at half past seven, go out onto the porch at the back door, and do the 'daily dozen' sequence of calisthenic exercises he had performed every day since 1920. While Ethel, always a late riser, was still upstairs in bed, Wodehouse would prepare his regular breakfast – toast and honey or marmalade, a slice of coffee cake and a mug of tea – and, as part of the early morning routine, he would read a 'breakfast book', for example a Rex Stout or Ngaio Marsh mystery. Then he would light the first pipe of the day, crumbling the cigars Peter Schwed sent him into the bowl in preference to pipe tobacco. At nine o'clock, after a short walk with some of the dogs, he would retire to his study, a spacious, pine-clad room overlooking the garden, for the morning's work. His writing methods had not changed in years. He would sit and brood in a favourite armchair, draft a paragraph or two in pencil, then move to the typewriter, sitting under a Victorian oil painting of the Hongkong and Shanghai Bank's Lombard Street offices. Even in old age, he was still translating the chaos of reality into the farcical stability of Blandings Castle. There is something both heroic and poignant about the octogenarian Wodehouse, in exile, pecking away at his typewriter.

In his last decade, Wodehouse could still average 1,000 words a day where, as a younger man, he had often written 2,500 words and more. The morning's work would be followed by lunch – usually meat and two veg, followed by an English pudding like apple crumble – at about one o'clock. If he was visiting Remsenburg, Bolton, now also in his eighties, would arrive at two for their daily walk, an hour-long circuit, a regular outing which would unfailingly bring Wodehouse back home in time for the all-important rendezvous with his favourite soap opera, *The Edge of Night*. At about four, he and Ethel would have tea, which was served, English style, on good china with cucumber sandwiches. After this, he might snooze a bit in his armchair, have a bath, and do some more work, before the evening cocktail (sherry for her, a lethal martini for him) at six, which they took in the sun parlour, overlooking the garden. This was followed by dinner, alone with Ethel, and eaten early to allow the cook to get home to her family. After dinner, Wodehouse would usually read, but occasionally he would play two-handed bridge with Ethel, a habit, he joked, that doubtless suggested he was senile.

His new decade as an octogenarian started with more sadness, the death of Bill Townend, alone in a nursing home in Folkestone. Their lifelong correspondence had petered out in the late 1950s as Townend became infirm and increasingly preoccupied with caring for his wife Rene, who was dying of cancer. When Rene finally passed away in September 1961, Townend was broken. He scribbled to his school friend, 'I can't write anymore. I feel old and shaken.' Townend, who shared

Wodehouse's interest in spiritualism, said he had nothing to look forward to, save to see his wife in the next world. He told his friend and mentor that 'the house is very lonesome and I dread the nights. I sleep very badly now.' A few weeks later he had a bad fall in the night and was not discovered until morning. Feeble, heartbroken, stone-deaf and almost destitute, Townend was moved to a nursing home, where he had another fall, lingered for a few weeks and then, mercifully, died. Townend's sad life had shadowed Wodehouse's for decades. It was only after he had gone that Wodehouse could bring himself to articulate what he must have known all along, that Townend's writing was, as he put it to the novelist Tom Sharpe, 'frightfully dull'. Wodehouse expressed no grief at his close friend's death. Apart from Ethel, who had always disapproved of Townend's sponging, there was no one left to confide in, even if he had wanted to.

Wodehouse himself was remarkably spry. He finished *Stiff Upper Lip, Jeeves*, spent the summer of 1962 plotting out *Frozen Assets* and continued to write regularly for *Punch*, as 'Our Man in America'. Although he rarely left Remsenburg, scarcely ever visited New York, saw no one, apart from Bolton, and had lost almost all contact with any literary or theatrical life that did not concern his writing, Wodehouse still managed to fashion an amusing column out of press clippings in a manner reminiscent of his work on the *Globe*, sixty years earlier. Although there was no shortage of political material to write about – Khrushchev's explosive visit to the United Nations; John F. Kennedy's election as President; Castro and the Cuban missile crisis – Wodehouse confined himself to the margin, the everyday doings of ordinary American citizens: 'The police in Grand Rapids, Michigan, are spreading a dragnet for a night-club entertainer who recently skipped out of town . . .'

Wodehouse also wrote about American sports, a subject that had always engaged his interest. In old age, he had become a devoted baseball fan, and he also loved to watch boxing matches on television. In anticipation of a Patterson–Liston bout, he told Frank Sullivan, 'I am rooting hard for Liston', and he enjoyed following the inept exploits of the newly formed New York Mets. Crime was another favourite topic. He retained a special affection for bungling criminals, botched robberies and failed jailbreaks, and would narrate the vicissitudes of American life outside the law, culminating in amusing courtroom scenes in which local justices would hand down sentences to obscure suburban miscreants, just as Sir Watkyn Bassett used to do from the bench in Bosher Street. Wodehouse told his editor at *Punch* he was apprehensive that 'these darned things aren't funny enough', but they have a light, autumnal charm and *Punch* was proud to be associated with Wodehouse's name.

Wodehouse's commitment to *Punch*, on top of steady work at his next novel, is all the more remarkable because towards the end of 1962 and during the first months of 1963 Ethel was unwell. In September 1962 she underwent a serious operation for cancer, and was given nine months to live, a diagnosis that proved mistaken. In the event, a prolonged convalescence was followed by many visits to the hospital for check-ups. Wodehouse found himself alone in Basket Neck Lane, looked after by Lynn Kiegiel, with just the dogs and cats for company. After a life-time of marriage, he was distressed by Ethel's absence. 'My own precious darling Bunny,' he wrote to her in hospital, 'this is just to tell you how much I am missing you and praying that you will soon come back safe to me. I love you, darling, more than a million bits.'

Writing was always his first refuge from pain. He continued to work hard on *Galahad at Blandings*, but the flow of inspiration was not what it had been. He confessed to his editor Grimsdick that, although he believed his new Blandings novel was one of the best of the series, he had cheated in its composition. 'For the American version I have put in one or two passages from old books, because nobody over here will remember them.' In the mid-1960s, professional uncertainty was mixed with his own ill-health. Wodehouse suffered from arthritis in both hands which, he told a Dulwich correspondent, was 'pretty bad hell'. He also admitted to Bolton that 'I have the greatest difficulty in getting the stuff down on paper. I do a couple of pages with terrific effort and then have to take a day off to think how to handle the next scene.' Age was one handicap; social change was another. It was hard to write with the same brio about Bertie and his manservant in the era of the Beatles, the Bomb, and the paperback edition of *Lady Chatterley's Lover*. Wodehouse had generally solved the problem of modernity in his fiction by ignoring twentieth-century progress. His characters still took liners rather than jumbos long after air travel had become commonplace, and it did not seem to matter. This was not always so. The scene in *Aunts Aren't Gentlemen* (1974) in which Bertie Wooster gets caught up in an anti-war demonstration is one of Wodehouse's very rare post-war narrative mis-steps.

After her illness, Ethel, who was now in her eighties, no longer had the energy to run the house as she had done throughout their married life. The solution, both practical and sentimental, was to invite Armine's widow, Nella, to come and live with them in Remsenburg. Nella arrived during the summer of 1964. Wodehouse told Bolton, 'we both like her very much, so I think the new arrangement will be a success. She will take a lot of work off Ethel's hands.' Sadly, his idea of Nella's role in the household would lead to bitter conflict with Ethel and hasten Nella's eventual return to England.

As the 1960s unfolded, inexorable change intruded more and more into Wodehouse's settled world, but he maintained a close and steady correspondence with J. D. Grimsdick at Herbert Jenkins in London and Peter Schwed at Simon & Schuster in New York. The even flow of author–editor business letters was mixed with occasional outbursts at his publishers' inanities. 'One feels that P. Schwed ought to rent a padded cell in some not too choosy lunatic asylum,' he wrote to Grimsdick, complaining about the American jacket for *Galahad at Blandings*, but in general his relations with his publishers were harmonious and profitable. His sales were steady but respectable, with each new title averaging 10,000 copies in the United States and about 30,000 in Britain, and he was still producing a book a year.

So it came as a shock to learn, in the spring of 1965, that Grimsdick had sold Herbert Jenkins to another company, Barrie and Rockliffe, now renamed Barrie and Jenkins. In the short term, Grimsdick continued to look after his author's interests, but the change of ownership and Wodehouse's advancing age affected his output. From 1965 to 1970, a succession of titles, some of them barely more than novelettes (Wodehouse's own description), show a marked falling off in quality as he approached ninety. It was now thirty years since he had set foot in England and his long exile was affecting his work. 'How difficult it is to write stories about a country when you aren't in it,' he exclaimed to Guy Bolton.

If his current work was faltering, his backlist was in rude good health. *The World of Wooster*, a BBC television adaptation of his Bertie Wooster stories, starring Dennis Price as Jeeves and Ian Carmichael as Bertie, was a great success in 1965 (Wodehouse himself greatly preferred Price's Jeeves to Carmichael's Bertie), and brought him a new generation of readers. He and Guy Bolton also spent hours in discussion of a new version of *Come On, Jeeves*, retitled *Win with Wooster*, and also a Jeeves musical, neither of which came to anything. Much of his time in these last years was taken up in a project dear to his and Ethel's heart: the P. G. Wodehouse Animal Shelter, known as the Bide-a-Wee Association.

All their lives, the Wodehouses had been touched by the plight of stray cats and dogs. In Remsenburg, their house had become an unofficial sanctuary for an ever-changing menagerie of homeless pets. New York families would come out to the Hamptons for the summer holidays, often bringing a puppy to amuse the children. When the season ended, faced with taking a now fully grown dog back to a Manhattan apartment, the visitors would simply abandon the animals on the beach, to scavenge among the dustbins of the nearest houses. In 1966 Wodehouse invested several thousand dollars to establish a home in West Hampton for a hundred of these strays. Ethel, particularly, would spend long periods almost every day visiting the inmates, feeding and caring for them, and even in extreme old age insisting on special Thanksgiving dinners for the animals. Wodehouse also made occasional visits, but remained more detached. In March 1969 he cannily refused an invitation to give money to Dulwich on account of his expenses for the animal shelter. Money was always on his mind: on a visit to Basket Neck Lane, his new British editor at Barrie and Jenkins, Christopher MacLehose, complimenting Wodehouse on his spectacular lawns, was disconcerted to be told how many dollars a month it was costing to maintain this vista of serenity.

Wodehouse continued to plug away, with the dedication that characterized his entire career. 'It always takes me six months and four hundred pages to get a book set,' he told Grimsdick, 'so it just means patience.' His work might be thinner now, and more anachronistic, but he still had his standards: '[*Company for Henry*] will definitely be a novelette,' he wrote. 'I don't want to spoil it by padding it.' In February 1966 he boasted that 'I have just done a record for me – viz. to get out a scenario of a novel in just a month. It looks good, too.' His hard work paid dividends. *The Girl in Blue*, published in 1970, marked a return to form noted by almost all the critics. In May 1970, greatly encouraged, he wrote to Christopher MacLehose, with whom he was establishing an excellent rapport, that 'I am now busy scenario-ing a new Jeeves novel [*Much Obliged, Jeeves*] . . . my difficulty being to get the characters and their relationship right.'

Occasionally, journalists still came to pay homage, finding their host courteous and hospitable. When Philip Norman, a young reporter on the *Sunday Times*, wangled an invitation to lunch in the summer of 1969, he encountered Wodehouse in a flowered shirt, heavy brogues and cavernous tweed jacket waiting to meet him on the grass verge at Remsenburg's solitary bus stop. To the young Norman, the eighty-seven-year-old Wodehouse was much taller than he expected; in the America of the late 1960s, the era of Bob Dylan, Richard Nixon and Johnny Carson, his voice was noticeably English, with that fruity timbre peculiar to middle-class Englishmen born before 1900, a timbre shared by Graham Greene. Wodehouse was somewhat dismayed by Norman's 'long yellow hair hanging down his back', but nonetheless gave him a warm welcome: lunch at a local restaurant; an inscribed copy of *A Prefect's Uncle*; conversation about the work-in-progress, *A Pelican at Blandings* ('It's going to be *awfully* good,' said Wodehouse); cocktails with Guy and Virginia Bolton, mixed by Ethel in a patent ice-making gadget, followed by dinner – leg of lamb accompanied by Mateus Rosé – and reminiscences about butlers, W. S. Gilbert, Florenz Ziegfeld and George Gershwin. The visit ended when, like so many before him, Norman found himself on the Long Island Railroad at Speonk, catching the last train to New York. More telling of Wodehouse's approval was the farewell gift, a box of cigars from 'Plum and Bunny Wodehouse', awaiting Norman in his cabin when he boarded the QE*2* for the voyage home. At one point in their conversation, Wodehouse told the young reporter that he did not mind where he was so long as the work was going right. Norman asked if he ever laughed out loud at what he was writing. 'Not much,' Wodehouse replied. 'When you're alone you don't do much laughing.'

Wodehouse had always been solitary, with an inner core of well-concealed sadness, but now he was facing the approach of his ninetieth birthday with almost all his old friends dead and Ethel increasingly bedridden and querulous. She loved parties and metropolitan life, and had made a considerable personal sacrifice to live in Remsenburg; in these last years she was not only fading but also profoundly bored. She would stay up in her bedroom until midday. Wodehouse, wheezing heavily with the effort, would climb the stairs to her room and watch the little television in the corner while she lingered in bed. Lynn Kiegiel also remembers Ethel feeding, and fussing over, the birds on the little balcony outside her bedroom. Edward Cazalet, visiting his grandfather for the last time, found that he had lost a lot of weight and was moving much more slowly. Ethel was still smoking and drinking hard, 'aglow with make-up and jewellery' in honour of the visitors. When Cazalet went to say goodbye, he found Wodehouse reading *Smokescreen* by Dick Francis. Wodehouse began to struggle up out of his chair, but Cazalet begged him not to move. 'Goodbye, old boy,' said Wodehouse. 'We have loved seeing you.' As he left the room, Cazalet says he could not resist looking back. 'Plum was already back in his book, fully absorbed.'

The solitude of these final years was punctuated by the inevitable media hoo-ha that greeted Wodehouse's ninetieth birthday. This time there was no question of hashing over the Berlin broadcasts. They were part of the record now and attitudes had softened. It was acknowledged that Wodehouse had been guilty of nothing worse than stupidity. He himself told the BBC that he had never felt bitter about his fate. 'I think if one has done a foolish thing you have got to take the consequences,' he said, looking miserably into the camera. 'I just feel that it was a pity it happened.' The anniversary was also marked, in Britain, by the publication of *Much Obliged, Jeeves*, which gave the reviewers a chance to pay tribute to his life and work. In a leader about Bertie Wooster, *The Times* said: 'To strike a comic vein thus far impervious to time and fashion is genius indeed . . . To the question where does he stand, the only answer is: apart,' adding that Wodehouse should receive an honour. Writing in the *Sunday Times*, John le Carré saluted Wodehouse's 'magic, his humour, his humanity, his sheer bubbling hilarity', and then also moved, as many other admirers were beginning to do, to address the English establishment's inexplicable failure to make reparation for what he called its 'disgraceful act of spiritual brutality' against him during the war. Le Carré noted bitterly that Wodehouse had not returned to England since the broadcasts. He went on: 'Wodehouse, for half a century a by-word for a certain kind of English wisdom, has never received so much as that OBE mysteriously bestowed on county librarians. Medals are fat-headed things, he would probably say. But at least they are a way of saying sorry. Better still, he might pop over to receive it.'

But Wodehouse had long ago given up on the idea of coming home. Now, at peace in his Long Island sanctuary, and advised by his doctor that a trip to England would strain his heart, he paid no attention to such efforts to lure him back. He was still doing his 'daily dozen', and told one correspondent: 'I feel pretty good for an old fossil of ninety – and I am going to try for that hundred.' In March 1972 he was invited to attend Sunday service with President Nixon, but turned it down as 'too much of a strain'. He had no desire to leave Basket Neck Lane and, apart from his year in Tost, had never bothered much with religion, remaining strenuously agnostic. He told one BBC interviewer that it was '*awfully* hard to say' if he had religious beliefs. 'It varies from day to day. Some days I have, and other days I haven't.' As to the matter of eternity, he advised another interviewer from the *Illustrated London News* that 'we'll have to wait and see'.

In fact, there was no question of waiting for the end, or the beginning, or whatever else it might turn out to be. All that mattered to Wodehouse at ninety, as always, was his work. 'I am sweating away at my new novel,' he told Christopher MacLehose. 'I am adopting a different policy this time. I know the story is all right up to about page 90, so I am writing the first chapters before sitting down and thinking what goes in the middle. The end is fine.' A year after his ninetieth birthday, he published *Pearls, Girls and Monty Bodkin*, an end-of-season outing for Hollywood tycoon Ivor Llewelyn, Chimp Twist and several characters from *The Luck of the Bodkins*, in a plot that bears some striking resemblances to *Money in the Bank*. Writing to Grimsdick, he described himself as 'mentally very fit', but having to hobble about with a stick. He told his regular correspondents that his legs had 'gone back' on him, but conceded philosophically, 'I suppose one has to expect a drawback or two at my age.'

Although he missed his daily outings with Guy Bolton, the two old partners continued to plan revivals of Princess shows like *Oh, Lady! Lady!!* and discuss ways of turning an abandoned Jeeves musical into a novel. Bolton and Wodehouse, ex-kings of Broadway, were no longer in demand, but were now an inspiration to a new generation. Hot from the success of *Jesus Christ Superstar*, Tim Rice and Andrew Lloyd Webber made the pilgrimage to Remsenburg with their next project, *Jeeves*. Wodehouse feared it would be a flop, but encouraged 'the boys' in a venture that, after his death, fulfilled his predictions. Such discussions were an agreeable distraction from the new tensions of life in Basket Neck Lane. Ethel and Nella, who had never really got along, probably because Nella's role in the house was, unhappily for her, an ambiguous one of indigent relative-cum-servant, had reached a kind of grudging truce, but the atmosphere in the house was far from sunny. At Christmas 1972, Wodehouse told his nephew Patrick that he had stayed at home with a book while the two women had gone off to feed the dogs at Bide-a-Wee, and 'We had cold lamb and baked beans for dinner!' Whenever he could, Wodehouse would struggle out of the house with a stick, but walking was no longer either a pleasure or a way to resolve plot problems, and there was the risk of a fall. The inexplicable dizzy spells of the 1950s had never quite gone away, and on one of his walks in the spring of 1973 he had found himself 'toppling over sideways and [coming] down a frightful purler'.

None of these difficulties, or even the trouble he was having with his latest typewriter, was allowed to stop the flow of composition. In November 1973 he told Grimsdick, with whom he continued to correspond, that he was three chapters from the end of a new Jeeves novel 'which looks like being one of my very best'. Then, just as he was coming to the end of the main draft, the news came from London that Christopher MacLehose, on whom he had come to depend, was leaving Barrie and Jenkins. 'As far as I was concerned,' he told Tom Sharpe, 'he [MacLehose] was the whole firm', and temporarily he lost the will to work on his new book with the old urgency. MacLehose's break with Barrie and Jenkins was a blow to Wodehouse's creative drive, but advanced old age was slowing him down in so many other ways, too. 'I sit in the old arm chair,' he confessed to Tom Sharpe, a new confidant and a comic writer he admired, 'and brood and I do get an occasional minor scene, but never anything I can build on. It doesn't matter to me financially, but how dull life will be if I can't write.'

Life and work had always been one with Wodehouse. He had suffered a mild heart attack just before his ninetieth birthday, but now, as his work faltered, he developed renewed heart trouble. His doctor, Leroy B. Davis, diagnosed a need for treatment. Wodehouse was unconcerned. In other respects, he felt pretty fit, and had got used to hobbling about with a stick, taking his manuscripts and letters to the post office as usual. Ever the Old Alleynian, he told a Dulwich correspondent that he was now 'exactly the weight I was when I was in the Fifteen in 1899'. To Tom Sharpe, he fussed over his new novel, as he had used to do with Bill Townend: 'I keep getting detached scenes but not a plot,' he admitted.

Two months later, in the summer of 1974, he was excited to report that 'my big news is that they are putting me in Madame Tussaud's, which I have always looked on as the supreme honour'. For Wodehouse, a child of late-Victorian England, Madame Tussaud's, with its bewigged historical celebrities and Chamber of Horrors, had a special place in his imagination, and he was thrilled to be part of it. Tussaud's sent a sculptor across the Atlantic to model Wodehouse, in several sittings. 'He has a whole tray of eyes, glass eyes,' he reported to David Jasen, whose biography was, after many vicissitudes, on the verge of publication. 'Then he looks at me very, very carefully and begins to match the glass eye with mine.'

There was one more tribute to come, England's final act of forgiveness. In the New Year's Honours of 1975, Wodehouse (like Charlie Chaplin) was awarded a knighthood by the Queen. With this belated honour, Sir Pelham Wodehouse joined the ranks of his patrician ancestors, Sir Constantine, Sir Bertram and Sir John, for services every bit as vital to his country, a lifetime's dedication to its literature, an enduring contribution to its distinctive humour. He was probably less thrilled by the decoration than by the waxwork, but he recognized that it was the establishment's gesture of reconciliation, as he put it, 'sort of their way of saying, that's that'.

As well as a mountain of fan-mail, which he was determined to answer himself as usual, he had to worry about whether to go to London for the ceremony. Ethel was keen, but his doctor advised that his heart would not stand the strain and, in the end, Peter Schwed and Scott Meredith came out to Remsenburg and knighted him, with a replica Japanese ceremonial sword, in a mock ceremony. (Ethel later received the honorary award on his behalf from the British consul.) There is also an apocryphal story that Queen Elizabeth the Queen Mother, a lifelong fan, had volunteered to go to Long Island to conduct a private investiture, but was forbidden by the authorities. Close examination of the record shows that, like Wodehouse's 'secret' post-war visit to London, this is a fanciful tale.

Towards the end of January, Wodehouse began recording short introductions to the stories in the BBC's *Wodehouse Playhouse*, starring John Alderton and Pauline Collins. The strain of this extra work took its toll. He developed pemphigus, a nasty rash so persistent that his doctor advised a brief period of hospitalization for treatment. In the second week of February 1975 he reported to the Southampton Hospital for tests, taking the manuscript of his latest, unfinished Blandings Castle novel with him. On the evening of 14 February, Ethel and Nella visited him in his room, and found him in good spirits. After they had seen that he was comfortable and bade him goodnight, they left him to take his dinner, after which he prepared to work on his manuscript. Even now, he was under deadline pressure from his publishers, who wanted the new typescript by the end of February. It was always a point of honour with him to fulfil such obligations. When the doctor, Bernard Berger, looked in on his famous patient at about eight o'clock he found him sitting in his armchair, with a pipe and tobacco pouch in his hands, and the manuscript nearby. He appeared to be asleep, but the doctor realized at once that P. G. Wodehouse was dead. His heart had failed at last. As St Valentine's Day, 1975, drew to a close, the news began to break on the international wires and the late-night radio bulletins. Another 'global howl' was about to begin, but this time there would be mourning, not recrimination.

The Afterlife of P. G. Wodehouse

If any young writer with a gift for being funny has got the idea that
there is something undignified and anti-social about making people laugh,
let him read this from the *Talmud*, a book which . . . was written in an
age just as grim as this one. '. . . And Elijah said to Berokah, "These two
will also share the world to come". Berokah then asked them, "What is
your occupation?" They replied, "We are merrymakers. When we see a
person who is downhearted, we cheer him up." These two were among
the very select few who would inherit the kingdom of Heaven.'
(*Over Seventy*)

The funeral took place at two o'clock in the afternoon of 18 February,
a fine late winter's day, at the Remsenburg Presbyterian church. The
post office, where Wodehouse had collected his mail for nearly thirty
years, flew the Stars and Stripes at half staff. There were about fifty
mourners, who picked their way to the chapel through patches of snow.
Ethel, who remained composed throughout the ceremony, was joined
by Edward and Sheran Cazalet, representing the family, Scott Meredith
and Peter Schwed, and some friends and neighbours from Remsenburg.

Before the service, there was one final moment of controversy. Ethel,
dominant and theatrical to the end, wanted Wodehouse laid out in an
open coffin so that the mourners could pay their last respects. Edward
Cazalet, representing a more discreet, English point of view, argued
against this and, after a fierce debate, persuaded his grandmother to let
'Plummie' rest in private in a massive cherrywood casket. Wodehouse's
own wishes were that he should be cremated. His ashes were later placed
beneath a monumental white marble tombstone, inscribed with the
names of Psmith, Mr Mulliner and Jeeves.

After the funeral, the mourners repaired to Basket Neck Lane, where
some parts of Wodehouse's life came together for the first time. David
Jasen met Scott Meredith. Peter Schwed spoke to the Cazalets. Guy
Bolton told the reporter from the *New York Times* that his old friend

'was, quite simply, the most humane and kind man I have ever known'. Ethel, probably still smarting from the row about the coffin, seemed angry and overwhelmed. The loyal retainers, Lynn Kicgicl and Margaret Zbrozak, who looked after Lady Wodehouse (as she liked to be known) until she died in 1984 at the great age of ninety-nine, believe that Ethel never really got over her husband's death. Her health deteriorated. Increasingly, she stayed up in her room, drinking sherry, surrounded by dogs and cats, dispatching scarcely legible notes to family and friends around the world and doing her best to administer the enormous responsibilities involved in the Wodehouse Estate. Her last public appearance of any consequence was at the Morgan Library in 1981 on the occasion of the Wodehouse centenary.

It is now a generation since Wodehouse's death. A succession of new Wodehouse landmarks is in view, the one-hundredth anniversaries of his first books: *The Pothunters*, *Love among the Chickens*, *Mike* and *Something Fresh*. These are all in print, and still admired by a new generation. Today, the wartime scandal, seen in a longer perspective, no longer clouds the reader's approach to his work; it can be seen as a disastrous blunder that reflects on the author but not on his books. Almost unique among his twentieth-century contemporaries, many of whom predeceased him, all his work is in print in various editions. He would probably be the first to be surprised at the sums of money for which first editions of his work change hands. Film and television producers continue to toy with adaptations of his work, generally proving the rule that the best literature makes the worst cinema. Nonetheless, Wodehouse is more popular today than on the day he died, and references to his characters appear somewhere in the English-speaking world almost every day. The *Oxford English Dictionary*, for instance, contains more than 1,600 quotations, from 'angel-face' to 'zippiness' by way of 'oompus-boompus' and 'squiggle-eyed'. His fame will never again reach the peaks of the 1930s, but his comic vision has an absolutely secure place in the English literary imagination. To have created not one but as many as five great characters (Bertie, Jeeves, Lord Emsworth, Aunt Agatha and Psmith) who require no introduction places him in a very select group of writers, led by Shakespeare and Dickens.

Some enthusiasts have tried to compare him to these, and other, great English writers, but this comparison does not really fly. Wodehouse was a miniaturist and his work is not like theirs. He is closer in spirit to

Jane Austen, who famously worked on a 'little bit (two inches wide) of ivory'. Her inspiration, however, was drawn from a near-contemporary world; Wodehouse placed his characters in a recently vanished society and one, moreover, whose reality was transformed by his remarkable powers of fantasy and imagination into something timeless – and permanent. The secret of that permanence lies in Wodehouse's surreptitious elegy for his country. Behind the Drones and the manor house weekends is a sweet, melancholy nostalgia for an England of innocent laughter and song.

Wodehouse's work has an undisputed place in the canon of English literature, and though his writing is less vulnerable to literary fashion than that of many twentieth-century contemporaries, as popular comedy it is likely to be undervalued. Wodehouse understood this. 'Humorists', he wrote towards the end of his life, 'are looked down on by the intelligentsia.' His work will continue to suffer the fate of so much light comic writing: it will rarely be treated with the seriousness it deserves or the seriousness accorded to many lesser writers. Wodehouse would not be dismayed. For him, the lightness was all. Seriousness was risky. Seriousness meant raising too many painful questions, either about himself or about his society. Seriousness was about finding answers, which were troubling things with painful consequences. Probably he sensed that there were no answers. Personally enigmatic and elusive, he was happy to let life remain a mystery. In lightness and lunacy, life could be bearable, and the unexamined life, left to its own devices, could go like a breeze, especially if crowded with incident, orchestrated by butlers and valets, and dedicated to helping old pals. Furthermore, it was Wodehouse's genius to execute the lightness of his stories in a language that danced on the page like poetry, marrying the English style of the academy with the English slang of the suburbs.

The lightness is also a sleight-of-hand. Behind the comic mayhem of Wodehouse's best work – horrifying as it might seem to those for whom his work is a blessed escape from seriousness and difficulty – there is an inspiration that gives it significance. Deprived in childhood of parental affection and unable, in adulthood, fully to express it in his own life, Wodehouse's lasting subject is universal: the foibles of the human heart. Coded more tightly than an Enigma cryptogram, the theme that animates Wodehouse's work, and gives it a moral purpose, is the quest for sweetness and light in the daily transactions of humanity, and for something approximate to love. As an Englishman of his class and generation, he has to make a joke of it, and place those who experience or suffer it in ludicrous situations – in one of the rare weddings in his work, the groom is plugged by a rotten tomato. The indomitable flippancy of his characters is a brilliant camouflage for an unassuaged longing for a condition that is almost beyond the reach of his characters' vocabulary: understanding and sympathy. Take away the Aberdeen terriers, the cocktail shakers, the banjos, the tartan spats, the pigs and the frantic telegrams, and you find the figure of the 'laughing love god'. There is hardly a sentimental line among the millions that he wrote, and his expression of this universal theme is constrained by the profound Englishness of his character, but the quest for human connection is the whirring flywheel that keeps the intricate clockwork of his plots ticking, and makes his world go round.

Wodehouse is often described as an innocent, and so he was, in many ways, but with the innocence came an exceptional good nature and a profound humanity. He believed in 'doing the square thing' by his fellow man, and in an understated tolerance of human frailty. His biggest trouble, the terrible wartime blunder, sprang from an admirable motive, the expression of gratitude to readers who liked his work.

Finally, it is the work, an extraordinary body of English prose – novels, stories, poems, plays, reportage, correspondence, lyrics and memoirs – that gives him consequence. Successive generations of readers will return again and again to his books, to admire his inimitable gifts, to laugh at the follies of the human comedy, and to celebrate the magic of an English prose caught at a singular moment between mass culture and high art. In the lives of most great writers, there are usually two lasting themes, love and work. With Wodehouse these are indistinguishable, and both prevail.

NOTES

AMPASL   Academy of Motion Picture Arts and Sciences Library, Beverly Hills, California

Berg   The Henry W. and Albert A. Berg Collection of English and American Literature, The New York Public Library

Black   A. & C. Black Archive, Eaton Socon

Bradshaw   Private collection

Caversham   BBC Written Archives Centre, Caversham, Reading

Chapel Hill   Louis Round Wilson Library, University of North Carolina, Chapel Hill, North Carolina

CNB   Camp Notebook, P. G. Wodehouse Archive, the Wodehouse Estate

Columbia   Rare Book and Manuscript Library, Columbia University, New York

Concordance   Tony Ring and Geoffrey Jaggard (eds.), *The Wodehouse Millennium Concordance*, 8 vols. (Maidenhead, 1994–2001)

Cornell   Division of Rare and Manuscript Collections, Cornell University Library, Ithaca, New York

Cussen   Major Cussen's 'Report on the Case of P. G. Wodehouse', 3 October 1944, PRO, HO 45/22385-66279

Dulwich   Special Collections, P. G. Wodehouse Library, Dulwich College, London

Emsworth   Emsworth Museum, Emsworth Maritime and Historical Trust, Emsworth, Hampshire

HSBC   HSBC Group Archive, Hongkong and Shanghai Banking Corporation Collection, London

King's   Modern Archive Centre, King's College Cambridge

MRFLW   P. G. Wodehouse, *Money Received for Literary Work*, P. G. Wodehouse Library, Dulwich College, London

Muggeridge   Malcolm Muggeridge Collection, Buswell Memorial Library, Wheaton College, Wheaton, Illinois

Orwell   George Orwell Archive, University College London

PAAA   Politisches Archiv des Auswärtigen Amts (German Foreign Office archive), Berlin

PRO   Public Record Office, Kew

Punch	Punch Cartoon Library Archive, Hans Crescent, London
Ransom	Harry Ransom Humanities Research Center, University of Texas at Austin, Texas
Sharpe	Tom Sharpe papers, Great Shelford, Cambridge
State Department	Archives of US State Department, Washington, DC
Wodehouse Archive	P. G. Wodehouse Archive, the Wodehouse Estate Archive
Young	Young Research Library, Arts Library Special Collections, UCLA, Los Angeles, California

Wodehouse's novels have been published in various unsatisfactory editions. The Everyman Library edition, co-published in the USA by the Overlook Press, is the first attempt at correct and authentic texts. This edition is cited where available and indicated in these notes.

PROLOGUE: 'Does aught befall you? It is good'

p. 1 *pet parrot*: the parrot, Coco, was owned by Lady Dudley, formerly Gertrude Millar, a friend and neighbour who had recently left Le Touquet for England. Ethel Wodehouse to Leonora Cazalet, 27 March 1940, Wodehouse Archive.

p. 2 *There was a sharp, indignant yap*: 'Apologia', Berg.

p. 2 *There for awhile . . .*: ibid.

p. 3 *'In the forty years . . .'*: ibid.

p. 3 *'This diversion . . .'*: ibid.

p. 4 *number more than a hundred*: fierce scholarly debate rages over the actual number of Wodehouse titles. Figures range from ninety-eight volumes upwards.

p. 4 *On the Indian subcontinent . . .*: see Shashi Tharoor, 'How the Woosters Captured Delhi', *Guardian*, 20 July 2002.

p. 5 *H. L. Mencken*: who observed that PGW had the best ear of any living writer.

p. 5 *two contrasting Adamses*: see Douglas Adams, *The Salmon of Doubt* (London, 2002), p. 67: 'He's up in the stratosphere of what the human mind can do, above tragedy and strenuous thought, where you will find Bach, Mozart, Einstein, Feynman, and Louis Armstrong, in the realms of pure, creative playfulness.' Gerry Adams told the author, during an interview, that he identified with Jeeves, sorting out the chaos created by 'mentally negligible' Englishmen.

CHAPTER 1: 'My childhood went like a breeze' (1881–1894)

p. 9 *Rooted in the English past, its pronunciation*: see PGW to John Starr, 16 January 1964: 'My name is pronounced Wood-house, though I have never discovered why.

Just one of those English Cholmondeley (sic) Marjoribanks things!' *Wooster Sauce*, December 2002, p. 21.

p. 9 *This sense appears punningly . . .*: A Midsummer Night's Dream, Act II, scene ii, line 192, 'wood within this wood'.

p. 9 *'If you ask me to tell you . . .'*: preface to *Something Fresh* (1915; London, 1969), p. viii.

p. 10 *'The first few rows were occupied . . .'*: The Inimitable Jeeves (1923; London, 1999), pp. 174–5.

p. 11 *Wodehouse himself had no title*: in *Laughing Gas* and *Service with a Smile*, Wodehouse has heroes who joke about inheriting earldoms through the untimely deaths of 'fifty-seven uncles and aunts'.

p. 11 *'his ancestors did dashed well . . .'*: Thank You, Jeeves (1934; Everyman, 2003), p. 19. I gladly acknowledge a special debt to the Wodehouse expert Lt. Col. N. T. P. Murphy for his tireless and generous assistance on the genealogical side of the Wodehouse family history. Murphy's *In Search of Blandings* (London, 1981) is the indispensable guide to this subject.

p. 11 *'Earls are hot stuff'*: 'Uncle Fred Flits By', in *Young Men in Spats* (1936; Everyman, 2002), p. 179.

p. 11 *'Is an Earl . . . ?'*: Laughing Gas (1936; Everyman, 2001), p. 21.

p. 12 *'the manly spirit . . .'*: PGW to Leonora Wodehouse, 28 November 1920, Wodehouse Archive.

p. 12 *Clear out? That is no way . . .*: Uncle Fred in the Springtime (1939; Everyman, 2004), p. 117.

p. 12 *served until his return in 1895*: two of Wodehouse's uncles also served in the British Empire, as colonels, respectively in the Indian Army and the Royal Iniskillings. (On his mother's side, Wodehouse also had naval connections through his uncles John and Gussie.) Another uncle (Walter) was a captain-superintendent in the Hong Kong police; and there were several cousins in the colonial service.

p. 12 *David Cannadine*: in *Ornamentalism* (London, 2001), p. 28.

p. 13 *devoted his energies to genealogy*: Deane died in 1897; his daughter Mary published his work posthumously as *The Book of Dene, Deane, Adeane: A Genealogical History* in 1899. Deane also wrote *The Worship of the Serpent, Traced Through the World and its Traditions Referred to in the Events in Paradise proving the Temptation and Fall of Man*.

p. 13 *One doesn't want . . .*: The Code of the Woosters (1938; Everyman, 2000), p. 161.

p. 13 *'Shanghai Lil'*: I am indebted to Patrick Wodehouse for this detail.

p. 13 *a book on whist*: Murphy, *In Search of Blandings*, p. 41.

p. 14 *hard on her servants*: Frances Donaldson, *P. G. Wodehouse* (London, 1982), p. 47.

p. 14 *a family of eccentrically named sons*: Ernest and Eleanor Wodehouse had a whimsical side. Philip Peveril was born on the Peak in Hong Kong, and owes his name to Walter Scott's novel, *Peveril of the Peak*.

p. 14 *'The last thing in the world . . .'*: Blandings Castle and Elsewhere (1935; Everyman, 2002), p. 23.

p. 14 *'it is a moot point . . .'*: 'Portrait of a Disciplinarian', in *Meet Mr Mulliner* (1927; Everyman, 2002), p. 133.

p. 15 *'We looked upon mother . . .'*: David Jasen, *P. G. Wodehouse: Portrait of a Master* (London, 1975), p. 5.

p. 15 *parallels between the respective childhoods . . .*: see Andrew Lycett, *Rudyard Kipling* (London, 1999), pp. 59–68.

p. 15 *his family went to extraordinary lengths . . .*: PGW's literary agent, Ella King-Hall, reported that when his stepdaughter Leonora was rushed from Sussex to London after the birth of her first child, Wodehouse, who was staying with her at the time, was not told of her condition, so well known was his horror of pain; John Hayward, interview with Ella King-Hall, King's.

p. 15 *'one has deliberately to school oneself . . .'*: CNB, 12 August 1940.

p. 16 *'my father was very indulgent . . .'*: Jasen, *Wodehouse*, p. 9.

p. 16 *A Freudian would say . . .*: see Paul Fussell, *Abroad* (Oxford, 1980), pp. 15–16.

p. 16 *The three essentials . . .*: *Over Seventy* (London, 1957), p. 16.

p. 16 *'I can't remember . . .'*: Jasen, *Wodehouse*, p. 9.

p. 16 *As a writer of light fiction . . .*: preface to *The Clicking of Cuthbert* (1922 (US edition 1924); Everyman, 2002), p. 9.

p. 17 *'The question [for Wodehouse] . . .'*: interview with Adam Phillips, 27 September 2000.

p. 17 *Describing William ('Bill') West's . . .*: *Bill the Conqueror* (London, 1924), p. 26.

p. 17 *'Show me a delicately nurtured female'*: *Stiff Upper Lip, Jeeves* (1963; London, 1966), p. 71.

p. 17 *'a refusal to know them'*: interview with Adam Phillips.

p. 17 *'the scourge of my childhood'*: PGW to Richard Usborne, 14 January 1955, Wodehouse Archive.

p. 18 *'There's about five-foot-nine of Aunt Agatha . . .'*: 'Aunt Agatha Speaks Her Mind', in *The Inimitable Jeeves*, p. 22.

p. 18 *'has an eye like a man-eating fish'*: 'Extricating Young Gussie', in *The Man with Two Left Feet* (London, 1917), p. 24.

p. 18 *'a large, genial soul . . .'*: 'Clustering Round Young Bingo', in *Carry On, Jeeves* (1925; London, 1999), p. 202.

p. 18 *'The Great Sermon Handicap'*: published in *The Inimitable Jeeves*.

p. 18 *one of his best stories*: 'Anselm Gets His Chance', in *Eggs, Beans and Crumpets*, (1940; Everyman, 2000), pp. 106–30.

p. 18 *There's something about evening service . . .*: 'The Purity of the Turf', in *The Inimitable Jeeves*, p. 151.

p. 18 *Ernest had been awarded a CMG*: see Sukhdev Sandhu, *London Calling* (London, 2003), p. 100.

p. 19 *housed in The Chalet*: a few hundred yards up the road was the home of Alfred Russel Wallace, the great Victorian biologist.

p. 19 *stealing a turnip*: Jasen, *Wodehouse*, p. 6.

p. 19 *'It is many years since . . .'*: 'Uncle Fred Flits By', in *Young Men in Spats*, p. 173.

p. 19 *Life in The Chalet*: see Barry Dighton, *Elmhurst: A School and Its Boys* (privately printed, 2000), pp. 17–21.

p. 19 *'Pev has written to father . . .'*: ibid., p. 21.

pp. 19–20 *'the great event of the year'*: Jasen, *Wodehouse*, pp. 7–8.

p. 20 *'We were left very much to ourselves . . .'*: ibid., p. 7.

p. 20 *'I had always wanted to be a writer'*: *Over Seventy*, p. 28.

p. 20 *O ah, that soryful day . . .*: quoted in Richard Usborne, *After Hours with P. G. Wodehouse* (London, 1991), p. 146. First published in facsimile in the *Captain*, April 1907, p. 90.

p. 21 *About five years ago . . .*: the story was reproduced in a *Chums* interview with Wodehouse in 1933, p. 215, and was first quoted in Jasen, *Wodehouse*, p. 7. It is also cited in Donaldson, *Wodehouse*, p. 46, and Barry Phelps, *P. G. Wodehouse: Man and Myth* (London, 1992), p. 42. The original MS apparently does not survive.

p. 21 *Memories of Cheney Court*: neighbouring villages include Brixton Deverill, Monkton Deverill, Kingston Deverill, Longbridge Deverill and Hill Deverill.

p. 21 *'Five?' . . .*: *The Mating Season* (1949; Everyman, 2001), p. 10.

p. 21 *passed from aunt to aunt*: Jasen, *Wodehouse*, pp. 7–8.

p. 22 *The largest occupational group*: see A. N. Wilson, *The Victorians* (London, 2002), p. 318.

p. 22 *'on the fringe of the butler belt'*: *Over Seventy*, p. 52.

p. 22 *'There always came a moment . . .'*: ibid., p. 54.

p. 22 *a weak chest . . . sea air*: see Jasen, *Wodehouse*, p. 8.

p. 22 *Elizabeth College, in Guernsey*: PGW's rare, forgotten, early novel *Not George Washington* (London, 1907) is partly set in Guernsey. PGW also won a prize there, now kept at Dulwich College.

p. 23 *Ernest Armine*: I am indebted to Dr Jan Piggott and Patrick Wodehouse for their help with information about Armine Wodehouse.

p. 23 *'I always felt so near . . .'*: PGW to Nella Wodehouse, 10 October 1936, private collection.

p. 24 *the Revd Aubrey Upjohn*: see references in *Joy in the Morning*, *The Mating Season*, *Jeeves in the Offing*, and 'The Inferiority Complex of Old Sippy', in *Very Good, Jeeves*.

p. 24 *their father, Ernest, had glimpsed . . .*: Jasen, *Wodehouse*, pp 8–9.

CHAPTER 2: 'The Boy, What Will He Become?' (1894–1900)

p. 25 *Wodehouse entered Dulwich College . . .*: the best account of Wodehouse's Dulwich career is Dr Jan Piggott's essay, 'Wodehouse and Dulwich College', in *Concordance*, vol. iii, pp. xix–lxiii.

p. 25 *'six years of unbroken bliss'*: *Over Seventy* (London, 1957), p. 16.

p. 25 *'seem like Heaven'*: PGW to William Townend, 7 March 1946, Dulwich.

p. 25 *a glimpse of St Paul's*: V. S. Pritchett, *A Cab at the Door* (London, 1979), p. 88.

p. 25 *'fragrant oasis'*: *Something Fishy* (London, 1957), p. 13.

p. 25 *'in the thirty-three years . . .'*: *Sam the Sudden* (London, 1972), pp. 9–10.

p. 25 *one of his favourite books*: PGW had several favourites among his work. He once said his favourite story was 'From a Detective's Notebook', *Punch*, 20 May 1959; see Frank Muir (ed.), *The Oxford Book of Humorous Prose* (Oxford, 1990), p. 1119.

p. 26 *'stucco Siamese twins'*: ibid., p. 23.

p. 26 *'apologetic flower beds . . .'*: ibid.

p. 26 *'The most deadly error . . .'*: *The Pothunters* (London, 1902), p. 64.

p. 26 *'it was . . . what you would call a middle-class school'*: David Jasen, *P. G. Wodehouse: Portrait of a Master* (London, 1975), p. 11.

p. 27 *'like a policeman'*: 'Under the Flail,' *Public School Magazine*, October 1901, pp. 304–5.

p. 27 *opportunity for making friends*: Jasen, *Wodehouse*, p. 11.

p. 27 *'elderly men who were at Dulwich . . .'*: William Townend's introduction to *Performing Flea* (London, 1953), p. 11.

p. 27 *'I was pretty friendly with everybody'*: Jasen, *Wodehouse*, p. 18.

p. 27 *Ivyholme was a mixture. . .*: see Jan Piggott's invaluable essay, 'Wodehouse and Dulwich College', in *Concordance*, vol. iii, pp. xix–xxxvi.

p. 28 *'conscious of an extraordinary feeling . . .'*: 'The Bishop's Move', in *Meet Mr Mulliner* (1927; Everyman, 2002), p. 78.

p. 28 *Each study expressed its owner's personality*: in *Right Ho, Jeeves*, Bertie Wooster reports with some distaste that Gussie Fink-Nottle kept newts 'in his study in a kind of glass tank, and pretty niffy the whole thing was, I recall': *Right Ho, Jeeves* (1934; Everyman, 2000), p. 13.

p. 28 *an exceptional games player*: on the cricket field, PGW's exploits are part of Dulwich legend, and include the seven Tonbridge wickets he took in June 1899.

p. 29 *Sport was an acceptable . . .*: interview with Adam Phillips, 27 September 2000.

p. 29 *first appearance in print*: in *Alleynian*, 22 (1894), pp. 239–40.

p. 29 *Wodehouse continued to attend . . .*: between 1920 and 1935, Wodehouse wrote some eighteen 1st XV and 1st XI match reports for the *Alleynian*. See Eileen McIlvaine, Louise Sherby and James H. Heineman (eds.), *P. G. Wodehouse: A Comprehensive Bibliography and Checklist* (New York, 1990), pp. 164–5.

p. 29 *Throughout the 1930s . . .*: S. C. 'Billy' Griffith (1914–93) correspondence: 10 autograph and 64 typed letters; private collection.

p. 29 *'Isn't it odd . . .'*: PGW to William Townend, 20 November 1946, Dulwich.

p. 29 *'"fixated" on his old school'*: George Orwell, 'In Defence of P. G. Wodehouse', *Windmill*, 2 (July 1945).

p. 29 *'a bad case of arrested mental development'*: *Performing Flea*, p. 214.

p. 29 *'the best form of education . . .'*: Jasen, *Wodehouse*, p. 11.

p. 29 *the classical greats*: among the Greek texts he studied were Aeschylus (*Agamemnon, Prometheus Bound*), Aristophanes (*Peace, Knights, Clouds*), Demosthenes, Euripides (*Heraclidae, Orestes*), Homer, Plato, Sophocles (*Electra, Philoctetes*) and Thucydides.

p. 30 *There certainly is a close resemblance . . .*: PGW to Peter Brown, 2 April 1969; private communication.

p. 30 *his adolescent library*: they included Kipling's *The Second Jungle Book* and *Stalky and Co.* (1899), Conan Doyle's *The Memoirs of Sherlock Holmes* (1894), F. Anstey's *Vice Versa* (1882) and Jerome K. Jerome's *Three Men in a Boat* (1889).

p. 30 *the Savoy operas*: Richard Usborne says that there are 172 echoes of W. S. Gilbert in Wodehouse's works; Usborne, *Wodehouse at Work to the End* (London, 1976), p. 21.

p. 30 *The first stage show*: PGW to William Townend, 3 March 1952, Dulwich.

p. 30 *'a new and exhilarating experience . . .'*: A. Smith, *Selected Essays and Addresses*, quoted *Concordance*, vol. iii, p. xxv.

p. 31 *Wodehouse learned to write Latin and Greek . . .*: Jasen, *Wodehouse*, p. 17. See also W. R. M. Leake, *Gilkes and Dulwich* (privately printed, London, n.d.).

p. 31 *'a sort of blend . . .'*: 'The Voice from the Past', in *Mulliner Nights* (1933; Everyman, 2003), p. 111.

p. 31 *'It was terrific'*: Jasen, *Wodehouse*, pp. 18–19.

p. 31 *At the age of forty, Ernest Wodehouse . . .*: he would draw a full pension from 1898 to his death in 1929. Some biographers have claimed that Ernest retired prematurely. In fact, it was quite usual for imperial civil servants who had served in gruelling foreign climates to come home in early middle age. See also Frances Donaldson, *P. G. Wodehouse* (London, 1982), p. 41.

p. 31 *to 'get to the only gents' lavatory . . .'*: PGW to William Townend, 2 April 1952, Dulwich.

p. 32 *It would be paltering with the truth . . .*: 'Noblesse Oblige', in *Young Men in Spats* (1936; Everyman, 2002), p. 157.

p. 32 *'visions of shady gardens . . .'*: *Psmith in the City* (1910; Everyman, 2000), p. 38.

p. 32 *several country houses*: these include Weston Park and Sudeley Castle. See N. T. P. Murphy, *In Search of Blandings* (London, 1981), pp. 202–31, for a useful discussion of their place in the Wodehouse *oeuvre*.

p. 32 *'my happiest days . . .'*: preface to *Something Fresh* (1915; London, 1979), p. viii.

p. 33 *'troubles are things . . .'*: *The Pothunters*, p. 69.

p. 33 *'The part played by relations . . .'*: 'Concerning Relations', *Public School Magazine*, March 1901, pp. 232–4.

p. 33 *'I was completely inarticulate . . .'*: PGW and Guy Bolton, *Bring on the Girls* (London, 1953), p. 213.

p. 33 *'one of the most important boys in the school'*: *Performing Flea*, p. 10. PGW returned the compliment in 'Old Bill Townend', in *Weekend Wodehouse* (London, 1939), p. 77.

p. 34 *'I pour out my heart . . .'*: PGW to William Townend, 24 March 1937, Dulwich.

p. 34 *Townend rejected the opportunity . . .*: during the First World War, hindered by his poor sight from full military service, he served in the ambulance corps, and later in Ireland with the Royal Welch Fusiliers. I am indebted to Jan Piggott and various members of the Townend family for their help with William Townend's biography.

p. 34 *a career as a commercial artist*: see 'The Spot of Art', in *Very Good, Jeeves* (London, 1957).

p. 35 *'I feel sort of responsible . . .'*: PGW to Paul Reynolds, 9 September 1920, Reynolds papers, Columbia.

p. 35 *'We talked incessantly . . .'*: Jasen, *Wodehouse*, pp. 18–19.

p. 35 *'a series of plays . . .'*: *Performing Flea*, p. 10.

p. 35 *Wodehouse was never funny to meet*: Richard Usborne, *After Hours with P. G. Wodehouse* (London, 1991), pp. 97–8.

p. 36 *was said by his stepdaughter . . .*: Leonora Wodehouse, 'P. G. Wodehouse at Home', *Strand*, January 1929.

p. 36 *Wodehouse played the part of Guildenstern . . .*: PGW's 'accompanying dance (exact species unknown)', ran the *Alleynian* review, 'was very striking, and the masterly way in which he twirled round the chambers of the revolver to shew Hamlet that it would really work was a very effective piece of by-play'.

p. 36 *his friend Eric 'Jimmy' George*: Eric Beardsworth George (1881–1961), known to PGW as 'Jeames', after a character in Thackeray's *Yellowplush Papers*; private collection and Wodehouse Archive.

p. 36 *'. . . I always knew it'*: PGW to 'Jeames', September 1899, private collection.

p. 36 *'. . . I would join him there'*: *Over Seventy*, p. 19.

p. 36 *'Friend of me boyhood . . .'*: PGW to 'Jeames', undated, private collection.

p. 36 *Only in old age was he fully reconciled*: private communication from Tom Sharpe, 23 August 2003.

p. 37 *For he heard the voice . . .*: *Public School Magazine*, June 1901.

p. 37 *a national joke, as Oscar Wilde . . .*: in *The Importance of Being Earnest*, Miss Prism instructs Cecily Cardew in political economy with the words, 'the chapter on the Fall of the Rupee you may omit. It is somewhat too sensational.'

p. 37 *'The rupee . . .'*: *Over Seventy*, p. 19.

p. 38 *cruelly arbitrating some sibling rivalry*: for speculations on this theme, see Barry Phelps, *P. G. Wodehouse: Man and Myth* (London, 1992), p. 62; and Usborne, *Wodehouse at Work*, p. 53.

p. 38 *'during my schooldays . . .'*: *Over Seventy*, p. 19.

p. 38 *'All through my last term'*: ibid.

p. 38 *Mike looked at him blankly . . .*: *Psmith in the City*, p. 22.

p. 39 *'I didn't want to do it'*: *Over Seventy*, p. 18.

p. 39 *He sat down on a bench . . .*: *Psmith in the City*, p. 29.

p. 39 *'I will have 2 yrs . . .'*: PGW to 'Jeames', undated, Wodehouse Archive.

p. 39 *'Some Aspects of Game Captaincy'*: *Public School Magazine*, February 1900, p. 127.

p. 39 *'Money Received for Literary Work'*: MRFLW.

p. 40 *'Better, I think, to skip childhood . . .'*: *Over Seventy*, p. 18.

CHAPTER 3: 'First-fruits of a GENIUS' (1900–1902)

p. 41 *'Banks . . . have a habit . . .'*: *Psmith in the City* (1910; Everyman, 2000), p. 24.

p. 41 *'The whole system of banking was a horrid mystery'*: ibid., p. 163.

p. 41 *'We are . . . in for a pretty rotten time of it . . .'*: ibid., p. 45.

p. 41 *very lost and forlorn*: PGW to G. O. W. Stewart, 13 November 1965, private collection.

p. 41 *'enjoyed my two years . . .'*: PGW to 'Mr Jones', 15 October 1954, HSBC.

p. 42 *'The difficulty now . . .'*: *Psmith in the City*, pp. 30–31.

p. 42 *To juniors like Wodehouse*: Frank H. H. King, *The History of the Hong Kong and Shanghai Banking Corporation* (Cambridge, 1988), p. 176.

p. 43 *'Conversation in a city office'*: *Psmith in the City*, p. 38.

p. 43 *steaks were ninepence*: see Jonathan Schneer, *London 1900* (New Haven, 1999), p. 68.

p. 43 *'I can still remember . . .'*: PGW to 'Mr Jones', 15 October 1954, HSBC.

p. 43 *a prospect that terrified Wodehouse*: *Over Seventy* (London, 1957), p. 24.

p. 43 *'This ain't a regular bank'*: PGW notebooks, Wodehouse Archive.

p. 43 *'Everybody except me . . .'*: David Jasen, *P. G. Wodehouse: Portrait of a Master* (London, 1975) p. 22.

p. 44 *On Sunday evenings, to save money*: William Townend to Richard Usborne, 22 March 1959, Wodehouse Archive.

p. 44 *'The work in the postage department . . .'*: *Psmith in the City*, p. 37.

p. 44 *'I was just a plain dumb brick'*: *Over Seventy*, pp. 19–24.

p. 44 *Wodehouse progressed steadily*: London standing order books, HSBC.

p. 45 *the informal choral society*: HSBC. See also King, *Hong Kong and Shanghai*, p. 151.

p. 45 *late morning attendance*: London standing order books, HSBC.

p. 45 *'One of the great sights . . .'*: *Over Seventy*, p. 20.

p. 45 *men from Tonbridge . . .*: *Psmith in the City*, p. 91.

p. 45 *Opening words of novel*: PGW notebooks, Wodehouse Archive. PGW's fellow trainee, V. M. Grayburn, who eventually rose to the very top of the bank, had affectionate memories of Wodehouse in 'Outward Bills'; HSBC.

p. 46 *'Jessop's Match'*: see Murray Hedgcock (ed.), *Wodehouse at the Wicket* (London, 1997), p. 13.

p. 46 *A new ledger came . . .*: Something Clever', galley proof, *Punch,* 8 September 1954, HSBC.

p. 47 *'at liberty to embark on the life literary'*: *Over Seventy*, p. 27.

p. 47 *magazines like Tit-Bits*: a highly successful Victorian penny weekly, aimed at the new suburban readership, that had published excerpts from the work of writers such as Thackeray, Scott, Trollope, Carlyle, Macaulay, Verne and Hugo.

p. 47 *'Where can he sell his stories?'*: PGW's list includes the *Royal, Red, Yellow,*

Cassell's, New, Novel, Grand, Pall Mall, Windsor, Blackwood, Cornhill and *Chambers's*; *Performing Flea* (London, 1953), p. 156.

p. 47 '*readers who had never before bought books . . .*': quoted in John Carey, *The Intellectuals and the Masses* (London, 1992), p. 6.

p. 47 *Alfred Harmsworth*: (1865–1922), the greatest of the press barons. He founded the Amalgamated Press in 1887, and launched both the *Daily Mail* (1896) and the *Daily Mirror* (1903). Deranged and megalomaniac, he was made Lord Northcliffe by Lloyd George.

p. 47 '*If Harmsworth pays . . .*': MRFLW, August 1901.

p. 48 '*dismal backwater*': *Ukridge* (London, 1924), p. 43.

p. 48 *glued to his chair*: *Over Seventy*, p. 23.

p. 48 '*I could have papered the walls. . . .*': ibid., p. 21.

p. 48 '*I wrote everything . . .*': Jasen, *Wodehouse*, p. 23.

p. 48 *Nothing was beneath his notice*: the *Weekly Telegraph* paid five shillings for a short article on 'Strange Requests Made of Doctors'; in *Fun*, he published a short poem entitled 'Morning Carol'; *Sandow's Physical Culture Magazine* accepted a piece entitled 'Physical Culture at Dulwich College'; *Answers* magazine took a story under the 'loathsome title' of 'When Papa Swore in Hindustani'; and *Universal and Ludgate Magazine* paid a guinea for a story entitled 'A Highway Episode'; MRFLW, August 1901. The range of PGW's freelance activities during these years is hard to overemphasize.

p. 48 '*Worse bilge . . .*': *Over Seventy*, p. 21.

p. 48 *Bus driver. Been 17 years . . .*: Wodehouse notebooks, Wodehouse Archive.

p. 49 '*I avoided the humorous story*': *Over Seventy*, p. 22.

p. 49 *At Ipswich recently . . .*: 'Men Who Have Missed Their Own Weddings', *Tit-Bits*, 24 November 1900, p. 206.

p. 49 '*rather a bad time*': MRFLW, February 1901.

p. 49 *nineteen short stories*: *Over Seventy*, p. 21.

p. 50 *the Edwardian magazine*: Eileen McIlvaine, Louise Sherby and James H. Heineman (eds.), *P.G. Wodehouse: A Comprehensive Bibliography and Checklist* (New York, 1990), pp. 143–87.

p. 50 '*roughly equivalent to . . . Order of the Garter*': *Over Seventy*, p. 29.

p. 50 *down-at-heel London*: N. T. P. Murphy, *In Search of Blandings* (London, 1981), p. 195.

p. 51 *A hundred years on*: from the *Globe*, 4 October 1904: 'Mr Rider Haggard's "She" was followed by a parody "He", by the author of "It". Mr Kipling has cut out both by a story in his new book entitled "They".'

p. 51 *Typical 'By the Way' paragraphs*: *Globe*, 6 and 11 January 1904. One contemporary at the bank, H. E. Nixon, remembers Wodehouse's brilliant little paragraphs composed in 'moments stolen from odd slack periods in the Inward Bills Dept.'; HSBC.

p. 51 '*They printed 7 of my pars*': MRFLW, September 1901.

p. 51 '*the most complete confidence*': *Over Seventy*, p. 22.

p. 51 *'When in due course Charon ferries me'*: ibid., p. 23.

p. 51 *'The Language of Flowers'*: MRFLW, October 1901.

p. 52 *absence of vanilla chocolate*: *Public School Magazine*, December 1900.

p. 52 *'the rules governing school stories'*: ibid., August 1901.

p. 52 *the only subject he knew*: Jasen, *Wodehouse*, p. 24.

p. 52 *'Awfully funny . . .'*: ibid.

p. 52 *typical of the five*: PGW's public school novels include *A Prefect's Uncle*, *The Gold Bat*, *The Head of Kay's*, *The White Feather* and *Mike*.

p. 53 *The serialization of The Pothunters was cut short . . .*: in the serial version, Wodehouse had to condense the plot of the last three chapters into an explanatory letter from one character to another.

p. 53 *still turning out potboiling articles*: MRFLW, January–March 1902.

p. 53 *a team of journalists*: HSBC.

p. 53 *cast-off frock coat and trousers*: preface to *Joy in the Morning* (London, 1974).

p. 53 *'naughty cousins'*: Queen Elizabeth the Queen Mother to Edward Cazalet, undated, Wodehouse Archive.

p. 53 *As an old lady, Effie . . .*: Wodehouse first met the Bowes-Lyon girls at Stableford: his parents rented The Old House from their uncle, a Mr Corbett.

p. 53 *'I occupy in your house . . .'*: PGW notebooks, Wodehouse Archive.

p. 54 *'marry a rich man'*: PGW notebooks, Wodehouse Archive.

p. 54 *'he used to propose . . .'*: quoted Murphy, *In Search of Blandings*, p. 132.

CHAPTER 4: 'My wild lone' (1902–1904)

p. 56 *'a young man's crossroads'*: PGW to Richard Usborne, 11 January 1952, Wodehouse Archive.

p. 56 *'This month starts my journalistic career'*: MRFLW, September 1902.

p. 56 *'I should think it extremely improbable . . .*: *Over Seventy* (London, 1957), p. 73.

p. 56 *droll smoking-room anecdote*: *Punch*, 17 September 1902, p. 182.

p. 57 *'I can generally improve . . .'*: PGW letter of 8 December 1902, Black.

p. 57 *He hardly ever went out*: David Jasen, *P. G. Wodehouse: Portrait of a Master* (London, 1975), p. 30.

p. 57 *'The early struggles . . .'*: Herbert Westbrook and P. G. Wodehouse, *Not George Washington* (London, 1907), p. 255.

p. 57 *free from the irritating chatter*: information supplied by Norman Murphy, from an interview with PGW's flatmate, Perceval Graves.

p. 57 *eight rejected manuscripts*: John Hayward, interview with Ella King-Hall, 16 March 1939, King's.

p. 58 *sitting at a table*: Jasen, *Wodehouse*, p. 29.

p. 58 *'some good advice . . .'*: ibid.

p. 58 *'Stinker' and 'Sport'*: John Hayward, interview with Ella King-Hall, 16 March 1939, King's.

p. 58 *eventually married her:* King-Hall family information supplied by Cdr. Richard Perceval Maxwell.

p. 59 *never a schoolmaster:* PGW to Richard Usborne, 11 January 1952, Wodehouse Archive.

p. 59 *headmaster breakfasting in bed:* Stephen King-Hall, *My Naval Life* (London, 1952), p. 25.

p. 59 *taking the school on a picnic:* 'Memories of Emsworth House School', *Wooster Sauce*, March 2002, p. 3.

p. 59 *helping Ella King-Hall:* she was no amateur, but had actually composed an Edwardian popular song, 'Forbearance'.

p. 59 *'Wodehouse appeared to keep . . .':* John A. Whitham, unpublished memoir, 1995.

p. 60 *the 'Pink 'Un':* see N. T. P. Murphy, *In Search of Blandings* (London, 1981), pp. 9–29.

p. 60 *'a short, trim, dapper little man . . .':* *Summer Lightning* (1929; Everyman, 2002), p. 26.

p. 60 *The Edwardian London . . .:* see Jerry White, *London in the Twentieth Century* (London, 2001), pp. 3–12.

p. 60 *'a mild, dreamy, absent-minded sort':* *Heavy Weather* (1933; Everyman, 2001), p. 27.

p. 61 *Wodehouse commentators:* Emsworth and Hampshire place-names that occur in the Wodehouse *oeuvre* include: Wickham, Rogate, Liss, Warblington, Hayling, Havant, Bosham, Southbourne and Bognor.

p. 61 *'A prep school in Hampshire . . .':* *Mike at Wrykyn* (1909; London, 1990), p. 29.

p. 61 *'wild lone':* MRFLW, September 1902.

p. 61 *a total of £215 18s. 1d.:* MRFLW, September 1903.

p. 61 *Still, when your ochred . . .:* 'To William (Whom We Have Missed)', *Punch*, 31 December 1902, p. 460.

p. 62 *Though other things . . .:* 'The Coming Saga', *Punch*, 29 July 1903, p. 63. See Peter Dickinson, 'Wodehouse's *Punch* Verse', in James H. Heineman and Donald R. Bensen (eds.), *P. G. Wodehouse: A Centenary Celebration* (New York, 1981), pp. 46–8.

p. 62 *Royal Magazine:* MRFLW, April 1903.

p. 62 *an interview with his literary hero:* V.C., 2 July 1903. The interview displays Wodehouse's instinctive grasp of popular literary taste. 'The public', he wrote, 'likes a man to resemble his books.'

p. 62 *'I shall always remember . . .':* Jasen, *Wodehouse*, pp. 30–31.

p. 62 *'I tell Westbrook . . .':* PGW notebooks, Wodehouse Archive.

p. 63 *'We have crushed the grapes . . .':* ibid.

p. 63 *'probably the best hand':* William Beach Thomas, *The Way of the Countryman* (London, 1944), p. 50.

p. 63 *the hours on the Globe:* ibid.

p. 64 *[Trevor] was looking forward . . .:* *The Gold Bat* (London, 1904), p. 213.

p. 64 *In the aftermath of the Boer War:* see Barbara Tuchman, *The Proud Tower* (New York, 1966), pp. 354–6.

p. 64 '*If you are to give preference* . . .': Parl. Debs. (series 4), vol. 123, col. 185 (28 May 1903).

p. 65 *Where the Cobden Club relaxes* . . .: *The Parrot and Other Poems* (London, 1988), p. 17.

p. 65 *Up at Oxford* . . .: *Daily Express*, 3 November 1903.

p. 66 *Dan Leno:* S. N. Behrman, *Portrait of Max* (New York, 1960), p. 159.

p. 67 *There can be no doubt that* . . .: *Daily Express*, 18 December 1903.

p. 67 '*One owner struck a sinister note* . . .': ibid.

p. 67 '*The parrot is dead*': ibid., 21 December 1903.

p. 67 *a close, lifelong friendship*: see PGW to Lillian Hill, unpublished correspondence, Emsworth.

CHAPTER 5: 'I have Arrived' (1904–1909)

p. 68 '*Why America?*': *Over Seventy* (London, 1957), pp. 29–32.

p. 68 *intention to visit Philadelphia*: *Alleynian*, February 1900.

p. 68 *heavyweight champion James 'Gentleman Jim' Corbett*: James Corbett, 1866–1933.

p. 68 '*shake the hand* . . .': *Over Seventy*, p. 30.

p. 69 *To say that New York* . . .: like London, the city was in the middle of a period of massive upheaval and reconstruction. The subway was under construction; the Flatiron Building had opened in 1902; Washington Square was undergoing refurbishment.

p. 69 '*worth many guineas* . . .': *MRFLW*, May 1904.

p. 69 '*In 1904, anyone* . . .': *Over Seventy*, p. 38.

p. 69 *he made Herbert Westbrook his deputy*: Westbrook rarely went to the *Globe's* office and posted his contributions from Emsworth. A hint of Wodehouse's irritation at the Westbrook work ethic creeps into his dedication to *The Gold Bat*, published by A. & C. Black in September 1904, 'To that Prince of Slackers, Herbert Westbrook'.

p. 70 *he was paid £60*: *MRFLW*, October 1904.

p. 70 *a witty reworking*: the colour illustrations to this sumptuous volume were by Philip Dadd and the accompanying verses by John W. Houghton, a would-be Gilbert. Those who argue that Wodehouse was obsessed with money point to the many sharp references to 'tax' scattered through the text of this exceedingly rare book. See Tony Ring, *You Simply Hit Them with an Axe: The Extraordinary True Story of the Tax Turmoils of P. G. Wodehouse* (Maidenhead, 1995), pp. 32–6.

p. 70 '*if you had £1 10s.* . . .': PGW to Richard Usborne, 11 January 1952, Wodehouse Archive.

p. 70 '*This is Fame*': *MRFLW*, December 1904.

p. 70 '*always quite at my ease* . . .': PGW notebooks, Wodehouse Archive.

p. 71 *'On this, the 13th December 1904 . . .':* MRFLW, December 1904.

p. 71 *as Evelyn Waugh wrote:* Sunday Times, 16 July 1961.

p. 71 *Wodehouse, sustaining a prodigious output . . .:* in January 1905, in addition to his daily stint at the *Globe*, he made contributions to *Pearson's*, the *Daily Chronicle* ('The Doyen', 'The New Order' and 'A Defence'), *Books of Today* ('New Year Resolutions', 'The Crease') and *Vanity Fair* ('The Road to Success', 'The Rhyme of the Bassinette', 'Mainly about Mush', 'Half Hours with a Ghost'), and noted 'royalties on 4 books' of £7 4s. 2d. MRFLW, January 1905.

p. 71 *A shabby man stops me . . .:* PGW notebooks, Wodehouse Archive.

p. 72 *Miss Congreve, met at Miss B-Ws:* ibid.

p. 72 *'What gory right has he . . .':* PGW to William Townend, 3 March 1905, Dulwich.

p. 73 *'Chapter one is good':* ibid.

p. 73 *Westbrook asks me . . .:* PGW notebooks, Wodehouse Archive.

p. 74 *'I'm a thorough Londoner':* ibid.

p. 74 *a rudimentary dramatis personae:* ibid.

p. 74 *told his French translator:* PGW to Benoît de Fonscolombe, 4 April 1952, Wodehouse Archive.

p. 74 *'that day in Brook's digs':* William Townend to PGW, 16 February 1957, Wodehouse Archive.

p. 75 *'write a book about our life . . .':* William Townend to PGW, 11 November 1952, Wodehouse Archive.

p. 75 *I've thought it all over . . .:* Love among the Chickens (1906; London, 2001), ˆ p. 11. For more details about the factual background to the novel, see *Wooster Sauce*, March 2004, p. 1.

p. 75 *'Ukridge Starts a Bank Account':* Playboy, July 1967, pp. 79, 136–41.

p. 75 *whispering J. B. Pinker:* see Leon Edel, *Henry James: The Treacherous Years* (London, 1969). See also James Hepburn, *The Author's Empty Purse and the Rise of the Literary Agent* (London, 1968).

p. 75 *rubicund, round-faced:* Frank Swinnerton's description, quoted Hepburn, *Author's Empty Purse*, p. 57.

p. 76 *special point of helping:* ibid., p. 58.

p. 76 *conceded that the editor of Fry's Magazine:* PGW to J. B. Pinker, 1 June 1905, Pinker papers, Berg.

p. 76 *Wodehouse hoped that Bill Townend . . .:* PGW told Townend that, contractually, this would be 'an absolutely rigid condition': PGW to William Townend, 3 March 1905, Dulwich.

p. 76 *selling a cricket story:* 'The Wire-Pullers', Strand, July 1905, pp. 29–34.

p. 76 *grand total of £500:* MRFLW, December 1905.

p. 76 *'I have made a sort of corner . . .':* PGW to J. B. Pinker, 16 January 1906, Pinker papers, Berg.

p. 77 *'wonderful summer':* introduction to *Performing Flea* (London, 1953), p. 12.

p. 77 *the Allahakbarries:* see Murray Hedgcock (ed.), *Wodehouse at the Wicket* (London, 1997), pp. 17–25.

p. 77 *long cricketing weekends*: PGW to 'Mollie', 2 August 1905, Ransom.

p. 77 *'My father was a professional cricketer'*: *Performing Flea*, p. 66.

p. 78 *'. . . giving me particular Hell'*: PGW to William Townend, 3 March 1905, Dulwich.

p. 78 *daze of exhilarated happiness*: David Jasen, *P. G. Wodehouse: Portrait of a Master* (London, 1975), p. 36. Hicks was the epitome of theatrical glamour, a West End celebrity who had known and worked with Oscar Wilde, and was also the most successful actor-manager of the Edwardian theatre.

p. 78 *He plays for Aston Villa . . .*: Kurt Ganzl, *The British Musical Theatre 1865–1914*, vol. i (London, 1986), p. 153.

p. 78 *'the little genius'*: David Ewan, *Great Men of American Popular Song* (New York, 1970), pp. 125–7.

p. 79 *'Here, I thought, was a young man . . .'*: Jasen, *Wodehouse*, p. 36.

p. 79 *Kern, for his part, did not forget . . .*: Lee Davis, *Wodehouse and Bolton and Kern: The Men Who Made Musical Comedy* (New York, 1993), pp. 30–31.

p. 79 *'open and happy nature'*: Ellaline Terriss, *Just a Little Bit of String* (London 1955), p. 181; see also *By Herself* (London, 1928).

p. 79 *Behind scenes at Chelsea Palace . . .*: PGW notebooks, Wodehouse Archive.

p. 80 *We all act through life . . .*: ibid.

p. 80 *He crashed the Darracq*: *MRFLW*, November 1906.

p. 80 *New York City in the 1920s*: cf. PGW to William Townend, 28 February 1920 and 27 June 1922, Dulwich.

p. 80 *'cricket, boxing, football, swimming'*: *Who's Who* entry, 1908, Black.

p. 80 *The experience of writing for the theatre*: Norman Murphy notes that between 1904 and 1954, Wodehouse contributed either the book or the lyrics to some fifty-one shows. Murphy has calculated that there are no fewer than eighty theatre characters in his novels, 'split equally between those who appear in novels about the theatre, and theatrical characters with whom other personae of the novels become involved'; N. T. P. Murphy, *In Search of Blandings* (London, 1981), p. 159.

p. 80 *living, salaried actors*: PGW to William Townend, 28 October 1924, Dulwich.

p. 81 *revised as a play (though never performed)*: in a quasi-amateur production, one version was finally performed, titled *Joy in the Morning*, at Ashburnham, Devon, in 1955.

p. 81 *'In addition to verses . . .'*: *Not George Washington* (London, 1907), p. 52.

p. 82 *'Westbrook and I . . .'*: PGW to J. B. Pinker, January 1907, Pinker papers, Berg.

p. 82 *'The central idea . . .'*: PGW to Cassells, 4 August 1907, Pinker papers, Berg.

p. 82 *'as far in that direction'*: PGW to J. B. Pinker, 23 March 1907, Pinker papers, Berg.

p. 82 *My Darling*: I am indebted to Tony Ring for this information. See British Library, 1907 F 690 p (3).

p. 82 *a Footlights May week musical*: Cambridge University Library, MS Tranchell.2.696(1).

p. 82 *contributed two lyrics*: 'Now That My Ship's Come Home' and 'You, You, You'.

p. 82 *walk-on part as a butler*: William Townend to PGW, 21 November 1949, Wodehouse Archive.

p. 82 *'a frost!'*: *MRFLW*, November 1907.

p. 84 *'the p . . . is silent . . .'*: *Leave It to Psmith* (1923; Everyman, 2003), p. 43.

p. 84 *'Psmith . . . is the Knut'*: Richard Usborne, *Wodehouse at Work to the End* (London, 1976), p. 92.

p. 84 *preceded by the 'masher'*: see George Orwell, 'Boys' Weeklies', in *Essays* (London, 1984), p. 87.

p. 84 *'the Beau, the Buck . . .'*: 'The Knuts o' London', *Vanity Fair*, September 1914, p. 43.

p. 85 *'Psmith is a major character . . .'*: PGW to William Townend, 13 May 1936, Dulwich.

p. 85 *'the only thing . . .'*: introduction to *The World of Psmith* (London, 1974).

p. 85 *beautifully dressed and very dignified*: ibid.

p. 85 *'I have made a big hit'*: PGW to J. B. Pinker, 20 January 1909, Pinker papers, Berg.

p. 85 *'Here's a go'*: PGW to William Townend, 6 May 1908, Dulwich.

p. 86 *'story of fun and adventure'*: *The Luck Stone* opens with young Jimmy Stewart alone at home at the end of the summer holidays from Marleigh College, recovering from mumps. His father, 'the Colonel', is big-game hunting in Africa, 'and when his father was away he never saw anybody to speak of during the holidays, except the servants'. A mysterious stranger 'from India' appears with a talisman belonging to the 'Maharajahs of Estapore' for Col. Stewart's safe keeping; *Chums*, September 1908.

p. 86 *three late-Victorian best-sellers*: Usborne, *Wodehouse at Work*, pp. 44–6.

p. 86 *paper-covered shilling books*: *Over Seventy*, p. 73.

p. 86 *Wodehouse the novelist . . .*: I am indebted to Prof. I. F. Clarke's unpublished paper on *The Swoop!* Other invasion-scare titles include *The Shock of Battle*, *The Enemy in Our Midst* and *The Swoop of the Vulture*.

p. 86 *a vigorous 'invasion-scare' literature*: begins with T. W. Offins, *How The Germans Took London* (London, 1900). In the Franco-Prussian War, George Chesney's short story 'The Battle of Dorking' had been the *succès fou* of the 1870s.

p. 86 *The appetite for war fantasies*: see Christopher Andrew, *Secret Service* (London 1985), pp. 37–56. Le Queux's effort was the most ludicrous and also the most popular example of a genre that ranged from distinguished adventure-writing like Erskine Childers' *The Riddle of the Sands* to H. G. Wells's *The War in the Air*.

p. 86 *advertised the story throughout London*: see Barbara Tuchman, *The Proud Tower* (New York, 1966), p. 380.

p. 87 *satirized invasion scares*: 'The Next Invasion', *Punch*, 17 June 1903.

p. 87 *'a great deal of fun . . .'*: *Over Seventy*, p. 73.

p. 87 *The 'bombardment of London'*: 'Thus was London bombarded. Fortunately it was August, and there was nobody in town. Otherwise there might have been loss of life': *The Swoop!* (reissue, New York, 1979), p. 19.

p. 87 *'could spoor, fell trees . . .'*: ibid., p. 4.

p. 88 *'the people who read it . . .'*: *Over Seventy*, p. 73.

p. 88 *'The First Time I Went to New York'*: ed. Theodora Benson (London, 1935), pp. 265–79.

CHAPTER 6: 'I want to butt into the big league' (1909-1914)

p. 89 *'after nineteen days . . .'*: *Over Seventy* (London, 1957), p. 39.

p. 89 *denouncing the devious Baerman*: to Kentucky writer Charles Neville Buck, author of *The Key to Yesterday*, PGW inscribed his copy of *Love among the Chickens* 'Death to Abe!' I gratefully acknowledge Gus Caywood's information.

p. 89 *a new literary agent*: Seth Moyle would be the future biographer of O. Henry.

p. 89 *rapidly sold both stories*: 'The Good Angel' (a humorous love story featuring a comic butler) to *Cosmopolitan* and 'Deep Waters' to *Collier's Weekly*.

p. 89 *'like suddenly finding a rich uncle from Australia'*: *Over Seventy*, p. 39.

p. 89 *Bubbling over with hope*: ibid., pp. 39–42.

p. 89 *'a seedy rookery'*: ibid.

p. 89 *an extraordinary knack*: David Jasen, *P. G. Wodehouse: Portrait of a Master* (London, 1975), p. 44.

p. 90 *'although he could always sell . . .'*: ibid.

p. 90 *His unflattering portrait . . .*: 'You will recognise "Jake" as a blend of Abe Baerman and Seth Moyle', PGW to Paul Reynolds, 5 April 1939, Reynolds papers, Columbia.

p. 90 *There is no question . . .*: 'The First Time I Went to New York', *The First Time I . . .* ed. Theodora Benson (London, 1935), pp. 265–79.

p. 90 *'the slightest, airiest sort . . .'*: *New York Times*, 29 May 1909.

p. 90 *a temperamental beast*: when the company which made the Monarch went out of business, the quest for spare parts became progressively more urgent. Only Wodehouse was allowed near the machine, and whenever he travelled always took charge of the typewriter's welfare. In 1935, the Monarch was replaced by a Royal; PGW to William Townend, 2 December 1935, Dulwich.

p. 91 *'Millionaire humorist . . .'*: George Wilson to PGW, 1 November 1909, Black.

p. 91 *the latest Psmith serialization*: the *Captain's* serialization ran from October 1909 to March 1910.

p. 91 *'The "gangs" of New York . . .'*: preface to *Psmith Journalist* (London, 1915).

p. 91 *'I like de kits and boids'*: Herbert Asbury, *The Gangs of New York* (New York, 1928), pp. 253–76.

p. 91 *Like Eastman . . .*: ibid.

p. 92 *'getting local colour . . .'*: *Captain*, March 1910.

p. 92 *'a second O. Henry'*: ibid.

p. 92 *'Use any public-school stuff . . .'*: PGW to L. H. Bradshaw, undated, May 1910, cited in Richard Usborne, *After Hours with P. G. Wodehouse* (London, 1991), p. 151.

p. 92 *'So far from wanting . . .'*: PGW to L. H. Bradshaw, November 1909, Bradshaw letters, Bradshaw.

p. 93 *'my middle period'*: draft preface to the 1971 edition of *The Man Upstairs*, Wodehouse Archive.

p. 93 *The Black Sheep*: an alternative title was *The Amateur*. It was finally published as *A Gentleman of Leisure* (US: *The Intrusion of Jimmy*).

p. 93 *renewed his lease on Threepwood*: some biographers (Jasen, Donaldson, Phelps) have suggested that PGW now 'bought' Threepwood for £200. This is not so.

p. 93 *a children's tea party*: PGW to 'Bubbles', undated, 1910, private collection.

p. 93 *'The Man Upstairs'*: *Strand*, March 1910.

p. 93 *Handicapped by knowing so little . . .*: *Over Seventy*, p. 46.

p. 93 *'I knew quite a lot . . .'*: ibid.

p. 94 *'nominally ruled over . . . Sir Thomas and Lady Julia Blunt'*: *A Gentleman of Leisure* (London, 1910), p. 61.

p. 94 *'I sort of shuttled . . .'*: Jasen, *Wodehouse*, p. 47.

p. 94 *In the dim cavern . . .*: *Piccadilly Jim* (1917; London, 1969), p. 79.

p. 95 *soothing on-board rituals*: I gratefully acknowledge John Maxtone-Graham's assistance with this paragraph.

p. 95 *There was a long line . . .*: *The Luck of the Bodkins* (1935; Everyman, 2002), p. 193.

p. 95 *started yet another new novel*: PGW to L. H. Bradshaw, 19 January 1911, Bradshaw.

p. 96 *halfway through the narrative . . .*: ibid. This strategy was possible because *Psmith Journalist* had been published as a serial in the *Captain*. Conventionally, the novel should also have appeared in volume form about a year later; in fact, its publication was now delayed until 1915.

p. 96 *he could get it done . . .*: PGW to L. H. Bradshaw, 19 January 1911, Bradshaw.

p. 96 *cheerfully cannibalized his own work*: to add to the textual complexity surrounding this novel a sentimental version of *The Prince and Betty* was published in the UK by Mills and Boon in May 1912.

p. 96 *he was getting good exercise playing soccer with the boys*: PGW to L. H. Bradshaw, 10 February 1911, Bradshaw.

p. 96 *'It will be ripping . . .'*: PGW to L. H. Bradshaw, 3 April 1911, Bradshaw.

p. 96 *the Lusitania, the pride of the Cunard line*: Diana Preston, *Wilful Murder: The Sinking of the Lusitania* (London, 2002), pp. 44–6.

p. 96 *His old sparring-partner*: Jasen, *Wodehouse*, p. 47.

p. 97 *the Authors against the Publishers*: Murray Hedgcock, *Wodehouse at the Wicket* (London, 1997), *passim*.

p. 97 *successive issues of the Strand*: Eileen McIlvaine, Louise Sherby and James H. Heineman (eds.), *P. G. Wodehouse: A Comprehensive Bibliography and Checklist* (New York, 1990), D133, 13, 14, 15.

p. 97 *'ginger up' Seth Moyle*: PGW to L. H. Bradshaw, 26 January 1912, Bradshaw.

p. 97 *The Little Nugget*: at the same time, he cancelled a planned trip to New York, to concentrate on dramatizing *The Little Nugget*, a project that languished for months and came to nothing. PGW to L. H. Bradshaw, 22 November 1912, Bradshaw.

p. 97 *After the Show*: see John Hayward papers, Kings.

p. 97 *Reggie Pepper*: Pepper is the prototype silly ass, or 'drone' (a term popularized by *The Drone*, a play by another young Englishman in New York, Guy Bolton, that had just opened at the 39th Street Theater).

p. 97 *'a chap who's supposed to be . . .'*: 'Disentangling Old Percy', *Strand*, August 1912.

p. 98 *The dim-witted upper-class stereotype*: see Jonathan Cecil, 'Bertie Wooster and the Silly Ass Tradition', *Wooster Sauce*, June 2002. See also *Concordance*, vol. vi, *passim*.

p. 98 *'full of Berties'*: BBC television interview, October 1971.

p. 98 *moonlighting for Punch's 'Charivaria' column*: with occasional digs at contemporary highbrow culture: 'Asbestos pockets for the accommodation of lighted pipes and cigars have been invented by an American tailor. Also useful for the modern novel'; *Punch*, 26 February 1913, p. 153.

p. 98 *write and rewrite till all the punch was lost*: PGW to L. H. Bradshaw, 6 May 1913, Bradshaw.

p. 98 *'I never saw such notices'*: PGW to L. H. Bradshaw, 6 May 1913, Bradshaw.

p. 98 *he had mastered the deadly practice . . .*: see preface to *The Man with Two Left Feet* (1917; London, 1971): 'Shortly after my arrival in New York an editor . . . [rejecting a story] told me he thought I would eventually amount to something. "But", he added, "don't try to write like everyone else." I did not take his advice. I knew better . . . I was mistaken.'

p. 99 *'I have started in already on a new novel. . .'*: PGW to L. H. Bradshaw, 6 May 1913, Bradshaw.

p. 99 *closed after only seven performances*: their series 'A Man of Means' was sold to the *Strand* and ran April–September 1914.

p. 99 *Alice Dovey*: PGW to L. H. Bradshaw, 13 May 1913, Bradshaw.

p. 100 *'anything in the nature of a sex joke'*: George Orwell, 'In Defence of P. G. Wodehouse', in Peter Davison (ed.), *The Complete Works of George Orwell* (London, 1998), vol. xvii, pp. 51-63.

p. 100 *Not only is there hardly any reference*: in a letter to Hesketh Pearson about his biography of Oscar Wilde, Wodehouse wrote, 'What a weird thing sexual perversion is. It seems something absolutely apart from the rest of a man's nature'; PGW to Hesketh Pearson, 16 June 1946, Wodehouse Archive.

p. 100 *the critic Christopher Hitchens*: see C. Hitchens, 'Between Waugh and Wodehouse', in Zachary Leader (ed.), *On Modern British Fiction* (Oxford, 2002), pp. 45–59.

p. 100 *a sensational case whose lurid details . . .*: see Graham Robb, *Strangers* (London, 2003), pp. 35–8.

p. 101 *'not a process for prolonging . . .'*: *The Small Bachelor* (1927; London, 1987), p. 53.

p. 101 *Broadly autobiographical*: see Usborne, *After Hours*, pp. 146–53.

p. 101 *Rutherford [Maxwell]'s salary . . .*: *The Man Upstairs* (1914; London, 1960), p. 276.

p. 102 *'Why don't you make your fortune . . .'*: ibid., p. 282.

p. 102 *'Don't you ever let up . . .'*: ibid., p. 284

p. 102 *'night after night . . .'*: ibid., pp. 287–8.

p. 102 *'Suddenly an intense desire . . .'*: ibid., p. 291.

p. 103 *the solitary hours of composition*: undated draft preface to *The Man Upstairs*, Wodehouse Archive.

p. 103 *'I love you, Peggy!'*: *The Man Upstairs*, p. 297.

p. 103 *'Life at present'*: PGW to L. H. Bradshaw, undated, September 1914, Bradshaw.

CHAPTER 7: 'An angel in human form' (1914-1915)

p. 107 *Wodehouse hardly ever referred to the First World War*: in an interview to promote the American edition of *Something Fresh*, Wodehouse argued that the democratizing effects of war would break down the class barriers of the English joke. See 'War Will Restore England's Sense of Humour', *New York Times Magazine*, 7 November 1915.

p. 107 *'How's the weather, Jeeves?'*: 'Jeeves in the Springtime' (first published in December 1921 in *Cosmopolitan* (USA) and *Strand* (UK), appears in *The Inimitable Jeeves* (London, 1923) as 'Jeeves Exerts the Old Cerebellum' and 'No Wedding Bells for Bingo'.

p. 107 *Furious, the officer called them over*: see Lawrence James, *The Rise and Fall of the British Empire* (London, 1995), pp. 346–7.

p. 108 *'This is a war of kings'*: see David Nasaw, *Hearst* (London, 2002), p. 241.

p. 108 *he did belatedly register for the draft*: PGW finally registered for military service on 12 September 1918. I gratefully acknowledge the assistance of Murray Hedgcock with this important new detail.

p. 108 *'age sixty-three, sole support of wife'*: PGW to William Townend, 18 February 1920, Dulwich.

p. 108 *with a touring repertory company*: William Townend to McCulloch 'Slacker' Christison, 16 May 1945, Dulwich.

p. 109 *'with a touch of Lady Macbeth thrown in'*: Malcolm Muggeridge, *Chronicles of Wasted Time* (London, 1973), vol. ii, pp. 255–6.

p. 109 *Ethel Newton was born . . .*: see PGW–Ethel Wayman marriage certificate, 30 September 1914, Little Church Around the Corner, New York City.

p. 109 *he died in obscure circumstances*: David Jasen, *P. G. Wodehouse: Portrait of a Master* (London, 1975), p. 52 attributes Rowley's death to 'drinking infected water', i.e. cholera.

p. 109 *Wayman went bankrupt*: John Wayman: Bankruptcy Petition, *London Gazette*, 3 July 1912, see Barry Phelps, *P. G. Wodehouse: Man and Myth* (London, 1992), p. 269.

p. 110 *It's a known fact that my aunt Julia . . .*: 'Extricating Young Gussie', in *The Man with Two Left Feet* (London, 1917), pp. 29–30.

p. 110 *courtship with its romantic visits to Long Island*: Jasen, *Wodehouse*, p. 53.

p. 110 *Long Island Railroad*: in those days the LIRR took its passengers down to the beach. PGW would later make affectionate reference to the Long Island Railroad in 'The Enchanted Train':

> There's a train that pulls out in the twilight,
> Quite the best on the list of all trains that exist . . .
> Dear magic train that brings you home again
> How I shall wish it could fly!

(*Sitting Pretty*, 1924).

p. 110 *'I remember bathing once . . .'*: Jasen, *Wodehouse*, p. 52.

p. 111 *youthful agonies of 'clap'*: PGW to Guy Bolton, 16 October 1959, Wodehouse Archive.

p. 111 *'The funny part . . .'*: PGW to L. H. Bradshaw, 1 September 1914, Bradshaw.

p. 111 *'Look here,' exploded Ginger . . .*: *The Adventures of Sally* (1922; London, 1986), p. 234.

p. 112 *'Dear little, dear little Church . . .*: 'The Church 'Round the Corner', a lyric in *Sally* (1920), a musical which is itself based on an unproduced Bolton and Wodehouse musical, 'The Little Thing'.

p. 112 *. . . he had yet to meet*: 'I have a little stepdaughter! I have not met her yet, but I hear she is delightful'; PGW to Lillian Hill, 2 December 1914, Emsworth.

p. 112 *'Excuse delay . . .'*: PGW to L. H. Bradshaw, 1 October 1914, private collection, Bradshaw.

p. 112 *Self-control came naturally*: by later standards, Wodehouse and his circle of ex-public schoolboys were astonishingly ill-informed about sex. Guy Bolton, a notorious gossip, liked to tell the story of Bill Townend, who, after several months of marriage, went to see his doctor and said, 'We have a perfect marriage. We go to dinner parties etc and walk the dog together. My friends tell me there is more to married life than this, but won't say what it is.' The doctor asked if he and his wife did anything in bed. Townend was bewildered. 'What should we do in bed?' The doctor gave him a book of sexual instruction and told him to read it. Townend returned after three months in a terrible state. 'Doctor, you've got to do something. We've followed the instructions in that awful book, and we find the whole business disgusting.' The doctor advised Townend to forget the whole subject, and they lived happily ever after. Tom Sharpe, letter to the author, 24 July 2001.

p. 113 *'a terror to work for'*: interviews with David Jasen, Patrick Wodehouse and Edward Cazalet.

p. 113 *'The right way of looking at marriage . . .'*: *Piccadilly Jim* (1917; London, 1969), p. 88.

p. 113 *'The only way of ensuring . . .'*: *Uncle Fred in the Springtime* (1939; Everyman, 2004), p. 225.

p. 113 *'an angel in human form'*: preface to *Something Fresh* (1915; London, 1979), p. vii.

p. 113 *'my best pal and severest critic'*: Jasen, *Wodehouse*, p. 98.

pp. 113–14 *he confided the nitty-gritty*: the opening lines of the following letter, written when Leonora was just sixteen, are typical: 'Darling Snorkles, We beat Sherborne yesterday after a very hot game, so that we wound up the season with five wins and one defeat. Pretty hot! I forgot to tell you in my last letter of the laughable imbroglio – or mix-up – which has occurred with Jerry Kern. You remember I sent my lyrics over, and then read in *Variety* that some other cove was doing the lyrics . . . I now hear that Jerry is bringing an action against me'; PGW to Leonora Wodehouse, 20 May 1921, Wodehouse Archive.

p. 114 *Leonora would grow up to be . . .*: see Godfrey Wynn, *The Infirm Glory* (London, 1967), pp. 298–301.

p. 114 *a variety of pseudonyms*: 'J. Walker Williams' was taken from America's celebrated Negro crosstalk act Walker and Williams. 'C. P. West' was inspired by PGW's apartment on Central Park West. 'Melrose Grainger' probably came from PGW's address in Bellport, Melrose Grange; he used this pseudonym to recycle a chapter from *Love among the Chickens* into a short story, 'The Eighteenth Hole', for *Vanity Fair*.

p. 114 *'hasty dashes'*: PGW to L. H. Bradshaw, 24 October 1914, Bradshaw.

p. 114 *'We have two cats . . .'*: PGW to Lillian Hill, 2 December 1914, Emsworth.

p. 114 *'Knowing me . . .'*: ibid.

p. 115 *his sweater, his heavy boots*: ibid.

p. 115 *After the publication of The Man Upstairs . . .*: in May, *Munsey's Magazine* had published a one-shot commissioned novel, 'The White Hope', published later as *The Coming of Bill* (US: *Their Mutual Child*), but Wodehouse knew that it was inferior work. In the theatre, there was frustrating talk about a dramatization of *The Little Nugget*, and Lawrence Grossmith was still hoping to stage a New York production of *Brother Alfred*, despite its failure in London. But both these projects had moved forward with agonizing slowness. 'Theatrical business makes me sick,' he exclaimed in his letter to Lillian Hill (2 December 1914, Emsworth). In addition to these irritations, he was plagued with agent trouble (he was using a 'hopeless incompetent', a Mrs Wilkening, at this time). Dealing with magazine editors was a nightmare, and good plots were always hard to come by. 'I have to have an author-proof plot,' he told Bradshaw, 'or I'm no good.' See also PGW to David Magee, 14 July 1964, quoted in Eileen McIlvaine, Louise Sherby and James H. Heineman (eds.), *P. G. Wodehouse: A Comprehensive Bibliography and Checklist* (New York, 1990), p. 34. He expressed the same opinion to a correspondent, Mrs Carroll, on 18 May 1965: '*The White Hope* was a very early one and I am not very proud of it. It was written to a plot suggested to me by Bob Davis . . . and needing the money badly I wrote it, though it wasn't my sort of story at all'; private collection.

p. 115 *'the war has sent . . .'*: PGW to Lillian Hill, 2 December 1914, Emsworth.

p. 115 *'Ethel has come out very strong . . .'*: PGW to L. H. Bradshaw, 24 October 1914, Bradshaw.

p. 115 *he was going to hit the jackpot*: *Over Seventy* (London, 1957), p. 46.

p. 115 *'the time of my life'*: PGW to William Townend, 9 February 1933, Dulwich.

p. 115 *'I have been working . . .'*: PGW to L. H. Bradshaw, 20 January 1915, Bradshaw.

p. 116 *'some of the funniest knockabout stuff'*: in its first serialization, parts of the novel were lifted, almost word for word, from *Mike*.

p. 116 *'From the restaurant . . .'*: *Something Fresh*, p. 47.

p. 116 *Wafted through the sunlit streets . . .*: ibid., p. 37.

p. 116 *We may say what we will . . .*: ibid., p. 44.

p. 117 *Kitchen maids . . .*: ibid., p. 96.

p. 117 *'Listen to me, Joan'*: ibid., p. 236.

p. 117 *'it seems to be one of those masterpieces'*: PGW to George Wilson, 28 March 1915, Black.

p. 117 *'didn't make one windy promise . . .'*: PGW to L. H. Bradshaw, 20 January 1915, Bradshaw.

p. 118 *His massive correspondence with Wodehouse*: see Reynolds papers, *passim* Columbia.

p. 118 *George Lorimer at the Saturday Evening Post*: Lorimer had transformed the *Post*'s circulation, from 1 million in 1908 to 2 million in 1919. When he retired in 1936, the magazine was selling 3 million copies. This was Wodehouse's regular American audience.

p. 118 *'an autocrat all right . . .'*: *Performing Flea* (London, 1953), p. 157.

p. 118 *'I had twenty-one serials in the Post'*: not true: PGW had just fourteen serials in the *Post*.

p. 118 *'these struggles ceased abruptly'*: *Over Seventy*, p. 70.

p. 119 *between seventy and eighty theatres*: Brooks Atkinson, *Broadway* (New York, 1970), pp. 167–77.

p. 119 *appetite for musicals*: one star-struck couple from Iowa was reported to have seen no fewer than twenty-nine shows in ten days.

p. 119 *part of the Herbert Reynolds song*: the American version of the song is 'Package of Seeds'; it was used again in *Oh, Boy!* in 1917. *90 in the Shade* opened at the Knickerbocker Theater on 25 January 1915 and ran for forty performances. See *Vanity Fair*, April 1915, p. 43.

p. 119 *another 'farce comedy in two acts'*: derived from a successful 1906 English comedy *Mr Popple of Ippleton*.

p. 119 *When we get to New York . . .*: *Uneasy Money* (1917; London, 1958), p. 189.

p. 120 *On the Sunday*: *Performing Flea*, pp. 91–2.

p. 120 *the dead included . . .*: see Diana Preston, *Wilful Murder: The Sinking of the Lusitania* (London, 2002), pp. 139–40.

p. 120 *I find it curious . . .*: introduction to *The World of Jeeves* (London, 1967).

p. 121 *'It was the soft cough of Jeeves's'*: *Joy in the Morning* (1974; Everyman, 2002), p. 177.

p. 121 *'Jeeves doesn't exactly smile . . .'*: *Joy in the Morning*, p. 190.

p. 121 *Wodehouse scholars*: see Phelps, *Wodehouse*, pp. 140–41; Richard Usborne, *Wodehouse at Work to the End* (London, 1976), pp. 223–38; and Frances Donaldson, *P. G. Wodehouse* (London, 1982), pp. 107–8.

p. 121 *Ruggles of Red Gap*: see Kristin Thompson, *Wooster Proposes, Jeeves Disposes* (New York, 1992), p. 121.

p. 122 *He told Lawrence Durrell*: PGW to Lawrence Durrell, 19 May 1948, Southern Illinois University Library.

p. 122 *In the early Jeeves stories*: Thompson, *Wooster Proposes*, p. 98.

p. 122 *'I must get a character . . .'*: *Performing Flea*, p. 83.

p. 123 *'I started writing about Bertie Wooster . . .'*: PGW to Denis Mackail, 11 August 1951, Wodehouse Archive.

p. 123 *Very Good Eddie*: in the Broadway fashion of the time, this show took its title from the popular catchphrase in a recent hit show, in which the comedian Fred Stone had played a ventriloquist whose stock response to his on-stage dummy had been 'Very good, Eddie'.

p. 123 *The Princess Theater*: it was not unique, but like the Belmont, the Punch and Judy and the Little theatres.

p. 123 *'dear, kindly, voluminous Bessie Marbury'*: PGW and Guy Bolton, *Bring on the Girls* (London, 1953), p. 5.

p. 123 *'devoid of all vulgarity'*: Elizabeth Marbury, *My Crystal Ball* (New York, 1920), pp. 252–7.

p. 123 *embark on a collaboration*: see Benny Green, *P. G. Wodehouse: A Literary Biography* (London, 1981), pp. 100–104.

CHAPTER 8: 'Musical comedy was my dish' (1916-1918)

p. 124 *They liked to tell the story*: *Bring on the Girls* (London, 1953), p. 7–12.

p. 124 *'To Kern's for supper'*: ibid., p. 18.

p. 124 *'We shall have to let truth go to the wall . . .'*: PGW to Guy Bolton, 4 November 1952, Wodehouse Archive.

p. 124 *Wodehouse already knew Kern*: he had reviewed *Nobody Home* for *Vanity Fair* in September, while the Broadway press reported a forthcoming Bolton, Wodehouse and Kern musical in November; *Dramatic Mirror*, 27 November 1915.

p. 125 *a mature and distinctive identity*: see Andrew Lamb, *150 Years of Popular Musical Theater* (New Haven, 2000), pp. 133–70.

p. 125 *Kern, 'the American Schubert'*: the description is the musicologist Steven Blier's.

p. 126 *Where a big Broadway production . . .*: Lee Davis, *Wodehouse and Bolton and Kern: The Men Who Made Musical Comedy* (New York, 1993), pp. 99–149.

p. 126 *Schuyler Greene*: ibid., pp. 87–92.

p. 127 *'Guy and I clicked . . .'*: *Performing Flea* (London, 1953), p. 14.

p. 127 *their collaboration was conducted*: Max Wilk, *They're Playing Our Song: Conversations with America's Songwriters* (New York, 1991), p. 34.

p. 127 *W. S. Gilbert had always said . . .*: David Jasen, *P. G. Wodehouse: Portrait of a Master* (London, 1975), p. 69.

p. 128 *I think you get the best results. . .*: ibid.

p. 128 *'How did you find out?'*: there are several versions of this story, which may be apocryphal.

p. 129 *'Musical comedy was my dish . . .'*: *Over Seventy* (London, 1957), p. 169.

p. 129 *'not a bit interested in music . . .'*: Leonora Wodehouse, 'P. G. Wodehouse at Home', *Strand*, January 1929.

p. 129 *put the telephone on the piano*: ibid.

p. 129 *Here, a composer . . .*: *Jill the Reckless* (London, 1921), pp. 253–4. *Jill the Reckless* was published in the USA as *The Little Warrior*.

p. 130 *a czar of the American theatre*: *Bring on the Girls*, p. 13.

p. 130 *'Episode of the Dog McIntosh'*: *Very Good, Jeeves* (London, 1957), p. 110.

p. 130 *'We don't have nothing little . . .'*: Davis, *Bolton and Wodehouse and Kern*, p. 104.

p. 131 *'Miss Springtime is a corker'*: *Vanity Fair*, December 1916.

p. 131 *had already caused the wolf . . .*: *Vanity Fair*, March 1917.

p. 131 *linked his massive Monarch typewriter*: the story is told in Guy Bolton's 'Working with Wodehouse', in Thelma Cazalet-Keir (ed.), *Homage to P. G. Wodehouse* (London, 1973), pp. 103–14. It is further mythologized in Douglas Adams's introduction to *Sunset at Blandings* (London, 2000), pp. xi–xii.

p. 131 *three more Jeeves stories*: 'Jeeves and the Unbidden Guest', Jeeves and the Hardboiled Egg' and 'Jeeves and the Chump Cyril'.

p. 131 *'the most wonderful child on earth'*: dedication to *Piccadilly Jim* (London, 1917).

p. 131 *When Leonora returned to school . . .*: the Wodehouses' movements are sometimes hard to follow during the early years of their marriage. Summers were spent on Long Island, but they wintered at 375 Central Park West, and spent part of the autumn of 1917 in the Beaux Arts Building near 41st Street. Wodehouse himself often wrote from other people's apartments, ships and hotels.

p. 132 *the mistress of William Randolph Hearst*: see David Nasaw, *Hearst* (London, 2002), p. 256.

p. 132 *to paraphrase Oscar Hammerstein*: Davis, *Wodehouse and Bolton and Kern*, p. 124.

p. 132 *As the musicologist Steven Blier has noted*: private communication. I gratefully acknowledge Steven Blier's assistance with this chapter.

p. 133 *a nice line in nice lines*: see Brooks Atkinson, *Broadway* (New York, 1970), p. 167.

p. 133 *'The excellence of Miss Springtime. . .'*: *New York Tribune*, 27 May 1917.

p. 133 *The Princess sold out*: six months later Comstock moved the show to the much bigger Casino Theater, where it completed a run of some 475 (estimates vary; some say 463) performances.

p. 134 *the potential of the series*: 'You can't write a series bang off . . . In 1916 I wrote the first Jeeves story. About a year later I wrote another. But it wasn't until I had done about six at long intervals that I realised I had got a series-character'; PGW to William Townend, 18 September 1935, Dulwich.

p. 134 *'The fellow who does the words . . .'*: 'On the Writing of Lyrics', *Vanity Fair*, June 1917.

p. 134 *'Every time I meet Guy Bolton . . .'*: ibid., September 1916.

p. 134 *no fewer than five shows running simultaneously*: *Bring on the Girls*, p. 76.

p. 134 *'a dead and gone turkey'*: *Bring on the Girls*, p. 249.

p. 135 *This is the way I see it . . .*: 'Fixing It for Freddie', in *Carry On, Jeeves* (1925; London, 1999), pp. 191–2.

p. 136 *As I recall . . .*: *Right Ho, Jeeves* (1934; Everyman, 2000), p. 13.

p. 136 *'everything is as rocky . . .'*: *Piccadilly Jim* (1917; London, 1969), p. 63.

p. 136 *At different spots . . .*: ibid., p. 107.

p. 137 *an unexpected hit*: Guy Bolton dramatized it in 1918. It was made into a silent movie in 1919; in 1934 film rights were sold to MGM for $5,000.

p. 137 *sale of more than 2,000 copies*: see PGW to William Townend, 1 April 1927, Dulwich; actually, about 9,000 copies in the British market.

p. 137 *'a monstrous freak with one verse . . .'*: 'Writing the Show at the Century', *Vanity Fair*, December 1917.

p. 138 *'Bill', the lyric for which . . .*: the number eventually found its way into Kern's landmark musical, *Show Boat*, in 1927.

p. 138 *Well, Wodehouse and Bolton . . .*: Dorothy Parker, 'A Succession of Musical Comedies', *Vanity Fair*, April 1918.

p. 139 *'I find I can do a lot of work here'*: PGW to Lillian Hill, 20 June 1918, Emsworth.

p. 139 *'If only I'd taken up golf . . .'*: Jasen, *Wodehouse*, p. 77.

p. 139 *'a stodgy and colourless Englishman'*: 'Crowninshield in the Cubs' Den', *Vogue*, 15 September 1944.

p. 139 *Wodehouse shut himself away*: Davis, *Wodehouse and Bolton and Kern*, pp. 150–51.

p. 140 *'The Land Where the Good Songs Go'*: from the musical *Miss 1917*, music by Jerome Kern.

p. 140 *'the pathfinder for Larry Hart . . .'*: Alan Jay Lerner, *The Street Where I Live* (London, 1978), p. 253.

p. 141 *Oh, My Dear!*: opened at the Princess on 27 November 1918.

p. 141 *Dorothy Parker wrote that . . .*: Davis, *Wodehouse and Bolton and Kern*, p. 197.

p. 141 *The defeated Kaiser . . .*: see Richard Usborne, 'Native Woodnotes Wild', in James H. Heineman and Donald R. Bensen (eds.), *P. G. Wodehouse: A Centenary Celebration* (New York, 1981), pp. 73–4.

p. 141 *Robert Lansing*: see Margaret MacMillan, *Peacemakers* (London, 2001), p. 11.

p. 141 *A Damsel in Distress*: the novel was twice made into a movie. The 1920 version was silent; in 1937 it was remade, starring Fred Astaire and Joan Fontaine, and with music and lyrics by George and Ira Gershwin.

CHAPTER 9: 'A bloke called Bertie Wooster' (1918–1923)

p. 142 *'the P. G. Wodehouse manner'*: PGW to Leonora Wodehouse, 7 August 1920, Wodehouse Archive.

p. 142 *'rather a blood these days'*: ibid.

p. 142 *never missing a day*: *Over Seventy* (London, 1957), p. 126; see also Walter Camp, 'Keeping Young at Forty', *Collier's*, 5 June 1920.

p. 142 *'watching humanity at work and play . . .'*: *Strand*, December 1921.

p. 142 *'I am much the same'*: PGW to William Townend, 28 February 1920, Dulwich.

p. 142 *'I'm not arrested . . .'* ibid.

p. 143 *Kipling and Conan Doyle*: see Andrew Lycett, *Rudyard Kipling* (London, 1999), and Daniel Stashower, *Teller of Tales: The Life of Arthur Conan Doyle* (London, 1999).

p. 143 *My Man Jeeves*: the four Jeeves stories are 'The Artistic Career of Corky', 'The Aunt and the Sluggard', 'Jeeves and the Unbidden Guest' and 'Jeeves and the Hard-boiled Egg'. All appear in *Carry On, Jeeves* (1925; London, 1999).

p. 143 *The Coming of Bill*: published in the USA as *Their Mutual Child*.

p. 143 *'a real dream boat . . .'* PGW and Guy Bolton, *Bring on the Girls* (London, 1953), p. 137.

p. 143 *Arthur Somers Roche*: the author of *The Eyes of the Blind*.

p. 144 *the big source of his income*: *Performing Flea* (London, 1953), p. 14.

p. 144 *'without a dude character . . .'*: PGW to Leonora Wodehouse, 27 September 1920, Wodehouse Archive.

p. 144 *'to rhyme with Bluffinghame'*: *Indiscretions of Archie* (1922; London, 1963), p. 19.

p. 144 *'Directly I was demobbed . . .'*: ibid., p. 10.

p. 144 *'It seemed to him as though New York . . .'*: ibid., p. 22.

p. 145 *'in the recent unpleasantness in France . . .'*: ibid., p. 101.

p. 145 *'the blood of generations . . .'* ibid., p. 119.

p. 145 *I did pick up a few . . .*: ibid., p. 153.

p. 145 *the designs of some twenty fiancées*: see *Concordance*, vol. vi, pp. 174–5, for the full catalogue which, notoriously, includes Daphne Braythwayt, Gwladys Pendlebury, Pauline Stoker, Cynthia Wickhammersley, Florence Craye, Honoria Glossop and, *fiancée-en-chef*, Madeline Bassett.

p. 145 *'The Haileybury match . . .'*: PGW to Leonora Wodehouse, 24 November 1920, Wodehouse Archive.

p. 145 *'confidential secretary and adviser'*: PGW to Leonora Wodehouse, 1 January 1921, Wodehouse Archive.

p. 145 *'Oh, by the way . . .'*: PGW to Leonora Wodehouse, 27 September 1920, Wodehouse Archive.

p. 146 *'Great excitement last night'*: PGW to Leonora Wodehouse, 24 November 1920, Wodehouse Archive.

p. 146 *busy moulding the Archie stories*: which were appearing in both the *Strand*, and *Cosmopolitan* in New York.

p. 147 *'I don't suppose the action . . .'*: PGW to Leonora Wodehouse, 28 November 1920, Wodehouse Archive.

p. 147 *'I'm off tomorrow . . .'*: PGW to William Townend, 21 February 1921, Dulwich. Occasionally, his inability to turn down a new commission led to crises. In March 1921 he found himself besieged in New York with offers to do a play, and returned to Britain to discover that four separate jobs had collided. In addition to a commitment to write some new lyrics for *The Blue Mazurka*, Col. Henry Savage's production of Franz Lehár's *Die blaue Mazur* (never performed), and a final script of *The Golden Moth*, he was being asked to revise a new novel, *The Girl on the Boat*, for *Woman's Home Companion*, and complete another, *The Adventures of Sally*, for serialization in *Collier's* (this last was published in the USA as *Mostly Sally*).

p. 147 *'On a novel . . .'*: PGW to William Townend, 28 February 1920, Dulwich.

p. 147 *wrote the delighted Mackail a fan letter*: PGW to Denis Mackail, 13 May 1921, Wodehouse Archive.

p. 147 *'he provided a considerable banquet . . .'*: Denis Mackail, *Life with Topsy* (London, 1942), p. 40.

p. 148 *Denis and his wife Diana*: see Ann Thwaite, *A. A. Milne: His Life* (London, 1990), pp. 391–3.

p. 148 *some new Jeeves stories*: these would become 'Jeeves Exerts the Old Cerebellum', 'No Wedding Bells for Bingo', 'The Pride of the Woosters Is Wounded', 'The Hero's Reward', 'Introducing Claude and Eustace', 'Sir Roderick Comes to Lunch', 'Comrade Bingo' and 'Bingo Has a Bad Goodwood'.

p. 148 *'a great rush of ideas . . .'*: PGW to Leonora Wodehouse, 21 December 1921, Wodehouse Archive.

p. 148 *'got out the plot of a new Jeeves story . . .'*: PGW to Leonora Wodehouse, 24 January 1922, Wodehouse Archive.

p. 148 *he would hide in the shrubbery of the school drive*: Frances Donaldson, *P. G. Wodehouse* (London, 1982), p. 124.

p. 149 *this second sequence of Jeeves and Wooster stories*: Kristin Thompson, *Wooster Proposes, Jeeves Disposes* (New York, 1992) pp. 159–203.

p. 149 *'Jeeves,' I said . . .*: 'The Pride of the Woosters Is Wounded', in *The Inimitable Jeeves* (1923; London, 1999), pp. 47–8.

p. 150 *The Inimitable Jeeves*: published as *Jeeves* in the USA in September 1923.

p. 150 *'I've found that writing musical comedy'*: PGW to William Townend, 29 December 1922, Dulwich.

p. 150 *'I think I'll do a series about Ukridge'*: PGW to William Townend, 27 June 1922, Dulwich.

p. 151 *'an epoch in my literary career . . .'*: introduction to *The Clicking of Cuthbert* (1932; Everyman, 2002), p. 9. The collection was published in the USA as *Golf without Tears*.

p. 151 *Golf links, especially the Sound View*: see *Concordance*, vol. i, pp. 143–9.

p. 151 *'the best golf-story I have ever done'*: PGW to William Townend, 24 August 1923, Dulwich.

p. 151 *the mid-1920s*: *The Heart of a Goof* (US: *Divots*) was published in April 1926.

p. 151 *Plummie, quite oblivious . . .*: George Grossmith, *'GG'* (London, 1933), pp. 175–7.

p. 152 *'Honestly, old egg . . .'*: PGW to Leonora Wodehouse, 20 September 1922, Wodehouse Archive.

p. 152 *the Duncan sisters*: see *Bring on the Girls*, pp. 156–8.

p. 152 *'I am weeping tears of blood. . .'*: PGW to William Townend, 16 December 1922, Dulwich.

p. 153 *'a straightforward narrative of . . .'*: *Leave It to Psmith* (1923; Everyman, 2003), pp. 257–8.

p. 153 *'that amiable and boneheaded peer'*: ibid., p. 11.

p. 153 *the significant variations in the text*: Wodehouse revised the ending first published in the *Saturday Evening Post* in March 1923 for the UK publication of the novel. For further details, see *Concordance*, vol. v, pp. 163–4.

p. 153 *'I have improved my golf. . .'*: PGW to Denis Mackail, 20 May 1923, Wodehouse Archive.

p. 153 *'Playing to a handicap of sixteen . . .'*: preface to *The Heart of a Goof*, p. xiii.

p. 153 *The Beauty Prize*: this was initially known as 'The First Prize'.

p. 153 *Lord and Lady Ilchester*: see David Jasen, *P. G. Wodehouse: Portrait of a Master* (London, 1975), p. 97.

p. 154 *Herbert Jenkins . . . had died*: PGW to William Townend, 23 July 1923, Dulwich. The publishing house remained a family business, controlled by John and, later, Derek Grimsdick.

p. 154 *'If I had been a trifle less fit'*: ibid.

p. 154 *a gazelle-like spring*: ibid.

p. 154 *periodical fits of depression*: ibid.

p. 154 *in a perfect agony of boredom*: PGW to William Townend, 24 August 1923, Dulwich.

p. 155 *The British literary diaspora*: see Paul Fussell, *Abroad* (Oxford, 1980), p. 11.

p. 155 *'a rotten piece'*: PGW to Denis Mackail, 5 December 1923, Wodehouse Archive.

p. 155 *'The dickens of a sweat . . .'*: ibid.

p. 155 *mad days of Prohibition*: see Ann Douglas, *Terrible Honesty: Mongrel Manhattan in the 1920s* (New York, 1995), pp. 62–4.

p. 156 *'I believe those stories . . .'*: PGW to Leonora Wodehouse, 14 November 1923, Wodehouse Archive.

p. 156 *Put all your troubles . . .*: the text of the lyric first appears in PGW to Leonora Wodehouse, 23 November 1923.

p. 156 *'America is only for visits'*: PGW to William Townend, 4 November 1923, Dulwich.

p. 156 *'easily the best stuff I have done'*: ibid.

p. 157 *'a sort of comic Uncle Tom's Cabin'*: *Performing Flea*, p. 25.

CHAPTER 10: 'All dizzy with work' (1924-1927)

p. 159 *Bert French . . . died suddenly during rehearsals*: PGW to Leonora Wodehouse, 4 February 1924, Wodehouse Archive.

p. 159 *'I am all dizzy with work these days'*: PGW to William Townend, 26 January 1924, Dulwich.

p. 159 *'This is certainly one swell story'*: PGW to Leonora Wodehouse, 4 February 1924, Wodehouse Archive.

p. 160 *'We have practically decided . . .'*: PGW to William Townend, 1 August 1924, Dulwich.

p. 161 *Sam in the Suburbs*: this was the title eventually accorded to *Sam the Sudden* when it was published in the USA.

p. 161 *'Mummie is the belle of the hotel'*: PGW to Leonora Wodehouse, 12 September 1924, Wodehouse Archive.

p. 161 *'the damned funniest idea . . .'*: PGW to William Townend, 1 October 1924, Dulwich.

p. 161 *a much-admired short story*: the philosopher Ludwig Wittgenstein was a particular fan of 'Honeysuckle Cottage'.

p. 161 *a popular guide to contemporary spiritualism*: H. Dennis Bradley, *Towards the Stars* (London, 1924).

p. 161 *According to Bradley . . .*: H. Dennis Bradley, *The Wisdom of the Gods* (London, 1929), p. 68.

p. 161 *At a third seance in April*: ibid., p. 378.

p. 161 *one of Leonora's childhood friends*: PGW to Armine Wodehouse, 17 March 1936, private collection.

p. 162 *'I think it's the goods'*: PGW to William Townend, 17 December 1925, Dulwich. Later, in March 1927, Wodehouse quizzed his friend about the results of another seance; spiritualism was a subject of great mutual interest.

p. 162 *He's like one of those weird birds . . .*: 'The Artistic Career of Corky', in *Carry On, Jeeves* (1925; London 1999), p. 31. See also *Right Ho, Jeeves* (1934; Everyman, 2000), p. 220.

p. 162 *firing off lists of research questions*: 'What did Sam see, hear and smell, as he stood outside the galley? Could he [Sam] have a cabin to himself? And do you call it a cabin or a state-room? Would it be ship's etiquette for him to chum up with the skipper as well as [Todhunter] the cook? etc.'; *Performing Flea* (London, 1953), pp. 28–30.

p. 162 *'even if the windows leak . . .'*: PGW to William Townend, 12 December 1924, Dulwich.

p. 162 *'You have to live with a novel . . .'*: ibid.

p. 163 *At about half-past ten . . .*: Denis Mackail, *Life with Topsy* (London, 1942), p. 41.

p. 163 *'That was the game of a lifetime'*: PGW to William Townend, 17 November 1924, Dulwich.

p. 163 *Ukridge*: published in the USA as *He Rather Enjoyed It*.

p. 163 *'I feel as if . . .'*: PGW to Denis Mackail, 14 December 1924, Wodehouse Archive.

p. 164 *'a weird bird'*: PGW to William Townend, 22 December 1924, Dulwich.

p. 164 *hobby of training prize Jersey cows*: Hunstanton Hall also boasted a large black pig, which is said by some to be the model for the Empress of Blandings (interview with Tom Mott, 24 June 2003).

p. 164 *Hunstanton Hall visitors' book*: courtesy of Michael M. Lestrange.

p. 164 *'that sound like a man with an unpleasant voice . . .'*: PGW to William Townend, 26 June 1926, Dulwich.

p. 164 *alone on a punt named Plum*: interview with Tom Mott.

p. 164 *'on a bed-table balanced on one of the seats'*: ibid. See also *Performing Flea*, p. 34.

p. 164 *the nearly complete typescript*: apart from a debate about the title (Lorimer favoured 'Sunshine Sam'), the typescript was virtually ready for serialization in the *Post*.

p. 164 *a strange, unnerving silence*: PGW to Leonora Wodehouse, 20 March 1925, Wodehouse Archive.

p. 164 *'Of all the poisonous, foul, ghastly places . . .'*: PGW to Leonora Wodehouse, 20 March 1925, Wodehouse Archive.

p. 165 *sketch ideas for a new novel*: ibid.

p. 165 *London . . . was loathsome*: PGW to William Townend, 28 April 1925, Dulwich.

p. 165 *'What rot all this social stuff is'*: PGW to William Townend, 27 May 1925, Dulwich.

p. 165 *a grey top hat*: PGW to Denis Mackail, 18 June 1925, Wodehouse Archive.

p. 165 *The Nightingale*: performed at Jolson's Theater in 1927 and ran for ninety-six performances.

p. 165 *'What a ghastly time . . .'*: PGW to William Townend, 2 November 1925, Dulwich.

p. 165 *'one of the few occasions . . .'*: PGW to William Townend, 28 March 1935, Dulwich.

p. 166 *'the sort of contract . . .'*: PGW to William Townend, 2 November 1925, Dulwich.

p. 166 *Lorimer was very angry*: Paul Reynolds papers, 29 December 1926, Columbia. The *Post* did not serialize another Wodehouse novel until 1933 (*Heavy Weather*), and between 1926 and 1932 published just two short stories.

p. 166 *a kind of delirium tremens*: see *Carry On, Jeeves*, pp. 96–7.

p. 166 *The Drones' terms for hangover*: see *The Mating Season* (1949; Everyman, 2001), p. 34.

p. 167 *For perhaps the split part of a second . . .*: *Right Ho, Jeeves*, p. 48.

p. 167 *A crusty roll . . .*: 'The Shadow Passes', in *Nothing Serious* (London, 1950), p. 9.

p. 167 *planning to buy a house in London*: PGW to William Townend, 2 November 1925, Dulwich.

p. 167 *'in the biggest bout of work . . .'*: PGW to William Townend, 29 January 1926, Dulwich.

p. 168 *the fashionable Russian designer-director*: a refugee Russian prince, Komisarjevsky was one of the theatrical phenomena of the 1920s, who would eventually leave his mark in Britain not so much on the stage but with his spectacular Moorish designs for the Granada cinemas in Woolwich, Clapham Junction and Tooting.

p. 168 *Hearts and Diamonds*: the show, starring Charles Stone and Lupino Lane, opened at the Strand Theatre on 1 June, but closed after forty-six performances.

p. 168 *The Play's the Thing*: see *Performing Flea*, pp. 35–6.

p. 168 *I was talking to Gilbert Miller . . .*: PGW to William Townend, 5 May 1927, Dulwich.

p. 169 *'She had everything'*: PGW and Guy Bolton, *Bring on the Girls* (London, 1953) p. 191. Miss Lawrence rapidly became a Broadway hit, starring in Charlot's *Revue* of 1924 and 1926.

p. 169 *'I am trembling on the verge . . .'*: PGW to William Townend, 26 June 1926, Dulwich.

p. 169 *'considerably hotter than blazes'*: David Jasen, *P. G. Wodehouse: Portrait of a Master* (London, 1975), p. 104.

p. 169 *Wodehouse played a larger part in the making of Oh, Kay!*: later, Wodehouse would also be responsible for anglicizing the lyrics for a triumphant London run at Her Majesty's Theatre.

p. 169 *'Heaven on Earth'*: co-written by Howard Dietz and Ira Gershwin.

p. 169 *'usually it is sufficient . . .'*: *New York Times*, 9 November 1926.

CHAPTER 11: 'I am planning a vast campaign' (1927–1929)

p. 171 *'the gol-darnedest house you ever saw'*: PGW to William Townend, 17 May 1927, Dulwich.

p. 171 *decorated with the Wodehouse crest*: interview with Patrick Wodehouse, 28 August 2000.

p. 171 *'My library . . . is magnificent . . .'*: PGW to William Townend, 12 February 1927, Dulwich.

p. 171 *Denis Mackail remembered . . .*: Denis Mackail, *Life with Topsy* (London, 1942), pp. 65–6.

p. 171 *'Isn't it curious . . .'*: PGW to William Townend, 12 February 1927, Dulwich.

p. 172 *some of his most memorable Bertie Wooster stories*: 'Jeeves and the Impending Doom'; 'Jeeves and the Song of Songs'; 'Jeeves and the Kid Clementina'; 'Jeeves and the Old School Chum'; 'Jeeves and the Spot of Art'. These would be published in *Very Good, Jeeves* (London, 1957).

p. 172 *'Pig-hoo-o-o-o-ey!'*: this story was first published in the *Strand* in August 1927.

p. 172 *'Lord Emsworth and the Girl Friend'*: first published in 1928 (*Liberty*; *Strand*) and later in *Blandings Castle and Elsewhere* (1935; Everyman, 2002; US: *Blandings Castle*).

p. 172 *A welcome coolness had crept . . .*: *Blandings Castle and Elsewhere*, p. 154.

p. 172 *It was, in itself, quite a trivial thing . . .*: ibid., p. 157.

p. 172 *Mr Mulliner*: *Meet Mr Mulliner* was published in the UK on 27 September 1927 and in the USA on 2 March 1928.

p. 173 *just under 30,000 students at university*: see A. J. P. Taylor, *English History 1914–1945* (Oxford, 1965), p. 308.

p. 173 *Gerald Gould*: see *Observer*, 30 April 1929 and *passim*; Guardian–Observer Archive Centre, Farringdon Road, London.

p. 173 *a yearning for escape*: 'Perhaps it is because the world is so sick and anxious and unhappy that Mr Wodehouse is so popular'; *Observer*, review of *Sam the Sudden*, October 1925.

p. 173 *Reconstruction, Restoration . . .*: Taylor, *English History*, p. 299.

p. 173 *sales of his books were rarely spectacular*: in 1934, at the height of his fame, Wodehouse's sales in the USA were 10,000–12,000 copies in the first edition, followed by numerous cheap reprints. The same pattern was repeated in Britain, on a smaller scale. See Paul Reynolds to Arthur Levenseller, 6 July 1934, Reynolds papers, Columbia.

p. 173 *incessant demands on Wodehouse's time*: PGW to William Townend, 10 October 1929, Dulwich.

p. 173 *bracing himself to start . . .*: PGW to Paul Reynolds, 11 April 1927, Reynolds papers, Columbia. This would become *Money for Nothing* (London, 1928).

p. 174 *'sweating blood'*: PGW to William Townend, 27 July 1927, Dulwich.

p. 174 *Wodehouse took a suite*: Guy Bolton, in the midst of an acrimonious divorce, had an apartment at the same address.

p. 174 *complaining that theatrical work was sapping his energy*: PGW to William Townend, 28 November 1927, Dulwich.

pp. 174–5 *Leonora was courted by many . . .*: see Godfrey Wynn, *The Infirm Glory* (London, 1967), pp. 298–301. See also John Millar's short memoir in *Wooster Sauce*, March 2003, p. 3.

p. 175 *'Hell's foundations . . .'*: PGW to William Townend, 28 November 1927, Dulwich.

p. 175 *'[we] seem to be doing jolly well . . .'*: ibid.

p. 175 *Only once in his life . . .*: *Money for Nothing* (London, 1928), p. 171.

p. 176 *the interruptions of London life*: PGW to William Townend, 22 March 1928, Dulwich.

p. 176 *'I am having a great time . . .'*: PGW to Denis Mackail, 30 April 1928, Wodehouse Archive.

p. 176 *had written 10,000 words*: PGW to William Townend, 26 July 1928, Dulwich.

p. 176 *Ian Hay*: Hay (pseudonym of Ian Hay Beith) also collaborated with PGW on a stage version of *Leave It to Psmith*, in 1930.

p. 176 *Wodehouse dabbled in theatrical business*: even with three shows (*Rosalie, The Three Musketeers* and *Good Morning, Bill!*) playing to excellent houses in London and New York, PGW could not resist acquiring an extra share in his adaptation of the Jacques Deval comedy *Her Cardboard Lover*, which opened in London shortly after *A Damsel in Distress*, starring Leslie Howard and Tallulah Bankhead. Acquiring the share involved buying out the director Al Woods for $10,000, but the investment paid off well; Reynolds papers, Columbia.

p. 177 *'must have done about a hundred thousand'*: PGW to William Townend, 28 September 1928, Dulwich.

p. 177 *'I am planning a vast campaign . . .'*: ibid.

p. 177 *'Dulwich have got a red-hot team . . .'*: PGW to William Townend, 18 October 1928, Dulwich.

p. 177 *According to Reynolds*: letter, 11 March 1929, Reynolds papers, Columbia.

p. 177 *'The fact is I cannot keep away from Blandings Castle'*: preface to *Summer Lightning*. Some of the new personnel in the Wodehousian paradise were recent arrivals. Hugo Carmody and Ronnie Fish had only just appeared in the recently published *Money for Nothing*. The loathsome Pilbeam was in *Bill the Conqueror*. The other characters, Lord Emsworth, the Efficient Baxter and Beach the butler, had all participated in *Something Fresh* and *Leave It to Psmith*, but this time their association within the castle walls was to be made more complex by the Empress of Blandings, making her majestic first appearance in a Blandings novel.

p. 178 *desire to be left alone with his pig*: see Michael Davie, ninetieth birthday interview, *Observer*, 10 October 1971. See also *Paris Review*, 64 (1975), pp. 150–71.

p. 178 *Evelyn Waugh recognized this . . .*: Mark Amory (ed.), *The Letters of Evelyn Waugh* (London, 1981), p. 36. The letter was to Henry Yorke (Henry Green).

p. 179 *'the air of romantic decay'*: PGW to William Townend, 12 May 1929, Dulwich.

p. 179 *Tom Mott, the chauffeur's son*: interview with Tom Mott, 24 June 2003.

p. 179 *trying to work up some new Jeeves plots*: PGW to William Townend, 13 April 1929, Dulwich. The other Jeeves stories he would complete in fulfilment of his contract with *Cosmopolitan* include 'Indian Summer of an Uncle' and 'Tuppy Changes His Mind'.

p. 179 *Kristin Thompson*: in *Wooster Proposes, Jeeves Disposes* (New York, 1992), pp. 182–200.

p. 179 *'to let it cool'*: PGW to William Townend, 12 May 1929, Dulwich.

p. 180 *reporting to Townend*: PGW to William Townend, 11 June 1929, Dulwich.

p. 180 *he always had to wrestle . . . before he could get started*: *Over Seventy* (London, 1957), p. 105.

p. 180 *'There always comes a moment . . .'*: ibid., p. 188.

p. 180 *'Pinch that scene from . . .'*: PGW notes, undated, Dulwich.

p. 180 *Father an actor . . . restored to Amer's aunt?*: 'Jeeves novel. Lay-out of story', Ransom.

p. 181 *'the actual core of a story . . .'*: PGW to William Townend, 26 July 1929, Dulwich.

p. 181 *a new musical comedy, East is West*: PGW's collaborator on this show, Billy Rose, was notable as the author of the song 'Does Your Chewing Gum Lose Its Flavor on the Bedpost Overnight?'

p. 181 *'brush up my American slang'*: PGW to William Townend, 17 August 1929, Dulwich.

p. 181 *a proposed revival of a 1918 show*: *Rose of China*.

p. 181 *'Plum is really the hardest of workers . . .'*: Leonora Wodehouse, *Strand*, January 1929, pp. 20–25.

p. 182 *ghost-writing for the best-selling mystery author*: interview with David Jasen, 7 June 2003.

p. 182 *'the brave old days . . .'*: PGW to Paul Reynolds, 5 February 1927, Reynolds papers, Columbia.

p. 182 *'keep a sharp eye on [Denby]. . .'*: PGW to Paul Reynolds, 6 February 1927, Reynolds papers, Columbia.

p. 183 *'without anyone knowing'*: PGW to Paul Reynolds, 11 November 1929, Reynolds papers, Columbia.

p. 183 *caught in the usual Ziegfeld nightmare*: PGW to William Townend, 10 October 1929, Dulwich.

p. 183 *According to George Cukor*: cited in A. Scott Berg, *Goldwyn* (London, 1989), p. 173.

p. 183 *curious about the opportunities*: PGW to William Townend, 10 October 1929, Dulwich.

p. 183 *By the Christmas season of 1928/9*: Berg, *Goldwyn*, p. 174.

p. 184 *got the brush-off*: Goldwyn tried to acquire the rights to Shaw's *Arms and the Man*. Shaw told Goldwyn that he was only interested in money where it was clear the producer was inspired by 'art'.

p. 184 *was in no hurry to commit*: PGW to William Townend, 10 October 1929, Dulwich.

p. 184 *'Millions are to be grabbed . . .'*: quoted in Ann Douglas, *Terrible Honesty: Mongrel Manhattan in the 1920s* (New York, 1995), p. 61.

p. 184 *'like one of those great race movements . . .'*: PGW and Guy Bolton, *Bring on the Girls* (London, 1953), p. 261.

p. 185 *a visit by Winston Churchill*: Roy Jenkins, *Churchill* (London, 2001), pp. 424–6.

p. 185 *Marion Davies's palatial 'bungalow'*: D. Nasaw, *Hearst* (London, 2002), p. 418.

p. 185 *'That was a very good speech . . .'*: quoted in *Performing Flea* (London, 1953), p. 49.

p. 185 *'I have reluctantly come to the conclusion . . .'*: ibid.

p. 186 *'I suppose it will come . . .'*: ibid., p. 50.

p. 186 *'in the chips'*: *Over Seventy*, p. 99.

CHAPTER 12: 'I altered all the characters to Earls and butlers'
(1930–1931)

p. 189 *While suit-cases, golf-bags . . .*: PGW and Guy Bolton, *Bring on the Girls* (London, 1953), pp. 271–2.

p. 189 *'a combination of Santa Claus . . .'*: *Over Seventy* (London, 1957), p. 160.

p. 189 *'I've always wanted . . .'*: *Los Angeles Examiner*, 9 May 1930.

p. 190 *'The slogan was . . .'*: *Over Seventy*, p. 160.

p. 190 *Although he was new to Hollywood . . .*: I gratefully acknowledge the research of Brian Taves at the Library of Congress on Wodehouse's work in films.

p. 190 *Wodehouse had sold the film rights . . .*: PGW to L. H. Bradshaw, 1 September 1914, Bradshaw.

p. 190 *Cecil B. De Mille*: the co-author of the dramatic version, John Stapleton, disputed these rights in an Authors' League case; PGW to L. H. Bradshaw, 10 October 1914, Bradshaw.

p. 190 *alludes to William Collier's performance*: *Psmith Journalist* (1915; London, 1970), p. 167.

p. 190 *'Ukridge's Accident Syndicate'*: first published as 'Ukridge, Teddy Weeks and the Tomato' in the *Strand*, June 1923.

p. 190 *'The Passing of Ambrose'*: *Mr Mulliner Speaking* (1929; London, 1999), p. 198. The story was first published in the *Strand* in July 1928.

p. 190 *Several novels . . .*: books that became films include *Uneasy Money* (1917), *Piccadilly Jim* (1919), *A Damsel in Distress* (1920), *The Prince and Betty* (1920), *Their Mutual Child* (1920) and *The Small Bachelor* (1927). Some 'Reggie Pepper' and 'Oldest Member' golfing stories had also been made into comedy shorts.

p. 191 *Sam Marx, the story editor*: see Samuel Marx, *Mayer and Thalberg: The Make-believe Saints* (Los Angeles, 1975), pp. 100–102.

p. 191 *'I get up, swim . . .'*: PGW to Denis Mackail, 26 June 1930, Wodehouse Archive.

p. 191 *'I motor over there . . .'*: ibid.

p. 191 *'This place is great'*: PGW to Paul Reynolds, 27 May 1930, Reynolds papers, Colombia.

p. 191 *'The actual work is negligible . . .'*: ibid.

p. 192 *'There is something . . .'*: PGW to William Townend, 26 June 1930, Dulwich.

p. 192 *'I fear I shall not be able. . .'*: PGW to Guy Bolton, 19 July 1930, Wodehouse Archive.

p. 192 *Thalberg had mistakenly believed*: see George F. Custen, *Twentieth Century's Fox: Darryl F. Zanuck and the Culture of Hollywood* (New York, 1997), p. 118.

p. 192 *Sam Marx later remembered . . .*: Marx, *Mayer and Thalberg*, p. 152.

p. 192 *'I don't see much . . .'*: PGW to William Townend, 26 June 1930, Dulwich.

p. 193 *'You have already arrived'*: Gerard Fairlie, *With Prejudice: Almost an Autobiography* (London, 1952), p. 211-12.

p. 193 *'story conference'*: notes on Story Conference, 18 October 1930, AMPASL.

p. 193 *Sadly, the memorandum in the studio's archive contradicts*: ibid. Thalberg's memorandum is complete, lucid and persuasive.

p. 193 *When he had finished . . .*: *Performing Flea* (London, 1953), p. 55.

p. 193 *vultures 'who had done . . .'*: 'The Castaways', in *Blandings Castle and Elsewhere* (1935; Everyman, 2002), p. 255.

p. 193 *'smiled sheepishly . . .'*: PGW to Denis Mackail, 28 December 1930, Wodehouse Archive.

p. 194 *MGM's plans to make a Jeeves film*: Marx, *Mayer and Thalberg*, p. 154.

p. 194 *two dreadful 'Jeeves' movies*: *Thank You, Jeeves* (1936) was made by Twentieth Century–Fox, starring Arthur Treacher and David Niven, who said he used the experience to enrich his acting repertory, 'from boggling my eyes to furrowing my brow' (Tom Hutchinson, *Niven's Hollywood*, Salem, NH, 1984, pp. 65–6). *Step Lively, Jeeves* (1937) was also filmed by Twentieth Century–Fox and again starred Arthur Treacher, an original script that was not based on any Wodehouse material and omitted all reference to Bertie. See also Graham Lord, *Niv: The Authorised Biography of David Niven* (London, 2003).

p. 194 *Wodehouse jibbed a bit*: for the unpublished text of the *Rosalie* novelization, see Turner–MGM script collection, file R880, AMPASL.

p. 194 *'about eight times . . .'*: PGW to William Townend, 28 October 1930, Dulwich.

p. 194 *he instructed Reynolds . . .*: PGW to Paul Reynolds, 23 November 1930, Reynolds papers, Columbia.

p. 194 *'the abode of the damned'*, PGW to Guy Bolton, 19 July 1930, Wodehouse Archive.

p. 194 *he tried hard to persuade*: PGW to William Townend, 28 October 1930, Dulwich.

p. 195 *'almost impossible to think of Plum . . .'*: *Performing Flea*, p. 90.

p. 195 *the long-lost days of Actors vs. Authors*: Aubrey Smith was also a former England cricket captain.

p. 195 *to found the Hollywood Cricket club*: together with the actor Ronald Colman. See invoice for life membership, 24 September 1931, Reynolds papers, Columbia. See also Murray Hedgcock (ed.), *Wodehouse at the Wicket* (London, 1997), pp. 44–5. I gratefully acknowledge Murray Hedgcock's advice on the cricketing passages of this chapter.

p. 195 *'The swim I enjoy most . . .'*: PGW to William Townend, 28 October 1930, Dulwich.

p. 195 *The American Spectator judged, perceptively, that Metro . . .*: 'All right in books, but not on screen' ran the headline.

p. 196 *Writing 'additional dialogue'*: 'The Nodder', in *Blandings Castle*, p. 215.

p. 196 *Both these scripts suggest . . .*: production files relating to *The Man in Possession* and *Men Call It Love* are held by AMPASL and USC Cinema–Television Library.

p. 196 *clearing the decks for a new full-length novel*: this became *Hot Water* (1932).

p. 196 *A Prince for Hire*: republished, with an introduction by Tony Ring, London, 2003.

p. 196 *a five-part serialization*: *Illustrated Love Magazine* was a monthly magazine published for sale within US and Canadian F. W. Woolworth's stores. Only Wodehouse could have contemplated a sale to such a publication. I gratefully acknowledge Tony Ring's invaluable assistance in elucidating this minor Wodehouse puzzle.

p. 196 *'a tremendous rush of work'*: PGW to William Townend, 16 January 1931, Dulwich.

p. 197 *'a ghastly job . . .'*: PGW to William Townend, 25 February 1931, Dulwich.

p. 197 *Meals are in an enormous room . . .*: *Performing Flea*, p. 57.

p. 197 *She starts by asking . . .*: PGW to Denis Mackail, 12 April 1931, Wodehouse Archive.

p. 198 *some blunt and sensible advice*: Maureen O'Sullivan, 'The Wodehouses of Hollywood', in James H. Heineman and Donald R. Bensen (eds.), *P. G. Wodehouse: A Centenary Celebration* (New York, 1981), pp. 15–18.

p. 198 *'really a sort of carbon copy . . .'*: PGW to William Townend, 19 May 1931, Dulwich.

p. 199 *On paper, Blair Eggleston . . .*: *Hot Water* (London, 1932), p. 223.

p. 199 *'Oddly enough, Hollywood hasn't inspired me. . .'*: PGW to William Townend, 16 August 1930, Dulwich.

p. 199 *'doing a lot of hearty sucking up'*: PGW to Denis Mackail, 12 April 1931, Wodehouse Archive.

p. 199 *'I've never been able to stay . . .'*: PGW to Denis Mackail, 10 May 1931, Wodehouse Archive.

p. 200 *'I haven't been able to get much . . .'*: ibid.

p. 200 *'I was lucky to get mine . . .'*: ibid.

p. 200 *a stream of Hollywood stories*: in addition to those mentioned in the text, 'Monkey Business' and 'The Juice of an Orange' were published in *Blandings Castle and Elsewhere*. These stories were followed by the novels *The Luck of the Bodkins* (1935) and *Laughing Gas* (1936).

p. 200 *'The Rise of Minna Nordstrom'*: in 1924, Marcus Loew had merged his Metro Picture Corporation with the Goldwyn Picture Corporation and Louis B. Mayer into MGM, under the ownership of Loew's Inc.

p. 200 *A bonfire had been started . . .*: 'The Castaways', in *Blandings Castle*, p. 301.

p. 200 *It is not easy to explain . . .*: 'The Nodder', in *Blandings Castle*, p. 215.

p. 201 *'God's Back Garden'*: *Over Seventy* (London, 1957), p. 162.

p. 201 *At his desk . . .*: 'The Juice of an Orange', in *Blandings Castle*, p. 236.

p. 201 *'He hasn't a heart . . .'*: *The Luck of the Bodkins* (1935; Everyman, 2002), p. 197.

p. 201 *'if you make a noise . . .'*: ibid., p. 26.

p. 202 *paid '$104,000 for loafing'*: *Los Angeles Times*, 7 June 1931.

p. 202 *MGM's profits halved . . .*: A. Scott Berg, *Goldwyn* (New York, 1989), p. 208.

p. 202 *in this piece*: he also told the story of 'my friend Roland Pertwee's' summary dismissal. Pertwee, a professional playwright with a career at stake in Hollywood, was not best pleased to read that he had been sacked by Warners when in fact he had been made redundant on generous terms by Jack Warner.

p. 202 *'the effect . . . of the late assassination'*: PGW to William Townend, 29 June 1931, Dulwich.

p. 202 *Townend loyally corroborated*: *Performing Flea*, pp. 60–61.

p. 203 *'I judge that your arrangement . . .'*: Paul Reynolds to PGW, 10 June 1931, Reynolds papers, Columbia.

p. 203 *required to do so little work*: *Over Seventy*, p. 160.

p. 203 *'I got away from Hollywood . . .'*: ibid., pp. 164–5.

p. 203 *a lot of resentment*: see O'Sullivan, 'The Wodehouses of Hollywood', p. 17.

p. 203 *'My career as a movie-writer . . .'*: PGW to William Townend, 26 August 1931, Dulwich.

p. 203 *'Honestly, this story is a corker'*: PGW to Paul Reynolds, 26 August 1931, Reynolds Papers, Columbia.

p. 203 *exceedingly pessimistic*: PGW to William Townend, 29 June 1931, Dulwich.

p. 204 *'We are toying with a scheme . . .'*: ibid.

p. 204 *planning to stay with a Maharajah*: Ethel Wodehouse to Denis Mackail, 8 October 1931, Wodehouse Archive.

p. 204 *I'm darned if I know*: PGW to William Townend, 26 August 1931, Dulwich.

p. 204 *he thought Collier's would snap it up*: Paul Reynolds to PGW, September 1931, Reynolds papers, Columbia.

p. 204 *'my brain doesn't seem to work properly . . .'*: PGW to William Townend, 14 September 1931, Dulwich.

p. 204 *'Americans aren't funny'*: ibid.

p. 204 *'a darned good mind . . .'*: ibid.

p. 205 *If I Were You was published*: it was later staged at the Duke of York's Theatre, London, in a collaboration with Guy Bolton, as *Who's Who*.

p. 205 *Charles Le Strange had given up Hunstanton Hall*: PGW to William Townend, 14 September 1931, Dulwich. Shortly after this, Le Strange was caught up in a sex scandal involving a guardsman. He died on 9 June 1933.

p. 205 *'I don't know how I shall get on . . .'*: PGW to William Townend, 14 September 1931, Dulwich.

CHAPTER 13: 'My worst year since I started writing' (1932–1934)

p. 206 *there was not much guidance*: see Tony Ring, *You Simply Hit Them with an Axe: The Extraordinary True Story of the Tax Turmoils of P. G. Wodehouse* (Maidenhead,

1995), p. xi. The income tax parts of this chapter owe an important debt to this invaluable monograph.

p. 206 *humorous references to taxation*: see 'Wheatless Days' in *Oh, Lady! Lady!!*, for example.

p. 207 *spending less than six months a year*: PGW to William Townend, 21 February 1921, Dulwich.

p. 207 *Some time ago . . .*: *Bill the Conqueror* (London, 1924), pp. 248–9.

p. 208 *atrociously handled from the first*: Paul Reynolds to PGW, 19 November 1929, Reynolds papers, Columbia.

p. 208 *suggested that Wodehouse owed . . .*: Halsey Malone to Paul Reynolds, 3 December 1929, Reynolds papers, Columbia.

p. 208 *'The only way seems . . .'*: Paul Reynolds to PGW, 6 December 1929, Reynolds papers, Columbia.

p. 208 *Ethel's involvement in this crisis*: Ethel Wodehouse's personal secretary, Vera Church, was partly involved in some of the preliminary work.

p. 208 *questionable decision*: for Margaret Matusch's role, see Reynolds papers, *passim*, Columbia.

p. 208 *highly irresponsible in financial matters*: Denby had advised Wodehouse that there was no need to mention the Famous Players' $5,000 in his tax returns for 1927.

p. 208 *'We shall be able . . .'*: Bobby Denby to PGW, 23 July 1932, Reynolds papers, Columbia.

p. 208 *took an instant dislike to Freeman and Greenberg*: Wodehouse especially loathed Greenberg, whom he considered to be dishonest.

p. 209 *uninspiring, cold and gloomy*: PGW to Paul Reynolds, 7 December 1931, Reynolds papers, Columbia.

p. 209 *a Provençal country estate*: PGW to William Townend, 6 March 1932, Dulwich.

p. 209 *'a German butler . . .'*: PGW to William Townend, 1 April 1932, Dulwich.

p. 209 *'We dined at the Casino . . .'*: ibid.

p. 209 *learning French*: see preface to *French Leave* (London, 1956): 'I never succeeded in speaking French, but I learned to read it all right, which is all I need.'

p. 209 *literary friends*: PGW to Denis Mackail, 24 August 1932, Wodehouse Archive.

p. 209 *he now wrote 64 pages*: PGW to William Townend, 1 April 1932, Dulwich.

p. 210 *To Reynolds, he boasted*: PGW to Paul Reynolds, 25 March 1932, Reynolds papers, Colombia.

p. 210 *'ought to be easy to write . . .'*: PGW to Denis Mackail, 8 April 1932, Wodehouse Archive.

p. 210 *The Wooster blood . . .*: *Thank You, Jeeves* (1934; Everyman, 2003), p. 19.

p. 211 *The attitude of fellows . . .*: ibid., p. 78.

p. 211 *a record $50,000*: PGW to William Townend, 13 August 1931, Dulwich.

p. 211 *J. B. Priestley*: *Evening Standard*, 18 August 1932. Priestley wrote: 'We do not grumble at Mr Wodehouse's almost impudent lack of inventive power. We are fascinated by the sublime idiocy of his comments on these puppets. . . . I am afraid that Mr Wodehouse, even though he has shaken a fist at Hollywood, is rapidly becoming an American humorist. He will have to be severely talked to by Jeeves.'

p. 211 *'Priestley was the worst of all . . .'*: PGW to Denis Mackail, 9 October 1932, Wodehouse Archive.

p. 211 *anxiety that he had written himself out*: see PGW to William Townend, 24 August 1932, Dulwich.

p. 211 *'unless it seems real . . .'*: ibid.

p. 212 *'I can't kid myself . . .'*: ibid.

p. 212 *'I always envy you . . .'*: PGW to Denis Mackail, 9 October 1932, Wodehouse Archive.

p. 212 *'My great trouble . . .'*: ibid.

p. 213 *'I'm so happy about it . . .'*: PGW to Leonora Wodehouse, 6 November 1932, Wodehouse Archive.

p. 213 *the wealth of Leonora's future father-in-law William Cazalet*: PGW to William Townend, 1 December 1932, Dulwich.

p. 213 *the groom was not a literary man*: Peter Cazalet was an Oxford cricket Blue, and a leading amateur race rider in the 1930s who became a highly successful racehorse trainer.

p. 214 *Graham Greene*: *Spectator*, 17 November 1933. The row is discussed in full in Ann Thwaite, *A. A. Milne: His Life* (London, 1990), pp. 391–5.

p. 214 *'a sort of stunned feeling'*: PGW to William Townend, 20 January 1936, Dulwich.

p. 214 *huge tax bills were looming*: 'vast sums to be paid out for both English and American income tax'; PGW to William Townend, 13 August 1932, Dulwich.

p. 214 *'Hell's foundations . . .'*: PGW to William Townend, 1 December 1932, Dulwich.

p. 215 *'the actual things you really want . . .'*: ibid.

p. 215 *Claud Cockburn*: 'Wodehouse All the Way', in Thelma Cazalet-Keir (ed.), *Homage to P. G. Wodehouse* (London, 1973), p. 31.

p. 215 *Gerald Fairlie*: in *With Prejudice: Almost an Autobiography* (London, 1952), p. 213.

p. 215 *When I first met him . . .*: Beverly Nichols, *Are They the Same at Home?* (London, 1927), pp. 248–52.

p. 216 *'his almost uncanny capacity for disappearances . . .'*: ibid., p. 249.

p. 216 *whose honesty he doubted*: 'I didn't like him, and am dubious about his honesty'; PGW to Paul Reynolds, 12 December 1932, Reynolds papers, Columbia.

p. 216 *'in many ways, I am not sorry'*: PGW to William Townend, 1 December 1932, Dulwich.

p. 216 *'getting on splendidly . . .'*: PGW to William Townend, 4 January 1932, Dulwich.

p. 217 *Wodehouse the unorthodox gambler*: E. Phillips Oppenheim, *The Pool of Memory* (London, 1941), p. 75.

p. 217 *'My idea . . . is to guarantee an overdraft'*: PGW to William Townend, 9 February 1933, Dulwich.

p. 217 *'a dead secret . . .'*: PGW to William Townend, 15 March 1933, Dulwich.

p. 217 *He joked to Mackail that he was planning . . .*: PGW to Denis Mackail, 9 October 1932, Wodehouse Archive.

p. 218 *'three novels and 10 short stories . . .'*: PGW to Denis Mackail, 10 September 1933, Wodehouse Archive.

p. 218 *the stars are 'God's daisy chain'*: *Right Ho, Jeeves* (1934; Everyman, 2000), p. 19.

p. 218 *Brinkley Court*: the US edition was given the title *Brinkley Court*.

p. 218 *'I fear that you inadvertently left Cannes . . .'*: *Right Ho, Jeeves*, p. 21.

p. 218 *The hell you say it's all right? . . .*: ibid., p. 238.

p. 219 *looking at the thing from every angle . . .*: ibid., p. 290.

p. 219 *working towards a settlement*: PGW to Paul Reynolds, 12 April 1933, Reynolds papers, Columbia.

p. 219 *'he . . . is quite impractical . . .'*: Paul Reynolds' deposition on PGW tax matters, January 1934, Reynolds papers, Columbia.

p. 219 *You have Mr Malone . . .*: Paul Reynolds to PGW, 26 April 1933, Reynolds papers, Columbia.

p. 220 *His advisers were divided*: PGW to Paul Reynolds, 15 June 1933, Reynolds papers, Columbia.

p. 220 *'is playing the devil with my work'*: ibid.

p. 220 *'If they would agree . . .'*: ibid.

p. 220 *'out of a clear blue sky'*: PGW to William Townend, 7 December 1933, Dulwich.

p. 220 *'To Raymond Needham KC, who put . . .'*: see Ring, *You Simply Hit Them*, pp. 88–9.

p. 221 *expressed his relief*: PGW to Paul Reynolds, 25 January 1934, Reynolds papers, Columbia.

p. 221 *'Even now, I can't see . . .'*: PGW to Leonora Cazalet, 3 April 1935, Wodehouse Archive.

p. 221 *'my income tax experts . . .'*: PGW to William Townend, 10 March 1934, Dulwich.

p. 221 *'my wife and I both want to make it our headquarters . . .'*: PGW to Paul Reynolds, 27 March 1934, Reynolds papers, Columbia.

p. 221 *'the foulest week of my career'*: PGW to William Townend, 10 March 1934, Dulwich.

p. 221 *Thank You, Jeeves was about to be published*: in the UK on 16 March and in the USA on 23 April 1934.

p. 222 *US authorities issuing a lien*: see Ring, *You Simply Hit Them*, pp. 94–5.

p. 222 *'my worst year . . .'*: PGW to William Townend, 12 September 1934, Dulwich.

p. 222 *'Things are not so bad as they seem . . .'*: PGW to William Townend, 16 August 1934, Dulwich.

CHAPTER 14: 'The one ideal spot in the world' (1934-1936)

p. 223 *the producers Alex Aarons and Vinton Freedley*: Freedley and Aarons had also produced *Oh, Kay!*

p. 223 *'one of those big musical comedies . . .'*: PGW to Paul Reynolds, 27 March 1934, Reynolds papers, Columbia. The new novel would become *The Luck of the Bodkins*.

p. 224 *completed a first draft*: see Lee Davis, *Wodehouse and Bolton and Kern: The Men Who Made Musical Comedy* (New York, 1993), p. 330.

p. 224 *Their meeting was interrupted . . .*: *New York Herald Tribune*, 13 May 1962.

p. 225 *'Cole had a reputation . . .'*: see David Grafton, *Red, Hot and Rich: An Oral History of Cole Porter* (New York, 1987), p. 106. See also George Eells, *The Life That Late He Led: A Biography of Cole Porter* (New York, 1967).

p. 225 *'a club you couldn't get into'*: see Grafton, *Red, Hot and Rich*, p. 108.

p. 225 *'if you said, "They're homosexual" . . .'*: ibid.

p. 226 *'the one ideal spot in the world'*: PGW to William Townend, 2 August 1934, Dulwich.

p. 226 *'what has become of [Cole Porter] . . .'*: ibid.

p. 226 *when Hitler interfered in Austrian politics*: see Ian Kershaw, *Hitler 1889–1936: Hubris* (London, 1998), pp. 522–3.

p. 226 *Bill, do you realise . . .*: PGW to William Townend, 2 August 1934, Dulwich.

p. 227 *'two pekes . . . is the right number'*: PGW to Denis Mackail, 15 October 1934, Wodehouse Archive.

p. 227 *'My particular trouble . . .'*: PGW to William Townend, 12 September 1934, Dulwich.

p. 227 *Guy Bolton played truant*: there is some mystery surrounding Guy Bolton's absence during August 1934. His illness may have been tactical. Two years later, in July/August 1936, he did indeed suffer a burst appendix, was rushed to Worthing Hospital and nearly died. Wodehouse, indeed, spent several days by his bedside (see PGW to William Townend, 23 July 1936, Dulwich). It now seems likely that, when he came to narrate his on-off involvement in the writing of *Anything Goes*, Bolton conflated the two episodes into a single crisis. See also Davis, *Wodehouse and Bolton and Kern*, pp. 330–32, for a version of events that takes Bolton's account at face value.

p. 227 *Bill and Rene Townend*: see *Performing Flea* (London, 1953), p. 89.

p. 227 *'an antic Hollywood satire'*: Davis, *Wodehouse and Bolton and Kern*, p. 330.

p. 228 *'had a ghastly cable . . .'*: PGW to Leonora Cazalet, 12 November 1934, Wodehouse Archive.

p. 228 *'Howard Lindsay . . . meant all along . . .'*: PGW to Guy Bolton, 8 March 1937, Wodehouse Archive. It is impossible now to establish the truth of this claim, but Lee Davis has argued convincingly that Freedley rejected the first script more for the fierceness of its satire on Hollywood and rather less for its similarity to the *Morro Castle* disaster.

p. 228 *prevented either from crossing the Atlantic*: both PGW and Bolton were also preoccupied with launching *Who's Who*, their comedy version of Wodehouse's novella, *If I Were You*, itself a version of a Bolton and Wodehouse play, at the Duke of York's Theatre in late September, a production that closed after nineteen performances.

p. 228 *whose title dropped into place during rehearsals*: an apocryphal story relates how it was the stage-doorman's casual 'Anything goes' that inspired the title.

p. 228 *Cole Porter described the show . . .*: Grafton, *Red, Hot and Rich*, p. 87.

p. 229 *'in melancholy mood'*: PGW to William Townend, 12 September 1934, Dulwich.

p. 229 *'Usually . . . when I get to the last fifty pages . .'*: PGW to William Townend, 4 December 1934, Dulwich.

p. 229 *far too long*: this draft was about 100,000 words. It was cut.

p. 229 *'I don't see a soul . . .'*: PGW to Denis Mackail, 15 October 1934, Wodehouse Archive.

p. 230 *The other night . . .*: PGW to Leonora Cazalet, 24 August 1934, Wodehouse Archive.

p. 230 *'most extraordinarily fit'*: PGW to William Townend, 15 October 1934, Dulwich.

p. 230 *'like a giant'*: PGW to Denis Mackail, 15 October 1934, Wodehouse Archive.

p. 230 *'eight months of terrific strain'*: PGW to Leonora Cazalet, 19 December 1934, Wodehouse Archive.

p. 230 *'a ghastly sweat'*: PGW to William Townend, 3 January 1935, Dulwich.

p. 230 *'what kills an author . . .'*: PGW to Leonora Cazalet, 19 December 1934, Wodehouse Archive.

p. 231 *'I believe there are two ways of writing . . .'*: PGW to William Townend, 23 January 1935, Dulwich. See *Performing Flea*, p. 78, for his revised version of this judgement.

p. 231 *Wodehouse transferred his British contracts*: Wodehouse drove a characteristically hard bargain on his new agent's commission, which was settled at 5 per cent, not 10 per cent; PGW to A. P. Watt, 20 March 1935, Wodehouse Archive.

p. 231 *rejected The Luck of the Bodkins*: the US edition of *The Luck of the Bodkins* is effectively a rewritten, shorter version of the British edition.

p. 231 *Needham wrote to say . . .*: PGW to William Townend, 3 April 1935, Dulwich.

p. 231 *Mr Mulliner, who had made his début . . .*: the first Mulliner stories were published in the *Strand* in 1926. They were collected in *Meet Mr Mulliner* (1927), *Mr Mulliner Speaking* (1929) and *Mulliner Nights* (1933). Peter Hollingsworth, of the Old House, Stableford, Salop, told the author that his researches in the county archive had revealed that the Wodehouse family gardener in the 1900s was a Mr Mulliner.

p. 232 *'How true it is . . .'*: 'The Story of Cedric', in *Mr Mulliner Speaking* (1929; London, 1992), p. 42.

p. 232 *'he had never contemplated matrimony . . .'*: ibid., p. 58.

p. 232 *'Well-bred and highly civilised . . .'*: 'Something Squishy', ibid., p. 126.

p. 232 *'Bobbie's mater might . . .'*: 'The Awful Gladness of the Mater', ibid., p. 146.

p. 232 *'a blend of Lucretia Borgia . . .'*: Portrait of a Disciplinarian', in *Meet Mr Mulliner* (Everyman, 2002), p. 136.

p. 232 *'you must have noticed . . .'*: 'Cats Will Be Cats', in *Mulliner Nights* (Everyman, 2003), p. 68.

p. 232 *'the march of civilisation . . .'*: ibid., p. 72.

p. 232 *'you are suffering from . . .'*: 'The Voice from the Past', ibid., p. 112.

p. 232 *'I come of a fighting line . . .'*: 'Gala Night', ibid., p. 228.

p. 232 *'Darkling, a threnody'*: 'Came the Dawn', in *Meet Mr Mulliner*, pp. 101–2.

p. 233 *'His idea of poetry'*: 'Unpleasantness at Budleigh Court', *Mr Mulliner Speaking*, (London, 1929), p. 89.

p. 233 *'Sensational news'*: PGW to Leonora Cazalet, 4 June 1935, Wodehouse Archive.

p. 233 *He and Ethel had been in a fever of indecision . . .*: ibid.

p. 234 *'frail, but not too bad'*: ibid.

p. 234 *did not die until 1941*: Eleanor Wodehouse died on 21 April 1941.

p. 234 *'used up all the plots'*: ibid.

p. 234 *'I won't write what isn't good enough . . .'*: PGW to A. P. Watt, 21 June 1935, Watt papers, Chapel Hill.

p. 234 *'I find the taste . . .'*: PGW to A. P. Watt, 15 September 1935, Watt papers, Chapel Hill.

p. 234 *'sweating like blazes'*: adapting an American play, *Three Men on a Horse*, for the London stage; PGW to William Townend, 1 July 1935 and 12 September 1935, Dulwich.

p. 234 *'the show looks v.g.'*: PGW to A. P. Watt, 21 October 1935, Watt papers, Chapel Hill.

p. 234 *'Uncle Fred Flits By'*: the story appeared in *Red Book* in July 1935 and the Christmas issue of the *Strand*. It was republished in *Young Men in Spats* (1936).

p. 234 *'in Uncle Fred I'm sure . . .'*: PGW to William Townend, 18 September 1935, Dulwich.

p. 235 *F. Anstey's Vice Versa*: published in 1882, the year after Wodehouse was born.

p. 235 *you can't heave a brick . . .*: *Laughing Gas* (1936; Everyman, 2001), p. 139.

p. 235 *'Sure', he said . . .*: ibid., p. 176.

p. 235 *'Ah Hollywood . . .'*: ibid., p. 114.

p. 236 *'I hold strong views on the films . . .'*: ibid., p. 214.

p. 236 *'White Hell'*: PGW to Leonora Cazalet, 26 February 1936, Wodehouse Archive.

p. 236 *'This is just a line . . .'*: PGW to Leonora Cazalet, 16 April 1936, Wodehouse Archive.

p. 236 *'My belief is . . .'*: PGW to William Townend, 29 May 1936, Dulwich.

p. 237 *'A thing we've got to remember . . .'*: PGW to William Townend, 3 July 1936, Dulwich.

p. 237 *I'll tell you what I feel . . .*: PGW to William Townend, 4 August 1936, Dulwich.

p. 237 *'so infernally intimate . . .'*: PGW to William Townend, 24 March 1937, Dulwich.

p. 237 *'You can imagine the relief'*: PGW to William Townend, 4 August 1936, Dulwich.

p. 237 *under contract to MGM*: this was organized by Bill Stevens, PGW's long-standing Hollywood film agent.

CHAPTER 15: 'I am leading a very quiet life here' (1936-1937)

p. 238 *'Now that the pay envelope has ceased . . .'*: PGW to Denis Mackail, 10 May 1931, Wodehouse Archive.

p. 238 *'as I am Public Enemy Number One'*: PGW to William Townend, 11 June 1934, Dulwich.

p. 238 *'rather gratifying after the way . . .'*: ibid.

p. 239 *was shooting films of . . .*: *Piccadilly Jim* was released in August 1936, starring Robert Montgomery.

p. 239 *a female puppy named Wonder*: Wonder, the most famous Wodehouse Pekinese, was originally named 'Teresa'; PGW to William Townend, 7 November 1936, Dulwich.

p. 239 *In his mercenary way*: the full story is told in *Performing Flea* (London, 1953), pp. 91–2.

p. 239 *The next day he was dead*: A. Scott Berg, *Goldwyn* (London, 1989), p. 286.

p. 239 *'Well, here we are . . .'*: PGW to William Townend, 7 November 1936, Dulwich.

p. 240 *Gaylord Hauser, the best-selling diet guru*: Hauser's belief in the healing powers of yoghurt and blackstrap molasses was so extreme that the FDA seized copies of his books from a healthfood store in Rochester, NY.

p. 240 *'Ethel and Plummie . . . as though no time at all had passed'*: Maureen O'Sullivan, 'The Wodehouses of Hollywood', in James H. Heineman and Donald R. Bensen (eds.), *P. G. Wodehouse: A Centenary Celebration* (New York, 1981), p. 17.

p. 240 *'a stunning blow'*: PGW to Nella Wodehouse, 10 October 1936, courtesy of Patrick Wodehouse.

p. 240 *Armine always described his brother's writing . . .*: interview with Patrick Wodehouse, 28 August 2000.

p. 240 *'how absolutely right . . .'*: PGW to Nella Wodehouse, 10 October 1936.

p. 241 *'Everything looks very bright'*: PGW to Leonora Cazalet, 28 December 1936, Wodehouse Archive.

p. 241 *'Have you ever done any picture work?'*: PGW to Claude Houghton, 7 January 1937, Ransom.

p. 241 *'being quietly frozen out'*: PGW to Guy Bolton, 8 March 1937, Wodehouse Archive.

p. 241 *Everything he turned in . . .*: ibid.

p. 241 *'There seems to be a curse . . .'*: PGW to William Townend, 24 March 1937, Dulwich.

p. 241 *which he swiftly sold . . .*: *Summer Moonshine* appeared in the *Saturday Evening Post* from 24 July to 11 September 1937.

p. 241 *'I am leading . . .'*: PGW to William Townend, 28 January 1937, Dulwich.

p. 242 *he had visited Hollywood and taken tea with her parents*: Paul Reynolds, jun., to Leonora Cazalet, Reynolds papers, 15 May 1937, Columbia.

p. 242 *'Helen Wills is getting a divorce!!'*: PGW to Leonora Cazalet, 13 July 1937, Wodehouse Archive. Wills was the eight-times Wimbledon tennis champion.

p. 242 *they go down to Los Angeles . . .*: PGW to Leonora Cazalet, 13 August 1937, Wodehouse Archive.

p. 242 *they would read and listen to the radio*: PGW to William Townend, 28 January 1937, Dulwich.

p. 242 *'My day starts . . .'*: ibid.

p. 242 *Ethel had accumulated quite a staff*: interview with Fran Ershler (née Mayer), 16 February 2002. No information survives about the nature of Ethel's surgery, but it may have been acute dental work.

p. 243 *very relaxed and congenial . . .*: interview with Fran Ershler.

p. 243 *'I am getting very fed up . . .'*: PGW to William Townend, 24 March 1937, Dulwich.

p. 244 *Kelland's The Stand-In*: released by UA as *Stand-In*, starring Leslie Howard with Joan Blondell (dir. Jay Garnett) in 1937.

p. 244 *'I turned it down'*: PGW to William Townend, 24 March 1937, Dulwich.

p. 244 *'I'm not worth the money . . .'*: PGW to William Townend, 6 May 1937, Dulwich.

p. 244 *Only the completion of a new novel*: 'If I can think out a story with a beginning, middle and end, it is simply a matter of technique to write it as a full length novel. Anyway, I have no ideas at present'; PGW to Paul Reynolds, 30 March 1937, Reynolds papers, Columbia.

p. 244 *'He told me the whole . . .'*: PGW to William Townend, 7 May 1937, Dulwich.

p. 244 *Wodehouse persuaded Allen . . .*: Murray Hedgcock (ed.), *Wodehouse at the Wicket* (London, 1997), pp. 45–9.

p. 244 *hoped to complete a new serial*: PGW to Paul Reynolds, 15 May 1937, Reynolds papers, Columbia.

p. 244 *'got out a very good plot'*: PGW to Paul Reynolds, 9 June 1937, Reynolds papers, Columbia.

p. 245 *an Ira Gershwin tribute to Wodehouse*: the lyrics included Wodehouse terms like 'chin up', 'old bean', 'dash it' and 'pip pip'.

p. 245 *'I must say . . .'*: PGW to Leonora Cazalet, 13 July 1937, Wodehouse Archive.

p. 245 *after a script conference*: see PGW's 'Analysis of Characters and Scenario of Story', 16 June 1937, RKO-S527, Young.

p. 245 *'What uncongenial work . . .'*: PGW to William Townend, 24 June 1937, Dulwich.

p. 245 *Everything is made very pleasant . . .*: PGW to Leonora Cazalet, 13 July 1937, Wodehouse Archive.

p. 246 *Everybody treated the thing . . .*: ibid.

p. 246 *'Gosh, I'm sick . . .'*: PGW to William Townend, 30 July 1937, Dulwich.

p. 246 *'I have really come across . . .'*: PGW to Leonora Cazalet, 13 August 1937, Wodehouse Archive.

p. 247 *only a passing resemblance to the original*: in later life, Wodehouse disowned *A Damsel in Distress* as 'a Mess [with a story] more suitable to retarded adults and children with water on the brain'; 1975 preface to *A Damsel in Distress*, see Wodehouse Archive.

p. 247 *'put my career back four years'*: see Benny Green, *P. G. Wodehouse: A Literary Biography* (London, 1981), p. 178.

p. 247 *'she's one of the funniest women I've ever met'*: 'Interview with P. G. Wodehouse', Hedda Hopper papers, AMPASL.

p. 247 *part of his first scenario*: see PGW's 'Analysis of Characters and Scenario of Story', Young.

p. 247 *When Wodehouse would occasionally show up . . .*: interview with Allan Scott, in Pat McGilligan (ed.), *Back Story: Interviews with Screenwriters of Hollywood's Golden Age* (Berkeley, 1986), p. 321.

p. 248 *'they were still the niggers of the studio system'*: see Nancy Lynn Schwartz, *The Hollywood Writers' Wars* (New York, 1982), p. 99.

p. 248 *the fiery young screenwriter*: Dunne's later credits included *The Count of Monte Cristo* and *How Green Was My Valley*.

p. 248 *accused Wodehouse of collaborating*: Dunne asked 'if he realised that he was consorting with scabs and scallawags . . . whose sole malign purpose was to break [the] Guild'; Philip Dunne, *Take Two* (New York, 1980), pp. 49–50.

p. 248 *Hammett, Hellman . . .*: Schwartz, *Hollywood Writers' Wars*, p. 105.

p. 249 *a film whose story he disliked*: PGW to William Townend, 4 September 1937, Dulwich.

p. 249 *'Bill, I hate this place!'*: ibid.

CHAPTER 16: 'I have become a biggish bug these days' (1937–1939)

p. 250 *'confronted with a programme . . .'*: Winston S. Churchill, *The Second World War* (London 1948–54), vol. i, p. 212.

p. 250 *Mussolini, to 'a Dictator on the point . . .'*: *The Code of the Woosters* (1938; Everyman, 2000), pp. 62, 46, 18, 43, 66.

p. 252 *'an imbroglio that would test the Wooster soul . . .'*: ibid., p. 10.

p. 252 *'"Man and boy, Jeeves" . . .'*: ibid., p. 38.

p. 252 *'Jeeves . . . stand by to counsel . . .'*: ibid., p. 104.

p. 252 *'when two men of iron will . . .'*: ibid., p. 8.

p. 253 *He spoke with . . . beneath the harrow*: ibid., pp. 9, 40, 48, 107.

p. 253 *'I call her a ghastly girl . . .'*: ibid., p. 15.

p. 253 *'red-hot sparks of pash'*: ibid., p. 220.

p. 253 *'I read her purpose . . .'*: ibid., p. 101.

p. 254 *The whole fact of the matter . . .*: ibid., p. 108.

p. 254 *'What the Voice of the People is saying . . .'*: ibid., p. 143.

p. 254 *'isn't it ghastly . . .'*: PGW to William Townend, 22 November 1937, Dulwich.

p. 254 *'It is working out as quite one of the best . . .'*: PGW to Paul Reynolds, 3 December 1937, Reynolds papers, Columbia.

p. 254 *'I imagine the trouble is that I have twice been stopped. . .'*: PGW to William Townend, 4 January 1938, Dulwich.

p. 255 *'I thought it would never be finished'*: Ethel Wodehouse to Paul Reynolds, 8 February 1938, Reynolds papers, Columbia.

p. 255 *'a sort of elderly Psmith'*: *Performing Flea* (London, 1953), p. 85. See also a less self-conscious description, PGW to William Townend, 2 December 1935, Dulwich.

p. 255 *'they are letting a rather neurotic kind of man . . .'*: *Uncle Fred in the Springtime*, p. 99.

p. 255 great sponge Joyeuse, *'one of the hottest earls'*: *Uncle Dynamite*, pp. 170, 204.

p. 255 an affectionate allusion: *Uncle Fred in the Springtime*, p. 16. The private investigator, Mustard Pott, gives Horace Davenport a precise description of Low Wood, 'a house with a hedge', opposite the fourteenth tee on the golf course, and 'two males, one with cocktail shaker'.

p. 256 *'I go off the rails . . .'*: PGW to William Townend, 13 November 1938, Dulwich.

p. 256 *'I can hardly bear . . .'*: PGW to William Townend, 28 November 1938, Dulwich.

p. 257 *'Do you know . . . a feeling'*: PGW to William Townend, 23 April 1938, Dulwich.

p. 258 *'I am rather stunned by this . . .'*: PGW to J. D. Grimsdick, 24 May 1939, private collection.

p. 258 *'Great excitement'*: PGW to Paul Reynolds, 3 June 1939, Reynolds papers, Columbia.

p. 258 *'Mark Twain appears to be . . .'*: Oxford had awarded Twain an honorary doctorate in 1907.

p. 258 *'proceedings open at 11.20 . . .'*: PGW to S. C. 'Billy' Griffith, 6 June 1939, Griffith papers, private collection.

p. 258 *'I have become a biggish bug these days'*: PGW to William Townend, 6 June 1939, Dulwich.

p. 258 *'there is no question that . . .'*: *The Times*, 22 June 1939.

p. 259 *In the spring of 1939 . . .*: the story is told in a letter from John Griffith to David Cartwright, 5 July 1989, Wodehouse papers, Dulwich.

p. 259 *'someone sophisticated and perhaps remote'*: George Gordon letter, Wodehouse papers, Dulwich.

p. 260 *He said to me . . .*: *Performing Flea*, p. 128.

p. 260 *'a terrific triumph'*: PGW to S. C. 'Billy' Griffith, 27 June 1939, Griffith papers, private collection.

p. 260 *In the procession through the Oxford streets*: see Letty Grierson, 'Honoris Causa', in James H. Heineman and Donald R. Bensen (eds), *P. G. Wodehouse: A Centenary Celebration* (New York, 1981), pp. 31–3. I am indebted to this account for some details of the Encaenia.

p. 260 *'tepid applause'*: PGW to S. C. 'Billy' Griffith, 27 June 1939, Griffith papers, private collection.

p. 261 *Petroniumne dicam . . . ?*: *Oxford University Gazette*, June 1939.

p. 261 *'The only catch . . .'*: PGW to S. C. 'Billy' Griffith, 27 June 1939, Griffith papers, private collection.

p. 261 *'We want Wode-house'*: see Frances Donaldson, *P. G. Wodehouse* (London, 1982), p. 162.

p. 261 *said goodbye to Wodehouse*: *Performing Flea*, p. 108.

p. 261 *a new Uncle Fred story*: Lord Ickenham 'pinches a villa on the Riviera, and the duke of Dunstable gets into trouble with the police at this Riviera town and has to lie low, so Uncle Fred makes him shave off his moustache and takes him on as a butler, in which capacity he falls in love with the cook, who turns him down because in her opinion he isn't quite a gentleman'; PGW to William Townend, 6 June 1939, Dulwich.

p. 262 *'now all I want is . . .'*: PGW to William Townend, 2 August 1939, Dulwich.

p. 262 *'Ethel was talking airily . . .'*: PGW to William Townend, 3 October 1939, Dulwich.

p. 262 *He had only a few qualms*: PGW to William Townend, 3 October 1939, Dulwich.

p. 262 *'Just what was needed . . .'*: ibid.

p. 262 *'Have you read them?'*: PGW to William Townend, 8 December 1939, Dulwich.

p. 263 *'everything [is] very quiet'*: PGW to Frank Sullivan, 16 October 1939, Sullivan papers, Cornell.

p. 263 *'I am glad Le Touquet is so peaceful . . .'*: Paul Reynolds, jun., to PGW, 17 November 1939, Reynolds papers, Columbia.

p. 263 *'My new novel Quick Service . . .'*: PGW to Paul Reynolds, jun., 1 December 1939, Reynolds papers, Columbia.

CHAPTER 17: 'The *hors d'oeuvre* in Fate's banquet' (1940)

p. 267 *'Young men, starting out . . .'*: PAAA. For the published texts of these broadcasts, see Iain Sproat, *Wodehouse at War* (New York, 1981). This ground-breaking and important book is still the indispensable guide to the many controversies surrounding Wodehouse's Berlin broadcasts. I gratefully acknowledge a profound debt to Mr Sproat, who has been very helpful in the research for this biography.

p. 267 *dreamed of getting away to America*: PGW to Guy Bolton, 23 December 1940, Wodehouse Archive.

p. 267 *Out-of-season Le Touquet*: ibid.

p. 267 *'desert island feeling'*: PGW to William Townend, 3 October 1939, Dulwich.

p. 267 *'running a doss house . . .'*: ibid.

p. 267 *two medical officers*: PGW, statement to Major E. J. P. Cussen, 9 September 1944, Cussen.

p. 267 *Ethel raced about . . .*: interview with Jacqueline Grant, 3 April 2001.

p. 267 *invite likely looking young British servicemen . . .*: Ethel Wodehouse to Denis Mackail, 26 June 1945, Wodehouse Archive.

p. 267 *pressed him to come to Low Wood*: Robert ('Rex') King-Clark, *Free for a Blast* (London, 1988), p. 114.

p. 268 *susceptible to what she called 'a flutter'*: interview with Jacqueline Grant, 3 April 2001.

p. 268 *'I spent several happy evenings . . .'*: King-Clark, *Free for a Blast*, pp. 114–15.

p. 268 *'Is everybody happy?'*: interview with Jacqueline Grant, 3 April 2001.

p. 268 *'I work in the morning . . .'*: PGW to William Townend, 23 January 1940, Dulwich.

p. 268 *'I had tea with [Wodehouse] . . .'*: King-Clark, *Free for a Blast*, p. 114.

p. 268 *There is a cosy fire . . .*: George Orwell, 'Boys' Weeklies', in *Inside the Whale and Other Essays* (London, 1962), pp. 189–90.

p. 269 *'I can't think what is going to happen . . .'*: PGW to William Townend, 23 January 1940, Dulwich.

p. 269 *the British naval blockade*: A. J. P. Taylor, *English History 1914–1945* (Oxford, 1965), p. 461.

p. 269 *'My only fear is . . .'*: PGW to William Townend, 23 January 1940, Dulwich.

p. 269 *make Hot Water into a musical*: Paul Reynolds to PGW, 14 May 1940, Reynolds papers, Columbia.

p. 269 *one of his favourite novels*: the *Post*'s serialization of *Quick Service* ran through May and June 1940.

p. 269 *Life wanted to commission a piece . . .*: Paul Reynolds to PGW, 31 May 1940, Reynolds papers, Columbia.

p. 269 *seven dogs . . . a stray cat*: PGW to William Townend, 6 April 1940, Dulwich.

p. 269 *plugging away at his new novel*: Paul Reynolds to PGW, 24 April 1940, Reynolds papers, Columbia.

p. 269 *'It's such a business getting started . . .'*: PGW to Paul Reynolds, 25 April 1940, Reynolds papers, Columbia.

p. 270 *I wrote a short story . . .*: ibid.

p. 270 *'Is it possible', he asked, 'for a hard-up young peer . . .'*: PGW to William Townend, 6 April 1940, Dulwich.

p. 270 *'I have nothing to offer . . .'*: quoted in Taylor, *English History*, p. 475.

p. 271 *the Dutch army had capitulated*: ibid. p. 485.

p. 271 *the opening lines of 'Buried Treasure'*: *Strand*, September 1936; *Lord Emsworth and Others* (1937; London, 1966), p. 71: 'The situation in Germany had come up for discussion in the bar parlour of the Angler's Rest, and it was generally agreed that Hitler was standing at the crossroads and would soon be compelled to do something definite.'

p. 271 *The front office was full . . .*: 'The Big Push', *Punch*, 13 December 1939.

Wodehouse's other pre-war reference to Hitler (in fact, to his moustache) comes in 'Buried Treasure'. See also 'Shock Dogs', *Punch*, 14 February 1940.

p. 271 *British vice-consul in Boulogne*: Cussen, p. 3.

p. 272 *'our Bible at that time'*: Ethel Wodehouse to Denis Mackail, 26 June 1945, Wodehouse Archive.

p. 272 *If he crossed the Channel . . .*: on 28 May the Foreign Office, prompted by Leonora, tried to enlist the help of the consul in Dieppe, saying 'money no object'. To no avail. 'Impossible to help Wodehouse from here', cabled the consul in reply; 30 May 1940, Wodehouse Archive.

p. 272 *hordes of French colonial troops*: 'Apologia', Berg.

p. 272 *'the general feeling was . . .'*: Cussen, p. 2.

p. 273 *Their flight was bungled . . .*: ibid., p. 3.

p. 273 *he and Ethel found Arthur Grant . . .*: see Ruth Grant's Le Touquet diary, 'The Flight', Wodehouse Archive.

p. 273 *a Mr Lawry*: through a mistranscription, Cussen refers to this man as 'Mr Barry'.

p. 273 *in flight from the invaders*: see Cussen, *passim*, and Ruth Grant's Le Touquet diary, 'The Flight', Wodehouse Archive.

p. 273 *dubbed the Exodus*: see Julian Jackson, *France: The Dark Years, 1940–1944* (Oxford, 2001), p. 120.

p. 273 *the complete disintegration of social order*: 'Apologia', Berg.

p. 274 *'The blazing sunshine . . .'*: ibid.

p. 274 *There was no possibility of escape*: William Townend and Leonora Cazalet did try to organize a cross-Channel escape by motor boat in early June, but no details of this abortive effort survive. See William Townend to the editor of the *Times Literary Supplement*, 31 July 1940, Dulwich.

p. 274 *'read P. G. Wodehouse . . .'*: Michael Davie (ed.), *The Diaries of Evelyn Waugh* (London, 1976), p. 470.

p. 274 *'My own first meeting . . .'*: 'Apologia', Berg.

p. 274 *The first time you see a German soldier . . .*: this passage, which appears in the 'Apologia', also features in almost identical terms in the first Berlin broadcast.

p. 275 *'invited the blighters . . .'*: PGW to William Townend, 18 April 1953, Dulwich.

p. 275 *'weeks went by and nothing happened . . .'*: 'Apologia', Berg.

p. 275 *'Afraid no news . . .'*: Leonora Cazalet to Paul Reynolds, 28 May 1940, Reynolds papers, Columbia.

p. 276 *'the whole experience . . .'*: Paul Reynolds to PGW, 31 May 1940, Reynolds papers, Columbia.

p. 276 *'a petition is being got up . . .'*: Paul Reynolds to Ethel Wodehouse, 12 June 1940, Reynolds papers, Columbia. This document, dated 4 June 1940, was delivered to the Chargé d'Affaires at the German embassy in Washington, and 'respectfully point[ed] out' that 'Mr Wodehouse is fifty-nine years of age, that he has never had any military or political connections and that without exception his writings are of a light, humorous order, completely free from propaganda.' The request that

Wodehouse should be returned to the USA illustrates the complexity of his position. He was, of course, a British, not an American, national and the USA was still technically neutral. Petition in Wodehouse Archive.

p. 276 *On the morning of Sunday, 21 July*: this is the date PGW gives in his 'Apologia'; in his statement to Major Cussen, possibly in a mistranscription, he refers to Sunday, 27 July.

p. 276 *'The old stomach did a double buck-and-wing'*: 'Apologia', Berg.

p. 276 *'I shook from base to apex . . .'*: ibid.

p. 276 *The Complete Works of Shakespeare*: Wodehouse made a particular point in his first Berlin broadcast of drawing this detail to his future biographers' attention. The volume in question is now in the Wodehouse Archive, inscribed with the dates of his internment under the heading 'One Man's War'.

p. 277 *a dozen other Le Touquet internees*: also in the party at this stage was Bert Haskins, with whom Wodehouse later developed an important relationship.

p. 277 *'looked like something out of a film . . .'*: second Berlin broadcast, PAAA.

p. 277 *Wodehouse's experience . . .*: I am indebted to Thomas Smith for his assistance with this information.

p. 277 *civilian internment camps . . .*: see I. C. B. Dear (ed.), *The Oxford Companion to World War II* (Oxford, 1995), pp. 569–70.

p. 277 *the air of a ragged regiment*: CNB.

p. 278 *'nearly insane'*: Ethel Wodehouse to Denis Mackail, 26 June 1945, Wodehouse Archive.

p. 278 *the address of a room*: Cussen, p. 19. See also Foreign Office to William Townend, 4 October 1940, Dulwich.

p. 278 *After about ten days . . .*: Ethel Wodehouse to Denis Mackail, 26 June 1945, Wodehouse Archive.

p. 278 *referred to as Wodehouse in Wonderland*: *Performing Flea* (London, 1953), p. 175.

p. 278 *'While this was a hell of a thing . . .'*: CNB.

p. 278 *12 foot long by about 8 foot wide . . .*: CNB.

p. 279 *a mixture of uncertainty and terrible monotony*: CNB.

p. 279 *'Prison brings out all that is best in us all'*: CNB.

p. 279 *'Thank you for Jeeves!'*: CNB.

p. 279 *Summing up my experience . . .*: second Berlin broadcast, PAAA.

p. 279 *no food and drink*: CNB.

p. 280 *I was first to alight . . .*: CNB.

p. 280 *'We spent a week at Liège . . .'*: third Berlin broadcast, PAAA.

p. 280 *bloodstained and dirty*: interview with Robert Whitby, 27 October 2001. I am indebted to Mr Whitby for his generous contribution to Chapters 17 and 18.

p. 280 *the same resemblance . . .*: third Berlin broadcast, PAAA.

p. 280 *'the latest news is . . .'*: Leonora Cazalet to A. P. Watt, 2 August 1940, Watt papers, Chapel Hill.

p. 280 *'The Citadel of Huy . . .'*: fourth Berlin broadcast, PAAA.

p. 281 *the right 'to communicate with our families'*: 21 August 1940, CNB.

p. 281 *'ragged and down at heels'*: 29 August 1940, CNB.

p. 282 *A wonderful day!*: 14 August 1940, CNB.

p. 282 *'with a jam tart wrapped round his chest. . .'*: 4 and 5 September 1940, CNB.

p. 283 *'horror . . . lurking round the corner'*: 8 August 1940, CNB.

p. 283 *'Neither can see the other . . .'*: fourth Berlin broadcast, PAAA.

p. 283 *'Their wives are down below . . .'*: 25 August 1940, CNB.

p. 283 *rumours that the war was about to end*: 31 August 1940, CNB.

p. 284 *'Subita Germanorum sunt concilia'*: 30 October 1940, CNB. The phrase echoes Caesar, *De Bello Gallico*, 3.8.

CHAPTER 18: 'Camp was really great fun' (1940-1941)

p. 285 *the three-day journey*: the train's route took in Neanderthal, Halle, Gottbus, Breslau (Wrocław), Gleiwitz (Gliwice) and terminated at Tost, where the internees had to walk for about half an hour from the station. See Max Enke's Tost memoir, Wodehouse Archive. Tost (the old German name) is now Toszek, about fifteen miles north of Gliwice, Poland. I gratefully acknowledge the assistance of Alan Stretton with the research for this chapter.

p. 285 *'looking like something the carrion crow had brought in'*: ibid. This description is corroborated by Albert Edward Forster (1910–77), an Anglo–Dutch translator interned with Wodehouse, who reported that when the Huy contingent arrived 'they looked like scarecrows'; unpublished memoir. I am grateful to Michael Forster for this information.

p. 285 *'frightful thing about these journeys. . .'*: 8 September 1940, CNB.

p. 285 *Bob Whitby*: interview with Robert Whitby, 27 October 2001.

p. 285 *'Some humorist on parade'*: 8 September 1940, CNB.

p. 285 *church bells had rung out*: A. J. P. Taylor, *English History 1914–1945* (Oxford, 1965), p. 499.

p. 285 *During the remaining ten months . . .*: ibid., pp. 498–506.

p. 285 *'We have air battles overhead . . .'*: Leonora Cazalet to Paul Reynolds, 26 October 1940, Reynolds papers, Columbia.

p. 286 *Ethel had been traced to the home . . .*: Foreign Office to William Townend, 4 October 1940, Dulwich. The address was Le Moulin, Saint-Georges par Le Parc, Pas de Calais.

p. 286 *'I have no news of Plummie'*: Leonora Cazalet to Paul Reynolds, 12 October 1940, Reynolds papers, Columbia. Reynolds explained (15 October 1940) that PGW's account did not actually have a thousand dollars, because Wodehouse had made his recent contracts directly with Doubleday, and that there was a problem with transferring funds to 'certain countries' without permission. He promised to try to solve the problem, but on 18 October 1940 the Federal Reserve Bank refused to transfer any money to Paris. Reynolds tried again on 28 October and 11 November, in vain. Reynolds papers, Columbia.

p. 286 *he had appealed to the Red Cross to intervene, and had been ignored*: Ernest J.

Swift, Vice-Chairman of American Red Cross to Paul Reynolds, 11 September 1940: 'The ICRC . . . cannot intervene, especially when the life of the person concerned does not seem in danger.' Reynolds papers, Columbia.

p. 286 *'is believed to be in a concentration camp . . .'*: Paul Reynolds to Mr L. B. Saunders, 19 September 1940, Reynolds papers, Columbia.

p. 286 *Goodness knows when you will get this . . .*: PGW to Paul Reynolds, 21 October 1940, Reynolds papers, Columbia. A second postcard, asking for $15 and $5 to be paid to two Canadians, a Ruth Chambers and a Stephen Enke, in repayment for money borrowed from a fellow internee, Max Enke, to whom Wodehouse had become very attached, arrived at Reynolds's office at the beginning of November. (Ruth Chambers was Enke's married daughter; Stephen was his son.) This has been described (Barry Phelps, *P. G. Wodehouse: Man and Myth* (London, 1992), p. 209) as a coded signal, circumventing the censor, to Enke's family that their father was alive and well and safe in Ilag VIII, but the story is apocryphal. The Germans were efficient in notifying the Red Cross of their internees' well-being, and such manoeuvres were not necessary. See PGW to Paul Reynolds, 1 November 1940, Reynolds papers, Columbia. These and other postcards are described by Reynolds's son in Paul R. Reynolds, jun., *The Middle Man: Adventures of a Literary Agent* (New York, 1971), pp. 106–13.

p. 287 *'in a room with fifty other men . . .'*: PGW to William Townend, 11 May 1942, Dulwich.

p. 287 *'two huge unblinking eyes of the palest blue . . .'*: *Money in the Bank* (London, 1946), p. 41. See also N. T. P. Murphy, *In Search of Blandings* (London, 1981), pp. 116–21.

p. 287 *the nostalgic and sentimental similarities*: Lord Uffenham's country seat is modelled on Fairlawne, the Cazalet family estate outside Tonbridge, Kent.

p. 288 *a 'lost feeling', evocative of his childhood*: 8 September 1940, CNB.

p. 288 *a converted mental hospital*: today, the internment camp is once again a mental hospital.

p. 288 *part of a network . . .*: the camp was originally Oflag 8D, and was used to house officers of the French, Dutch and Belgian armies captured during the blitzkrieg. It was redesignated as Internierungslager VIII in October 1940. Wodehouse was among the first internees. See Jonathan F. Vance, 'Tost Internment Camp', unpublished thesis, University of Western Ontario.

p. 288 *'The thing about Tost . . .'*: fifth Berlin broadcast, PAAA.

p. 288 *'. . . the local lunatic asylum'*: first Berlin broadcast, PAAA.

p. 288 *'the cream of the camp we think'*: 19 October 1940, CNB.

p. 288 *'White frost on roofs. I am lying on my bed . . .'*: CNB.

p. 289 *governed by 'rumours and potatoes'*: fifth Berlin broadcast, PAAA.

p. 289 *At Liège and Huy . . .*: ibid.

p. 289 *'Camp was really great fun'*: PGW to William Townend, 11 May 1942, Dulwich.

p. 289 *'without women . . . we relapse into boyhood . . .'*: CNB.

p. 289 *'The great advantage [of Tost] . . .'*: CNB.

p. 290 *he only saw the Kommandant on one occasion*: Cussen, p. 3.

p. 290 *'The really important thing is the inner camp'*: cf. 'The inner life of a boarding house is the real life of a Public School', *The Pothunters* (London, 1902).

p. 290 *'presided over by a Lagerführer . . .'*: fifth Berlin broadcast, PAAA.

p. 290 *'the answer to an internee's prayer'*: *Performing Flea* (London, 1953), pp. 201–2. The final section of this book, 'Huy Day by Day', contains a meticulous, but essentially innocent, account of the workings of the camp. If Wodehouse was aware of the darker side of camp life, he did not record it.

p. 290 *'was working all the time in our interests'*: fifth Berlin broadcast, PAAA.

p. 290 *'Germans are swell guys'*: 30 October 1940, CNB.

p. 290 *this unexceptionable comment*: 'Having regard to the circumstances in which this journal was written, I do not think any very great exception can fairly be taken . . . The [*entry quoted*] above may contain sentiments with which one definitely disagrees, but Wodehouse is not the first person to have expressed such views'; Cussen, p. 6.

p. 290 *'The morale of the men . . .'*: PGW to William Townend, 11 May 1942, Dulwich.

p. 291 *Their sense of betrayal . . .*: an unidentified correspondent has described 'quite a rumpus in the Camp when [PGW] left to go to the Adlon hotel in Berlin. A deputation of . . . the 200% British . . . [demanded] that all the Wodehouse books be removed from the Camp library and destroyed'; Wodehouse Archive.

p. 291 *'Home Before Christmas'*: interview with Robert Whitby, 27 October 2001.

p. 291 *there were several American journalists in Berlin*: see William L. Shirer, *'This is Berlin': Reporting from Nazi Germany 1938–1940* (London, 1999), and Harry W. Flannery, *Assignment to Berlin* (London, 1942).

p. 292 *Thuermer advised that 'Money for Jam . . .'*: Cussen, p. 5.

p. 292 *'He [Wodehouse] Declines Favors*: see Iain Sproat, *Wodehouse at War* (New York, 1981), pp. 45–8, for a penetrating analysis of this phase of the controversy.

p. 293 *'Plum is in an internment camp . . .'*: Leonora Cazalet to Paul Reynolds, 14 January 1941, Reynolds papers, Columbia.

p. 293 *a concerted operation run from the Foreign Office*: Ilag VIII was monitored by the Prisoner of War department in the Foreign Office from the early days of the war. The presence in Tost of several war graves gardeners ensured that the Imperial War Graves Commission was active in lobbying the Foreign Office about the internees' conditions soon after the fall of France. PRO, Kew, FO 916 2596.

p. 293 *Red Cross and Swiss embassy representatives*: PRO, Kew, FO 916 524, 1 January 1943.

p. 293 *a German-run paper, the Camp*: Cussen, p. 4.

p. 293 *elegant young lecturers*: CNB.

p. 294 *Reynolds unwittingly contributed to the excitement*: Paul Reynolds to an unidentified correspondent: 'So much interest was expressed in what had happened to [PGW] that we went ahead and let that postal card be published'; 10 January 1941, Reynolds papers, Columbia.

p. 294 *Prince Albert tobacco as requested*: Paul Reynolds to PGW, 15 January 1941, Reynolds papers, Columbia.

p. 294 *'not only laughed, but applauded . . .'*: PGW to Wesley Stout, 29 November 1941, Reynolds papers, Columbia.

p. 294 *a report that Wodehouse had spirited his novel out*: Paul Reynolds to Leonora Cazalet, 6 March 1941, Reynolds papers, Columbia.

p. 294 *a Daily Express journalist*: 6 April 1941, Reynolds papers, Columbia. The journalist, Fraser, subsequently had a nervous breakdown, and fades from view.

p. 294 *'a likelihood that [Ethel] has been interned'*: Paul Reynolds to Leonora Cazalet, 7 February 1941, Reynolds papers, Columbia.

p. 295 *not even the British embassy*: 'Nothing is known here as yet concerning Mrs Wodehouse', 3 April 1941, Reynolds papers, Columbia.

p. 295 *living at 241 rue Nationale, Lille*: Leonora Cazalet to Paul Reynolds, 6 April 1941, Reynolds papers, Columbia.

p. 295 *'a charming house with a huge park'*: Ethel Wodehouse to Denis Mackail, 26 June 1945, Wodehouse Archive.

p. 295 *staying with a Madame de Rocquigny*: 14 May 1941, Reynolds papers, Columbia.

p. 295 *Coco, the parrot, meanwhile, had learned*: PGW to Denis Mackail, 7 August 1945, Wodehouse Archive.

p. 295 *'Mummie and Plum evidently get news of each other'*: Leonora Cazalet to Paul Reynolds, 6 April 1941, Reynolds papers, Columbia.

p. 295 *Lagerführer Buchelt launched . . .*: Cussen, p. 7.

p. 295 *When Buchelt discovered that . . .*: Leonora Cazalet to Paul Reynolds, 10 June 1941, Reynolds papers, Columbia.

p. 295 *shipped to America*: George Kennan was the no. 2 Counselor in the American embassy in Berlin from 1939 to December 1941. He remembers meeting PGW and recalls what he supposed was his normal mood 'of lighthearted charm and amused detachment'. Private letter to the author, 23 March 2001.

p. 295 *through the proper channels*: the manuscripts were *Joy in the Morning*, *Full Moon*, 'Tangled Hearts' and 'Excelsior'. *Money in the Bank* was shipped separately.

p. 295 *'appears to be in terrific form . . .'*: Leonora Cazalet to Paul Reynolds, 10 June 1941, Reynolds papers, Columbia.

p. 295 *I'm not absolutely certain . . .*: 'Jeeves and the Unbidden Guest', in *Carry On, Jeeves* (1925; London, 1957), p. 46. See also the story 'Fate', in *Young Men in Spats* (1936; Everyman, 2002): 'it just shows what toys we are in the hands of Fate', p. 9.

p. 296 *As he reported it later*: see Cussen, p. 7.

p. 296 *A copy of the Saturday Evening Post*: the *Post* had serialized the novel from May to June 1940. This detail is reported by Wodehouse in Cussen.

p. 296 *'Why don't you do some broadcasts . . . he reported to Berlin'*: Cussen, p. 7.

p. 296 *Other Tost internees, for instance, reported*: Albert Edward Forster, unpublished memoir.

p. 297 *'The release of Wodehouse . . .'*: George Orwell, 'In Defence of P. G. Wodehouse', in Peter Davison (ed.), *The Complete Works of George Orwell* (London, 1988), vol. xvii, p. 60.

p. 297 *'was precisely that he was not . . .'*: Sproat, *Wodehouse at War* p. 65.

p. 297 *Hitler's English-language interpreter*: confusingly, the head of von Ribbentrop's private office was also called Paul Schmidt. Hitler's Paul Schmidt is more significant, and later published a memoir, *Hitler's Interpreter* (London, 1951).

p. 297 *a stout, red-cheeked civil servant . . .*: Flannery, *Assignment to Berlin*, p. 32.

p. 298 *left the United States it was under suspicion of espionage*: *Report of US Army Pearl Harbor Board*. Werner Plack was identified as an associate of Hans Wilhelm Rohl, a high-living man-about-town in Los Angeles and Hollywood, well known for his Nazi sympathies, and who left the USA in 1940 'under suspicion of being a German agent'.

p. 298 *the self-styled English-speaking go-between*: Plack's other responsibilities included baby-sitting William Joyce (Lord Haw-Haw) and Julian Amery, who were both later hanged for treason.

p. 298 *According to Iain Sproat*: Sproat, *Wodehouse at War*, p. 58.

p. 298 *Wodehouse's circumstances during May and June . . .*: George Kennan, for instance, remembers seeing Wodehouse in an unidentified camp outside Berlin; private letter to the author, 23 March 2001.

p. 299 *In 1933 Goebbels, who was one of the first*: see John Carver Edwards, *Berlin Calling* (New York, 1991), pp. 1–40.

p. 299 *Hitler was enraged*: Ian Kershaw, *Hitler 1936–1945: Nemesis* (London, 2000), pp. 369–81.

p. 299 *In a widespread joke*: ibid., p. 375.

p. 299 *felt terrific and looked like Fred Astaire*: *Performing Flea*, p. 211.

p. 299 *apparently uncensored*: Paul Reynolds to Leonora Cazalet, 13 June 1941, Reynolds papers, Columbia.

p. 300 *'My War with Germany'*: this was published by the *Post* on 19 July 1941.

p. 300 *when it was published internationally*: it was also published in an abridged form in Britain by the *Daily Mail* on 17 July 1941.

p. 300 *It should be simple to arrive . . .*: 'My War with Germany', *Saturday Evening Post*, 19 July 1941.

p. 300 *As his MI5 interrogator would correctly observe*: Cussen, p. 3.

p. 300 *[his] main idea . . .*: Orwell, 'In Defence of P. G. Wodehouse', p. 54.

CHAPTER 19: 'It was a loony thing to do' (June 1941)

p. 301 *leaving the unfinished manuscript of Full Moon behind*: Cussen, p. 8.

p. 301 *Mackenzie*: Noel Barnard Teesdale Mackenzie was a Yorkshire schoolmaster who had left England in 1939 to live in France to avoid arrest on charges of homosexuality. He remained in Berlin, and was employed as a translator for the International Social Economic Institute, and later the German Foreign Office's Language Service, supplementing his income by giving bridge lessons and betting on horses.

p. 301 *night train to Berlin*: see 'Now That I Have Turned Both Cheeks', pp. 1–12,

Wodehouse Archive. PGW gave various, mutually consistent, accounts of his movements 21–28 June. I have drawn this account from a range of sources.

p. 301 *As recently as 14 June*: Cussen, pp. 5–6.

p. 301 *'attributed . . . to the efforts'*: 'Now That I Have Turned Both Cheeks', p. 8, Wodehouse Archive.

p. 301 *On 12 January she had written*: ibid., pp. 9–10.

p. 302 *'a sketchy breakfast'*: ibid., p. 11.

p. 302 *In mid-1941, Berlin was buoyant*: Alexandra Ritchie, *Faust's Metropolis: A History of Berlin* (London, 1998), p. 497.

p. 302 *there was a cup-final match*: the game was played on Sunday, 22 June 1941. Rapid Wien lost 4–3.

p. 302 *'was the pinnacle . . .'*: Ritchie, *Faust's Metropolis*, p. 475.

p. 302 *Baron Raven von Barnikow*: in a letter to Guy Bolton, Wodehouse wrote: 'Barnikow [was] one of my oldest friends . . . I had never looked on him as a German at all, as he was so entirely American'; PGW to Guy Bolton, 1 September 1945, Wodehouse Archive. It is said that the discovery of his opposition to Hitler contributed to von Barnikow's suicide outside his Pomeranian hunting lodge in 1942.

p. 303 *to get Wodehouse exchanged for a German businessman*: Cussen, pp. 8–9. The businessman was described by PGW as a 'screw-manufacturer'; he was probably joking.

p. 303 *Von Barnikow loaned him . . .*: 'Apologia', Berg.

p. 303 *chatting about life . . .*: ibid., p. 12.

p. 303 *Wodehouse always said . . .*: PGW to Michael Joseph, 16 July 1945, Wodehouse Archive.

p. 303 *'It was during this conversation . . .'*: Cussen, pp 11–12.

p. 304 *'anxious to perform a service . . .'*: Report to US Secretary of State, 28 July 1941, *Foreign Service of the USA*; State Department.

p. 304 *published shortly after the events*: 'In Defence of P. G. Wodehouse' was first published in *Windmill* in July 1945.

p. 305 *'to broadcast on Nazi radio . . .'*: 'In Defence of P. G. Wodehouse', in *Essays* (London, 1984), p. 297.

p. 305 *Evelyn Waugh, who knew him*: Evelyn Waugh, *Sunday Times*, 15 July 1961.

p. 306 *'it was a loony thing to do'*: *Performing Flea* (London, 1953), p. 115.

p. 306 *'I can now, of course, see that this was an insane thing to do'*: PGW to Foreign Office, 21 November 1942, Wodehouse Archive.

p. 306 *'Isn't it the damnedest thing . . .'*: PGW to Guy Bolton, 1 September 1945, Wodehouse Archive.

p. 306 *'every country in the world'*: these words were reported by Harry Flannery in his exceedingly dubious *Assignment to Berlin* (London, 1942), p. 247, but they accurately reflect PGW's sense of bewilderment during this first week of freedom.

p. 306 *began 'to get blurred'*: Cussen, p. 8.

p. 306 *'I told them I was going to broadcast'*: Cussen, p. 8.

p. 306 *a magazine article about camp life*: this was published in *Cosmopolitan* in October 1941 as 'My Years behind Barbed Wire'.

p. 306–7 *'I had received a great number of letters . . .'*: 'Now That I Have Turned Both Cheeks', p. 12. See also 'Apologia', Berg.

p. 307 *'how a little group of British people . . .'*: 'Now That I Have Turned Both Cheeks', p. 13.

p. 307 *'My motive . . . in doing the talks'*: 'Apologia', Berg.

p. 307 *A cheery cable to Maureen O'Sullivan*: 'Listen in tonight,' ran the message, quoting the frequency on which she could hear the broadcast. See Maureen O'Sullivan, 'The Wodehouses of Hollywood', in James H. Heineman and Donald R. Bensen (eds.), *P. G. Wodehouse: A Centenary Celebration* (New York, 1981), p. 17.

p. 307 *'Hope broadcasts will be of such nature . . .'*: Paul Reynolds to PGW, 26 June 1941, Reynolds papers, Columbia.

p. 307–8 *'we felt very far from our snug homes . . .'*: first Berlin broadcast, PAAA.

p. 308 *'I never was interested in politics'*: *New York Times*, 26 June 1941.

p. 308 *a mixture of dupe and collaborator*: see Flannery, *Assignment to Berlin*, pp. 240–56.

p. 309 *I believe you wrote a book . . .*: the text of the CBS interview and Elmer Davis's conclusion is found ibid., pp. 246–7.

p. 309 *'I'm living here at the Adlon'*: ibid.

p. 310 *a vicious attack on Wodehouse*: published in *Saturday Review of Literature*, August–September 1944, Reynolds papers, Columbia.

p. 310 *Mr Wodehouse's many friends . . .*: Flannery, *Assignment to Berlin*, p. 248.

p. 310 *urgently tried to telephone his client in Berlin*: calls from neutral countries were delayed by as much as half an hour for military censorship; it is not clear if he was able to speak to his client. Reynolds papers, Columbia.

CHAPTER 20: 'The global howl' (June 1941)

p. 312 *He was introduced . . .*: first Berlin broadcast, PAAA

p. 312 *Denis Mackail was one*: Mackail, *Life with Topsy* (London, 1942), p. 384.

p. 312 *Mackail was not indignant*: ibid.

p. 313 *a crowd of super-patriotic Englishmen*: 'Apologia', Berg.

p. 313 *'I remember', he wrote later . . .*: ibid.

p. 314 *'Impossible you to realise American . . .'*: Wesley Stout to PGW, 30 June 1941, Reynolds papers, Columbia.

p. 314 *'At all costs to ourself . . .'*: Leonora Cazalet to PGW, 4 July 1941, Reynolds papers, Columbia.

p. 314 *'a great deal of mental pain'*: Cussen, p. 12.

p. 314 *The press assumption that Wodehouse . . .*: *Daily Mirror*, 28 June 1941.

p. 314 *a vehement correspondence*: *Daily Telegraph*, 1–13 July 1941.

p. 315 *Most wounding of all*: A. A. Milne letter, *Daily Telegraph*, 3 July 1941; see Ann Thwaite, *A. A. Milne: His Life* (London, 1990), pp. 441–9.

p. 315 '*The trouble with P. G. . . .*': William Townend to 'Slacker' Christison, 16 April 1945, Dulwich.

p. 315 *noises of outrage from parliamentary patriots*: Hansard, HC (series 5), vol. 372, cols. 1344–5 (2 July 1941); col. 1518 (3 July 1941); vol. 373, col. 32 (8 July 1941); cols. 145–6 (9 July 1941)

p. 315 '*lent his services to the Nazi . . .*': Hansard HC (series 5), vol. 373, col. 145 (9 July 1941).

p. 316 '*I do not want to see Wodehouse shot . . .*': Harold Nicolson, diary, 4 January 1944, private papers. I am most grateful to Nigel Nicolson for sharing this information.

p. 316 *had entertained a number . . .*: see Charles Graves, *Off the Record* (London, 1942), pp. 193–9. Graves claims that Michael Foot was present, representing the *Evening Standard*, but Foot told the author that this was not so.

p. 316 *moved even Churchill to regret*: see Ruth Dudley Edwards, *Newspapermen: Hugh Cudlipp, Cecil Harmsworth King and the Glory Days of Fleet Street* (London, 2003), p. 154.

p. 316 *According to Hugh Cudlipp*: in Hugh Cudlipp, *Publish and be Damned! The Astonishing Story of the Daily Mirror* (London, 1953), pp. 132–3, cited in Edwards, *Newspapermen*, p. 101.

p. 316 *the minister being accused*: Francis Williams, *Nothing So Strange* (London, 1970), pp. 164–6. See also John Charmley, *Duff Cooper* (London, 1987), pp. 151–3.

p. 316–7 *fuelled with a vicious yellow vodka*: Graves, *Off the Record*, pp. 193–9.

p. 317 '*blue pencils, censors, the Ministry . . .*': BBC internal memo, 6 July 1941, R 34/271, Caversham.

p. 317 *argued strongly against broadcasting it as a 'postscript'*: ibid.

p. 317 *This meeting instructed . . .*: 'it was undesirable to broadcast this script (a) because of Counsel's opinion and the use of the BBC to broadcast material so described [*and*] (b) because of the possibility that this script with its many exaggerations might provoke reactions in America and at home opposite to those desired'; confidential BBC internal memo of 15 July 1941, R 34/271, Caversham.

p. 317 *Cassandra made the broadcast . . .*: there were in fact two versions transmitted, a domestic script, and a longer version for the United States; R 34/271, Caversham.

p. 318 *The BBC duty log . . .*: R 34/271 Policy, Caversham.

p. 318 '*I have never heard anything like this . . .*': Dorothy L. Sayers to Stephen Tallents, 15 July 1941, R 34/271, Caversham.

p. 318 *it was Cassandra's 'postscript' which intensified . . .*: Orwell, 'In Defence of P. G. Wodehouse', in Peter Davison (ed.), *The Complete Works of George Orwell* (London, 1998), vol. xvii, p. 61.

p. 319 *was the sole responsibility for the broadcast . . .*: *The Times*, 22 July 1941. This was almost his last act as Minister for Information. In a government reshuffle the following week, he left the government and was sent on a special mission to

Singapore on Churchill's behalf. It is significant that Cooper makes no reference to this episode in his memoirs, *Old Men Forget* (London, 1953).

p. 319 *'expressed the view that . . .'*: Duff Cooper to W. D. Connor, 23 July 1941, copy in Wodehouse Archive.

p. 319 *As George Orwell pointed out . . .*: Orwell, 'In Defence of P. G. Wodehouse', p. 70.

p. 320 *'The Press and Public of England . . .'*: fourth Berlin broadcast, PAAA.

p. 320 *Rebutting the charge . . .*: ibid.

p. 320 *I can honestly say . . .*: 'Apologia', Berg.

p. 321 *'I have heard records . . .'*: Leonora Cazalet to Paul Reynolds, 16 July 1941, Reynolds papers, Columbia.

p. 321 *'a bit like a mother with an idiot child . . .'*: Leonora Cazalet to Denis Mackail, 21 July 1941, Wodehouse Archive.

p. 321 *Reynolds was dismayed . . .*: see Paul Reynolds to Leonora Cazalet, 16 July, 28 July, 11 August 1941, Reynolds papers, Columbia.

p. 321 *We must have Mr Wodehouse's express promise . . .*: Wesley Stout to Paul Reynolds, 21 July 1941, Reynolds papers, Columbia.

p. 322 *'Money in Bank good . . .'*: Wesley Stout to PGW, 23 July 1941, Reynolds papers, Columbia.

p. 322 *To Reynolds, Stout was brutally frank*: Wesley Stout to Paul Reynolds, 23 July 1941, Reynolds papers, Columbia. See also letter of 31 July 1941.

p. 322 *'why his broadcasts are folly'*: Paul Reynolds to Sumner Welles, 28 July 1941, Reynolds papers, Columbia.

p. 322 *'Those letters in the Daily Telegraph . . .'*: PGW to William Townend, 11 May 1942, Dulwich.

p. 322 *'a great deal of mental pain'*: Cussen, p. 12.

p. 322 *In every difficult situation . . .*: *Full Moon* (1947; London, 1961), p. 216.

p. 323 *funded partly by the sale of Ethel's jewellery*: 'Statement by Ethel Wodehouse', Cussen.

p. 323 *his behaviour was incredibly stupid, but it was not treacherous*: ibid.

p. 323 *'Being an enemy . . .'*: notes from Anga von Bodenhausen, 22 September 1941, Wodehouse Archive.

p. 323 *kept the German Foreign Office at arm's length*: it is said by her daughter Reinhild that Anga von Bodenhausen played a decisive role in breaking Wodehouse's connection with the German Foreign Office.

p. 324 *delighted to offer sanctuary*: Anga von Bodenhausen did claim a state subsidy for the cost of Wodehouse's stay in Degenershausen; it is unclear if Wodehouse knew this.

CHAPTER 21: 'Now I shall have nothing to worry about until 1944'
(1941-1943)

p. 325 *'shuffling their feet nervously . . .':* PGW to William Townend, 5 April 1945, Dulwich.

p. 325 *The old house was perfectly suited . . .:* I am exceptionally grateful to Reinhild von Bodenhausen, who agreed to be interviewed about her recollections of PGW, for her invaluable assistance with this part of the chapter.

p. 326 *leeches, wild geese, fiction, spiritualism . . .:* notes from Anga von Bodenhausen, 22 September 1941, Wodehouse Archive.

p. 326 *'a very kind and light and large personality . . .':* ibid.

p. 326 *He had already given a written commitment:* Wesley Stout confirmed PGW's undertaking to Reynolds, 31 July 1941, Reynolds papers, Columbia.

p. 326 *'considerable doubt as to . . .':* Wesley Stout to Paul Reynolds, 14 August 1941, Reynolds papers, Columbia.

p. 326 *the Ministry of Propaganda's transmission:* the broadcasts were transmitted direct to Britain, for the first time, on 9, 10, 11, 12 and 14 August.

p. 327 *'When you have problems . . .':* interview with Reinhild von Bodenhausen, 12 November 2001.

p. 327 *'very religious in camp':* PGW to William Townend, 11 May 1941, Dulwich.

p. 328 *'he is a child . . .':* notes from Anga von Bodenhausen, 22 September 1941, Wodehouse Archive.

p. 328 *'Degenershausen is just like a dream':* ibid.

p. 328 *'I haven't heard from Plum . . .':* Leonora Cazalet to Paul Reynolds, 1 October 1941, Reynolds papers, Columbia.

p. 328 *When Reynolds tried to telephone Germany:* Paul Reynolds cable to Leonora Cazalet, 11 November 1941, Reynolds papers, Columbia.

p. 328 *'Hope well received':* PGW cable to Paul Reynolds, 19 November 1941, Reynolds papers, Columbia.

p. 328 *'the supreme Jeeves novel of all time':* PGW to Wesley Stout, 29 November 1941, Reynolds papers, Columbia.

p. 328 *'The super-sticky affair . . .':* Joy in the Morning (1974; Everyman, 2002), p. 10. The following quotations in this paragraph are from pp. 20, 81, 83, 259, 139, 27, 274, 147.

p. 330 *'How would it be', I suggested . . .:* ibid., pp. 295–6.

p. 330 *'Joy cometh in the morning':* Psalm 30:5.

p. 330 *'My Art is flourishing like the family of an Australian rabbit':* PGW to Wesley Stout, 29 November 1941, Reynolds papers, Columbia.

p. 330 *'Life . . . jogs along quite peacefully':* PGW to Anga von Bodenhausen, 24 December 1941, Wodehouse Archive.

p. 330 *Vermehren, who was born in Lübeck . . .:* interview with Michael Vermehren, 28 May 2001.

p. 331 *'When I was in Berlin . . .'*: PGW to William Townend, 30 December 1944, Dulwich.

p. 332 *the circumstances in which Wodehouse and Ethel found themselves . . .*: for Ethel's life in Berlin, see Iain Sproat, *Wodehouse at War* (New York, 1981), pp. 73–4.

p. 332 *'I wish I could learn German'*: PGW to Reinhild von Bodenhausen, 4 February 1942, Wodehouse Archive.

p. 333 *Isabel Russel Guernsey*: in her *Free Trip to Berlin* (New York, [n.d.]), pp. 175–80. I am indebted to Timothy Garton Ash for this citation.

p. 333 *Pro-Nazi Americans*: Delaney was the *nom de guerre* of E. D. Ward. See John Carver Edwards, *Berlin Calling: American Broadcasters in Service to the Third Reich* (New York, 1991), pp. 2–40. For further evidence of Wodehouse's association with Delaney, see Paul R. Reynolds, jun., *The Middle Man: Adventures of a Literary Agent* (New York, 1971), pp. 110–12.

p. 333 *as an informal club*: the American news correspondent Howard Smith reports that he saw Wodehouse in the company of government officials; Howard Smith, *Last Train from Berlin* (London, 1943).

p. 333 *the Wodehouses never went to the theatre*: Sproat, *Wodehouse at War*, p. 73.

p. 334 *Rationing was relaxed in Berlin . . .*: Alexandra Ritchie, *Faust's Metropolis: A History of Berlin* (London, 1998), p. 489.

p. 334 *I find that the best way to get my type of story . . .*: PGW to William Townend, 29 September 1951, Dulwich.

p. 334 *very quiet and regular life*: PGW to Anga von Bodenhausen, 14 March 1942, Wodehouse Archive.

p. 334 *'We have had quite a pleasant winter'*: ibid.

p. 334 *'Now I shall have nothing to worry about . . .'*: ibid.

p. 334 *a substantial sum*: ibid. See also PGW to E. J. P. Cussen, 14 September 1944, Cussen, p. 14, for PGW's defence of this remuneration. PGW says he turned down 'several offers to write' and two specific film contracts.

p. 334 *'about as good as I have done'*: PGW to Wesley Stout, 11 May 1942, Reynolds papers, Columbia.

p. 335 *'I am mulling over the plot . . .'*: ibid. He added: 'I suppose after the war Lord Emsworth will have to sell Blandings Castle and come to America and live on his son Freddie.'

p. 335 *making the most of the Adlon*: Ethel Wodehouse to PGW, 8 August 1942, Wodehouse Archive. She also took the opportunity to discuss a possible film contract with the Tobis Film Co.

p. 335 *'The children are too sweet for words'*: PGW to Raven von Barnikow, 26 July 1942, Wodehouse Archive.

p. 335 *trying to think out a novel*: ibid.

p. 335 *'It has come out very funny'*: ibid.

p. 335 *'I'd like to murder Master Flannery'*: Leonora Cazalet to Paul Reynolds, 24 September 1942, Reynolds papers, Columbia.

p. 335 *Reynolds picked up a rumour*: Paul Reynolds to Leonora Cazalet, 27 August 1942, Reynolds papers, Columbia.

p. 335 *The typescripts of Joy in the Morning and Full Moon*: memorandum for Mr Ladd, 24 August 1942, US Department of Justice, FBI 40-HQ-82394.

p. 355 *'the happiest time in all my life'*: notes from Anga von Bodenhausen, undated, 1942, Wodehouse Archive.

p. 336 *happy to be with Ethel again*: PGW to Reinhild von Bodenhausen, 9 November 1942, Wodehouse Archive.

p. 336 *'Every time we sit down to a meal . . .'*: PGW to Anga von Bodenhausen, 20 November 1942, Wodehouse Archive.

p. 336 *'people in Sweden don't think badly of me . . .'*: PGW to 'Mr Soderburgh', 14 December 1942, private communication.

p. 336 *'I made the broadcasts . . .'*: ibid.

p. 336 *'mapped out the plot . . .'*: ibid.

p. 336 *'I feel quite happy these days'*: PGW to Anga von Bodenhausen, 23 December 1942, Wodehouse Archive.

p. 336 *After Stalingrad*: see Antony Beevor, *Stalingrad* (London, 1998), pp. 398–401.

p. 337 *'an extraordinary sight. Large fires . . .'*: PGW to Anga von Bodenhausen, 5 March 1943, Wodehouse Archive.

p. 337 *'look at the corpses . . .'*: PGW to Anga von Bodenhausen, 15 April 1943, Wodehouse Archive.

p. 337 *the library was full of English books*: PGW to William Townend, 24 February 1945, Dulwich.

p. 337 *'practically no woods, just corn fields and beet fields'*: PGW to Anga von Bodenhausen, 11 June 1943, Wodehouse Archive.

p. 337 *'it is trying to write a novel . . .'*: ibid.

p. 338 *'very different from the last war . . .'*: ibid.

p. 338 *The American tax authorities*: 'Notice of Tax Lien under Internal Revenue Laws', 15 June 1943, Reynolds papers, Columbia.

p. 338 *'the arbitrary seizure of property'*: Paul Reynolds to Senator Walter F. George, 24 June 1943, Reynolds papers, Columbia.

p. 338 *'How sickening about the jeopardy tax . . .'*: Leonora Cazalet to Paul Reynolds, 17 August 1943, Reynolds papers, Columbia.

p. 338 *'a very dangerous spot at the moment!'*: Ethel Wodehouse to Anga von Bodenhausen, 13 August 1943, Wodehouse Archive.

p. 338 *permission to go to Sweden, Lisbon or Switzerland*: Ethel Wodehouse to Anga von Bodenhausen, 19 June 1943, Wodehouse Archive.

p. 338 *'If it is old Werner . . .'*: Anga von Bodenhausen to PGW, 5 September 1943, Wodehouse Archive.

p. 339 *In a valedictory letter to 'Dearest Anga', he reported . . .*: PGW to Anga von Bodenhausen, 1 September 1943, Wodehouse Archive.

CHAPTER 22: 'I made an ass of myself, and must pay the penalty' (1943-1947)

p. 340 *Paul Schmidt continued to write*: PGW to Anga von Bodenhausen, 21 November 1943, Wodehouse Archive.

p. 340 *the Nazi hotel*: at the beginning of the war, the Bristol had been the head-quarters of the American Red Cross.

p. 340 *'The manager has been charming . . .'*: PGW to Anga von Bodenhausen, 21 November 1943, Wodehouse Archive.

p. 340 *'thoroughly bad'*: secret dispatch no. 3237, from 'PEP', 21 December 1944, from US embassy, Madrid, to the Foreign Service of the USA, State Department.

p. 341 *'I shall not be surprised . . .'*: Cussen, p. 4.

p. 341 *'having a very pleasant time in Paris'*: PGW to Anga von Bodenhausen, 21 November 1943, Wodehouse Archive.

p. 341 *In contrast to his failure . . .*: ibid.

p. 341 *reading Colette and even translating . . .*: PGW to Reinhild von Bodenhausen, 22 November 1943, Wodehouse Archive.

p. 341 *violent street battles*: see Antony Beevor and Artemis Cooper, *Paris After the Liberation 1944–1949* (London, 1994), pp. 150–79.

p. 341 *attracting the suspicious attention . . .*: secret dispatch no. 3737, from 'PEP', 21 December 1944, from the US embassy, Madrid, to the Foreign Service of the USA, State Department.

p. 341 *'the favourite reading of Princess Elizabeth'*: PGW to Anga von Bodenhausen, 21 November 1943, Wodehouse Archive.

p. 342 *Ethel, particularly, found it very stressful*: 'The only consolation', Wodehouse wrote, 'is that it is unlikely they [the Allies] would deliberately bomb the centre of Paris'; PGW to Anga von Bodenhausen, 3 May 1944, Wodehouse Archive.

p. 342 *the subject of controversy*: see PRO, FO 369/3509, 369/3786c.

p. 342 *'oasis of safety and happiness'*: PGW to Anga von Bodenhausen, 8 February 1944, Wodehouse Archive.

p. 342 *'Mister Bwana and Mrs Goat . . .'*: ibid. (also 3 May 1943).

p. 342 *an unexplained post-operative collapse*: the mystery surrounding what exactly Leonora was being treated for is compounded by the fact that there is no surviving death certificate.

p. 342 *Peter Cazalet immediately cabled Reynolds*: 'Know you will be grieved to hear that dear Nora [sic] is dead', 17 May 1943, Reynolds papers, Columbia.

p. 342 *this dreadful news was first broken*: David Jasen, *P. G. Wodehouse: Portrait of a Master* (London, 1975), p. 184; Frances Donaldson, *P. G. Wodehouse* (London, 1982), p. 260; Barry Phelps, *P. G. Wodehouse: Man and Myth* (London, 1992), p. 219.

p. 342 *'We are quite crushed . . .'*: PGW to William Townend, 24 October 1944, Dulwich.

p. 343 *'Nothing much matters now'*: ibid.

p. 343 *'I shall never recover'*: Ethel Wodehouse to Denis Mackail, 26 June 1945, Wodehouse Archive.

p. 343 *The Americans liberated Paris*: Julian Jackson, *France: The Dark Years 1940–1944* (Oxford, 2001), pp. 561–7.

p. 343 *'It was all very exciting'*: PGW to William Townend, 30 December 1944, Wodehouse Archive.

p. 343 *he asked an American colonel . . .*: see Hubert Cole, 'I've Been a Silly Ass', *Illustrated Magazine*, 7 December 1946, p. 9.

p. 343 *'British subjects in enemy occupied territory . . .'*: Cussen, p. 1.

p. 344 *'a bald, amiable-looking large man . . .'*: Malcolm Muggeridge, 'Wodehouse in Distress', in Thelma Cazalet-Keir (ed.), *Homage to P. G. Wodehouse* (London, 1973), pp. 87–99. The details of the meeting with PGW are taken from this account, and from Muggeridge's unpublished papers. I gratefully acknowledge the generous assistance of Sally Muggeridge.

p. 344 *Muggeridge always found him elusive*: Malcolm Muggeridge, *Sunday Times*, October 1953.

p. 345 *'a spirited and energetic lady . . .'*: Malcolm Muggeridge, *Chronicles of Wasted Time* (London, 1973), vol. ii, p. 231.

p. 345 *'Darling sweet adoreable [sic] Malcolm'*: Ethel Wodehouse to Malcolm Muggeridge, 27 August 1945, Muggeridge.

p. 345 *the news of Leonora's death*: Muggeridge always claimed to have broken the news, and to have been the first to hear PGW's response, but it is improbable that, in the four months since Leonora's death, the Wodehouses had not been informed.

p. 345 *Both Wodehouses loved Muggeridge*: Ethel Wodehouse (undated) to Malcolm Muggeridge; PGW to Muggeridge, 16 April 1945, Muggeridge.

p. 345 *a letter came from Paul Reynolds, junior*: Paul Reynolds, jun., to PGW, 8 September 1944, Reynolds papers, Columbia.

p. 345 *his 'frame of mind while in internment at Tost'*: Cussen, p. 1.

p. 346 *Cussen's fifteen-page report might have . . .*: see Cussen, *passim*.

p. 346 *or spoke, officially, to Werner Plack*: the most valuable investigation of Plack's role was conducted informally by Iain Sproat and Richard Usborne (see *Wodehouse at War* and *Wodehouse at Work to the End*), who have together played a crucial role in helping to clarify the ambiguities of this story.

p. 346 *'there is not sufficient evidence . . .'*: Director of Public Prosecutions memo, 23 November 1944, PRO, HO 45/22385/865098/2.

p. 347 *When Duff Cooper . . .*: interview with John Julius Norwich, 4 April 2003. I am most grateful to John Julius Norwich for his help with some details of this paragraph.

p. 347 *a keen Wodehouse reader*: 'When [Duff Cooper] was ambassador in Paris, I asked Malcolm Muggeridge, who was going to London, to bring me back a copy of my *Quick Service*. He did, and Duff Cooper met him on his return, said "Ah, *Quick Service*? I want to read that" and pinched it.' PGW to Denis Mackail, 6 May 1952, Wodehouse Archive.

p. 347 *'the press have already got hold of it'*: Duff Cooper diary, 28 September 1944; 3 October 1944; private collection. See also Duff Cooper to FO, 29 September 1944: 'I am trying to arrange for Wodehouse to be moved to another hotel'; PRO, HO 45/22385/865098/2. For Duff Cooper's troubled relationship with PGW, see John Charmley, *Duff Cooper* (London, 1987).

p. 347 *everyone commented on his low spirits*: Dorothy Bess told Reynolds's son that she had been to a birthday party given in Wodehouse's honour and had found him 'rather dispirited'; Dorothy Bess to Paul Reynolds, jun., 16 October 1944, Reynolds papers, Columbia.

p. 347 *a very sad message*: Thelma Cazalet-Keir to Paul Reynolds, jun., 17 October 1944, Reynolds papers, Columbia.

p. 348 *'eventually things will straighten themselves out'*: PGW to William Townend, 30 December 1944, Dulwich.

p. 348 *'I meet English and American soldiers . . .'*: PGW to William Townend, 15 February 1945, Dulwich. He wrote in similar terms to Guy Bolton on 30 May 1945.

p. 348 *'exactly like a movie'*: Ethel Wodehouse to Denis Mackail, 4 January 1945, Wodehouse Archive.

p. 348 *According to Muggeridge*: Muggeridge, 'Wodehouse in Distress', pp. 96–7. The 'English guest', probably a woman, remains unknown.

p. 348 *we are absolutely fainting with hunger . . .*: PGW to Malcolm Muggeridge, 22 November 1944, Muggeridge.

p. 348 *'a lot of phonus-bolonus'*: PGW to Guy Bolton, 30 May 1945, Wodehouse Archive.

p. 349 *'pretty foul to be cooped up'*: PGW to William Townend, 30 December 1944, Dulwich.

p. 349 *Wodehouse's arrest made new headlines in Britain . . .*: Hansard, HC (series 5), vol. 406, cols. 499–502 (6 December 1944); cols. 1582–8 (15 December 1944).

p. 349 *complex and serious legal aspects*: the two Acts that exercised the Commons in relation to Wodehouse were the Treason Act of 1351 and the Trading with the Enemy Act of 1939.

p. 349 *It was only now, after the press coverage . . .*: I gratefully acknowledge the assistance of Major Tom Smith with this passage.

p. 349 *'we ought to know what he is accused of doing'*: Churchill minute, M1163/4, 28 November 1944, PREM 4/39/4B, PRO.

p. 349 *'if you are shy . . . I will telegraph de Gaulle myself'*: Churchill memo to Duff Cooper, 3 December 1944, PREM 4/39/4B, PRO.

p. 349 *'We would prefer not ever . . .'*: Churchill minute to Foreign Secretary, 7 December 1944, M1193/4, PREM 4/39/4B, PRO.

p. 350 *I generally wake up at four a.m.*: PGW to William Townend, 30 December 1944, Dulwich.

p. 350 *a comic book about his adventures . . .*: PGW to William Townend, 24 February 1945, Dulwich.

p. 350 *he would be making a mistake . . .*: 'The one thing against a serious treatment is the fact that everybody in England has been through such hell these last years that . . . it would be simply ludicrous if I were to try to make heavy weather over the really quite trivial things that happened to me'; ibid.

p. 351 *Living costs were high and food so scarce*: PGW to Guy Bolton, 17 May 1945, Wodehouse Archive.

p. 351 *a Danish friend in Neuilly*: PGW to Denis Mackail, 16 April 1945, Wodehouse Archive. It is not known who this was.

p. 351 *'Do you find that your private life . . .'*: PGW to William Townend, 24 February 1945, Dulwich.

p. 351 *'relying on technique instead of exuberance'*: PGW to Denis Mackail, 16 April 1945, Wodehouse Archive.

p. 351 *'writing about unpleasant experiences . . .'*: PGW to William Townend, 5 April 1945, Dulwich.

p. 351 *Revere Reynolds broke the bad news*: Paul Reynolds, jun., to PGW, 14 June 1945, Reynolds papers, Columbia.

p. 352 *'I suppose you are apt . . .'*: PGW to William Townend, 30 June 1945, Dulwich.

p. 352 *Wodehouse was delighted*: PGW to Malcolm Muggeridge, 22 April 1945, Muggeridge.

p. 352 *'We are now safe . . . stay there for years'*: ibid.

p. 352 *a long letter of self-justification*: *Alleynian*, 73 (1945), pp. 90–91.

p. 352 *'My trouble'*: PGW to William Townend, 13 September 1945, Dulwich.

p. 352 *H. D. Ziman*: it is clear from Ziman's comments that some of 'the camp book's' contents were redrafted into 'Now That I Have Turned Both Cheeks' and 'Apologia', and also used in *Performing Flea*.

p. 352 *Chatty, well-informed and judicious . . .*: I gratefully acknowledge the assistance of Selina Hastings with this passage.

p. 353 *a self-assured stranger's opinion of the book*: Ziman's frank analysis is of particular interest because the typescript was later lost or destroyed.

p. 353 *Ziman had two main criticisms*: H. D. Ziman to PGW, 20 September 1945, Wodehouse Archive. I am grateful to Ziman's daughter, Naomi Roberts, for her kind help with this section.

p. 353 *the awkward facts*: (a) that 'there were many English people who made more effort to escape being overrun by the Germans', and (b) that 'you were the only reputable Englishman who broadcast from a German radio'.

p. 353 *sold for serial publication*: the editor of *Liberty* had expressed strong interest in serializing 'the camp book'; PGW to Guy Bolton, 1 September 1945, Wodehouse Archive.

p. 353 *When I was in Berlin . . .*: PGW to H. D. Ziman, 26 September 1945, Wodehouse Archive. Ethel Wodehouse expressed the same point in a letter (29 September 1945) to Malcolm Muggeridge: 'Mr Ziman thought he should write about our life in Germany. The only trouble about that is that nothing really interesting happened, just meals and taking the dog for a walk, and Plummie doing his daily dozen and working on his novel. All very dull, but I suppose he could make a chapter of it.' Muggeridge.

p. 353 *'what has hampered me is the difficulty . . .'*: PGW to H. D. Ziman, 26 September 1945, Wodehouse Archive.

p. 354 *'things are beginning to stir . . .'*: PGW to Guy Bolton, 1 September 1945, Wodehouse Archive.

p. 354 *He told Townend*: PGW to William Townend, 13 September 1945, Dulwich.

p. 354 *a letter of brutal abruptness*: PGW to Paul Reynolds, jun., 14 September 1945, Reynolds papers, Columbia.

p. 354 *'I was a new personality . . .'*: Paul R. Reynolds, jun., *The Middle Man: Adventures of a Literary Agent* (New York, 1971), p. 108.

p. 354 *the consensus of opinion*: PGW to Denis Mackail, 7 November 1945, Wodehouse Archive.

p. 354 *'until this Belsen business . . .'*: PGW to William Townend, 8 November 1945, Dulwich.

p. 354 *This one reference to the Holocaust*: see Robert Hall's invaluable 'Was Wodehouse Anti-Jewish?', in his *Papers on Wodehouse* (Ithaca, NY, 1985). The question is also discussed in Kristin Thompson, *Wooster Proposes, Jeeves Disposes* (New York, 1992), pp. 36–7.

p. 354 *'Aren't the Jews extraordinary people'*: PGW to William Townend, 22 September 1947, Dulwich; another example of Wodehouse's idiosyncratic perception of contemporary events.

p. 355 *Herbert Jenkins were now proposing to print . . .*: *Money in the Bank* sold 26,000 copies in its first month. This reflected the wartime sales pattern. Some 450,000 copies of all Wodehouse's books were sold between 1941 and 1945.

p. 355 *'If I can get by with that one . . .'*: PGW to William Townend, 7 December 1945, Dulwich.

p. 355 *'a tremendous success'*: ibid.

p. 355 *'I have great hopes of the Spring'*: PGW to Guy Bolton, 11 December 1945, Wodehouse Archive.

p. 355 *'I wish I could get a glimmering . . .'*: PGW to Denis Mackail, 7 December 1945, Wodehouse Archive.

p. 356 *'I look on myself as a historical novelist'*: PGW to Denis Mackail, 23 December 1945, Wodehouse Archive.

p. 356 *'the day before yesterday . . .'*: PGW to Denis Mackail, 28 March 1946, Wodehouse Archive.

p. 356 *They lunched at a dingy little restaurant*: PGW to George Orwell, 25 July 1945, Orwell; PGW to William Townend, 29 April 1946, Dulwich. See also Peter Davison (ed.), *The Complete Works of George Orwell*, 20 vols. (London, 1998), vol. xvii, p. 63. It was during a meeting with Muggeridge and Orwell that PGW told the former he considered *Mike* his best book; see Muggeridge, *Chronicles of Wasted Time*, vol. ii, p. 257.

p. 356 *Wodehouse later said that . . .*: PGW to Richard Usborne, 3 June 1955, Wodehouse Archive.

p. 356 *the two men got on very well*: when Orwell was tragically widowed in the spring of 1945, Wodehouse wrote, with rare sympathy, that 'my wife and I are feeling for you with all our hearts, the more so as a year ago we lost our daughter and so can understand what it must be for you'; PGW to George Orwell, 1 August 1945, Orwell. Evelyn Waugh was also in correspondence with Orwell about Wodehouse's broadcasts; see Mark Amory (ed.), *The Letters of Evelyn Waugh* (London, 1981), p. 299.

p. 356 *at the time, Wodehouse was grateful*: later, Wodehouse changed his mind, describing Orwell's essay as 'practically one long roast . . . Don't you hate the ways these critics falsify the facts in order to make a point?' PGW to Denis Mackail, 11 August 1951, Wodehouse Archive.

p. 356 *'I don't think I have ever read . . .'*: PGW to George Orwell, 25 July 1945, Orwell. Writing to William Townend, Wodehouse described Orwell's essay as 'masterly'; 29 April 1946, Dulwich.

p. 356 *a revival of Oh, Boy!*: PGW to Guy Bolton, 11 December 1945, Wodehouse Archive.

p. 356 *I've suddenly got the most terrific idea*: PGW to Guy Bolton, 21 January 1946, Wodehouse Archive.

p. 357 *'What the hell? If a section of the press . . .'*: PGW to Denis Mackail, 7 May 1946, Wodehouse Archive.

p. 357 *He monitored the sales*: PGW to Guy Bolton, 17 June 1946, Wodehouse Archive.

p. 357 *You can probably imagine . . .*: PGW to V. S. Pritchett, 15 June 1946, Wodehouse Archive.

p. 358 *Up till now, of course . . .*: PGW to Guy Bolton, 6 April 1946, Wodehouse Archive.

p. 358 *after protracted negotiations*: see PGW to Guy Bolton, 19 May 1946, 17 June 1946, 5 July 1946, 13 July 1946, Wodehouse Archive. For the Foreign Office side of these negotiations, see FO minutes, 3 June 1946 and 26 July 1946, FO 369/3509, PRO.

p. 358 *the visa came through*: PGW to Guy Bolton, 13 July 1946: 'Isn't it marvellous about the visa'; Wodehouse Archive. The Foreign Office view was that 'Mr Wodehouse is rather a nuisance in France and, as we feel the United States is a bigger country and less collaboration-conscious . . . it would be a step in the right direction for Mr Wodehouse to go there'; 3 June 1946, FO 369/3509, PRO.

p. 358 *Wodehouse toyed with settling in Switzerland*: PGW to William Townend, 27 August 1946, Wodehouse Archive.

p. 358 *'My heart is in France'*: PGW to Benoît de Fonscolombe, 28 November 1947, Wodehouse Archive.

p. 358 *'I used to write a novel . . .'*: PGW to Guy Bolton, 24 January 1947, Wodehouse Archive.

CHAPTER 23: 'My world has been shot to pieces' (1947-1951)

p. 361 . . . *to plant the garden in November?*: PGW to William Townend, 14 February 1947, Dulwich.

p. 361 *a secret post-war return to Britain*: among some Wodehouse fans, this apocryphal story has shown exceptional resilience, but there is no evidence to support it.

p. 361 *he planned to stay in America*: PGW to Guy Bolton, 17 April 1947, Wodehouse Archive.

p. 362 *'frightfully rich, as if I had just been left $19,000 . . .'*: PGW to Guy Bolton, 31 March 1947, 17 April 1947, Wodehouse Archive.

p. 362 *US bank deposits of about $100,000*: Cussen, p. 5.

p. 362 *he would write the final chapter on the boat*: PGW to William Townend, 12 April 1947, Dulwich.

p. 362 *'a sensational triumph'*: PGW to William Townend, 11 May 1947, Dulwich.

p. 362 *a left-leaning evening paper*: ibid.

p. 362 *there was no acrimony*: British newspaper hostility to PGW had inspired a memorable letter of support from Evelyn Waugh, writing from White's: 'I hope you will not think it impudent of me to write to you and express my great indignation at the way in which the newspapers have reported your arrival in America. I should like you to know that the admiration your fellow writers have for your work is entirely unaffected by the campaign of misrepresentation, that we have nothing but sympathy for your misfortunes during the war, and look forward eagerly to your future books.' Evelyn Waugh to PGW, 10 May 1947, Wodehouse Archive.

p. 363 *'Final Score – everything in the garden is lovely'*: PGW to William Townend, 11 May 1947, Dulwich.

p. 363 *'simply incredible. About five times larger . . .'*: PGW to William Townend, 5 May 1947, Dulwich.

p. 363 *'Everything has gone marvellously well . . .'*: PGW to Guy Bolton, 25 May 1947, Wodehouse Archive.

p. 363 *was exerting himself in the manner customary to . . .*: 'Over here,' Wodehouse wrote to Townend in June, with premature optimism, 'things are booming . . . this new agent of mine is making things hum.' PGW to William Townend, 6 June 1947, Dulwich.

p. 363 *landing $3,000 contracts*: the stories were 'Joy Bells for Barmy' (*A Few Quick Ones*) and 'Birth of a Salesman' (*Nothing Serious*).

p. 363 *he and Ethel began to feel depressed*: PGW to William Townend, 6 June 1947, Dulwich.

p. 364 *he missed the old-time Broadway manager*: ibid.

p. 364 *'It's so damned difficult . . .'*: PGW to Guy Bolton, 6 July 1947, Wodehouse Archive.

p. 364 *'Oscar Hammerstein and Richard Rodgers . . .'*: PGW to William Townend, 4 July 1947, Dulwich.

p. 364 *He had always preferred the hustle of Broadway*: PGW to William Townend, 18 June 1947, Dulwich.

p. 364 *'There are too many women in the world . . .'*: ibid.

p. 364 *'the remotest flicker . . .'*: ibid.

p. 365 *'they couldn't use comic stories . . .'*: PGW to William Townend, 13 August 1947, Dulwich.

p. 365 *Privately, Hibbs described Wodehouse*: Ben Hibbs to Watson Washburn (PGW's lawyer), 25 January 1950, Wodehouse Archive.

p. 365 *Between 1947 and 1951*: Kristin Thompson, *Wooster Proposes, Jeeves Disposes* (New York, 1992), p. 356. This bleak picture is softened by the serialization of *Full Moon* and *Uncle Dynamite* (in *Liberty*); *The Mating Season* (in *Star Weekly*, Toronto) and *Phipps to the Rescue* (US: *The Old Reliable*) (in *Collier's*).

p. 365 *he told his French translator*: PGW to Benoît de Fonscolombe, 18 November 1947, Wodehouse Archive.

p. 365 *'I am hopeless unless I'm creating . . .'*: PGW to William Townend, 21 November 1947, Dulwich.

p. 365 *'selling terrifically in England'*: PGW to William Townend, 13 December 1947, Dulwich.

p. 365 *'it's a bit thick, of course . . .'*: PGW to William Townend, 13 August 1947, Dulwich.

p. 365 *'a sort of loathing for short stories'*: ibid.

p. 366 *a rewrite of a melodrama*: *Don't Lose Your Head*, a play about headhunters, by E. P. Conkle (and Irving St John), was performed in England in 1950, but flopped. See Wodehouse letters to E. P. Conkle, Ransom.

p. 366 *'I haven't really got going yet . . .'*: PGW to Guy Bolton, 7 September 1947, Wodehouse Archive.

p. 366 *declared the new address . . . a great success*: PGW to William Townend, 15 November 1947, Dulwich.

p. 367 *'so I can nip across . . .'*: ibid.

p. 367 *the Molnár hit comedy*: this was later adapted by Tom Stoppard as *Rough Crossing*.

p. 367 *'Let's suppress Stephen Powys . . .'*: PGW to Guy Bolton, 15 October 1948, Wodehouse Archive.

p. 367 *He had plenty of money in England*: PGW to William Townend, 13 December 1947, Dulwich.

p. 367 *another unresolved income tax case*: Tony Ring, *You Simply Hit Them with an Axe: The Extraordinary True Story of the Tax Turmoils of P. G. Wodehouse* (Maidenhead, 1995), pp. 149–94. See also PGW to William Townend, 24 February 1948, Dulwich.

p. 367 *'Oh, Architect of the Universe'*: PGW to Guy Bolton, 17 June 1948, Wodehouse Archive.

p. 368 '*very weary of wandering . . .*': Malcolm Muggeridge, *Diaries* (London, 1981), p. 300.

p. 368 *too many* '*things cooking*': a Lengyel play; another Molnár adaptation; 'two adaptations of novels of mine'; the Puccini musical. PGW to William Townend, 7 September 1948, Dulwich.

p. 368 '*I don't feel a bit older . . .*': PGW to William Townend, 5 October 1948, Dulwich.

p. 368 '*I can find practically nothing to read now*': ibid.

p. 368 *obsessive analysis of the Dulwich team's prospects*: PGW to William Townend, 24 December 1947, Dulwich.

p. 368 '*the Doubleday organisation*': PGW to Derek Grimsdick, 27 November 1947, private collection.

p. 369 '*in the Inspecteur's room in the Palais de Justice*': *Performing Flea* (London, 1953), p. 118.

p. 369 '*All I do now is sit in a tree . . .*': PGW to William Townend, 7 September 1948, Dulwich.

p. 369 '*it's crazy to spoil a play . . .*': PGW to Guy Bolton, 13 November 1950, Wodehouse Archive.

p. 369 *the controversy surrounding Guitry's name . . .*: see Lee Davis, *Wodehouse and Bolton and Kern: The Men Who Made Musical Comedy* (New York, 1993), pp. 381–3.

p. 370 *Evelyn Waugh, visiting New York*: Selina Hastings, *Evelyn Waugh* (London, 1994), p. 535.

p. 370 '*Dr Wodehouse*', *as he liked to call him*: Mark Amory (ed.), *The Letters of Evelyn Waugh* (London, 1981), pp. 435–6.

p. 370 '*the awful flat dreariness . . .*': Hastings, *Evelyn Waugh*, p. 509.

p. 370 *He looked exactly the same*: Alec Waugh, 'Lunching with Plum', in James H. Heineman and Donald R. Bensen (eds.), *P. G. Wodehouse: A Centenary Celebration* (New York, 1981), pp. 10-12..

p. 371 *Evelyn Waugh later described . . .*: Evelyn Waugh, *Sunday Times*, 16 July 1961.

p. 371 '*hew to the butler line*': PGW to Denis Mackail, 23 December 1945, Wodehouse Archive.

p. 371 '*an enormous roof . . .*': PGW to William Townend, 20 June 1949, Dulwich.

p. 372 '*I am absolutely out of touch . . .*': PGW to William Townend, 21 July 1949, Dulwich.

p. 372 '*the physical act of writing . . .*': PGW to William Townend, 14 October 1949, Dulwich.

p. 372 *accepted for a '*quota visa*'*: the US Immigration Act of 1924, known as the Quota Act, determined strict percentages for the number of immigrants admitted annually from overseas countries. Visas were issued by the consul in the country of origin, and would-be immigrants 'on the quota' had to enter the USA at a designated point and be inspected. According to the Immigration Act of 1917, immigrants could be excluded on a wide range of grounds, from illiteracy to prostitution. I gratefully acknowledge the help of Katherine Bucknell with this information.

p. 372 *'To think . . . in 1914 I came over . . .'*: PGW to William Townend, 8 December 1949, Dulwich.

p. 372 *'perhaps the Wodehouse tale . . .'*: Christopher Hitchens, introduction to *The Mating Season* (London, 1999), p. v.

p. 372 *described as 'nauseous productions'*: *The Mating Season* (1949; Everyman, 2001), p. 106.

p. 372 *'Christopher Robin going hoppity-hoppity-hop'*: ibid., pp. 107 and 206.

p. 373 *'the planned Americanisation' of England*: ibid., p. 259.

p. 373 *reproaches Bertie's 'Dickensy' sentimentalism*: 'It all comes of letting that Dickens spirit creep over you, Bertie. The advice I give to every young man starting life is Never get Dickensy'; ibid., p. 202.

p. 373 *Jeeves, wanly philosophical, quotes Marcus Aurelius*: ibid., p. 47.

p. 373 *His brow was sicklied o'er . . .*: ibid., p. 15.

p. 373 *'who chews broken bottles . . .'*: ibid., p. 8.

p. 373 *'Not a single loose end left over'*: ibid., p. 268.

p. 373 *'I wish to God I could be with you'*: PGW to Denis Mackail, 18 November 1949, Wodehouse Archive.

p. 374 *'I know those blank periods . . .'*: PGW to Denis Mackail, 15 April 1950, Wodehouse Archive.

p. 374 *'which tots up to quite a bit'*: PGW to Guy Bolton, 22 May 1950, Wodehouse Archive.

p. 374 *There is the problem . . .*: PGW to William Townend, 26 August 1950, Dulwich.

p. 374 *'My only trouble . . .'*: PGW to William Townend, 25 December 1950, Dulwich.

p. 374 *The news that the Strand . . .*: the magazine finally closed in March 1952.

p. 375 *his 1925 screwball comedy*: this became *Barmy in Wonderland*; the American edition, *Angel Cake*, carried a dedication: 'To the Onlie Begetter of These Ensuing Sonnets, Mr G. S. K.' In fact, the first third of the novel was loosely based on a short story which had already appeared in two earlier versions. See *Concordance*, vol. vii, pp. 343–4.

p. 375 *'If I'd known what I was letting myself in for . . .'*: PGW to Guy Bolton, 22 August 1950, Wodehouse Archive.

p. 375 *'this has cured me . . .'*: PGW to Denis Mackail, 22 August 1950, Wodehouse Archive.

p. 375 *'never been in such form . . .'*: PGW to William Townend, 25 December 1950, Dulwich.

p. 375 *'a sort of freak whom age could not touch'*: PGW to William Townend, 8 March 1951, Wodehouse Archive.

p. 375 *'two cocktails, dollops of Burgundy'*: PGW to Guy Bolton, 11 May 1951, Wodehouse Archive.

p. 375 *'I started to walk down town . . .'*: PGW to William Townend, 8 March 1951, Dulwich.

p. 376 *B. H. Kean, by chance a celebrity doctor*: Frances Donaldson, *P. G. Wodehouse* (London, 1982), p. 300.

p. 376 *'for the first time almost since I can remember. . .'*: PGW to William Townend, 31 January 1951, Dulwich.

p. 377 *'there is life in the old dog yet'*: PGW to William Townend, 6 July 1951, Dulwich.

p. 377 *the dialogue in the novel*: see David Jasen, *P. G. Wodehouse: Portrait of a Master* (London, 1975), p. 226.

p. 377 *'I shan't bother again about serial publication'*: PGW to William Townend, 3 August 1951, Dulwich.

p. 377 *Not one of Wodehouse's later novels*: *French Leave* and *Something Fishy*, and *Jeeves in the Offing*, much edited, appeared in *John Bull*. *Frozen Assets* and *Stiff Upper Lip, Jeeves*, also reduced, appeared in *Playboy*.

p. 377 *'she suddenly broke up'*: PGW to Denis Mackail, 11 August 1951, Wodehouse Archive.

p. 377 *'more lovable every day'*: ibid.

p. 378 *the British authorities continued to equivocate*: David Maxwell-Fyfe, the Home Secretary, wrote to Thelma Cazalet-Keir on 20 May 1952 to inform her that the Attorney General had said that 'it would not be right for him [the Attorney General] to give any undertakings in regard to possible proceedings against Mr Wodehouse, should he return home'; Wodehouse Archive.

CHAPTER 24: 'Our slogan must be Entertainment' (1951–1954)

p. 379 *British Baronets, like British pig men*: *Pigs Have Wings* (1952; Everyman, 2000), p. 142. Wodehouse makes the same point about the resilience of 'pig men' earlier in the plot: 'It has been well said of pig men as a class that though crushed to earth, they will rise again' (p. 110).

p. 379 *he had completed Pigs Have Wings*: he had first mapped out a scenario for this novel in 1950.

p. 379 *I have suddenly started . . .*: PGW to William Townend, 16 October 1951, Dulwich.

p. 379 *'first-class ancestral home . . .'*: *Pigs Have Wings*, p. 8.

p. 380 *an unprecedented third time*: in the lyrical and triumphant words of the *Bridgnorth, Shifnal and Albrighton Argus*, incorporated with the *Wheat Growers' Intelligencer and Stock Breeders' Gazette*, 'a hurricane of rousing cheers from the nobility and gentry acclaimed the Blandings Castle entry'; ibid., p. 253.

p. 380 *mocking echoes of 'the global howl'*: 'Apologia', Berg. The phrase recurs throughout PGW's correspondence during these years.

p. 380 *'What is life but . . .'*: *Uneasy Money* (1917; London, 1958), p. 96. Albert Peasemarch in *The Luck of the Bodkins* endeavours to encourage Monty Bodkin with 'The way to look at these things, sir, is to keep telling yourself that's just Fate. Somehow, if you know a thing has been fated from the beginning of time . . . it doesn't seem so bad'; *The Luck of the Bodkins* (1935; Everyman, 2002), p. 80.

p. 381 *she would protest his innocence*: interview with Christopher MacLehose, 12 June 2000. MacLehose describes Wodehouse irritably terminating Ethel's discussion of the 'German troubles' by thumping his hand down on the lunch table in a very rare flash of anger. MacLehose described Ethel Wodehouse as 'fragile, repetitive, and irritating to Plum'.

p. 381 *'Thelma makes me sick'*: PGW to Denis Mackail, 6 May 1952, Wodehouse Archive.

p. 381 *it was Townend who revived the idea*: PGW to William Townend, 3 July 1936, Wodehouse Archive.

p. 382 *'I think the letters scheme is terrific'*: PGW to William Townend, 16 October 1951, Dulwich.

p. 382 *felt too self-conscious*: ibid.

p. 382 *'The great thing . . .'*: ibid.

p. 382 *'It should be clear to anyone . . .'*: William Townend to Evelyn Waugh, 15 February 1952, Dulwich.

p. 383 *'my letters need a bit of polishing . . .'*: PGW to William Townend, 4 December 1951, Dulwich.

p. 383 *The trouble is that I can't . . .*: PGW to William Townend, 3 March 1952, Dulwich.

p. 383 *'I found myself getting more and more angry . . .'*: William Townend to PGW, 4 March 1952, Dulwich.

p. 383 *'I want to edit the stuff . . .'*: PGW to William Townend, 21 March 1952, Dulwich.

p. 384 *The two things I want to avoid . . .*: PGW to William Townend, 15 April 1952, Dulwich.

p. 384 *'This book is going through . . .'*: PGW to William Townend, 21 April 1952, Dulwich. He made the same point in a letter to Grimsdick.

p. 384 *'My one hope of fame . . .'*: William Townend to PGW, 19 April 1952, Dulwich.

p. 384 *efforts to justify his wartime conduct*: Derek Grimsdick to PGW, 13 May 1952 and 15 August 1952, private collection.

p. 384 *'I want the reader . . .'*: PGW to William Townend, 6 May 1952, Dulwich.

p. 384 *He was grateful to Townend*: apropos a formal autobiography, he said he could not imagine what he could have written about. 'After 1920 the only really interesting things that happened to me were the Hollywood trouble and the German trouble'; PGW to William Townend, 18 May 1952, Dulwich.

p. 385 *'our slogan must be Entertainment'*: PGW to William Townend, 13 August 1952, Dulwich.

p. 385 *'Ethel has bought a house!!!'*: PGW to William Townend, 18 May 1952, Dulwich.

p. 385 *decided to cut the broadcasts*: PGW to William Townend, 29 July 1952, Dulwich. The broadcasts were, however, included in the Penguin Books edition of 1961.

p. 385 *'I have gone for entertainment'*: PGW to William Townend, 11 March 1953, Dulwich.

p. 385 *'We are calling the book . . .'*: ibid.

p. 386 *'With Sean O'Casey's statement . . .'*: *Performing Flea* (London, 1953), p. 217.

p. 386 *'I have tried to keep the whole thing . . .'*: PGW to William Townend, 16 May 1953, Dulwich.

p. 386 *'shuddering over some . . .'*: PGW to William Townend, 8 July 1953, Dulwich.

p. 386 *a commission from the new editor of Punch*: 'This Is New York' appeared in *Punch* on 15 July 1953.

p. 386 *'I think we shall have to let truth go to the wall . . .'*: PGW to Guy Bolton, 2 and 4 November 1952, Wodehouse Archive.

p. 386 *well aware that co-authored reminiscences . . .*: PGW confided to Townend that Bolton's 'dialogue gets very strained and trying-to-be-funny at times . . . Of course, it's awfully difficult writing a book about ourselves and having to say "said Bolton", "said Wodehouse". You don't like to put in good lines because you feel that the reader will say "Thinks he's damned funny, this bird, doesn't he!"' PGW to William Townend, 4 November 1952, Dulwich.

p. 387 *'to go to blazes'*: PGW to William Townend, 31 January 1953, Dulwich. The relationship with Doubleday, Doran had started with the publication of *Meet Mr Mulliner*.

p. 387 *His agent had always been a fan of his*: see Kristin Thompson, *Wooster Proposes, Jeeves Disposes* (New York, 1992), pp. 50–58.

p. 387 *When, wondering what had happened . . .*: see Peter Schwed, 'Wodehouse's Editor', in James H. Heineman and Donald R. Bensen (eds.), *P. G. Wodehouse: A Centenary Celebration* (New York, 1981), pp. 13–15.

p. 387 *'delivering a new . . .'*: ibid. Interview with Peter Schwed, 18 July 2000.

p. 387 *The sales of these late Wodehouse books . . .*: see Kristin Thompson, *Wooster Proposes*, pp. 50–58.

p. 387 *'I think P. G. . . .'*: William Townend to 'Mr Joscelyne', 1 November 1954, Dulwich.

p. 388 *so the score now is one foxhound . . .*: *Performing Flea*, p. 171.

p. 388 *waiting breathlessly for the first reviews*: PGW to William Townend, 14 October 1953, Dulwich.

p. 388 *The British press was almost universally favourable*: *Times Literary Supplement, Scotsman, Book of the Month, New Statesman*.

p. 389 *answering every letter*: he would collect his mail at the Remsenburg post office, weed out and destroy any letters that referred to the broadcasts, and take the balance of his post back to his desk.

p. 389 *'I had better spend my last days . . .'*: PGW to Derek Grimsdick, 25 April 1953, private collection.

p. 389 *'have to admit this in public'*: *Performing Flea*, p. 217.

p. 389 *Connor was in New York*: *Daily Mirror*, 9 October 1953.

p. 389 *his charm and likeability*: *Daily Mirror*, 17 July 1961.

p. 389 *they had got on like a couple of sailors*: PGW to William Townend, 25 November 1953, Dulwich.

p. 390 *'to bury the whole story . . .'*: *Daily Mirror*, 17 July 1961.

p. 390 *In April 1947, the Attorney General*: Hartley Shawcross to McCulloch 'Slacker' Christison, 22 April 1947, Dulwich.

p. 390 *'it would not be right . . .'*: David Maxwell-Fyfe to Thelma Cazalet-Keir, 20 May 1952, Wodehouse Archive.

p. 390 *'I don't want to come to England'*: PGW to William Townend, 3 June 1952, Dulwich.

CHAPTER 25: 'I keep plugging away at my Art' (1955–1961)

p. 391 *left alone with his characters*: 'I want to be alone to think about my characters'; PGW to William Townend, 6 July 1951, Dulwich.

p. 391 *never a dull moment*: PGW to Frank Sullivan, 27 September 1956, Sullivan papers, Cornell.

p. 391 *'a sort of autobiography'*: PGW to William Townend, 27 June 1955, Dulwich.

p. 392 *'I have always had the idea . . .'*: PGW to William Townend, 7 October 1956, Dulwich.

p. 392 *the New Yorker writer Frank Sullivan*: Sullivan (1896–1972), a regular correspondent, was a journalist, humorist and member of the Algonquin Round Table; Cornell.

p. 392 *'makes up for our loss . . .'*: Frank Sullivan to PGW, 17 December 1955, Sullivan papers, Cornell.

p. 392 *'I see myself directing the destinies . . .'*: PGW to Frank Sullivan, 29 December 1955, Sullivan papers, Cornell.

p. 393 *'Do I prefer living in the country . . . ?'*: *Over Seventy* (London, 1957), p. 131.

p. 393 *no newspapers in the morning*: PGW to Denis Mackail, 18 May 1955, Wodehouse Archive.

p. 393 *once Lynn Kiegiel, a Polish girl . . .*: interview with Lynn Kiegiel, 19 April 2001.

p. 393 *no mistaking his persistent grouchiness*: PGW letters to Denis Mackail, 27 November 1953, 21 March 1954, 1 May 1954, 24 June 1954, 21 December 1954, 15 September 1955, 2 July 1956, 8 June 1957, 17 August 1957, 22 April 1959, and 1 and 23 November 1962, Wodehouse Archive.

p. 393 *To Townend, he wrote that Graham Greene . . .*: PGW to William Townend, 29 November 1955, Dulwich.

p. 394 *delivered it to Spender*: see Evelyn Waugh to Ann Fleming, in Mark Amory (ed.), *The Letters of Evelyn Waugh* (London, 1981), p. 550.

p. 394 *'the idea of finally seeing . . .'*: *Encounter*, October 1954. See also Iain Sproat, 'Wodehouse's War', *Encounter*, September–October 1982.

p. 394 *The version published . . .*: *Encounter*, October 1954, pp. 17–24, November 1954, pp. 39–47.

p. 396 *It was typical of Wodehouse that he should amend*: later editions of *Performing Flea* include the *Encounter* version of the broadcasts.

p. 396 *based on a Bolton plot*: Bolton's play was *Three Blind Mice*, and it, in turn, owed much to Michel Perrin's *The Man Who Lost His Keys*. PGW actually *bought* the English rights to the plot and the Bolton–Wodehouse combination eventually inspired no fewer than three films – *Moon over Miami, Three Little Girls in Blue* and *Three Blind Mice*. Wodehouse wrote to Bolton that 'nobody except you and me and Watt knows that *French Leave* is not my own unaided work . . . [the novel] deviates so much from your original that I don't think it is necessary to say anything'; PGW to Guy Bolton, 6 July 1962, Wodehouse Archive. See also Bolton's note to PGW's copy of *The Man Who Lost His Keys*, Wodehouse Archive.

p. 396 *'Rather an experiment'*: PGW to William Townend, 27 February 1955, Dulwich.

p. 396 *'Years and years ago . . .'*: Evelyn Waugh, 'Dr Wodehouse and Mr Wain', *Spectator*, 24 February 1956.

p. 396 *a prolonged and bruising correspondence*: Wodehouse cheered Waugh from the touchline: 'It really was wonderful of you to come to my rescue like that'; PGW to Evelyn Waugh, 11 March 1956, Wodehouse Archive.

p. 396 *'I shall certainly keep the flag flying . . .'*: PGW to Mrs Sherwood, 21 May 1956, Sullivan papers, Cornell.

p. 397 *'Ethel and I never see a soul . . .'*: PGW to Denis Mackail, 6 June 1960, Wodehouse Archive.

p. 397 *'Dogs and cats'*: PGW to Denis Mackail, 17 August 1959, Wodehouse Archive.

p. 397 *Edward Cazalet recalls that . . .*: interview with Edward Cazalet, 25 September 2000.

p. 398 *'too difficult and too distressing'*: ibid.

p. 398 *One young Englishman*: private communication from John Hughes, 16 January 2002.

p. 398 *an Englishman of the old school*: ibid.

p. 398 *In September 1958*: interview with David Jasen, 7 June 2003.

p. 399 *'Any newspapermen who want to interview me . . .'*: PGW to William Townend, 26 July 1956, Dulwich.

p. 399 *joined with a set of comic verses*: 'The Visitors' is reproduced in *Over Seventy*, pp. 90–91.

p. 399 *His artful modesty*: *Over Seventy*, p. 89.

p. 399 *Wodehouse found Usborne's questioning*: PGW to Denis Mackail, 25 January 1956, Wodehouse Archive.

p. 400 *'The awful part of the writing game'*: PGW to Denis Mackail, 15 August 1957, Wodehouse Archive.

p. 400 *'a hell of a time with my novel'*: PGW to Denis Mackail, 7 October 1957, Wodehouse Archive.

p. 400 *Wodehouse wrote broodingly*: PGW to the Editor, *Punch*, 25 July 1958.

p. 401 *'I keep plugging away at my Art'*: PGW to Denis Mackail, 17 August 1959, Wodehouse Archive.

p. 401 *'I've just finished my new novel'*: PGW to Denis Mackail, 28 February 1960, Wodehouse Archive.

p. 401 *Was it, he wondered . . .*: PGW to Denis Mackail, 6 June 1960. Wodehouse Archive. At home in his imaginary paradise, inspiration eventually flowed. Within weeks of fussing about giving up, he was writing to Frank Sullivan that he had 'just got out a plot for an Uncle Fred and Blandings Castle novel' (*Service with a Smile*); PGW to Frank Sullivan, 11 July 1960, Sullivan papers, Cornell.

p. 401 *'having my octogenarianism hurled at me . . .'*: PGW to Denis Mackail, 7 January 1960, Wodehouse Archive.

p. 401 *'I suppose my work . . .'*: *New Yorker*, 15 October 1960, pp. 36–7.

p. 402 *'an inimitable international institution . . .'*: *New York Times*, 14 October 1960.

p. 402 *Waugh's remarks, which were published . . .*: *Sunday Times*, 16 July 1961.

p. 402 *When Wodehouse got wind of it*: 'I am hoping you will see your way to make your talk not so personal'; PGW to Evelyn Waugh, 10 May 1961, Wodehouse Archive.

CHAPTER 26: 'The Grand Old Man of English Literature'
(1961–1975)

p. 403 *'At eighty things begin to get a bit serious'*: PGW to Frank Sullivan, 20 October 1960, Sullivan papers, Cornell.

p. 403 *'I'm beginning to dislike . . .'*: PGW to Guy Bolton, 24 September 1961, Wodehouse Archive.

p. 403 *Sheran Cazalet, who happened . . .*: PGW to Denis Mackail, 16 October 1961, Wodehouse Archive; interview with Sheran Hornby, 6 October 2003.

p. 403 *several hundred column inches*: PGW to Guy Bolton, 28 October 1961, Wodehouse Archive.

p. 403 *'I got a good press'*: PGW to Denis Mackail, 16 October 1961, Wodehouse Archive.

p. 403 *'the Grand Old Man . . .'*: PGW to Guy Bolton, 28 October 1961, Wodehouse Archive.

p. 403 *Alistair Cooke, reporting . . .*: 'The Hermit of Remsenburg', *Manchester Guardian*, 19 October 1961. See also Cooke, *Memories of the Great and the Good* (London, 2000), pp. 35–47.

p. 404 *On most days, he would get up at half past seven*: see Herbert Warren Wind, 'Chap with a Story to Tell', *New Yorker*, 15 May 1971.

p. 405 *dinner, alone with Ethel*: interview with Lynn Kiegiel, Anne Smith and Margaret Zbrozak, 19 April 2001.

p. 405 *'I can't write anymore'*: William Townend to PGW, 6 September 1961, Wodehouse Archive.

p. 405 *Townend, who shared Wodehouse's interest in spiritualism*: William Townend to PGW, 21 and 27 September 1961, Wodehouse Archive.

p. 406 *A few weeks later*: PGW to Mrs Carroll, 28 February 1962, private collection.

p. 406 *Townend's writing was . . .*: letter to the author from Tom Sharpe, 2001.

p. 406 *plotting out Frozen Assets*: the novel's working title was 'Great Possessions'. It was published in the USA as *Biffen's Millions*.

p. 406 *'The police in Grand Rapids . . .'*: *Punch*, 1 November 1961, quoted in Robert Persing, 'The Punch Columns of P. G. Wodehouse', *Plum Lines*, 1997.

p. 406 *'I am rooting hard for Liston'*: PGW to Frank Sullivan, 25 September 1962, Sullivan papers, Cornell.

p. 407 *Wodehouse told his editor*: PGW to Bernard Holloway, 29 April 1962, *Punch*.

p. 407 *Punch was proud to be associated . . .*: PGW had been invited to carve his name on the *Punch* table in 1957. When the New York newspaper strike of 1963 cut off the flow of press clippings on which Wodehouse relied for his material, 'Our Man in America' fell silent.

p. 407 *In September 1962 she underwent a serious operation*: interview with Sheran Hornby, 6 October 2003.

p. 407 *'My own precious darling Bunny'*: PGW to Ethel Wodehouse, undated, Wodehouse Archive.

p. 407 *Galahad at Blandings*: published in the USA as *The Brinkmanship of Galahad Threepwood*.

p. 407 *'For the American version I have put in . . .'*: PGW to Derek Grimsdick, 2 March 1964, private collection.

p. 407 *'pretty bad hell'*: PGW to McCulloch 'Slacker' Christison, 1 March 1969, Wodehouse Archive.

p. 407 *'I have the greatest difficulty . . .'*: PGW to Guy Bolton, 7 June 1964, Wodehouse Archive.

p. 407 *Bertie Wooster gets caught up in an anti-war demonstration*: *Aunts Aren't Gentlemen* (London, 1974), pp. 5–12. Similarly, 'Bingo Bans the Bomb', in *Plum Pie* (a collection of stories), has Bingo Little being arrested in Trafalgar Square at a Ban-the-Bomb rally.

p. 408 *'we both like her very much'*: PGW to Guy Bolton, 16 July 1964, Wodehouse Archive.

p. 408 *'One feels that P. Schwed . . .'*: PGW to Derek Grimsdick, 27 November 1964, private collection.

p. 408 *His sales were steady but respectable*: see Kristin Thompson, *Wooster Proposes, Jeeves Disposes* (New York, 1992), pp. 50–52.

p. 408 *barely more than novelettes*: for example, *Company for Henry* (US: *The Purloined Paperweight*), *Do Butlers Burgle Banks?* and *A Pelican at Blandings* (US: *No Nudes Is Good Nudes*).

p. 408 *'How difficult it is to write stories . . .'*: 'One keeps getting up against facts. I have just got to a point in my novel where a man with a guilty conscience thinks the hero is a private detective trailing him, and they both start for London from somewhere in Sussex which might be Horsham . . . Now here's where you can rally round. Do you go to Victoria from Horsham or Haywards Heath or whatever it is?' PGW to Guy Bolton, 19 August 1966, Wodehouse Archive.

p. 408 *a BBC television adaptation*: for the details of *Win with Wooster* see Thompson, *Wooster Proposes*, pp. 270–71.

p. 409 *Wodehouse invested several thousand dollars*: estimates vary. Some say $20,000; others claim $35,000.

p. 409 *'It always takes me six months . . .'*: PGW to Derek Grimsdick, 18 April 1964, private collection.

p. 409 *'[Company for Henry] will definitely be a novelette'*: PGW to Derek Grimsdick, 18 May 1965, private collection.

p. 409 *'I have just done a record . . .'*: PGW to Derek Grimsdick, 6 February 1966, private collection.

p. 409 *'I am now busy scenario-ing . . .'*: PGW to Christopher MacLehose, 12 May 1970, private collection.

p. 410 *Wodehouse was somewhat dismayed . . .*: PGW to Guy Bolton, 31 July 1969, Wodehouse Archive.

p. 410 *profoundly bored*: Frances Donaldson, *P. G. Wodehouse* (London, 1982), p. 338.

p. 411 *Edward Cazalet, visiting his grandfather*: Edward Cazalet, unpublished memoir, September 1974, Wodehouse Archive.

p. 411 *The solitude of these final years*: see Michael Davie, 'Wodehouse at Ninety', *Observer*, 10 October 1971.

p. 411 *'I think if one has done a foolish thing . . .'*: BBC television interview, October 1971.

p. 411 *Much Obliged, Jeeves*: published in the USA as *Jeeves and the Tie That Binds*.

p. 411 *The Times said*: 'It must be all the fish he eats', *The Times*, 15 October 1971.

p. 411 *John le Carré saluted Wodehouse's 'magic, his humour . . .'*: *Sunday Times*, 10 October 1971.

p. 412 *'I feel pretty good for an old fossil . . .'*: PGW to P. D. Hancock, 20 October 1971, private collection.

p. 412 *'too much of a strain'*: PGW to Herbert Mitgang, 21 October 1971, Berg. Mitgang, of the *New York Times*, had written asking if Wodehouse would write a piece about President Nixon.

p. 412 *'It varies from day to day . . .'*: 'Pilgrimage to P. G. Wodehouse', BBC radio interview, 13 October 1974.

p. 412 *he advised another interviewer*: *Illustrated London News*, February 1973.

p. 412 *'I am sweating away . . .'*: PGW to Christopher MacLehose, 13 September 1972, private collection.

p. 412 *Pearls, Girls and Monty Bodkin*: this was published in the USA as *The Plot That Thickened*.

p. 412 *his legs had 'gone back'*: PGW to Derek Grimsdick, 25 October 1972, private collection.

p. 412 *the two old partners continued to plan*: PGW to Christopher MacLehose, 5 December 1972, private collection.

p. 412 *an abandoned Jeeves musical*: entitled *Betting on Bertie*; see Thompson, *Wooster Proposes*, pp. 272–4.

p. 412 *Wodehouse feared it would be a flop*: PGW to Guy Bolton, 8 August 1972, Wodehouse Archive.

p. 412 *encouraged 'the boys' in a venture*: interview with Peter Brown, 7 April 2001.

p. 413 *'We had cold lamb and baked beans for dinner!'*: PGW to Patrick Wodehouse, 27 December 1972, private collection.

p. 413 *'toppling over sideways . . .'*: PGW to Derek Grimsdick, 10 November 1973, private collection.

p. 413 *'which looks like being one of my very best'*: ibid.

p. 413 *'As far as I was concerned . . .'*: PGW to Tom Sharpe, 31 December 1973, Sharpe.

p. 413 *'I sit in the old arm chair'*: PGW to Tom Sharpe, 7 May 1974, Sharpe. He told the *Paris Review*, 'I love writing. I never feel really comfortable unless I am either actually writing or have a story going. I could not stop writing'; *Paris Review*, 64 (1975), pp. 150–71.

p. 413 *Ever the Old Alleynian*: PGW to Mr Lloyd, 21 May 1974, private collection.

p. 413 *'I keep getting detached scenes . . .'*: PGW to Tom Sharpe, 25 May 1974, Sharpe.

p. 414 *'my big news is that . . .'*: PGW to Tom Sharpe, 27 July 1974, Sharpe.

p. 414 *'He has a whole tray of eyes . . .'*: David Jasen, *P. G. Wodehouse: Portrait of a Master* (London, 1975; revised edition, 2002), p. 253.

p. 414 *There was one more tribute to come*: interview with Robert Armstrong, 11 February 2004.

p. 414 *'sort of their way of saying . . .'*: Jasen, *Wodehouse*, p. 254.

EPILOGUE: The Afterlife of P. G. Wodehouse

p. 416 *There were about fifty mourners*: interview with Sheran Hornby, 6 October 2003.

p. 416 *a massive cherrywood casket*: *New York Times*, 19 February 1975.

p. 416 *Guy Bolton told the reporter . . .*: ibid.

p. 417 *The Oxford English Dictionary . . .*: of these, nearly two hundred are principal citations, indicating the first, or only, use of the word in that nuance.

p. 418 *'Humorists', he wrote towards the end of his life*: 'A Note on Humour', in *Plum Pie* (London, 1966), p. 282.

BOOKS BY P. G. WODEHOUSE

This is a list of books published by Wodehouse during his lifetime, with one important *caveat*: there is absolutely no agreement, and much lively debate, among Wodehouse scholars about the number of his titles. Some collections of short stories published in the United States differ significantly from the nearest equivalent collection in the United Kingdom; other collections of short stories and some fiction serials have been published posthumously. Then there are the Omnibus Volumes . . . In the list that follows, I have cited the UK publication details, unless otherwise noted; and where the US title differed from the UK one I have listed this also.

The Pothunters (A. & C. Black, 1902).
A Prefect's Uncle (A. & C. Black, 1903).
Tales of St Austin's (A. & C. Black, 1903).
The Gold Bat (A. & C. Black, 1904).
William Tell Told Again (A. & C. Black, 1904).
The Head of Kay's (A. & C. Black, 1905).
Love Among the Chickens (George Newnes Ltd., 1906 and Herbert Jenkins, 1921; US: Circle Publishing Co., 1909).
The White Feather (A. & C. Black, 1907).
Not George Washington (with Herbert Westbrook) (Cassell & Company, 1907).
The Globe By the Way Book (with Herbert Westbrook) (Globe Publishing Co., 1908).
The Swoop! (Alston Rivers Ltd., 1909).
Mike★ (A. & C. Black, 1909).
A Gentleman of Leisure (Alston Rivers Ltd., 1910; US: *The Intrusion of Jimmy*, W. J. Watt & Co., 1910).
Psmith In the City (A. & C. Black, 1910).
The Prince and Betty (Mills & Boon, 1912; US: W. J. Watt & Co., 1912).
The Little Nugget (Methuen, 1913; US: W. J. Watt & Co., 1914).
The Man Upstairs and other Stories (Methuen, 1914).
Something Fresh (Methuen, 1915; US: *Something New*, D. Appleton & Co., 1915).
Psmith Journalist (A. & C. Black, 1915).
The Man with Two Left Feet (Methuen, 1917; US: A. L. Burt & Co., 1933).
Uneasy Money (Methuen, 1917; US: D. Appleton & Co., 1916).
Piccadilly Jim (Herbert Jenkins, 1918; US: Dodd, Mead & Co., 1917).
My Man Jeeves (George Newnes Ltd., 1919).

★ subsequently published in two parts in UK and USA: *Mike at Wrykyn* (1953); and *Enter Psmith* (1935) and *Psmith and Mike* (1953)

A Damsel in Distress (Herbert Jenkins, 1919; US: George H. Doran, 1919).

The Coming of Bill (Herbert Jenkins, 1920; US: *Their Mutual Child*, Boni & Liveright, 1919).

Jill the Reckless (Herbert Jenkins, 1921; US: *The Little Warrior*, George H. Doran, 1920).

Indiscretions of Archie (Herbert Jenkins, 1921; US: George H. Doran, 1921).

The Clicking of Cuthbert (Herbert Jenkins, 1922; US: *Golf without Tears*, George H. Doran, 1924).

The Girl on the Boat (Herbert Jenkins, 1922; US: *Three Men and a Maid*, George H. Doran, 1922).

The Adventures of Sally (Herbert Jenkins, 1922; US: *Mostly Sally*, George H. Doran, 1923).

The Inimitable Jeeves (Herbert Jenkins, 1923; US: *Jeeves*, George H. Doran, 1923).

Leave it to Psmith (Herbert Jenkins, 1923; US: George H. Doran, 1924).

Ukridge (Herbert Jenkins, 1924; US: *He Rather Enjoyed It*, George H. Doran, 1926).

Bill the Conqueror (Methuen & Co. Ltd, 1924; US: George H. Doran, 1925).

Carry On, Jeeves (Herbert Jenkins, 1925; US: George H. Doran, 1927).

Sam the Sudden (A. & C. Black, 1925; US: *Sam in the Suburbs*, George H. Doran, 1925).

The Heart of a Goof (Herbert Jenkins, 1926: US: *Divots*, George H. Doran, 1927).

The Small Bachelor (A. & C. Black, 1927; US: George H. Doran, 1927).

Meet Mr Mulliner (Herbert Jenkins, 1927; US: Doubleday, Doran & Co., 1928).

Money for Nothing (Herbert Jenkins, 1928; US: Doubleday, Doran & Co., 1928).

Mr Mulliner Speaking (Herbert Jenkins, 1929; US: Doubleday Doran, 1930).

Summer Lighting (Herbert Jenkins, 1929; US: *Fish Preferred*, Doubleday Doran, 1929).

Very Good, Jeeves (Herbert Jenkins, 1930; US: Doubleday Doran, 1930).

Big Money (Herbert Jenkins, 1931; US: Doubleday Doran, 1931).

If I Were You (Herbert Jenkins, 1931; US: Doubleday Doran, 1931).

Louder and Funnier (Faber & Faber, 1932).

Doctor Sally (Methuen, 1932).

Hot Water (Herbert Jenkins, 1932; US: Doubleday Doran, 1932).

Mulliner Nights (Herbert Jenkins, 1933; US: Doubleday Doran, 1933).

Heavy Weather (Herbert Jenkins, 1934; US: Little, Brown & Co., 1933).

Thank You, Jeeves (Herbert Jenkins, 1934; US: Little, Brown & Co., 1934).

Right Ho, Jeeves (Herbert Jenkins, 1934; US: *Brinkley Manor*, Little, Brown & Co., 1934).

Blandings Castle and Elsewhere (Herbert Jenkins, 1935; US: *Blandings Castle*, Doubleday Doran, 1935).

The Luck of the Bodkins (Herbert Jenkins, 1935; US: Little, Brown & Co., 1936).

Young Men in Spats (Herbert Jenkins, 1936; US: Doubleday Doran, 1936).

Laughing Gas (Herbert Jenkins, 1936; US: Doubleday Doran, 1936).

Lord Emsworth and Others (Herbert Jenkins, 1937; US: *The Crime Wave at Blandings*, Doubleday Doran, 1937).

Summer Moonshine (Herbert Jenkins, 1938; US: Doubleday Doran, 1937).

The Code of the Woosters (Herbet Jenkins, 1938; US: Doubleday Doran, 1938).

Uncle Fred in the Springtime (Herbert Jenkins, 1939; US: Doubleday Doran, 1939).

Eggs, Beans and Crumpets (Herbert Jenkins, 1940; US: Doubleday Doran, 1940).

Quick Service (Herbert Jenkins, 1940; US: Doubleday Doran, 1940).

Money in the Bank (Herbert Jenkins, 1946; US: Doubleday Doran, 1942).

Joy in the Morning (Herbert Jenkins, 1947; US: Doubleday Doran, 1946).

Full Moon (Herbert Jenkins, 1947; US: Doubleday Doran, 1947).

Spring Fever (Herbert Jenkins, 1948; US: Doubleday Doran, 1948).

Uncle Dynamite (Herbert Jenkins, 1948; US: Didier, 1948).

The Mating Season (Herbert Jenkins, 1949; US: Didier, 1949).

Nothing Serious (Herbert Jenkins, 1950; US: Doubleday Doran, 1951).

The Old Reliable (Herbert Jenkins, 1951; US: Doubleday Doran, 1951).

Barmy in Wonderland (Herbert Jenkins, 1952; US: *Angel Cake*, Doubleday & Co., 1952).

Pigs Have Wings (Herbert Jenkins, 1952; US: Doubleday & Co., 1952).

Performing Flea (Herbert Jenkins, 1953; US: *Author! Author!*, Simon & Schuster, 1962).

Ring for Jeeves (Herbert Jenkins, 1953; US: *The Return of Jeeves*, Simon & Schuster, 1954).

Bring on the Girls! (with Guy Bolton) (Herbert Jenkins, 1954; US: Simon & Schuster, 1953).

Jeeves and the Feudal Spirit (Herbert Jenkins, 1954; US: *Bertie Wooster Sees It Through*, Simon & Schuster, 1955).

French Leave (Herbert Jenkins, 1956; US: Simon & Schuster, 1959).

Over Seventy (Herbert Jenkins, 1957; US: *America I Like You*, Simon & Schuster, 1956).

Something Fishy (Herbert Jenkins, 1957; US: *The Butler Did It*, Simon & Schuster, 1957).

Cocktail Time (Herbert Jenkins, 1958; US: Simon & Schuster, 1958).

A Few Quick Ones (Herbert Jenkins, 1959; US: Simon & Schuster, 1959).

Jeeves in the Offing (Herbert Jenkins, 1960; US: *How Right You Are, Jeeves*, Simon & Schuster, 1960).

Ice in the Bedroom (Herbert Jenkins, 1961; US: *The Ice in the Bedroom,* Simon & Schuster, 1961).

Service With A Smile (Herbet Jenkins, 1962; US: Simon & Schuster, 1961).

Stiff Upper Lip, Jeeves (Herbert Jenkins, 1963; US: Simon & Schuster, 1963).

Frozen Assets (Herbert Jenkins, 1964; US: *Biffen's Millions*, Simon & Schuster, 1964).

Galahad at Blandings (Herbert Jenkins, 1965; US: *The Brinkmanship of Galahad Threepwood*, Simon & Schuster, 1964).

Plum Pie (Herbert Jenkins, 1966; US: Simon & Schuster, 1967).

Company for Henry (Herbert Jenkins, 1967; US: *The Purloined Paperweight*, Simon & Schuster, 1967).

Do Butlers Burgle Banks? (Herbert Jenkins, 1968; US: Simon & Schuster, 1968).

A Pelican at Blandings (Herbert Jenkins, 1969; US: *No Nudes is Good Nudes*, Simon & Schuster, 1970).

The Girl in Blue (Barrie & Jenkins, 1970; US: Simon & Schuster, 1971).

Much Obliged, Jeeves (Barrie & Jenkins, 1971; US: *Jeeves and the Tie That Binds*, Simon & Schuster, 1971).

Pearls, Girls and Monty Bodkin (Barrie & Jenkins, 1972; US: *The Plot That Thickened*, Simon & Schuster, 1973).

Bachelors Anonymous (Barrie & Jenkins, 1973; US: Simon & Schuster, 1974).

Aunts Aren't Gentlemen (Barrie & Jenkins, 1974: US: *The Cat-Nappers*, Simon & Schuster, 1975)

Sunset at Blandings★ (Chatto & Windus, 1977; US: Simon & Schuster, 1977).

★ published posthumously

SELECT BIBLIOGRAPHY

Douglas Adams, *The Salmon of Doubt* (London, 2002).

Hedda Adlon, *The Life and Death of a Great Hotel* (London, 1958).

Mark Amory (ed.), *The Letters of Evelyn Waugh* (London, 1981).

Christopher Andrew, *Secret Service* (London, 1985).

Herbert Asbury, *The Gangs of New York* (New York, 1928).

Brooks Atkinson, *Broadway* (New York, 1970).

William Beach Thomas, *The Way of the Countryman* (London, 1944).

Antony Beevor, *Stalingrad* (London, 1998).

—— and Artemis Cooper, *Paris After the Liberation 1944–1949* (London, 1994).

A. Scott Berg, *Goldwyn* (London, 1989)

Gerald Boardman, *Jerome Kern: His Life and Music* (Oxford, 1980).

H. Dennis Bradley, *The Wisdom of the Gods* (London, 1929).

Ian Bradley (ed.), *The Complete Annotated Gilbert & Sullivan* (Oxford, 1996).

Ruth Brandon, *The Spiritualists: The Passion for the Occult in the 19th and 20th Centuries* (New York, 1983).

David Cannadine, *Ornamentalism* (London, 2001).

John Carey, *The Intellectuals and the Masses* (London, 1992).

Thelma Cazalet-Keir (ed.), *Homage to P. G. Wodehouse* (London, 1973).

John Charmley, *Duff Cooper* (London, 1987).

Joseph Connolly, *P. G. Wodehouse: An Illustrated Biography* (London, 1979).

Alistair Cooke, *Memories of the Great and the Good* (London, 2000).

Alfred Duff Cooper, *Old Men Forget* (London, 1953).

George F. Custen, *Twentieth Century's Fox: Darryl F. Zanuck and the Culture of Hollywood* (New York, 1997).

Michael Davie (ed.), *The Diaries of Evelyn Waugh* (London, 1976).

Lee Davis, *Wodehouse and Bolton and Kern: The Men Who Made Musical Comedy* (New York, 1993).

Peter Davison (ed.), *The Complete Works of George Orwell*, 20 vols. (London, 1998).

I. C. B. Dear (ed.), *The Oxford Companion to World War II* (Oxford, 1995).

Frances Donaldson, *P. G. Wodehouse* (London, 1982).

Ann Douglas, *Terrible Honesty: Mongrel Manhattan in the 1920s* (New York, 1995).

Philip Dunne, *Take Two* (New York, 1980).

Leon Edel, *Henry James: The Treacherous Years* (London, 1969).

David Edmonds and John Eidinow, *Wittgenstein's Poker* (London, 2001).

John Carver Edwards, *Berlin Calling: American Broadcaster in Service to the Third Reich* (New York, 1991).

Owen Dudley Edwards, *P. G. Wodehouse* (London, 1977).

Ruth Dudley Edwards, *Newspapermen: Hugh Cudlipp, Cecil Harmsworth King and the Glory Days of Fleet Street* (London, 2003).

George Eells, *The Life That Late He Led: A Biography of Cole Porter* (New York, 1967).

Gerard Fairlie, *With Prejudice: Almost an Autobiography* (London, 1952).

Harry W. Flannery, *Assignment to Berlin* (London, 1942).

R. B. D. French, *P. G. Wodehouse* (Edinburgh, 1966).

Paul Fussell, *Abroad* (Oxford, 1980).

Kurt Ganzl, *The British Musical Theatre 1865–1914*, vol. i (London, 1986).

David Gilmour, *The Long Recessional: The Imperial Life of Rudyard Kipling* (London, 2002).

Robert Gottlieb and Robert Kimball (eds.), *Reading Lyrics* (New York, 2000).

David Grafton, *Red, Hot and Rich: An Oral History of Cole Porter* (New York, 1987).

John Maxtone Graham, *The Only Way to Cross* (New York, 1972).

Charles Graves, *Off the Record* (London, 1942).

Benny Green, *P. G. Wodehouse: A Literary Biography* (London, 1981).

Stanley Green, *Broadway Musicals Show by Show* (London, 1985).

Selina Hastings, *Evelyn Waugh* (London, 1994).

Murray Hedgcock (ed.), *Wodehouse at the Wicket* (London, 1997).

James H. Heineman and Donald R. Bensen (eds.), *P. G. Wodehouse: A Centenary Celebration* (New York, 1981).

James Hepburn, *The Author's Empty Purse and the Rise of the Literary Agent* (Oxford, 1968).

Richard Ingrams, *Muggeridge* (London, 1995).

Julian Jackson, *France: The Dark Years, 1940–1944* (Oxford, 2001).

Lawrence James, *The Rise and Fall of the British Empire* (London, 1995).

David Jasen, *P. G. Wodehouse: Portrait of a Master* (London, 1975).

—— *The Theatre of PG Wodehouse* (London, 1979).

Ian Kershaw, *Hitler 1889–1936: Hubris* (London, 1998).

—— *Hitler 1936–1945: Nemesis* (London, 2000).

Frank H. H. King, *The History of the Hong Kong and Shanghai Banking Corporation* (Cambridge, 1988).

R. King-Clark, *Free for a Blast* (London, 1988).

Stephen King-Hall, *My Naval Life* (London, 1952).

Hugh Kingsmill, *Progress of a Biographer* (London, 1949).

Andrew Lamb, *150 Years of Popular Musical Theatre* (New Haven, 2000).

Zachary Leader (ed.), *On Modern British Fiction* (Oxford, 2002).

Alan Jay Lerner, *The Street Where I Live* (London, 1978).

Mary Lutyens, *Krishnamurti: The Years of Awakening* (New York, 1975).

Andrew Lycett, *Rudyard Kipling* (London, 1999).

Pat McGilligan (ed.), *Back Story: Interviews with Screenwriters of Hollywood's Golden Age* (Berkeley, 1986).

Eileen McIlvaine, Louise Sherby and James H. Heineman (eds.), *P. G. Wodehouse: A Comprehensive Bibliography and Checklist* (New York, 1990).

Denis Mackail, *Life with Topsy* (London, 1942).

Margaret MacMillan, *Peacemakers* (London, 2001).

Samuel Marx, *Mayer and Thalberg: The Make-believe Saints* (Los Angeles, 1975).

Scott Meredith, *George S. Kaufman and His Friends* (New York, 1974).

Malcolm Muggeridge, *Chronicles of Wasted Time*, 2 vols. (London, 1973).

N. T. P. Murphy, *In Search of Blandings* (London, 1981).

David Nasaw, *Hearst* (London, 2002).

Beverly Nichols, *Are They the Same at Home?* (London, 1927).

E. Phillips Oppenheim, *The Pool of Memory* (London, 1941).

Barry Phelps, *P. G. Wodehouse: Man and Myth* (London, 1992).

Diana Preston, *Wilful Murder: The Sinking of the Lusitania* (London, 2002).

V. S. Pritchett, *A Cab at the Door* (London, 1979).

Paul R. Reynolds, jun., *The Middle Man: Adventures of a Literary Agent* (New York, 1971).

Tony Ring, *You Simply Hit Them with an Axe: The Extraordinary True Story of the Tax Turmoils of P. G. Wodehouse* (Maidenhead, 1995).

Alexandra Ritchie, *Faust's Metropolis: A History of Berlin* (London, 1998).

Jonathan Schneer, *London 1900* (New Haven, 1999).

Nancy Lynn Schwartz, *The Hollywood Writers' Wars* (New York, 1982).

Iain Sproat, *Wodehouse at War* (New York, 1981).

Daniel Stashower, *Teller of Tales: The Life of Arthur Conan Doyle* (London, 1999).

Mark Steyn, *Broadway Babes Say Goodnight* (London, 1997).

A. J. P. Taylor, *English History 1914–1945* (Oxford, 1965).

Ellaline Terriss, *By Herself* (London, 1928).

—— *Just a Little Bit of String* (London, 1955).

Kristin Thompson, *Wooster Proposes, Jeeves Disposes* (New York, 1992).

Ann Thwaite, *A. A. Milne: His Life* (London, 1990).

Barbara Tuchman, *The Proud Tower* (New York, 1966).

Richard Usborne, *Wodehouse at Work to the End* (London, 1976).

—— *After Hours with P. G. Wodehouse* (London, 1991).

Tyler Whittle, *The Last Kaiser* (New York, 1977).

Max Wilk, *They're Playing Our Song: Conversations with America's Songwriters* (New York, 1991).

A. N. Wilson, *The Victorians* (London, 2002).

Angus Wilson, *The Strange Ride of Rudyard Kipling* (London, 1977).

Among magazines devoted to P. G. Wodehouse, the two most important are *Wooster Sauce*, the quarterly journal of the P. G. Wodehouse Society (UK), and *Plum Lines*, the quarterly journal of the Wodehouse Society (USA). Both publications are indispensable to the Wodehouse student.

Index